Angelomorphic Christology

Library of
Early Christology

Larry W. Hurtado
David B. Capes
April D. DeConick
Editors

SERIES INTRODUCTION

Over the past forty years or so, there has been a renewed interest in the origins and early developments of belief in Jesus, many of these studies sometimes referred to as loosely forming a kind of "new religionsgeschichtliche Schule" (new history of religion school). This body of work both resembles and differs from the German scholarship of the original "Schule," particularly in emphasizing more the roots of early Jesus-devotion in the rich and varied Jewish traditions of the Greco-Roman era.

Available from the Library of Early Christology Series

Bousset, Wilhelm. *Kyrios Christos: A History of the Belief in Christ from the Beginnings of Christianity to Irenaeus*

Capes, David B. *Old Testament Yahweh Texts in Paul's Christology*

DeConick, April D. *Seek to See Him: Ascent and Vision Mysticism in the Gospel of Thomas*

Fossum, Jarl E. *The Name of God and the Angel of the Lord: Samaritan and Jewish Concepts of Intermediation and the Origin of Gnosticism*

Gieschen, Charles A.. *Angelomorphic Christology: Antecedents and Early Evidence*

Hengel, Martin. *Between Jesus and Paul: Studies in the Earliest History of Christianity*

Hurtado, Larry W. *Ancient Jewish Monotheism and Early Christian Jesus-Devotion: The Context and Character of Christological Faith*

Juel, Donald H. *Messianic Exegesis: Christological Interpretation of the Old Testament in Early Christianity*

Newman, Carey C. *Paul's Glory-Christology: Tradition and Rhetoric*

Newman, Carey C., James R. Davila, and Gladys S. Lewis, editors. *The Jewish Roots of Christological Monotheism: Papers from the St Andrews Conference on the Historical Origins of the Worship of Jesus*

Segal, Alan F. *The Other Judaisms of Late Antiquity: Second Edition*

Segal, Alan F. *Two Powers in Heaven: Early Rabbinic Reports about Christianity and Gnosticism*

Stuckenbruck, Loren T. *Angel Veneration and Christology: A Study in Early Judaism and in the Christology of the Apocalypse of John*

Angelomorphic Christology

Antecedents and Early Evidence

Charles A. Gieschen

BAYLOR UNIVERSITY PRESS

Published in 1998 by E. J. Brill. Copyright © 1998 Koninklijke Brill NV, Leiden, The Netherlands
Reprinted in 2017 by Baylor University Press, Waco, Texas

All rights reserved. No part of this publication may be reproduced, stored in a retrieval system, or transmitted in any form or by any means. electronic, mechanical, photocopying, recording, or otherwise, without the prior permission of the publisher, E. J. Brill.

Authorization to photocopy items for internal or personal use is granted by E. J. Brill provided that the appropriate fees are paid directly to The Copyright Clearance Center, 222 Rosewood Drive, Suite 910, Danvers, MA, 01923, USA. Fees are subject to change.

Cover design Savanah N. Landerholm

Library of Congress Cataloging-in-Publication Data

Gieschen, Charles A.
    Angelomorphic christology: antecedents and early evidence / by Charles A. Gieschen.
    xvi, 403 p. ; 25 cm.
    Originally published: Leiden: Brill, 1998, in series: Arbeiten zur Geschichte des antiken Judentums und des Urchristentums, 42
    ISBN 9-0041-0840-0 (alk. paper)
    Includes bibliographical references and index.
    1. Jesus Christ—Person and offices—History of doctrines—Early church, ca. 30-600. 2. Angels—History of doctrines—Early church, ca/ 30-600. 3. Angels (Judaism)—History of doctrines I. Title. II. Series.

BT198.G485   1998
232

97050045

Baylor University Press ISBN: 978-1-4813-0794-9 (paper)

TABLE OF CONTENTS

Acknowledgements.. xiii
Abbreviations... xv

PART I

INTRODUCTION

Prologue: Christ as an Angel?... 3

1. *History of Research*.. 7
   A. Early Historical Research: Angelology and
      Intermediation... 8
   B. A Revival of Research: Angel Christology.................. 12
   C. Recent Research: The Influence of Divine Mediator
      Figures on Early Christology....................................... 16

2. *Nomenclature and Methodology*.. 26
   A. Religious Group Nomenclature.................................. 26
   B. Angel Nomenclature.. 27
   C. Divinity Nomenclature.. 30
   D. Veneration Nomenclature... 33
   E. Hypostasis Nomenclature.. 36
   F. Methodology.. 46

PART II

ANTECEDENTS

3. *An Angelomorphic God*... 51
   A. Interpretative Approaches.. 53
   B. Angel of the Lord Traditions in the Old Testament.. 57
   C. Conclusion... 67

4. *Angelomorphic Divine Hypostases*.................................... 70
   A. The Name... 70
      1. The Name as a Divine Hypostasis of Presence...... 71
      2. The Name as the Cosmogenic Agent..................... 74

    3. The Name Hypostatized as an Angelomorphic
       Figure 76
  B. The Glory.. 78
    1. The Glory at Sinai, the Tabernacle, and the
       Temple 78
    2. The Glory as an Angelomorphic Man, Especially
       in Ezekiel 1 80
    3. The Angelomorphic Glory in Texts after
       Ezekiel 1 84
    4. The Identification of the Glory with a Human 88
  C. Wisdom.. 89
    1. Wisdom as an Hypostasis and Cosmogenic
       Agent.. 89
    2. Wisdom and the Divine Throne 93
    3. Wisdom and the Angel of the Lord 98
  D. The Word.. 103
    1. The Word of YHWH Appears to the Patriarchs
       and Prophets.. 103
    2. The Word, Wisdom, and the Angel of the Lord ... 105
    3. The Angelomorphic Roots of Philo's *Logos*........... 107
    4. *Memra* and the Angel of the Lord............................ 112
  E. The Spirit... 114
    1. Spirits as Angels.. 114
    2. The Spirit as an Angel 116
  F. The Power... 119
    1. Power as a Designation for an Angel..................... 119
    2. Power as a Designation for God............................ 120
  G. Conclusion... 122

5. *The Principal Named Angels*.. 124
  A. Michael.. 126
  B. Gabriel... 131
  C. Raphael.. 135
  D. Uriel... 136
  E. Israel... 137
  F. Yahoel... 142
  G. Eremiel... 145
  H. Metatron 146
  I. Other Interpretations of the Principal Angels 148
  J. Conclusion.. 150

6. *Angelomorphic Humans*	152
A. Patriarchs	153
1. Adam	153
2. Abel	155
3. Enoch	156
4. Noah	158
5. Jacob	159
B. Prophets	161
1. Introduction	161
2. Moses	163
3. Elijah	167
4. Other Prophets	168
C. Priests	169
1. Introduction	169
2. Levi	170
3. Melchizedek	171
4. The Priests of the Qumran Literature	173
D. Kings	175
E. Apostles	176
F. Elect Ones	180
G. Conclusion	183

PART III

EARLY EVIDENCE

7. *Angelomorphic Christology at Nicea and Before*	187
A. Angel Christology at Nicea	187
B. Representative Evidence from Justin to Eusebius	188
1. Justin Martyr	189
2. Theophilus of Antioch	190
3. Irenaeus of Lyons	191
4. Tertullian	193
5. Clement of Alexandria	194
6. Hippolytus of Rome	194
7. Origen	195
8. Novatian	196
9. Lactantius	197
10. Eusebius of Caesarea	198
11. The Apostolic Constitutions	198
C. An Introduction to Early Evidence (Pre-150 CE)	199

CONTENTS

8. *The* Pseudo-Clementines 201
   A. The True Prophet as Adam and the Glory 202
   B. The True Prophet as Wisdom and the Spirit 205
   C. The True Prophet as the Chief Archangel 209
   D. The True Prophet as the Angel of the Lord 211
   E. Conclusion 212

9. *The* Shepherd of Hermas 214
   A. The Various Angelomorphic Figures 215
   B. The Relationship Between Pneumatology,
      Christology, and Ecclesiology 220
   C. The Son as the Angel of the Lord, the Name, and
      the Glory 225
   D. Conclusion 228

10. *The* Ascension of Isaiah 229
    A. The Angel of the Holy Spirit 231
    B. The Beloved 236
    C. The Great Glory 241
    D. Conclusion 244

11. *The Revelation to John* 245
    A. One Like a Son of Man 246
    B. The Word of God and the Name of God 252
    C. The Mighty Angel with the Scroll 256
    D. God and His Angel 260
    E. Conclusion 269

12. *The Gospel of John* 270
    A. The Word, the Name, and the Glory 271
    B. The Descending and Ascending Son of Man 280
    C. The Apostle 284
    D. The Paraclete(s) 286
    E. Conclusion 293

13. *The Epistle to the Hebrews* 294
    A. Creator, Name, Firstborn, Glory, and Enthroned
       Son 295
    B. Apostle, High Priest, and Son of God's House 303
    C. A High Priest After the Order of Melchizedek 307

D. The Word of God	311
E. Conclusion	314
14. *The Pauline Epistles*	315
A. God's Angel	315
B. The Destroyer	325
C. The Heavenly Man	329
D. The Power of God and the Wisdom of God	331
E. The Glory, the Image of God, and the Spirit	333
F. The Form and the Name of God	337
G. The Body	339
H. The Image of the Invisible God, the Head of the Body, the Firstborn, and the Beginning	343
I. Conclusion	346

PART IV

CONCLUSION

15. *Implications for the Study of Early Christology*	349
Bibliography	352
Ancient Literature Index	371
Modern Author Index	399

ACKNOWLEDGEMENTS

This book represents the culmination of several years of historical and theological education focused on biblical literature. Several individual teachers have made a lasting impact on the shape of that education. James Voelz, then of Concordia Theological Seminary in Fort Wayne, first instilled in me a passion for rigorous exegesis. His encouragement led me to spend an invaluable year at Princeton Theological Seminary where I was cultivated primarily by James Charlesworth and Martinus de Boer. My years at the University of Michigan were influenced by Jarl Fossum and Gabriele Boccaccini. Professor Fossum, under whose guidance much of what follows was first submitted as a dissertation in 1995, has been an abundant source of scholarly insight, as is apparent throughout this book. I also benefited from conversations with Christopher Rowland during my months at the University of Oxford in 1994. It is to each of these teachers, especially my *Doktorvater*, that I am profoundly indebted and herewith express my sincere gratitude.

Several other people and events have also shaped the dissertation stage of this book. April De Conick, a treasured friend and scholar, led me to doctoral studies and offered encouragement along the way. Several lectures by Christopher Morray-Jones in Ann Arbor and at the National SBL Meetings were insightful and stimulating. I benefited from the opportunity to present portions of this research at the National Meetings of the Society of Biblical Literature in 1992-1996. I was the thankful recipient of Michigan's Radcliffe-Ramsdell Fellowship in 1993-94 which assisted in six months of study at the University of Oxford. While there I presented a portion of my Pauline chapter to the Oxford New Testament Graduate Seminar and to the Ehrhardt Seminar at the University of Manchester. An afternoon conversation with Gilles Quispel during my visit to the Netherlands clarified several questions in my research. I also benefited from the environment of Westfield House in Cambridge where I resided and wrote the formative chapters of this study. The time in England as well as the years at the University of Michigan would not have been feasible without the generous financial support of the Wiebe Mission Trust Fund

Scholarship and the patient understanding of the members of Trinity Lutheran Church of Traverse City, Michigan whom I served as pastor during the years of my doctoral studies.

The opportunity to focus on the revision of my disseration would not have been possible without the support of my esteemed colleagues, Dean Wenthe and William Weinrich of Concordia Theological Seminary, who have provided me with a wonderful environment for teaching and research. I am very indebted to Chad Bird, our Graduate Assistant for Exegetical Theology, who tirelessly read the entire manuscript and offered numerous helpful suggestions. Grant Knepper, Duane Bamsch, and Christopher Esget also provided valuable assistance with the indices and proofing. Lastly, I extend my sincere thanks to Martin Hengel and the editoral staff of Brill Academic Publishers for accepting this into the *Arbeiten zur Geschichte des Antiken Judentums und des Urchristentums* series.

No person in this process has been more important than my wife, Kristi. Her unfailing love and daily encouragement have inspired my every effort. Therefore, it is to her that I dedicate this work.

Charles A. Gieschen

ABBREVIATIONS

With the exception of those listed below, the abbreviations used in this book are those listed in alphabetical order in the front of any volume of *The Anchor Bible Dictionary* (6 vols.; ed. David Noel Freedman; New York: Doubleday, 1992). The full name of abbreviated titles of ancient literature is provided in the Ancient Literature Index.

DDD	*Dictionary of Deities and Demons in the Bible*
Frag.	fragment
m.	*Mishnah*
NumenSup	Supplements to *Numen*
Rec.	Recension
SSEJC	Studies in Scripture in Early Judaism and Christianity
TSAJ	Texten und Studien des Antiken Judentums

Use of Primary Sources

OT Hebrew quotations are from *Biblia Hebraica Stuttgartensia* (Stuttgart: Deutsche Bibelgesellschaft, 1984). NT Greek quotations are from *Novum Testamentum Graece* (26th ed.; Stuttgart: Deutsche Bibelgesellschaft, 1979). LXX Greek quotations are from *Septuaginta* (ed. A. Rahlfs; Stuttgart: Deutsche Bibelgesellschaft, 1979). English quotations of the OT, NT, and OT Apocrypha are my own translations or from the *Revised Standard Version* (2d ed.; 1971; copyright by Division of Christian Education of the National Council of Churches of Christ in the United States of America). Quotations of the Old Testament Pseudepigrapha, unless otherwise noted, are from *Old Testament Pseudepigrapha* (2 vols.; New York: Doubleday, 1983/1985). Greek and English texts from Philo and Josephus are from the *Loeb Classical Library* (Cambridge, MA: Harvard University Press). Qumran Literature translations are my own or from *The Dead Sea Scrolls Translated* (Leiden: Brill, 1994). New Testament

Apocrypha quotations are from *New Testament Apocryha* (Cambridge: James Clarke & Co., 1991). Quotations from the Nag Hammadi Codices are from *The Nag Hammadi Library in English* (Leiden: Brill, 1988). The source of other ancient texts that are referenced or quoted in this book are listed under "Primary Sources" in the Bibliography. Please note that all references to the *Prayer of Joseph* are to the lines of Frag. A as in *OTP* 2.713.

PART ONE

INTRODUCTION

PROLOGUE
CHRIST AS AN ANGEL?

> So far as we can tell then *no NT writer thought of Christ as an angel*, whether as a pre-existent divine being who had appeared in Israel's history as the angel of the Lord, or as an angel or spirit become man, or as a man who by exaltation after death had become an angel.[1]

This sweeping statement by James Dunn in *Christology in the Making* concludes his consideration of evidence that Jewish angelology had influence on the origin and development of early Christology. Almost a decade later, after his reflection on the most recent research about angelomorphic traditions, he expressed in his foreword to the second edition that he did not give this area ample consideration previously and that this topic is much more involved than merely whether any NT writer thought of Jesus as an angel.[2] In spite of these corrective comments, he concludes in a similar manner:

> [. . .] the angelomorphic description of the exalted Christ, which is certainly a feature of Revelation, and which certainly came to powerful lasting expression in the Byzantine Pantocrator, does not seem otherwise to have provided the highroad for developing christological thought in the intervening period.[3]

Dunn is not alone in this assertion. His conclusion is reflective of the pervasive position on the matter in biblical scholarship that will be challenged in the pages ahead.[4]

---

[1] J. Dunn, *Christology in the Making: An Inquiry into the Origins of the Doctrine of the Incarnation* (London: SCM, 1980) 158, emphasis his.

[2] "Angelomorphic" is an inclusive term which means having some of the various forms and functions of an angel, even though the figure may not be explicitly called an "angel" or considered to have the created nature of an angel; see discussion on 27-29 below.

[3] *Christology in the Making: An Inquiry into the Origins of the Doctrine of the Incarnation* (2d ed.; London: SCM, 1989) xxvi. He makes this statement in spite of his acquaintance with the research of Segal, Rowland, Fossum, and Hurtado; see the summary of their work on 17-25 below.

[4] The now classic refutation of Angel Christology in the NT is W. Michaelis, *Zur Engelchristologie im Urchristentum* (Basel: Heinrich Majer, 1942). See also the dogmatic rebuttal of "an angel-Christ" by W. McDonald, "Christology and 'The Angel of the Lord'", *Current Issues in Biblical and Patristic Interpretation: Studies in Honor of Merrill C. Tenney Presented by His Former Students* (ed. G. Hawthorne; Grand Rapids: Eerdmans, 1975) 324-335. Very few scholars advocate the importance of angelomorphic traditions for early Christology.

The study of Angelomorphic Christology has been plagued by two foundational misconceptions. First, the lack of much overt "angel" terminology in first century Christology has misdirected our understanding of its influence far too long. Christopher Rowland laments this situation:

> That early christologies owed much to angelomorphic categories is not now disputed, at least as far as the post-New Testament period is concerned. Nevertheless the fact that the New Testament writings do not contain any passage which speaks of Christ as an angel has persuaded many that, if there was an angel christology, it was merely a peripheral phenomenon, rapidly rejected by mainstream Christianity (e.g. Heb. 1-3; cf. Col. 2.28). It is the implicit threat both to the uniqueness and divinity of Christ involved in the attribution of the title angel that has lead to suspicion of this particular development.[5]

The relative lack of labeling Christ as an angel in the pages of the NT does not warrant the conclusion that he was understood and depicted by NT writers without the significant influence of Jewish angelology.[6] For this reason "angelomorphic" is a more helpful term to broaden the discussion beyond overt "angel" terminology. Furthermore, "angel" terminology also raises the ontological question that has moved some interpreters to dismiss *a priori* the impact of such concepts on early Christology. It is crucial to understand that distinctions which early Christian documents make between Christ and the "created" angels do not preclude the use of angelomorphic traditions in expressing Christology. Angelic forms and functions do not of necessity imply a nature that is less than divine. This conclusion is evident from the OT texts which equate God and his angel.[7]

The second major misconception plaguing the study of Angelomorphic Christology is that many scholars believe that it developed at a later date and could not have influenced the origin and very early expression of Christology. Its seeds are often seen as sprouting through the soil in Revelation (ca. 95 CE), then vividly blossoming in Justin Martyr (ca. 150 CE) and those ante-Nicene fathers who follow him.[8] This flawed position is founded on an

---

[5] "A Man Clothed in Linen: Daniel 10.6ff. and Jewish Angelology", *JSNT* 24 (1985) 99.

[6] Although "angel" is not a significant title of Christ in the NT, neither is it without some overt use; see Gal 4.14; Rev 10.1; 14.14-15; 20.1. These texts are discussed in detail in Part III below.

[7] See discussion on 51-69 below.

[8] For an extensive treatment of second through fourth century evidence, see J.

inadequate model for discussions of early Christology: the development of early Christology is seen as beginning with simple concepts (Jesus as a prophet in 30 CE) and developing to more complex concepts (Jesus as the preexistent Son and one with God by 100 CE).[9] Martin Hengel has exposed this fallacy and convincingly emphasized that much more happened in the development of Christology during the first two decades after the crucifixion of Jesus than took place in the next seven centuries.[10] Therefore, the development and expression of Christology should not be traced primarily through the pages of the New Testament which were written in relatively close chronology, but from the formative pre-Christian Israelite and Jewish angelomorphic traditions which were adopted and adapted by authors to express their understanding of Jesus Christ. As Rowland states:

> [. . .] early Christianity may itself offer testimony in its christological reflection more to the theological complexity already inherent within contemporary Jewish religion rather than to the unique inventiveness of its adherents.[11]

The complex and multi-faceted "Angel of the Lord" traditions are part of ancient Israelite literature. This means these textual traditions are not only important in their own right as an influence on early Christology, but they are also noteworthy for their influence on other Jewish traditions which impacted Christology. For example, Wisdom traditions tend to dominate discussions of early Christology. Very seldom, however, is the dependence of Wisdom traditions on Angel of the Lord traditions ever discussed.[12] This study will demonstrate that at the root of Wisdom Christology, Spirit Christology, Name Christology, Glory Christology, Son of Man Christology, Image Christology, and Anthropos

---

Barbel, *Christos Angelos: Die Anschauung von Christus als Bote und Engel in der gelehrten und volkstümlichen Literatur des christlichen Altertums* (Bonn: Hanstein, 1941; Nachdruck 1964 mit einem Anhang); see also the summary on 187-189 below.

[9] Such a progression can be seen in P. Casey, *From Jewish Prophet to Gentile God: The Origins and Development of New Testament Christology* (Philadelphia: Westminster/John Knox, 1991).

[10] *The Son of God: The Origin of Christology and the History of Jewish-Hellenistic Religion* (trans. J. Bowden; London: SCM, 1976) 2; see also his *Between Jesus and Paul* (trans. J. Bowden, London: SCM, 1983) 30-47, and his most recent *Studies in Early Christology* (Edinburgh: T&T Clark, 1995).

[11] *Christian Origins: From Messianic Movement to Christian Religion* (Minneapolis: Augsburg, 1985) 38-39.

[12] An exception to this is J. Fossum, "Kyrios Jesus as the Angel of the Lord in Jude 5-7", *NTS* 33 (1987) 236-237.

Christology are angelomorphic traditions. The central root from which these so-called Christologies grew is the angelomorphic tradition in which the Angel of the Lord is God appearing in the form of a man. Therefore, the essential form of the revelation of God in Israelite and Jewish literature is as an angelomorphic figure.

Ignorance concerning the influence of angelomorphic traditions has also plagued scholarship on early Pneumatology.[13] This study will have implications for research on early Pneumatology because the same or similar angelomorphic traditions also influenced teaching about the Holy Spirit.[14] These implications grow out of the close interrelationship between Pneumatology and Christology as portrayed in many texts.[15]

Already in 1977 Alan Segal issued a call for further study of the impact of angel traditions on early Christology:

> Continued study is needed in almost every area [. . .]. Of particular interest is the relationship of the angelic figure to early christology. Perhaps angelic christologies will turn out to be more important to the thought of the first century than the New Testaments leads us to believe.[16]

Much research that assists in addressing Seyal's challenge has been done in this field over the past two decades. This research will be reviewed in the next chapter. There remains a need, however, to join together this variegated research for a coherent presentation of ideological antecedents to this Christology and a fresh exegesis of early texts which evince the influence of these angelomorphic traditions. This study will address this need by arguing the following thesis: *Angelomorphic traditions, especially those growing from the Angel of the Lord traditions, had a significant impact on the early expressions of Christology to the extent that evidence of an Angelomorphic Christology is discernible in several documents dated between 50 and 150 CE.*

---

[13] It is quite surprising to read R. Menzies' recent study on the development of early Christian Pneumatology only to find it completely lacking a discussion of Angel Pneumatology, especially when the Holy Spirit is identified as "an angel of the Lord" in Acts 8.26-29; see *The Development of Early Christian Pneumatology: With Special Reference to Luke-Acts* (JSNTSup 54; Sheffield: Sheffield Academic Press, 1991). Contrast the work of J. Levison who gives much attention to the role of angelology in expressions of pneumatology; see "The Angelic Spirit in Early Judaism", *SBLSP* 34 (1995) 464-493, and *The Spirit in First Century Judaism* (AGJU 29; Leiden: Brill, 1997).

[14] This will be demonstrated primarily in the study below of the Paraclete in John and the Holy Spirit in Revelation.

[15] See: 2 Cor 3.15-18; Rom 8.9-11; Acts 16.6-8; Phil 1.18-19; *Ign. Magn.* 16.

[16] *Two Powers in Heaven: Early Rabbinic Reports About Christianity and Gnosticism* (SJLA 25; Leiden: Brill, 1977) 266.

CHAPTER ONE

HISTORY OF RESEARCH

The contribution that angelomorphic traditions made to the development of Christology occurred primarily in the first three centuries before the Council of Nicea in 325 CE.[1] In this richly generative period there were exegetical efforts to express Christ's preexistence, as well as to affirm his divinity, through the use of traditions found in Israelite and Jewish literature. Culminating in the Arian controversy and the formulations of Nicea, ontological questions were raised which effectively stifled further discussion of the relationship between overt angel traditions and Christ.[2] Therefore, the Arian Christological debate served to veil and bury the important contribution that angelomophic traditions made to the early expression of Christology. Furthermore, until recent decades Jewish and Christian scholars alike have often portrayed the diverse wealth of angelomorphic traditions in extra-canonical Jewish literature of this period as esoteric and not representative of the so-called "Normative Judaism" in the first century CE.[3] This, in turn, impacted the weight that most pre-twentieth century interpreters and historians placed on the influence these traditions exerted upon early Christology.[4]

---

[1] See Barbel, *Christos Angelos*. He does not, however, assert or document the crucial impact of Jewish angelomorphic traditions upon the expression of Christology in the first century.

[2] R. Lorenz has gathered convincing data to demonstrate the background of Arian Christology in these traditions; see *Arius judaizans? Untersuchungen zur dogmengeschlichtlichen Einordnung des Arius* (Göttingen: Vandenhoeck & Ruprecht, 1979) esp. 141-180.

[3] Many scholars have worked to dispel the myth of a normative Judaism in the first century CE, but none as prolifically as Jacob Neusner; see his "The Formation of Rabbinic Judaism: Yavneh (Jamnia) from A.D. 70-100", *ANRW* II.19.2 (1979) 3-42. See also G. Boccaccini, "Middle Judaism and Its Contemporary Interpreters (1986-1992): Methodological Foundations for the Study of Judaisms, 300 BCE to 200 CE", *Henoch* 15 (1993) 207-233.

[4] This is shown most clearly with respect to *1 Enoch*, which went from an obscure document in most scholarly circles for centuries to a widely-read centerpiece of the apocalyptic tradition in the past century.

This does not mean that Christian exegetes after Nicea discontinued their interest in the relationship between Christ and figures like the Angel of the Lord. Such exegesis, however, typically was done within clear dogmatic bounds which limited its focus to canonical documents and carefully distinguished the ontology of the Angel of the Lord from that of created angels.[5] Furthermore, the focus of this exegesis was not primarily on how these ancient traditions influenced early Christology, but rather on how the carefully articulated Christology of later Christianity (Nicea and Chalcedon) could be found in OT texts. Even the angelomorphic depictions of Christ within canonical books like Revelation were usually understood as "theophanies" rather than "angelophanies" because of the dogmatic and ontological problems involved in referring to Christ as "an angel". This situation, however, began to change with the growth of historical research and its use of extra-biblical literature.

A. *Early Historical Research: Angelology and Intermediation*

Historical research on the existence of angelomorphic traditions and their influence on the origins of Christology budded in the closing decades of the nineteenth century and blossomed in the twentieth century. The focus of this period was angelology and intermediation. It is characterized by a growing awareness of the vast variety of angel traditions in Jewish and Christian literature, especially in documents outside the biblical canon(s). During these decades dogmaticians and exegetes, such as ADOLPH VON HARNACK, had a more inclusive methodology in recording various divergent traditions from a variety of extra-canonical sources that contributed to the expression of Christian doctrine.[6]

The scholar who made the greatest impact on this period of research was WILHELM BOUSSET, whose name is synonymous with the well-known *Religionsgeschichtliche Schule* ("History-of-Religions School"). Bousset made a substantive departure from the

---

[5] E. Hengstenberg, *Christologie des Alten Testaments und commentar über die Messianischen Weissagungen* (3 vols.; Berlin: L. Oehmigke, 1854-1857), and H.P. Liddon, The Divinity of Our Lord and Savior Jesus Christ (6th ed.; London: Rivingtons, 1872).

[6] See his *History of Dogma* (trans. N. Buchanan; 6 vols.; London: Williams and Norgate, 1894-97).

scholarly norm in his depiction of Judaism at the turn of the Common Era. He showed much less reliance on Rabbinic sources than his contemporaries while drawing heavily upon documents of the OT Apocrypha and Pseudepigrapha (in the limited state that the latter collection existed at his time), especially apocalyptic literature.[7] This led him to place the limited data on angels found in the OT within a much broader literary context. He was one of the first scholars to document and discuss extensively the concept of intermediary beings (*Mittelwesen*) as the primary means of access to God in this period of Judaism.

Bousset's research does have deficiencies. He asserted that the primary Christological development which led to Jesus being viewed as a divine mediator happened late in the first century through contact with the imperial cult, the mystery religions, and Oriental religion in the Greco-Roman world. This position has been proven false. This perspective is especially visible in the writing of Bousset's friend and *religionsgeschichtliche* associate, RICHARD REITZENSTEIN.[8] More attention needed to be paid to Jewish evidence in the earliest years of Christianity which provided the conceptual background for understanding Jesus as a divine mediator. Bousset is also criticized for his assertion that the development of intermediary beings in Judaism is reflective of an increased sense of God's transcendence and a degeneration of monotheism.[9]

---

[7] The influence of Bousset can be seen in the prolonged use of his *Die Religion des Judentums im Späthellenistischen Zeitalter* (4th ed.; Tübingen: Mohr/Siebeck, 1966), which was first published in 1903, then updated by H. Gressmann in 1924. Note also the durability of his *Kyrios Jesus* (trans. J. Steely; 5th ed.; Nashville: Abingdon, 1970).

[8] See esp. *Hellenistic Mystery-Religions: Their Basic Ideas and Significance* (trans. J. Steely; 3d ed.; Pittsburgh Monograph Series 15; Pittsburgh: Pickwick, 1978).

[9] See the critque of this position by L. Hurtado, "New Testament Christology: A Critique of Bousset's Influence", *TS* 40 (1979) 306-317; see also his *One God, One Lord: Early Christian Devotion and Ancient Jewish Monotheism* (Philadelphia: Fortress, 1988) 24-36. Although Bousset used language that reflects a bias towards such a development (in contrast to the immanence of Jesus' relationship with God as Father), Hurtado does not adequately acknowledge that this literature does reflect significant changes in how Jews viewed God's interaction with the world. The exalted mediator traditions certainly indicate a greater complexity in the Jewish monotheism of some groups. See also the criticism of Bousset's paradigm by S. Olyan, *A Thousand Thousands Served Him: Exegesis and the Naming of Angels in Ancient Judaism* (TSAJ 36; Tübingen: Mohr/Siebeck, 1993) 8, 89-90.

WILHELM LUEKEN, a student of Bousset, followed his teacher's model for tradition history studies of particular angelic figures by producing a volume on the archangel Michael.[10] Lueken collated data from a wide range of extant literature, including later patristic and rabbinic evidence, to depict the traditions that developed around this angel. Although Lueken did not find much direct influence of "Michaelology" on Christology, his study was one of the first to argue for a close connection between angelology and the development of Christology, especially the concept of preexistence as is visible in the Colossians hymn (Col 1.15-19), the Philippians hymn (Phil 2.5-11), and the opening chapter of Hebrews.[11]

Christology was not the only area where the study of angel traditions was having an impact. HANS WINDISCH, another *religionsgeschichtliche* scholar of this period, was among the first to demonstrate the importance of Jewish angelology for Pneumatology. For example, in his studies of the Johannine Paraclete he argued that the historical antecedents of this figure are to be found in angelic advocate traditions such as the interceding angel of Job 33.23-25 and the intercessory *Logos* in Philo (e.g., *Heres* 205).[12]

GEORGE FOOT MOORE, a highly respected American scholar of Judaism, affected the direction of research on Jewish intermediation with two influential articles in 1921-22 that are still cited in scholarly literature with some frequency.[13] In these articles he levels pointed criticism against the manner in which Christian authors often characterize Judaism, especially those researchers who were seeking to mine Jewish literature for Christological or

---

[10] *Michael: Eine Darstellung und Vergleichung der jüdischen und der morgenländisch-christlichen Tradition von Erzengel Michael* (Göttingen: Vandenhoeck & Ruprecht, 1898). For Bousset's methodological approach to tradition history that guided Lueken, see his *Der Antichrist in der Überlieferung des Judentums, des neuen Testaments, und der alten Kirche: Ein Beitrag zur Erklärung der Apocalypse* (Göttingen: Vandenhoeck & Ruprecht, 1895).

[11] Lueken, *Michael*, 133-166.

[12] "Die fünf johanneischen Parakletsprüche", *Festgabe für Adolf Jülicher* (Tübingen: Mohr/Siebeck, 1927), and "Jesus und der Geist im Johannesevangelicum", *Amicitiae Corolla* (London: University of London Press, 1933), are translated and published in *The Spirit-Paraclete in the Fourth Gospel* (trans. J. Cox; Philadelphia: Fortress, 1968).

[13] "Christian Writers on Judaism", *HTR* 14 (1921) 197-254, and "Intermediaries in Jewish Theology: Memra, Shekinah, Metatron", *HTR* 15 (1922) 41-85. The continued influence of these articles can be seen, for example, in Hurtado, *One God*, 136 n.1, and Olyan, *A Thousand Thousands*, 6 n.12, 8 n.23.

Trinitarian dogma.[14] Bousset was one of the primary "anti-Jewish Christian writers" whom Moore targeted in his critique of scholars who use sources that are not representative of the so-called orthodox position of Judaism at the time.[15] While his criticism was justified in several cases, he also misconstrued the evidence through his exclusive focus on Rabbinic literature to understand first century Judaism and his avoidance of texts concerning Jewish mediator figures.[16] The impact which Moore had on twentieth century scholarly understandings of intermediation in Judaism hardly can be overstated.

Solid historical research in this field was also being conducted by British scholars who were united by their study and translation of documents included in the publication of *The Apocrypha and Pseudepigrapha of the Old Testament* which served as the standard English translation for several decades.[17] Most notable is the editor of the project, R. H. CHARLES. His research in extra-canonical apocalyptic literature, such as *1 Enoch* and the *Ascension of Isaiah*, prompted him to utilize these angel traditions in his exegesis, especially in his commentary on Revelation.[18] With respect to the impact of angelology on the Christology of Revelation, his conclusions remained cautious: "Christ is never designated as an angel in the Apoc. [. . .]".[19]

G. H. BOX was of assistance to Charles in this translation project and made a significant contribution to the discussion of intermediation with an article that responded to G. F. Moore's depiction of intermediation in the Judaism of the first centuries CE.[20] He emphasized the "hostility" of Rabbinism to discussions of intermediation, since such discussions threaten the traditional rabbinic understanding of God. He argued that the significance of revisions

---

[14] E.g., studies that would posit the *Skekinah* to be the second or third person of the Trinity; see "Intermediaries in Jewish Theology", 41-42.
[15] "Christian Writers", 241-248.
[16] "Intermediaries in Jewish Theology", 52-53.
[17] *The Apocrypha and Pseudepigrapha of the Old Testament* (2 vols.; Oxford: OUP, 1913). These English translations of the Pseudepigrapha were finally superseded and replaced by publication of *The Old Testament Pseudepigrapha*, ed. J. H. Charlesworth (2 vols.; Garden City: Doubleday, 1983 and 1985).
[18] *The Revelation to St. John* (ICC; 2 vols; Edinburgh: T & T Clark, 1920).
[19] *Revelation*, 1.259.
[20] "The Idea of Intermediation in Jewish Theology: A Note on Memra and Shekinah", *JQR* 23 (1932/33) 103-119; see also "The Jewish Environment of Early Christianity", *Exp Tim* 42 (1916) 1-25.

within the targumic tradition is evidence of attempts by rabbis to safeguard so-called orthodoxy.[21] HUGO ODEBERG, a student of Box, also contributed significant studies on *3 Enoch* and John which furthered scholarly understanding of Jewish mysticism and its implications for early Christology.[22]

G. H. DIX, another British scholar, contributed several articles to the study of Jewish angelology and the development of early Christology in the decade following World War I.[23] He argues, although much too simplistically, that Jewish messianism was founded upon the Angel of the Lord traditions and included the expectation that this angel would come in the form of a man.[24] He also stated that the Jewish roots of later Trinitarian dogma are to be found in the *Logos* (Son) and Wisdom (Spirit) of apocalyptic literature.[25]

An article by ADOLPINE BAKKER is characteristic of this growing awareness of angel traditions coupled with a hesitation to assert that some of the earliest Christians understood Christ as an angel.[26] Bakker quickly surveys a small amount of representative evidence from the Pentateuch, the Targumim, Justin, the *Shepherd of Hermas*, Hebrews, Lactantius, and Tertullian. This article's primary assertion is that the opening chapters of Hebrews are an anti-docetic argument which was constructed to counteract a Jewish-Christian understanding of Christ as an angel.

B. *A Revival of Research: Angel Christology*

With the decade of the 1940s came a revival of research in this field, but with a distinctly new focus: a conviction that angel

---

[21] "The Idea of Intermediation", 105.
[22] *3 Enoch or The Hebrew Book of Enoch* (Cambridge: CUP, 1928; reprint with new prolegomenon by J. Greenfield, New York: KTAV, 1973) and *The Fourth Gospel Interpreted in Its Relation to Contemporaneous Religious Currents in Palestine and the Hellenistic-Oriental World* (Chicago: Argonaut, 1929).
[23] "The Heavenly Wisdom and the Divine Logos in Jewish Apocalyptic", *JTS* 26 (1924) 1-12; "The Influence of Babylonian Ideas on Jewish Messianism", *JTS* 27 (1925) 241-256; and "The Seven Archangels and the Seven Spirits", *JTS* 28 (1927) 233-250.
[24] "Influence of Babylonian Ideas", 250.
[25] "Heavenly Wisdom", 1-12.
[26] "Christ an Angel? A Study of Early Christian Docetism", *ZNW* 32 (1933) 255-265.

traditions are of the very earliest strata in the origin and development of Christology. MARTIN WERNER, in his synthetic history of Christian doctrine, published the bold thesis that Angel Christology was the first Christology of Christianity.[27] Werner discusses evidence which demonstrates that many of the so-called messianic expectations dealt with a heavenly or angelic being (e.g., Elect One/Son of Man in *1 Enoch*). His documentation for this in the first decades of Christianity is meager. For example, he asserts that Angel Christology is evident in the Gospels' depiction of Christ as the Prince of angels in various texts and even goes so far as to assert that Paul's use of κύριος for Christ is not based upon its use in the LXX as a translation of the Tetragrammaton, but is based upon the understanding that angels were designated as κυριοί.[28] He placed too much emphasis on post-resurrection Angel Christology and did not discuss ways in which angelomorphic traditions shaped Christian teaching concerning the pre-incarnate and fleshly Jesus.

Werner's assertion received a hasty and damaging response from the influential pen of WILHELM MICHAELIS.[29] He argued against the presence of any form of Angel Christology in the New Testament. His primary contention was that the messianic figure in Jewish and Christian literature is carefully distinguished from the ranks of angels.[30] Although this is often the case, Michaelis failed to see that such distinguishing does not preclude that the messianic figure is a distinct exalted angel or, at the very least, angelomorphic in his depiction. Very few scholars challenged Michaelis' critique.[31] Therefore, it effectively crippled any sub-

---

[27] *Die Entstehung des christlichen Dogma* (Tübingen: Katzmann, 1941). This volume was abbreviated by the author for translation; see *The Formation of Christian Dogma: An Historical Study of its Problem* (trans. S. Brandon; London: Adam & Charles Black, 1957).

[28] Werner, *Formation of Christian Dogma*, 121-125. His position resulted in the logical conclusion that Arius actually was expressing the earliest and most authentic Christology. Such a position is overstated and was, naturally, attacked with vigor.

[29] *Zur Engelchristologie im Urchristentum* (Basel: Heinrich Majer, 1942).

[30] *Engelchristologie*, 187.

[31] Exceptions are: K. Goetz, *Das antichristliche und das christliche, geschichtliche Jesusbild von heute* (Basel: Helbing & Lichtenhahn, 1944) 29-32; F. Scheidweiler, "Novatian und die Engelchristologie", *ZKG* 66 (1954/55) 126-139; and F. Scheidweiler, "Zur Christologie des Paulus", *Deutsches Pfarrerblatt* 10/11 (1952) 292. Scheidweiler belittled Michaelis' criticism and asserted that Angel-Christology, with its combination of exaltation and preexistence, is the key to Paul's Christology and it solves many problems of origin and analysis; see "Novatian", 138-139.

stantial contribution that Werner, and others in the years that followed, hoped to make to the discussion.

It is most unfortunate that Werner's volume and Michaelis' reply overshadowed and negatively impacted how scholars received the invaluable research of JOSEPH BARBEL.[32] Although Barbel did not advocate Angel Christology as part of the earliest Christology, his work is the most carefully documented account to date of Angel Christology in Christian literature of the second through fourth centuries. Furthermore, the appendix to the reprint of his book provides invaluable insights into the two decades of scholarly debate spawned by Werner's thesis.[33]

HANS JOACHIM SCHOEPS also recognized the presence of Angel Christology in early Jewish Christianity.[34] His research draws primarily, though too narrowly, on the *Pseudo-Clementines* (3d-4th century CE) as the crucial document for understanding earlier traditions and beliefs of Jewish Christians, especially the Ebionites.[35] Schoeps exposes much of the complexity of the True Prophet figure as an amalgamation of several traditions. His scholarship in this question is the major reason that the *Pseudo-Clementines* is given respectable mention in discussions of early Christology, even though it was often discounted among fellow German scholars.[36]

One of the most important analyses of how angelomorphic traditions impacted the development of Trinitarian dogma is that of historian GEORG KRETSCHMAR.[37] In contrast to earlier scholarship, which focused primarily on expressing second and third century developments, Kretschmar searched for the pre-Christian ante-

---

[32] *Christos Angelos: Die Anschauung von Christus als Bote und Engel in der gelehrten und volkstümlichen Literatur des christlichen Altertums* (Bonn: Hanstein, 1941).

[33] *Christos Angelos*, 335-352.

[34] *Theologie und Geschichte des Judenchristentums* (Tübingen: Mohr/Siebeck, 1949). See also *Urgemeinde-Judenchristentum-Gnosis* (Tübingen: Mohr/Siebeck, 1956) or his *Jewish Christianity: Factional Disputes in the Early Church* (trans. D. Hare; Philadelphia: Fortress, 1969). The latter work is an abridged and translated form of *Theologie and Geschichte*.

[35] In this emphasis Schoeps returned to the Tübingen School's position that the *Pseudo-Clementines* corpus is based on a much earlier Jewish Christian document identified for scholarly discussion as Κηρύγματα Πέτρου ("Preaching of Peter"); see the discussion on 201-213 below.

[36] See G. Quispel, "The Discussion of Judaic Christianity", *Gnostic Studies* (2 vols; Istanbul: Nederlands Historisch-Archaeologisch Istituut, 1975) 2.148-149.

[37] *Studien zur frühchristlichen Trinitätstheologie* (BHT 21; Tübingen: Mohr/Siebeck, 1956).

cedents of both the Christology and Pneumatology of these centuries. He explored the impact that the traditions about the two Seraphim (cf. Isa 6.1-3) had on the Alexandrian contributions to Trinitarian formulations.[38] He also detailed evidence of Jewish traditions surrounding a pair of angels influencing Christology and Pneumatology outside of Egypt and in Palestine.[39]

The more inclusive terms "angelomorphic" and "Angelomorphic Christology" originated with the influential French scholar JEAN DANIÉLOU.[40] In the volume on Jewish Christianity from his trilogy on early Christian thought, Daniélou details how early Jewish Christians drew on angelomorphic traditions in order to articulate their understandings of Christ and the Holy Spirit.[41] While he is open to the criticism that he labels almost every pre-150 CE Christian document as "Jewish Christian", his synthetic work demonstrates the continued vitality of Jewish influences on Christianity far beyond the first century and is overflowing with insightful proposals about relationships between various ideas. The implications of his research for early Christology were developed further by RICHARD LONGENECKER, who also promulgated the term Angelomorphic Christology.[42]

A. T. HANSON argued for the significance of the OT Angel of the Lord traditions for early Christology, including the NT.[43] Although this research interest was fostered by the abundant second and third century evidence, his exegesis centers on NT texts which speak of, or allude to, Christ's presence in OT events or with OT persons (e.g., 1 Cor 10.1-11). He argues that Christ's presence was not conceptualized typologically by some NT writers, but Christ was understood to be present as the Angel of the Lord who is closely associated with traditions about the Destroyer (cf. 1 Cor 10.9; Jude 5; Rev 19.11-13) and the Glory (cf. Jas 2.1; John 5.44).[44] His

---

[38] *Trinitätstheologie*, 62-93.
[39] *Trinitätstheologie*, 94-124.
[40] *The Theology of Jewish Christianity* (trans. J. Baker; Philadelphia: Westminster, 1964) 146.
[41] *Jewish Christianity*, esp. 117-142. Kretschmar and Quispel influenced his work.
[42] "Some Distinctive Early Christological Motifs", *NTS* 14 (1968) 526-545. This article with revisions forms a portion of his *The Christology of Jewish Christianity* (Grand Rapids: Baker, 1970). "Angelomorphic Christology" is discussed on 26-32.
[43] See esp. *Jesus Christ in the Old Testament* (London: SPCK, 1965).
[44] *Jesus Christ in the OT*, 10-47, 104-138.

passionate advocacy of the idea that the Angel of the Lord in the OT is Christ impacted his exegesis and did little to endear his insights to other scholars.

GILLES QUISPEL, the source of several of Daniélou's insights, represents a scholarly bridge from this period to the more recent research that has transpired in the past two decades on both sides of the Atlantic. He is a pioneering advocate of the hypothesis that the origins of Gnosticism, including the roots of Gnostic intermediation, are to be found primarily in very early forms of Jewish Mysticism.[45] He used Jewish angel traditions, especially those dealing with the angel who possesses the Divine Name, to illuminate Christian and Gnostic Christology.[46] He has also affirmed the central importance of Ezekiel's opening vision for understanding the origins and development of Christology.[47] There the prophet records that he saw the כבוד יהוה ("the Glory of YHWH") seated upon the chariot-throne and describes him as a "likeness as the appearance of a man" (1.26). Furthermore, Quispel has explained some of the complexities of Paul's Christology in light of traditions which grew in conjunction with the angelomorphic "Man" upon the throne in this vision of Ezekiel and related traditions.[48] The primary theses of his prolific and varied publications have been a foundation for further exploration in recent years.

C. Recent Research: The Influence of Divine Mediator Figures on Early Christology

The past two decades have witnessed a vigorous study of Jewish angelomorphic traditions which exalt various figures as divine mediators, even though much of NT scholarship remains

---

[45] See esp. his collected essays in *Gnostic Studies* (2 vols.; Istanbul: Nederlands Historisch-Archaeologisch Instituut, 1974 and 1975). Quispel's understanding of the role of Jewish Mysticism in the origins of Gnosticism (as well as Christianity) was influenced by G. Scholem; see esp. *Major Trends in Jewish Mysticism* (reprint of 3d ed.; New York: Schocken, 1974) 1-79.

[46] E.g., "Het Johannesevangelie en de Gnosis", *NedTTs* 11 (1956/57) 173-202.

[47] E.g., "Ezekiel 1:26 in Jewish Mysticism and Gnosis", *VC* 34 (1980), 1-13; "Judaism, Judaic Christianity and Gnosis", *The New Testament and Gnosis: Essays in Honour of Robert McL. Wilson* (eds. A. Logan and A. Wedderburn; Edinburgh: T&T Clark, 1983) 47-68; "Hermes Trismegistus and the Origins of Gnosticism", *VC* 46 (1992) 1-19.

[48] "Ezekiel 1:26 in Jewish Mysticism", 9-13, and "Hermetism and the New Testament, Especially Paul", *ANRW* II.22, forthcoming.

unconvinced about the crucial role these traditions played in the origin and development of Christology.[49] This research has been driven by four factors. First, there is a greater scholarly consensus concerning the diversity of first century Jewish religious thought and groups. Second, and intimately connected with this first point, a renewed interest in what were once considered sectarian, esoteric, and obscure Jewish texts has promoted new research directions. Updated translations of the OT Pseudepigrapha have been a significant boon to this interest.[50] Third, the plethora of new texts which have come to light in the past fifty years, especially from Qumran and Nag Hammadi, has given scholars a wider literary base from which to understand the Christological formulations of the NT and later Christianity. Four, a broader understanding of the "angel" or "angelomorphic" category has developed which includes less overt angel traditions (e.g., the "man" of Ezek 1.26, the "one like a son of man" in Dan 7.13, and exalted patriarchs like Enoch in *1 Enoch* 71). These factors have led several scholars to a more nuanced examination of the evidence.

In his slim volume on Son of God Christology, MARTIN HENGEL reviewed the various *Religionsgeschichtliche Schule* solutions that have been set forth over the years for the origins of Christology.[51] It is well-known from this study and others that Hengel is justifiably critical of many of these solutions, especially the late date for a developed Christology that is often advocated. Nevertheless, Hengel's historical rigor led him to affirm the importance of seeking the origins of Christological expressions in Jewish mediator figures which include the ideas of pre-existence, mediation at creation, and being sent into the world.[52]

---

[49] This topic has even become the focus of the newly formed SBL Group "Divine Mediators in Antiquity" each year since 1991 at the National meetings in the United States; see J. Fossum, "The New *Religionsgeschichtliche Schule*: The Quest for Jewish Christology", *SBLSP* 30 (1991) 638-646.

[50] E.g., the English translation of the *Old Testament Pseudepigrapha* edited by Charlesworth in 1983 and 1985.

[51] *The Son of God: The Origin of Christology and the History of Jewish-Hellenistic Religion* (trans. J. Bowden; London: SCM, 1983). For his most recent research, see *Studies in Early Christology* (Edinburgh: T&T Clark, 1995). His significant contributions to the study of Judaism are visible in *Judaism and Hellenism: Studies in their Encounter in Palestine in the Early Hellenistic Period* (trans. J. Bowden; 2 vols; Philadelphia: Fortress, 1974).

[52] *Son of God*, 66-76.

The question of the pivotal influence of Ezekiel 1 upon later authors who wrote about God's throne was the subject that brought CHRISTOPHER ROWLAND squarely to the question of how angelomorphic traditions impacted early Christology.[53] Among other things, his research has pointed out the development of an exalted angel tradition which is evidence for a bifurcation of God. Rowland points to the following texts as key expressions of this tradition: Ezek 1.26-28 depicts the Glory appearing on the divine throne as a man; Ezek 8.2 shows the Glory separating from the divine throne to act as a quasi-angelic mediator; Dan 7.9-13 portrays the Ancient of Days giving his power and authority to the "one like a son of man"; Dan 10.5-10 describes an angelic figure who is greater than other angels; Rev 1.13-17 pictures Christ with features of both the Glory and the Ancient of Days; and *Apoc. Ab.* 11.2-4 indicates that the angel Yahoel shares the divine throne in some fashion but functions as an divine agent.[54] Furthermore, Rowland has convincingly argued that the origins of Jewish apocalypses and later mystical literature lie primarily in the foundational prophetic visions of the heavenly world.[55]

In his examination of the *Sendungschristologie* in the Fourth Gospel, JAN-A. BÜHNER has carefully argued that the "sending" concept in John is founded upon the fusion of prophet and angel traditions.[56] Bühner posits that the tradition that influenced John centered around the belief in the Son of Man as an exalted angelic mediator who descended from heaven. He then argues that this idea was later combined with a prophetic portrait of Jesus as a

---

[53] "The Influence of the First Chapter of Ezekiel on Judaism and Early Christianity" (Ph.D. diss., University of Cambridge, 1975). Rowland builds on the research of O. Procksch, "Die Berufungsvision Hesekiels", *Karl Budde Festschrift* (BZAW 34; Giessen: Töpelmann, 1920), 141-149. Rowland's dissertation gave much impetus to his *The Open Heaven: A Study of Apocalyptic in Judaism and Early Christianity* (New York: Crossroad, 1982). See also: "The Visions of God in Apocalyptic Literature", *JSJ* 10 (1979) 137-154; "The Vision of the Risen Christ in Rev. i. 13ff.: The Debt of an Early Christology to an Aspect of Jewish Angelology", *JTS* 21 (1980) 1-11; "Apocalyptic Visions and the Exaltation of Christ in the Letter to the Colossians", *JSNT* 19 (1983) 73-83; "John 1.51, Jewish Apocalyptic and Targumic Tradition", *NTS* 30 (1984) 498-507; "A Man Clothed in Linen: Daniel 10.6ff. and Jewish Angelology", *JSNT* 24 (1985) 99-110.

[54] *Open Heaven*, esp. 94-113.

[55] *Open Heaven*, 199; see Isa 6.1-4, 1 Kgs 22.19, Ezek 1.1-28 (cf. Zech 1.1-6.15, Ezek 40.1-48.35).

[56] *Der Gesandte und sein Weg im 4. Evangelium* (WUNT 2/2; Tübingen: Mohr/Siebeck, 1977).

visionary who was about to ascend and experience transformation.[57] CHARLES TALBERT furthered research on the question of the "myth of a descending-ascending redeemer" by advocating Jewish angelology as important pre-Christian and pre-Gnostic evidence of such a pattern.[58] JOHN ASHTON has used Brühner's research recently to argue for the importance of the Angel of the Lord traditions in understanding the Gospel of John.[59] ROBERT PASCHAL, who also deals with the Fourth Gospel, has persuasively detailed the importance of angelic mediator traditions for understanding the technical terminology in John 17, such as "Glory" and "Name".[60]

Whereas Daniélou emphasized the relationship between Michael and Gabriel as the soil whence the Angelomorphic Christ and the Angel of the Spirit traditions grew, GEDALIAHU STROUMSA attempted to account for their angelomorphic character in the *Ascension of Isaiah* and in the teaching of Elchasai as a development from Jewish traditions surrounding the two cheribum upon the Ark of the Covenant.[61] Drawing on Philonic and rabbinic evidence, Stroumsa shows that the Ark was understood to be the Divine throne. Therefore, he argues that these two angels or powers who were part of the Ark were understood to share the throne of God and were the impetus for the Angel of the Son and the Angel of the Spirit. In other intriguing research, he argued for the value of *Shi'ur Qomah* ("Measure of the Body") mysticism in understanding descriptions of the Body of Christ present in the Pauline epistles.[62]

Although NIHLS DAHL has published very little on the subject, he has been an advocate for the importance of angelomorphic traditions in the early development of Christology.[63] One of his

---

[57] *Gesandte und sein Weg*, 341-370.
[58] "The Myth of a Descending-Ascending Redeemer in Mediterranean Antiquity", *NTS* 22 (1976) 418-439.
[59] *Studying John: Approaches to the Fourth Gospel* (Oxford: OUP, 1994) 71-89.
[60] "The Farewell Prayer of Jesus: A Study of the Gattung and the Religious Background of John 17" (Ph.D. diss., University of Cambridge, 1983).
[61] "Le couple de l'ange et de l'esprit: traditions juives et chrétiennes", *RB* 88 (1981), 42-61. For an alternate derivation for this tradition, see J. Fossum, "Jewish-Christian Christology and Jewish Mysticism", *VC* 7 (1983) 276-280.
[62] "Form(s) of God: Some Notes on Metatron and Christ", *HTR* 76 (1983) 269-288.
[63] An essay from years ago that advocates this idea, "Sources of Christological Language", has been published in his *Jesus The Christ: The Historical Origins of Christological Doctrine* (ed. D. Juel; Minneapolis: Fortress, 1991) 113-

students, ALAN SEGAL, has been much more prolific in this field of study. In his dissertation he probed the rabbinic polemic against "Two Powers in Heaven". His study led him through a labyrinth of texts which document evidence for an angelic being who was considered to be a "Power" sharing God's divinity and throne.[64] He argues that interpretations involving figures other than God on the throne in Jewish apocalyptic literature are the basis for later polemics and declarations of a "Two Powers" heresy. Furthermore, he has made substantial contributions to research on Jewish mystical traditions about heavenly ascent.[65] This research has also led him to demonstrate the influence of these traditions on both Paul's conversion and Christology.[66]

In a wide-ranging revision of his dissertation dealing with Samaritan and Jewish texts about intermediation, JARL FOSSUM developed and bore out the theory of his *Doktorvater*, Gilles Quispel, that the Gnostic demiurge developed from Jewish ideas about the hypostasized Divine Name and the Angel of the Lord (who possesses the Divine Name) as the agent of creation.[67] In more recent publications he has shown the pervasive influence of angel traditions within Jewish Christian Christology, including that of some NT documents.[68] His research on this subject has engaged

---

136, esp. 120-121. Dahl argues for the background of John in Jewish Mysticism in "The Johannine Church and History", *Current Issues in New Testament Interpretation: Essays in Honor of Otto A. Piper* (ed. W. Klassen and G. Snyder; New York: Harper, 1962) 124-142, esp. 131.

[64] *Two Powers in Heaven*; see also his collection of essays, *The Other Judaisms of Late Antiquity* (BJS 127; Atlanta: Scholars Press, 1987).

[65] "Heavenly Ascent in Hellenistic Judaism, Early Christianity, and Their Environments", *ANRW* II.23.2 (1980) 1332-1394.

[66] *Paul the Convert: The Apostolate and Apostasy of Saul the Pharisee* (New Haven: Yale University Press, 1990); see also "The Risen Christ and Angelic Mediator Figures in Light of Qumran", *Jesus and the Dead Sea Scrolls* (ed. J. H. Charlesworth; New York: Doubleday, 1992) 302-328.

[67] *The Name of God and the Angel of the Lord: Samaritan and Jewish Concepts of Intermediation and the Origin of Gnosticism* (WUNT 1/36; Tübingen: Mohr/Siebeck, 1985).

[68] E.g., "Jewish-Christian Christology and Jewish Mysticism", *VC* 37 (1983) 260-287; "Kyrios Jesus as the Angel of the Lord in Jude 5-7", *NTS* 33 (1987) 226-243; "Colossians 1.15-18a in the Light of Jewish Mysticism and Gnosticism", *NTS* 35 (1989) 183-201; "Son of God", *ABD* 6.128-137; "Son of God", *DDD* 659-668; "Glory", *DDD* 1486-1498. The Jude and Colossians articles have been revised and included with other essays in *The Image of the Invisible God: Essays on the Influence of Jewish Mysticism on Early Christology* (NTOA 30; Universitätsverlag Freiburg, Schweiz, and Vandenhoeck & Ruprecht, Göttingen, 1995).

the vast and often overlooked literature of Samaritanism, Jewish Mysticism, and Gnosticism. Fossum has been the leading advocate for a renewed religio-historical approach to the study of Christology among several scholars whom Martin Hengel has labeled the "New *Religionsgeschichtliche Schule*".[69]

LARRY HURTADO was in conversation with Segal, Rowland, and Fossum while researching and writing concerning early Christology and Jewish monotheism.[70] Although expressing disagreement with these scholars on their understanding of hypostases and the bifurcation of God (or incipient binitarianism), he nevertheless is in partial agreement with their approach.[71] Hurtado's work has emphasized that Jewish "divine agency" traditions were crucial for early Christian understandings of Jesus' exaltation. He argues that their understanding of Jesus as God's chief agent produced a "distinctive" modification in Jewish monotheism which is visible in the worship of Jesus alongside God.[72] He has been an untiring advocate for the role that divine agency played in assisting early Jewish Christians to understand and worship the exalted Jesus.

CHRISTOPHER MORRAY-JONES, one of Rowland's students, has argued carefully and convincingly that the Hekhalot literature contains evidence of earlier mystical traditions dating from the first and second centuries CE.[73] His research is foundational in establishing the value of this literary corpus for NT exegesis. Through some substantial articles that show the background of an important element of Paul's thought in Jewish transformational mysticism, he has also shown how his research can be applied to the NT.[74]

---

[69] See Fossum's discussion in "New *Religionsgeschichtliche Schule*"
[70] See esp. his *One God, One Lord: Early Christian Devotion and Ancient Jewish Monotheism* (Philadelphia: Fortress, 1988).
[71] For these differences see *One God*, esp. 36-38, 85-90, and "What Do We Mean by 'First Century Jewish Monotheism'?", SBLSP 32 (1993) 348-368.
[72] *One God*, 12. Evidence of such veneration is visible, according to Hurtado, in early texts (e.g., Rom 1.3-4; 10.9-10; 8.15; 1 Cor 16.22; Gal 4.6; Col 1.15-20; Phil 2.5-11). In his emphasis on worship as the distinctive evidence of mutation in monotheism he follows R. Bauckham, "The Worship of Jesus in Apocalyptic Christianity", NTS 27 (1980-81) 322-341.
[73] "Merkabah Mysticism and Talmudic Tradition" (Ph.D. diss., University of Cambridge, 1988); see also "Transformational Mysticism in the Apocalyptic-Merkabah Tradition", JJS 43 (1992) 1-31.
[74] "Paradise Revisited (2 Cor 12:1-12): The Jewish Mystical Background of Paul's Apostolate" HTR 86 (1993) 177-217 ("Part 1: The Jewish Sources") and 265-292 ("Part 2: Paul's Heavenly Ascent and Its Significance").

Along a similar research direction is the substantial article by ANDREW CHESTER which argues that mediatoral figures are an important part of the background of Pauline Christology.[75] The strength of Chester's discussion is his citation of Jewish messianic and mediatorial texts; unfortunately, his demonstration of their impact on Pauline Christology is very terse. Also helpful is his critique of Hurtado on three points: Hurtado's emphasis on functional categories in discussing mediatorial figures to the exclusion of ontological status; worship as the sole criterion of divinity to the exclusion of divine functions and appearance; and the universality of strict monotheism within first century Judaism because the situation is not that clear, based upon present evidence.[76]

The published dissertation of CAREY NEWMAN carefully explores the semantic background, origin, and use of "Glory" terminology in the Pauline corpus.[77] He begins with a detailed tradition history of the concept "Glory" to demonstrate that it became a defined concept full of semantic signification before the time of Paul (i.e., the presence of God as a man-like figure). He convincingly proves that Paul identified Christ as "the Glory" and proposes that the experience of Paul's conversion Christophany was the primary motivation for this understanding.[78]

Insights into Paul's identification of Christ as the visible manifestation of God have been furthered by the research of DAVID CAPES on Paul's use of OT YHWH texts in expressing his Christology.[79] Capes shows that in several instances Paul applied OT texts to Jesus which originally had YHWH as their referent. Furthermore, he draws on the research of Segal and others to assert that the license for this conceptual overlap is found in Jewish angel traditions and in Paul's identification of Christ as the Glory. CARL DAVIS took a similar research direction by examining the use of Isa 40.3 ("prepare the way of the LORD") and Joel 2.32[3.5]a ("call on the name of the LORD") in pre-Christian Judaism and then

---

[75] "Jewish Messianic Expectations and Mediatorial Figures and Pauline Christology", *Paulus und das antike Judentum* (eds. M. Hengel and U. Heckel; Tübingen: Mohr/Siebeck, 1991) 17-89.

[76] Chester, "Jewish Messianic Expectations", 63-65.

[77] "Glory of God in the Face of Jesus" (Ph.D. diss., Baylor University, 1989). It has been revised and published as *Paul's Glory-Christology: Tradition and Rhetoric* (NovTSup 69; Leiden: Brill, 1992).

[78] *Paul's Glory-Christology*, 241-47.

[79] *Old Testament Yahweh Texts in Paul's Christology* (WUNT 2/47; Tübingen: Mohr/Siebeck, 1992).

compared this usage with the NT application of these texts to Jesus.[80] He affirms the importance of "second figures" such as the Angel of the Lord, Glory of the Lord, Word of the Lord, and Wisdom for understanding first century monotheism and the acknowledgement of Jesus as God.[81] Davis misses the key points, however, that Jesus was understood as the Angel of the Lord and the hypostatized Divine Name by several first century Christians.[82]

With insightful assertions that are peppered with generalizations about a vast array of evidence for binitarianism in Jewish and early Christian literature, MARGARET BARKER advocates a relatively uniform "Great Angel" tradition which has its origin in YHWH as the lesser deity under the supreme God of Ancient Israel (El Elyon, El, Elohim).[83] This construct is problematic since YHWH and El were clearly united in Jewish literature long before the first century. In spite of this problem, her provocative research centers on many of the crucial texts and questions of Angelomorphic Christology.

JONATHAN KNIGHT, another student of Rowland, made a welcome contribution to the study of Angelomorphic Christology through his research on the *Ascension of Isaiah*, a second century Jewish Christian document which draws heavily on Jewish angelology.[84] He demonstrates that the Beloved One (Jesus) is presented as an angelomorphic being who both shares God's divinity and is subordinate to God.[85] In this process he also argues for the broader thesis that these same angelomorphic antecedents are important factors in earlier first century Christology.[86]

PETER CARRELL and LOREN STUCKENBRUCK both wrote dissertations recently that dealt with the Angelomorphic Christology in

---

[80] *The Name and Way of the Lord: Old Testament Themes, New Testament Christology* (JSNTSup 129; Sheffield: Sheffield Academic Press, 1996).

[81] *Name and Way*, esp. 28-60.

[82] *Name and Way*, esp. 38 and 180. For much evidence of Jesus as the hypostatized Divine Name in early Christian texts, see 187-346 below.

[83] *The Great Angel: A Study of Israel's Second God* (Louisville: Westminster/John Knox, 1992).

[84] His 1991 Ph.D. dissertation (University of Cambridge) was revised and published as *Disciples of the Beloved One: The Christology, Social Setting and Theological Context of the Ascension of Isaiah* (JSPSup 18; Sheffield: Sheffield Academic Press, 1996). He also wrote a brief introduction to this apocalypse entitled *The Ascension of Isaiah* (Sheffield: Sheffield Academic Press, 1995).

[85] *Disciples of the Beloved One*, 71-185.

[86] *Disciples of the Beloved One*, 74, 125-139.

Revelation.[87] Stuckenbruck researched the phenomenon of angel worship based upon a form-critical study of the angel worship prohibitions in Revelation and other literature.[88] His conclusion, which is of substantial significance, is that the veneration of angels in some Jewish groups "may have provided an underlying model behind the accommodation of monotheistic belief to Christology" in Revelation.[89] Carrell's study of Jewish antecedents and select texts of Revelation affirms the conclusion that Jewish angelology influenced the Christology of this apocalypse.[90] The value of his study, however, is weakened substantially by his emphasis on the "temporary" nature of these angelic depictions of Christ in Revelation.[91] In contrast to Carrell's cautious approach, ROBERT GUNDRY argues that Angelomorphic Christology is found not only in Rev 1.13-16, 14.1, and 19.11-16, but also in Rev 10.1-11, 18.1-3, 18.21-24, and 20.1-3.[92]

Crispin Fletcher-Louis, under the guidance of Rowland, has broken new ground by using angelomorphic traditions to understand the Christology and soteriology of Luke-Acts.[93] He goes far beyond the well-used transfiguration and resurrection narratives to argue for the angelomorphic depiction of the earthly Jesus in Luke-Acts. A significant amount of his research focuses on Jewish traditions about angelomorphic humans and the assistance they provide in understanding Lukan soteriology in terms of angelic transformation. In his discussion of both Christology and

---

[87] Both dissertations are now published: P. Carrell, *Jesus and the angels: Angelology and the christology of the Apocalypse of John* (SNTSMS 95; Cambridge: CUP, 1997), and L. Stuckenbruck, *Angel Veneration and Christology: A Study in Early Judaism and in the Christology of the Apocalypse of John* (WUNT 2/70; Tübingen: Mohr/Siebeck, 1995).

[88] For a helpful list of these texts, see the appendix in *Angel Veneration and Christology*, 275-283; see also his "An Angel Refusal of Worship: The Tradition and Its Function in the Apocalyse of John", *SBLSP* 33 (1994) 679-696.

[89] *Angel Veneration and Christology*, 273.

[90] Carrell sees the influence of angelology in Rev 1.13-16, 14.14, and 19.11-16; see *Jesus and the angels*, 129-219.

[91] *Jesus and the angels*, 224-226. Visions are "temporary" by their very nature. These visions, however, were meant to be written down so that they would give "enduring" insight into the person and work of Christ.

[92] "Angelomorphic Christology in the Book of Revelation", *SBLSP* 33 (1994) 662-678.

[93] *Luke-Acts: Angels, Christology and Soteriology* (Wunt 2/94; Tübingen: Mohr/Siebeck, 1997).

Soteriology, Fletcher-Louis is careful to emphasize Luke's own peculiar adaptation of angelomorphic traditions.[94]

The past two decades have witnessed a substantial growth in research and publication on the subject of angelomorphic traditions and their impact on first century Christology. The examination of antecedents and early evidence of Angelomorphic Christology which follows will evaluate, build upon, and make additional contributions to this growing body of research.[95]

---

[94] *Luke-Acts*, esp. 248-250.
[95] Although this manuscript was originally a dissertation written prior to 1995, I have attempted to bring the bibliography up-to-date and integrate recent publications where possible. The work of Carrell and Fletcher-Louis, unfortunately, reached me very late in this process.

CHAPTER TWO

NOMENCLATURE AND METHODOLOGY

Various methodologies and uses of terminology have become apparent through the discussion of past research. False conclusions and confusion can result from imprecise nomenclature and poor methodology. Therefore, the determinative nomenclature and methodology for this study will be set forth in this chapter. Because of current debate about the "divinity" of angelomorphic figures, the veneration of angels, and the use of the word "hypostasis", these three topics will be given separate and more extensive attention. The discussion of methodology will conclude with a brief preview of the scope of this study.

A. *Religious Group Nomenclature*

Scholars have used the term "Judaism" in a very confused manner during the past several decades. What was biasly titled "Late Judaism" a few decades ago (leading into "Early Christianity") is now titled by various scholars: "Early Judaism", "Ancient Judaism", "Second Temple Judaism", or "Middle Judaism".[1] A solution to this diverse nomenclature is not easy. For purposes of this study we will use JUDAISM to denote that religious phenomenon that began with the Babylonian Exile (586 BCE) and continued beyond the destruction of the Second Temple (70 CE), after which it gave birth to Rabbinism.[2] To use the language of taxonomy, Judaism properly denotes the *genus* which is made up of various *species*, or JUDAISMS, which are competing movements or groups (such as first century Pharisaism, Essenism, Samaritanism, and Christianity). ISRAELITE RELIGION is the *genus* out of which Judaism originally grew and it encompasses the multi-faceted phenomenon "Israel" from the time of Abraham to the Babylonian Exile. The

---

[1] See G. Boccaccini, *Middle Judaism: Jewish Thought 300 BCE to 200 CE* (Philadelphia: Fortress, 1991) 7-25.
[2] A. Segal, *Rebecca's Children: Judaism and Christianity in the Roman World* (Cambridge, MA: Harvard University Press, 1986).

adjective JEWISH will be used to designate the diverse literature and culture of people who identified themselves in some way with Judaism. There are three primary *branches* which grew out of Judaism in the first and second centuries CE: Samaritanism, Christianity, and Rabbinism (the term "Rabbinic Judaism" will not be used in order to prevent the impression that it is the only legitimate "child" of Judaism). Each of these *branches* became its own *genus*. RABBINISM took shape after the destruction of the temple in 70 CE and expresses itself through allegiance to the Dual Torah (the Pentateuch and the Mishnah). The term CHRISTIANITY is used with the understanding that it was closely related to Judaism in its earliest decades as it became its own *genus*.

B. Angel Nomenclature

ANGEL is an English term that has the basic meaning "messenger" and the technical meaning "a spirit or heavenly being who mediates between the human and divine realms". It typically will be used in the latter sense within this study, with sensitivity to pluralistic usage within the texts that will be examined. Several theophanies of the OT identify God as an angel, but not always with the same phrase.[3] To prevent confusion amid the various ways that these traditions can be referred to in English translation (e.g., the mal'ak YHWH, the Angel of YHWH, the Angel of the LORD, the Angel of God), this study will refer to this figure associated with these variegated traditions as THE ANGEL OF THE LORD unless making a point regarding the original language of the text(s). The presentation of Hebrew texts in English, however, will transliterate the divine names rather than translate them (e.g., YHWH, El, Elohim).

ANGELOLOGY will be used in a very general sense to refer to the diverse ideas about angels. Its usage in this study does not imply the existence of a uniform doctrinal system concerning angels. ANGELOMORPHIC is an inclusive adjective which describes a phenomenon that has the variegated form and functions

---

[3] The Angel of YHWH is most frequent (Gen 16.7-14; 22.11-15; Exod 3.1-14; 14.19-20; Num 22.22-35; Judg 2.1-4; 5.23; 6.11-24; 13.3-21), but there are several occurrences of the Angel of Elohim (Gen 21.17; 31.11; Exod 14.19; Judg 6.20; 13.6, 9); see discussion on 51-69 below.

of an angel, even though the figure may not be explicitly identified as an angel. In Jewish and early Christian thought an angel often manifests himself in the form of a man, but also may take on some other form, such as a winged creature (Isa 6.2-7; Ezek 1.4-14), a fire (Exod 3.2), or a cloud (Philo, *Vita Mos* 1.166; cf. Exod 14.19). Furthermore, angels are sometimes pictured from a cosmological perspective as stars, especially in apocalyptic literature.[4] Because angels often appear in the form of men, the distinction between what is anthropomorphic and what is angelomorphic is difficult to maintain. What one person may interpret as an anthropomorphism, another could see as a concrete description of an angelomorphic figure (e.g., "YHWH is a *man* of war" in Exod 15.3).

ANGEL CHRISTOLOGY is the explicit identification of Jesus Christ as an angel. ANGELOMORPHIC CHRISTOLOGY is the identification of Christ with angelic form and functions, either before or after the incarnation, whether or not he is specifically identified as an angel. Christopher Rowland has asserted the value of such a distinction:

> It is probably a mistake simply to talk of angel-christology, at least in the primitive period, without further qualification. It is, in my view, more appropriate to speak of angelomorphic christology in the earliest period. This kind of description in no way implies that Christ was identified entirely with the created order. There is an implicit recognition, that, while there may indeed be a *prima facie* case for the transference of angelomorphic categories in passages like Mark 9.2ff. and Rev. 1.13ff this need not necessarily mean that Christ was identified as an angel, if by that is meant a being ontologically distinct from God.[5]

Rowland emphasizes the fact that angelic form, function, or terminology does not of necessity imply created ontology. Tertullian appears to be the first Christian to write about this distinction.[6] For him Christ was an angel according to function, but not ontology, since angels were generally understood to be created beings. One should note, however, that the ontological distinction between angel and deity is not consistently clear in many texts. This is especially apparent because several texts identify the figure of the

---

[4] E.g., 1 Kgs 22.19 (cf. 2 Chr 18.18); Ps 103.21; Neh 9.6; Dan 8.10, 12.1; *1 En.* 18.14, 104.2-6; Rev 1.16, 12.4; *L.A.B.* 15.2, 31.1, 32.14-18; see also F. Lelli, "Star", *DDD* 1530-1540.
[5] "A Man Clothed in Linen", 100.
[6] *De carne Christi* 14.

theophany as the Angel of the Lord.[7] Therefore, angelomorphic depictions of Christ, and even texts which explicitly identify him as an angel, do not signify that the author understood him to be from the ranks of created angels or even ontologically distinct from God.

There is some inconsistent use in scholarship of the terms ANGELOPHANY (a manifestation of an angel), THEOPHANY (a manifestation of God), EPIPHANY (a manifestation, especially of a supernatural figure), and CHRISTOPHANY (a manifestation of Christ. Distinguishing between angelophanies and theophanies is at times very difficult. Furthermore, it is also important to distinguish between epiphanic texts which present a tangible manifestation of God on earth and those texts which present a vision of God to the visionary while he is on earth or after he has been mystically transported to heaven. An *ANGELUS INTERPRES* is an angel who interprets a vision or dream for someone and may function as a guide or revealer during a visionary or mystical experience (e.g., Uriel in *4 Ezra*).

APOCALYPTICISM is concerned with the disclosure of divine mysteries about what is above and below as well as what has happened and will happen.[8] One of the focal points of Apocalyptic literature is the realm of heaven, especially the divine throne room. JEWISH MYSTICISM developed from this aspect of apocalypticism since it focuses on the mysteries of heaven and ways that one can gain knowledge of these mysteries.[9] There are two types of Jewish Mysticism that will be encountered in the pages ahead. *MERKABAH* ("chariot") Mysticism has the divine throne-chariot featured in Ezekiel 1 as its focus.[10] *SHI'UR QOMAH* ("measure of the stature") mysticism focuses on the body of the Glory that may become visible during mystical experiences.[11]

---

[7] See discussion on 51-69 below.

[8] See Rowland, *Open Heaven*, 271. Rowland correctly emphasizes that apocalyptic literature is much more than eschatology.

[9] For an introduction to the field, see Scholem, *Major Trends*, 1-79. For the use of Jewish Mysticism in NT studies, see Fossum, *Image of the Inivisble God*, 1-11.

[10] See I. Gruenwald, *Apocalyptic and Merkavah Mysticism* (AGJU 4; Leiden: Brill 1980), and P. Schäfer, *The Hidden and Manifest God: Some Major Themes in Jewish Mysticism* (trans. A. Pomerance; Albany: SUNY, 1992). This type of literature also has concerns for the *hekhaloth* ("palaces") one must pass through before viewing the *Merkabah*.

[11] See the works by M. Cohen: *The Shi'ur Qomah: Liturgy and Theurgy in Pre-Kabbalistic Jewish Mysticism* (New York: University Press of America, 1983),

C. *Divinity Nomenclature*

Using the term MONOTHEISM to describe first century CE Jewish belief in one God can be problematic.[12] Several scholars have acknowledged the difficulty in asserting a blanket "strict monotheism" among Jews of this period, given the textual evidence of intermediation:

> Much attention has been devoted to mediatorial figures in Judaism, because of the possible contribution they may have made to nascent Christology. What is becoming clear is that we cannot blithely assume that there was a clear-cut monotheistic theology which was adhered to by all Jews. The gap between early Christian theology and pre-Christian Jewish theology is not as wide as is sometimes assumed.[13]

Some scholars have argued that the criteria for distinguishing divine status should be based solely on worship or cultic veneration.[14] No one disputes the grave importance of worship practices as a definite signal of divinity, nor can one disagree that the worship of Jesus by Jewish Christians was a significant development within so-called Jewish monotheism. Most scholars also agree that flexibility existed within at least some expressions of Jewish monotheism which allowed for very exalted mediator figures.[15]

It is not proper, however, to force depictions of angelomorphic mediators to fit our categories. These texts testify to a *variety* of imagery and language used to describe the relationship between God and these angelomorphic mediators. Rather than limiting the ascription of divinity to mediators who are cultically venerated, we must allow the texts themselves to define what ideas are significant indicators of divinity. As will be demonstrated through the analysis of texts in the chapters below, there are five CRITERIA OF

---

and *The Shi'ur Qomah: Texts and Recensions* (Tübingen: Mohr/Siebeck, 1985).

[12] See esp. Stuckenbruck, *Angel Veneration and Christology*, 15-21.

[13] Rowland, *Christian Origins*, 36.

[14] See: Bauckham, "The Worship of Jesus", 322-341, revised and reprinted in *The Climax of Prophecy* (Edinburgh: T&T Clark, 1993) 118-149; Hurtado, *One God*, 93-124; and Olyan, *A Thousand Thousands*, 91-98.

[15] Hurtado does not acknowledge any significant modifications of Jewish monotheistic belief and practice before Christian veneration of Jesus; see *One God*, 36-38, 85-90. He argues against the textual evidence of Jewish veneration of agents such as divine attributes, exalted angels, or exalted patriarchs (e.g., Moses in *Ezekiel the Tragedian*). He appears to have softened his position recently by at least acknowledging the "flexibility" of pre-Christian Jewish monotheism; see "First Century Jewish Monotheism", 355.

DIVINITY that are used in texts. These criteria may be used either individually or in combination to assert the divinity of a mediator alongside God, a mediator who usually is not completely separate from God.

First, the *Divine Position* criterion: Is the angelomorphic mediator positioned with or near God or his throne? Segal's research on the "Two Powers in Heaven" controversy has helped to emphasize the interest that exegetes had in a second figure sharing the divine throne in Judaism, Christianity, and Rabbinism.[16] The divine throne belonged to God alone. Therefore, divine status is usually accorded to the sole occupant sitting on the divine throne, the one who sits on the divine throne with God, or the one who sits on a similar throne that is alongside the divine throne.[17]

In contrast, *standing* around God's throne is the typical position of angels in Jewish apocalyptic literature.[18] Standing is also the posture of the righteous who receive angelic status.[19] "Standing Ones" is even a title for angels in Samaritanism.[20] There is, however, some evidence that standing next to God, or the divine throne, is an action that may signify more than angelic status. God, especially in Philonic and Samaritan literature, is described as "the Standing One" (קים; ὁ ἑστώς).[21] Thus, some texts may indicate a position of divinity through the position of standing near God.[22]

---

[16] *Two Powers in Heaven*, 3-32.

[17] E.g., Moses takes over the throne in *Ezek. Trag.* 68-80; Jesus shares the throne in Rev 7.15-17; the "one like a son of man" is probably seated in a throne near the Ancient of Days due to the mention of "thrones" in Dan 7.9; and the Beloved and the Angel of the Holy Spirit are seated in thrones alongside the Great Glory in *Ascen. Is.* 11.32-33.

[18] E.g., *1 En.* 39.12, 40.1, 47.3, 68.2; *2 En.* 21.1; *T. Ab.* 7.11, 8.1; cf. *1 En.* 49.2.

[19] E.g., *Ascen. Is.* 9.9-10; *2 En.* 22.10. This posture of the angels also influenced the description of the encratites found in the *Gospel of Thomas* as "standing" (L. 16, 18); see A. De Conick, *Seek to See Him: Ascent and Vision Mysticism in the Gospel of Thomas* (SupVC 33; Leiden: Brill, 1996) 89-93.

[20] *The Samaritan Liturgy* 54.31 (ed. A.E. Cowley) contains this title for the angels and describes Moses as "standing" with them; see esp. Fossum, *Name of God*, 55-58, 120-124, 139-141.

[21] This title probably originates from Deut 5.31 where God invites Moses to "stand" by him as he delivers the Law. Whereas Philo uses this title as a philosophical concept to emphasize the immutability of God (*Post* 27-31), Samaritanism uses it to emphasize God's eternal nature (*Samaritan Liturgy* 27.18 and *Memar Marqa* IV.12), from which Simonianism and Dositheans adapted this divine title for respective leaders (*Ps-Clem. Hom.* II.22); see Fossum, *Name of God*, 55-58; 120-130.

[22] E.g., Stephen sees the Glory of God, namely Jesus, "standing" at the right hand of God (Acts 7.55-56).

Second, the *Divine Appearance* criterion: Does the angelomorphic figure have the physical characteristics of God's visible form as depicted in various theophanies? For example: Isa 6.1-4 shows the Lord sitting on a throne, with a long train, and smoke is swirling around; Ezek 1.26-28 shows the Glory of YHWH in the likeness of a man with a gleaming bronze upper torso and firey lower parts, with a bright rainbow round about him; Dan 7.9 describes the Ancient of Days with raiment as white as snow and hair like pure wool. When these kinds of distinctive descriptions of God's visible form are used to describe an angelomorphic figure, divinity may be implied.

Concerning appearance, it is also possible that the *size* of an angelomorphic figure had some impact on his status. The huge form that an angel can assume is apparent in the depiction of the Angel of the Lord in 1 Chr 21.16. Other angelomorphic figures are portrayed as gigantic: the Word/the Destroyer (Wis 18.15-21); the Watchers (*T. Reu.* 5.7; cf. CD 2.19); the Son of God (Rev 10.1-11, 14.14; *Hermas Sim.* VII.1.2, IX.2.1, IX.3.1, IX.6.1; *Gos. Pet.* 40; *Ascen. Is.* 3.17); the Angel of the Son and the Angel of the Spirit (Book of Elchesai in Hippolytus, *Ref.* 9.13.2-3); and Metatron (*3 En.* 9.5). The relationship of some of these accounts to Jewish mystical literature that portrays the vastness of the visible form or body of God, such as implied by God's assertion through Isaiah that "the heavens are my seat and the earth my footstool" (66.1), suggests that some of these angelic figures are depicted with divine status.[23] These ideas about the large form or body of God are portrayed very vividly in *Shi'ur Qomah* Mysticism.[24]

Third, the *Divine Functions* criterion: Does the angelomorphic figure carry out an act, or actions, typically ascribed to God? There are many actions associated with God that are often carried out by angels: providential care of the cosmos, protecting the righteous, punishing evil, answering prayers, and similar activity. Other functions are typically limited to God himself; these include creating the world, absolving sins, and pronouncing eschatological judgment. The assigning of one or more of these typically divine functions to an angelomorphic figure is a significant statement about his identity and status.

---

[23] See also Pss 29.1-11, 95.3-5, 96.6, and Isa 40.12.
[24] See discussion on 29 above. Isa 66.1 is a key text in the *Shi'ur Qomah*.

Fourthly, the *Divine Name* criterion: Does the mediator possess the Name of God or is he seen as an hypostasis of the Divine Name? The Divine Name YHWH is of the essence of Israel's God. Therefore, the one who is identified as possessing this Divine Name should be understood as sharing in the very authority and essence of YHWH (Exod 23.20-21). As will be shown, this is a very prominent idea in the portrayal of Jewish and Christian angelomorphic mediators. Furthermore, one should also be sensitive to the possibility of the personal name of the angelomorphic mediator implying a divine status (e.g., Yahoel in *Apocalypse of Abraham*).

Fifthly, the *Divine Veneration* criterion: Is the angelomorphic figure the object of some form of veneration? We are limited to literary evidence, which usually does not reveal a group's religious praxis concerning angel veneration. Several textual details, however, may indicate veneration. Is there a worship posture shown towards the angelomorphic figure? Are praise and prayer offered to him (solely or in conjunction with God)? Does the angelomorphic figure accept or refuse the veneration? Is his name given cultic status alongside the Divine Name? One should remember that there may be various degrees of veneration in these texts.

The presence of one or more of these five criteria in a text may indicate that the angelomorphic mediator figure was understood to share God's status, authority, and nature. The Jewish understanding of God during this period was certainly more complex than the issue of worshiping one God. Because of the weight given to the Divine Veneration criterion by some scholars, this criterion merits further attention and detail.

D. *Veneration Nomenclature*

The general consensus among scholars has been that there is very little significant evidence for veneration of angels within Judaism, early Christianity, and Rabbinism. Separate studies by Loren Stuckenbruck and Clinton Arnold, which were published in 1995, masterfully present evidence that successfully refutes this consensus.[25] Neither of these scholars argue that there is evidence in first

---

[25] See C. Arnold, *The Colossian Syncretism: The Interface Between Christianity and Folk Belief in Colossae* (WUNT 2/77; Tübingen: Mohr/Siebeck, 1995) 8-102, and Stuckenbruck, *Angel Veneration and Christology*, 47-204.

and second century CE Judaism and Christianity for the worship of angels taking the place of the worship of God. Both conclude, however, that there were *specific* individuals and groups who venerated angels, sometimes privately, in a manner that usually was not seen as a substitute for the worship of God.[26] Thus, both speak of the *veneration*, instead of the *worship*, of angels.

Stuckenbruck's interest in the refusal tradition in Revelation led him on an extensive journey through polemical and non-polemical texts, primarily Jewish or Christian, related to angel veneration. After carefully surveying this textual evidence, he summarizes three basic types of venerative activity that are found in extant texts:

> (1) Invocation of angels for assistance, vengeance or protection.
> (2) Reverence of angels whose heavenly worship is exemplary.
> (3) Expressions of thanksgiving in response to various functions or activities attributed to angels.[27]

Arnold's interest in understanding the "Colossian heresy", especially the meaning of "worship of angels" in Col 2.18, led him to cover some similar ground. Because he is studying angel veneration in Asia Minor in the first-third centuries CE, he examines more magical and pagan texts than Stuckenbruck, but does no analysis of the refusal tradition in apocalyptic texts. Although they disagree on their understanding of the worship of angels mentioned in Col 2.18, Arnold draws similar conclusions about the Jewish evidence.[28] He finds substantial evidence that some Jews invoked or called upon angels for help, often without reference to YHWH. Moreover, these Jews who called upon angels were asking for more than deliverance from evil spirits; they also sought revelation about the future and specific answers to life (such as how to find a mate or curse an enemy). Arnold characterizes this practice of "apotropaic magic" as *private* and argues that it is the result of a pervasive fear of malevolent powers. Michael was by far the most frequently invoked angel, but Arnold did not find evidence that Michael or any of the other angels became the center of cultic veneration jointly with God.

Struckenbruck also examined the important evidence that cautions against angel veneration and deduces from it that particular "[. . .] contexts were thought to be capable of breeding an

---

[26] Stuckenbruck, *Angel Veneration and Christology*, 201-202.
[27] *Angel Veneration and Christology*, 200-201.
[28] For these conclusions see his *Colossian Syncretism*, esp. 59-60.

unhealthy posture which threatened monotheistic belief".[29] He outlines four such contexts:

>   (1) The invocation of a prominent angel "in a time of distress".
>   (2) Observation of, or participation in, angel worship.
>   (3) An angelophany during an ascent to the divine throne.
>   (4) Settings with "cultic" overtones.[30]

The bulk of the evidence that Stuckenbruck examined involves the refusal tradition (i.e., where an angel informs the human not to worship him).[31] It is reasonable to opine that such prohibitions ostensibly presuppose the practice in some form. Stuckenbruck offers this balanced conclusion on this probability:

> These observations do not leave much room for a conclusion that the refusal tradition constitutes evidence for a polemic against a veritable angel "cult." But it is possible to suggest that it may have functioned as *a critique from within* which recognized a danger of angels thought to be encountered in heavenly journeys. Since the application of the refusal tradition leaves no trace that the notion of an angel's striking appearance is being questioned, we may assume that the author and the position being opposed shared common angelological ideas. At the same time, the intensity of the refusal is hard to explain without positing some form of underlying venerative behavior which may have been deemed appropriate towards God's messengers, an attitude which at least the proponents would probably not have considered destructive to a belief in God. We may suppose that the refusal tradition found its *Sitz im Leben* as a response to such a posture. Hence in the refusal tradition we encounter a form which—if its use in Revelation, the *Apocalypse of Zephaniah*, and the *Ascension of Isaiah* and its varied adaption in further early Jewish and Christian writings are any indication— was well-known, indeed, was flourishing among various Jewish and Christian circles by the late first-early second century CE.[32]

Therefore, veneration of an angelomorphic figure alongside God may involve various degrees or combinations of the following: an exalted portrayal that ascribes divinity, in some manner, to an angelomorphic figure; the assumption of a worship posture before the angel (a posture which results from more than initial fear); the invocation of an angel for help; a fascination for, or participation in, the worship offered by angels to God; expressions of

---

[29] *Angel Veneration and Christology*, 202.
[30] *Angel Veneration and Christology*, 202.
[31] See Stuckenbruck's helpful summary of the evidence in *Angel Veneration and Christology*, 275-283.
[32] *Angel Veneration and Christology*, 102-103.

thanksgiving directed to an angel; and a song of praise about an angel.

E. *Hypostasis Nomenclature*

The complex relationship between God and the Angel of the Lord, or the relationship between God and some of his divine attributes, has brought the term hypostasis into use for the past century. Many scholars have used it as a label for a divine attribute that is identified with God and yet has some degree of independent identity. A significant debate over defining this phenomenon and its usage has developed among biblical scholars in recent decades.[33] The discussion centers on whether particular divine attributes of God in Israelite Religion and Judaism (e.g., the Name, the Glory, Wisdom) are essentially linguistic personifications or whether they take on a relatively independent identity in certain texts. While hypostasis has a long history of usage, several recent studies strongly question its value in the discussion of divine attributes. For example, Saul Olyan asserts that "[. . .] these expressions [hypostasis and hypostatization] are best avoided in light of the history of their use and abuse in biblical scholarship".[34]

The result has been the introduction of generalized nomenclature, such as "personified divine attributes" or "special figurative treatment of divine attributes". This nomenclature, however, is not adequate to describe the *independent identity* of divine attributes which is present in many texts and also in the later exegesis of those texts.[35] Although we may be convinced that a particular text contains personification according to our literary and theological categories, we still need to be historians who look at how earlier exegetes understood this phenomenon. Then we need to use terminology that is descriptive of their—not our own—understanding. It is often more profitable to refine terminology than to discard it and create new nomenclature. Thus, the extended discussion which follows reviews the debate and defines "hypostasis" for this study.

Hypostasis (ὑπόστασις) in the philosophical context has the basic meaning of "a reality" and in practice often means "an *individual*

---

[33] E.g., Hurtado, *One God*, 41-50, 85-90.
[34] *A Thousand Thousands*, 88; see also 89-115.
[35] Olyan, *A Thousand Thousands*, 88.

reality or thing".³⁶ This word is most familiar to theologians in the context of the development of Trinitarian thought, although it has some biblical usage.³⁷ Its usage underwent modification by Origen who no longer used the term for God as an hypostasis ("individual reality"), but rather spoke of the three hypostases ("individual persons") of God.³⁸ J. N. D. Kelly states:

> *Hupostasis* and *ousia* were originally synonyms, the former Stoic and the latter Platonic, meaning real existence or essence, that which a thing is; but while *hupostasis* retains this connotation in Origen, he more frequently gives it the sense of individual subsistence, and so individual existence.³⁹

After the Arians emphasized the teaching of three distinct hypostases at Nicea (325 CE), Athanasius and others counteracted this understanding by treating ὑπόστασις and οὐσία ("substance") as virtual synonyms.⁴⁰ A later compromise at the Council of Alexandria (362 CE) allowed for talk of three hypostases, provided that there was no emphasis on distinct substances between the three. The Cappadocian Fathers taught that an hypostasis is a person (i.e., the special form in which the divine substance exists). The Greek ὑπόστασις was later replaced by the Latin *persona* ("person, individual being"). This varied usage in Christian dogma, no doubt, has contributed to some rejection of hypostasis nomenclature in the discussion of divine attributes.

The scholar who furthered usage of hypostasis nomenclature in biblical studies is Wilhelm Bousset. He understood hypostases as intermediary beings, much like angels:

> Die »Hypostasen« sind wie die Engel Mittelwesen zwischen Gott und Welt, die sein Wirken auf die Welt ermöglichen. Sie sind nur abstrakter, schemenhafter, schwerer zu fassen, als die derben und anschaulichen Gestalten des volkstümlichen Engelglaubens. Sie erscheinen also Mitteldinge zwischen Personen und abstrakten Wesen, nicht so losgelöst von Gott wie die konkreten Engelgestalten, mehr mit seinem Wesen verschmolzen und zu ihm gehörig, aber doch wieder gesondert gedacht, seltsame Zwitterbildungen eines kindlichen, zur vollen Abstraktion noch unfähigen Denkens.⁴¹

---

36 C. Stead, *Divine Substance* (Oxford: OUP, 1977) ix.
37 See 2 Cor 9.4; 11.17; Heb 1.3; 3.14; 11.1; Wis 16.21.
38 See the discussion by J.N.D. Kelly, *Early Christian Doctrines* (rev. ed.; San Francisco: Harper, 1978) 129-140.
39 *Early Christian Doctrines*, 129.
40 Kelly, *Early Christian Doctrines*, 240-247.
41 *Religion des Judentums*, 342-343.

G. F. Moore led the attack against Bousset's emphasis on intermediation in Judaism.⁴² Moore justly criticized Bousset's crude characterizations of Judaism as the deterioration of Israelite Religion. The basis for some of Moore's critique, however, was not without fault of its own. He emphasized that Bousset was not primarily using the "normative" literary sources of Judaism (i.e., he used too many apocalypses and not enough Rabbinic literature).⁴³ Moore's criticism has caused many scholars to ignore Bousset's correct emphasis that there was a significant change after the exile in the nature of Israelite monotheism and the depiction of God's interaction with the world. So-called hypostases and angels certainly illustrate God's activity and control of all creation, yet these beings depict that divine activity in a manner substantially different from earlier traditions. Martin Hengel has responded to this criticism of Bousset's understanding:

> The remarks by Bousset and Gressmann on the historical reasons for this development are still valid today, and have simply been confirmed by the dominant role of the doctrine of angels in Qumran [. . . .] The objections of G. Pfeifer, that there had always been hypostasis-like conceptions in Judaism, but that on the whole they had been rare and that an awareness of God constantly active in the world had always been preserved, cannot conceal the fact that in the hellenistic period the middle-forms—whether as 'hypostases', like wisdom in Prov. 8,22ff., Job 28, etc, or angels, as the boundary is a fluid one—increased in both Palestinian Judaism and that of the Diaspora.⁴⁴

Helmer Ringgren has promulgated the use of hypostasis terminology more than any other scholar of this century. In his major monograph on the subject he discussed this phenomenon in several Near East religions, with primary focus given to Israelite Religion and Judaism.⁴⁵ He works with the following definition of hypostasis:

> Those scholars who have denied that Wisdom is a hypostasis have taken the term in its later theological sense of >>person in the Trinity>>, or the like. I have chosen a wider definition of the term, mainly in accordance with OESTERLEY-BOX and MOWINCKEL. A

---

⁴² "Intermediaries in Jewish Theology" and "Christian Writers on Judaism". Bousset is specifically critiqued in the latter article, 241-248.
⁴³ "Christian Writers on Judaism", 243-244.
⁴⁴ *Judaism and Hellenism*, 1.155.
⁴⁵ *Word and Wisdom: Studies in the Hypostatization of Divine Qualities and Functions in the Ancient Near East* (Lund: Hakan Ohlssons, 1947).

hypostasis is a »quasi-personification of certain attributes proper to God, occupying an intermediate position between personalities and abstract beings» [*The Religion and Worship of the Synagogue* (London, 1911), 169]. According to Mowinckel, the hypostases represent »a personification of qualities, functions, limbs etc. of a higher god» ["Hypostasen", *RGG* (2d ed.; 1928), cols. 2066-2067]. But the personal character should not be stressed too much. In fact there are cases when a divine quality is spoken of as an independent entity without it being personified, and I should like to use the term 'hypostasis' in these cases as well. But it should be kept in mind that the result of a personification is not always an hypostasis; it may very well be an allegory or a poetic metaphor.[46]

In a separate analysis of Israelite beliefs, Ringgren submits this explanation:

> In many, perhaps most, cases, what we are dealing with here is merely a stylistic device, a substitute for the divine name and God's activity. Occasionally, however, the abstract concept becomes semi-autonomous, appearing as an almost independent entity, half personified. This process is called hypostatization. Among the concepts discussed above, this tendency operates most noticeably on the word; but other concepts were personified to an even greater degree. This is especially true of the spirit and wisdom.[47]

One can see from these quotations that a definition of this complex religious phenomenon is difficult to articulate (i.e., "quasi-personification" or "semi-autonomous"). What is sometimes missed in Ringgren's approach is the acknowledgement and caution that personification of attributes does not automatically imply or lead to hypostatization. Unlike Bousset, Ringgren was more careful in dealing with individual texts to determine whether hypostatization was depicted (e.g., rather than seeing a concept like Wisdom as an hypostasis wherever it appears).

A critique of Ringgren's monograph written by Ralph Marcus in 1950 has been used in recent discussion to discourage use of hypostasis terminology.[48] It is noteworthy that Marcus is not very

---

[46] *Word and Wisdom*, 8.
[47] *Israelite Religion* (trans. D. Green; London: SPCK, 1966) 309; see also 89-94, 307-312. For a similar definition, see his "Hypostasen", *RGG* (3d ed.; 1959 3.504.
[48] "On Biblical Hypostases of Wisdom", *HUCA* 23 (1950-51) 157-171. This article is used frequently by Hurtado in *One God*; see 143 n.77, 146 n.20, 147 n.21, 152 n.42. Others who argue against Ringgren include: B. Gemser, *Sprüche Salomos*, (HAT 16; Tübingen: Mohr/Siebeck, 1963) 48; R. N. Whybray, *Wisdom in Proverbs: The Concept of Wisdom in Proverbs 1-9.45* (SBT 45; London: SPCK, 1965) 103; and G. Pfeifer, *Ursprung und Wesen der Hypostasen vorstellungen*

negative with regard to Ringgren's work.⁴⁹ His criticism centers on Ringgren's description of Wisdom as an hypostasis. After praising Ringgren's willingness to acknowledge diverse conceptualizations of attributes within Israelite Religion (i.e., hypostases, personifications, metaphors), Marcus states that he understands Wisdom in biblical literature as "[. . .] essentially and uniformly a poetic personification" and "[. . .] the work of a particular group of thinkers, all [sic] of whom seem to have regarded the Torah as the embodiment of divine Wisdom."⁵⁰ It is important to note that it is Marcus, and not Ringgren, who asserts a uniformity of perspective which simply does not exist in the texts. Marcus' primary contribution to the discussion is his nuancing of Ringgren's hypothesis that hypostatization of attributes tends to lead to polytheism.⁵¹

Hypostasis has become a prominent part of the vocabulary of several scholars researching mediator figures in Israelite Religion, Samaritanism, Early Christianity, and Rabbinism. For example, in his volume on the "Two Powers in Heaven" controversy in early Rabbinism, Alan Segal asserts that "[. . .] angelic or hypostatic creatures were considered independent enough [of God] to provide definite targets for the the 'Two Powers' polemic."⁵² He offers no definition of hypostasis; he uses the term as understood from previous biblical scholarship. Jarl Fossum specifically cites the inclusive definition of Ringgren as he uses "hypostasis" terminology extensively in his discussion of the Name, the Angel of the Lord, the Glory, and Wisdom in Jewish, Samaritan, and Gnostic literature.⁵³ Fossum gathers this textual evidence to show how "the hypostasized Name" which was invested in the Angel of the Lord (Exod 23.20) provides important data for asserting the Jewish origin of the Gnostic demiurge. In discussing the human figure on the throne in Ezek 1.26-28, 8.2-4, and Dan 10.5-9, Christopher Rowland sees "[. . .] the beginning of a hypostatic development similar to that connected with divine attributes like word and wisdom."⁵⁴ He

---

im Judentum (Arbeiten zum Theologie 31; Stuttgart: Calwer, 1967) 66, 102-103. See the comments of Hengel against these objections in *Judaism and Hellenism*, 1.153-155.

⁴⁹ With regard to the monograph he states: "[. . .] for which I have high regard and from which I have learned much"; "Biblical Hypostases", 167.
⁵⁰ "Biblical Hypostases", 167.
⁵¹ "Biblical Hypostases", 168-171.
⁵² *Two Powers in Heaven*, 201; see also 22 n.53, 137 n.6, 185-189, 192.
⁵³ *Name of God*, 85-86; see also 24, 106-108, 112, 315-316.
⁵⁴ *Open Heaven*, 100; see also 96-103.

also argues that the angel Yahoel of the *Apocalypse of Abraham* is portrayed as an hypostasis of the enthroned deity. After Rowland cautions against the identification of these figures as a "second power" in the heavenly world, he adds: "But having said all this, it is difficult to resist the impression that beliefs like this were susceptible of complete misunderstanding."[55]

Other recent discussions of Christology, such as those of Dunn and Hurtado, have not only avoided hypostasis nomenclature, but also downplay the idea of intermediation.[56] Hurtado has been one of the more outspoken and stinging critics of the use of hypostasis nomenclature, as can be seen in the following quotations:

> I find attempts to define or justify the use of this term as a description of personified attributes of God in Jewish tradition neither very clear nor compelling [....] The use of descriptions of such items as divine Wisdom for evidence of a belief in actual quasi-divine entities distinct from God is a failure to understand the language used by ancient Jews to describe God's activities and powers, taking literally what is in fact best understood as a vivid idiom of ancient Jewish religious expression.[57]

> That the divine Name, divine Wisdom or Word, and other divine attributes are referred to in ancient texts in language of personification is not sufficent reason to conclude that these items were understood by ancient Jews as personal beings or as things somewhere in "between personalities and abstract beings" (e.g., hypostases). While personified divine attributes behave in the linguistic world of ancient Jewish texts as personal beings, this is not necessarily indicative of the function of divine attributes in the conceptual world and religious life of the people who created the texts.[58]

Hurtado levels criticism at Fossum for furthering the influence of Ringgren's position.[59] He emphasizes that Ringgren's interpretation of divine attributes was designed to support his theory that hypostatization played an important role in the origin and growth of polytheism.[60] Furthermore, he cautions against the exaggeration of this phenomenon in Judaism and emphasizes that the major mutation within Jewish monotheism happened with the cultic

---

[55] *Open Heaven*, 111.
[56] E.g., see Dunn's discussion of Wisdom in *Christology in the Making*, 161-176, esp. 170; see also Hurtado, *One God*, 41-50.
[57] *One God*, 37.
[58] *One God*, 47.
[59] *One God*, 146 n.21.
[60] See Ringgren's theory in *Word and Wisdom*, 193.

veneration of Jesus. In place of hypostasis he suggests "personified divine attributes as divine agents".[61] Such a statement, however, is a misnomer; the language "divine agent" implies an independence that goes far beyond "personification". Furthermore, in his discussion of Wisdom he cites the depiction of Penitence (or Repentance) in *Jos.Asen.* 15.7-8 as a personification similar to Wisdom in some texts and concludes: "Surely this text shows the prevalence of personification in the religious language of ancient Jews and is a warning against much that has been concluded on the basis of such vivid rhetoric."[62] It is very probable, however, that his sure illustration of personification is actually a depiction of Repentance as an angel.[63]

Convinced by the argument of Hurtado, Saul Olyan has recently contributed a critique of the hypostasis nomenclature.[64] The alternative he offers to describe "hypostatization" is the term "special figurative treatment". He cites three reasons for this change. First, such language emphasizes the figurative nature of the words used. Secondly, it avoids the associations with the Trinitarian debate and dogma that "hypostasis" carries. Thirdly, it is a more general and inclusive term. If an attribute receives cultic devotion, then Olyan uses the term "divinization". Although Olyan's attempt to introduce new nomenclature is understandable, his grouping together of the so-called special figurative treatment of "Wisdom" with such things as "Plague" and "Disease" in Hab 3.5 adds further confusion to the situation. Are we to think that Prov 8:22-30 and Hab 3.5 are similar phenomena? Such over-generalized catagorization hardly proves helpful in distinguishing between the developments of various attributes.

---

[61] It is puzzling that Newman, who draws heavily on the works of Segal and Fossum to argue for his understanding of Glory theology, follows Hurtado on this issue; see his *Paul's Glory-Christology*, 97.

[62] *One God*, 47.

[63] Repentance is depicted as an angel who intercedes for the repentent in these verses: she is in "the heavens"; she entreats her father, the Most High God, on behalf of all who repent; she prepares a resting place in heaven for them; the angels are in awe of her beauty; the angel (Michael) calls her his "sister" (15.8). An Angel of Repentance is also found in contemporaneous literature (e.g., *1 En.* 40.9 and *Hermas Vis.* V.8); see also Paschal, "Farewell Prayer", 240.

[64] Olyan, *A Thousand Thousands*, 88-98.

Both Hurtado and Olyan cite the semantic treatments of hypostatization by James Barr and Arthur Gibson as authoritative testimony that the term should be avoided.[65] Barr and Gibson do not, however, attempt to withdraw "hypostasis" from discussion; instead, they urge a recognition of the difference between "linguistic hypostatization" and "attributive hypostatization". Barr notes the importance of this distinction:

> There is a well-known phenomenon of religious hypostatization, which occurs when something like "the Wisdom of God" or "the Word of God" comes to be regarded as rather more than a characteristic or an activity of God, as something indeed which may "come" or "act" or "create", for example. Many may wish to regard certain biblical cases of "the Word" as cases of hypostatization of this kind. This however is not hypostatization of a linguistic phenomenon, but hypostatization in the sense of attribution of some kind of independent being to that which might otherwise have been thought of as only the characteristic or the action of another being, and in particular of God.[66]

Gibson especially highlights the very real danger of hypostatizing linguistic terminology (i.e., Word) and asserting hypostases apart from, or in spite of, their linguistic context.[67] He also notes the value of seeing differing grades of "attributive hypostatization" at linguistic and ontological levels. These semantic discussions further clarify, and note dangers of, hypostasis terminology; they do not hinder its continued usage.

Andrew Chester examined Hurtado's understanding of "personified divine attributes" and set forth a critique which merits our attention:

> Certainly it seems scarcely adequate to describe Wisdom and Logos (at least in the fully developed form of the Wisdom traditions) as merely speaking of God's immanent activity in the world; equally, it seems difficult to avoid designating them as hypostatizations, although the misleading implications and false claims often associated with the use of this term are of course rejected. Thus, for example, I would not want this term (or the term 'intermediary' either) to be taken to imply that there is by this stage in

---

[65] See J. Barr, "Hypostatization of Linguistic Phenomena in Modern Theological Interpretation", *JSS* 7 (1962) 85-92, and A. Gibson, *Biblical Semantic Logic: A Preliminary Analysis* (Oxford: Blackwell, 1981) 92-96. Gibson is cited by Hurtado (*One God*, 143 n.77, 146 n.16, 147 n.23) and both are cited by Olyan (*A Thousand Thousands*, 91 n.10).

[66] "Hypostatization", 93.

[67] *Biblical Semantic Logic*, 92-96.

> Judaism a doctrine of God as remote from the world and unable to be active directly within it (although the question of exactly *how* God comes into contact with the world is certainly involved). One important issue is how these developed concepts, as also the elevated and angelic figures, stand in relation to God; whether, for example, any of them are to be seen as identical, in being, role or function; whether they represent a challenge or complement to God's sole rule and supreme position, and how precisely we are to conceive of the situation in the heavenly world, with the co-existence of exalted beings alongside God.[68]

Chester identifies the central dilemma: these "concepts" or figures are more than personifications or figurative treatments of divine attributes and should be identified as such. The hypostasis nomenclature presents problems, but the alternatives proposed are inadequate and misleading. Given this current situation, six caveats are in order to guide the future usage of hypostasis nomenclature. First, the variegated textual evidence should be emphasized in research rather than the slotting of the evidence into particular modern scholarly categories. Nomenclature should be descriptive for grouping similar phenomena; it should neither limit nor embellish the significance of the evidence.

Second, the past problems in the usage of hypostasis nomenclature, as noted above, must be acknowledged in order that these problems can be avoided in the future. These problems include: the presupposition that hypostases *a priori* emphasize God's transcendence or a degeneration in Jewish monotheism; the confusion between linguistic and attributive hypostatization; the insensitivity of some to linguistic context for understanding different depictions of the same divine attributes; and the tendency towards a multiplicity of hypostases.

Third, critics of hypostasis nomenclature tend to argue that this terminology emphasizes the separateness of the attribute(s) from the deity, rather than noticing the continued connection between the deity and the hypostatized aspect(s) of the deity precisely because of the nomenclature. The presence of hypostases does not destroy or even weaken so-called monotheism; it increases the complexity of monotheism because the hypostases continue to remain aspects of the deity.

---

[68] "Jewish Messianic Expectations", 63; see also 23 above.

Fourth, proponents of hypostasis nomenclature tend to imply that there is a sharp line between personification and hypostatization. In reality we must confess a significant "gray area" that demands we speak of degrees of personification or hypostatization. Three possible gradations or degrees of hypostatization in the Jewish evidence are: an hypostasis functioning as an instrument of God's action; an hypostasis that is the visible manifestation of God; and an hypostasis that is a distinct agent of God.

Fifth, hypostasis nomenclature has developed because personification does not adequately describe what is asserted about certain divine attributes in particular texts. In this study, PERSONIFICATION is the literary representation of a divine aspect as a deity without implying independent personhood from the deity.[69] The fact that personification does not adequately describe what is depicted in some of the textual evidence related to divine attributes and concepts is merely asserted here; its inadequacy will be demonstrated in the exegesis of texts in Chapter 4.

Sixth, we should bear in mind the difference between an author's intention and later exegetical reflection. Some authors may not have intended to have their depictions interpreted in a particular way, but their depictions gave impetus to later exegetes developing ideas more sharply in particular directions. No matter how cogent the arguments are that the Jewish authors of the texts in question understood their depictions as merely vivid personifications, later exegetes indisputably read a number of these depictions as much more than a species of literary metaphor.

In light of these caveats, this study will use hypostasis nomenclature according to the following definition: an HYPOSTASIS is an aspect of the deity that is depicted with independent personhood of varying degrees.[70] The textual evidence shows that an hypostasis shares the nature, authority, and will of the deity since it remains an aspect of the deity.

---

[69] Fossum, who uses hypostasis terminology extensively, does confuse the issue by speaking of Moses as "the personified Divine Name"; see *Name of God*, 112. Because personification is typically understood as a literary device or species of metaphor, it would be better to use terminology such as hypostasis or manifestation (i.e., Moses as "the hypostatized Divine Name" or "the manifestation of the Divine Name").

[70] "Aspect" is used here in a wide sense that is inclusive of realities like "the Word of the Lord".

F. Methodology

The overwhelming focus of this study will be the exegesis and comparison of texts using the religio-historical method. This method assumes that although ideas may be adopted, adapted, and shaped by different authors, there is a degree of consistency that is maintained in the meaning or presence of the idea. The fact that the religio-historical method was brought into widespread usage by the *Religionsgeschichtliche Schule* does not mean that this study is based upon the presuppositions of this school. Subsequent research has shown a number of them to be problematic.[71]

Two frequent criticisms of this method need to be addressed. First, the comparison of numerous texts to demonstrate the development of a particular idea sometimes brings on a charge of "parallelomania".[72] The concern with parallelomania grows from excessive attempts to chart direct dependence of one author upon another. This study will be concerned primarily with showing evidence of the same or similar ideas; it will not be advocating direct (geneological) dependence between documents in most comparisons. Standard criteria for determining quotations, allusions, and echos will be followed.[73] Secondly, the use of later texts in the discussion of an earlier text is often considered methodologically unsound. While later texts should not be the sole pillar upon which an argument is built, it should also be recognized that later texts can, and often do, contain earlier ideas. If the idea in a document can be dated, there is legitimacy in using a later text as an expression and record of that idea from an earlier period.

Lest this approach only focus on parts of documents without a sensitivity for how those parts function within the whole, this study will also use systemic analysis.[74] This method assumes that

---

[71] Fossum, "New *Religionsgeschlichtliche Schule*", 638-46.

[72] See the discussion by S. Sandmel related to the QL and NT in "Parallelomania", *JBL* 81 (1962) 1-13.

[73] See the criteria and methodology outlined by M. Thompson, *Clothed with Christ: The Example and Teaching of Jesus in Romans 12.1-15.13* (JSNTSup 59; Sheffield: Sheffield Academic Press, 1991) 28-36. Thompson does not spell out the gradations of judgment that will be used in this study: a) certain/virtually certain; b) probable/possible; c) unlikely/doubtful.

[74] This basic method has been articulated and practiced most widely by J. Neusner; see his discussion in *The Systemic Analysis of Judaism* (Atlanta: Scholars Press, 1988). See also G. Boccaccini, "Middle Judaism and Its Contemporary Interpreters", 207-33.

the different ideas of a document are organized by an author into a hierarchy and that the individual parts derive an important aspect of their significance from their position in the system of ideas which make up the document. Although the amount of diverse literature discussed in Part II militates against much detailed systemic analysis, this study will be sensitive to the significance that ideas have in the document within which they are found. This method will be more visible in Part III where ideas are traced through individual documents.

The combination of these methodologies will be used to bear out the thesis that angelomorphic traditions, especially those growing from the Angel of the Lord traditions, had a significant impact on the early expressions of Christology to the extent that evidence of an Angelomorphic Christology is discernible in several documents dated between 50 and 150 CE. Support for this thesis will be examined in the two major parts: Antecedents (Part II) and Early Evidence (Part III).

Part II will be an examination of antecedents from varied Israelite and Jewish literature in order to understand the existence and development of angelomorphic traditions before the middle of the first century CE (Chapters 3-6). The first subject to be explored will be angelomorphic traditions associated with the so-called Angel of the Lord. Attention will then turn to the angelomorphic aspects of various Divine hypostases: the Name, the Glory, Wisdom, the Spirit, the Word, and the Power. The phenomenon of principal named angels is another significant development that will be explored. This part will conclude with a chapter examining how particular humans were considered to be angels, to have an angel inside them, or to be like an angel. It must be emphasized that the numerous texts in these chapters are selective and representative for the specific purpose of highlighting angelomorphic traditions so that the evidence of Part III can be understood in a broader historical context. Therefore, the lack of a comprehensive portrait of the pluralistic traditions associated with some of the complex topics discussed in Part II should not be interpreted as the lack of an acute awareness of this pluralism in the sources.

Part III, the examination of early evidence of Angelomorphic Christology, will be the heart of this study (Chapters 8-14). After a brief introductory chapter about second and third century evidence, seven early Christian documents or groupings of documents will be perused to demonstrate the presence of angelomorphic traditions used in developing Christology: *Pseudo-Clementines*, the *Shepherd of Hermas*, the *Ascension of Isaiah*, the Revelation to John, the Gospel of John, the Epistle to the Hebrews, and the Pauline Epistles, including those sometimes considered Deuteropauline.[75] Evidence from these texts will demonstrate that the use of angelomorphic traditions in Christology is more prevalent and much earlier than often thought by scholars. Traditions within these documents will be analyzed to demonstrate that a coherent, if varied, Angelomorphic Christology existed in early Christianity.

Part IV will be a brief concluding chapter which outlines implications of this research for the origins and study of Christology (Chapter 15). These substantial implications will be drawn from a wide scope of textual evidence. It is to the textual antecedents of Angelomorphic Christology that we now turn our attention.

---

[75] The ordering of these chapters is intentional. The later documents will be considered first before moving to the first century NT documents.

PART TWO

ANTECEDENTS

CHAPTER THREE

AN ANGELOMORPHIC GOD

It is a well documented and ancient tradition of the OT that in several of the narratives where God communicates with humans, the form from which God speaks is identified as מלאך.[1] The Hebrew term מלאך is the nominal construct form from לאך, which means "to send" or possibly "to send on a comission".[2] The basic meaning of the nominal, "one who is sent", has led to the common definition: "messenger". Well-defined messenger activity was prominent in the ancient Near East.[3] The OT uses מלאך for both human messengers (e.g., 1 Sam 11.4) and supernatural messengers (e.g., Ps 103.20). The Greek term ἄγγελος also signifies "a messenger". The use of מלאך or ἄγγελος as a designation for supernatural messengers caused these terms to carry more ontological significance and to become associated with more functions than message delivery, especially in the Second Temple Period. Therefore, by the first century CE, among Jews and Christians, both מלאך and ἄγγελος usually signified the broader technical meaning of "a spirit who mediates in various ways between the human and divine realms".[4] This description retains the basic idea of "one sent (with a commission)", but the role of messenger becomes less dominant. Furthermore, this technical meaning has led to the frequent English translation of both מלאך and ἄγγελος in biblical and related literature as "angel" when the referent is supernatural, and "messenger" when the referent is human.

---

[1] For a survey of scholarship see H. Röttger, *Mal'ak Jahwe - Bote von Gott* (Regensburger Studien zur Theologie 13; Frankfurt: Peter Lang, 1978), i-xxii, 12-32. For a treatment of the Angel of the Lord in the context of Jewish angelology, see M. Mach, *Entwicklungstadien des jüdischen Engelglaubens in vorrabbinisher Zeit* (TSAJ 34; Tübingen: Mohr/Siebeck, 1992). See also S. Meier, "Angel", *DDD* 81-90, and S. Meier, "Angel of Yahweh", *DDD* 96-108.
[2] G. von Rad, "ἄγγελος" (D. מלאך in the OT), *TDNT* 1.76-80.
[3] See S. Meier, *The Messenger in the Ancient Semitic World* (HSM 45; Atlanta: Scholars Press, 1988), and L. Handy, *Among the Host of Heaven* (Winona Lake, IN: Eisenbrauns, 1994).
[4] von Rad, "ἄγγελος", 77; see also J. van Henten, "Angel II", *DDD* 90-96.

What מלאך or ἄγγελος signifies becomes more complicated when they are used with a divine name in biblical texts where God speaks to humans and often has a visible form as well. These literary accounts are found with some regularity in the Pentateuch and Judges, although the designation מלאך יהוה ("the Angel of YHWH") does not appear in each one.[5] The identity of this "angel" has been the subject of much scholarly debate.[6] The depictions in the texts which seem to have him as their referent are by no means uniform or homogeneous, to the point where scholars question if we should even speak of the existence of "the Angel of the Lord".[7] Samuel Meier, an authority on the use of messengers in the ancient Near East, writes of the exacerbation that these texts can cause the exegete:

> It must be underscored that the angel of YHWH in these perplexing biblical narratives does not behave like any other messenger known in the divine or human realm. Although the term 'messenger' is present, the narrative itself omits the indispensable features of messenger activity and presents instead the activities which one associates with Yahweh and the other gods of the ancient Near East.[8]

The discussion which follows will not attempt to sort out all the perplexities of these texts or debate their origins in biblical history. The focus of this chapter is much simpler: to discuss tersely the basic content of the foundational texts related to "the Angel of the Lord" in order to demonstrate their formative influence on later angelomorphic traditions.

---

[5] This figure is identified in various ways. "The Angel of YHWH" or "an Angel of Kyrios" (MT: מלאך יהוה; LXX: [ὁ] ἄγγελος κυρίου) is found in: Gen 16.7-14; 22.11-15; Exod 3.1-14; 14.19-20; Num 22.22-35; Judg 2.1-4; 5.23; 6.11-24; 13.3-21. "The (an) Angel of God" (MT: מלאך אלהים; LXX: ἄγγελος τοῦ θεοῦ) is found in: Gen 21.17; 31.11; Exod 14.19; Judg 6.20 (not LXX); 13.6, 9. "The Angel" (MT: מלאך; LXX: ὁ ἄγγελος) is present in Gen 48.16. "The three men" of Gen 18.1-33 (MT: אנשים; LXX: ἄνδρες) are clearly angelomorphic (cf. Gen 19.1). "The man" (MT: איש; LXX: ἄνθρωπος/ἀνήρ) is used interchangably with other titles for this angel in Gen 32.24-30 and Judg 13.3-22. An exception to the LXX following the MT in these various designations is Judges 6.11-23: מלאך אלהים (6.20) and יהוה (6.14, 16) are rendered ὁ ἄγγελος κυρίου (which is already present in 6.11, 12, 22). There are other texts which refer to "the Angel of YHWH/Kyrios", but this "angel" is not directly related to the earlier theophanic traditions in Genesis through Judges (e.g., Hag 1.13).

[6] Meier, "Angel of Yahweh", 96-108.

[7] V. Hirth prefers to identify this manifestation as "a messenger of YHWH"; see *Gottes Botten im Alten Testament* (Theologische Arbeiten 32; Berlin: Evangelische Verlagsanstalt, 1975) 25-31.

[8] "Angel of Yahweh", 88.

A. *Interpretative Approaches*

The first important problem that the exegete must confront in examining these texts is how one understands the relationship between this angel and God where this angel is the form in which God appears in order to speak or act.[9] For example, this difficulty is readily apparent in YHWH's appearance to Moses in the Burning Bush:

> [Exod 3.2] And the Angel of YHWH appeared to him in a flame of fire out of a bush; and he looked, and lo, the bush was burning, yet it was not consumed. [3] And Moses said, "I will turn aside and see this great sight, why the bush is not burnt." [4] When YHWH saw that he turned aside to see, Elohim called to him out of the bush, "Moses, Moses!" And he said, "Here am I." [5] Then he said, "Do not come near; put off your shoes from your feet, for the place on which you are standing is holy ground." [6] And he said, "I am the Elohim of your father, the Elohim of Abraham, the Elohim of Isaac, and the Elohim of Jacob." And Moses hid his face for he was afraid to look at Elohim. [7] Then YHWH said, "I have seen the affliction of my people who are in Egypt, and have heard their cry because of their taskmasters; I know their sufferings."

The Angel of YHWH appeared in a flame of fire and YHWH/Elohim spoke. In spite of the testimony in 3.2 that it was the Angel of YHWH who appeared (וירא) to Moses, God commands him to tell the elders that "YHWH, the Elohim of your ancestors [. . .] has *appeared* [נראה] to me" (Exod 3.16).[10] Several interpretative approaches have been proposed by scholars in order to understand this question of the indistinguishability between God and this angel, here and in several other texts from Genesis through Judges.[11]

---

[9] E.g., Gen 16.7-14, Gen 31.2-13, Exod 3.1-14, Judg 6.11-24; see the discussion on 57-67 below.

[10] The indistinguishability element of Exod 3.2-7 is less clear in Stephen's speech in Acts. He proclaims that Moses saw "an angel" in the Burning Bush and heard "the voice of the Lord" (7.30, 35). Some distinction between this angel and the Lord seems to be indicated a few verses later when Stephen mentions "the angel who *spoke* to him [Moses] at Mount Sinai".

[11] For an review of the various theories of interpretation, see A. S. van der Woude, "De *Mal'ak Jahweh*: Een Godsbode", *Nederlands Theologisch Tijdschrift* 18 (1963/64) 1-13; Hirth, *Gottes Botten*, 13-21; W. Heidt, *Angelology of the Old Testament: A Study in Biblical Theology* (Studies in Sacred Theology 2/24; Washington: Catholic University of America Press, 1949) 69-101.

One of the most prominent approaches to this problem has been the *interpolation theory*. It asserts that the Angel of the Lord figure was added by redactors to soften the bold anthropomorphisms of very old textual traditions that presented God appearing in the form of a man.[12] Gerhard von Rad, who championed this approach, explains it in this manner:

> The naive immediacy of the relationship to God was broken somewhat by the introduction of this mediating figure, in such a way that nothing of the directness of the divine address to man and the divine saving activity for man was lost.[13]

The problems with this approach have been ably exposed by James Barr in an article on anthropomorphism in the OT that is worthy of attention:

> When we come to the *mal'ak* of the old stories, it seems to me even more doubtful whether we can understand the purpose of its introduction and development as a mitigation of the direct anthropomorphic theophany. For this there are several reasons. Firstly, the introduction of the *mal'ak* is too extremely spasmodic, and leaves too many fierce anthropomorphisms untouched, for its purpose to be understood in this way. The voice and presence of the *mal'ak* alternates in a number of stories so much with the voice and appearing of Yahweh that it is hardly possible to understand his place as a substitute for the latter. Secondly, far from the *mal'ak* representing a later and more sophisticated feature, it is found deeply embedded in stories of great antiquity; the best example is the J story of Gen. xviii, where to be sure the term *mal'ak* does not appear until xix 1 and there in the plural, but where it is indisputable that we have the same general phenomenon as the *mal'ak* of other stories. In general, the *mal'ak* passages do not do anything explicit to assert the remoteness or the transcendence of Yahweh or to combat a primitive anthropomorphism. If anything, the *mal'ak* might be better understood as the accompaniment of the anthropomorphic appearance rather than as a dilution of it.[14]

The *representation theory* asserts that the Angel of the Lord is a messenger spirit who represents God as his ambassador. Thus, this angel speaks and acts for God, but is not God.[15] Although this approach can be used to explain some texts that show the Angel of

---

[12] G. von Rad, *Genesis* (trans. J. Marks; 3d rev. ed.; London: SCM, 1972) 193-94. This theory has been endorsed (more recently) by S. Meier; see "Angel of Yahweh", 106.
[13] *Genesis*, 194.
[14] "Theophany and Anthropomorphism in the Old Testament", *Congress Volume: Oxford 1959* (VTSup 7; Leiden: Brill, 1960) 33-34.
[15] Heidt, *Angelology of the OT*, 97-99.

the Lord as distinct from God (e.g., 1 Chr 21.15-30), there is no support for this theory in the numerous texts that present this angel as indistinguishable from God. Even where this angel is depicted as a person distinct from God, it should still be remembered that there is, in some sense, a sharing in the divine substance through the angel's possession of the Divine Name (cf. Exod 23.20-21).

The *identity theory* asserts that the Angel of the Lord is a manifestation of God himself. This approach defines the Angel of the Lord as "[. . .] the visible or audible phenomenon through which God manifests himself and communicates with the person or persons concerned."[16] What, however, is the reason for this phenomenon? W. Eichrodt argues that the Angel of the Lord safeguards God's transcendent nature while also maintaining his immanent presence through temporary incarnations.[17] This cannot be correct. The earliest Angel of the Lord traditions have little to do with God's transcendence. The answer must center on the holiness of God which makes his normal visible form something that brings death to the viewer.[18] Therefore, when God manifests himself in these ancient Angel of the Lord traditions, he visibly appears as an angel (in the form of a man, fire, or a cloud) so as not to destroy those who see him.

The *logos theory* asserts that the Angel of the Lord is God's means of communication with the world.[19] This angel, like Philo's *Logos*, manifests himself in many different forms and circumstances. He can be identified with various different angels and persons. This theory affirms both the unity and differences in the various accounts of the so-called Angel of the Lord.

The *hypostasis theory*, championed by Helmer Ringgren, holds that the Angel of the Lord is an aspect of God's personality that has taken on a distinct, but not separate, identity.[20] This phenomenon is seen most prominently in texts which depict the Name, the Glory, or Wisdom as an hypostasis of God. Ringgren argues that

---

[16] Heidt, *Angelology of the OT*, 70.

[17] W. Eichrodt, *Theology of the Old Testament* (trans. J. Baker; 2 vols.; London: SCM, 1967) 2.27-29.

[18] E.g., Exod 33.20 and Gen 32.20; this is argued by Barr, "Theophany and Anthropomorphism", 31-38.

[19] Heidt, *Angelology of the OT*, 96-97. Eichrodt considers this view to be obsolete among scholars; see *Theology of the OT*, 2.6.

[20] "Geister, Dämonen, Engel", *RGG* (3d ed.) 2.1301-1302, and "Hypostasen", *RGG* (3d ed.) 3.503-506.

the Angel of the Lord remains associated with God as an aspect of God's personality. Therefore, the Angel of the Lord shares God's nature and can speak or act as God himself.

The *l'âme extérieure theory* is the creation of Adolphe Lods.[21] This theory holds that elements of a personality can detach themselves without ceasing to be connected with the person (i.e., an exterior or external soul). He attempts to garner evidence that this idea helped people of various religious cultures to understand the presence of the deity in different locations. Lods proposed, by analogy, that one could explain the presence of the Angel of the Lord as an aspect of God's personality that became manifest. Concrete evidence of this concept in Israelite religion or Judaism, however, is never shown.

The *messenger theory*, proposed by A. S. van der Woude, emphasizes that the best conceptual background for understanding these texts is the idea of the union between the sender and the messenger in the Near East.[22] He argues that the angel in these accounts should not be interpreted as a being distinct from God. The figure identified as the angel is an extension of God himself who speaks, protects, and punishes. Therefore, van der Woude prefers to avoid translations which use the definite article "*the* Angel of the Lord". The evidence supporting a translation free of the article, however, is inconclusive.[23]

This difficulty in understanding the indistinguishability between God and his angel in several texts leads us to a second problem. Other texts do not reflect this indistinguishability and present the Angel of the Lord as a mediator who is distinct from God. Therefore, we do not find a uniform Angel of the Lord tradition which leaves the same footprint in each text in which it appears; rather, we find variable traditions, including those in which the Angel of the Lord appears to be an angel who is distinct from God. The key text for seeing this distinguishability between God and his angel is Exod 23.20-21:

> [20] Behold, I send an angel in front of you, to guard you on the way and to bring you to the place that I have prepared. [21] Be

---

[21] "L'Ange de Yahvé et l'âme extérieure", BZAW 27 (1913) 265-278.
[22] "*Mal'ak Jahweh*", 6-13.
[23] He bases his preference for a translation without the article in part upon the LXX accounts which often omit the Greek article; see n.5 above.

attentive to him and listen to his voice; do not rebel against him, for he will not pardon your transgression; for my Name is in him.

Although this angel is not referred to as the Angel of the Lord, the Exodus events lead one to see this angel as part of the Angel of the Lord traditions. Unlike the texts involving the Angel of the Lord in which he is the manifestation of God, the angel that is spoken of here is clearly distinct from God, but not completely separate from him. Because the Name of God is synonymous with his divine nature, the angel or being who has his Name should be regarded as a person possessing his full divine authority and power.[24]

Even though modern scholarship points to the great diversity in these textual traditions, such was usually not the case with ancient interpretation in Jewish and Christian circles. The Divine Name Angel textual tradition influenced the interpretation of the Angel of the Lord texts in the direction of seeing this angel as distinct from God. This fact must be kept in mind because it is what allows us to speak of "the Angel of the Lord" in a manner that is not anachronistic.

B. *Angel of the Lord Traditions in the Old Testament*

As noted above, there are two striking features in several of these texts. The first feature is their depiction of the Angel of the Lord as God's visible form or God's voice in his epiphanies. When God is seen and/or heard by a human, the human sees and/or hears the Angel of the Lord. This does not mean that the human has seen and/or heard a being distinct from God. On the contrary, the second feature of several texts is that both God and the Angel of the Lord are often identified as the same being; they are presented as indistinguishable. For example, the first occurence of the Angel of the Lord happens after Hagar has been cast out by Sarai:

> [Gen 16.7] The Angel of YHWH found her by a spring of water in the wilderness, the spring on the way to Shur. [8] And he said, "Hagar, maid of Sarai, where have you come from and where are you going?" She said, "I am fleeing from my mistress Sarai." [9] The Angel of YHWH said to her, "Return to your mistress, and

---

[24] For the significance of the Divine Name, especially as an hypostasis of God, see 70-78 below, and Fossum, *Name of God*, 76-191, esp. 84-87.

submit to her." [10] <u>The Angel of YHWH</u> also said to her, "<u>I will greatly multiply</u> your descendants that they cannot be numbered for multitude." [11] And <u>the Angel of YHWH</u> said to her, "Behold, you are with child, and shall bear a son; you shall call his name Ishmael; because <u>YHWH</u> has given heed to your affliction. [12] He shall be a wild ass of a man, his hand against every man and every man's hand against him; and he shall dwell over against all his kinsmen." [13] So she called <u>the name of YHWH</u> who spoke to her, "<u>You are an El of seeing</u>" [ותקרא שם־יהוה הדבר אליה אתה אל ראי]; for she said, "<u>Have I really seen him</u> and remained alive after seeing him?" [14] Therefore the well was called Beerlahairoi [לבאר באר לחי ראי]—the well of one who sees and lives]; it lies between Kadesh and Bered.

Although this text does not specifically identify the Angel of YHWH as YHWH, it certainly gives that impression. This angel speaks and blesses in the first person as God did in his earlier theophanies with Abram (16.10; cf. Gen 12.2), but he also speaks of YHWH's actions in the third person (16.11). It is noteworthy that this angel does not identify himself, yet Hagar is convinced that she has seen God (16.13).[25] This is brought out by her acknowledgment of the widely-known maxim that one cannot see God's face and live (Exod 33.20; cf. Gen 32.30) and by the name that is given to the well (16.14). This paradox of being able to see God in some way and still live is present in several of these texts (cf. Gideon in Judg 6.11-23).

A question that naturally arises from these narratives is: What does the Angel of the Lord, or God's visible form, look like? Sometimes that question is not answered in a way that fully satisfies our curiosity. For example, it was shown above that the visible appearance of God is a flame of fire in a bush in the theophany to commission Moses (Exod 3.1-15). A vital aspect of this account is the revealing of God's personal name by the Angel of the Lord (Exod 3.13-14), which is very significant for the understanding of the Divine Name Angel of Exod 23.20-21.

---

[25] Gen 21.17-19 records that Hagar hears, but does mention her seeing the angel. A similar phenomena is at work in the Sacrifice of Isaac account where the Angel of YHWH calls from heaven (22.11, 15) and speaks as YHWH (22.16). These details, however, do not mean that there was no visible encounter. Note Gen 22.14 MT: ויקרא אברהם שם־המקום ההוא יהוה יראה; LXX: καὶ ἐκάλεσεν Αβρααμ τὸ ὄνομα τοῦ τόπου ἐκείνου Κύριος εἶδεν. The translation of יהוה יראה as "the Lord will provide" appears to be based more on the context (the ram being provided for the sacrifice) than on the typical meaning of ראה as "to see, appear" (cf. Gen 16.13).

The presence of the Angel of the Lord in a fire calls to mind one of the prominent theophanies of God as a pillar of fire leading Israel by night and a pillar of cloud leading them by day. That God himself was in these pillars is clear from Exod 13.21-22 and 14.24 (cf. Isa 52.12). In this same context, however, one finds mention of the Angel of the Lord in close proximity with this pillar of cloud[26]:

> [Exod 14.19] Then the Angel of Elohim who went before the host of Israel moved and went behind them; and the pillar of cloud moved from before them and stood behind them, [20] coming between the host of Egypt and the host of Israel. And there was the cloud and the darkness; and the night passed without one coming near the other all night.

This association leaves the door open to identification of the angel with the pillar.[27] In fact, both Num 20.15-16 and Judg 2.1 witness that the angel led Israel out of Egypt.

Still other texts address the intriguing issue of God's visible form and indicate that the Angel of the Lord appeared as a man on several occasions. Probably the most well-known theophany that presents God appearing as a man is the visit of the three men to Abraham (Gen 18.1-19.1). This text is very complex and has generated a great variety of interpretation by both Jewish and Christian exegetes.[28] It relates these fundamental details: YHWH appeared to Abraham (18.1; cf. 18.13, 22); Abraham sees three men (18.2); and two of the figures are specifically identified as angels (19.1). The natural deduction is that one of the men was YHWH (18.1, 13, 22), but it is possible that YHWH was in some sense all

---

[26] The Targumim substitute "Angel of the Lord" for "Angel of God" in their treatment of this text; see *Tg. Ps-J.* Exod 14.19, *Tg. Onq.* Exod 14.19, and *Tg. Neof.* Exod. 14.19.

[27] Philo states that the pillars of cloud and fire enclosed "one of the commanders [ὑπάρχων] of the Great King, an unseen angel [ἀφανὴς ἄγγελος]" (*Vita Mos* 1.166; cf. *Heres* 201-205). Later Jewish tradition identified this figure with Michael (*Pirqe R. El.* 73), as did some Christian writers (*Acts of Andrew and Matthias* 30).

[28] See the extensive discussion and bibliography in J. Loader, *A Tale of Two Cities: Sodom and Gomorrah in the Old Testament, Early Jewish and Early Christian Traditions* (Contributions to Biblical Exegesis and Theology 1; Kampen: Kok, 1990). One of the difficulties in identifying these men as angels or as divine is their apparent consumption of food (18.6-8; cf. Josephus, *Ant* 1.122, Philo, *Abr* 118, and Tob 12.19); see D. Goodman, "Do Angels Eat?", *JJS* 37 (1986) 160-175.

three men.[29] This account also contains the intriguing reference to two YHWHs: "YHWH" as the one (on earth) who destroys by raining down fire from "YHWH out of heaven" (Gen 19.24).[30]

A second pivotal text in identifying God's visible form as a man is the episode of Jacob wrestling with a man whom Jacob later realizes is Elohim:

> [Gen 32.24] And Jacob was left alone; and <u>a man</u> wrestled with him until the breaking of the day. [25] When <u>the man</u> saw that he did not prevail against Jacob, he touched the hollow of his thigh; and Jacob's thigh was put out of joint as he wrestled with him. [26] Then he said, "Let me go, for the day is breaking." But Jacob said, "I will not let you go, unless you bless me." [27] And he said to him, "What is your name?" And he said, "Jacob." [28] Then he said, "Your name shall no more be called Jacob, but Israel, for <u>you have striven with Elohim and with men</u>, and have prevailed." [29] Then Jacob asked him, "Tell me, I pray, your name." But he said, "Why is it that you ask my name?" And there he blessed him. [30] So Jacob called the name of the place Peniel, saying, "For <u>I have seen Elohim face to face</u>, and yet my life was preserved."

In a manner similar to Genesis 18, this text follows the pattern of God appearing in the form of a man even though there is no specific mention of the Angel of the Lord. Several details in the text indicate the divine status of this man who wrestled with Jacob. First, he is able to bless Jacob, one of God's select sons (32.26-28). Second, he indicated that Jacob had striven against God (32.28). Third, when Jacob asks for his name, he does not answer (32.29); this implies that Jacob should have known the unspeakable name of this being (i.e., the Name of God). Finally, as with other texts, Jacob acknowledges in his naming of the place that he has seen God face-to-face and is surprised to be alive (32.30; cf. Exod 33.20). This "man" is probably the "angel" whom Jacob identifies as God in his blessing of Ephraim and Mannaseh (Gen 48.15-16).

---

[29] See von Rad, *Genesis*, 1.199. Note the common question asked by these men to Sarai in 18.9. Philo conceives of the three in some sense of a divine unity in *Abr* 121: they are the Father of the Universe and his senior potencies or angels, the creative (God) and the kingly (Lord). *T. Ab.* 2.10 [B] identifies these three as angels, and one of them as Michael (cf. 6.1-18 [A] and 6.4 [B]).

[30] Jewish and Christian interest in this text is evident in Justin, *Dial. Trypho* 56. Gen 19.21 indicates that one of the two angels would carry out the destruction. *Gen. R.* 51.2 identifies this angel as Gabriel, who was understood to be the Divine Name Angel of Exod 23.20-21 in some Jewish exegesis. See the discussion of Gen 19.24 in Fossum, *Image of the Invisible God*, 45-50.

Hosea 12.3-4, through its parallel structure, appears to affirm that the man with whom Jacob strove was God in the form of the angel:

> [3] In the womb he took his brother by the heel, and in his manhood he strove with Elohim. [4] He strove with the angel and prevailed, he wept and sought his favor. He met Elohim at Bethel, and there Elohim spoke with him.

The Targumim on this incident, however, contain a clear polemic emphasizing that this man was an angel distinct from God.[31]

The most extensive theophany involving the Angel of the Lord takes place with the parents of Samson preceding his birth:

> [Judg 13.3] And the Angel of YHWH appeared to the woman [Manoah's wife] and said to her, "Behold, you are barren and have no children; but you shall conceive and bear a son."
>
> [13.6] Then the woman came and told her husband, "A man of Elohim came to me, and his countenance was like the countenance of the Angel of Elohim, very terrible; I did not ask him where he was from, and he did not tell me his name [. . .].
>
> [13.8] Then Manoah entreated the Lord, and said, "O Lord, I pray you, let the man of Elohim whom you did send come to us again, and teach us what we are to do with the boy who will be born." [9] And Elohim listened to the voice of Manoah, and the Angel of Elohim came again to the woman as she sat in the field; but Manoah her husband was not with her. [10] And the woman ran in haste and told her husband, "Behold, the man who came to me the other day has appeared to me." [11] And Manoah arose and went after his wife, and came to the man and said to him, "Are you the man who spoke to this woman?" And he said, "I am." [12] And Manoah said, "Now when your words come true, what is to be the boy's manner of life, and what is he to do?" [13] And the Angel of YHWH said to Manoah, "Of all that I said to the woman let her beware."
>
> [13.15] Manoah said to the Angel of YHWH, "Pray, let us detain you, and prepare a kid for you." [16] And the Angel of YHWH said to Manoah, "If you detain me, I will not eat of your food; but if you make ready a burnt offering, then offer it to the Lord." For Manoah did not know that he was talking with the Angel of YHWH. [17]

---

[31] *Tg. Onq.* Gen 32.29 explains the new name Israel as "for you are a prince before the Lord". *Tg. Onq.* Gen 32.31 changes "I have seen God" to "I have seen an angel of the Lord" (*Tg. Ps-J.* and *Tg. Neof.*: "angels of the Lord"). *Tg. Ps-J.* Gen 32.25 also asserts that it was "an angel in the form of a man" who wrestled with Jacob and specifically identifies this angel as "Michael" (it also explains that Michael had to leave at dawn to offer praise). *Tg. Neof.* gives a similar explanation, but identifies the angel as "Sariel". *Tg. Ps-J.* Gen 33.29 asserts that Jacob had gained superiority over the angels of the Lord. Codex D of the LXX also indentifies this man as an angel.

And Manoah said to the Angel of the Lord, "What is your name, so that, when your words come true, we may honor you?" [18] And the Angel of YHWH said to him, "Why do you ask my name, seeing it is wonderful?" [19] So Manoah took the kid with the cereal offering, and offered it upon the rock to YHWH, to him who works wonders. [20] And when the flame went up toward heaven from the altar, the Angel of YHWH ascended in the flame of the altar while Manoah and his wife looked on; and they fell on their faces to the ground. [21] The Angel of YHWH appeared no more to Manoah and to his wife. Then Manoah knew that he was the Angel of YHWH. [22] And Manoah said to his wife, "We shall surely die, for we have seen Elohim."

There appears to be a conscious effort in this text to pull together and unify diverse strands of the Angel of the Lord traditions. Notice that in these verses the same figure is identified as the Angel of YHWH, the Angel of Elohim, YHWH, Elohim, the man, and the man of Elohim. This text clearly unites elements found in earlier theophanies and smoothes out some of the diverseness to which these differing elements testify. One of the primary foci of this text is that God appears in the form of a man. It also implies, however, that the appearance of the Angel of the Lord was quite distinctive (cf. 13.6). Again in this text there is evidence that this angel is the angel who bears the Name of God [13.18; MT: ויאמר לו מלאך יהוה למה זה תשאל לשמי והוא־פלאי]. In addition, the flame of fire is probably related to previous theophanies (Exod 3.2; 19.18; 24.16-17), especially to the Glory being connected with the altar fire that consumed the sacrifices offered at the tabernacle (cf. Lev 9.23-24).

This phenomenon of a figure identified as the Angel of the Lord appearing as a man and speaking as God is also found in Zech 1.7-21. The "Angel of the Lord" figure in Zechariah does not seem to have many ideological links with the figure found earlier in the OT, yet this text has several significant features. As with several prophetic texts, the introductory formula notes that "the Word of YHWH came".[32] We are then introduced to "the man" in 1.8 who is also "the angel of YHWH" in 1:11. These titles are interchangable (cf. Judg 13.6; Ezek 9.2; Dan 10.5) and both of these figures are located among "the myrtle trees" which Zechariah sees (1.8, 10, 11). This angel of the Lord seems distinct from God: he leads the

---

[32] This phrase should sometimes be understood in a more visible and tangible manner: the hypostatized Word of YHWH manifest as an angel who communicates with the prophet. See the discussion on 103-114 below.

patrol mounted on horses (1:11); he intercedes with God (1:12); he communicates to humans (1.9, 14-17; 3:6-10); and he also presides over the divine council in 3:1-10, representing God as the judge.[33] What makes this text more notable than other examples of angels in vision interpretation is that the angel's mediatorial functions are taken over by God himself in the text. In 1.20-22 it is YHWH who shows Zechariah a vision and speaks to him.

Although some of the depictions of the Angel of the Lord as a man indicate that he could not be easily identified as distinct from other men, several texts give evidence that the Angel of the Lord's visible presence was very imposing and distinct. For example, it was mentioned above that in Judg 13.6 Samson's mother recognized the man who appeared to her since "his countenance was like that of the Angel of Elohim, terrible" [MT: ומראהו כמראה מלאך האלהים נורא מאד]. Such characterizations of the Angel of the Lord probably reflect the understanding of this angel as a warrior.[34] The warrior angel has its origins in the depiction of YHWH as "the Destroyer" who carried out the dreadful destruction of the Tenth Plague against the Egyptians:

> [Exod 12.21] Then Moses called all the elders of Israel, and said to them, "Select lambs for yourselves according to our families, and kill the passover lamb. [22] Take a bunch of hyssop and dip it in the blood which is in the basin, and touch the lintel and the two doorposts with the blood which is in the basin; and none of you shall go out of the door of his house until the morning. [23] For <u>YHWH will pass through to slay the Egyptians</u>; and when he sees the blood on the lintel and on the two doorposts, <u>YHWH will pass over the door</u>, and will not allow <u>the Destroyer</u> [MT: המשחית; LXX: τὸν ὀλεθρεύοντα] <u>to enter your houses to slay you</u>. [24] You shall observe this rite as an ordinance for you and for your sons for ever. [25] And when you come to the land which YHWH will give you as he has promised, you shall keep this service. [26] And when your children say to you, 'What do you mean by this service?' [27] you shall say, 'It is the sacrifice of <u>YHWH's passover</u>, for he passed over the houses of the people of Israel in Egypt, when <u>he slew the Egyptians</u> but spared our houses.'" And the people bowed their heads and worshipped. [28] Then the people of Israel went and did so; as the Lord had commanded Moses and Aaron, so they did. [29] At midnight <u>YHWH smote all the firstborn in the land of Egypt</u>,

---

[33] In spite of this, Zech 12.3 espouses a likeness between this angel and God: "the house of David shall be like Elohim, like the angel of YHWH."

[34] YHWH is often portrayed as a warrior (e.g., Exod 15.3-18; Deut 32.39-42; Ps 18.6-15); see P. Miller, *The Divine Warrior in Early Israel* (Cambridge, MA: Harvard University Press, 1973).

from the firstborn of Pharaoh who sat on his throne to the firstborn of the captive who was in the dungeon, and all the firstborn of the cattle.

This text assigns the killing of the firstborn to God himself (12.23, 27, 29), with one minor exception: the mention in Exod 12.23 of "the Destroyer" being controlled by God from entering to kill. It was this minor exception that proved to be an important detail contributing to the depiction of the Angel of the Lord as a destructive warrior in other texts.[35] In a similar fashion, the destruction of the Egyptian army in the Red Sea is attributed to YHWH in Exodus (14.24; 15.10, 19, 21). It is apparent, however, that the description of YHWH as "a man of war" in Exod 15.3 led to some speculation that this "man of war" was distinct or separate from YHWH.[36] In fact, Exod 15.3 is a centerpiece for the derivation of the second "Power" in the "Two Powers in Heaven" controversy found in Rabbinic literature.[37]

Evidence of the Angel of the Lord visibly appearing as an imposing warrior wielding a sword is found in several OT texts.[38] One of the most vivid is Joshua's encounter with an imposing angelomorphic being:

> [Josh 5.13] When Joshua was by Jericho, he lifted up his eyes and looked, and behold, <u>a man stood before him with his drawn sword in hand</u>; and Joshua went to him and said to him, "Are you for us, or for our adversaries?" [14] And he said, "No; but as <u>commander of the army of YHWH</u> I have now come." And Joshua fell on his face to the earth, and worshipped, and said to him, "What does <u>my adonai</u> bid his servant?" [15] And <u>the commander of YHWH's army</u> said to Joshua, "Put off your shoes from your feet; for the place where you stand is holy." And Joshua did so.

---

[35] Gen 3.24, Num 22.21-38, Josh 5.13-15, 2 Sam 24.16-17 = 1 Chr 21.15-16, 2 Kgs 19.35 = Isa 37.33-37, and Wis 18.15; see the discussion of many of these texts immediately below. *Ezekiel the Tragedian* 159 attributes this killing to "the fearsome angel" (cf. 187). *Jub.* 49.2 ascribes it to all the powers of Mastema. *Tg. Ps.-J.* Exod 12.29 assigns this action to the Memra YHWH. Rabbinic literature emphasizes that God did not use an angel for this task; see *Mek. Pisha* 7 and 13, *y. Sanh.* 2.1, *y. Hor.* 3.1. For further discussion, see J. Goldin, "Not by Means of an Angel and not by Means of a Messenger", *Religions in Antiquity: Essays in Memory of Erwin Ramsdell Goodenough* (ed. J. Neusner; NumenSup 14; Leiden: Brill, 1968) 412-424.

[36] Segal discusses the pivotal role of this text in his *Two Powers in Heaven*, 34-47, 52-59; see also Fossum, *Image of the Invisible God*, 62 n.72.

[37] Segal, *Two Powers in Heaven*, esp. 34-47.

[38] Num 22.21-38; 2 Kgs 19.32-35 (cf. Isa 37.33-37); 1 Chr 21.14-30 (cf. 2 Sam 24.15-17).

This angel identifies himself (5.14) and is identified in the narration (5.15) with the uncharacteristic title: "the Prince of the army of YHWH" [MT: שׂר־צבא—יהוה; LXX: ἐγὼ ἀρχιστράτηγος δυνάμεως κυρίου (5.14); ὁ ἀρχιστράτηγος κυρίου (5.15)]. Although there has been a tendency by later interpreters to identify this angel as Michael because of his title (שׂר or ἀρχιστράτηγος), he is described in the same manner as some earlier manifestations of the Angel of the Lord.[39] His appearance as someone wielding a sword in 5.13 parallels the description of the Angel of the Lord before Balaam in Num 22.23.[40] Futhermore, the exhortation of 5.15 parallels the words of the Angel of the Lord in the burning bush of Exod 3.5. This figure is to be interpreted in the context of the Angel of the Lord traditions, even as he adds to the warrior element of these traditions.[41]

The Angel of the Lord as "the Destroyer" is present in the following incident involving King David:

> [1 Chr 21.14] So YHWH sent a pestilence upon Israel; and there fell seventy thousand men of Israel. [15] And Elohim sent <u>the Angel</u> to Jerusalem to destroy it, but when he was about to destroy it, YHWH saw, and he repented of the evil; and he said to <u>the Destroying Angel</u>, "It is enough; now stay your hand." And <u>the Angel of YHWH</u> was standing by the threshing floor of Ornan the Jebusite. [16] And David lifted his eyes and saw <u>the Angel of the Lord standing between earth and heaven, and in his hand a drawn sword</u> stretched out over Jerusalem. Then David and the elders, clothed in sackcloth, fell upon their faces [See also 1 Chr 21.17-30; cf. 2 Sam 24.15-17].

Although this text has similarities with others given above, "the Destroying Angel" who is also "the Angel of the Lord" is depicted as distinct from God in this text: God must speak to him to stop the destruction (24.26). Furthermore, David *sees* the angel, but *speaks* to God (24.27). In spite of this testimony, 2 Chr 3.1-2 states: "Solomon

---

[39] The identification of Michael as שׂר (LXX: ἄρχων) in Daniel (10.13, 21; 12.1) and his role as the guardian of Israel influenced some interpreters to identify the angel Joshua encountered as Michael; see Lueken, *Michael*, 104, 157-166. Lueken does not note that Aphraates, a third century Christian, identifies this angel and the angel in Exod 23.20-21 as Michael in his *Tract on Fasting*.

[40] The angel's actions and words in the Balaam incident are nothing less than God's words and actions; compare 22.35 with 22.38, and 23.12 with 23.16.

[41] Josh 23.3, 9-10 may allude to this warrior angel of 5.13-14 when it says that "YHWH, your Elohim" fought for Israel.

began to build the house of YHWH in Jerusalem on Mount Moriah, where *YHWH had appeared* to his father David [. . .] on the threshing floor of Ornan, the Jebusite". This "Destroyer" tradition is most likely also the basis for the figure titled "the Avenger of Blood" in 2 Sam 14.11 and the model for the tradition of six destroying angels who carry out a "passover" style purge in the vision Ezek 9.1-11.[42]

This warrior tradition is related to the important text where God speaks of the angel that bears his Name and whom he will send before Israel to guard and admonish them through the wilderness and into Canaan:

> [Exod 23.20] Behold, <u>I send an angel in front of you</u>, to guard you on the way and to bring you to the place that I have prepared. [21] Be attentive to him and listen to his voice; do not rebel against him, for he will not pardon your transgression; for <u>my Name is in him</u> [MT: כי שמי בקרבו]. [22] But if you listen attentively to <u>his voice</u> and do all that <u>I say</u>, then I will be an enemy to your enemies and an adversary to your adversaries. [23] When <u>my Angel goes before you</u>, and brings you in to the Amorites, and the Hittites, and the Perizzities, and the Canaanites, the Hivites, and the Jebusites, and I blot them out, [24] you shall not bow down to their gods [. . .].

The primary link between this text and Angel of the Lord traditions is the angel going before Israel (23.20); we noted above that this action was understood to have been performed by the Angel of the Lord. In this text he is given the function of Israel's "guardian" angel, acting as an enemy against Israel's enemies as she enters Canaan (23.20, 22; cf. Exod 32.34, 33.2; Pss 34.7, 35.5-6). This angel is also entrusted with some judgment functions over Israel.[43] Both the guarding and punishing functions help paint this angel in warrior armour. The tradition that the Angel of the Lord would speak to Israel as a nation is confirmed in later texts (Judg 2.1-4; 5.23; cf. Job 33.23). His voice conveys the words of God: "if you listen attentively to *his voice* and do all that *I say* " (23.22).

The status and authority of this angel is derived from his possession of the Name of God: "my Name is in him" [כי שמי בקרבו].

---

[42] For a discussion of this text's importance in the development of an archangel heirarchy, see 138-139 below. The "Destroyer Angel" tradition also is visible in the fantastic accounts of warrior horsemen in 2 Maccabees (11.6-13, 10.24-32; 3.1-40) and the end-time angelic avenger in *T. Mos.* 10.1-5.

[43] The lack of pardoning by an angel is also evident in Eccl 5.6 with reference to judgment: "Let not your mouth lead you into sin, and do not say before the Angel that it was a mistake" (cf. Gen 48.15-17).

The noun קרב ("inner") with the pronomial suffix and locative ב prefix signifies "in his inner"; thus, "in him" or "inside him". Jarl Fossum unpacks the laden significance of this attribution:

> When God promises to send his angel carrying his own Name in order to guide Israel to the land he has appointed for them, this means that he has put his power into the angel and thus will be with his people through the agency of the angel. The Angel of the Lord is an extension of YHWH's personality, because the proper Name of God signifies the divine nature. Thus, the Angel of the Lord has full divine authority by virtue of possessing God's Name: he has the power to withhold the absolution of sins.[44]

As noted in the introduction to this chapter, Exod 23.20-21 is an extremely significant part in the Angel of the Lord traditions. Most of the texts that reference the Angel of the Lord depict him as a manifestation of God who is indistinguishable from God. The angel of this text is a personal being clearly distinguishable from God, yet he remains closely associated with God through the possession of the Divine Name. Here we have important evidence that a divine attribute of God, nothing less than his powerful Name, was hypostatized as a particular angel. Exod 23.20-21 was obviously very influential in the development of angels whose exalted status was determined by virtue of their possession of the Name of God.[45]

C. *Conclusion*

This perusal of texts has demonstrated the variegated nature of traditions associated with the Angel of the Lord figure. There is not a uniform pattern for these theophanies or angelophanies, nor are there uniform designations used for the visible manifestions described in these texts. This, in itself, is an important conclusion. It is crucial, however, to read these texts with sympathy to how later interpreters, in the centuries before and after the beginning of the Common Era, understood and harmonized these traditions. This harmonious reading of these texts as speaking about the same

---

[44] *Name of God*, 86.
[45] Yahoel in the *Apoc. Ab.* 10-11, with his twice-theophoric name (YHWH + El), was considered to be this angel of Exod 23.20-21. Metatron is called "the little YHWH" in *3 En.* 10.9. The angel Israel who tabernacled in Jacob according to the *Pr. Jos.* 9 possessed the Name of God.

angelomorphic being is the precedent for why this study draws these diverse texts together and treats them holistically. With this important caveat in mind, three primary conclusions will now be set forth that speak for the foundational importance of these texts for early Christology.

First, these texts present indisputable evidence of the understanding that God can manifest himself in visible form ranging from a fire, to a cloud, to a man. When manifest as a man—which is by far the most prominent part of these epiphanic traditions—the angelomorphic figure appears either as a rather normal male or as an imposing warrior, sometimes quite large in size. The two primary reasons for these epiphanies were to speak revelatory words to someone or to offer visible assurance of God's guardianship and protection. These epiphanies, especially of God as a man, are fundamental to later conceptions of the figure upon the divine throne in Jewish apocalyptic and mystical literature. It is amazing that these startling epiphanic depictions exist alongside the prominent textual traditions that one cannot see God and live.[46]

Second, one of two primary understandings of the Angel of the Lord is found in each of these texts: the angel is either indistinguishable from God as his visible manifestation or the angel is a figure somewhat distinct from God, yet who shares God's authority. In the texts where God and the angel are indistinguishable, the Angel of the Lord is understood to be God's visible form, but not distinct, in any substantive way, from God. In other texts this angel is a distinct figure who functions with divine authority and power. The pivotal text that led to this second understanding is Exod 23.20-21. When God declared that the angel who would watch over Israel had his Name in him, this angel was seen as a figure distinct from God who still shared in God's power by virtue of his possession of the Divine Name. This tradition, which understood the Angel of the Lord to be a figure distinct from God, caused other Angel of the Lord traditions to be read in this same manner by later interpreters.

Third, the significance of the Angel of the Lord traditions as developed in this exegetical direction centers on the angel's

---

[46] See esp. Gen 16.13; 32.31; Exod 20.19 (cf. Deut 5.21; 18.16); Exod 33.20; Deut. 4.24; Isa 6.5; 33.14 (cf. Heb 12.29). Contrast the visibility/invisibility of God (or his form) in: Exod 24.10-11 and Deut 4.12-15; Num 12.8 and Exod 33.20; Isa 6.1 and Ezek 1.26-28.

possession of the Divine Name. To use language familiar from later Trinitarian discussion, this promoted an understanding that this angel was a "person" distinct from God who, in a significant way, shared in God's "substance" through the possession of the Divine Name. The presence of the Divine Name in the Angel of the Lord is a concept that became the center of much interest with regard to angelomorphic figures in the Second Temple period.

CHAPTER FOUR

ANGELOMORPHIC DIVINE HYPOSTASES

Since the concept of divine hypostases was introduced thoroughly in chapter two, now specific texts will be perused in which evidence is found for the hypostatization of the following aspects of God: the Name; the Glory; Wisdom; the Word; the Spirit; and the Power.[1] The purpose of this chapter is to give a concise presentation of each of these hypostases with primary attention given to their relationship to angelomorphic traditions, especially those relating to the Angel of the Lord. The dependent relationship of these hypostatizations on earlier angelomorphic traditions, as well as the help angelology offers in understanding how these hypostatizations may have been understood by ancient Jews, is a field of study that often has been neglected.[2] This survey narrowly focuses on select evidence that brings angelomorphic traditions to light. It, however, does not attempt to present a comprehensive picture of the pluralistic nature of the traditions associated with these ideas. The focus on evidence of these ideas as hypostases certainly should not lead one to infer that the evidence of these ideas as non-hypostatic is either sparse or unimportant.

A. *The Name*

> When it is believed that the nature of a thing is comprehended in its name, then on the one hand emphasis is laid on the idea that knowledge of the name mediates a *direct relationship with the nature*, and on the other the name is regarded as to such an extent an *expression of the individual character* of its owner that it can, in fact, stand for him, become a concept interchangable with him.[3]

---

[1] See discussion on 47-60 above. An hypostasis is an aspect of the deity that is depicted with a degree of independent personhood.
[2] Daniélou, Quispel, Segal, and Fossum are notable expections to this general neglect among biblical scholars, expecially those who specialize in the Hebrew Bible; see 8-25 above.
[3] Eichrodt, *Theology of the OT*, 2.40 (emphasis his).

With these words Walter Eichrodt notes the significance that names, especially God's name, have in biblical documents. The phrases שֵׁם יהוה or שֵׁם אֱלֹהִים ("Name of YHWH" or "Name of Elohim") appear in a variety of ways which are not always easily understood or categorized.[4] These phrases sometimes appear in poetic parallelism with יהוה as a synonym or alternate title for יהוה, especially in various psalms. For example, Ps 20.1 states: "YHWH answer you in the day of trouble; the Name of the Elohim of Jacob protect you!" These phrases are also used in an instrumental sense: people can access or praise God and he can benefit his people by means of his Name. For example, Ps 54.3 asks God's help by means of his Name: "O God, help me by your Name and save me by your Power" (cf. Pss 54.6-7; 44.5; 118.10-14; 148:13; Joel 2.26; Mal 1.11). This later usage may reflect the paradox of how individuals articulated the immanent involvement of a transcendent God with his people on earth. In these texts the Divine Name is not an hypostasis, but such usage contributed to the development of a Name theology and to its hypostatization in some later texts.

1. *The Name as a Divine Hypostasis of Presence*

In several texts the phrases שֵׁם יהוה or שֵׁם אֱלֹהִים or merely שֵׁם are more than synonyms for יהוה or instruments through which God acts in the world; they appear as independent subjects of divine action. In such cases the Name should be understood as an hypostasis.[5] A cursory examination of the OT texts where this usage occurs in the OT shows that they are found primarily in Deuteronomy, the so-called Deuteronomistic History, and Jeremiah.[6] In fact, there is significant evidence that during a period of Israel's history an extensive Name theology developed in which God's presence with his people was described through expressions

---

[4] See the extended explanation which serves as the basis of this discussion in Fossum, *Name of God*, 84-87. I disagree, however, with some of the examples in which he sees the Name as an independent hypostasis.

[5] See the fundamental studies of O. Grether, *Name und Wort Gottes im Alten Testament* (BZAW 64; Giessen: Töpelmann, 1934) 1-58, and T. N. D. Mettinger, *The Dethronement of Sabaoth: Studies in the Shem and Kabod Theologies* (ConBOT 18; Lund: CWK Gleerup, 1982) 129-132.

[6] In Deuteronomy God dwells in heaven (4.36; 26.36), but his Name dwells on earth (12.5, 11; 14.23; 16.11), especially in the sanctuary (2 Sam 7.13; 1 Kgs 3.2; 5.7; 8.12; 9.3, 7; 2 Kgs 21.7; 2 Chr 20.8; Ps 74.7). For a more comprehensive discussion, see Mettinger, *Dethronement of Sabaoth*, 38-79.

involving the dwelling of his שם, especially in the sanctuary.[7] The cultic roots of the hypostatized Name concept are noted by Tryggve Mettinger:

> Accordingly, we conclude that the choice of *shem* as a central theological term in Deuteronomistic theology must be seen in the light of the proclamation of the divine Name in the cultic theophany, and in part as a result of the tendency towards personification or hypostatization of the divine Name. In selecting *shem*, a term was found which was suitable for expressing both the presence of God at the cult site and the distinction between God's being in heaven and his representation on Mount Zion.[8]

There are five verbs commonly used in connection with שם to express this conception of the Name being localized[9]:

1. לשכן and שם ("the Name dwells")[10]

[Deut 12.11] Then you shall bring everything that I command you to the place that YHWH your Elohim will choose, to make <u>his Name to dwell there</u>.

2. לשום and שם ("the Name is put")[11]

[Deut 12.5] But you shall seek the place which YHWH your Elohim will choose out of all your tribes <u>to put his Name</u> and make his dwelling there.

3. היה and שם ("the Name is, exists")[12]

[1 Kgs 8.16] I chose no city in all the tribes of Israel in which to build a house, that <u>my Name might be there</u>; but I chose David to be over my people Israel [cf. 2 Chr 6.5].

---

[7] For a summary of research on the Name Theology, see Mettinger, *Dethronement of Sabaoth*, 41-45, and I. Wilson, *Out of the Midst of Fire: Divine Presence in Deuteronomy* (SBLDS 151; Atlanta: Scholars Press, 1995) 1-15.

[8] Mettinger, *Dethronement of Sabaoth*, 132. Mettinger overemphasizes the idea that God is no longer present in the temple, but only in heaven. The Name is not a theological abstraction; it was an aspect of YHWH that, in some real way, conveyed his presence.

[9] These texts are presented by Mettinger, *Dethronement of Sabaoth*, 38-40. The texts that do not fit into these five categories and yet reflect this Name theology include 2 Chr 20.9; Ps 74.7; Isa 18.7; 60.9; Jer 3.17; 33.9; 1 Chr 22.5.

[10] See also Deut 14.23; 16.2, 6, 11; 26.2. There are reflexes of this phrase in Jer 7.12; Ezra 6.12 (cf. Ezra 1.3); Neh 1.9.

[11] See also Deut 14.24. In conjunction with the Temple: 1 Kgs 9.3; 2 Kgs 21.7 = 2 Chr 33.7 (cf. 2 Chr 6.20). In conjunction with Jerusalem: 1 Kgs 11.36; 1 Kgs 14.21 = 2 Chr 12.13; 2 Kgs 21.4 (cf. 2 Kgs 21.7 = 2 Chr 33.7).

[12] With the Temple, see also: 2 Kgs 8.29; 2 Kgs 23.27; 2 Chr 7.16. In conjunction with Jerusalem, see 2 Chr 6.6 and 33.4.

4. בית לשם יהוה ("a house for the Name of YHWH")[13]

[1 Kgs 5.5 (MT: 5.17)] So I intend to build <u>a house for the Name of YHWH my Elohim</u>, as YHWH said to my father David, 'Your son, whom I will set on your throne in your place shall build <u>the house for my Name</u>'.

5. נקרא and שם ("the Name is called" upon the ark, temple or city)[14]

[1 Kgs 8.43] In order that all the peoples of the earth may know your Name and fear you, as do your people Israel, and that they may know that this house which I have built <u>is called by your Name</u>.

A natural question arises: What motivated or led to this theological development? In one of the most influential analyses of the Name theology, von Rad argues that: "Deuteronomy is replacing the old crude idea of Jahweh's presence and dwelling at the shrine by a theologically sublimated idea".[15] This basic understanding, although it has been nuanced, continues to influence scholarship. Some scholars have argued against the "crudeness" of such ancient concepts and instead speak of the changes that were necessitated by the historical and theological circumstances in Israel.[16] Moreover, Ian Wilson has persuasively argued against the scholarly consensus by demonstrating that the Name theology does not indicate God's transcendence because Deuteronomy contains much evidence of the presence of YHWH on earth.[17]

---

[13] See also: 2 Sam 7.13; 1 Kgs 3.2;1 Kgs 8.17 = 2 Chr 6.7; 1 Kgs 8.18 = 2 Chr 6.8; 1 Kgs 8.19 = 2 Chr 6.9; 1 Kgs 8.20 = 2 Chr 6.10; 1 Kgs 8.44 = 2 Chr 6.34; 1 Kgs 8.48 = 2 Chr 6.38; 2 Chr 6.38; 1 Chr 22.7, 8, 10, 19; 28.3; 29.26; 2 Chr 1.18; 2.3. Note the similar expressions in 1 Kgs 9.17 = 2 Chr 7.20, and 2 Chr 20.8.

[14] It is also used of the Temple in 2 Chr 6.33; Jer 7.10, 11, 14, 30; 32.34; 34.15 (cf. 1 Macc 7.37; Bar 2.26). It is used of the Ark in 2 Sam 6.2 = 1 Chr 13.6. It is used of Jerusalem in Jer 25.29 and Dan 9.18-19.

[15] *Studies in Deuteronomy* (London: SCM, 1953) 39.

[16] E.g., Mettinger postulates that the Name theology was developed to interpret the invasion by the Babylonians which climaxed with the disastrous destruction of the temple in 586 BCE; see *Dethronement of Sabaoth*, 78-79.

[17] *Out of the Midst of Fire*, 199-217. He focuses much of his examination on the phrase לפני יהוה (before "YHWH").

2. *The Name as the Cosmogenic Agent*

Not only is the significance of Name theology seen in texts that speak of the cultic presence of God, but the Name is also accorded other important actions. For example, Isa 30.27 depicts the Name coming to judge: "Behold! The Name of Elohim is coming from afar: burning is his anger, his lips are full of indignation, and his tongue is like a devouring flame!" On the other end of the spectrum, Prov 18.10 implies that the Name is an entity in itself in which protection is found: "The Name of YHWH is a strong tower; the righteous man runs to it and is safe."

Even more significant is the cosmogenic activity assigned to the Name in some Jewish, Samaritan, and Christian literature. For example:

> [Ps 124.8] Our help is in the Name of YHWH who made heaven and earth.
>
> [Pr Man 2] You have made heaven and earth with all their order; you have shackled the Sea by your word of command; [3] you have confined the Deep and sealed it with your terrible and glorious Name.
>
> [*Memar Marqa* IV.2] ה [ה = יהוה] is the Name by which all creatures arose.
>
> [*1 Clem.* 59.3] Your Name, which is the primal source of all creation.
>
> [*Hekaloth Rabbati* 9] Great is the Name through which heaven and earth have been created.

The cosmogenic significance of the Name probably resulted from its association with the creative command, יהי ("let there be"), spoken in the act of creation (Gen 1.3, 6, 14). Both Macdonald and Fossum have compiled evidence from Samaritan literature that shows this to be the case.[18] This association results from the presence of the letters *Yod* and *He* in the creative command יהי; these letters were also used as an abbreviation for the Divine Name יהוה. Fossum has also shown Jewish evidence for this understanding from *Tg. Neof.* and *Frg. Tg.* Exod 3.14 and *Gen. Rab.* 12.10.[19] These texts, as well as those quoted above, present the Name as the instrument used by God to create the world.

---

[18] J. Macdonald, "The Tetragrammaton in Samaritan Liturgical Compositions", *TGUOS* 17 (1959) 37-47, and Fossum, *Name of God*, 76-94.

[19] *Name of God*, 77-80, 253-254.

There is pre-Christian evidence, however, that the Name as an hypostasis actually did the creating. *Jubilees* (ca. second century BCE) records Isaac calling his sons to swear an oath by the Name to which he honorifically ascribes all of creation:

> [36.7] And now I will make you swear by the great oath—because there is not an oath which is greater than it, by the glorious and honoured and great and splendid and amazing and mighty Name which created heaven and earth and everything together—that you will fear and worship him.

1 Enoch 69 (ca. first century CE) also contains evidence of this phenomenon in a lengthy enigmatic discussion of an oath that single-handedly created and sustains the whole universe[20]:

> [69.13] And it was he who reckoned up the number of the Chief of Days for Kasbeel, who revealed the sum of the oath to the angels when he dwelt above in glory, and its name is BIQA [14] This (satan) told to Michael to show him the hidden Name, that they pronounce it in the oath, so that those who revealed all that was secret to the children of men might tremble before that Name and oath. [15] And this is the power of this oath, for it is powerful and strong, and he (God) placed this oath 'AKA' in the hand of Michael. [16] And these are the secrets of this oath:
>
>> 'Through his oath the firmament and the heavens were suspended before the world was created and for ever.
>
> [17] And through it the earth was founded upon the waters;
> And from the secret recesses of the mountains comes sweet water, for the creation of the world and unto eternity.
>
> [18] And through that oath the sea was created and its foundations;
> For the time of its wrath he placed for it the sand as a barrier,
> And it does not pass beyond its boundary from the creation of the world to eternity.
>
> [19] And through that oath are the depths made firm;
> And abide and do not move from their place from eternity to eternity.
>
> [20] And through that oath the sun and the moon complete their course, And do not deviate from their ordinance from eternity to eternity.
>
> [21] And through that oath the stars complete their course;
> And he calls them by their names,
> And they answer him from eternity to eternity.

---

[20] This is the translation of M. Black, *The Book of Enoch or 1 Enoch* (SVTP 7; Leiden: Brill, 1985). This translation is preferable for this text to the one in *OTP* 1.48-49.

> [22] And likewise with regard to the waters, to their winds, and to all spirits and their courses from all regions of spirits;'
>
> [23] And there are kept the storehouses of the thunder-peals and the flashes of the lightning: and there are kept the storehouses of the hail and of the hoar-frost, and the storehouses of the storm-cloud, and the storehouses of the rain and of the dew. [24] And all those who give thanks and praise before the Lord of the Spirits, and glorify (him) with all their power; and their sustenance is in all (their) thanksgiving; they will praise and glorify and extol the Name of the Lord of the Spirits for ever and ever.
>
> [25] And this oath is binding upon them;
> And by it they shall be kept, and they shall keep to their paths,
> And their course shall not be spoiled.

The significance of the "oath" discussed here is "the hidden Name" which is passed on to Michael. The only name that could possibly effect what is ascribed to this oath is the שם המפורש ("the Ineffable Name"): יהוה.[21] The verses which follow this text mention that "the name of that Man was revealed to them" (69.26-27). This implies that in *1 Enoch* there is a connection between the Divine Name and the name of the Son of Man/Elect One. That the name of the Son of Man/Elect One existed before creation is confirmed elsewhere in *1 Enoch* (48.2; cf. 62.7).[22]

3. *The Name Hypostatized as an Angelomorphic Figure*

Especially significant for our subject is the tradition in *1 En.* 69.13-26 that the Name is possessed by the angel Michael. This idea is dependent on the prominent biblical tradition of Exod 23.20-24, as introduced in the previous chapter, where the Name of God is "in" the Angel of the Lord who goes before Israel:

> [Exod 23.20] "Behold, I send an angel in front of you, to guard you on the way and to bring you to the place that I have prepared. [21] Be attentive to him and listen to his voice; do not rebel against him, for he will not pardon your transgression; for my Name is in him.

---

[21] See Fossum, *Name of God*, 257-259. Michael also appears as the possessor of the Divine Name in the *T. Sol.* 1.6 where he brings Solomon the ring with the seal that has power over all demons (i.e., the ring contains the Divine Name). The cosmological significance of the Name is also implied in Psalm 8.

[22] Segal notes the significance of the Name as a weapon of the Son of Man/Elect One against demons and fallen angels; see *Two Powers in Heaven*, 195-196.

This text is pivotal to our thesis because it offers justification for connecting the Name of God with angelomorphic traditions, especially those involving the Angel of the Lord.[23] Exod 23.21 supports the deduction that this important aspect of God—the Divine Name—could be hypostatized as an angel. This profound assertion stimulated differing directions in later exegesis of texts referring to the Divine Name. First, as noted in the previous chapter, there was further speculation about the identity of this Divine Name Angel of Exod 23.20-21. Various texts identify this angel as Michael (*1 En.* 69.15), Yahoel (*Apoc. Ab.* 10.3-8), Metatron (*3 En.* 12.5-13.1), Israel/Jacob (*Pr. Jos.* 9), the Word (Philo, *Migr* 174), Moses (*Samaritan Targum* Exod 23:20-21), or Christ (Clement of Alexandria, *Paid.* I.7). Second, this union of Name and Angel caused later exegetes to read one tradition in light of the other. They reasoned that because an angelomorphic figure bears the Divine Name, those texts which speak of the hypostatized Name can also be read as angelomorphic traditions. For example, Name and Angel became two of the leading traditions and titles that make up the complex *Logos* in Philo (*Conf* 146). Third, because in some circles the Name was seen as the cosmogenic agent, one naturally expects traditions to develop which place an exalted angel who possesses the Name in the cosmogenic role. The Angel of the Lord, including both Gabriel and Michael, have such functions in various texts.[24] Fourth, thought about the Name of God having an existence before creation naturally led to thought about the preexistence of the angelomorphic figure who possessed the Divine Name.[25]

Another probable result of this union of Angel and Name traditions is that it served as the impetus towards speculation, especially in Samaritan circles, that Moses was this angel since God invested

---

[23] Not only this text, but other Angel of the Lord accounts acknowledge that this angel possessed the Divine Name since he is not distinguished from God in these texts; e.g., Gen 32.29, Exod 3.13-14, and Judg 13.17-18.

[24] This is the major thesis of Fossum, *Name of God*; see esp. 192-238, 257-338.

[25] *1 En.* 48.2 speaks of the Son of Man, an angelomorphic being, receiving "a Name" before the creation of the world (cf. *1 En.* 48.7 which speaks of his pre-existence in hiddeness). Surely this is the same Name that existed before creation and brought everything into being (*1 En.* 69.16). The preexistence of the Divine Name is also found in some rabbinic writings; e.g., *Pirqe R. El.* 3 states that only God and his Name existed before the world, and *b. Pesharim* 54a notes that the name of the Messiah is one of the seven things which preceded creation.

Moses with the Divine Name when he revealed it to him (cf. Exod 3.14)[26]:

> [*Memar Marqa* IV.1] Where is there a prophet like Moses, and who can compare with Moses, whose name was made the Name of his Lord (דאתעבד שם מרה שמה)?

As we shall see below, Moses was not the only human to be accorded the honorific status due to the investiture of the Divine Name.[27] This phenomenon prompted rabbinic prohibitions about associating the Divine Name with any created being or thing (e.g., *b. Suk.* 45b; *b. Sanh.* 63a; *Exod. Rab.* 43.3).

B. *The Glory*

Although the כבוד יהוה ("the Glory of YHWH") possesses a wide range of meaning in Israelite and Jewish literature, our focus here is on those texts in which the Glory of YHWH is a signifier of the visible presence of God.[28] The origin of כבוד יהוה as an hypostatized attribute or aspect of God lies in the theophanic texts of the Pentateuch that are commonly associated with the so-called Priestly concern for the temple cult.[29] These texts depict God's presence as a cloud and/or fire that leads Israel, appears to her, or dwells with her, during the Exodus, at Sinai, or in the Tabernacle.

1. *The Glory at Sinai, the Tabernacle, and the Temple*

In the account of the Exodus, for example, some texts depict the pillar of cloud/fire which led Israel out of Egypt and through the

---

[26] Fossum, *Name of God*, 87-94.
[27] See 152-183 below and the abundant evidence of Christ as the Name in Part III of this study.
[28] For a discussion of the semantic field of the כבד word group, see Newman, *Paul's Glory-Christology*, 19-24.
[29] For a more thorough discussion of the biblical evidence and a survey of scholarship on the Glory theology, see Mettinger, *Dethronement of Sabaoth*, 81-115. For a thorough tradition-history of Glory in the MT and LXX that also dialogues with current scholarly research on the subject, see Newman, *Paul's Glory-Christology*, 25-153. For terse and perceptive tradition-history, see Fossum, "Glory", *DDD* 659-668. The discussion below draws primarily on the insights of these scholars.

wilderness as God himself (Exod 13.21-22; 14.24) while others link these manifestations with the Angel of the Lord (Exod 14.19-20; 23.20; Num 20.16). In addition to these two designations, the narrative after the Exodus offers a third way to identify God's presence with Israel:

> [Exod 16.9] And Moses said to Aaron, "Say to the whole congregation of the people of Israel, 'Come near before <u>YHWH</u>, for he has heard your murmurings.'" [10] And as Aaron spoke to the whole congregation of the people of Israel, they looked toward the wilderness, and behold, <u>the Glory of YHWH</u> appeared in <u>the cloud</u>.

The identification of "the Glory of the Lord" as God visibly present in cloud and fire is also made at the Sinai theophany (Exod 24.9-18). In a pattern very similar to the theophany at Moses' commissioning in Exodus 3 where God appears as the Angel of the Lord in the burning bush, God manifests himself on Sinai in a fire as the Glory of the Lord:

> [Exod 24.9] Then Moses and Aaron, Nadab, and Abihu, and seventy of the elders of Israel went up, [10] and <u>they saw the Elohim of Israel</u>; and there was under his feet as it were a pavement of sapphire stone, like the very heaven for clearness. [11] And he did not lay his hand on the chief men of the people of Israel; <u>they beheld Elohim</u>, and ate and drank. [12] YHWH said to Moses, "Come up to me on the mountain, and wait there."

> [24.15] Then Moses went up on the mountain, and <u>the cloud</u> covered the mountain. [16] <u>The Glory of YHWH</u> settled on Mount Sinai, and <u>the cloud</u> covered it six days; and on the seventh day <u>he called</u> to Moses out of the midst of the cloud. [17] Now <u>the appearance of the Glory of YHWH was like a devouring fire</u> on the top of the mountain in the sight of the people of Israel. [18] And Moses entered <u>the cloud</u> and went up on the mountain.[30]

The first part of this narrative records a very startling event: Moses and several others saw God, but he did not lay his hand on them. The problematic nature of this assertion in the MT is undoubtably the reason for the LXX translation in 24.10-11 which eliminates the theophany: εἶδον τὸν τόπον, οὗ εἱστήκει ἐκεῖ ὁ θεὸς τοῦ Ισραηλ [. . .] ὤφθησαν ἐν τῷ τόπῳ τοῦ θεοῦ ("they beheld the place where the God of Israel stands [. . .] they were seen in the place of God").[31] Although no description of God's form is given, it

---

[30] Fire in the cloud at night is mentioned in Exod 40.38.
[31] Philo also emphasizes that they saw the place where God stands, which is the Word (e.g., *Conf* 95).

does mention the clarity of the sapphire stone pavement under God's "feet"; this clear surface became part of later theophanies that feature the divine throne room.[32]

The curiosity sparked by this theophany is satisfied in part by the next verses which include some physical description of YHWH's visible form: "Now the appearance of the Glory of YHWH was like a devouring fire on the top of the mountain" (24.17). These appearances occur directly before God gives Moses instructions for the tabernacle.[33] The visible presence of God as cloud and fire in the Exodus and Sinai events is then linked to the tabernacle later in the narrative:

> [Exod 40.34] Then <u>the cloud</u> covered the tent of meeting, and <u>the Glory of YHWH</u> filled the tabernacle. [35] And Moses was not able to enter the tent of meeting, because <u>the Glory of YHWH</u> filled the tabernacle. [36] Throughout all their journeys, whenever <u>the cloud</u> was taken up from over the tabernacle, the people of Israel would go onward; [37] but if <u>the cloud</u> was not taken up, then they did not go onward till the day that it was taken up. [38] For throughout all their journeys <u>the Cloud of YHWH</u> was upon the tabernacle by day, and <u>fire</u> was in it by night, in the sight of all the house of Israel [cf. Lev 9.22-24].

This same phenomenon of the Glory of the Lord "filling" the sanctuary happens at the dedication of the temple in 1 Kgs 8.10-11. There it serves a legitimating function by demonstrating a continuity of divine presence between the nomadic Exodus-Sinai tabernacle worship with Moses and the now centralized Jerusalem temple worship of the Davidic monarchy.[34]

2. *The Glory as an Angelomorphic Man, Especially in Ezekiel 1*

The texts in which the Glory of the Lord has the form of a man are especially important for our study of angelomorphic traditions. Evidence in the previous chapter showed that the primary angelomorphic manifestation of God in the texts related to the Angel of the Lord is as a man. While several of the texts above depict the Glory as a cloud or fire, the vivid theophany in Exod 33.17-34.8

---

[32] E.g., Ezek 1.22, 26; *1 En.* 14.17-18; Rev 4.2; 22.1.
[33] The dwelling of the Glory in the tabernacle/temple was of great concern to the sacerdotal tradition of Israel. Adherents of the Documentary Hypothesis assign these references about "the Glory of the Lord" to the Priestly Document (P); see Fossum, "Glory", 660.
[34] Newman, *Paul's Glory-Christology*, 44.

gives evidence that God manifested himself in human form (mention is made of his "face", "back", "hand" and of him "standing"):

> [33.18] Moses said, "I ask you, show me your Glory." [19] And he said, "I will make my Glory[35] pass before you, and will proclaim before you my Name "YHWH"; and I will be gracious to whom I will be gracious, and will show mercy on whom I will show mercy." [20] "But," he said, "you cannot see my face; for man shall not see me and live." [21] And YHWH said, "Behold, there is a place by me where you shall stand upon the rock; [22] and while my Glory passes by I will put you in a cleft of the rock, and I will cover you with my hand until I have passed by; [23] then I will take away my hand, and you shall see my back; but my face shall not be seen."
>
> [34.5] And YHWH descended in the cloud and stood with him there, and proclaimed the Name of YHWH. [6] YHWH passed before him, and proclaimed, YHWH, YHWH, an Elohim merciful and gracious [...].

This theophany indicates the severe consequence which results from seeing the visible form of God: death (33.20). This maxim is qualified by the assertion that seeing God's face is not possible; God does allow Moses to see his backside. Fossum makes the following pointed observations on this intriguing episode:

> The picture emerging from this story is that of the indistinguishability between the divine Glory and the anthropomorphous Deity. The relationship between God and his Glory is here thus comparable to that between God and the Angel of Yahweh, the human-like Messenger of God.[36]

Isaiah's call vision is the "patriarch" of visions focused on the *enthroned* YHWH: "I saw the Lord sitting upon a throne, high and lifted up; and his train filled the temple" (Isa 6.1). The dire consequences of seeing God are captured in Isaiah's panicked response: "Woe is me! For I am lost [...] for my eyes have seen the King, YHWH of hosts!" (Isa 6.5). The *Isaiah Targum* could not leave such an assertion stand. Instead, it states that Isaiah saw "the Glory of YHWH":

> [6.1] In the year that King Uzziah was struck with it, the prophet said, I saw <u>the Glory of YHWH</u> resting upon a throne, high and

---

[35] The reading of the MT (כל-טובי; "all my goodness") appears to downplay the theophany, especially in light of כבוד in Exod 33.18, 22. This translation follows the reading of τῇ δόξῃ μου ("my Glory") in the LXX.

[36] "Glory", 661.

lifted up on the heavens of the height; and the temple was filled with the brillance of his glory [. . .]. [6.5] And I said, "Woe is me! For I have sinned; for I am a man liable to chastisement, and I dwell in the midst of people that are defiled with sins; for my eyes have seen <u>the Glory of the Shekinah of the eternal king, YHWH of hosts!</u> [6.6] Then there was given to me one of the attendants and in his mouth there was a speech which he took before him whose Shekhinah is upon the throne of glory in the heavens of the height, above the altar.

The most significant text which identifies the Glory as having the form of a man is Ezekiel's elaborate vision of the moving heavenly *Merkabah* (chariot-throne) in the opening chapter of his prophetic writings (ca. 593 BCE). After an elaborate description of the chariot-throne scene, he proceeds to offer this description of the figure upon the throne:

> [1.26] And above the dome over their heads there was something like a throne, in appearance like sapphire; and <u>seated above the likeness of a throne was the likeness as the appearance of a man</u>. [27] Upward from what appeared like the loins I saw something like gleaming amber, something that looked like fire enclosed all around; and downward from what looked like the loins I saw something that looked like fire, and there was a splendor all around. [28] Like the bow in a cloud on a rainy day, so was the appearance of the brightness round about. Such was <u>the appearance of the likeness of the Glory of YHWH.</u>

This text communicates the mystery of the unseen God with uncharacteristic detail in comparison with glimpses of the divine throne in earlier texts.[37] The figure on the throne was doubtlessly understood to be the Glory (1.28); there is no other occupant of the throne or divine figure in the area of throne. The seated figure was "the likeness as the appearance of a man" [MT: דמות כמראה אדם; LXX: ὁμοίωμα ὡς εἶδος ἀνθρώπου]. This description of the Glory is related to the Angel of the Lord theophanies, especially where God appeared in the form of a man, and the limited description of the Glory found in Exod 33.17-34.8. The Glory then speaks to Ezekiel as he commissions him to prophesy (2.1-11). Afterwards, the *Merkabah* rumbles off with "the sound of a great earthquake" (2.11-13).

---

[37] Exod 24.10 only mentions the "pavement of sapphire stone" and Isa 6.1-13 gives only a few more details (the throne being up high, the garment of the Lord filling the temple, the seraphim above him, and the smoke).

There are two other portraits of the Glory in Ezekiel that are important for our understanding of this figure. The first is the appearance of the Glory in Ezekiel 3:

> [22] And the hand of YHWH was there upon me; and he said to me, "Arise, go forth into the plain, and there I will speak with you." [23] So I arose and went forth into the plain and, lo, the Glory of YHWH stood there, like the Glory which I had seen by the river Chebar; and I fell on my face. [24] But the Spirit entered into me, and set me upon my feet; and he [the Glory] spoke with me and said to me [...].

This depiction indicates that the Glory is appearing to Ezekiel *apart from* the *Merkabah* upon which he was seated earlier (1.26): the Glory is standing in this depiction (3.23) and there is no mention of the throne's presence or departure. As in Ezekiel 2, the Glory speaks to the prophet (3.24-5.17).

The man-like Glory reappears in Ezekiel 8. Even though this figure is not specifically identified as the Glory, his visible similarity to the figure on the throne in Ezek 1.26-27 is unmistakable[38]:

> [8.2] Then I looked, and, lo a form that had the appearance of a man[39]; below what appeared to be his loins it was fire, and above his loins it was like the appearance of brightness, like gleaming bronze.

The throne and its accompanying elements are not present. Instead, the Glory functions here as *an angelus interpres* who puts out his "hand" (3.22) and transports the prophet Ezekiel via "the Spirit" (3.24) to Jerusalem for visionary experiences (8.3).

The next time the chariot-throne appears is in chapter 10 where the Glory is above the throne and then takes a position in another portion of the sanctuary (10.4, 18; cf. Ps 99.1). Rowland sees this appearance of the man-like Glory apart from the divine throne in Ezekiel 8 as a very significant depiction and one that represents "[...] the separation of the form of God from the divine throne-

---

[38] These shared features are: both figures have the appearance of a man (1.26b and 8.2a); both have fire as their lower body (1.27b and 8.2b); both have a torso that is like gleaming bronze (1.27a and 8.2b). See the discussion by W. Zimmerli, *Ezekiel* (Hermenia; 2 vols.; Philadelphia: Fortress, 1979) 1.236. In spite of this evidence, Carrell argues that these two figures are distinct (YHWH and a heavenly messenger); see *Jesus and the angels*, 28-35.

[39] This translation follows the reading of the LXX (ὁμοίωμα ἀνδρός) since the MT (דמות כמראה אש "a form that had appearance of fire") may have been emended (איש to אש); see Rowland, *Open Heaven*, 464 n.38.

chariot to act as quasi-angelic mediator".[40] In light of the Angel of the Lord traditions discussed above, however, the separation of the Glory from the throne in both Ezekiel 3 and 8 is not so much of a new development as it is a reflection of older angelomorphic conceptions of God.[41] God is more consistently depicted on his throne in visions after Isaiah's dramatic call, especially in Jewish mystical texts. What is amazing about Ezekiel 1 is that the figure on the divine throne is described as appearing as a man; one would not expect to see any significant visible features if the Merkabah is viewed from the front (cf. Exod 33.18-23). Therefore, what is significant in these depictions is not that the man-like Glory appears apart from the throne, *but that he appears seated on the throne in the powerful opening vision.* This man-like Glory is on the sacred heavenly domain of God himself: the divine throne.

These brief observations reveal some of the complexities present with the Glory figure of Ezek 1.26. The danger of an improper exegesis of this mystery in Ezekiel made it a forbidden text by the second century CE for the inexperienced rabbi to interpret.[42] Concerning this situation Rowland states:

> In particular, the subject which seems to have intrigued some, to such a degree that a warning was necessary, was speculation about the nature of God himself: interest, in other words, in the holy God, whom it was not possible for man to look upon without death (Exod 33.20). It is hardly surprising that in a religion which prohibited images and seemed to cultivate a belief in the invisibility of God, a passage like Ezekiel 1 should quickly assume an important position as the basis for discussion about the form and character of the unseen God.[43]

3. *The Angelomorphic Glory in Texts After Ezekiel 1*

Ezekiel 1 became a very influential text in the ensuing apocalyptic and mystical traditions concerning the form of God seated upon

---

[40] Rowland, *Open Heaven*, 97. This position is criticized by Hurtado, *One God*, 87-88.

[41] The pattern in Ezek 9.3-4 is similar to that in several Angel of the Lord texts: "the Glory of God [. . .] called [. . .] and YHWH said".

[42] See the rabbinic discussion in *m. Meg.* 4.10 and *m. Hag.* 2.1; cf. Rowland, *Open Heaven*, 271-281, esp. 277.

[43] Rowland, *Open Heaven*, 280. Rowland also notes that there was a movement away from describing the human-like figure on the throne in texts that used Ezekiel 1, such as *1 En.* 71, *Apoc. Sedr.* 2, *Apoc. Ab.* 18, Rev 4, (cf. *4 Ezra* 9-13; *2 Bar.* 36, 53); see *Open Heaven*, 86-87.

the divine throne. The most well-known of these texts is Dan 7.9-13. Although its content is closely related to Ezekiel 1, this vision is distinct in that at least two thrones are depicted (7.9) and the "one like a son of man" is a second figure distinct from God (i.e., the Ancient of Days in 7.13). In this text the angelomorphic figure comes alongside the Ancient of Days and becomes the representative of divine rule:

> [13] I saw in the night visions, and behold, with the clouds of heaven there came one like a son of man, and he came to the Ancient of Days and was presented before him. [14] And to him was given dominion and glory and kingdom, that all peoples, nations, and languages should serve him; his dominion is an everlasting dominion, which shall not pass away and his kingdom one that shall not be destroyed.

By examining Dan 7.13 in light of Ezek 1.27, one could conclude that "the one like a son of man" is the Glory. This would mean that there are two divine figures present in Daniel 7. An attempt to resolve this problem was made in the LXX of Dan 7.13 which states "there came one like a son of man, and he came as [ὡς] the Ancient of Days".[44]

Alan Segal has carefully documented evidence of the controversy that the existence of a second enthroned being or "Power" brought to early rabbinic circles.[45] He points to the following second or third century CE rabbinic text involving Rabbi Akiba (ca. 110-135 CE) that sheds more light on the controversy that Daniel 7 and a second figure on God's throne could cause:

> [b. Hag. 14a] One passage says: "His throne was fiery flames" (Dan. 7:9); and another passages says: "Till thrones were placed, and One that was ancient of days did sit"—there is no contradiction: One (throne) for Him, and one for David. This is the view of Rabbi Akiba. Said Rabbi Yosi the Galilean to him: Akiba, how long will you treat the Divine Presence as profane! Rather, one for justice and one for grace. Did he accept (this explanation) from him or did he not accept it?—come and hear: One for justice and one for grace; this is the view of R. Akiba [cf. b. Sanh. 38b].

This text shows that Rabbi Akiba had linked Dan 7.13 with the enthronement of the Davidic Messiah in Ps 110.1. However plausible this may have been, Akiba's colleagues did not agree. The

---

[44] Segal, *Two Powers in Heaven*, 202.
[45] *Two Powers in Heaven*, 3-59.

note that he changed his mind is probably a later emendation to help Akiba appear more orthodox. With regard to enthronement, Segal also notes that "the rabbis are determined to refute the whole idea of heavenly enthronement by stating that such things as 'sitting' and other anthropomorphic activities are unthinkable in heaven".[46] He cites the following later rabbinic text which gives insight into the controversy of another one *sitting* on the throne of God:

> [*b. Hag.* 15a] Aher mutilated the shoots. Of him Scripture says: (Ecc. 5:5). Suffer not thy mouth to bring thy flesh into guilt. What does it refer to?—He saw that permission was granted to Metatron to sit and write down the merits of Israel. Said he: "It is taught as a tradition that on high there is no sitting and no emulation, no back and no weariness." Perhaps God forfend!—there are two divinities (powers). Thereupon they led Metatron forth, and punished him with sixty fiery lashes, saying to him: "Why didst thou not rise before him when thou didst see him?" Permission was (then) given to him to strike out the merits of Aher. A Bath Kol went forth and said: "Return, ye backsliding children" (Jer. 3:22)—except Aher [cf. *3 En.* 16.1-5].

Even though this evidence is from a later period, it helps our understanding of the type of controversy that two or more enthroned powers could cause in earlier periods of the discussion.

The myopic focus on Dan 7.13 has often led attention away from the intriguing angelomorphic figure in Dan 10.5-9. Ezek 1:26-28 and 8.3-4 as well as the description of the primal man in Ezek 28.13, appear to have influenced the way this figure is described[47]:

> [10.5] I lifted up my eyes and looked, and behold, a man clothed in linen, whose loins were girded with gold of Uphaz. [6] His body was like beryl, his face like the appearance of lightning, his eyes like flaming torches, his arms and legs like the gleam of burnished bronze and the sound of his words like the noise of a multitude. [7] And I, Daniel, alone saw the vision, for the men who were with me did not see the vision, but a great trembling fell upon them, and they fled to hide themselves. [8] So I was left alone and saw this great vision, and no strength was left in me; my radiant appearance was fearfully changed, and I retained no strength. [9] Then I heard the sound of his words; and when I heard the sound of his words, I fell on my face in a deep sleep with my face to the ground.

---

[46] *Two Powers in Heaven*, 60-66.
[47] This is argued convincingly by Rowland, *Open Heaven*, 98-100.

From the exalted description of this figure and Daniel's reaction, this angelomorphic figure is of some status; on the basis of Ezek 1.27 and 8.2, he also could be identified as the Glory. Although it is not possible to state conclusively the identity of this angelomorphic figure, it is most logical to identify him as the angel Gabriel because Gabriel carries out a similar function for Daniel in Dan 8.15-26 and 9.21.[48] One can easily see how the angelomorphic figures in Daniel added further complexities to the identity and appearance of the Glory.

The appearances of the Glory in *1 Enoch* (ca. second century BCE to first century CE) betray influence from the powerful first chapter of Ezekiel, Exodus 24, and Isaiah 6, each of which predate all portions of this Enochic pentateuch.[49] One of the older portions of this document contains a theophany of the enthroned Glory who is described in this manner:

> [14.20] And the Great Glory was sitting on it [the throne]—as for his gown, which was shining more brightly than the sun, it was whiter than any snow. [21] None of the angels was able to come in and see the face of the Excellent and the Glorious One; and no one of the flesh can see him—[22] the flaming fire was round about him, and a great fire stood before him. No one could come near unto him from among those that surrounded the tens of millions (that stood) before him.

The injunction of Exod 33.20 is echoed here: neither angel nor human can see the *face* of the Great Glory. This text also portrays how privileged one must be to come near the throne (14.22).

Unlike this picture of God as the Great Glory alone upon his throne, the Similitudes (*1 En.* 37-71) show influence from Daniel 7 by depicting two figures: the Ancient of Days (also called the Lord of the Spirits) and the Elect One/Son of Man. That the Elect One/Son of Man is to be identified with the Glory of Ezek 1.26 is clear from how he is introduced in the Similitudes: "whose countenance had the appearance of a man" (46.1). This angelomorphic figure is seated on "the throne of Glory" of the Ancient of Days.

---

[48] Rowland, *Open Heaven*, 98-102, and Fossum, *Name of God*, 279 n.61. Fossum has even suggested that the "one like a son of man" in Dan 7.13 could have been understood as Gabriel. For further discussion about Gabriel, see 131-134 below.

[49] The Book of the Watchers (*1 Enoch* 1-36) is usually dated to the second century BCE. The Similitudes (*1 Enoch* 37-71) is dated to the first century CE, and probably pre-70; see *OTP* 1.7.

This text gives further evidence of the Glory being understood as an angelomorphic figure who has some distinctness from God and yet shares or occupies his throne.

The *Sibylline Oracles* also contains a text in Book 5 (ca. second century CE) which displays the savior figure as "a man" from heaven:

[414] For <u>a blessed man came from the expanses of heaven</u>
[415] with a scepter in his hands which God gave him,
[416] and he gained sway over all things well, and gave back the wealth
[417] to all the good, which previous men had taken.
[418] He destroyed every city from its foundations with much fire
[419] and burned nations of mortals who were formerly evildoers.
[420] And the city which God desired, this he made
[421] more brillant than stars and sun and moon,
[422] and he provided ornament and made a holy temple,
[423] exceedingly beautiful in its fair shrine, and he fashioned
[424] a great and immense tower over many stadia
[425] touching even the clouds and visible to all,
[426] so that all faithful and all righteous people could see
[427] <u>the Glory of eternal God, a form desired</u>.

In a manner similar to *1 En.* 46.1, the reference to "a blessed man from the expanses of heaven" is more than a subtle allusion to the Glory in Ezek 1.26.[50] This is substantiated by the visibility of "the Glory of the eternal God" as "a form desired" (5.427).

4. *The Identification of the Glory with a Human*

Although the Glory on the throne in Ezekiel 1 is angelomorphic, it is not surprising that creative attempts were made to identify this figure with an actual human being sharing God's throne. For example, in the closing chapter of the Similitudes of *1 Enoch* the mysterious Son of Man is identified as the man Enoch (71.14). The *Testament of Abraham* (ca. first or early second century CE) testifies that both Adam and Abel are radiant enthroned figures.[51] In *Ezekiel the Tragedian* (ca. second century BCE) the Glory upon the throne (line 70: "a man [φώς] of noble mien"; cf. Ezek 1.26) even steps down from the throne which is then given over to the man Moses. Here again, a human figure is seated upon the throne of the Glory.

---

[50] See J. Fossum, "The Figure of the Heavenly Man in Recent Research", *ANRW* II.22, forthcoming.
[51] Adam is on a "throne of Great Glory" in *T. Ab.* 11.4-12 (Rec. A). Abel has a throne and a fearsome appearance like the Lord as he shines like the sun in *T. Ab.* 12.4-13.3 (Rec. A). Both participate in the judgment process.

C. *Wisdom*

The personification of Wisdom [Heb: חכמה; Gk: σοφία] is widely recognized as an important antecedent for early Christology.[52] Whether Wisdom is an hypostatized attribute is a much more debated subject.[53] The following perusal will demonstrate that some depictions of Wisdom go beyond the bounds of literary personification and present her as an hypostatized aspect of God. Moreover, as with the Name and the Glory, it will become apparent in this examination that some Wisdom traditions are dependent upon and were shaped by angelomorphic traditions.[54]

1. *Wisdom as an Hypostasis and Cosmogenic Agent*

Proverbs 1-9 is the primary fountainhead for later elaboration about Wisdom.[55] Several aspects of Proverb's discussion of Wisdom gave impetus to such ideological thought and literary activity. First, portions of these chapters detail how Wisdom is to be held in the highest esteem; according to Prov 3.13-18 she is more precious than any possession in the world (cf. Job 28.12-28). Second, in several places she is vividly personified as a woman whose speech is recorded in the first person (Prov 1.20-33, 8.1-36, and 9.3-6). Third, she is described as a primordial figure who enjoyed a close relationship with God in the act of creating the world (8.22-31). She is shown to be a figure fairly distinct from God and the rest of his

---

[52] Dunn notes how Wisdom became much more prominent in discussions of Christology the past 35 years since the Gnostic Redeemer Myth lost adherents; see *Christology in the Making*, 161-167. Hengel argues for the importance of Wisdom traditions in early Christology; see *Studies in Early Christology*, 73-117. For a broader introductions to the Wisdom literature, see G. von Rad, *Wisdom in Israel* (trans. J. Martin; London: SCM, 1972), and L. Perdue, *Wisdom and Creation: The Theology of Wisdom Literature* (Nashville: Abingdon, 1994).

[53] Dunn is so bold as to state: "Language which denoted a hypostasis or independent deity in polytheism would certainly have a different connotation within a monotheistic religion"; see *Christology in the Making*, 170.

[54] Wisdom's dependence upon angel traditions has been noted by Fossum, but not extensively worked out; see "Kyrios Jesus", 237.

[55] See: W. McKane, *Proverbs* (OTL; London: SCM, 1970) 342-359; von Rad, *Wisdom in Israel*, 149-173; Hengel, *Judaism and Hellenism*, 1.153-174; Perdue, *Wisdom and Creation*, 77-122; and Whybray, *Wisdom in Proverbs*.

creation (Prov 8.22-31; cf. Sir 1.9). Fourth, she is also pictured as intimately involved in the act of creating the world, even having cosmogenic functions (Prov 8.27-31, cf. 3.19-20).

These latter three elements are present in the most exalted presentation of Wisdom found in Proverbs:

[8.22] YHWH begot me [MT: קנני; LXX: ἔκτισέν με] as the beginning [MT: ראשית; LXX: ἀρχήν] of his ways, the first of his acts of old.[56]

[23] Ages ago I was installed, at the first, before the beginning of the earth.

[24] When there were no depths I was brought forth, when there were no springs abounding with water.

[25] Before the mountains had been shaped, before the hills, I was brought forth;

[26] before he made the earth with its fields, or the first of the dust of the world.

[27] When he established the heavens, I was there, when he drew a circle on the face of the deep,

[29] when he assigned to the sea its limit, so that the waters might not transgress his command, when he marked out the foundations of the earth,

[30] then I was beside him, like a master craftsman [MT: אמון; LXX: ἁρμόζουσα]; and I was daily his delight, rejoicing before him always,

[31] rejoicing in his inhabited world and delighting in the sons of men.

Unlike other personifications of Wisdom in Proverbs, the assertions in this text portray her as an hypostasis, an aspect of God that has a degree of independent personhood.[57] Wisdom speaks in the first person and refers to God in the third person several times (8.22-29). A distinction exists between the origins of Wisdom and those of God; Wisdom is also distinct from the rest of creation (8.22). She is God's companion, even a participant ("master crafts-

---

[56] The language of this verse is very important for later use of Wisdom theology. The MT קנני is translated with the procreative "begot" because there is an emphasis in this text on Wisdom's presence with God before creation began; contra ἔκτισέν με "he created me" of the LXX. On the LXX translation, see Hengel, *Judaism and Hellenism*, 1.162-163; cf. Sir 1.4, 9; 24.3. This procreative thrust is also found in the use of חוללתי ("I was brought forth [in labor]") twice in 8.24-25. The designation of Wisdom as "the beginning" (MT: ראשית; LXX: ἀρχήν) is probably the antecedent of its use as an important Christological title in Col 1.18 and Rev 3.14; see the important discussion of Daniélou, *Theology of Jewish Christianity*, 166-168, and C. Burney, "Christ as the ΑΡΧΗ of Creation", *JTS* 27 (1926) 161-177.

[57] See Hengel, *Judaism and Hellenism*, 1.153-169.

man" [MT: אָמוֹן; LXX: ἁρμόζουσα]), in the creation.⁵⁸ Furthermore, the position of Wisdom in relation to God also indicates a degree of independent personhood: Wisdom is "beside him" and "in his presence" (8:30). The latter position is typical of descriptions of angels standing before God (e.g., Dan 7.10).

Wisdom's place with the angels is discussed also in *1 Enoch* 42, which is an encapsulation of the Wisdom descent tradition⁵⁹:

> [1] Wisdom could not find a place in which she could dwell;
> but <u>a place was found (for) her in the heavens</u>.
> [2] Then Wisdom went out to dwell with the children of the people,
> but she found no dwelling place.
> (So) Wisdom returned to <u>her place</u>
> and <u>she settled permanently among the angels</u>.

Sirach also depicts Wisdom in the midst of God's angelic host: "In the assembly of the Most High she will open her mouth, and in the presence of his host she will glory" (24.2).

The preposition "beside him" [אֶצְלוֹ] in Prov 8.30a, however, is indicative of more than the position of a typical angel (cf. Sir 1.8-9). Such language is used of one's position next to, or on, the throne of God in Jewish and Christian literature.⁶⁰ The force of the verb נסך ("pour out, anoint, install"; cf. Ps. 2.6) in Prov. 8.23 supports the understanding of Wisdom's enthronement. Her honored position certainly substantiates the claims made about her value. This brief examination of Proverbs 8 confirms R.N. Whybray's conclusion: "in the mind of the author wisdom had assumed a degree of reality as a being distinguishable from, though not independent of, God, a divine agent rather than merely a divine characteristic".⁶¹

---

⁵⁸ God is depicted as the creator in these verses until one attempts to interpret 8.30. It is possible to understand אָמוֹן as a passive participle translated as "darling" or "ward" (cf. Aquila) and argue that Wisdom is depicted here as a child on God's lap. "Craftsman" (cf. Jer 52.15), however, is a very viable translation which explains the cosmogenic role that Wisdom has in later texts (e.g., Wis 7.22; 8.1, 5; 9.1-2). See the discussion by McKane, *Proverbs*, 356-358.

⁵⁹ *2 Bar.* 3.14-15, 29; Sir 24.1-7; *4 Ezra* 5.9-10; see also G. MacRae, "The Jewish Background of the Gnostic Sophia Myth", *NovT* 12 (1970) 86-101.

⁶⁰ Wisdom's position relative to God's throne is made explicit in Wis 9.4, 11; see the discussion on 93-97 below, and Hengel, *Studies in Early Christology*, 212-214. Sirach 24.4 mentions that Wisdom's throne is in a "pillar of cloud". The Lamb in Revelation is "standing" at the right hand of the throne (5.6-7). Because he has triumphed he then "sits" with God on the throne (7.15-17; 22.1-3) and can invite others to sit with him (3.21).

⁶¹ *Wisdom in Proverbs*, 13.

These characteristics of Wisdom were developed in an even more pronounced way by other writers, as can be seen from the Egyptian Jewish document Wisdom of Solomon (ca. first century BCE or early first century CE):

> [6.22b] I will trace her course from the beginning of creation.
> [7.21] I learned both what is secret and what is manifest, for Wisdom, the Fashioner of all things, taught me.
> [22] For in her there is a spirit that is intelligent, holy, unique, manifold, subtle, mobile, clear, unpolluted, distinct, invulnerable, loving the good, keen, irresistible,
> [23] beneficent, humane, steadfast, sure, free from anxiety, all-powerful, overseeing all, and penetrating through all the spirits that are intelligent and pure and most subtle.
> [24] For Wisdom is more mobile than any motion; because of her pureness she pervades and penetrates all things.
> [25] For she is a breath of the Power of God, and a pure emanation of the Glory of the Almighty; therefore nothing defiled gains entrance into her.
> [26] For she is a reflection of eternal light, a spotless mirror of the working of God, and an image of his goodness[. . .].
> [29] For she is more beautiful than the sun, and excels every constellation of the stars. Compared with the light she is found to be superior.
> [8.3] She glorifies her noble birth by living with God, and the Lord of all loves her.

This text exudes with profound ascriptions to Wisdom that are unparalleled in Wisdom literature.[62] An important part of these ascriptions is the cosmogenic role of Wisdom which grew from Proverbs 8: she is declared to be "the Fashioner of all things" [ἡ πάντων τεχνῖτις] (7.21; cf. 8.6). Her cosmogenic role is reinforced by the epithets "all powerful" (7.23) and "a breath of the Power of God" (7.25). In 9.1-2 she is identified as the "Word" that creates all things.

Philo also developed the idea of Wisdom's assistant role in creation.[63] For Philo, Wisdom is the cosmic principle, a being who

---

[62] For discussion of the Hellenistic background for the 21 epithets and the five-fold descriptive metaphor of Wisdom, see D. Winston, *The Wisdom of Solomon* (AB 43; Garden City: Doubleday, 1979) 178-190; see also Winston, "Wisdom in the Wisdom of Solomon", *In Search of Wisdom: Essays in Memory of John G. Gammie* (eds. L. Perdue, B. Scott, and W. Wiseman; Louisville: Westminster/John Knox, 1993) 149-164.

[63] Segal, *Two Powers in Heaven*, 79, 83, 114, 129, 188.

existed before creation and was instrumental in "birthing" the creation and "mothering" it (*Ebr* 30-31; *Fug* 109; *Quod Det* 54; cf. *Virt* 62). Although Philo melds Wisdom with *Logos* in some places (*Conf* 146; *Leg All* 1.43), in *Ebr* 30-31 he calls Wisdom the mother of *Logos* with the implication that God is her husband. In other texts he indicates that Wisdom is the model from which the physical world is copied (*Leg All* 1.43; cf. *Leg All* 2.49).

Wisdom of Solomon and Philo are by no means the only examples of the development of this cosmogenic role of Wisdom.[64] Another example, specifically in the creation of man, is found in *2 Enoch* (ca. first century CE):

> [30.8] And on the sixth day I commanded my Wisdom to create man out of the seven components. [11] And on earth I assigned him [man = Adam] to be a second angel, honored and great and glorious. [12] And I assigned him to be a king, to reign on the earth, and to have my Wisdom.

Wisdom may be considered the "first angel" who then created Adam. This description is very similar to the creation of man described in Wisdom of Solomon:

> [9.1] "O God of my fathers and Lord of mercy, who hast made all things by your Word, [2] and by your Wisdom has formed man to have dominion over the creatures you have made [...]".

This role of Wisdom in creation is also evidenced in the Targumim and some of the Jewish prayers that are incorporated into the *Apostolic Constitutions*.[65]

2. *Wisdom and the Divine Throne*

One of the most intriguing angelomorphic aspects of Wisdom in Wisdom of Solomon is her relationship to the divine throne. This detail is especially significant for establishing Wisdom's relationship with God and with the rest of the heavenly host. Texts in which a figure shares the divine throne with God, or is its sole

---

[64] For a discussion of this development, see Quispel, "From Mythos to Logos", *Gnostic Studies* 1.161-165.

[65] *Tg. Neof.* Gen 1.1 indicates an instrumental role for Wisdom (cf. *Gen. Rab.* 1.1). *Frg. Tg.* goes further by modifying בראשית ("In the beginning") to בחכמה ("In his Wisdom"). Wisdom is the one who creates in *Apos. Con.* 7.34.5-6, 8.12.7-8, and 8.12.16. For the Jewish background to these portions of the *Apostolic Constitutions*, see *OTP* 2.671-673.

occupant, make a profound theological statement in a Jewish context: divinity could be ascribed to the enthroned figure.[66] It will now be shown how Wisdom's position on the divine throne reflects her divinity.

The two primary references to Wisdom's position of sharing the throne are from Wisdom of Solomon:

[9.4]   give to me Wisdom, she who sits by you on your throne
        [δός μοι τὴν τῶν σῶν θρόνων πάρεδρον σοφίαν]
[9.10] Send her [Wisdom] forth from the holy heavens,
        and from the throne of your Glory send her,
        [ἐξαπόστειλον αὐτὴν ἐξ ἁγίων οὐρανῶν
        καὶ ἀπὸ θρόνου δόξης σου πέμψον αὐτήν]
        that she may be with me and toil,
        and that I may learn what is pleasing to you.

From these two verses it is clear that Wisdom has the very privileged position of sharing the divine throne. In Sir 24.4 we find Wisdom enthroned in a pillar of clouds (cf. Exod 14.19; 14.24; 19.9). The "all-powerful Word", who is closely linked with Wisdom in Wis 9.1-2, is described as leaping from "the royal throne [θρόνων βασιλείων]" in 18.15. In spite of the supposed abstractness of an attribute like Wisdom, still she is conceived of as "sitting" by God upon his throne (Wis 9.4), specifically "the throne of your Glory" (Wis 9.10). Both of these ideas, "thone of Glory" and "sitting", merit futher attention.

According to Jewish traditions, the divine throne was sometimes understood as preexistent or as one of the first acts in the creation of the world.[67] Wisdom tradition in the LXX text of Prov 8.27, which certainly influenced the Greek-speaking author of Wisdom of Solomon, implies that Wisdom existed even before the creation of the throne. Note the difference of the MT and LXX as translated here:

MT: בהכינו שמים שם אני בחוקו חוג על־פני תהום
When he established the heavens, I was there,
When he drew a circle on the face of the deep [. . .].

---

[66] See the criteria of divinity, 30-33 above.
[67] 2 *En.* 25.4 depicts the creation of the throne as following the creation of light. *b. Pesah* 54a asserts that the throne was among those things created before the world. Rabbi Aba b. Kahana (ca. 300 CE) reflects the uncertainty of about the priority of preexistent things like the throne and Torah in *Gen. Rab.* 1.4. See the discussion by Rowland, *Open Heaven*, 148-150.

LXX: ἡνίκα ἡτοίμαζεν τὸν οὐρανόν, συμπαρήμην αὐτῷ,
καὶ ὅτε ἀφώριζεν τὸν ἑαυτοῦ θρόνον ἐπ' ἀνέμων.
When he made the heavens, I was a partner with him,
And when he separated his throne on the wind.

The phrase "throne of *your* Glory [θρόνου δόξης σου]" in Wis 9.10 may allude to an identification of Wisdom as the Glory who is seated upon the throne (cf. Ezek 1.26). Similar designations are used extensively in the Similitudes of *1 Enoch* when identifying the throne.[68] When the Ancient of Days (47.3; 60.2) or the Lord of the Spirits (62.2,3) sits on the divine throne, it is identified as "the throne of *his* glory" (cf. a variant of *1 En.* 55.4 "throne of *my* Glory"). When the mysterious figure of the Similitudes (identified as the Elect One, the Son of Man, or the Righteous One) is seated on this throne, it is usually identified as the "throne of glory", "my throne" [God is the subject], and also "throne of his glory". For example, the Elect One sits on the "throne of glory" in contexts in which he exercises his role as judge (45.3; 51.3; 55.4). The Son of Man is placed on the "throne of glory" by the Lord of Spirits (61.8). Like the Lord of the Spirits, however, the Son of Man also sits on the "throne of *his* glory" (62.5; 69.29).

The evidence definitely affirms that this throne is the divine throne which is shared by both the Lord of the Spirits/Ancient of Days and the Elect One/Son of Man. Furthermore, it is possible that "glory" is not an adjective modifying throne, but a noun referring to the occupant of the throne. Therefore, although the "throne of my Glory" in Wis 9.10 is certainly referring to the divine throne, it could also be linking Wisdom with the image of the enthroned Glory discussed above. This is also indicated by the Prayer of Enoch in *1 En.* 83.3: "Wisdom does not elude you and retreats neither from the 'place' of your throne nor from your presence".[69]

"Sitting" on the throne is a very exalted depiction full of significance. The sitting or enthronement of a figure alongside God or on his throne is a subject that reappears in several Jewish documents during the centuries immediately preceding the Common Era. The central significance of Ezekiel 1 and Daniel 7 has already been discussed. The Similitudes of *1 Enoch* (31-72) are also very

---

[68] See also Jer 17.12; *1 En.* 9.4; *Jub.* 31.20; 4Q405 Frags. 20-22.
[69] Hengel, *Studies in Early Christology*, 213.

instructive in showing the interpretation of Daniel 7 within a Jewish group. There are many references to one "whose face was like the appearance of a man" (46.1; cf. the Glory in Ezek 1.26) who will be *seated* on the throne (45.3; 51.3; 55.4; 61.8; 62.5-6; 70.27). The climactic scene of enthronement occurs in *1 Enoch* 62. From other portions of the Similitudes as well as from the discussion above, it is evident that Daniel 7 inspired this text. Both the Lord of the Spirits sits on the throne of glory (also identified as the Ancient of Days in *1 En.* 46.1, 47.3, 48.2, and elsewhere) and the Son of Man or Elect One sits on the throne of glory preparing to judge.[70]

Another significant detail from the Similitudes is that the author who wrote them (or later edited them) was not content in leaving this enthroned man-like figure as an exalted angelic being (46.1-2; cf. Ezek 1.26). *1 En.* 71.14 goes on to identify this enthroned figure, the Glory, as none other than the righteous *man* Enoch. Also instructive in this context is *3 Enoch* (ca. 5th century CE) which contains further evidence of Enoch's enthronement as the angel Metatron (*3 En.* 12.1-16.5). This is the response that Metatron receives from the heavenly hosts after being crowned:

> [14.5] They all fell prostrate when they saw me and could not look at me because of the majesty, splendor, beauty, brightness, brilliance, and radiance of the glorious crown which was on my head.

The connection between Wisdom and this enigmatic figure in *1 Enoch* can be made more distinct. There is evidence that Wisdom has been assimilated into the Son of Man/Elect One:

> [48.6] For this purpose he became the Elect One; he was concealed in the presence of (the Lord of the Spirits) prior to the creation of the world, and for eternity. [7] And <u>he has revealed the wisdom of the Lord of the Spirits to the righteous</u> because they have hated and despised this world of oppression.
>
> [49.1] So <u>wisdom flows like water and glory is measureless before him forever and ever</u>. [2] For his might is in all the mysteries of righteousness, and oppression will vanish like a shadow having no foundation. The Elect One stands before the Lord of the Spirits; his glory is forever and ever and his power is unto all generations. [3] <u>In him dwells the spirit of wisdom</u>, the spirit which gives thought-

---

[70] The Son of Man/Elect One is also described as the "Righteous One" and "His Messiah" in the Similitudes. For a discussion of these varied designations, see J. VanderKam, "Righteous One, Messiah, Chosen One, and Son of Man in 1 Enoch 37-71", *The Messiah: Developments in Early Judaism and Christianity* (ed. J.H. Charlesworth; Minneapolis: Fortress, 1992) 169-191.

fulness, the spirit of knowledge and strength, and the spirit of those who have fallen asleep in righteousness.

These texts portray Wisdom, who had looked for a dwelling place earlier (*1 En.* 42.1-2), now dwelling in the Elect One who is about to be enthroned (*1 En.* 62.1-6). Thus, there are conceptual links in *1 Enoch* between these two figures and their respective enthroned position.

A prominent example of a figure sharing the throne is found in Revelation 4-7. God, who is seated on the throne in the heavenly Throne Room, hands the scroll to the Lamb with the result that all the hosts erupt in worship (Rev 5.7-14). The Lamb is decidedly divine in this text. Of particular significance for our discussion is the Lamb's position at the center of the throne in which God is seated:

> [7.15]"For this reason they are before <u>the throne of God,</u>
> worship him day and night within his temple,
> and <u>the One [God] who is seated on the throne will shelter them.</u>
> [16]They will hunger no more, and thirst no more;
> the sun will not strike them, nor any scorching heat;
> [17] for <u>the Lamb at the center of the throne will be their shepherd</u>,
> and he will guide them to springs of the water of life,
> and God will wipe every tear from their eyes."

The question of whether the Lamb is truly *sitting* on the throne is answered earlier in the promise Christ makes to the Laodiceans: "He who conquers, I will grant him to sit with me on my throne, as I myself have conquered and *sat down with my Father on his throne*" (Rev 3.21).

Although the significance of Wisdom being enthroned next to God may not be apparent to modern exegetes, it would be to Jews living at the beginning of the Common Era.[71] The controversy evoked by the sharing of the divine throne is evident in the blasphemy charge in the trial of Jesus. This charge was probably a response to his claim of enthronement (Matt 26.64; Mark 14.64; Luke 22.69). Therefore, in light of this evidence, the depiction of Wisdom as an enthroned angelomorphic figure in Wisdom of Solomon is a profound theological statement of her divinity.

---

[71] See the polemics about enthronement in *b. Hag.* 15a and *Mid. Ps.* 72.2; cf. Segal, *Two Powers in Heaven*, 84-97. The concern about someone usurping YHWH's throne is very ancient. It is seen already in Isa 14.12-15.

3. *Wisdom and the Angel of the Lord*

In addition to the enthronement language, there is further evidence in Wisdom of Solomon that Wisdom has roots in angelomorphic traditions. The historical review in 10.1-21 of Wisdom's involvement in the lives of the patriarchs and Moses provides evidence that some actions associated with angelomorphic traditions in the Pentateuch have been reinterpreted and assimilated to Wisdom. The first and most blatant example is Wis 10.6, where Wisdom is credited with the rescue of Lot. In contrast, Gen 18.1-19.23 states the rescue was the work of the two angels who accompanied God:

> [Wis 10.6] Wisdom rescued a righteous man [Lot] when the ungodly were perishing; he escaped the fire that descended on the Five Cities.

> [Gen 19.16] But he [Lot] lingered; so the men [the two men=angels in Gen 19.1] seized him and his wife and his two daughters by the hand, YHWH being merciful to him, and they brought him forth and set him outside the city.

Second, Wisdom is said to be the one who led Israel out of Egypt in a pillar of cloud/fire:

> [Wis 10.17] She gave to holy men the reward of their labors; she guided them along a marvelous way [ὡδήγησεν αὐτοὺς ἐν ὁδῷ θαυμαστῇ], and became a shelter to them by day, and a starry flame [φλόγα ἄστρων] through the night. [18] She brought them over the Red Sea, and led [διήγαγεν] them through deep waters; [19] but she drowned their enemies and cast them up from the depth of the sea.

God himself guided by a pillar of cloud/fire according to some Exodus texts (13.21-22; 14.24). This is also true of leading Israel through the Red Sea and the destruction of the Egyptian army there (Exod 15.1-19). These same actions, however, are often ascribed to the Angel of the Lord in the OT:

> [Exod 14.19] Then the Angel of Elohim who went before the host of Israel moved and went behind them; and the pillar of cloud moved from before them and stood behind them.

> [Exod 23.20] Behold I send an angel before you, to guard you on the way [ἐν τῇ ὁδῷ] and to bring [εἰσαγάγῃ] you to the place which I have prepared.

> [Num 20.15] You know how our fathers went down to Egypt, and we dwelt in Egypt a long time; and the Eyptians dealt harshly with us and our fathers; [16] and when we cried to YHWH, he heard

our voice and sent an angel and brought [ἐξήγαγεν] us forth out of Egypt.

[Judg 2.1] Now the Angel of YHWH went up from Gilgal to Bochim. And he said, "I brought [ἀνεβίβασεν] you up from Egypt, and brought [εἰσήγαγεν] you into the land which I swore to give your fathers.

These examples in the OT and Wisdom of Solomon are not the only precedents for ascribing divine actions to an angelomorphic figure. Samaritan tradition regularly assigns the annihilation of evil-doers, including the Egyptians of the Exodus event, to the Angel of the Lord, who is also known as the Glory or Regent:

[*Memar Marqa* III.5] The Glory too seemed to be saying: "O congregation, keep yourself from me, for is there not before me a mighty deed? I slew, I oppressed, I destroyed, I made alive; and, with you, I did all this when I was at the sea and showed you every wonder and made you cross with great marvels by the mighty power of God.

Those who revered Wisdom as a mediator probably engaged in similar exegesis to give their mediator historical grounding in Israel's past. It is reasonable to assert that the author of Wisdom of Solomon was aware of angelomorphic Exodus traditions when he assigned these actions to Wisdom. Furthermore, the identification of these events with the Angel of the Lord most likely preceded and legitimated the assignment of these actions to Wisdom.[72]

Philo articulates his awareness of traditions that associated the pillar with Wisdom as well as those that linked it with the Angel of the Lord. He makes an allegorical interpretation of Wisdom's presence in the pillar of cloud:

[*Heres* 203] And I marvel still more, when listening to the sacred oracles I learn from them in what manner "a cloud came in the midst" [Exod 14.19] between the army of the Egyptians and the company of the children of Israel; for the cloud no longer permitted the race, which is temperate and beloved by God, to be persecuted by that which was devoted to the passions and a foe to God; being a covering and a protection to its friends, but a weapon of vengeance and chastisement against its enemies; [204] for it gently showers down wisdom on the minds which study virtue—wisdom which cannot be visited by any evil. But on those minds which are

---

[72] Fossum concludes that Wisdom's role in the Exodus as depicted in Wis 10.15-17 "[. . .] clearly absorbed the figure of the Angel of the Lord"; see *Image of the Invisible God*, 62.

ill-disposed and unproductive of knowledge, it pours forth a whole body of punishments, bringing upon them the most pitiable destruction of the deluge.

The cloud which "showers down wisdom", pouring forth punishment is responsible for protecting Israel and for vengefully destroying the Egyptian army. Philo's assertion about the cloud containing wisdom may be dependent upon Sir 24.4., where Wisdom states "my throne was in a pillar of cloud". Nevertheless, there is no specific evidence that Wisdom of Solomon or Sirach are his source because Wisdom is not personified in Philo. Philo, however, was aware of a special angel in this cloud who could not be seen with the naked eye:

> [*Vita Mos* 1.166] For a cloud, fashioned into the form of a vast pillar, went before the multitude by day, giving forth a light like that of the sun, but by night it displayed a fiery blaze, in order that the Hebrews might not wander on their journey, but might follow the guidance of their leader along the road, without any deviation. Perhaps, indeed, this was one of the lieutenants [ὑπάρχων] of the Great King, an unseen angel [ἀφανὴς ἄγγελος], a guide of the way [cf. Exod 23.21] enveloped in this cloud, whom it was not lawful for men to behold with the eyes of the body.

Philo taught that God's actions in the world were done through mediating powers (δυνάμεις or λόγοι), identified as angels (ἄγγελοι) in the OT.[73] Philo, therefore, illustrates the type of exegesis found in Wis 10.17-19 by providing evidence in his writings that the cloud was linked to both Wisdom and Angel of the Lord traditions.

In its depiction of the Exodus, Wis 10.17-21 seems to draw primarily on the Song of Moses (Exod 15.1-18). There is a direct reference to this song in Wis 10.20-21. The Song of Moses appears to have been the center of much exegetical discussion. The description of YHWH as "a man of war" in Exod 15.3 was a centerpiece in the derivation of the second angelomorphic "Power" in the "Two Powers in Heaven" controversy later found in rabbinic literature.[74]

---

[73] See *Leg All* 3.177 and the discussion in the revised edition of E. Schürer, *The History of the Jews in the Age of Jesus Christ* (eds. G. Vermes, F. Miller, M. Goodman; 4 vols; Edinburgh: T&T Clark, 1983) 3.881-885. Philo also taught that God was only the cause of good (*Agr* 128-29); he could not do evil, even in justified punishment (*Fuga* 66). Thus, the destruction of the Exodus events was wrought by God's "angels".

[74] Segal discusses the pivotal role of this text in his *Two Powers in Heaven*, 34-47, 52-59.

The reference to "your defending hand" in Wis 10.20 is especially intriguing. God's "hand" is frequently mentioned as the instrument of deliverence in the Song of Moses ("my hand" in Exod 15.9; "your right hand" in 15.6a, 6b, 12; "your arm" in 15.16).[75]

This "Hand" seems to be related to the creative "Hand of God" that is portrayed in Wis 11.17.[76] A comparison of this text with Wis 9.1-2 indicates that Hand is another title for Wisdom:

> [11.17] For your all-powerful Hand, which created the world out of formless matter, did not lack the means to send upon them a multitude of bears, or bold lions [...].

> [9.1] "O God of my fathers and Lord of mercy, who hast made all things by your Word, [2] and by your Wisdom has formed man to have dominion over the creatures you have made [...].

Moreover, Wisdom 10 contains echoes of other vivid language from Exodus 15 ("cast ... sea" Exod 15.4/Wis 10.19; "depths" Exod 15.5/ Wis 10.18-19; "enemies" Exod 15.6/Wis 10.6). Based upon this evidence, the author of Wisdom 10 understood the "Hand of YHWH" in Exodus 15, and possibly even YHWH as "a man of war" (Exod 15.3; cf. Wis 18.15), to be Wisdom. It has already been shown that the destruction of the Egyptians often was assigned to the Angel of the Lord in Jewish and Samaritan circles.[77]

The third example of Wisdom of Solomon 10 building its depiction of Wisdom on Pentateuchal angelomorphic traditions involves what is said about Jacob:

> [10] When a righteous man fled from his brother's wrath, she guided him on straight paths; she showed him the kingdom of God, and gave him knowledge of holy ones [ἁγίων]; she prospered him in his labors, and increased the fruit of his toil. [11] When his oppressors were covetous, she stood by him and made him rich. [12] She protected him from his enemies, and kept him safe from those who lay in wait for him; so that he might learn that godliness is more powerful than anything.

---

[75] For mention of Hand/Arm, see: Wis 3.1; 5.16-23; 7.16; 10.20; 11.17, 21; 14.6; 19.8. Ezek 10.8 mentions that "the cherubim appeared to have the form of a human hand under their wings".

[76] See Fossum, *Name of God*, 288. This idea was taken up by early Christians: *2 Clem.* 14.2-4; Irenaeus, *Adv. haer.* IV.20.1, V.5.1; *Ps-Clem. Hom.* XI.22, *Rec.* VI.7; Theophilus, *Autolycus* 2.18; Lactantius, *Institutiones* 4.6.

[77] The "Hand" as an angelomorphic designation is clear in 1QM 13.14: "Your Mighty Hand is with the poor! And which angel or prince is like you [Michael] for aid?" (cf. 1QS 3.20). J. Duhaime proposes such a connection between the Prince of Light and the Hand of God in 1QM 10-19; see "Dualistic Reworking in the Scrolls from Qumran", *CBQ* 49 (1987) 45, 48.

One can see from the Genesis narrative that most of the events related in Wis 10.10-12 involved the actions of God as the Angel of the Lord. Genesis relates that God spoke to Jacob in his dream at Bethel (28.12-17), that God told him in a dream to leave when Laban's family becomes covetous (31.1-3), and that God told Laban in a dream not to harm Jacob (31.24). This, however, does not preclude, however, the association of the Angel of the Lord with these actions. Indeed, when Jacob relates to his wives the dream in which God told him to leave Laban, he mentions the Angel of the Lord as the one who spoke to him in that dream:

> [31.11] Then the Angel of Elohim said to me in the dream, "Jacob", and I said, "Here I am!" [12] And he said, "Lift up your eyes and see, all the goats that leap upon the flock are striped, spotted, and mottled; for I have seen all that Laban is doing for you. [13] I am the God of Bethel, where you anointed a pillar and made a vow to me. Now arise, go forth from this land, and return to the land of your birth."

In this account the Angel identifies himself with the dream at Bethel and the blessing of Jacob's herds. These actions are assigned to Wisdom in Wis 10.10-11. Moreover, Jacob's safety in his encounter with Esau is assigned to Wisdom in Wis 10.12, whereas Gen 32.1-2 relates that before Jacob encountered Esau he met "angels of God" whom he declared to be "God's army". Finally, Wis 10.12 relates that Wisdom "awarded" a mighty contest to Jacob, whereas Gen 32.24-30 indicates that the angelomorphic man who wrestled with Jacob gave him a prize: the name "Israel".[78]

There is one remaining example of angelomorphic traditions in Wisdom 10. Concerning Abraham's near sacrifice of Isaac, Wisdom is said to have kept Abraham "[. . .] strong in the face of his compassion for his child" (10.5b). The only figure we find with Abraham and Isaac in the Genesis narrative is the Angel of the Lord (22.11, 15).

This cumulative evidence shows how this chapter built its depiction of Wisdom on pentateuchal angelomorphic traditions in

---

[78] The text of Wis 10.12 reads: καὶ ἀγῶνα ἰσχυρὸν ἐβράβευσεν αὐτῷ ("and she awarded a mighty contest to him" or even "and [in] a mighty contest she awarded [a prize to] him"). Βραβεύω generally means "be judge, decide, control, rule", but in the context of a contest (ἀγῶν) it means "award prizes"; see BAGD (2d ed.) 146. Philo's brief discussion of the incident in *Somn* 127-132 is also instructive. He speaks of it as a contest of virtue for the soul in which the winner is crowned with the garland of victory: a name.

an effort to give Wisdom firm historical grounding in the Angel of the Lord traditions. As has been seen in several examples, angelomorphic traditions were instrumental in the Jewish adaptation of Wisdom before she was identified with Torah (Sir 24.23; 2 Bar. 2.9-4.4).

D. *The Word*

Our concern now turns to the relationship that the Word (Heb: דבר; Gk: ὁ λόγος) shares with angelomorphic traditions. In his treatment of the "Word of God" in the OT, Terrance Fretheim emphasizes the importance of identifying the "Word of God" closely with the OT theophanies:

> The most important critique for these purposes is that the word of God as verbal event, particularly associated with the theophany, has been neglected. Theophanies are in fact the vehicle for the most common and most articulate revelations from God. Usually this entails the speaking of words by God, appearing often if not always in human form (cf. Genesis 18; Judg 6:11-18; Isaiah 6; Jeremiah 1), even in those contexts where the divine presence is veiled by fire or cloud (cf. Exod 3:2; 24:9-11).[79]

1. *The Word of YHWH Appears to the Patriarchs and Prophets*

There is a very early precedent for YHWH's visible form in a theophany being identified as "the Word of YHWH":

> [Gen 15.1] After these things <u>the Word of YHWH came to Abram in a vision</u>, "Fear not, Abram, I am your shield; your reward shall be very great." [2] But Abram said, "O Lord Elohim, what will you give me, for I continue childless, and the heir of my house is Eliezer of Damascus?" [3] And Abram said, "Behold, you have given me no offspring; and a slave born in my house will be my heir." [4] And behold, <u>the Word of YHWH came to him</u>, "This man shall not be your heir; your own son will be your heir."

The phenomenon described seems to begin with a vision (15.1), then progresses to a manifestation that comes to Abram in order to speak and lead him outside to see the stars (15.4-6), then concludes with the smoking fire pot and flaming torch going between the

---

[79] "Word of God", *ABD* 6.965. Grether gives the most extensive OT background discussion; see *Name und Wort Gottes*, 59-158.

sacrifices that Abram prepared (15.7-21). There is good reason to compare this theophany to those involving the Angel of YHWH in subsequent portions of the OT. Thus, the Word of YHWH could be considered to be an angelomorphic figure, especially by later interpreters in the first century CE.

The visual aspect of the Word of YHWH as a theophany is also prominent in the Samuel call narrative. Consider these select portions:

> [1 Sam 3.1] Now the boy Samuel was ministering to YHWH under Eli. And <u>the Word of YHWH</u> was rare in those days; there was not frequent <u>vision</u>.
>
> [3.6] And <u>YHWH called</u> again, "Samuel!" And Samuel arose and went to Eli, and said, "Here I am, for you called me." But he said, "I did not call, my son; lie down again." [7] Now Samuel did not yet know YHWH, and <u>the Word of YHWH had not yet been revealed to him</u>.
>
> [3.10] <u>YHWH came and stood</u> forth, calling as at other times, "Samuel! Samuel!"
>
> [3.21] And <u>YHWH appeared again at Shiloh</u>, for <u>YHWH revealed himself to Samuel at Shiloh by the Word of YHWH</u>.

Although the angelomorphic appearance of God to a prophet, such as those to Moses in Exodus 3 and 33, is less prominent in prophetic literature, this earlier theophanic model appears to be the basis of the expression "the Word of YHWH came to the prophet". Note, for example, the way that the Word of YHWH is depicted in the call of Jeremiah:

> [1.4] Now <u>the Word of YHWH came to me</u> saying, [5] "Before I formed you in the womb I knew you, and before you were born I consecrated you; I appointed you a prophet to the nations." [6] Then I said, "Ah, Adonai Elohim! Behold I do not know how to speak, for I am only a youth." [7] But <u>YHWH says to me</u>, "Do not say, 'I am only a youth'; for to all to whom I sent you, you shall go, and whatever I command you, you shall speak. [8] Be not afraid of them, for I am with you to deliver you, says YHWH" [9] <u>Then YHWH put forth his hand and touched my mouth</u>; and YHWH said to me, "Behold, I have put my words in your mouth. [10] See, I have set you this day over nations and over kingdoms: to pluck up and to break down, to destroy and to overthrow, to build and to plant." [11] And the Word of YHWH came to me saying, "Jeremiah, what do you see?" And I said, "I see a rod of almond." [12] Then <u>YHWH said to me</u>, "You have seen well, for I am watching over my word to perform it." [13] The <u>Word of YHWH came to me a second time</u>, saying, "What do you see?"

This narrative follows the basic call *Gattung*.[80] Here "the Word of YHWH" came to Jeremiah and spoke in the first person as YHWH (1.4, 11, 13; cf. 2.1). After Jeremiah's objection (1.6) and YHWH's verbal reassurance (1.7-8), Jeremiah relates that "then YHWH put forth his hand and touched my mouth" (1.9). What was the appearance of this "Word of YHWH" who was "YHWH" (1.7, 9a, 9b, 12; cf. 1.8, 15, 19) if he could be described as putting forth his hand to touch Jeremiah's mouth (1.9)? Is this not more than anthropomorphism? Here "word of YHWH" is most likely a figure in continuity with angelomorphic traditions that depict God appearing in the form of a man to a human.

The presence of an Angel of YHWH tradition alongside a tradition about the Word of YHWH coming to, and speaking with, a prophet is found in 1 Kings 19, where Elijah's rescue is described:

> [4] But he himself went a day's journey into the wilderness, and came and sat down under a broom tree; and he asked that he might die, saying, "It is enough; now, O Lord, take away my life; for I am no better than my fathers." [5] And he lay down and slept under a broom tree; and behold, <u>an angel</u> touched him, and said to him, "Arise and eat." [6] And he looked, and behold, there was at his head a cake baked on hot stones and a jar of water. And he ate and drank, and lay down again. [7] And <u>the Angel of YHWH came again a second time</u>, and touched him, and said, "Arise and eat, else the journey will be too great for you." [8] And he arose, and ate and drank, and went in the strength of that food forty days and forty nights to Horeb the mount of God. [9] And there he came to a cave, and lodged there; and behold, <u>the Word of YHWH came to him</u>, and said, "What are you doing here, Elijah?"

A similar combination of these Angel and Word traditions is also present in *Jub.* 2.1: "And the angel of the presence spoke to Moses by the word of the Lord". Furthermore, the subsequent theophany of YHWH in "a still small voice" (1 Kgs 19.11-18), should be read in light of the theophany in Exodus 33.

2. *The Word, Wisdom, and the Angel of the Lord*

One of the most distinctive depictions of the Word that is drawn from angelomorphic traditions appears in Wisdom of Solomon 18 concerning the Destroyer who carried out the 10th Plague (cf. Exod 12.21-29):

---

[80] Newman, *Paul's Glory-Christology*, 70.

> [14] For while gentle silence enveloped all things, and night in its swift course was now half gone, [15] your all-powerful Word leaped from heaven, from the royal throne, into the midst of the land that was doomed, a stern warrior [16] carrying the sharp sword of your authentic command, and stood and filled all things with death, and touched heaven while standing on the earth.

This vivid depiction is most assuredly based upon the descriptions of the Angel of the Lord as a warrior.[81] The account of the plague upon Israel that follows (18.20-25; cf. Num 16.41-49) even labels the figure carrying out the destruction as "the Punisher" (18.22) and "the Destroyer" [ὁ ὀλεθρεύων] (18.25). This account of the angelomorphic Word as the Destroyer has profound implications for the penetrating NT descriptions of the Word of God as an eschatological judge.[82]

The description of the Word in Wis 18.15 is probably based upon a depiction of the Destroyer Angel in 1 Chr 21.15-16, who is also identified as the Angel of YHWH, (note the correspondence between reaching to "heaven" while "standing" on "earth")[83]:

> [21.15] And <u>God sent the angel</u> to Jerusalem to destroy it; but when he was about to destroy it, YHWH saw, and he repented of the evil; and he said to <u>the Destroying Angel</u> [εἶπεν τῷ ἀγγέλῳ τῷ ἐξολεθρεύοντι], "It is enough; now stay your hand." And <u>the Angel of YHWH</u> was standing by the threshing floor of Ornan the Jebusite. [16] And David lifted his eyes and saw <u>the Angel of YHWH</u> standing between earth and heaven, and in his hand a drawn sword stretching over Jerusalem.

Little else is said about the hypostatized Word in Wisdom of Solomon. Given the overtness of the angelomorphic tradition in Wis 18.15, however, it is important to clarify the nature of the relationship between Wisdom and the Word in Wisdom of Solomon. An identification between these two concepts is intimated in Wis 9.1-2:

---

[81] See the discussion 63-67 above.
[82] See 252-256 (Rev 19.11-16) and 311-314 (Heb 4.11-13) below.
[83] Winston argues that this gigantic angelic warrior tradition was influenced by Hellenistic traditions: "She [Discord] plants her head in heaven, while her feet tread on earth" (*Iliad* 4.443); "She mounts up to heaven, and walks the ground with head hidden in the clouds" (Virgil, *Aeneid* 4.177); "God is firmly set in brazen heaven on his golden throne, and plants his feet upon the earth" (*Testament of Orpheus* 33-34). Much more likely is his secondary suggestion that 1 Chr 21.16 influenced Wis 18.16; see *Wisdom of Solomon*, 319.

> O God of my fathers and Lord of mercy, who has made all things by your word, and by your wisdom has formed man.

A subtle distinction between the creation of the world ("all things") and the forming of man appears to be made here (cf. Ps 33.6; *4 Ezra* 6.38). This distinction, however, may be more apparent than real because the Word is closely identified with Wisdom elsewhere: he is "all-powerful" like Wisdom (7.23) and he occupies the divine throne like Wisdom (9.4,10).

The antiquity of identifying angelomorphic traditions of Israel's past with "the Word of God" is affirmed by *Ezekiel the Tragedian* (c. second century CE). In his *Exāgōge* the playwright reshapes the words God spoke at the Burning Bush theophany: "Stay, Moses, best of men, do not come near until you have loosed the bindings from your feet; the place on which you stand is holy ground, and from this bush God's Word [θεῖος λόγος] shines forth to you" (lines 96-99). "The Angel of YHWH" in Exod 3.2 is here identified as "God's Word".[84]

Not only were the older Angel of the Lord traditions sometimes associated with the Word, but other angelomorphic figures were identified with this title as well. For example, the Son of Man/Elect One of the Similitudes is also called "the First Word" (*1 En.* 61.7), and Melchizedek is christened "the Word and Power of God" (*2 En.* 71:34 [Rec. J]; cf. Philo, *Leg All* 3.79-82).

3. *The Angelomorphic Roots of Philo's* Logos

Philo presents the Word as a divine hypostasis by melding together Jewish and Greek tradition in a very complex way.[85] Philo, as a faithful Jew, affirmed the revelation of God in the Scriptures as he knew them. In keeping with Middle Platonic thought, however, he also emphasized the utter transcendence of God as one who is not *directly* implicated in the material world. In order to reconcile these two beliefs, Philo drew on the λόγος traditions in both philosophy and the LXX to develop his wide-ranging concept

---

[84] Fossum has used this text to enlighten the background of the Word in the Johannine Prologue; see *Image of the Invisible God*, 113.

[85] For an excellent introduction to Philo's *Logos* in light of Middle Platonism, see D. Winston, *Logos and Mystical Theology in Philo of Alexandria* (Cincinnati: Hebrew Union College Press, 1985) 9-26; see also D. Runia, "Logos", *DDD* 988-989, and T. Tobin, "Logos", *ABD* 4.348-356.

of the Word as the mediator through whom God *indirectly* orders and sustains the material world.[86] All of God's activity, beginning with creation, is understood to be carried out by the Word who is the visible image of the High God above (*Fuga* 101). Philo carefully, and somewhat dangerously, *distinguishes* between God and the Word without totally *separating* them.[87] Therefore, Philo's concept of the Word allows him to affirm both the philosophical transcendence of God as well as the scriptural portrait of God's immanence.

Our primary interest in the Philonic corpus is the relationship of the Word to angelomorphic traditions. Usually the background of Philo's Word in Middle Platonism dominates discussions. The Jewish elements—especially in Jewish mysticism—are viewed too often as marginal. Because Philo's allegorical exegesis focused on the Pentatuech, however, the scriptural accounts of angelomorphic theophanies played a fundamental role in his development and depiction of the Word.[88] As Alan Segal states: "Philo wants the *logos*, the goal of the mystical vision of God, to serve as a simple explanation for all the angelic and human manifestations of the divine in the Old Testament".[89] For example, Philo writes the following account of the visit of the three men in Genesis 18:

> [*Migr* 173] Now he that follows God has of necessity as his fellow-travellers the words and thoughts that attend Him, angels as they are often called. What we read is that "Abraham travelled with them, joining with them in escorting them on their way" (Gen 18.16). What a glorious privilege to be put on a level with them! The escort is escorted; he gives what he was receiving; not one thing in return for another, but just one thing only that lies ready to be passed backwards and forwards from one to the other. [174] For as long as he falls short of perfection, he has the Divine Word as his

---

[86] See Tobin, "Logos", 350-351. Philo emphasizes the Word's role in ordering creation (*Leg All* 3.96; *Sacr* 8; *Quod Deus* 57; *Fuga* 94; *Spec Leg* 1.81; *Op* 20; *Cher* 127), but still affirms God as the creator (*Op* 72).

[87] Although Philo speaks about the Word as "divine" (ὁ θειὸς λόγος; *Somn* 1.62) or as "God"(θεός; *Somn* 1.228-230), he also details how to distinguish between the "two Gods" (*Somn* 1.228-230) and on one occasion calls the Word "the second God" (ὁ δεύτερος θεός; *Quaes Gen* 2.62). Segal has detailed how some of the issues and texts of the rabbinic "Two Powers" heresy are already visible in Philo's efforts to distinguish between God and his Word; see *Two Powers in Heaven*, 159-181.

[88] ὁ κύριος who revealed himself to Moses and Jacob was, for Philo, the *Logos* who is also the Angel of the Lord (*Migr* 174, *Agr* 51, *Leg All* 3.217-19); cf. Segal, *Two Powers in Heaven*, 162, 170, and Fossum, *Name of God*, 110.

[89] *Two Powers in Heaven*, 169.

leader: since there is an oracle which says: "Lo, I send My messenger before your face, to guard you in your way, that he may bring you into the land which I have prepared for you: give heed to him, and listen to him, do not disobey him; for he will by no means withdraw from you; for My Name is in him" (Exod 23.20-21).

This text demonstrates that Philo not only interpreted YHWH (i.e., the Word) as an angel in Genesis 18, but that he also harmonized the various angelomorphic traditions: the Divine Name Angel of Exod 23.20-21 is the same angel who visited Abraham in Genesis 18. This angelomorphic Word functions as a guide to lead Abraham (and others) to the knowledge that faciliates a mystical ascent and vision of God which, in turn, bestows immortality.[90] Segal argues that Philo played an important role in developing "the tradition of a single angelic messenger" from the LXX.[91]

The Jewish roots of Philo's Word in OT angelomorphic traditions are also laid bare through his use of the ascriptions "angel" or "archangel":

> [*Heres* 205] The Father, the Creator of the universe, gave to His archangel and most ancient Word the privilege of standing on the confines separating the creature from the creator. This same Word is continually suppliant to the immortal God on behalf of the mortal race which is exposed to affliction and misery; and is the ambassador sent from the Ruler to the subject.

> [*Agr* 51] This hallowed flock He leads in accordance with right and law, setting over it His true Word and First-born Son who shall take upon Him its government like lieutenant of a great king; for it is said in a certain place: "Behold I AM, I send My Angel before your face to guard you in the way" (Exod 23.20).

> [*Conf* 146] But if there be any as yet unfit to be called a son of God, let him press to take his place under God's First-born, the Word, who holds the eldership among the angels, an archangel as it were. And many names are his for he is called: the Beginning, the Name of God, His Word, the Man after His Image, and "He that sees", namely, Israel.

The striking thing about *Conf* 146 is that it attributes the various designations—Word, Angel, Name, Man—to one hypostasis: the

---

[90] *Somn* 1.68-69, 86; *Leg All* 3.169-178; *Quod Deus* 143; *Fuga* 63. See also: Winston, *Logos and Mystical Theology*, 43-55; Segal, "Heavenly Ascent", 1354-1358; and P. Borgen, "Heavenly Ascent in Philo: An Examination of Selected Passages", *The Pseudepigrapha and Early Biblical Interpretation* (eds. J.H. Charlesworth and C. Evans; JSPSup 14; Sheffield: Sheffield Academic Press, 1991) 246-268.
[91] *Two Powers in Heaven*, 170.

Word. These designations each merit a brief exposition because they enlighten our understanding of the Word's angelomorphic roots.

The title "Firstborn" (ὁ πρωτόγονος) prompts the question: When did this firstborn come to be?[92] This "firstborn" nomenclature has been shown to be dependent on the Jewish and pre-Christian tradition of the φῶς in the Greek translation of Gen 1.3 (τὸ φῶς = "light" and ὁ φώς = "man"): the φῶς in 1.3 is the creation of "the Glory" or God's physical man-like appearance (cf. Ezek 1.26).[93] This tradition is recorded in the non-Christian *Eugnostos the Blessed* found at Nag Hammadi (ca. third century CE):

> [NHC III.76.15-24] The First who appeared before the universe in infinity is self-grown, self-constructed Father, full of shining, ineffable light. In the beginning He decided to have His likeness come into being as a Great Power. Immediately the beginning of that Light was manifested as an immortal, androgynous Man.

Philo is aware of this tradition and identifies this light, "who is the archetype of every other light", as the Word (*Somn* 1.75; cf. *Op* 29-31).[94] This is where the Word, "the Man after His Image", came to be and then ordered creation. Philo affirms that the Word is the Image of God after which earthly man was created (*Quaes Gen* 2.62; cf. *Conf* 41; *Fuga* 101; *Leg All* 3.96).

A logical question arises: If the genesis of "the Man according to His Image" (ὁ κατ' εἰκόνα ἄνθρωπος) took place with the bringing forth of the light, what about the well-known accounts in Philo which speak of Gen 1.26 referring to the heavenly man being created after the Image of God, and Gen 2.7 referring to the creation of the earthly man?[95] Fossum notes a logical inconsistency within the Philonic corpus and concludes:

> On one hand, the heavenly Man, even the Logos, is said to have been created *after* the image and likeness of God; on the other hand, the Man-Logos *is* that Image, after which the earthly man was created. There can be little doubt that the former interpretation is absurd and secondary.[96]

---

[92] This title is also found in: *Conf* 62-63; *Agr* 51; *Somn* 1.215.
[93] Fossum, *Image of the Invisible God*, 15-28. See also the polemic against Adam as the φῶς in *b.Sanh.* 38a: "He [Adam] was created on the eve of Sabbath".
[94] Fossum, "Jewish Christian Christology", 266-267.
[95] E.g., *Op* 134; *Leg All* 1.31, 53-55; see Fossum, *Name of God*, 268-269.
[96] *Name of God*, 269.

This conclusion is supported by another designation given to the Word. "The Beginning" (ἀρχή) is usually associated with Wisdom due to its use in Prov 8.22.[97] It is a designation that reflects existence before creation and participation in creation. The LXX version of Prov 8.22 indicates that Wisdom is the first "creation": "The Lord created me as the beginning of his ways" (κύριος ἔκτισέν με ἀρχὴν ὁδῶν αὐτοῦ). *Tg. Kit.* Prov 8.22 reads in a similar manner: "God created me [Wisdom] at the beginning of his creation". The grounding of Philo's Wisdom figure in angelomorphic traditions has already been demonstrated.[98] Philo identifies Wisdom with the Word by using the same titles for both (*Conf* 146; *Leg All* 1.43), even though he also calls Wisdom the "mother" of the Word (*Ebr* 30-31). Philo's writings offer much evidence of the Word's active participation in creation.[99]

The Word is described in very explicit angel nomenclature: "the Ruler of the Angels, being as an Archangel" (τὸν ἀγγέλων πρεσβύτατον, ὡς ἂν ἀρχάγγελον). Heirarchies and archangel rankings of principal angels were quite developed by the first century CE.[100] This particular title appears to be very similar to the one given to the Angel Israel in *Pr. Jos.* 5: "A Ruling Spirit". The exalted ranking of this angel is revealed in another title with abundant angelic associations: "the Name of God" (ὄνομα θεοῦ). Philo's adaptation of this title for the Word comes from the Divine Name Angel of Exod 23.20-21. This is one of Philo's favorite texts to describe how the Word leads one to a mystical ascent and vision (cf. *Quaes Ex* 2.13).[101]

"He that Sees, Israel" (ὁ ὁρῶν,'Ισραήλ) is a frequent designation for the Word in Philo's writings, used 23 times and implied in 26 other places.[102] Its origins lie with the wrestling incident that Jacob

---

[97] See discussion on 90 above.
[98] See discussion on 92-93 above.
[99] *Leg All* 3.96; *Sacr* 8; *Quod Deus* 57; *Fuga* 94; *Spec Leg* 1.81; *Op* 20; *Cher* 127.
[100] See Chapter 5 on 124-151 below.
[101] This title is also related to Philo's belief that the Word is the angelomorphic High Priest who bears the Name of God (*Vita Mos* 2.114; cf. *Migr* 103); see the discussion about the priesthood on 306-307 below.
[102] See J. Smith, "The Prayer of Joseph", *Religions in Antiquity: Essays in Memory of Erwin Ramsdell Goodenough* (ed. J. Neusner; NumenSup 14; Leiden: Brill, 1968) 266 n.1. P. Borgen discusses this Philonic ascription and its relationship to *Merkabah* mysticism in *Bread From Heaven: An Exegetical Study of the Concept of Manna in the Gospel of John and the Writings of Philo* (SupNovT 10; Leiden: Brill, 1965) 115-118, 175-179.

had with "a man" in Gen 32.24-32. Philo understood the Word to be the Angel Israel who bestowed his own name upon Jacob, whom Philo holds up as a model of visionary ascent (cf. Gen 28.12-17). The content of the *Prayer of Joseph* confirms that Philo is not the only one to make such assertions; similar exegesis about angelomorphic figures was going on in other Jewish groups.[103]

Based upon this evidence, it is indisputable that OT angelomorphic traditions served an important role in development and expression of Philo's Word. Furthermore, although the Word is not completely *separate* from God, Philo does use language that indicates the Word is a divine hypostasis with a degree of *distinct* personhood. David Winston characterizes Philo's Word as "[. . .] a vivid and living hypostatization of an essential aspect of Deity, the face of God turned toward creation".[104] David Runia comes to a similar conclusion and also captures the difficulty of expressing the relationship between God and the Word in Philo:

> It cannot be denied that Philo personifies the Logos when talking about him, but it remains difficult to interpret the extent to which he accords him separate existence. In many texts the Logos represents God's presence or activity in the world, so that the distinction between God and Logos is more conceptual than real. There are other texts, however, in which the Logos is presented as an *hypostasis* separate from and ontologically inferior to God Himself.[105]

4. Memra *and the Angel of the Lord*

Margaret Barker has put forth evidence to support the old thesis that Philo's understanding of the Word was probably influenced by the targumic traditions concerning *Memra*.[106] Therefore, it is important to explore briefly the influence that these traditions could have exercised upon Philo and other exegetes of his time.

There has been considerable scholary debate concerning the meaning of *Memra* (Aramaic: מימרא) in the Targumim. The major figure in the debate earlier this century was G. F. Moore who argued that *Memra* was merely a "verbal buffer" for references to God.[107] This conclusion was soon challenged by G. H. Box

---

[103] See discussion of *Prayer of Joseph* on 137-142 below.
[104] *Logos and Mystical Theology*, 49-50.
[105] "Logos", 989.
[106] *The Great Angel*, 146-48.
[107] "Intermediaries in Jewish Theology", 41-61.

who asserted that it was an identification for God himself in a "certain mode of self-manifestation".[108] D. Muñoz Leon has argued that *Memra* is a substitution for the Divine Name YHWH, but also proposes that it may be a substitutive attribute of God like Name or Wisdom.[109] More recently, Robert Hayward has argued that *Memra* is an exegesis of the Name of God that gives expression to a theology of Divine Presence in the Targumim.[110] Andrew Chester has lent support to G. F. Moore's position by arguing that *Memra* is a phenomenon of translation and not a change motivated by theology.[111] His research has been criticized by Bruce Chilton who reasserts a theological understanding of *Memra* by emphasizing its relationship to God's speaking activity.[112]

Scholars are well aware that *Memra* is used as a periphrastic designation for the Divine Name and presence: "And they shall put my Name, my *Memra*, upon the children of Israel, and I, in my *Memra*, will bless them" (*Tg. Neof.* Num 6.27), or "Whoever despises the Name of the *Memra* of YHWH shall be killed" (*Tg. Neof.* Lev. 24.16).

A point often missed in the scholarly debate is the fact that *Memra* is also substituted for hypostatic theophanies of YHWH like "the Angel of YHWH". This OT figure sometimes becomes "My *Memra*" in the Targumim. For example, "the Destroyer" or "Angel of YHWH" in the Exodus Passover is substituted with "My *Memra*" in the Targumim: "And I, in My *Memra* will pass by over the land of Egypt on this Passover night" (*Tg. Neof.* Exod 12.12; cf. *Tg. Neof.* Exod 11.4; 12.13). The Angel of YHWH who guided Israel in the desert is also reinterpreted: "And the *Shekinah* of the *Memra* of YHWH will go before you" (*Tg. Ps-J.* Deut 31.6). The "Angel of the Covenant" in Mal 3.1 becomes "My *Memra*" (*Tg. Neb.* Mal 3.1).

This substitution demonstrates the possibility that *Memra* could have been interpreted as a divine hypostasis by some Jewish exegetes. This conclusion brings added significance to the abundant

---

[108] "The Idea of Intermediation", 118.
[109] *Memra en los Targumim del Pentateuco* (Institucion San Jerónimo 4; Granda, 1974) 106.
[110] *Divine Name and Presence: The Memra* (Oxford: Allanheld & Osum, 1991).
[111] *Divine Revelation and Divine Titles in the Pentateuchal Targumim* (TSAJ 14; Tübingen: Mohr/Siebeck, 1986) 308-309.
[112] "Recent and Prospective Discussion of *Memra*", *From Ancient Israel to Modern Judaism: Intellect in Quest of Understanding* (ed. J. Neusner; BJS 173; Atlanta: Scholars Press, 1989) 119-137.

targumic evidence that assigns the work of creation to the *Memra*. For example, *Tg. Neof.* Gen 1.1: "From the beginning with Wisdom the *Memra* of the Lord created and perfected the heavens and the earth".

E. *The Spirit*

Although the Spirit (Heb: רוח; Gk: πνεῦμα) is widespread in the OT, it is generally not presented as a divine hypostasis. This phenomenon, however, is found in some Jewish texts. The Wisdom of Solomon identifies the Spirit with the hypostatized Wisdom: "Who has learned your counsel, unless you have given wisdom and sent your holy Spirit from on high" (9.17; cf. 1.4-6; 7.7, 22; 12.1).[113] The Spirit appears to be a hypostatized agent of creation in Judith 16.14: "You sent forth your Spirit, and it formed them". The focus of the discussion below will be to show that the identification of the (holy) Spirit with a particular angel—especially a named angel—contributes to the understanding of the Spirit as a distinct divine hypostasis.[114]

1. *Spirits as Angels*

The link between Spirit and Angel traditions can best be demonstrated by looking at some representative examples of how spirits were understood to be angels since the angel and spirit nomenclature are closely related in Jewish and Christian writings. Ps 104.4 (LXX 103.4) unites these two terms in a manner that may have exercised some influence on later interpreters:

MT: עשה מלאכיו רוחות
Translation: he makes his angels spirits.[115]
LXX: ὁ ποιῶν τοὺς ἀγγέλους αὐτοῦ πνεύματα
Translation: the one who makes the angels his spirits.

---

[113] For a discussion of the hypostatization of the Spirit in Wisdom of Solomon, see Ringgren, *Word and Wisdom*, 168.

[114] See esp. Levison, "The Angelic Spirit in Early Judaism", 464-493. Levison draws upon the work of P. Volz, *Der Geist Gottes und die verwandten Erscheinungen im Alten Testament und im anschliessenden Judentum* (Tübingen, Mohr/Siebeck, 1910).

[115] Most translate this verse "who makes the winds your messengers" (RSV). This fits with the context, but by the first century CE these terms had technical meanings that could be read out of the text (e.g., the use of Ps 104.4 in Heb 1.7).

A very vivid example is found in the *Prayer of Joseph* where the Angel Israel/Jacob identifies himself as both "a Ruling Spirit" and "an Archangel of the Power of the Lord".[116] *Jubilees* speaks of "the spirits" who minister before God and then lists various groups of angels (2.1). The QL also contains several examples in which רוח is understood to be an angel (or demon).[117] The parallel usage of "angels" and "spirits" is present in this text from the War Scroll (1QM):

> [12.8] The heros of the army of his angels [צבא מלאכים] are listed with us;
> [12.9] the war hero is in our congregation; the army of his spirits [צבא רוחין] with our infantry and our calvary.

Also worthy of attention in this context is the frequent title that is given to God in *1 Enoch*: "Lord of the Spirits".[118] Matthew Black notes that this title probably developed from a modified translation of the יהוה צבאות in Isaiah 6.3 as is found in *1 En.* 39.12:

> The vigilant ones bless Thee,
> They stand before thy Glory, saying:
> Holy, Holy, Holy, is the Lord of Spirits;
> He filleth the earth with spirits.[119]

The title given to the central figure of the spectacular angelophany recounted in 2 Macc 3.24 also reflects the understanding that the angelic hosts are spirits: παρόντος ὁ τῶν πνευμάτων καὶ πάσης ἐξουσίας δυνάστης ("the Ruler of the Spirits and Every Powerful Authority").

The author of the Epistle to the Hebrews had a similar idea in mind when he writes of being subject to τῷ πατρὶ τῶν πνευμάτων ("the Father of Spirits"; 12.9). This conclusion is supported by the opening chapter of this epistle which contains an extensive discussion about Christ's superiority over the many "angels" (1.4, 5, 7, 13)

---

[116] See discussion on 137-142 below.
[117] A. Sekki contends that there are 58 occurences; see *The Meaning of Ruah at Qumran* (SBLDS 110; Atlanta: Scholars Press, 1989) 145-171.
[118] It occurs 104 times in *1 Enoch* (cf. 2 Mac 3.24). For a discussion of this title as a reference to the angelic hosts see: Charles, *The Apocrypha and Pseudepigrapha*, 2.209; Rowland, *Open Heaven*, 104-5; and M. Black, "Two Unusual Nomina Dei in the Second Vision of Enoch", *The New Testament Age: Essays in Honor of Bo Reicke* (ed. W. Weinrich; 2 vols.; Macon, GA: Mercer, 1984) 1.53-59.
[119] This is Black's translation; see "Two Unusal Nomina Dei", 55.

and states in 1.14: "Are they all not ministering spirits [λειτουργικὰ πνεύματα] sent forth to serve, for the sake of those who are to obtain salvation?" He also identifies these two in his quotation of Ps 104.4: "the one who makes his angels spirits" (1.7).

2. *The Spirit as an Angel*

It is not a big step to go from angels identified as spirits to an Angel identified as *the* Spirit. Even as the Spirit could manifest itself in humans as a temporary or permanent indwelling, so it could manifest itself as an angel. For example, the angelic Prince of Lights (1QS 3.20; CD 5.18; 1QM 13.10) is identified in the Dead Sea Scrolls as both "the Angel of His Truth" (1QS 3.24) and "the Spirit of Truth" (1QS 3.19; 4.21; cf. 1QM 13.10). This angel is usually identified with Michael and probably also Melchizedek.[120]

Both Philo and Josephus provide interesting examples of identifying an angel as the Divine Spirit in conjunction with the incident of Balaam meeting the Angel of the Lord in Numbers 22-24.[121] Unlike the biblical narrative, which attributes the inspiration of Balaam's oracles to God or the Spirit of God, Philo frames the narrative so that it is the angel who gives prophetic utterance (*Vita* 1.269-279). The angel makes these claims about inspiring Balaam:

> [*Vita* 1.274] I shall prompt the needful words without you mind's consent, and direct your organs of speech as justice and convenience require. I shall guide the reins of speech, and, though you understand it not, employ your tongue for each prophetic utterance.

This angel is then later identified as "the truly prophetic spirit" who possesses Balaam temporarily in order to deliver oracles (*Vita.* 277, 283). Josephus handles this narrative in a similar way, but specifically labels "the angel of God" with the title "the Divine Spirit" (*Ant* 4.108). Like Philo, Josephus speaks of Balaam being possessed by the Spirit of God who then gives utterances (*Ant* 4.118-121). Both authors are melding their Jewish angelology with the Hellenistic understanding of a mediating daemon who possesses

---

[120] See the discussion of 11QMelch on 171-172 below.
[121] See the articles by J. Levison: "The Prophetic Spirit as an Angel According to Philo", *HTR* 88 (1995) 189-207; "The Debut of the Divine Spirit in Josephus's Antiquities", *HTR* 87 (1994) 123-138; "Josephus' Interpretation of the Divine Spirit", *JJS* 47 (1996) 234-255.

the speaker, alters his state of consciousness, and then produces a prophetic utterance.[122] Therefore, both Philo and Josephus present an understanding that the Spirit is active as an angel who, like a daemon, can enter and inspire the speaker.

Isa 63.9-10 (MT) is especially important for this discussion of the Spirit as an angelomorphic hypostasis. This text identifies "the Angel of the Presence" who rescued Israel as "his holy Spirit" and "the Spirit of the Lord":

> [9] In all their affliction he was afflicted, and <u>the Angel of His Presence</u> [ומלאך פניו הושיעם] saved them; in his love and in his pity he redeemed them; he lifted them up and carried them all the days of old. [10] But they rebelled and grieved <u>his holy Spirit</u> [את־רוח קדשו]; therefore he turned to be their enemy, and himself fought against them. [11] Then he remembered the days of old, of Moses his servant. Where is he who brought up out of the sea the shepherds of his flock? Where is he who put in the midst of them <u>his holy spirit</u> [את־רוח קדשו], [12] who caused <u>his glorious arm</u> to go at the right hand of Moses, who divided the waters before them to make for himself an everlasting name, [13] who led them through the depths? Like a horse in the desert, they did not stumble. [14] Like cattle that go down into the valley, <u>the Spirit of YHWH</u> [רוח יהוה] gave them rest.

There is testimony in Exodus that the exit from Egypt and the wilderness journey were guided by an angel.[123] Isaiah's discussion of "the Angel of the Presence" is probably primarily based upon the tradition of the Divine Name Angel who would guard Israel and bring her to Canaan (Exod 23.20-24).[124] The title given to this angel (מלאך פניו) indicates that Isa 69.9-10 is uniting the tradition of the Divine Name Angel with the tradition of Exod 33.14-15 where God promises that his "Presence" (פני) would go with Israel.[125] Thus, Isa 63.9 interpreted the Divine Name Angel

---

[122] Levison, "Prophetic Spirit", 192.

[123] Exod 14.19-20 (cf. Judg 2.1-4) and Exod 23.20-23; see discussion on 66 and 98-99 above, as well as Levison, "Angelic Spirit", 471-472.

[124] Note esp. the mention in Exod 23.22 that if they listened to this angel, YHWH would be "an enemy to their enemies". Isa 63.10 echoes this language in stating that the opposite took place: "they rebelled and grieved his holy Spirit; therefore he turned to be their enemy, and himself fought against them".

[125] This union of these two traditions flows logically from their context. God repeats his promise of Exod 23.20-21 to Moses in Exod 32.34 and 33.2 that he will have an angel go "before you" [לפניך] and then directly afterwards promises that his Presence will go "with you" [ילכו] (Exod 33.14); see Levison, "The Angelic Spirit in Early Judaism", 471. This text probably prompted

who went *before* Israel to be God's Presence *with* Israel. This conclusion apparently did not fit with the understanding of some Jews. The LXX reveals a polemic against angelic mediation by replacing the MT reading ומלאך פניו הושיעם with οὐ πρέσβυς οὐδὲ ἄγγελος, ἀλλ' αὐτὸς κύριος ἔσωσεν αὐτούς ("Neither messenger nor angel, but the Lord himself saved them").[126]

The identification of this Angel of the Presence as את־רוח קדשו ("his holy Spirit") and רוח יהוה ("the Spirit of YHWH") is of central importance to this discussion.[127] Through this identification the Spirit of the Lord is depicted as the angel who is distinguished from God: he possesses the Divine Name by which he guards, guides, speaks, and punishes. Therefore, even though the Spirit is linguistically linked as belonging to YHWH, its identification as the Angel of the Presence of Exod 23.20-21 gives it some degree of its own personhood. These same Exodus angel traditions appear to be the basis for mention of God's Spirit in both of these texts[128]:

> [Haggai 2.5] Yet now take courage, O Zerubbabel, says YHWH; take courage, O Joshua, son of Jehozadak, the high priest; take courage, all you people of the land, says YHWH; work, for I am with you, says YHWH of Hosts, <u>according to the promise that I made you when you came out of Egypt: My Spirit stands in your midst</u>. Do not fear.

> [Neh 9.20] <u>You gave your good Spirit to instruct them</u>, and did not withhold your manna from their mouths, and gave them water for their thirst.

After reviewing widely diverse evidence for the Angelic Spirit in ancient Israel and early Judaism, John Levison offers this conclusion:

> Discussions of the spirit of God in Early Juduaism and Christianity, therefore, ought to consider that interpretations of the spirit as an

---

the expression of other "Angel of the Presence" traditions in Second Temple Judaism which often focused on multiple Angels of the Presence who minister before God in heaven; see C. Seow, "Face", *DDD* 612.

[126] The MT reading is supported by 1QIsa. This polemic is also found in rabbinic literature concerning the Exodus narrative; see Goldin, "Not By Means of an Angel", 412-423.

[127] This identification is clear from the context and confirmed by the allusions to Exod 23.21 (Isa 63.10: "they rebelled") and Exod 33.14 (Isa 63.14: "rest"); see Levison, "Angelic Spirit", 471. Presence and Holy Spirit are also linked together in Ps 51.11.

[128] "Angelic Spirit", 471-474.

angelic presence are not necessarily the product of a growing hypostatization of the inner spirit or breath of God, as appears to be the case in texts such as Jud. 16:14; the רוח or πνεῦμα of God could also be, and often was, interpreted as an angelic emissary of God.[129]

Although depictions of God's Spirit as an angel are not necessarily the *result* of "a growing hypostatization" of the spirit of God, they certainly can and should be considered *evidence* of hypostatization.

F. The Power

"The Power" (Heb: כה; Gk: ἡ δύναμις) does not appear as a divine hypostasis in the OT. It is an aspect of God through which he accomplishes deliverance: "God help me by your Name and save me by your power" (Ps 54.3; cf. Jer 27.5). It is in the Hellenistic context that δύναμις is used more pervasively.[130] The *Letter of Aristeas* (c. first century BCE) portrays God's Power as "filling" the universe (132) as well as effecting and sustaining creation: "[Everything] is being sustained as well as having been created by the Power of God" (157). In the Hellenistic world Power developed into a title for cosmic agents in whom power is hypostatized (e.g., angels, demons, stars, spirits). This development contributed to the extensive practice of magic to control these powers.

The purpose of the following brief discussion of the Power is to demonstrate that "Power" was used as a designation or title for angels and for God, especially as a synonym for the Glory.

1. *Power as Designation for an Angel*

In a manner similar to rendering "angels" as "spirits", "powers" became another designation sometimes used in place of "angels", especially due to the interaction of Hellenism with Judaism.[131] This can be seen already in the LXX where יהוה צבאות is sometimes translated κύριος ὁ θεὸς τῶν δυνάμεων ("Lord God of the Powers"; e.g., 3 Kgms 17.1; 18.15; Ps 42.12; cf. Ps 24.9-10). H. D. Betz asserts that this kind of translation tendency in the LXX results

---

[129] "Angelic Spirit", 492-493.
[130] H.D. Betz, "Dynamis", *DDD* 509-515.
[131] E.g., Rom 8.38; 1 Cor 15.24; Eph 1.21; 1 Pet 3.22; cf. 2 Thess 1.7; 2 Pet 2.11; Rev 1.16. Philo identifies the "powers" who helped God in creation and who are used to carry out punishment as "angels" (*Conf* 168-182).

from the desire of Hellenistic Jews to depict the God of the OT more in terms of "a cosmic deity in control of all natural and supernatural forces".[132]

There are also many examples of principal angels being identified as a Power (or "the Power"). Yahoel, the exalted angel in the *Apocalypse of Abraham* (ca. first century CE), makes this declaration concerning the title given him by God: "I am Yahoel and I was called by him [. . .] a Power through the medium of his Ineffable Name in me" (10.8). Here it is the possession of the Divine Name that is the basis for his exalted status as "a Power". In the *Prayer of Joseph*, the Angel Israel/Jacob declares himself to be "the Archangel of the Power of the Lord"; this is another way of calling himself "the Power of the Lord".[133] In the *Ascension of Isaiah*, the "angel of iniquity", Beliar, is identified with the titles "Power of the World" (2.4) and "Prince of the World" (1.3; 10.29). In *2 Enoch* the angelomorphic priest Melchizedek is called "the Power of God" (71.34 [Rec. J]). Michael is called "a Mighty Power" and "the Power" in the Jewish Christian *Gospel of the Hebrews* (frag. 1).

The popularity of using "Power" as a designation for either angel or God is vividly portrayed in Philo's writings. For example, Philo identifies two of the three men that visited Abram (Gen 18) as ἄγγελοι (*Abr* 115) and later as δυνάμεις (*Abr* 143-145). These Powers are aspects of Philo's complex λόγος figure: the Creative Power (associated with goodness and θεός) and the Ruling Power (associated with justice and κύριος).[134] Both Powers are connected with the visible manifestation of the divine. The Ruling Power appears to those who are to be punished (e.g., Pharoah). The Creative Power manifests itself to those who are earnest strivers (e.g., Moses). Both Powers, who together comprise the Word, appear to the perfected (e.g., Jacob).[135] Philo also calls Wisdom the "highest and chiefest" of God's Powers (*Leg All* 2.86).

2. *The Power as a Designation for God*

This evidence demonstates that "Power" could be used as a designation for a variety of spiritual beings of various ranks. Power also

---

[132] "Dynamis", 510.
[133] *Pr. Jos.* 7; see discussion on 140-141 below.
[134] *Vita Mos* 2.99-199; *Cher* 27-30.
[135] Segal, *Two Powers in Heaven*, 174-178.

began to be used as a designation for God. This usage is apparent in in the trial of Jesus recorded in Mark and Matthew:

> [Mark 14.62] And Jesus said, "I am; and you will see the Son of Man seated at the right hand of the Power [τῆς δυνάμεως], and coming with the clouds of heaven" [cf. Matt 26.64].

These words are meant to call to mind the enthronement scene of Dan 7.13-14. Thus, the Power is used here as an alternate designation for the Ancient of Days. A similar usage is found in the report of the martyrdom of James the Just, who in his moment of death saw Jesus sitting in heaven "at the right of the Great Power" (τῆς μεγάλης δυνάμεως; Eusebius, *Hist. Eccl.* II.23.13). In the *Ascension of Isaiah*, however, the visionary Isaiah sees Christ "[. . .] sit down at the right hand of the Great Glory" (11.32). This difference can be understood by the observation that the Power is used interchangably with the Glory in some texts of Jewish mysticism and Jewish Christianity.[136]

Therefore, it is not surprising to find that the Power is a name of God in Samaritanism. The *Samaritan Targum* replaces אל with חילה ("the Power") or חיולה ("the Mighty One"). God is often praised as "the Great Power" in the *Defter* and *Memar Marqa*.[137] This Samaritan usage provides background for the use of this title by Simon Magus, who had followers in Samaria and was known as "the Great Power": οὗτός ἐστιν ἡ δύναμις τοῦ θεοῦ ἡ καλουμένη μεγάλη ("This man is the Power of God, the one who is called 'Great'"; Acts 8:10). The testimony of *Pseudo-Clementines* affirms the probability that Simon claimed divine status through the use of this title: "[. . .] he wished to be regarded as a certain highest Power, even above the god who made the universe" (*Hom.* II.22).

This designation was not isolated to Samaria and Simon Magnus. We find it also in use among the Elchasaites, a Jewish Christian sect in the early second century. Epiphanius writes that the name of the sect leader, Elchasai, means "Hidden Power" (*Pan.* 19.2.10). This appears to be an alternate designation for the Glory, since Elchasai believed himself to be the last manifestation of Christ, whom many Jewish Christians identified as the Glory.[138]

---

[136] See examples in Fossum, *Name of God*, 175-181, and *Image of the Invisible God*, 25-28.
[137] This discussion is based upon *Fossum*, "Sects and Movements", 364.
[138] Fossum, *Name of God*, 181.

G. Conclusion

Three fundamental conclusions can now be set forth. First, it has been affirmed through textual analysis that it is valid to speak of hypostases as aspects of God that have degrees of distinct personhood. It should be emphasized that our modern ways of conceptualization often resist giving a degree of personhood to these divine attributes or aspects. In spite of this, the textual evidence leads us to understand a world view that is based much more on *tangible forms* than *abstract concepts*. Thus, Name, Glory, Wisdom, Word, Spirit, and Power are not primarily abstract concepts in this world view; they are realities with visible forms.

Second, the angelomorphic aspect of these divine hypostases has been demonstrated. The importance of the Angel of the Lord traditions for understanding the origins of these hypostases has also become apparent. It has been demonstrated that the Pentateuchal accounts involving the Angel of the Lord contain foundational ideas that continued to influence later interpreters and writers. These ideas include: the Divine Name as the possession of a personal entity distinct from God; the invisibility of God; the visibility of God in some form (usually a man, fire, or cloud); and God's presence and activity apart from the Divine throne.

Third, we have seen that these six hypostases do not remain distinct and separate, but are intimately interrelated as aspects of one God. Name and Glory, Wisdom and Word, Glory and Power, Wisdom and Spirit, are woven together in many texts; for this reason they were treated together under the umbrella of this chapter. The close interrelationship between these aspects of God is seen most vividly when they are united to describe a single figure, such as the Word in the writings of Philo or Christ in the writings of Justin Martyr.

The impact of these traditions on Christology remains to be detailed as early evidence of Angelomorphic Christology is presented in Part III of this study. We will emphasize that it was not solely one of these hypostases that was adopted by early Christians in their Christologies, but often various combinations of them. This phenomenon is abundantly evident in both of these texts:

[Justin, *Dial. Trypho* 61.1] God has begotten of Himself a certain rational Power as a Beginning before all other creatures. The Holy Spirit indicates this Power by various titles, sometimes the Glory of the Lord, at other times Son, or Wisdom, or Angel, or God, or Lord, or Word.

[*Teachings of Silvanus* NHC VII.106.21-28] For the Tree of Life is Christ. He is Wisdom. For he is Wisdom; he is also the Word. He is the Life, the Power, and the Door. He is the Light, the Angel, and the Good Shepherd.

The identification of Jesus with one or more of these angelomorphic divine hypostases was distinctive in many ways, but not a unique phenomenon. There were several principal angels, as shall now be shown, who were accorded the very exalted status that accompanies the investiture of the Name or the outward marks of the Glory.

CHAPTER FIVE

THE PRINCIPAL NAMED ANGELS

Jewish literature of the centuries immediately before the Common Era testifies to a general cosmological development that emphasized God is enthroned in heaven while carrying out his work in the world by means of angelic leaders who have myriads of other angels at their command. In spite of the development of several leading angels, the idea of a principal angel of God among these angelic leaders remained. Chapter three detailed how the Angel of the Lord, who is indistinguishable from God as his visible manifestation in many early texts, came to be understood as a figure fairly distinct from God in later interpretation.[1] It is not surprising, therefore, that there were later texts which gave this unnamed angel his own distinct name.

The giving of a personal name to an angel is significant. It further distinguishes or separates the angel as an individual figure distinct from God. Some texts exalted a particular angel over other angels. Indeed, as amazing numbers of angels in service to God were depicted (e.g., Dan 7.10 or *1 En.* 71.8), a hierarchy of angelic leaders also was depicted and labeled as "Angels of the Presence" or "Archangels".[2] This hierarchy usually consisted of four to seven angels, with one of them often identified as the highest of these leaders.[3] Michael, Gabriel, and Raphael are primarily

---

[1] The key text for the assertion that the Angel of the Lord was a being distinct from God is Exod 23.20, where God speaks of the angel who has his Name.

[2] Tob 12.15; *T. Levi* 8.2; *Jub.* 1.27, 29; 2.1-2, 18; 15.27; *1 En.* 9.1; 10.1-11; 20.1-7; 40.1-10; 54.6; 71.9-13; 81.5; 87.2; 88.1; 90.21-22; *3 Bar.* 10.1; 11.7; 1QM 9.14-16; 1QSb 4.25; 1QH 6.13; *L.A.E.* 48.1; *Gk. Apoc. Ezra* 6.2; *T.Sol.* 2.4; Rev 8.2; see P. Schäfer, *Rivalität zwischen Engeln und Menschen* (SJ 8; Berlin: de Gruyter, 1975) 20-22, and J. van Henten, "Archangel", *DDD* 150-153.

[3] The idea of four Angels of the Presence comes from Ezek 1.5-11 where four winged creatures are mentioned as positioned around the divine throne. *Jubilees* speaks of the angels being created on the first day, including "the Angels of the Presence" (2.2). The author of *Jubilees* also changes the name of "the Angel of the Lord" to "the Angel of the Presence"; this angel is distinct from YHWH and imparts revelation to Moses. The idea of seven archangels, with one functioning as a leader, probably also originates from Ezekiel. In 9.1-11 the Glory shows Ezekiel a vision where a group of six armed men (angels) led by a man (angel) clothed in linen is commanded to mark the

associated with this group; Uriel (also known as Suru'el), Phanuel, and others are included with less consistency.[4] Michael often serves as the leader of this elite group, but Gabriel appears to have held this position in earlier tradition.[5] Furthermore, there are other angels not mentioned as part of such a group, but who are presented in some documents as God's leading mediator.[6] Even though there are similar ideas about several of these principal angels in different documents, these ideas are by no means uniform because each document presents the ideas peculiar to the author or group who produced it.

This chapter will examine several of these select principal angels, some of whom were considered to be the Angel of the Lord, or even the Glory, by those who esteemed them.[7] This discussion will focus narrowly on evidence of their highly exalted status that could, in turn, impact early understandings of Jesus. The five criteria of divinity discussed earlier will be used in evaluating the nature of these depictions: Divine Position; Divine Appearance; Divine Functions; Divine Name; and Divine Veneration.[8]

---

penitent and to kill all the unmarked in a "Passover" style purge (cf. Exod 12.1-30). The tradition of a leading archangel, usually identified as Gabriel or Michael, was also influenced by the tradition of an angelic commander of God's army (cf. Josh 5.14). In Rabbinic tradition, the names of the archangels originated in Babylon during the exile (*Gen. Rab.* 18.1; *b. Ber.* 48.9). Their names, however, are West Semitic (mostly compounds of the divine named 'El); see J. J. Collins, *Daniel* (Hermenia; Philadelphia: Fortress, 1993) 337. For a discussion of the background of seven archangels in Ezekiel and also in Babylonian ideas, see Dix, "Seven Archangels", 233-244.

[4] See the texts in note 2 above. Other names of angels who may have been considered archangels by some groups include: Sariel or Surafel (*1 En.* 9.1); Asuryal (*1 En.* 10.1); Raguel, Saraqa'el (*1 En.* 20.1-7); Eremiel (*4 Ezra* 4.36); Dokiel (*T. Ab.* 13.10 [Long Rec.]); Gabuthelon, Aker, Arphugitonos, Beburos, Zebuleon (*Gk. Apoc. Ezra* 6.2); see also G. Barton, "The Origin of the Names of Angels and Demons in the Extra-Canonical Apocalyptic Literature to 100 A.D.", *JBL* 31 (1912) 156-167.

[5] For Michael's leadership of the archangels or functions as chief commander, see also: *Ascen. Is.* 3.16; *2 En.* 22.6 [J]; 33.10; 71.28; 72.5; Jude 9; Rev 12.7-8. This topic is discussed by Lueken, *Michael*, 32-43. For Gabriel's status above Michael, see Bousset, *Religion des Judentum*, 328, and Fossum, *Name of God*, 259, 279 n.61.

[6] E.g., Angel Israel in the *Prayer of Jospeh*; Yahoel in the *Apocalypse of Abraham*; Eremiel in the *Apocalypse of Zephaniah*; Metatron in *3 Enoch*; see the discussion of these angels in sections E-H on 137-148 below.

[7] Angels who are intimately linked with human figures will be discussed in Chapter 6 on 152-183 below (e.g., Enoch, Melchizedek, Jacob).

[8] See the discussion on 30-33 above.

A. Michael

The principal angel that is most widely mentioned in the Jewish and Christian literature of 300 BCE to 200 CE is Michael (מיכאל), which means "Who is like God".[9] The theophoric element in his name, is very telling of the significance that this angel enjoyed. He is one of only two named angels in the OT, the other being Gabriel, with whom he is sometimes depicted. Michael's primary role in the literature of this period is guardian, commander, or warrior for the nation of Israel.[10] For example, in Daniel he is called: "one of the chief princes" [Heb: אחד השרים הראשנים; Gk: εἷς τῶν ἀρχόντων τῶν πρώτων] (10.13), "your [Israel's] prince" (10.21), and "the great prince standing over your people [Israel]" (12.1).[11] *1 Enoch* details his role in binding the fallen watchers (10.11-16) and in carrying out the eschatological destruction (54.6). The QL testifies to the fact that he played a significant role in guiding the Dead Sea community and giving them eschatological victory.[12] Early Christians understood him in similar roles. The church, rather than Israel, was understood to be the benefactor of his warrior skills and guardianship.[13]

Michael is often blandly discussed in dictionary and commentary entries with little sensitivity to the tradition history of his role as the guardian of Israel. This role was influenced by two important traditions originating from OT texts. First, at some point Michael became identified as the Divine Name Angel of Exod 23.20-21. The pivotal significance of this text has already been discussed at length. The evidence in *1En.* 69.15 that Michael

---

[9] For more detail see: Lueken, *Michael*; J. P. Rohland, *Der Erzengel Michael: Arzt und Feldherr* (Leiden: Brill, 1977); D. Watson, "Michael", *ABD* 4.811; M. Mach, "Michael", *DDD* 1065-1072.

[10] See Dan 10.13, 21; 12.1; *1 En.* 20.5; 90.14; *T. Mos.* 10.2; 2 Macc 11.6-8; 1QM 13.10; 17.6-8; 1QS 3.20. For Rabbinic evidence, see *b.Yoma* 77a; *Tg. Ket. Ps* 137.7; *Pesika R.* 44.10. Michael is given the title "chief commander" (ἀρχιστράτηγος) in Dan 8.11 (LXX and Theod.); *2 En.* 22.6 [J]; 33.10; *T. Ab.* 1.4; 2.1-6; and *3 Bar.* 11.1 (cf. *Jos. Asen.* 14.8). For further discussion this warrior role, see Lueken, *Michael*, 13-30.

[11] "Prince" (שר) is a title for the leading angels in Daniel (cf. Josh 5.14). In this role Michael fights for Israel against Persia and delivers her in the last days (Dan 10.13-21; 12.1).

[12] 1QM 13.10; 17.6-8; 1QS 3.20; CD 5.15, 18. Michael and Melchizedek appear to have very similar roles in the QL (cf. 11QMelch).

[13] Rev 12.7-8; cf. Jude 9.

possessed the Divine Name has been noted.[14] The Divine Name Angel was the guardian or punisher of Israel and was linked ideologically with the manifestation of the Angel of the Lord as "Commander of God's Army" to Joshua (Josh 5.13-15).[15] With the identification of Michael as this angel it is natural to expect that Michael was interpreted to be the Angel of the Lord in other OT texts that speak of this angel. For example, *Tg. Ps-J.* Gen 32.25 identifies the man who wrestled with Jacob as Michael (Gen 32.24-30). The primary man of the "three men" in Genesis 18 who is identified as YHWH is understood to be Michael by some later exegetes, both Jewish (*Pirqe R. El.* 73) as well as Christian (*Acts of Andrew and Matthias* 30). Moreover, the appearance of Michael to Abraham in *T. Ab.* 2.1-3.12 is patterned after the visit of the "three men" in Genesis 18. This phenomenon supports the important conclusion noted above that the Angel of the Lord traditions were widely interpreted as presenting an individual angel who was distinct from God. Furthermore, because some Jewish groups understood that Michael possesses the Divine Name, they assigned him cosmogenic and even demiurgic functions.[16]

The second foundational text for this guardian role of Michael is Deut 32.8-9, a text in which some exegetes found the appointing of angels to watch over nations[17]:

> When the Most High gave to the nations their inheritance, when he separated the sons of men, he fixed the bounds of the peoples according to the number of the sons of God.[18]

---

[14] See discussion on 96-98 above.

[15] For evidence of Michael's identification as the "Commander" Angel of Josh 5.13-15, see Lueken, *Michael*, 104, 157-166. Lueken does not note that Aphraates, a third century Christian, identifies this angel and the angel in Exod 23.20-21 as Michael in his *Tract on Fasting*.

[16] The Gnostic Satornil taught that the world was made by the god of the Jews, the demiurgic Michael, and his angelic associates; see the discussion by Fossum, *Name of God*, 216-217. Regarding Michael's demiurgic role in Ophite tradition, see *Name of God*, 323-326. This demiurgic role of Michael should be understood as founded upon earlier Jewish tradition that Michael was the possessor of the Divine Name which carried the creative power (cf. *1 En.* 69.14-26 and 74-76 above).

[17] See also: Isa 24.21-22; *1 En.* 20.5; 89.59-62; Dan 10.13; 10.20-21; Sir 24.12; *Jub.* 15.31; *2 Bar.* 3.16; *Ascen. Is.* 7.9-10. *Tg. Ps-J.* Deut 32.9 identifies Michael as the angel of the people Israel. For a broader discussion of angels of nations, see I. P. Culianu, "The Angels of the Nations and the Origins of Gnostic Dualism", *Studies in Gnosticism and Hellenistic Religions: Presented to Gilles Quispel* (eds. R. van den Broek and M. J. Vermaseren; Leiden: Brill, 1981) 78-91.

[18] Collins notes that the MT reads "sons of Israel", but the LXX reading

Some Jewish groups did not believe that this assignment of nations to "the sons of God" applied also to Israel. It appears that there was actually a reaction against the exalted role of "guardian over Israel" that was assigned to Michael in some texts. Note this nuanced interpretation of Deut 32.8-9 that is found in *Jubilees*:

> [15.31] And he sanctified them and gathered them from all the sons of man because [there are] many nations and many people, and they all belong to him, but over all of them he caused spirits to rule so that they might lead them astray to follow him. [32] But over Israel he did not cause any angel or spirit to rule because he alone is their ruler and he will protect them and he will seek for them at the hand of his angels and at the hand of his spirits and at the hand of his authorities so that he might guard them and bless them and they might be heirs henceforth and forever.

It is clear that for this author Israel was not the domain of Michael, but of God himself. Ben Sira (ca. second century BCE) also clarifies what is said in Deuteronomy 32: "He appointed a ruler over every nation, but Israel is the Lord's own portion" (Sir 17.17).

In addition to functioning as Israel's guardian, a second important role associated with Michael is that of intercessory angel.[19] Although it appears that each of the archangels was evidently understood to be an intercessor for humans with God (Tob 12.5; *1 En*. 9.1-3), Michael was probably considered the principal intercessory angel by some because of his exalted status.[20] Michael

---

ἀγγέλων θεοῦ is supported by a 4QDeut fragment which reads בני אלהים; see *Daniel*, 374 n.39.

[19] For the intercessory angel of Israel tradition, see *T. Levi* 5.5-6 and *T. Dan* 6.1-6 (cf. Job 16.19; 33.23-25; Zech 3.1-4). For Michael in this role see: *1 En*. 68.1-5; *2 En*. 33.10; 1QM 13.9-14; Jude 9; Rev 12.7. Michael also functions as an *angelus interpres* (e.g., for Abraham in the *Testament of Abraham*).

[20] Based upon Michael's leadership of the archangels and the reference in Dan 12.1 to his defense of those whose names are written in "the book", he appears to have been understood as the man with the writing case in Ezek 9.1-11 who supervises the work of the six executioners. *Ascen. Is*. 9.19-23 records the tradition of a glorious angel who keeps the heavenly books for the children of Israel. Two MSS add that Isaiah asked about the identity of this angel and was told: "This is the great angel Michael, ever praying on behalf of humanity" (see Burchard's translation, *OTP* 2.171, note e2). The glorious man who appears to Aseneth, often understood as Michael, had written Aseneth's name in the heavenly book (*Jos. Asen*. 15.4). Michael is also associated with the angelic mediation of the Law (*L.A.E.* [*Apoc.*] Preface; cf. *Herm. Sim.* VIII.3.3; *Jub*. 1.27-2.1; Acts 7.38, 53; Gal 3.19); see Lueken, *Michael*, 18-19, and Fossum, *Name of God*, 259-260. For Gabriel as a principal intercessory angel, see 131-134 below.

traditions are, no doubt, behind these two depictions of intercessory angels in the Testament literature:

> [*T. Levi* 5.5] And I [Levi] said to him [the angel], "I beg you, Lord, teach me your name, so that I may call on you in the day of tribulation." [6] And he said, "<u>I am the angel who makes intercession</u> for the nation Israel, that they might not be beaten."

> [*T. Dan.* 6.1] And now fear the Lord, my children, be on guard against Satan and his spirits. [2] Draw near to God and to <u>the angel who intercedes for you</u>, because he is the mediator between God and men for the peace of Israel. [3] He shall stand in opposition to the kingdom of the enemy.

Some Rabbinic evidence strongly suggests that this role of Michael as an intercessory angel led to prayers being directed to him instead of directly to God.[21]

Several of the characteristics of Michael's mediator roles are visible in the angel who appears in an intriguing text from the document *Joseph and Aseneth* (ca. first century BCE to second century CE). Aseneth knows that her repentant prayer has been heard as she sees the movement of one of the stars in heaven:

> [14.2] And Aseneth kept on looking, and behold, <u>next to the morning star, the heaven was torn open, and a great and unutterable light appeared</u>. [3] And Aseneth saw, and fell on her face on the ashes. [4] And <u>a man came to her from heaven</u>, and stood by her head; and he called to her and said, "Aseneth, Aseneth." [5] And she said, "Who is he that calls me, because the door of my chamber is closed, and the tower is high, and how then did he come into my chamber?" [6] And the man called her a second time and said, "Aseneth, Aseneth." [7] And she said, "Behold, (here) I (am), Lord. Tell me who you are." [8] <u>And the man said, "I am the chief captain of the house of the Lord and the commander of the whole host of the Most High.</u> Rise and stand on your feet, and I will tell you what I have to say. [9] And Aseneth lifted her head and saw, and behold, (there was) a man like Joseph in every respect, with a robe and a crown and a royal staff, except that his face was like lightning, and his eyes were like the light of the sun, and the hairs of his head like flames of fire from a burning torch, and his hands and feet like iron shining forth from a fire, and sparks shot forth from his hands and feet. [10] And Aseneth saw, and fell on her face at his feet on the ground.

---

[21] E.g., *y. Ber.* 13a contains a polemic against crying out to Michael and Gabriel, and *Abod. Zar.* 42b denounces offerings made to Michael. See also: Lueken, *Michael*, 4-12; Fossum, *Name of God*, 193; Stuckenbruck, *Angel Veneration and Christology*, 51-76; and Arnold, *Colossian Syncretism*, esp. 87.

Although this angelomorphic being is not named anywhere in this document, his titles ("the chief of the house of the Lord" and "commander of the whole host of the Most High") certainly put this account in the trajectory of Michael traditions.[22] His physical description appears to be built upon a combination of traditions, primarily the figure of the enthroned Glory in Ezek 1.26 ("a man [. . .] from heaven", "hands and feet like iron shining forth from a fire, and sparks shot forth from his hands and feet"), the angel in Dan 10.5-6 ("his face was like lightning"), and the φῶς of Gen 1.3 ("a great and unutterable light appeared").[23] His regal attire (crown, robe, staff) and identification as a man of light (ἄνθρωπος φωτός) call to mind a similar description of the Glory in *Ezekiel the Tragedian* 70-71: "Upon it [the great throne] sat a man of noble mien [ἐν τῷ καθῆσθαι φῶτα γενναῖόν τινα], becrowned, and with a scepter in one hand". The description of this "Man of Light from Heaven" leaves the reader with the impression that he is the enthroned visible form of God.

This deduction is strengthened by Aseneth's response when he finishing talking: she "prostrates herself" before him in an act of worship and even asks for his name so that she may "praise and glorify" him forever:

> [15.11] And when the man had finished speaking these words, Aseneth rejoiced exceedingly with great joy about all these words and <u>fell down at his feet and prostrated herself face down to the ground before him</u>, and said to him, [12] "Blessed be the Lord your God the Most High who sent you out to rescue me from the darkness and to bring me up from the foundations of the abyss, and blessed be your name forever." <u>What is your name, Lord; tell me in order that I may praise and glorify your for ever (and) ever</u>." And the man said to her, "Why do you seek this, my name, Aseneth? <u>My name is in the heavens in the book before all (the others), because I am chief of the house of the Most High</u>. And all names written in the book of the Most High are unspeakable, and man is not allowed to pronounce nor hear them in this world, because those names are exceedingly great and wonderful and laudable."

---

[22] When Aseneth tries to ascertain his name, he states that his is the first name in the heavenly book and that none of these names can be pronounced or heard in this world because they are "exceedingly great and wonderful and laudable" (15.12). Burchard, among others, identifies him as Michael; see *OTP* 1.225 note p. He is not Joseph or Joseph's angel, even though his initial kingly appearance (robe, crown, and staff) is like that of Joseph (14.9).

[23] See Fossum, *Image of the Invisible God*, 22-23; see also 156n.14 below.

Although her reaction of prostration to the first sight of this man was prompted by fear (14.11), this prostration is one of vereration.[24] The request for the angel's name (15.12) and the angel's consumption of the honeycomb by fire later in the narrative (17.3) are patterned after the Angel of the Lord accounts in Judges (6.20-21; 13.15-20).[25] This angel implies that he possesses the Divine Name since the name he has is "before all" (15.12). Furthermore, the angel departs in nothing less than a chariot of fire (17.8).[26] The comments of Aseneth as she witnesses this departure are very telling of the exalted status of this angel:

> [17.9] "What a foolish and bold woman I am, because I have spoken with frankness and said that a man came into my chamber from heaven; and <u>I did not know that (a) god came to me</u>.[27] And behold, now he is traveling back into heaven to his place." [10] And she said in herself, Be gracious, <u>Lord</u>, to your slave, and spare your maidservant, because I have spoken boldly <u>before you</u> all my words in ignorance.

The veneration of this angel is vivid: Aseneth offers a prayer to the "god" who has just visited her.

B. *Gabriel*

The name of the other well-known principal angel, Gabriel [גבריאל], means "Man of God" or "Power of God" or "God has shown himself mighty".[28] The last six chapters of Daniel are

---

[24] The prostration does not prompt the angel to speak a prohibition formula against angelic worship (cf. *Apoc. Zeph.* 6.15; Rev 19.10); see Stuckenbruck, *Angel Veneration and Christology*, 168-170. Hurtado (*One God*, 81, 84), followed by Bauckham (*Climax of Prophecy*, 126), see the refusal of telling the name as an oblique refusal of worship. This is not the case. Refusal to tell the name is evidence of the hidden or secret Divine Name which the angel possesses; see Fossum, *Image of the Invisible God*, 113-116 (cf. Judg 13.17-18).

[25] Bauckham, *Climax of Prophecy*, 126-127.

[26] This appears to be based upon the Elijah tradition in 2 Kgs 2.11 (cf. *T. Ab.* 10.1). It is not a depiction of the *Merkabah* throne depicted in Ezekiel since the description of it is brief and the man was "standing" on it as it departed (*Jos. Asen.* 17.8), rather than "seated" above it as in Ezek 1.26.

[27] Other readings for this verse are "God" and "an angel of the Lord"; see translation by Burchard, *OTP* 2.231 note k. See also *Jos. Asen.* 22.3, where Aseneth refers to Jacob in a similar manner and where Jacob has the appearance of an angel. On the basis of this scene as well as the link between the angel and Joseph, there appear to be some clear ideological links between this document and the *Prayer of Joseph*; see 137-142 below.

[28] M. Noth, *Die israelitischen Personennamen im Rahmen der gemeinsemitischen*

central to discussions of Gabriel and undoubtedly contributed to the growth of traditions about this angel. Although Michael is mentioned in these chapters, it is Gabriel who is prominently visible and active as the *angelus interpres* for the visions that Daniel receives (7.16-18, 23-27; 8.15-26; 9.21-27; 10.4-12.13). Gabriel is not specifically identified as the one with whom Daniel talked in Dan 7.16-27 and 10.5-12.13. Nevertheless, because of his interpretations and appearance in Daniel 8-9 where he is identified by name (8.16; 9.21), it is reasonable to conclude that he is the interpreter of these scenes as well.[29]

Because the angel in Daniel 10-12 can be identified as Gabriel, the exalted description given of him at the beginning of this vision deserves special attention:

> [10.4] On the twenty-fourth day of the first month, as I was standing on the bank of the great river, that is, the Tigris, [5] I lifted up my eyes and looked, and behold, a man clothed in linen, whose loins were girded with gold of Uphaz. [6] His body was like beryl, his face like the appearance of lightning, his eyes like flaming torches, his arms and legs like the gleam of burnished bronze, and the sound of his words like the noise of a multitude.

This is a very special angelomorphic figure. On account of the indisputable links with the appearance of the Glory in Ezek 1.26-28 and 8.2, Gabriel may appear like the Glory in Ezekiel in order to emphasize his exalted status or he may have been understood to be the Glory of Ezekiel.[30] One of the primary descriptions of Gabriel

---

Namengebung (BWANT 3/10; Stuttgart: Kohlhammer, 1928) 190. This name almost certainly is related to the descriptions of the Angel of the Lord in ancient tradition.

[29] It is difficult to prove conclusively that the interpreter in Dan 7.16-27 is Gabriel because so little information is given in 7.16. The identification of Gabriel as the man in 10.5-12.13 is more certain because of the appearance of Gabriel in 8.15 ("one having the appearance of a man") and 9.21 ("the man Gabriel") is linked with the descriptions of the angel in Daniel 10-12: "a man clothed in linen" (10.5); "one in the likeness of the sons of men" (10.16); "one having the appearance of a man" (10.18); "the man clothed in linen" (12.6, 7). Especially important is the parallel between 8.15 and 10.18. The references to Michael assisting him in battle also support this conclusion (10.13, 21; cf. the depiction of Gabriel as a warrior in *1 En.* 10.9-10 and working in tandem with Michael in *2 En.* 21.1-22.16). See Collins, *Daniel*, 373-374, and Fossum, *Name of God*, 279 n.61; for a contrary view, see Rowland, *Open Heaven*, 98-99.

[30] Daniel also appears to draw on the description of the primal man in Ezek 28.13. See Rowland, *Open Heaven*, 99, and Collins, *Daniel*, 373-374; see also Rowland, "A Man Clothed in Linen", who discusses the influence of

in Daniel 10-12, however, is his linen clothing (10.5; 12.6, 7). This is the distinguishing feature of the angelomorphic figure with the writing case in Ezekiel 9-10 who supervises the six destroying angels (9.2, 3, 11; 10.2, 6, 7). Perhaps the best way to understand Gabriel's splendor in Daniel 10 is to see it as a phenomenon similar to Ezek 8.2. There a very exalted angelomorphic figure, which one would expect to see upon the divine throne, functions as a revealer.[31] This understanding of Gabriel being identified as the Glory has led to the possibility of the rather controversial interpretation identifying Gabriel as the "one like a son of man" of Dan 7.13.[32]

Gabriel's role as a revealer in Daniel is performed in response to Daniel's fervent prayer and fasting. Gabriel's revelatory activity is related to his role as an intercessory angel because he is one of the archangels. Gabriel is entrusted, however, with a unique activity according to *1 Enoch*:

> [40.6] And the third voice I heard interceding and praying on behalf of those who dwell upon the earth and supplicating in the Name of the Lord of the Spirits.
>
> [40.9] The third, who is set over all exercise of strength, is Gabriel [...].

One may feasibly argue that Gabriel became known as the *angelus interpres* who responded to prayer with revelation. If he was the angel who gave interpretation to Daniel, he would understandably be looked upon as the spiritual being who had revealed prophecy to other prophets of God. We see Jewish traditions about Gabriel developed in this particular manner in Jewish Christianity, Mandeism, Manicheism, and Islam.[33]

Perhaps the most exalted of Gabriel's roles is his association with creation. Quispel and Fossum have both argued for a connection between the Mandean and Jewish evidence about Gabriel's role in

---

Daniel 10 on other texts.

[31] One sees a similar phenomenon with Michael in *Jos. Asen.* 14.1-17.10 and Yahoel in the *Apoc. Ab.* 10.1-17.21.

[32] Fossum, *Name of God*, 279 n.61.

[33] See Fossum, "The Apostle Concept in the Qur'ān and Pre-Islamic Near Eastern Literature", *Literary Heritage of Classical Islam: Arabic and Islamic Studies in Honor of James A. Bellamy* (eds. M. Mir and J. Fossum; Princeton: Darwin, 1993) 149-167.

creation.³⁴ In the third book of the Mandean *Right Ginza* the demiurge Ptahil is given hidden names (which held the power to create) and is also identified as Gabriel:

> [93.19] He called Ptahil-Uthra, embraced him, and kissed him like a mighty one. He bestowed names on him which are hidden and protected in their place. He gave him the name Gabriel the Apostle; and he called him, gave command, and spoke to him: "Arise, go, and descend to the place where there are no shekinas or worlds. Call forth and create a world, establish a world for yourself and make uthras in it [. . .]."

Fossum argues that this teaching was probably derived from Jewish tradition about Gabriel as God's apostle (שליח) functioning as his associate (שותף) in creation. He points to the rabbinic polemics against the angels as God's "associate" (שותף) in creation:

> [*Gen. Rab.* 1.3] R. Luliana ben Tabri said in the name of R. Isaac: Whether we accept the view of R. Haniuna or of R. Yohanan, all agree that none [of the angels] were created on the first day, lest you should say: "Michael stretched forth in the south of the firmament, and Gabriel in the north, while the Holy One, blessed be He, measured it in the middle." "But I am the Lord who makes all things, who stretched forth the heavens alone, who spread abroad the earth מאתי" (*Is.* xliv.24). It is written מי אתי: "Who was associated with Me in the creation of the World?" [cf. *Gen. Rab.* 3.8]

The polemic against Michael's role in creation presupposes the teaching within some Jewish group(s).³⁵ Fossum spells out the significance of this evidence:

> [. . .] it seems justified to conclude that the Mandean concept of the demiurge Gabriel שליהא derives from a Jewish teaching about the angel Gabriel being God's שליח and שותף, "apostle" and "associate", in creation by virtue of his possession of the Divine Name.³⁶

One final observation about Gabriel is important. With the presence of two principal angels in Daniel, neither of whom appears to dwarf substantially the other in significance, a noteworthy development has taken place: the idea of a single principal angel has become less distinct. What was "God and his Angel" has become "God and his angels" (usually two from among the four Angels of the Presence or seven Archangels).

---

³⁴ *Name of God*, 259-266. The texts and discussion that follow are based upon the more detailed and substantiated argument of Fossum.
³⁵ See Segal, *Two Powers in Heaven*, 137.
³⁶ *Name of God*, 266.

C. Raphael

The third angel who is featured with some regularity in lists of archangels is Raphael (רפאל: "God Healed").[37] Our knowledge of traditions about this angel is greatly enhanced by his presence in Tobit (ca. third or second century BCE). His name undoubtedly originated from his function as the healer of Tobit's blindness. This heart-warming Jewish story led to his characterization as the angel "[. . .] set over all disease and every wound of God's people" (*1 En.* 40.9).[38]

Several aspects of the depiction of Raphael found in Tobit are noteworthy developments that have implications for Christology. First, Raphael appears in human form to Tobias and others, yet remains undetected until he reveals himself and departs (12.15). Humans did not detect his nature because they saw a vision while Raphael was with them (12.19). Yet he is nothing less than one of the seven archangels who "stand before the Glory of the Lord" (12.12, 15).

Second, the concept of individual guardian angels is a prominent feature of this document. For example, Tobit blesses his son Tobias for his journey with the words: "Go with this man; God who dwells in heaven will prosper your way, and may his angel attend you" (5.16). Tobit comforts the fears of his wife a little later with this assurance: "Do not worry [. . . .] a good angel will go with him [. . .]" (5.20-21). Raphael also indicates that he is Tobit's intercessory angel because he brought and read Tobit and Sarah's prayer to God (12.12). Raphael also tells them that he had been with them as they did the good deed of burying the dead (12.12-13).

Third, Raphael is specifically identified as "the Angel of the Lord" (12.22). Here, again, is evidence that shows how the Angel of the Lord was considered to be an angel distinguishable from

---

[37] He is variously identified as one of the seven Archangels or Angels of God's Presence (Tob 12.15; *1En.* 20.3; ἀρχιστράτηγος in *Gk. Apoc. Ezra* 1.4), as one of the four angels carrying punishment against the fallen watchers (*1 En.* 10.4-9; 54.6), and as one of the four Angels of the Throne or Presence (*1 En.* 40.9; 71.8-9; *Sib. Or.* 2.215). His role as a binder of Azazel (*1 En.* 10.1-11) may be based on his binding of the demon Asmordaeus (Tob 8.3). He is infrequently linked with interpretation (*1 En.* 22.3; 32.6), the consummation (*Gk. Apoc. Ezra* 6.1-2), and judgment (*Sib. Or.* 2.215). See also M. Mach, "Raphael", *DDD* 1299-1300.

[38] Raphael's reputation as a healer led to his prominence in rabbinic and magical texts; see Mach, "Raphael", 1299-1300.

God. This is significant evidence that an angel bearing this designation has been identified with a personal name.

Fourth, there is a pattern of descent and ascent in this story: Raphael descends to help (12.14) and then ascends again to God who sent him (12.20). Because of the early date of this document, it may have played a paradigmatic role for the descent-ascent patterns in later literature.[39]

Finally, the veneration of angels in this document merits examination. The text that deserves special attention in this regard is the doxology in Tobit 11.14-15. Loren Stuckenbruck has made a significant contribution by arguing that the recension in Codex *Sinaiticus* is older and more original than the text typically used.[40] He further states that it may be an earlier doxological tradition that was incorporated into the prayer. This recension is in the third person and includes at least two doxological ascriptions to angels:

> [14] Blessed God
> and blessed his great Name
> and blessed all his holy angels;
> may his great Name be upon us,
> and blessed all the angels unto all ages.
> [15] for he has afflicted me
> but now I see my son Tobias!

Stuckenbruck readily recognizes the significance of the parallel blessings to God and his angels. What he fails to note in this blessing to God, His Name, and all the angels, is the possible identification of the Divine Name Angel who may be addressed in this prayer as "His Name". This would mean that Tobit is not only praising all the angels, but possibly praises an angel individually as the hypostatized Name. This doxology indicates that individuals did not only worship with angels, but they also offered them veneration along with God.

D. *Uriel*

Uriel (יראל: "God is My Light"), who is often understood to be one of the four archangels (*1 En.* 9.1), receives his name from the

---

[39] Knight, *Disciples of the Beloved One*, 146-153 (cf. John 3.13; 6.62; 1 Pet 3.22; Heb 10.19-20; 4.14; *Ascen. Is.* 3.13-18; 10.17; 11.23).
[40] *Angel Veneration and Christology*, 164-167.

dominant role he plays as commander over the celestial lights in the Astronomical Book (*1 En.* 72-82).[41] He has an important role in this document as an *angelus interpres* for Enoch (*1 En.* 72.1; 74.2; 75.3-4; 78.10; 79.6; 82.7). Another portion of *1 Enoch* assigns him the role of guiding Enoch to the prison house of the rebellious angels (*1 En.* 18.14-19.2; 21.5-6.9; cf. *Sib.Or.* 2.215-35).

Other documents continue to highlight Uriel's role as guide. In some documents he becomes the *angelus interpres par excellence* (e.g., *4 Ezra* 4.1; 5.20; 10.28). John Ashton has noted that the indistinguishability between God and his angel in *4 Ezra* is a pattern that is continued from the ancient Angel of the Lord texts.[42] This indistinguishability is visible in Uriel's first-person speech as God (5.40, 42; 6.6; 8.47; 9.18-22), the exalted address given to Uriel (4.38; 5.41; 7.45, 58, 75), Ezra addressing his reply to God when he is talking to Uriel, and Uriel responding to Ezra's prayer (13.37).

E. *Israel*

The most vivid depiction of the Angel Israel is found in the fragments of the *Prayer of Joseph* (first or second century CE).[43] The primary fragment of this prayer describes him as the angel who manifested himself in Jacob:

> [1] "I, Jacob, who is speaking to you, am also Israel, an angel of God and a ruling spirit. [2] Abraham and Isaac were created before any work. [3] But, I, Jacob, who men call Jacob but whose name is Israel am he who God called Israel which means, a man seeing God, because I am the firstborn of every living thing to whom God gives

---

[41] C. Newsom, "Uriel", *ABD* 6.769.

[42] "Bridging Ambiguities", *Studying John: Approaches to the Fourth Gospel* (Oxford: OUP, 1994) 83-85.

[43] Only three fragments of the 1st century CE *Prayer of Joseph* exist to date, which amount to about 16 lines of a document that reportedly contained 1100 *stichoi* (cf. the *Stichometry* of Nicephorus). The major Greek fragment of 15 lines (Frag. A) is found in Origen's *Comm. in Ioann.* II.31. Frag. B is only a single line that is cited in Gregory and Basil's *Philocalia* 23.15, Eusebius' *The Preparation of the Gospel* 6.2, and by Procopius of Gaza in his commentary *On Genesis*. Frag. C, also from *Philocalia*, is a paraphrase of content found in Frag. A and it includes the content of Frag. B. All of our comments here will based upon on the lines of Frag. A as in *OTP* 2.713. The major analysis of this text is by J. Smith, "The Prayer of Joseph", *Religions in Antiquity: Essays in Memory of Erwin Ramsdell Goodenough* (ed. J. Neusner; NumenSup 14; Leiden: Brill, 1968) 253-94. This document may be the referent of "the words of righteous Joseph" mentioned in *Ascen. Is.* 4.22.

life. [4] And when I was coming up from Syrian Mesopotamia, Uriel, the angel of God, came forth and said that I had descended to earth and I had tabernacled among men and that I had been called by the name of Jacob. [5] He envied me and fought with me and wrestled with me saying that his name and the name that is before every angel was to be above mine. [6] I told him his name and what rank he held among the sons of God. [7] 'Are you not Uriel, the eighth after me? and I, Israel, the archangel of the Power of the Lord and the chief captain among the sons of God? [8] Am I not Israel, the first minister before the face of God?' [9] And I called upon my God by the Inextinquishable Name."

The extant text appears to be a midrash on the Jacob narrative in Genesis, especially his incident of wrestling with the man at Peniel (Gen 32.24-32).[44] The speaker, Jacob/Israel, makes some remarkable claims about his identity through the use of several titles. Jonathan Smith, who has written a weighty article on this fragment, articulates the significance of these titles for the study of Jewish and Christian mediator figures:

> There is remarkable consistency to the titles given Jacob-Israel in the *PJ*. Indeed, it is striking that many of Jacob-Israel's titles are applied by Philo to the *Logos*, by rabbinic literature to Michael, by Jewish mystical literature to Metatron and by Jewish Christianity to Jesus. This suggests, without arguing direct literary dependence, a community and continuity of tradition. It would appear that the center of this continuity must be located within hellenistic mystical Judaism [. . .].[45]

The speaker of the prayer begins by acknowledging his earthly name Jacob and quickly indicates that he is "also Israel, an angel of God" (*Pr. Jos.* 1). Although the title "Israel" was one given to

---

[44] Smith suggests that this midrash follows the form of testament literature in which the patriarch is addressing his son; see "Prayer", 255-256. This would explain why Jacob is speaking in the first person in a "prayer" of Joseph (cf. Gen 48.9–49.28). The wrestling appears to represent the fraternal conflict between Jacob and Esau or between their angels (*Pr. Jos.* 5; cf. Smith, "Prayer", 276). Such rivalry gives us evidence of competing principal angel traditions (both Uriel and Israel are clearly angels from the heights of the celestial hierarchy). For other examples of this theme, see Smith, "Prayer", 279-280.

[45] "Prayer", 259. This document's importance for Christology was introduced by H. Windisch, "Die göttliche Weisheit der Juden und die paulinische Christologie", *Neutestamentliche Studien für G. Heinrici* (UNT 6; Leipzig, 1914) 225 n.1. More recently this has been discussed by Hengel, *Son of God*, 47-48; Segal, *Two Powers in Heaven*, 199-200; Rowland, *Christian Origins*, 39; Fossum, "Colossians", 190-193; and J. Ashton, *Understanding the Fourth Gospel* (Oxford: OUP, 1991) 343-345.

Jacob by the man with whom he wrestled (Gen 32.29), no mention is made there of the man's name. Such an association could be based on an exegesis of שׂרית עם־אלהים ("you have striven with God") or that the angel gave his own name to Jacob.[46] The title, ἀνὴρ ὁρῶν θεόν ("a man seeing God"), comes from Jacob's exclamation: "I have seen God!" (Gen 32.31). What is noteworthy here is that the author explains this designation as the meaning of the name "Israel" (*Pr. Jos.* 3). Such an exegesis of the name Israel is relatively rare, but is also found in abundance among the writings of Philo.[47] In *Conf* 146 the title Israel is linked with other significant titles which are also found in the *Prayer of Joseph*:

> [*Conf* 146] But if there be any as yet unfit to be called a son of God, let him press to take his place under God's First-born, the Word [ὁ λόγος], who holds the eldership among the angels, an archangel as it were. And many names are his for he is called: the Beginning, the Name of God, His Word, the Man after His Image, and "He that sees", namely, Israel.

This background helps us to understand how a Christian like Justin Martyr could posit the existence of the Son long before the incarnation by directly identifying "the man" with whom Jacob wrestled as the "Angel Israel" who is the Son of God:

> [*Dial. Trypho* 125.3] And that Christ would act so when He became man was foretold by the mystery of Jacob's wrestling with Him who appeared to him, in that He ministered to the will of the Father, yet nevertheless is God, in that He is the Firstborn of all creatures [. . .] But Israel was his name from the beginning, to which He altered the name of the blessed Jacob when He blessed him with His own name, proclaiming thereby that all who through Him have fled for refuge to the Father, constitute the blessed Israel.

Furthermore, the fact that Philo uses "Name of God" as a title for the Word alerts us to the probability that it was another designation for Jacob/Israel who, as stated in verse 9, calls "upon my God by

---

[46] Smith especially notes that varying traditions about an Angel Israel are found in Jewish mystical literature, including the tradition of an angel named Israel standing in the center of heaven leading the heavenly chorus; see "Prayer", 262. The antiquity of this *Merkabah* tradition is known by its presence in "On the Origin of the World", NHC II.105.20-25. There "[. . .] a firstborn whose name is Israel, the man who sees God [. . .]" stands in the midst of the heavenly hosts. The tradition that the wrestling angel gave Jacob his own name is found in *Pirqe R. El.* 37.

[47] Smith, "Prayer", 265; see also 109-112 above.

the Inextinguishable Name".[48] Once again, such evidence leads to the conclusion that this angel was understood to be the Angel of the Lord and more specifically the Divine Name Angel of Exod 23.20.

Israel/Jacob also designates himself πνεῦμα ἀρχικόν ("a ruling spirit").[49] This may be a synonym for "archangel" (cf. *Pr. Jos.* 7), a title that implies both ruling authority and spiritual nature.[50] It is instructive to see the prominent link between angel and spirit here and in the Angel of the Holy Spirit traditions of early Jewish Christianity.[51]

In the process of contrasting his own origins with those of the patriarchs who preceded him, the Angel Israel/Jacob gives himself another elevated title: "Abraham and Isaac were created before any work. But I [. . .] am the firstborn [πρωτόγονος] of every living thing to whom God gives life" (*Pr. Jos.* 2-3). Smith argues that the origin of the "firstborn" idea is a literalistic interpretation of Exod 4.22 where Israel (the nation) is declared God's firstborn son (cf. Ps 89.27).[52] The more probable and immediate background for the use of πρωτόγονος in the *Prayer of Joseph*, however, is the "firstborn" tradition that Philo employed for his *Logos* (*Conf* 62-3; 146; *Agr* 51; *Somn* 1.215).[53]

As the Angel Israel/Jacob is discussing his rank with Uriel (*Pr. Jos.* 7-8), he further asserts his authority with several titles: "Are you not Uriel, the eighth after me? and I, Israel, the Archangel [ἀρχάγγελος] of the Power of the Lord and the Chief Captain [ἀρχιχιλίαρχος] among the sons of God?" These designations

---

[48] This important detail is not seen by Smith, who tends to focus on connections with Michael-Gabriel-Metatron, but has been observed by Segal, *Two Powers in Heaven*, 200, and Fossum, *Name of God*, 314.

[49] Smith is somewhat puzzled by this description and links it with the idea of a national angel like Michael (cf. *Jub.* 35.17); see "Prayer", 265.

[50] Some common background may exist for this title and that given to (the angel) Satan, "the Ruler of the World", who is cast down (John 12.31; 16.11; Rev 12.7-9).

[51] The Angel of the Spirit, or Angel of the Holy/Prophetic Spirit, is prominently featured in *Ascension of Isaiah* (3.15; 4.21; 7.23; 8.14; 9.36, 39, 40; 10.4; 11.4, 33), *Herm. Man.* XI.9, and Elchasai (fragment in Hippolytus, *Ref.* 9.13.2-3); see also 116-119 above.

[52] Some rabbis interpreted Exod 4.2 to refer to the patriarch Israel (*Ex. Rab.* 19.7). This, Smith argues, developed into the tradition that the patriarchs were formed before creation (a tradition we see nuanced in *Pr. Jos.* 2); see "Prayer", 268. While Wisdom traditions may have given some impetus to this title, Wisdom is nowhere identified as the πρωτόγονος.

[53] See the discussion on 110-111 above.

(ἀρχάγγελος and ἀρχιχιλίαρχος) are often linked with Michael in Jewish literature.⁵⁴ The qualifier ("of the Power of the Lord"), however, is significant here in setting the Angel Israel apart as an archangel distinct from others. Fossum, following the lead of Daniélou, sees this title as a construction like "Angel of the Holy Spirit", which is synonymous with "Holy Spirit".⁵⁵ Thus, "Archangel of the Power of the Lord" is another expression for "the Power of the Lord". He finds further support in a Coptic magical papyrus where Jesus identifies himself with this threefold designation: "I am Israel-El, the Power of Iao Sabaoth, the Great Power of Barbaraoth".⁵⁶ Furthermore, it has already been shown that "the Power of the Lord" is another designation for "the Glory of the Lord" in Jewish mysticism.⁵⁷ Therefore, there is evidence to conclude that Jacob/Israel is identified in this text as the Glory.⁵⁸

The last title in the extant *Prayer of Joseph*, ὁ ἐν προσώπῳ θεοῦ λειτουργὸς πρῶτος ("the first minister before the face of God"), comes from the tradition that there are four or seven "Angels of the Face/Presence" who serve immediately before the divine throne in heaven.⁵⁹ The designation "first minister" identifies Israel as the leading Angel of the Presence, possibly even the High Priest of the heavenly temple.⁶⁰ The same Coptic magical papyrus quoted

---

⁵⁴ Dan 8.11; 12.1; *2 En.* 22.6[A]; 33.10[A]; *3 Bar.* 11.6; 13.3; *Jos. Asen.* 14.7; *Gk. Apoc. Ezra* 1.4; 4.24; *T. Ab.* 1.4[A] et.al. ἀρχιχιλίαρχος appears to be the same as the more common ἀρχιστράτηγος. The Angel of the Lord appears to Joshua as the ἀρχιστράτηγος of God's army (Josh 5.14 LXX).
⁵⁵ *Image of the Invisible God*, 25.
⁵⁶ *Image of the Invisible God*; 25; cf. A. M. Kropp, *Ausgewählte koptische Zaubertexte* (3 vols.; Bruxelles: Fondation Egyptologique Reine Elisabeth, 1930-1931) 1.48.
⁵⁷ See discussion of "The Power" on 119-123 above.
⁵⁸ See further evidence compiled by Fossum, *Image of the Invisible God*, 135-151.
⁵⁹ The Heb פנים signifies "face" or "presence". The Angel or Angels of the Presence probably developed from the single "Angel of the Presence" in Isa 63.9 (MT); see Seow, "Face", 612. "Angel of the Presence" is found with regularity in *Jubilees*, both in singular and plural forms. The singular use indicates the leading Angel of the Presence who lead Israel out of Egypt (1.29) and spoke as Moses wrote (1.27; 2.1). This angel is clearly separate from YHWH and replaces the "Angel of the Lord" of the MT as Genesis is retold in *Jubilees*; see discussion on 148-149 below. The plural is used with reference to the highest ranking group of angels who serve before the throne (cf. *Jub.* 2.2, 18; 15.27; 31.14; cf. 1QSb 4.25). Their work is described in *T. Levi* 3.5-7 (cf. *T. Judah* 25.2) and esp. *Songs of the Sabbath Sacrifice*. *T. Levi* 3.5 identifies these archangels with similar terminology to the *Prayer of Joseph*: οἱ λειτουργοῦντες [...] πρὸς κύριον.
⁶⁰ The Prince of Lights/Michael/Melchizedek has this role in the QL (cf.

above states that the Great Power Barbaraoth is "the Power that stands before the face of the Father". The Angel Israel holds the same type of exalted role and title that is given to Metatron, who is frequently called "the Prince of the Divine Presence" in Jewish mystical texts (e.g., *3 En.* 12.1). This angelomorphic being is not one from among the myriads of created angels of God which fill the heavens; his many honorific titles testify to his distinctiveness from the rest of creation, including other angels, for the Jewish group(s) that revered him.

F. *Yahoel*

One of the most exalted and remarkable depictions of an angelomorphic figure is found in the *Apocalypse of Abraham* (ca. first or early second century CE). In this document God sends an angel by the name of Yahoel to lead Abraham on a journey to heaven. Although Yahoel is not found in various lists as one of the archangels, he is considered to be the leading angel of God by the author(s) of this apocalypse. He offers a veritable resumé of his authority when he encounters the frightened Abraham:

> [10.3] And while I was still face down on the ground, I heard the voice speaking, "Go, Yahoel of the same Name, through the mediation of my Ineffable Name, consecrate this man for me and strengthen him against his trembling." [4] The angel he sent to me in the likeness of a man came, and he took me by my right hand and stood me on my feet. [5] And he said to me, "Stand up, Abraham, friend of God who has loved you, let human trembling not enfold you! [6] For lo! I am sent to strengthen you and to bless you in the Name of God, creator of heavenly and earthly things, who has loved you. [7] Be bold and hasten to him. [8] I am Yahoel and I was called so by him who causes those with me on the seventh expanse, on the firmament, to shake, a Power through the medium of his Ineffable Name in me. [9] I am the one who has been charged, according to his commandment, to restrain the threats of the living creatures of the cherubim against one another, and I teach those who carry the song through the medium of man's night of the seventh hour. [10] I am appointed to hold the Leviathans, because through me is subjugated the attack and menace of every evil reptile. [11] I am ordered to loosen Hades and to destroy those who wondered at the dead. [12] I am the one who

---

2 En. 22.6). The Word is the angelomorphic High Priest in Philo; see texts and discusssion on 306-307 below.

ordered your father's house to be burned with him, for he honored the dead. [13] I am sent to you now to bless you and the land which he whom you have called the Eternal One has prepared for you. [14] For your sake I have indicated the way of the land. [15] Stand up, Abraham, go boldly, be very joyful and rejoice. And I (also rejoice) with you, for a venerable honor has been prepared for you by the Eternal One. [16] Go, complete the sacrifice of the command. Behold, I am assigned (to be) with you and with the generation (to be born) from you. [17] And with me Michael blesses you forever. Be bold, go!"

A number of the items in this description indicate that Yahoel was understood to be the Angel of the Lord found in the Genesis narrative.[61] First and foremost, he is the hypostasis of the Divine Name (10.3, 6, 8) and he is the Divine Name Angel of Exod 23.20-21 whom God would send with Israel in the wilderness (10.16). Not only is it stated that he possesses the Divine Name, but he has a twice-theophoric personal name.[62] Furthermore, this name is one of the names used in worship according to *Apoc. Ab.* 17.13. Second, he enjoys a position in close proximity to the divine throne and leads the angelic chorus (10.9; 18.10-11).[63] Third, he has sweeping divine functions that include restraining angelic forces and holding "the Leviathans" (10.9-10; cf. Job 41.1-34) as well as controlling and punishing evil (10.10-12). Fourth, the mention of Michael in 10.17 is intriguing because it acknowledges the existence and importance of this leading angel who is often identified as the Guardian of Israel, even as the Angel of the Lord who possesses the Divine Name. One can speculate that Michael is mentioned here to prevent the possible criticism from some readers that Yahoel was "replacing" Michael. Fifth, chapter 12 is patterned after the Genesis 22 account, where specific interaction between Abraham and the Angel of the Lord is recorded.

---

[61] This exegesis follows that of both Rowland (*Open Heaven*, 101-102) and Fossum (*Name of God*, 318-21). Hurtado argues against their interpretation; see *One God*, 89-91.

[62] Yahoel (יהואל) is a compound of the Divine Names יהוה and אל. This tradition is a precursor of the one we find in *3 En.* 12.5; there Enoch is called the "the Little YHWH".

[63] Rowland's proposal that the throne found in *Apoc. Ab.* 18.12-14 is empty because Yahoel is not presently sitting on it, is speculative; see *Open Heaven*, 102-103, and Fossum, *Name of God*, 320. Instead, the throne appears to be occupied by the invisible God (16.3) who is shrouded in fire and light (18.13; 19.1; 20.1).

Yahoel is described here as "the likeness of a man" (10.4). As seen with other angelomorphic beings, this appears to be an allusion to the depiction of the Glory in Ezek 1.26-28. If so, then Yahoel is being presented as the Glory. This conclusion can be affirmed from the striking physical appearance of Yahoel:

> [*Apoc. Ab.* 11.2] The appearance of his body was like sapphire, and the aspect of his face was like chysolite, and the hair of his head like snow. [3] And a kidaris (was) on his head, its look that of a rainbow, and the clothing of his garments (was) purple; and a golden staff (was) in his right hand.

The bright appearance of Yahoel probably was developed from Ezekiel, especially the reference to the rainbow on his head.[64] It is quite interesting—even shocking—that the hair of Yahoel's head "was like snow" (11.2). This imagery, certainly dependent upon the portrayal of the Ancient of Days (Dan 7.9), presents Yahoel as a divine being. The high-priest type of turban, the purple garment, and the golden scepter all help define Yahoel's exalted status.[65]

Yahoel is especially significant because he is not one of the archangels or angels of the presence mentioned in other documents. He represents a development to establish a principal angel distinct from the other named angels because he possesses two of God's Names, distinguishing him from Michael (cf. 10.17). In light of his divine appearance, functions, and name, it is extremely significant that the name Yahoel is in the hymn of praise which Abraham leads: "Most Glorious El, El, El, El, Yahoel, you are he who my soul has loved, my protector" (17.13). This is evidence for some veneration of Yahoel, but not in a manner which displaces worship of God.[66] In spite of his exalted position, it should be observed that Yahoel does join Abraham in worshipping God (17.1-21).

---

[64] The Glory in Ezek 1.26-28 has a radiant body and a distinctive rainbow. Dan 10.6 may also be exercising some influence. Some details appear to be drawn from Ezek 28.13 (sapphire/chrysolite).

[65] The turban is important because of the plate upon which God's Name was inscribed; cf. Exod 28.4, 36. For the scepter, see *Ezek.Trag.* 74.

[66] Capes criticizes Hurtado's downplaying of the Yahoel evidence; see *OT Yahweh Texts*, 168-173.

G. *Eremiel*

There is some variation in the names and functions by which this principal angel is known. He is called Jeremiel in *4 Ezra* 4.36 where he responds to Ezra's question about the coming of the new age. His duty in *4 Ezra* is to watch over the souls in Hades. In *2 Baruch* he is identified as Ramiel, the angel who "presides over true visions" (55.3; cf. 63.6). In one manuscript of *1 En.* 20.8 he is said to be Remiel, "one of the holy angels that God set over them that rise" (cf. *Sib. Or.* 2.214-219).

The name Eremiel is the name given him in the *Apocalypse of Zephaniah* (ca. first century BCE to first century CE).[67] There he is the angel who assists in judgment by showing Zephaniah his sins and declaring his triumph. This apocalypse contains the following exalted depiction of this angel:

> [6.4] Then I [Zephaniah] thought that the Lord Almighty had come to visit me. [5] Then when I saw, I fell on my face before him in order to worship him. [6] I was very much afraid, and I entreated him that he might save me from this distress. [7] I cried out, saying, "Eloe, Lord, Adonai, Sabaoth, I beseech you to save me from this distress because it has befallen me" [he then proceeds to see the accuser angel of Hades in 6.8-10].
>
> [6.11] Then I arose and stood, and I saw a great angel standing before me with his face shining like the rays of the sun in its glory since his face was like the face of a man perfected in its glory. [12] And he had what looked like a golden girdle upon his breast, and his feet were like bronze melted in a fire. [13] And when I saw him, I rejoiced, for I thought that the Lord Almighty had come to visit me. [14] I fell on my face and worshiped him. [15] He said to me, "Take heed. Do not worship me. I am not the Lord Almighty, but I am the great angel, Eremiel, who is over the abyss and Hades."

The description of this angel is founded primarily upon that of Gabriel in Dan 10.5-6: the "golden girdle" (Dan 10.5 has it on the loins), the feet like gleaming bronze (Dan 10.6), and the bright face (Dan 10.6 mentions "lightning" not "sun").[68] The author is probably not using the description in Daniel to identify the angel

---

[67] The etymology of Yeremiel is probably related to the prophet Jeremiah (even as Uriel is related to the prophet Uriyahu in Jer 26.20); see Culianu, "Angels of the Nations", 91.

[68] The reference to the brightness of an angelomorphic face as the sun is found in *2 En.* 1.4-5; *Jos. Asen.* 14.9; Rev 1.16; 10.1.

of Daniel 10 with Eremiel. In all likelihood, he draws on Daniel's description with minor modifications to record the appearance of an angel whom he believes to be of similar status and authority.

The reaction of Zephaniah is emphatic: he states "the Lord Almighty had come" and he worships Eremiel (6.13-14). As with other texts, this account shows how the appearance of a principal angel could easily be mistaken for that of God himself.[69] The refusal formula found here is paralleled in early Jewish and Christian literature and is further polemical evidence which presupposes some form of angel veneration.[70]

H. *Metatron*

Metatron is one of the most exalted principal angels, especially in Jewish mystical texts, whose origins lie in the Tannaitic period (50-220 CE).[71] Although these written traditions are often of a later date, Metatron is an angel whose roots are exceedingly complex and reach back beyond exalted Enoch traditions.[72] *3 Enoch* (ca. fifth century CE) is a primary fountainhead for traditions about Metatron. This document purports to be a record of the mystical ascent visions of Rabbi Ishmael, one of the second generation Tannaim (120-140 CE). It contains this vision of Metatron's crowning as the principal angel of God:

> [12.1] R. Ishmael said: Metatron, Prince of the Divine Presence, said to me: Out of the love which he had for me, more than for all the denizens of the heights, the Holy One, blessed be he, fashioned for me a majestic robe, in which all kinds of luminaries were set, and he clothed me in it. [2] He fashioned for me a glorious cloak in which brightness, brilliance, splendor, and luster of every kind were fixed, and he wrapped me in it. [3] He fashioned for me a

---

[69] Culianu argues that a similiar idea is present in *4 Ezra* 7.3 and *2 Bar.* 75.1; see "Angels of the Nations", 89-91.

[70] Rev 19.10; 22.8-9; *Ascen. Is.* 7.21; cf 8.5; 9.31, 36; *Apocryphal Gospel of Matthew* 3.3; *2 En.* 1.4-8; *3 En.* 1.7; 16.1-5. For further discussion see Bauckham, "Worship of Jesus", 322-341, and Stuckenbruck, *Angel Veneration and Christology*, 87-103; cf. 33-36 above.

[71] See G. Scholem, "Metatron", *EncJud* 11.1443-1446. For Metatron in *3 Enoch*, see P. Alexander's introduction and translation in *OTP* 1.223-315, and his "The Historical Setting of the Hebrew Book of Enoch", *JJS* 28 (1977) 156-180. The translation by H. Odeberg, *3 Enoch or The Hebrew Book of Enoch*, is still very useful due to its generous notes.

[72] See Morray-Jones,"Transformational Mysticism", 10.

kingly crown in which 49 refulgent stones were placed, each like the sun's orb, [4] and its brillance shone [. . .] into the four quarters of the world. [5] He set it upon my head and he called me, "The Lesser YHWH" in the presence of his whole household in the height, as it is written, "My name is in him."

Metatron is unequivocally identified here as the Divine Name Angel of Exod 23.20-21. By virtue of his possession of God's Name, he is called יהוה הקטן ("the Lesser YHWH"), a title of great status.[73] His common title in *3 Enoch*, שר הפנים ("the Prince of the Divine Presence"), indicates that the functions that previously belonged to the seven archangels and the four angels of the presence are now distilled into one angelic High Priest. He is the sole conveyor of requests to God and his commands carry divine authority (*3 En.* 10.4-5). Moreover, God places a royal robe and crown on him that testify to his exalted position. He even has his own glorious throne patterned after the throne of glory (*3 En.* 10.1). After listing the names and duties of several significant angels, *3 En.* 14.5 relays their reaction to Metatron, especially to the crown on his head that bore the Divine Name: "They all fell prostrate when they saw me and could not look at me because of the majesty, splendor, beauty, brightness, brilliance, and radiance of the glorious crown which was on my head."

Saul Lieberman, among others, has argued that the name Metatron possibly developed from a title that reflected his enthroned position with God (μετάθρονος = σύνθρονος).[74] Even more intriguing and probable is Stroumsa's suggestion that the name Metatron may be related to μέτρον ("measure"), since Metatron could be considered the measure of God's Body as in *Shi'ur Qomah* mysticism.[75] For example, Enoch had become very large in the process of his transformation into the angel Metatron according to *3 Enoch*:

> [9.2] I [Metatron] was enlarged and increased in size till I matched the world in length and breath. [3] He made to grow on me 72 wings, 36 on one side and 36 on the other, and each single wing covered the entire world. [4] He fixed in me 365,000 eyes and each eye was like the Great Light.

---

[73] Scholem draws a conceptual link between Yahoel and Metatron based upon this designation "the Little YHWH", whereby the characteristics of the Yahoel were transferred to the Metatron; see his "Metatron", 1444.

[74] "Metatron, the meaning of his name and his functions", Appendix 1 in I. Gruenwald, *Apocalyptic and Merkavah Mysticism* (AGJU 14; Leiden: Brill, 1980) 235-241.

[75] "Form(s) of God", 287.

In light of this and similar evidence, Rowland draws this poignant conclusion about Metatron:

> Indeed, so similar is Metatron to God and so alike the trappings of his authority and power, that one is left with the impression that we have a figure here who is so like God that he virtually acts as the very embodiment of divinity.[76]

This exalted status must have caused problems for many Jewish interpreters. This led to polemics against Metatron's enthronement which are vividly depicted in *3 En.* 16.1-5 and rabbinic texts.[77]

I. *Other Interpretations of the Principal Angel(s)*

In order to present a balanced picture of the evidence, one must acknowledge that there were Jewish groups that produced significant documents which did not share this emphasis on developing principal angels with specific personal names. Nevertheless, they sought to interpret the Angel of the Lord traditions in some manner. For example, *Jubilees*, in its narrative rewriting of the early history of Israel, removes confusion about the indistinguishability between God and the Angel of the Lord by changing the depictions of this angel in the recorded events and by substituting terminology: the Angel of the Lord is called "the Angel of the Presence".[78] Therefore, in some OT accounts where the Angel of the Lord appeared to human beings and spoke as YHWH, *Jubilees* records the Angel of the Presence speaking and acting as a separate agent of God.[79] Therefore, Jubilees shows an awareness of the Angel of the Lord traditions (*Jub.* 1.29), yet they are generally downplayed. For example, the wrestling incident of Gen 32.24-30

---

[76] *Open Heaven*, 111.

[77] *1 En.* 16.1-5 contains a polemical account similar to *b. Hag.* 15a, (cf. *b.Sanh.* 38b) which is discussed on 125 above; see also Rowland, *Open Heaven*, 334-338, and Morray-Jones, "Transformational Mysticism", 7, and Segal, *Two Powers in Heaven*, 33-158.

[78] This designation further distinguishes this angel from God. A similar change of designation may be present in Mal 3.1 which refers to "the Angel of the Covenant". This angel is instructed by God to write the Pentateuch as he dictates its contents to Moses (*Jub.* 1.27; 2.1).

[79] E.g., *Jub.* 16.1 has "we appeared to Abraham" for "YHWH appeared to Abraham" (Gen 18.1). Unlike Gen 22.11 where the Angel of the Lord stops Abraham from sacrificing Isaac, *Jub.* 18.9-10 records God speaking to the Angel of the Presence to stop Abraham.

is transformed into a simple blessing of Jacob by God and an elaborate vision of the future in *Jub.* 32.16-26. Other incidents, like the call of Moses, are not even discussed.

The Samaritan literature also testifies to the modification of the OT Angel of the Lord traditions. In his discussion of the Angel of the Lord in Samaritanism, Fossum documents how their literature testifies to a melding of traditions about כבוד ("the Glory") and the Angel of the Lord. For example, the following understanding of Exod 23.21 is found in *Memar Marqa*:

> [III.5] The Glory said: "The Great Name (שמה רבה) is within me, and I do not shun him who is rebellious in action. When a man deviates, I forfeit him; and thus it is said of me: 'For he will not pardon your transgression, since My Name is in him'".

Furthermore, Fossum demonstrates that another designation for the Angel of the Lord/Glory in *Memar Marqa* is שלטן ("Regent"), which also functions as a substitute designation for the Destroyer.[80] This complex angelomorphic figure is responsible for the killing of Egyptians during the Passover and in the Red Sea.[81] Therefore, when the Pentateuch narrates that God has annihilated and punished evil-doers, the Samaritans ascribed these actions to the Angel of the Lord.[82]

The extensive reinterpretion of the Angel of the Lord traditions that is found in Philo has already been discussed.[83] The historian Josephus (ca. late first century CE), however, was not as intrigued with the exegetical possibilities of these traditions. He does relate some of the Angel of the Lord incidents in his retelling of Israelite history.[84] He once identifies the angel that confronted Balaam as "the divine spirit" (*Ant* 4.108) and he also avoids some uses of ἄγγελος by replacing this term with φάντασμα (e.g., *Ant* 5.213; 5.277). Furthermore, rather than depicting specific angelic beings with an emphasis on their communication with humans, Josephus focuses on the Law as God's means of communication and

---

[80] *Name of God*, 225.
[81] See *Memar Marqa* I.9 and III.5; cf. Fossum, *Name of God*, 225-228.
[82] Fossum, *Name of God*, 226-228.
[83] See discussion on 140-147 above.
[84] See the incidents with: Hagar in *Ant* 1.189.1; Abraham and Lot in *Ant* 1.196.2, 1.198.4 and 1.200.1; Ishmael in *Ant* 1.219.1; Jacob in 1.332.3 and 1.333.2-3; Balaam in *Ant* 4.108.1; 4.109.2; 4.110.2; Samson's parents in *Ant* 5.279.1; 5.280.3-4; 5.284.3; the angel sending a plague during David's reign in *Ant* 7.327.1-5; the angel destroying Sennacherib's army in *JW* 5.388.1.

also substitutes angels with the Hellenistic concept of daemons (divine providential spirits) who guide individuals and events of the day.[85]

Liber Antiquitatum Biblicarum (ca. 70 CE), also know as *Pseudo-Philo*, depicts angels as intermediaries who communicate with people, but are subordinate to God and the elect of Israel. It has a more elaborate hierarchy of angelic names, but little more than a few remnants of the OT Angel of the Lord traditions.[86] The relative prominence of angels and the mention of additional angels with specific functions or names shows the links between developed apocalypticism and the development of Rabbinism since Pseudo-Philo emphasizes the Law as the key to Israel's survival.

Evidence from the Magaharians, a pre-Christian Jewish group, is often not considered or is dismissed because it is preserved in the documents of historians outside this group who wrote centuries after the group existed.[87] The Magaharians developed the Angel of the Lord traditions, especially with regard to the angel's cosmogenic role. After sifting this scattered evidence carefully, Fossum concludes that the "Magharians could therefore argue that every anthropomorphic description of God in the Bible did not pertain to God in his essence but to his viceregent".[88]

J. *Conclusion*

This evidence records several developments in angelomorphic traditions that are significant for the origins of Christology. First, there is an increased emphasis in this literature on interpreting the principal angel as a distinct figure alongside God. No longer do we

---

[85] For a discussion of Josephus' apologetic purpose in adapting this biblical narrative, see J. Levison, "Josephus' Inspiration of the Divine Spirit", *JJS* 46 (1996) 234-255.

[86] See *L.A.B.* 19.9 (Moses sees God's angel but hears God); there are other incidents not paralleled in the OT where God speaks and/or acts through a distinct angel: 25.1-2; 30.2; 35.1-7; 38.4; 60.8-9 (cf. 26.4; 30.2).

[87] Evidence for this group and its ideas is preserved in scattered references by historians writing around 1000 CE; see J. Fossum, "The Magharians: A Pre-Christian Jewish Sect and Its Significance for the Study of Gnosticism and Christianity", *Henoch* 9 (1987) 303-343. See also H. Wolfson, "The Pre-Existent Angel of the Magharians and Al-Nahāwandi", *JQR* 91 (1960-61) 89-106.

[88] "The Magharians", 329.

encounter the indistinguishability between God and his angel as we found imbedded in the OT Angel of the Lord traditions. This does not mean, however, that these figures are completely separate from God and lack any criteria of divinity.

A second development witnessed in these texts is the interpretation of the hypostatized Glory, the visible likeness of God (cf. Ezek 1.26-28 and related texts), as a principal named angel distinct from God. Christopher Morray-Jones analyzes the far-reaching import of this development:

> While the motivation behind this development seems to have been to safeguard the transcendence and unity of God, it opened the way for two different but (from the rabbinic point of view) equally heretical aberrations: on the one hand, the Glory could be identified as a subordinate, created being (the beginning of the process that culminated in Gnosticism) and, on the other, a created being could be identified with the *kabod* (as in orthodox Christianity).[89]

Third, the Divine Name Angel tradition of Exod 23.20-21 is given great prominence in many of these texts. Its importance is difficult to overstate. The possession of the Divine Name is the key attribute that bestows divine authority, and in a qualified manner, a sharing in divine substance.

Not only do several of these principal angels possess the Divine Name, but often they are given a personal name as well. This fourth development makes these beings more distinct from God with their own personhood. Fossum spells out these implications:

> The identification of the Angel of the Lord and the Glory of God by means of a personal name, whether that of one of the archangels or that of a human being, was a very significant step. Whereas God's agent formerly was not clearly distinguishable from God himself and had existence only as long as the situation for which he was required lasted, he acquired a distinct personality and permanent existence through a personal name.[90]

---

[89] "Transformational Mysticism", 6-7.
[90] Fossum, *Name of God*, 337.

CHAPTER SIX

ANGELOMORPHIC HUMANS

The fact that angels are depicted as appearing in human form on earth leads to a natural question: Could a human be an angel? It is widely known that several Jewish texts depict life-after-death as an angelic state.[1] There has been less discussion, however, of the idea that some humans are angels, or become angels, without physical death.[2] Ontological questions have often stifled our exegesis of Jewish texts that depict exalted human beings, or the elect in general, as angels. These depictions vary widely in their content. Sometimes the person's angelomorphic state is the result of a transformation through a mystical ascent to heaven or upon assumption to heaven without physical death.[3] Other times humans are depicted as angels on earth, or as having an angel within them, without an explanation of how this came about.[4] Becoming an angel is not always viewed as the attainment of a new state; sometimes it is depicted as the return to the primordial state (*1 En.* 69.11; Luke 20.36). These variegated traditions will be examined according to the following categories of exalted humans, even though these groupings are not mutually exclusive: Patriarchs, Prophets, Priests, Kings, Apostles, and Elect Ones. Once again, the goal here is not a comprehensive catalog of the pluralistic traditions about angelomorphic humans. Rather, representative evidence will be given to demonstrate that several humans were understood to be, and were depicted as, angels. This evidence has

---

[1] E.g., Dan 12.3; *2 Bar.* 51.5, 10, 12. This will not be a focus of this chapter, although some evidence of humans becoming principal angels after death will be presented.

[2] This topic has been addressed by Bühner, *Gesandte und sein Weg*, 270-398, and in a limited manner by J.H. Charlesworth, "The Portrayal of the Righteous as an Angel", *Ideal Figures in Ancient Judaism* (eds. G. Nickelsburg and J.J. Collins; SCS 12; Chico, CA: Scholars Press, 1980) 135-151. More recently, Morray-Jones has explored this theme in Talmudic tradition in "Transformational Mysticism", 1-31.

[3] This is especially found in traditions about Enoch, Elijah, and Moses.

[4] E.g., the *Prayer of Joseph* depicts Jacob as the Angel Israel who "tabernacles" within him.

obvious implications for how the human Jesus could be understood and depicted in angelomorphic categories.

A. *Patriarchs*

1. *Adam*

In light of Adam's involvement in the origin of evil according to Genesis 3, the degree to which the first man is extolled in some Jewish documents may appear surprising.[5] The honor that Adam was accorded in some Jewish groups is founded primarily upon his status as the first human being and the one created in the image of God (Gen 1.26-27). His angelic nature is closely linked with the idea that he had a luminous angelic body before the fall.[6] Several texts enhance his status by not implicating him with the fall into sin.[7] Ben Sira closes his lengthy tribute to the OT worthies with this exalted assertion about Adam: "Shem and Seth were honored among men, and Adam above every living being in the creation" (Sir 49.16).

Such reverent ascriptions border on asserting that these individuals were suprahuman or angelic. *2 Enoch* (ca. first century CE) takes the role of Adam as guardian of God's creation to a more pronounced degree. It explicitly identifies Adam as one of God's principal angels over creation, probably by means of an exegesis of Psalm 8:

> [30.11] And on earth I [God] assigned him to be a second angel, honored and great and glorious. [12] And I assigned him to be a king, to reign [on] the earth, [and] to have my wisdom. And there

---

[5] See further: B. Murmelstein, "Adam, ein Beitrag zur Messiaslehre", *WZKM* 35 (1928) 242-275 and 36 (1929) 51-86; W. Staerk, *Die Erlösererwartung in den östlichen Religionen* (Berlin: Kohlhammer, 1938) 41-61; J. Levison, *Portraits of Adam in Early Judaism: From Sirach to 2 Baruch* (JSPSup 1; Sheffield: Sheffield Academic Press, 1988); M. Stone, *A History of the Literature of Adam and Eve* (Atlanta: Scholars Press, 1992); J. Fossum, "The Adorable Adam of the Mystics and the Rebuttals of the Rabbis", *Geschichte-Tradition-Reflexion: Festschrift für Martin Hengel zum 70. Geburtstag* (eds. H. Cancik, H. Lichtenberger, and P. Schäfer; Tübingen: Mohr/Siebeck, 1996) I.529-539.

[6] See G. Kittel, "εἰκών, E. The Divine Likeness in Judaism", *TDNT* 2.392-97. For a discussion of Moses being vested with this glorious image of Adam in Samaritan literature, see Fossum, *Name of God*, 93-94.

[7] E.g., *L.A.E. Vita* 3.1 indicates that it is because of Eve that God is angry with Adam.

was nothing comparable to him on the earth, even among my creatures that exist.

Although this text is found in the longer recension of 2 *Enoch* which is difficult to date, nevertheless there is other pre-first century CE testimony to the exalted status of Adam as God's vice-regent over creation.⁸ Wis 10.1 may be exalting Adam even further by bestowing upon him the title of "First-formed Father of the world", a designation which has obvious cosmogenic associations.⁹

Adam's status is notably higher than a principal angel in the Jewish document the *Life of Adam and Eve* (ca. first century CE). The Latin text (*Vita*) contains an account which explains the fall of Satan as due to his refusal to follow Michael's command and example in venerating Adam: "Worship the image of God" [i.e., Adam] (*Vita* 14.2). Although the text gives no physical description of Adam, he is called the "image" or visible likeness of God, and thus, is worthy of angelic worship (*Vita* 13.1-15.3). A clear development has taken place: Adam, who was made "in the image of God" (Gen 1.26) is considered here to be "the image of God".¹⁰ The injunction for the angels to worship Adam is striking and evinces once more the veneration of an angelomorphic figure in a Jewish context.¹¹

This veneration of the first man should not be seen as a new phenomenon that originated in the first century BCE and blossomed in Gnosticism. It has already been demonstrated that Jewish exegetes had long been intrigued with the idea of God's visible manifestation in the form of a man, both in early pentateuchal texts and especially with the angelomorphic figure of the Glory in Ezek 1.26. It would not be surprising, then, to find

---

⁸ E.g., Philo, *Quaes Gen* 2.56; see also Fossum, *Name of God*, 273.
⁹ This was the name of the creator in hellenistic literature; see A. Dupont-Sommer, "Adam. 'Père du Monde' dans la Sagesses de Solomon (10,1.2)", *RHR* 119 (1939) 182-191, and Fossum, "The Adorable Adam", 534-535.
¹⁰ Fossum, *Name of God*, 278.
¹¹ D. Steenburg argues that the worship of Adam here is evidence that the worship of the "visible manifestation" of God is within the bounds Jewish monotheism (contra Hurtado); see "The Worship of Adam and Christ as the Image of God", *JSNT* 39 (1990) 95-109. He also states that this principle is what legitimated early worship of Christ, who is the visible manifestation of God. For more evidence of the worship of Adam, see Fossum, *Name of God*, 271-272.

examples of Adam being glorified and enthroned after his death.[12] The *Testament of Abraham* [Rec. A] (ca. first century CE) gives evidence of such contemplation. In *T. Ab.* 11.4 Abraham is taken into heaven where he is shown a man "seated on a golden throne" who observes the results of judgment and has a "terrifying" appearance "like the Master's". Then Abraham asks his guide, Michael, about the identity of this figure:

> [11.8] "My lord Commander-in-chief, who is this most wonderous man, who is adorned in such glory, and sometimes he cries and wails while other times he rejoices and exults?" [9] The incorporeal one said, "This is the first-formed Adam who is in such glory, and he looks at the world, since everyone has come from him."

2. *Abel*

The *Testament of Abraham*, through a very creative exegesis of Dan 7.13-27, posits more than one glorious enthroned figure who is involved in judgment.[13] Consequently, Adam is not the only human described in such an elevated fashion in this document. An interesting aspect of this exegesis is that the "one like a son of man" in Dan 7.13 is understood literally to be the son of Adam (אדם = man), namely Abel:

> [12.4] And between the two gates there stood a terrifying throne with the appearance of terrifying crystal, flashing like fire. [5] And upon it sat a wondrous man, bright as the sun, like unto a son of God.

> [13.2] The Commander-in-chief [Michael] said, "Do you see, all-pious Abraham, the frightful man who is seated on the throne? This is the son of Adam, the first-formed, who is called Abel, whom Cain the wicked killed. [3] And he sits here to judge the entire creation, examining both righteous and sinners.

This text has striking features one would typically associate with

---

[12] The *Testament of Adam* (ca. second-fifth century CE), a Christian document, gives evidence of Adam having his desire to be a "god" fulfilled in heaven where he will be at God's right hand (3.4).

[13] There are four figures who are part of the judgment process in the *Testament of Abraham* 11.1-13.7: Adam (all souls pass him), Abel (the judge of those passing by Adam), the Twelve Tribes of Israel (who assist in the final end-time judgment), and the "Master God of all" (the final judge). For a complete discussion of these traditions, see P. Munoa, "Four Powers in Heaven: Exegesis of Daniel 7 in the *Testament of Abraham*" (Ph.D. diss., University of Michigan, 1993). This work will soon be published by Sheffield in JSPSup.

a theophany: Abel is described as "a wonderous man", "bright as the sun", "like a son of God", "seated on a throne", "judging the entire creation". He is plainly depicted as an angelomorphic being.[14] Abel has taken on the functions performed in other texts by principal angels or God himself. The conclusion that Abel is depicted here as an angel is supported by a scene in the *Ascension of Isaiah* where it states that Abel and Enoch "[. . .] were like the angels who stand there in great glory" (9.9).

3. *Enoch*

Because Enoch, of the seventh generation from Adam, was widely understood to have been assumed into heaven, based on the testimony of Gen 5.24, he was the focus of much wonderment about the heavenly realms. These traditions are especially visible in the Enochic literature. The earliest extant account of Enoch's visionary ascent to behold "the Great Glory" upon his throne is recorded in *1 En.* 14.8-16.3. There is no specific mention of Enoch's status in this account. Later ascent accounts, however, testify more overtly to the transformation of the human Enoch into an exalted angel.[15] Evidence of this phenomenon is the identification of Enoch as the Son of Man/Elect One in the throne room scene at the conclusion of the Similitudes of *1 Enoch* (ca. first century CE):

> [71.14] Then an angel came to me and greeted me and said to me, "You, son of man, who are born in righteousness and upon whom righteousness has dwelt, the righteousness of the Antecedent of Time will not forsake you." [15] He added and said to me, "He shall proclaim peace to you in the name of the world that is to become. For from here proceeds peace since the creation of the

---

[14] Dokiel, an angel who appears to have a lower status than Abel, is described here as "the sunlike angel" (*T. Ab.* 13.1, 10). Angelophanies often mention the brightness of the sun (*2 En.* 1.4-5; *Jos. Asen.* 14.9; 18.9; *Apoc. Zeph.* 6.11) or lightning (Dan 10.6; Matt 28.3) or chrysolite (*Apoc. Ab.* 11.2) or bright/ white apparel (Matt 28.3; Mark 16.5; Luke 24.3; Acts 1.10). Note also the brightness of sun in the face of Christ during the transfiguration (Matt 17.2 only) and visions (Rev 1.16; 10.1; Acts 9.3; 22.6; 26.13).

[15] Enoch also plays an important role in the *Testament of the Twelve Patriarchs* (*T. Sim.* 5.4; *T. Levi* 10.5; 14.1; *T. Judah* 18.1; *T. Zeb.* 3.4; *T. Dan.* 5.6; *T. Naph.* 4.1; *T. Benj.* 9.1) and *Jubilees* (4.17-26; 10.17; 21.10). Enochic traditions exercised influence in early Christianity; for evidence see W. Adler, "Enoch in Early Christian Literature", *SBLSP* 17 (1978) 271-276, and J. Vanderkam, "1 Enoch, Enochic Motifs, and Enoch in Early Christian Literature", *The Jewish Apocalyptic Heritage in Early Christianity* (eds. J. VanderKam and W. Adler; CRINT III.4; Minneapolis: Fortress, 1996) 33-101.

world and so it shall be unto you forever and ever. [16] Everyone that will come to exist and walk shall (follow) your path, since righteousness never forsakes you. Together with you shall be their dwelling places; and together with you shall be their portion. They shall not be separated from you forever and ever and ever." [17] So there shall be length of days with that Son of Man, and peace to the righteous ones; his path is upright for the righteous, in the name of the Lord of the Spirits forever and ever.

Although there is disagreement about whether chapters 70-71, which include this identification of Enoch as the Elect One/Son of Man, form an original part of the Similitudes (*1 En.* 37-71), the majority of specialists argue that these chapters are not an appendix.[16] This account demonstrates the remarkable phenomenon that a human could be identified with an exalted angelomorphic being: the Elect One/Son of Man.

2 Enoch 22 [Rec. A] also provides vivid evidence of an actual transformation of the human Enoch into an angelic being. This takes place after Michael brings Enoch before the divine throne in the tenth heaven:

> [5] And the LORD, with his own mouth, called to me, "Be brave, Enoch! Don't be frightened! Stand up, and stand in front of my face forever." [6] And Michael, the Lord's greatest archangel, lifted me up and brought me in front of the face of the LORD. And the LORD sounded out his servants. The LORD said, "Let Enoch join in and stand in front of my face forever!" [7] And the glorious ones did obeisance and said. "Let him come up!" [8] The LORD said to Michael, "Take Enoch, and extract (him) from the earthly clothing. And anoint him with the delightful oil, and put (him) into the clothes of glory." [9] And Michael extracted me from my clothes. He anointed me with the delightful oil; and the appearance of that oil is greater than the greatest light, its ointment is like sweet dew, and its fragrance like myrrh; and its shining like the sun. [10] And I gazed at all of myself, and I had become like one of the glorious ones, and there was no observable difference.

---

[16] See M. Black, "The Messianism of the Parables of Enoch: Their Date and Contribution to Christian Origins", *The Messiah: Developments in Early Judaism and Christianity* (ed. J.H. Charlesworth; Minneapolis: Fortress, 1992), 145-68; see also J. VanderKam, "Righteous One, Messiah, Chosen One, and Son of Man in 1 Enoch 37-71", 169-191, and M. Knibb, "The Date of the Parables of Enoch: A Critical Review", *NTS* 25 (1975) 345-359, esp. 352. These scholars argue against the position that *1 En.* 70-71 is a later appendix that is not closely related to the earlier chapters of the Similitudes. For a contrary opinion, see J.J. Collins, "The Heavenly Representative: The 'Son of Man' in the Similitudes of Enoch", *Ideal Figures in Ancient Judaism* (eds. G. Nickelsburg and J.J. Collins; SCS 12; Chico, CA: Scholars Press, 1980) 122-124.

In addition to his brilliant appearance as an angel, Enoch will be "standing" in front of the face of the Lord forever. This indicates the status of a principal angel.[17] Furthermore, he returns for one month to earth where his angelomorphic nature continues as he appears glorious (37.2) and lives without food or sleep (56.2).

4. *Noah*

Noah is also depicted as angelomorphic according to the peculiar account of his birth that is found in the so-called "Book of Noah", which is appended to *1 Enoch*:

> [106.2] And his [Noah's] body was white as snow and red as a rose; the hair of his head as white as wool and his *demdema* beautiful; and as for his eyes, when he opened them the whole house glowed like the sun—(rather) the whole house glowed more exceedingly. [3] And when he arose from the hands of the midwife, he opened his mouth and spoke to the Lord with righteousness. [4] And his father, Lamech, was afraid of him and fled and went to Methuselah his father; [5] and he said to him, "I have begotten a strange son: He is not like an (ordinary) human being, but he looks like the children of the angels in heaven to me; his form is different, and he is not like us. His eyes are like the rays of the sun, and his face glorious. [6] It does not seem to me that he is of me, but of the angels; and I fear that a wonderous phenomenon may take place upon the earth in his days.[18]

Several details of this description support the conclusion that Noah is presented as an angelomorphic being. He is twice described as having an appearance like "an angel" (106.5-6). He is identified as a glorious being of light. This light is manifested through his eyes which shine forth with the brilliance "of the sun" (106.2, 5). The brightness of the sun, especially associated with the face or eyes, is a prominent characteristic of theophanies and angelophanies.[19] For example, the angel (Michael) who appeared

---

[17] Testimony to the standing posture of angels is abundant; see 31 above. Those who stand immediately before the throne are usually the principal angels (i.e., the Angels of the Presence; cf. 124-151 above).

[18] E. Isaac explains that the Ethopic word *demdema* in vs. 2 refers to "long curly hair combed up straight"; see note in *OTP* 1.86.

[19] The description of the eyes of Gabriel as "flaming torches" in Dan 10.6 influenced other angelomorphic depictions emphasizing the eyes (e.g., Rev 1.14; 19.12). The brightness and glowing, usually associated with fire, are part of several theophanies (e.g., Exod 24.27; Ezek 1.26-28). Angelophanies often mention brightness; see 155-156 above, esp. n. 14.

to Aseneth has "eyes like sunshine" (*Jos. Asen.* 14.9). Even though Noah is a newborn in this text, he has hair "as white as wool". This is an unmistakable allusion to the Ancient of Days in the prominent theophany of Dan 7.9 (cf. *1 En.* 46.1). This hair, which is a marker of divinity in Dan 7.9, is surprisingly also a characteristic of the principal angel Yahoel in *Apoc. Ab.* 11.2. This birth narrative bears some similarities to the supernatural birth of Melchizedek depicted in *2 En.* 71.17-21. These accounts witness to a fascination with ante-deluvian mediator figures and a willingness to use known theophanic characteristics in the depiction of angelomorphic figures.

5. *Jacob*

The most striking example of a patriarch who is an angel is found in the *Prayer of Joseph* in which the Angel Israel manifests himself in Jacob.[20] A significant aspect of this document that was not discussed above is the descent tradition it presents: "Uriel, the angel of God, came forth and said that I had descended to earth and I had tabernacled among men and that I had been called by the name Jacob." Smith announces that this descent tradition "[. . .] clearly derives from the Jewish Wisdom-*Shekinah* theology [. . .]."[21] Although Smith recognizes that the descent pattern is certainly present in Wisdom traditions (e.g., Sir 24.8; *1 En.* 42), he does not see that such traditions are based upon earlier angelomorphic traditions.[22] Furthermore, it is the *Angel* Israel that becomes incarnate in Jacob, not Wisdom.[23]

The *Prayer of Joseph*, in all of the rich brevity of this fragment, does not satisfy our curiosity about Jacob/Israel's physical appearance. The *Prayer of Jacob*, which identifies Jacob as "an earthly

---

[20] See the discussion on 137-142 above.
[21] "Prayer", 282.
[22] Talbert has demonstrated that angelomorphic traditions are the most fruitful area for understanding the background of this pattern; see "Descending-Ascending Redeemer", esp. 425-426.
[23] The relationship between this descent myth and the stairway Jacob saw to heaven is also very intriguing (Gen 28.10-27), especially in light of the targumic tradition that Jacob's image was engraved on the throne (*Tg. Ps.-J.* Gen 28.12) or that Jacob, as the image of God (the Glory) was on the throne. See Rowland, "John 1.51", 497-508, and esp. Fossum, *Image of the Invisible God*, 135-151.

angel" and "immortal" (line 19), does not speak of his appearance. The Egyptian Jewish document *Joseph and Aseneth* (ca. first century BCE-second century CE), however, presents Jacob's son Joseph as an angelomorphic human whose physical appearance was so striking that when the angel (Michael) comes to Aseneth, she thinks he looks like Joseph (14.9).[24] Joseph is given the titles "son of God" (6.3, 5; 13.13), "his [God's] firstborn son" (18.11; 21.4) and "like the firstborn son" (23.10).[25] Furthermore, the narrative records this remarkable physical description of Jacob and the noteworthy reaction of Aseneth:

> [22.6] And they [Joseph and Aseneth] went into Jacob. And Israel was sitting on his bed, and he was an old man in comfortable old age. [7] And Aseneth saw him and was amazed at his beauty, because Jacob was exceedingly beautiful to look at, and <u>his old age was like the youth of a handsome young man</u>, and <u>his head was all white as snow</u>, and the hairs of his head were all exceedingly close and thick like those of an Ethiopian, and his beard was white reaching down to his breast, and <u>his eyes were flashing and darting flashes of lightning</u>, and his sinews and his shoulders and his arms were <u>like those of an angel</u>, and his thighs and his calves and his feet were like those of a giant. And Jacob was like a man who had wrestled with God. [8] <u>And Aseneth saw him and was amazed, and prostrated herself before him face down to the ground.</u>

The primary manner in which God appeared in the ancient theophanic traditions, as discussed above, was as a man (e.g., Gen 18.2; Ezek 1.26). This text emphasizes the youthful appearance and beauty of Jacob, which is also a characteristic of angels.[26] In spite of this youthful appearance, he is given the pronounced characteris-

---

[24] Joseph's appearance is certainly royal (5.5-6) and could even be considered divine (6.2). For the relationship between these royal and divine characteristics, see W. Meeks, "Moses as God and King", *Religions in Antiquity: Essays in Memory of Erwin Ramsdell Goodenough* (ed. J. Neusner; NumenSup 14; Leiden: Brill, 1968) 361-362.

[25] The significance of these designations should not be overemphasized since the elect are designated the "sons of God" elsewhere in the document (16.14; 19.8). This narrative also may indicate that Aseneth became an angelomorphic human. After eating the honeycomb from the angel (Michael) and while preparing for her marriage to Joseph, her face becomes "like the sun" and she has strikingly youthful beauty (18.9).

[26] Josephus describes the two men/angels who rescued Lot as "young men of remarkably fair appearance [. . .] with youthful beauty" (*Ant* 1.198; cf. Gen 19.1-22) and the Angel of the Lord that visits Samson's parents as "a comely and tall youth" (*Ant* 5.277; cf. Judg 13.3-22).

tic of hair that is "all white as snow" (22.7).²⁷ Jacob's eyes are also described in a manner characteristic of theophanies or angelophanies: "his eyes were flashing and darting flashes of lightning".²⁸ The description of Michael earlier in this document is especially noteworthy: "his face was like lightning, and his eyes were like the light of the sun" (14.9). Jacob is portrayed as an angelomorphic human on earth who possesses a degree of divinity which Aseneth acknowledges by means of her veneration.²⁹

B. *Prophets*

1. *Introduction*

There are pericopes in the OT that contain a close association, or actual identification, of an angel with a biblical prophet.³⁰ For example, 2 Chr 36.15-16 links together the angels and prophets whom God sent to Israel as one and the same: "[. . .] but they [Israel] kept mocking the *angels* of God, despising his [YHWH's] words, and scoffing at his *prophets* [. . .]" (cf. Isa 44.26).³¹ Hag 1.12-13 takes the relationship between the Angel of the Lord and the prophet one step further by actually uniting the two in the personage of Haggai:

---

²⁷ See also the "hair as white as *snow*" upon Yahoel (*Apoc. Ab.* 11.2). "Hair as white as *wool*" is the unmistakable characteristic of the Ancient of Days (Dan 7.9; cf. *1 En.* 46.1) that is also present on Noah (*1 En.* 106.2) and Christ (Rev 1.14). For parallelism between snow and wool, see Isa 1.18. Michael has hair "like flames of fire" in *Jos. Asen.* 14.10.
²⁸ Gabriel has *eyes* "like flaming torches" (Dan 10.6; cf. Rev 1.14; 19.12), but a *face* in the "appearance like lightning" (Dan 10.6).
²⁹ Jacob's veneration in Rabbinism is visible in traditions about his image being on the throne of God (e.g., *Gen. R.* 68.12); see also Rowland, "John 1.51", 498-507, and Fossum, *Image of the Invisible God*, 135-151.
³⁰ Josephus, who typically uses ἄγγελος either in the biblical sense of an angel or in the sense of a (human) messenger, employs this term in *Ant.* 15.136 when referring to the prophets. The context is the discussion of the payment of tribute to the Arabs and the injustices experienced by the envoys, whom he likens to the biblical prophets as envoys who also went through rejection and death. See this discussion of W. D. Davies, "A Note on Josephus, Antiquities 15.136", *HTR* 47 (1954) 135-40.
³¹ One could argue, with good reason, that מלאכיו simply signifies "messengers" in this context, but our primary concern is how this text could be understood by later interpreters.

> Then Zerubbabel son of Shealtiel, and Joshua son of Jehozadak, the high priest, with all the remnant of the people, obeyed the voice of the Lord their God, and the words of <u>the prophet Haggai</u>, as the Lord their God had sent him, and the people feared the Lord. Then <u>Haggai, the angel of the Lord</u>, spoke to the people with the Lord's message, saying, I am with you, says the Lord.

Rather than the Angel of the Lord speaking the word of the Lord to the prophet, here the prophet Haggai speaks as the Angel of the Lord. This concept may also be the idea behind Malachi's name.[32]

That other Jews interpreted these pericopes in this manner can be seen from exegesis in Rabbinic literature. J.-A. Bühner has collated evidence which shows this Prophet-Angel union.[33] For example, *Lev. Rab.* 1.1 reads:

> Prophets are also called angels. This is what stands written: "And he sent an angel and led us out of Egypt" (Num 20.16). Why is the speech about an angel, where, after all, Moses is meant? Why do the Scriptures call him angel? The prophets become labeled angels much more after this time. For instance: 'An Angel of God led the men from Gilgal to Bochim.' Was it then an angel? Wasn't it Phinehas? Why did the Scriptures call him angel? R. Simon [c. 280 CE] said: "As the Holy Spirit rests on Phinehas, there burnt his countenance as a torch. . . ." R. Jochanan said, "From the very beginning the prophets also became described as angels, as it says in Hag 1.13: "And Haggai, the angel of the Lord, said as the messenger of God. . . ." There you are forced to conclude that the prophets from the very beginning are also called angels."[34]

The motivation for this *literary* union of prophet and angel can be found in the following *functional* development: after Moses and the establishment of the Sinai covenent, prophets began to occupy the mediator role between God and humans which was usually held by God himself or his Angel. As noted above, in early traditions we see an angelomorphic God appearing to people and/or speaking with them on earth. This mode of revelation becomes less prominent in the prophetic literature. Rather than God appearing to and speaking with the prophet "on earth", the prophet is

---

[32] Malachi (מלאכי) means "My Angel". Therefore, YHWH's Angel, the prophet Malachi, could be understood as the Angel of YHWH.
[33] *Gesandte und sein Weg*, 270-374.
[34] Phinehas is understood to be the referent of "the Angel of YHWH" in Judg 2.1-4 (cf. *Judg. Rab.* 16.1).

(mystically) included with angels in a divine council "in heaven".[35] Note these words of YHWH in Jeremiah 23:

> [18] For who has stood in the council of YHWH so as to see and to hear his word? Who has given heed to his word so as to proclaim it? [19] Look, the storm of YHWH! [. . .]. [21] I did not send the prophets, yet they ran; I did not speak to them, yet they prophesied. [22] But if they had stood in my council, then they would have proclaimed my words to my people, and they would have turned them from their evil way, and from the evil of their doings.[36]

Here the prophet functions as an angel who is then "sent" to deliver the word from God. This functional development, in turn, impacted ontological assertions about human prophets as angels.

2. Moses

Traditionally Moses has been considered the first and greatest prophet of Israel. Because of his position as Israel's leader in the Exodus and the wilderness and his role as the receiver and deliverer of the Torah when he was in communion with God upon Sinai, he was the subject of many traditions that exalted his status, even to the point where one can view him as angelomorphic or divine.[37] Sir 45.1-5 blatantly states that he is "equal in glory to the holy ones".[38]

The most vivid example of Moses' exalted state is found in the *Ezekiel the Tragedian* (ca. second century BCE). This drama relates a dream of Moses in which he is enthroned and worshiped as a monarch over all creation[39]:

---

[35] 1 Kgs 22.13-23 (cf. 2 Chr 18.18-22); Job 1.6-12; 2.1-7; Amos 3.7; 9.1-4; Zech 3.1-7; Isa 6.1-13. See also E. Mullen, "Divine Assembly", *ABD* 2.214-217. For further discussion of these modes of revelation in Ancient Israel, see D. Aune, *Prophecy in Early Christianity and the Ancient Mediterranean World* (Grand Rapids: Eerdmans, 1983) 81-101.

[36] For the inclusion of the prophet in the heavenly council see also 1 Kgs 22.19; Isa 6.1-8; Ezek 40.3; Zech 1.9; 2 Kgs 6.16.

[37] W. Meeks details traditions in Jewish and Samaritan sources in *The Prophet-King: Moses Traditions and the Johannine Christology* (SupNovT 14; Leiden: Brill, 1967) 100-285; cf. his "Moses as God and King".

[38] There is evidence that the author of the original Hebrew text may have intended to compare the glory of Moses with that of God himself (cf. Exod 4.16; 7.1); see discussion by Hurtado, *One God*, 56.

[39] For introductory questions about this document in its present fragmentary state, see H. Jacobson, *The Exagoge of Ezekiel* (Cambridge: CUP, 1983) esp. 89-97. Jacobson, however, is incorrect in his argument that this depiction speaks against the apocalyptic-mystical traditions surrounding Moses; see P.

[68] On Sinai's peak I saw what seemed a throne
    so great in size it touched the clouds of heaven.
[70] Upon it sat a man of noble mien [ἐν τῷ καθῆσθαι φῶτα
    γενναῖόν τινα],
    becrowned, and with a scepter in one hand
    while with the other he did beckon me.
    I made approach and stood before the throne.
    He handed o'er the scepter and he bade
[75] me mount the throne, and gave to me the crown;
    then he himself withdrew from off the throne.
    I gazed upon the whole earth round about;
    things under it, and high above the skies.
    Then at my feet a multitude of stars
[80] fell down, and I their number reckoned up.
    They passed by me like armed ranks of men.

The roots of this drama lie in this early and remarkably simple theophany depicted in Exodus 24:

> [9] Then Moses and Aaron, Nadab, and Abihu, and seventy of the elders of Israel went up, [10] and they saw the Elohim of Israel; and there was under his feet as it were a pavement of sapphire stone, like a very heaven for clearness. [11] And he did not lay his hand on the chief men of the people of Israel; they beheld God, and ate and drank.

The depiction of God as a man (φῶς) on a throne in *Exāgōge* indicates the roots of this text are in Jewish apocalyptic and mystical traditions surrounding the "man-like" כבוד on the *Merkabah* (Ezek 1.26).[40] In a way similar to Enoch's exaltation in *3 Enoch* 10-14, Moses is given the scepter, mounts the throne, is crowned, and God (the Man) vacates his throne to him.[41] The latter detail leaves no doubt that Moses will not merely stand by God and assist; he will sit on God's throne in order to rule. Furthermore, worship by the angelic hosts after the enthronement demonstrates the significance of what is being proposed: a human being exalted to God's throne and receiving the adoration due to God.[42] As Wayne

---

van der Horst, "Moses' Throne Vision in Ezekiel the Dramatist", *JJS* 34 (1983) 19-29, and his "Some Notes on the *Exagoge* of Ezekiel", *Essays on the Jewish World of Early Christianity* (NTOA 14; Universitätsverlag Freiburg, Schwiez, and Vandenhoeck & Ruprecht, Göttingen, 1990) 72-93.

[40] Note the sapphire imagery connection between Exod 24.10 and Ezek 1.26

[41] This similarity is discussed by van der Horst, "Moses' Throne Vision", 24-25. Enthronement here also parallels that of Son of Man/Elect One of *1 Enoch* (45.3; 51.3; 55.4; 61.8).

[42] The angelic hosts are commonly symbolized as "stars" in apocalyptic literature. Here Moses is able to count the stars; such divine ability is ascribed

Meeks and Pieter van der Horst properly point out, this depiction of Moses implies deification.[43]

Philo has a very exalted depiction of Moses which goes far beyond his prophetic role.[44] Philo is attracted to the content of Exod 7.1 as he points out that Moses is considered worthy to be called אלהים ("god") by God himself (*Vita Mos* 1.158; *Somn* 1.189; *Mut* 128-129). Other writings of Philo make it clear that he did not consider Moses to be God in the sense that he is divine like the highest God.[45] Moses' mystical ascent where he beheld God (Exod 24.12), however, plays an important role in bringing Moses into a unity with God which divinized him, making him the ultimate paradigm of godliness, as can be seen in these texts:

> [*Vita Mos* I.58] Did he [Moses] not also enjoy an even greater partnership with the Father and Maker of the universe, being deemed worthy of the same title? For he was named god and king of the whole nation. And he was said to have entered into the darkness where God was, that is, into the formless and invisible and incorporeal archetypal essence of existing things, perceiving things invisible to mortal nature. And, like a well-executed painting, openly presenting himself and his life, he set up an altogether beautiful and God-formed work as an example for those who are willing to imitate it.
>
> [*Quaes Ex* 2.29] But he who is resolved into the nature of unity, is said to come near God in a kind of family relation, for having given up and left behind all mortal kinds, he is changed into the divine, so that such men become kin to God and truly divine.
>
> [*Quaes Ex* 2.40] This [Exod 24.12] signifies that a holy soul is divinized by ascending not to the air or to the ether or to heaven (which is) higher than all but to (a region) above the heavens. And beyond the world there is no place but God.

---

to God in Ps 147.4 (cf. *3 En.* 46.1-2 where Metatron knows the names of all the stars)

[43] Meeks, *The Prophet-King*, 148-149, and van der Horst, "Moses' Throne Vision", 25.

[44] See the masterful analysis of Philo's assertions about Moses in Meeks, *Prophet-King*, 100-31. An important reason for Philo's fascination with Moses, no doubt, is Moses' intimate connection with Egypt and the model he could be for Philo's fellow Egyptian Jews as they dealt with the political-religious situation in the first century CE.

[45] *Quod Det* 162; *Leg All* 1.40-41; *Migr* 84. See also C. Holladay, *Theios Aner in Hellenistic Judaism* (SBLDS 40; Missoula, MT: Scholars Press, 1977) 103-198. He argues that Philo's language of deification is controlled by his allegorical approach in which Moses is used as the model of godliness and philosophical virtues.

"Standing" is an angelic position and function. "Standing by God" can imply an even more exalted status.[46] Philo reads Deut 5.31 as speaking of such "standing" and uses this tradition in his discussion about Moses receiving a divine nature:

> [*Post* 27-28] But Abraham the wise, being one who stands, draws near to God the Standing One [συνεγγίζει τῷ ἑστῶτι θεῷ]; for it says "he was standing before the Lord and he drew near and said" [Gen 28.22]. For only a truly unchanging soul has access to the unchanging God, and the soul that is of such a disposition does in very deed stand near to the Divine Power. But what shows in the clearest light the firm steadfastness of the man of worth is the oracle communicated to the all-wise Moses which runs thus: "But as for you stand here by me" [Deut 5.31]. This oracle proves two things: first, that the Existent Being who moves and turns all else is himself exempt from movement and turning; and secondly that he makes the worthy man sharer of his own nature [τῆς ἑαυτοῦ φύσεως], which is repose [cf. *Gig* 49]

Because of the transformation effected by Moses' mystical ascent, Philo argues against any possiblity of his physical death. This is demonstrated in the following text which also indicates that God "sent" Moses as a loan to the earthly sphere:

> [*Sacr* 8-10] There are still others, whom God has advanced even higher, and has trained them to soar above species and genus alike and stationed them beside himself. Such is Moses to whom he says, "Stand here with me" [Deut 5.31]. And so when Moses was about to die we do not hear of him "leaving" or "being added" like those others. No room is in him for adding or taking away. But through the Word of the Supreme Cause he is translated [Deut 34.5], even through that Word by which also the whole universe was formed. Thus you may learn that God prizes the Wise Man as the world, for that same Word, by which he made the universe, is that by which he draws the perfect man from things earthly to himself. And even when he sent him as a loan to the earthly sphere and caused him to dwell there, he gifted him with no ordinary excellence, such as that which kings and rulers have, wherewith to hold sway and sovereignty over the passions of the soul, but he appointed him as god, placing all the bodily region and the mind which rules it in subjection and slavery to him. "I give you," he says, "as god to Pharoah" [Exod 7.1]; but God is not susceptible of addition or diminution, being fully and unchangeably himself. And therefore we are told that no man knows his grave [Deut 34.6]. For who has powers such that he could perceive the passing of a perfect soul to him that "is"?

---

[46] See discussion of Divine Position on 31 and 93-97 above. Moses is called ὁ ἀρχάγγελος ("the archangel" or "the chief messenger") in *Quaes Gen* 4.8 (cf. *Vita Mos* 1.155-159).

Samaritan literature applies angelomorphic language to Moses even more overtly.[47] In the *Samaritan Liturgy*, Moses is vested with the Name of God: "He [Moses] was worthy to put on the Name whereby the world came into being".[48] Due to the equation of "angel" and "apostle", some of the texts speaking about the Angel of the Lord leading Israel were applied to Moses as the "Apostle" *par excellence* in Samaritanism.[49] This indicates that Moses had the status of the Angel of the Lord or a principal angel, and therefore carried divine authority.

3. *Elijah*

The prophet Elijah, because he was assumed into heaven by a chariot of fire (2 Kgs 2.1-11; cf. Sir 48.1-11), was also accorded angelic status in many groups.[50] According to Jewish tradition, he joined Enoch and Moses as the only three men who entered the company of angels without facing death. Elijah's "angelic" status with Moses is also reflected in early Christianity, especially in the accounts of Jesus' Transfiguration.[51]

Although this angelic status was generally understood to have begun with his assumption, there is evidence that Elijah would return to earth as an angel. Mention of Elijah's return as an angel is explicit in the message of Malachi, which includes a prophecy where he warns of an eschatological prophet who will come:

> [3.1] See, I am sending my angel [MT: שלח מלאכי; LXX: ἐξαποστέλλω τὸν ἄγγελόν μου] to prepare the way before me, and the Lord whom you seek will suddenly come to his temple. The angel of the covenant [MT: ומלאך הברית; LXX: ὁ ἄγγελος τῆς διαθήκης] in whom you delight—indeed he is coming, says YHWH of hosts.

מלאך and ἄγγελος are often translated here as signifying the non-technical meaning of "messenger" (e.g., RSV, NRSV, NIV). What is often missed in translation and interpretation is the significance of the sequence and the identification of "the Angel of the

---

[47] See the discussion of Meeks, *Prophet-King*, 216-257, and Fossum, *Name of God*, 87-94, 112-156.
[48] A. E. Cowley, *The Samaritan Liturgy* (Oxford: OUP, 1909) 54.2. This assertion is also found in *Memar Marqa* I.1, 3, 9; II.12; VI.6, 7; see Fossum, *Name of God*, 87-94.
[49] Fossum, *Name of God*, 144-147; see texts on 305-306 below.
[50] J. Jeremias, "Ἠλ(ε)ίας", *TDNT* 2.928-941.
[51] See Matt 17.1-8; Luke 9.28-36; Mark 9.2-8 and the two witnesses in Rev 11.3-13. See also Fossum, *Image of the Invisible God*, 86-89.

Covenant" in 3.1b. The text, however, is clear: God's angel, known more specifically as "the Angel of the Covenant", will prepare the way and then the Lord himself will come into his temple (cf. 3.2-5). There is also an allusion here to the function of the Divine Name Angel whom God sent to lead his people through the Wilderness (Exod 23.20). The propriety of translating Mal 3.1 in a manner that emphasizes a *heavenly angel* who will come to prepare the way is made explicit when Malachi later identifies this "Angel of the Covenant" as "Elijah the prophet" who had already been translated to heaven:

> [4.5; MT 3.23] Behold, I will send you Elijah the prophet before the coming of the great and dreadful day of the Lord: [6] and he shall turn the hearts of the fathers to the children, and the heart of the children to the fathers, lest I come and smite the earth with a curse.

The willingness of Jews and early Christians to identify John the Baptist or Jesus as Elijah shows that this belief in the angelomorphic Elijah was strong in the first century.[52] There is evidence that the prophet John the Baptist was considered to be an angel. Some apparently thought him to be Elijah *redivivus* (John 1.21). The prophecy of Mal 3.1 (ἰδοὺ ἐγὼ ἐξαποστέλλω τὸν ἄγγελόν μου) is specifically ascribed to John the Baptist (Mark 1.2; Matt 11.10) as well as the prophecy in Mal 4.5 (Matt 11.14).[53] Origen used Frag. A of the *Prayer of Joseph* as evidence of "human angels" to prove that John the Baptist was an angel who became incarnate to be the precursor of Christ (*Comm. in Ioann.* II.31).

4. *Other Prophets*

There are other examples of prophets who were understood to be angels or who were transformed into angels. The *Ascension of Isaiah*, a second century Jewish Christian document, offers an extended account of Isaiah's visionary ascent that includes this reference to his transformation: "[. . .] the glory of my face was being transformed as I went from heaven to heaven" (7.25; cf. Isa

---

[52] John 1.21, 25; Mark 6.15 (Luke 9.8); Mark 8.28 (Matt 16.14; Luke 9.19). See also: Jeremias, "Ἠλ(ε)ίας", 935-938; J. Martyn, *The Gospel of John in Christian History* (New York: Paulist, 1978) 9-54; and Segal, *Two Powers in Heaven*, 70-71.

[53] Matt 11.11 claims that there is none greater than John, but then states that "he who is least in the kingdom of heaven is greater than he". This reveals something of the status of Jesus and his followers.

6.1-13).[54] *The Apocalypse of Zephaniah* (ca. first century CE) speaks of this angelic transformation involving both physical and mental aspects of Zephaniah during his ascent: "I, myself, put on an angelic garment [. . .] I myself prayed together with them, I knew their language, which they spoke with me" (8.3-4). *The Lives of the Prophets* (ca. first century CE) records that Malachi's name bespoke his nature. His angelic status is reflected in his appearance, behavior, and the tradition that an angel confirmed—rather than gave—his prophecy:

> [16.2] And since the whole people honored him as holy and gentle, it called him Malachi, which means "angel"; for he was indeed beautiful to behold. [3] Moreover, whatever he himself said in prophecy, on the same day an angel of God appeared and repeated (it).

C. *Priests*

1. *Introduction*

Israel's prophets were generally very closely associated with the Temple cult. Some even served as priests.[55] Such a connection appears to be in the background of Malachi 2.7: "For the lips of a priest should guard knowledge, and men should seek instruction from his mouth, for he is the angel [MT: מלאך LXX: ἄγγελος] of YHWH of hosts". This also may be the background for the blessing of Jacob upon Levi in *Jub.* 31.14: "May he [the Lord] draw you and your seed near to him from all flesh to serve in his sanctuary as the angels of the presence and the holy ones".

Furthermore, there are several texts that suggest a close relationship between earthly priests and heavenly angels. Zechariah's visionary account involving the High Priest Joshua illustrates this:

> [3.3] Now Joshua was standing before the Angel, clothed with filthy garments. [4] And the Angel said to those who were standing before him, "Remove the filthy garments from him." And to him he said, "Behold, I have taken your inquity away from you, and I will clothe you with rich apparel." [5] And I said, "Let them put a clean turban on his head." So they put a clean turban on his head and clothed him with garments; and the Angel of

---

[54] *Ascen. Is.* 11.35 indicates that Isaiah returned to an unglorified state after his visionary ascent.
[55] See Aune, *Prophecy*, 84 (e.g., Ezekiel and Jeremiah were prophets associated directly with the priesthood; cf. Ezek 1.1; Jer 1.1).

YHWH was standing by. [6] And the Angel of YHWH enjoined Joshua, [7] "Thus says YHWH of hosts: If you will walk in my ways and keep my charge, then you shall rule my house and have charge of my courts, and I will give you the right of access among those who are standing here.

The changing of apparel indicates forgiveness rather than angelic transformation as it does in other texts.[56] Especially intriguing is mention of "the right of access among those who are standing here" (3.7). This is a reference to the High Priest functioning as an Angel of the Presence (note the mention of angelic "standing" in 3.7).

2. *Levi*

A similar event is described by Levi. The event occurred during a visionary ascent which is recorded in the *Testament of the Twelve Patriarchs*[57]:

[*T. Levi* 8.1] Then I again saw the vision as formerly, after we had been there seventy days. [1] And I saw seven men in white clothing, who were saying to me, [3] "Arise, put on the vestments of the priesthood, the crown of righteousness, the oracle of understanding, the robe of truth, the breastplate of faith, the miter for the head, and the apron for prophetic power." [4] Each carried one of these and put them on me and said, "From now on be a priest, you and all your posterity."

This text shows the angelic nature of the office of the High Priest, but it does not specifically indicate that Levi was transformed into an angelomorphic human. Such transformation, however, usually occurred in conjunction with standing before the *Merkabah*.[58] In *T. Levi* 2.10 the *angelus interpres* tells Levi that he will stand near the Lord and be his priest:

"And when you have mounted there [i.e., the highest heaven], you shall stand near the Lord. You shall be his priest and you shall tell forth his mysteries to men."

The *Testament of Levi* holds out hope that an eschatological priest will come whose priesthood will endure forever (18.1-14). This priest is spoken of in angelomorphic language: "And his star shall rise in heaven like a king [. . .] this one shall shine forth like the

---

[56] See Morray-Jones, "Tranformational Mysticism", 1-31.
[57] See also M. Barker, *The Gate of Heaven* (London: SPCK, 1991) 162-163.
[58] See Morray-Jones, "Transformational Myticism", 1-31.

sun in the earth [. . .] the angels of glory of the Lord's presence will be made glad by him" (18.3-5). Ben Sira's praise of Simon also tends in this direction by ascribing suprahuman or even angelic status to a priest (Sir 50.1-24).

3. *Melchizedek*

Genesis 14.18-20 records a brief incident when the priest-king Melchizedek of Salem received Abraham's tithe and bestowed a blessing upon him. These sparse and intriguing details about the first priest mentioned in the Pentateuch prompted further writing about him among both Jews and Christians.[59] This interest was stimulated, to a large degree, by the exalted view of a so-called Melchizedek priesthood, which is reflected already in Psalm 110.[60] There YHWH declares the future Davidic king, who will execute eschatological judgment and rule, to be "a priest forever according to the order of Melchizedek" (110.4).

Especially intriguing among the texts that developed from Genesis 14 and Psalm 110 is the Qumran fragment 11QMelch.[61] This fragment portrays the priest Melchizedek as a divine rescuer who will bring eschatological judgment against the forces of Beliel. The application of the divine names to Melchizedek in a portion of this fragment is especially noteworthy:

> [2.7-14] And the day of atonement is the end of the tenth jubilee in which atonement will be made for all the sons of God and for the men of the lot of Melchizedek. And on the heights he will declare in their favour according to their lots; for it is the time of the "year of grace" for Melchizedek, to exalt in the trial the holy ones of God through the rule of judgment, as it is written about him in the songs of David, who said, "Elohim will stand up in the assembly of God [אל], in the midst of the gods he judges" [Ps 82.1]. And about him he said: "Above it return to the heights, God [אל] will judge

---

[59] For the development of Melchizedek traditions see F. Horton Jr, *The Melchizedek Tradition: A Critical Examination of the Sources to the Fifth Century A.D. and in the Epistle to the Hebrews* (Cambridge: CUP, 1976), and C. Gianotto, *Melchisedek e la sua tipologia: tradizioni guidaiche, cristiane e gnostiche* (Brescia: Paideia Editrice, 1984). See Gianotto for an extensive bibliography (281-298).

[60] See esp. D. Hay, *Glory at the Right Hand: Psalm 110 in Early Christianity* (Nashville: Abingdon, 1973).

[61] See esp. M. de Jonge and A. van der Woude, "11Q Melchizedek and the New Testament", *NTS* 12 (1966) 310-326, and P. Kobelski, *Melchizedek and Melchireša'* (CBQMS 10; Washington: Catholic Biblical Association of America, 1981).

the peoples" [Ps 7.8-9]. As for what he said: "How long will you judge unjustly and show partiality to the wicked? *Selah*" [Ps 82.2]. Its interpretation concerns Belial and the spirits of his lot, who were rebels all of them turning aside from the commandments of God to commit evil. But Melchizedek will carry out the vengeance of God's judgments on this day, and they shall be freed from the hands of Belial and from the hands of all the spirits of his lot. To his aid shall come all the gods of justice; he is the one who will prevail on this day over all the sons of God, and he will preside over this assembly.[62]

Melchizedek is clearly more than an earthly priest in this fragment, even though his status as priest is clear from the context of "the Day of Atonement" and the proclaimer of "liberty" (2.6). Both his function as the eschatological judge and the application of the divine names אלוהים and אל from Psalms 82 and 7 indicate that he is considered to be divine. Furthermore, 11QMelch 2.15-16 quotes Isa 52.7 and interprets the referent of "Your Elohim is king" to be Melchizedek. This exalted status leads one to wonder why there are not more references to Melchizedek in the QL. This question can be answered by the evidence that suggests Melchizedek should be identified with Michael who is also known as the Angel or Prince of Light in the QL.[63] Therefore, the Qumran community understood Melchizedek to be an angelomorphic figure of the highest rank and possibly even a divine hypostasis.

Melchizedek is also characterized as an angelomorphic figure in the closing chapters of *2 Enoch*. While the Melchizedek tradition does not dominate the content of *2 Enoch* as a whole, it is the major focus of chapters 69-73. Here we find a grave concern for a priestly mediator between God and humans. The evil that would necessitate the worldwide flood is growing (70.23), but hope is restored through the birth of a unique priest: Melchizedek. Several details highlight the miraculous nature of this birth: his mother had no sexual contact with a man (71.2); the child delivers himself

---

[62] This represents a reconstruction of the fragmentary text; see the critical edition of the text in Kobelski, *Melchizedek and Melchirešaʿ*, or the translation in *The Dead Sea Scrolls Translated* (ed. F. Martínez; Leiden: Brill, 1994) 139-140.

[63] Kobelski argues, on the basis of reconstructing 4QʿAmram[b], that the three names of the angelomorphic deliverer in the QL are Michael, Melchizedek, and Prince of Light; *Melchizedek and Melchirešaʿ*, 36. Melchizedek's action against Belial is parallel to that of Michael in 1QM 13.10-12 and 17.5-8. See also the succinct summary of current scholarship on this question in Davis, *Name and Way*, 44, esp. n.72.

after his mother dies (71.17); and the child is born as a fully developed three year old boy who is already speaking (71.18). These details are included to emphasize the purity of this child. He was not the product of a sinful sexual union or a bloody birth experience; he is a pure priest who could atone for sins. This appendix of *2 Enoch* reflects a very degenerative view of the Levitical priesthood, and possibly the whole temple cult, which was probably still functioning at the time when this document was written.[64]

Three other details of the Melchizedek in *2 Enoch* support the conclusion that he is an angelomorphic figure. This child's appearance is "glorious" because of "the badge of the priesthood on his chest" (71.19). This is a reference to him as a bearer of the Divine Name, the central aspect of the priestly garb.[65] The narrative also mentions that he will be "hidden" with the angel Michael until the proper moment of his revelation as a priestly messiah (72.9). A similar theme is found in *1 Enoch* with the Elect One/Son of Man (62.7). Moreover, in Rec. J, which may be as late as the 6th or 7th century CE, he is given an angelomorphic designation: "the Word and Power of God" (71.34). Even though the text is late, this title may reflect much earlier exegesis. Philo's allegorical treatment of Genesis 14 had identified Melchizedek as the Word (*Leg All* 3.79-82; cf. *Congr* 99, *Abr* 235).

4. *The Priests of the Qumran Literature*

The communion between human priests and heavenly angels is nowhere more prominent than in the Qumran literature. Several

---

[64] F. Anderson dates *2 Enoch* as late first century CE; see *OTP* 1.91, and "Enoch, Second Book of", *ABD* 2.522. P. Sacchi asserts that the ideology of *2 Enoch* as well as the content of chapters 69-73 affirms that the document was written before the destruction of the Jerusalem temple in 70 CE and that its Melchizedek traditions predate Hebrews. Based upon the content, style, and vocabulary of 69-73, Sacchi also argues that they were written by a different, yet contemporary, Jewish author (or authors) who sought to assimilate the priestly mediator Melchizedek into the Enochian tradition represented by chapters 1-68 and *1 Enoch*. See *Apocrifi dell'Antico Testamento* (ed. P. Sacchi; 2 vols.; Turin: Union Tipografico-Editrice Torinse, 1989) 2.495-507 and note on 2.580-581.

[65] There was a golden plate on the turban which contained the words "Holy to YHWH" (Exod 28.36). Philo records that it was simply the Tetragrammaton that was inscribed on this plate (*Vita Mos* 2.114; cf. *Migr* 103). Note the impact of Aaron bearing the Divine Name against the Destroyer in Wis 18.21-25.

texts testify to community members enjoying fellowship with angels who serve with them.[66] For example, as the blessing of these Zadokite priests in 1QSb 4.25-26 states: "May you be as an Angel of the Presence [MT: כמלאך פנים] in the Abode of Holiness to the glory of the God of [Hosts . . .] May you attend upon the service in the Temple of the Kingdom and decree destiny in the company with the Angels of the Presence" (cf. Zech 3.7). While this does not indicate that the community members were angelomorphic, there is nevertheless a functional identity between these human priests and their heavenly counterparts. This functional identity seems to be taken even further in this fragment where the priests, at least some of them, are identified as angels:

> [4Q511, Frag. 35] God shall sancti[fy] (some) of the holy as an everlasting sanctuary for himself, and purity shall endure among the cleansed. They shall be priests, his righteous people, his host, servants, the angels of his glory. They shall praise him with marvelous prodigies.

This exalted status of a human, even to the point of deification, is documented very clearly in the Dead Sea Scrolls text 4Q491 Frags. 20-22, which speaks of the mystical ascent and exaltation:

> [El Elyon gave me a seat among] those perfect forever, a mighty throne in the congregation of the gods. None of the Kings of the east shall sit in it and their nobles shall not [come near it]. No Edomite shall be like me in glory, and none shall be exalted save me, nor shall come against me. For I have taken my seat in the [congregation] in the heavens and none [find fault with me]. I shall be reckoned with gods and established in the holy congregation. I do not desire [gold,] as would a man of flesh; everything precious to me is the glory of [my God]. [The status of a holy temple,] not to be violated, has been attributed to me, and who can compare with me in glory? What voyager will return and tell [of my equivalent.] Who [laughs] at griefs as I do? And who is like me [in bearing] evil? Moreover, if I lay down the law in a lecture [my instruction] is beyond comparison [with any man's]. And who will attack me for my utterances? And who will contain the flow of my speech? And who will call me into court and be my equal? In my legal judgment [none will stand against] me. I shall be reckoned with gods, and my glory, with [that of] the king's sons. Neither refined god, nor gold of Ophir [can match my wisdom].

---

[66] 1QH 3.21-23; 4.24; 6.13; 11.10-12; 1QS 11.7; 1QSa 2.3-11.

Morton Smith has brought this fragment to scholarly attention by challenging M. Baillet's attribution of this poem to the angel Michael.[67] From the content of this text it is clear that a human being is speaking of his own exaltation following a heavenly ascent. The writer speaks of kings, Edomites, gold, men of the flesh, the teaching occupation, and the court; all of these are human relationships or experiences. Thus, it appears that in this text a Jew claims an exaltation due to his enthronement with the Divine Council.

D. *Kings*

The nature of the earthly kingships of Adam and Moses were noted above. Here we ask the question: Were kings from Israel's monarchy, especially David, considered to be angelomorphic? There is some evidence to indicate such an understanding.[68] There are, for example, a few texts that make a functional comparison between King David and God's Angel:

> [2 Sam 14.17; the woman of Tekoa is speaking] And your handmaid thought, 'The word of my adonai the king will set me at rest', for my adonai the king is as the Angel of Elohim to discern good and evil. YHWH your Elohim be with you! [cf. 2 Sam 14.20 and 19.27]

> [Zech 12.7; an oracle of YHWH delivered by Zechariah] "And the Lord will give victory to the tents of Judah first, the glory of the house of David and the glory of the inhabitants of Jerusalem may not be exalted over that of Judah. [8] On that day YHWH will put a shield about the inhabitants of Jerusalem so that the feeblest among them on that day shall be like David, and the house of David shall be like God, like the Angel of YHWH, at their head. [9] And on that day I will seek to destroy all the nations that come against Jerusalem."

These comparisons are probably expressions of the phenomenon of the unique nature of the Israelite king as YHWH's divinely selected representative. This position meant that the king could be seen to share YHWH's throne (e.g., 1 Chr 28.5; 29.20; 2 Chr 9.8; Ps

---

[67] "Two Ascended to Heaven—Jesus and the Author of 4Q491", *Jesus and the Dead Sea Scrolls* (ed. J.H. Charlesworth; New York: Doubleday, 1992) 290-301. 4Q491 is printed here as it is translated and edited in this article.

[68] Fletcher-Louis has gathered a substantial number of texts on this subject and offers an insightful analysis; see *Luke-Acts*, 110-118.

80.1) and be "divine" in some sense (as a "god", but not YHWH or equal to him; cf. Ps 45.7).

The comparison of the king to an angel also impacted future expectations of the ideal Davidic king, as can be seen from the LXX text of the well-known Isaiah 9.6 (9.5 MT) which rendered יועץ פלא ("Wonderful Counselor") as Μεγάλας Βουλῆς Ἄγγελος ("the Angel of Great Counsel").[69] This translation may have been motivated by the understanding that at least two of the other titles could be interpreted as angelic.[70] Already in the early part of this century, Gregory Dix argued that this phrase indicates that some of the Jewish expectations for a deliverer were formulated around the coming of the "Messianic Angel of Yahweh".[71]

Such an angelomorphic deliverer is reflected in the Jewish, and possibly pre-Christian, content of a prayer of praise in *Apostolic Constitutions*. After beginning with a call to sing a hymn to God, the hymn begins by listing God's actions and includes the following:

> [8.12.9] (You are) the one who brought everything into being out of non-being, through your only Son[72], and gave him birth before all ages, by purpose, and power, and unmediated goodness—an only Son, a divine Word, a living Wisdom, a firstborn of all creation, <u>an angel of your great purpose</u>, your high priest; both king and lord of all intelligible and perceptible nature, the one before all things, through whom are all things!

E. *Apostles*

One area in the question of the origin of the apostle concept that needs to be explored further is the sending (ἀποστέλλω) of God's

---

[69] For the impact of this text on Origen and others early Church Fathers, see J. Trigg, "The Angel of Great Counsel: Christ and the Angelic Hierarchy in Origen's Theology", *JTS* 42 (1991) 35-51. See also Justin, *Dial. Trypho* 126.1, and Novatian, *On the Trinity* 18.

[70] E.g., "Mighty God" is a title similar to Gabriel ("God has shown himself mighty"). "Prince" is an angelic title used with regularity. Michael was "the Prince of Lights" at Qumran (1QS 3.20; CD 5.18) and Metatron is called "the Prince of the Divine Presence" (*3 En.* 1.4; et. al.).

[71] "Influence of Babylonian Ideas", 245-48; see also Barker, *The Great Angel*, 35-36.

[72] This may be an interpolation into a Jewish text; see *OTP* 2.690. For Jewish origins of these prayers, see discussion and bibliography in *OTP* 2.671-676.

angels or prophets.[73] J.-A. Bühner has argued from Jewish texts that the Hebrew concept of שליח ("sent one") should be used to explain or parallel מלאך and the union of prophet and angel.[74] There is evidence from Samaritanism that shows the substitution of "Apostle" for "Angel" in relationship to Moses, the שליח *par excellence*.[75] For example, the *Samaritan Targum* Exod 23.20-22 makes this substitution:

> Behold! I send My Apostle [משלכ שלחי] before you in order to keep you and protect you on the way, and to bring you into the place which I have prepared. Give heed to him and obey his voice. Do not rebel against him, because he will not pardon your transgressions; for My Name is in him. But if you hearken attentively to his voice and do all that I say, then I will be an enemy to your enemies and an adversary to your adversaries. For My Apostle [שלחי] shall go before you [. . .].

Jarl Fossum has shown the close connection between the Angel and Apostle designations in the writings of Justin Martyr and their parallel application to Christ.[76] These two texts are pivotal to his argument:

> [*I Apol.* 63.5] Now the Word of God is His Son, as we have said before. And he is called "Angel" and "Apostle", for he declares whatever we ought to know and is sent forth to declare whatever is revealed. As our Lord himself says: "He who hears me hears Him who has sent me."

> [*Dial. Trypho* 75] Now Isaiah shows that those prophets who are sent to publish tidings from God are called His "angels" and "apostles", for Isaiah says in a certain verse: "Send me" [Is. 6.6]. And that the Prophet whose name was changed [cf. Num. 13.16], Jesus, was strong and great, is manifest to all.

---

[73] Much of recent scholarship has searched for its origin in the rabbinic institution of the שליח, in Syrian Gnosticism, in Cynic self-understandings, or in envoys of ancient diplomacy. For a recent summary of the longstanding debate, see F. H. Agnew, "The Origin of the NT Apostle-Concept: A Review of Research", *JBL* 105 (1986) 75-96; see also K. Rengstorf, "ἀπόστολος", *TDNT* 1.407-447.

[74] *Gesandte und sein Weg*, 281-282, 323-334, 326-329. See also the Jewish text *Gk. Apoc. Ezra* 2.1: "Michael, Gabriel, and all the apostles came [. . .]".

[75] Fossum, *Name of God*, 144-155, esp. 146-148.

[76] *Name of God*, 146-149. For the possible background of the Angel and Apostle ideas in an early Christian testimony book, see D. Pooij, *Studies in the Testimony-Book* (Verhandelinger der Koninklijke Akademie van Wetenschappen te Amsterdam 32/2; Amsterdam, 1932) 45-48.

Two different levels of Angel-Apostle union need to be recognized in this second text. Fossum perceptively concludes:

> Thus, Justin apparently reflects two different views of the concept of angel-apostle: on the one hand, the Jewish notion of the prophets as "angels", as explained by the term of apostle, and, on the other hand, the idea of a special Prophet who really is the Angel of the Lord, that is, a heavenly being, and is called God's "Apostle".[77]

It is plausible that the parallelism between angels and prophets in Logion 88 of the *Gospel of Thomas* may reflect a tradition where angels and apostles were equated:

> Jesus said: "The angels [ⲚⲦⲦⲈⲖⲞⲤ] and the prophets will come to you and give to you those things you (already) have. And you too, give them those things which you have, and say to yourselves, 'When will they come and take what is theirs?'"

It is clear from several early Christian texts that "apostles" is the implied referent of "angels" in this text.[78] The *Sitz im Leben* of this logion is the hospitable welcoming of traveling *apostles* and prophets of early Christianity. This setting, as well as the exalted status of apostle over prophet, can be deduced from the instructions given in the *Didache*:

> [11.3] And concerning the Apostles and Prophets, act thus according to the ordinance of the Gospel. [4] *Let every Apostle who comes to you be received as the Lord*, but let him not stay more than one day, or if need be a second as well; but if he stays three days, he is a false prophet. [5] And when an Apostle goes forth let him accept nothing but bread till he reach a night's lodging; but if he asks for money, he is a false prophet. [6] Do not test or examine any prophet who is speaking in a spirit, "for every sin shall be forgiven, but this sin shall not be forgiven." [7] But not everyone who speaks in a spirit is a prophet, except he have the behavior of the Lord. [8] From his behavior, then, the false prophet and the true prophet shall be known. [9] And no prophet who orders a meal in a spirit shall eat of it: otherwise he is a false prophet.

From this text it is apparent that apostles were also considered prophets (the apostle could be labeled a 'false *prophet*'), but there must have been many prophets who were not accorded the apostle designation since there is specific distinguishing between apostles *and prophets*, with apostles usually having first position in this pair. Also noteworthy is that the apostles should be received "as the Lord

---

[77] *Name of God*, 148-149.
[78] 1 Cor 12.28; Eph 2.20, 3.5; Luke 11.49; Acts 6.15; Rev 18.20; *Did.* 11.3; *Ps-Clem. Rec.* X.72.

himself" (11.4). This is not merely a continued honoring of Jesus' words in Matt 10.40, "He who receives you receives me"; it is an intensification of them.[79]

During and after the first century CE the apostle is generally accorded a higher status than the prophet.[80] The exalted or angelic nature of this designation is visible in early Christainity. In its contrast between Moses and Jesus, Heb 3.2 acknowledges "apostle" as an exalted title of Jesus, who is "[. . .] the apostle and high priest of our confession [. . .]".[81] It is employed frequently in the *Acts of Thomas*. Because of the mighty works that Thomas does, and that he is the "twin" of Christ, the people express how exalted this title is by exclaiming: "This man is *either* God or the Apostle of God" (*Acts Thom.* 9).

The influence of this concept is seen outside Judaism and Christianity. In Manichean texts one finds the name "Apostle of Light" as a prominent designation of the heavenly revealer.[82] According to the Coptic *Homilies* of Mani, this figure is an angel who inspires him.[83] The angelic Apostle, according to Mani, is also the Spirit of God: "[Mani says,] The Spirit of the Paraclete is it who has been sent to me from the Father of Greatness. What has happened and will happen is revealed to me".[84] The angelic Apostle figure is also found in Mandeism: in the *Right Ginza* he is the "Apostle Gabriel".[85] Muhammad, the founder of Islam, drew on this conceptual and

---

[79] For further implications of this for Paul's apostleship, see the exegesis of Gal 4.14 in Chapter 14 on 315-325 below.

[80] Examining evidence of the Apostle idea in later religious development is very fruitful for understanding its Jewish origins; see A. J. Wensick, "Muhammad und die Propheten" *Acta Orientia* 2 (1924) 168-198, and Fossum, "The Apostle Concept", 149-167. Geo Widengren has also authored several studies in this field: *The Great Vohu Manah and the Apostle of God: Studies in Iranian and Manichean Religion* (Uppsala: Almqvist & Wiksell, 1950); *The Ascension of the Apostle and the Heavenly Book* (Uppsala: Almqvist & Wicksell, 1950); *Muhammad, the Apostle of God, and His Ascension* (Uppsala: Almqvist & Wicksell, 1955); *The Gnostic Attitude* (trans. B. Pearson; Santa Barbara: University of CA, 1973).

[81] Fossum discusses the relationship of this passage as a polemic against Samaritanism; see *Name of God*, 150-52, and discussion on below.

[82] See discussion of these texts by Fossum, "The Apostle Concept", 152-154.

[83] *Manichäishe Homilien* (ed. and trans. H. J. Polotsky; Manichäische Handschriften der Sammlung A. Chester Beatty I; Stuttgart, 1934), 47.

[84] *Kephalaia* I (ed. and trans. A. Böhlig and H. J. Polotsky; Manichäische Handschriften der Staatlichen Museen Berlin I; Stuttgart, 1940) 16.

[85] *Thesaurus sive Liber Magnus, vulgo "Liber Adamai" appellatus* (ed. H. Peterman; Leipzig, 1867) 12, 93.

literary milieu in developing his understanding of himself as "the Apostle of God".[86] He had been inspired by a "heavenly Apostle" who is identified both as the angel Gabriel and the Spirit of God.[87]

F. *Elect Ones*

The concept of the Elect of Israel is an ancient one that grows primarily from the nationalistic idea of Israel being God's chosen people for whom he will care.[88] This idea is expressed in Deuteronomy 7.6: "For you are a people holy to YHWH, your Elohim; YHWH your Elohim has chosen you to be a people for his own possession, out of all the peoples that are on the face of the earth". This choosing or election meant that God had adopted them as his "sons"; therefore, the title "sons of God" is used of the people of Israel.[89] They were also considered God's "righteous ones" or "holy ones" on the earth (e.g., *1 En.* 38.2-5, 41.2, 48.1, 61.13, 70); such titles are also designations for angels in Jewish literature.[90] The status of the Elect meant that they were considered distinct from the "sinners" of the world since they were obedient to God (e.g., Isa 65.9, 15). At the Eschaton they would be with, and like, angels in heaven (e.g., Dan 12.3; *1 En.* 39.6-7; 104.2, 4, 6; *2 Bar.* 51.10-13; Matt 22.30) In some Jewish groups only the so-called "faithful remnant" of Israel was considered to be the Elect.[91]

---

[86] See Wensick, "Muhammad", 168-198, and Fossum, "The Apostle Concept", 148-167.
[87] Fossum cites ample evidence of this in the Qurʾān; see "The Apostle Concept", 149-151.
[88] See H. Rowley, *The Biblical Doctrine of Election* (London, 1950), and A. De Conick, *Seek to See Him*, 86-93.
[89] Exod 4.22-23; Deut 14.1, 32.5, 19; Isa 43.6, 45.11; Jer 31.9, 10; Hos 2.1; cf. Deut 32.6, 18; Jer 3.4.
[90] For a discussion of the corresponding use of these titles for the human elect and their angelic counterparts, see P. Decock, "Holy ones, sons of God, and the trascendent future of the righteous in 1 Enoch and the New Testament", *Neot* 17 (1983) 70-82. "Righteous One" and "Holy One" are also messianic and Christological titles (e.g., Jer 23.6; *1 En.* 46.3; 71.14; Mark 1.24; Luke 1.35, 49; 4.34; John 6.69; Acts 2.27; 13.35).
[91] De Conick notes this in: *Jub.* 1.29; *Sib. Or.* 3.69; Wis 3.9; *4 Ezra* 2.38; 16.74-78; *1 En.* 51.1-5; 62.8; *2 Bar.* 30.2; 75.5; *Apoc. Ab.* 29.17; cf. *Seek to See Him*, 87. For this phenomenon in the QL, see: CD 3.20; 4.2b-4; 1QS 3.13-17; 8.5-9; 11.7-8; 1QpHab 5.4; 9.12a.

Because of this special status, as well as the use of angelic titles, the Elect began to be identified closely with the community of the heavenly angels. As noted above (section C), this phenomenon is visible in the literature of the Dead Sea Scrolls. The following texts are representative of the close relations that the Elect enjoyed with the angels:

> [1QS 11.7-8] God has given them to His elect ones as an everlasting possession, and has caused them to inherit the lot of the Holy Ones. He has joined their assembly to the Sons of Heaven.

> [4Q181, Frag. 1.3-4] He has caused some of the sons of the world to draw near [...] to be counted with Him in the com[munity of the "g]ods" as a congregation of holiness in service for eternal life and sharing the lot of his holy ones.

This communion of the Elect with the angelic realm in the Qumran community is faciliated by worship. This is nowhere more apparent than in the *Songs of the Sabbath Sacrifice* (4QShir-Shab).[92] Although there appears to be a distinction between the human and angelic realms, nevertheless that distinction is blurred. There is virtually no reference to the human community in this document, yet its implications are significant for Qumran's human priesthood. Carol Newson cogently explains:

> The language of the *Sabbath Shirot*, especially in its second half, does more than invite an analogy [between angelic and human priests]. It is extraordinarily vivid, sensuous language, both aurally and visually. What this does is to create and manipulate a virtual experience, the experience of being present in the heavenly temple and in the presence of the angelic priests who serve there. It is, I suspect, in order to create and maintain this sense that the text avoids explicit reference to the human community after the one brief reference early in the cycle. The result, then, is to provide the community that recites and hears these songs not only with a model for their priesthood but also with an experiential validation of their legitimacy as those permitted to share the experience of heavenly worship.[93]

---

[92] For a summary of research on the *Sabbath Shirot* as well as an overview of its content, see C. Newsom, "'He has Established for Himself Priests': Human and Angelic Priesthood in the Qumran *Sabbath Shirot*", *Archaeology and History in the Dead Sea Scrolls* (ed. L. Schiffman; JSPSup 8; Sheffield: Sheffield Academic Press, 1990) 101-120. For text, see her *Songs of the Sabbath Sacrifice: A Critical Edition* (HSS 27; Atlanta: Scholars Press, 1985).
[93] "He has Established for Himself Priests", 115-116.

April De Conick has demonstrated that the *Gospel of Thomas* also contains evidence that the Elect were understood to be angels.⁹⁴ De Conick builds her case around the testimony that the Elect are celibates (ⲙⲟⲛⲁⲭⲟⲥ) who stand (ⲱϩⲉⲉⲣⲁⲧ⸗).⁹⁵ Drawing on the research of Klijn, she shows that the single encratite status of the Elect is a prominent theme in the *Gospel of Thomas*.⁹⁶ This status reflects the prelapsarian Adam in Paradise and may also be related to the celibate status of angels. The link with angels is most visible in the frequent references to the "standing" posture of the encratite.⁹⁷ For example, Logion 16 states:

> For there will be five in a house: Three will be against two, and two against three, the father against the son, and the son against the father. And they will stand solitary [ⲥⲉⲛⲁϩⲉ ⲉⲣⲁⲧⲟⲩ ⲉⲩⲟ ⲙ̄ⲙⲟⲛⲁⲭⲟⲥ].

De Conick points to the angel's posture of constantly "standing" before God's presence as the certain background for this description.⁹⁸ She concludes:

> It is notable that this condition [a standing encratite] set them [the Thomasites] on par with the celibate angels who stand before God [...] Thus the Thomasites probably understood their "standing encratite" status to be a condition of the people of the resurrection who were already "equal to the angels" and "sons of God" (cf. L. 3; L. 50).

This status among the elect Thomasites resulted from individual mystical ascent. Later Rabbinic literature even testifies to the nation of Israel as a whole experiencing an angelomorphic transformation through mystical ascent with Moses at Sinai.⁹⁹

---

⁹⁴ *Seek to See Him*, 86-93.
⁹⁵ *Seek to See Him*, 89. For the link between the Elect as celibates, see *Gos. Thom.* 49. The celibacy status (ⲙⲟⲛⲁⲭⲟⲥ) mentioned in *Gos. Thom.* 16, 49, and 75 is synonymous with the single status espoused in logia 4, 22, and 23 (ⲟⲩⲁ ⲟⲩⲱⲧ) as well as logia 11, 22, 106 (ⲟⲩⲁ).
⁹⁶ A. F. J. Klijn, "The 'Single One' in the Gospel of Thomas", *JBL* 81 (1962) 271-78; cf. *Seek to See Him*, 89.
⁹⁷ See esp. *Gos. Thom.* 23, 16, 18.
⁹⁸ See the discussion about the "standing" posture on 31 above.
⁹⁹ I. Cherus, *Mysticism in Rabbinic Judaism* (SJ 11; Berlin: de Gruyter), 1982.

G. *Conclusion*

Although this chapter focused evidence that is very diverse, common understandings or perspectives do appear and reappear. Many of these texts testify that humans can be, or become, angelomorphic while still alive on earth.[100] This can happen before or without death. Most of these texts, however, point to assumption to heaven, or mystical ascent, as the event that leads to an angelic state for the human. This indicates that an angelomorphic transformation results from the person coming into the presence of the enthroned God.

As with principal angels, there is some evidence that angelomorphic humans also have distinctive physical characteristics that set them apart. Divine functions, however, are a much more important catagory in these texts. Angelomorphic humans were understood as those who acted or spoke for God: Patriarchs, Kings, Prophets, Priests, Apostles. Furthermore, human ontology is not a question that troubles the writers of this literature. These texts push the reader to a broader understanding of what an angel was considered to be in first century Judaism and Christianity. The implications of this conclusion for early Christology will now be explored.

---

[100] See esp. Fletcher-Louis, *Luke-Acts*, 109-215.

PART THREE

EARLY EVIDENCE

CHAPTER SEVEN

ANGELOMORPHIC CHRISTOLOGY AT NICEA AND BEFORE

The vast and variegated evidence of angelomorphic traditions has been reviewed. A series of important questions now confront the researcher that must be addressed in these chapters focusing on early evidence. Did some early Christians use these angelomorphic traditions in formulating their understanding of Christ and in articulating Christology? If so, when and by whom were they used? Lastly, what angelomorphic tradition, or combination of traditions, did these early Christian writers use? A positive answer to the first question is readily apparent. The primary focus of the chapters in Part III will be to clarify the "when", "who", and "what" questions concerning the usage of these traditions. The present chapter will tersely introduce representative evidence of Angelomorphic Christology during the period 150-325 CE in order that the more detailed evidence of Chapters 8-14 may be interpreted in its broader historical context.

A. *Angel Christology at Nicea*

The Council of Nicea in 325 CE marks a very significant date for the study of Angelomorphic Christology. Several historians have investigated the thesis that Arius' metaphysically grounded subordinationism was influenced by Angel Christology or that, at the very least, Arius used angelomorphic terminology in support of their emphasis on the created nature of the Son. Martin Werner attempted to draw a line of continuity from early Christological uses of angel categories to Arianism as an authentic expression of this "earliest Christology" of the church.[1] Joseph Barbel, in his thorough documentation of angel traditions in the Christology of

---

[1] This is the thesis of his 1941 book *Die Entstehung des christlichen Dogma*. The stinging critique of W. Michaelis' *Zur Engelchristologie im Urchristentum* had a significant impact on talk among scholars of Angel Christology in the NT or early Christianity; see discussion on 14-15 above.

the Church Fathers of the second through fourth centuries, argues against such continuity. Contrary to Werner, his research demonstrated the absence of a strict Angel Christology in the early church that Arianism could have readily employed (i.e., an Angel Christology that emphasizes the created nature of the Son as an angel).[2] Georg Kretschmar supported Barbel's position by arguing that the particular use of angelic categories in Arianism, with the emphasis on the Son's created nature, was already recognized as inadequate by NT authors.[3]

Nevertheless, Rudolf Lorenz has convincingly argued Arius' Christology was influenced by use of angel traditions in the Christology of some Jewish Christian groups.[4] Unlike many of Arius' predecessors who used angel traditions to support Christ's pre-existence and divinity, he used them to argue for the created and subordinate aspect of the Son (e.g., Prov 8.22-31). In other words, traditions and texts that had been used to express a pre-existent creator Christology were now being employed to assert a subordinate first-created Christology. This association with Arianism, through the emphasis on Christ having the created nature of an angel, is a primary reason that overt angel traditions no longer played a major part in Christological discussions after Nicea. The gradual distancing of Christianity from its Jewish roots, no doubt, also contributed to the decreased use of angelomorphic traditions in expressing Christology.

B. *Representative Evidence from Justin to Eusebius*

Angelomorphic Christology was by no means a new development that surfaced with Arianism. Neither was it confined to heterodox church leaders, sects, or Gnosticism.[5] Even though Barbel steers clear of saying there was a true "Angel Christology" in the early church which confessed Christ as a created angel, he has carefully documented the abundant evidence that the most prominent

---

[2] *Christos Angelos*, 18-63, 344-347. Note his subtitle: *Zugleich ein Beitrag zur Geschichte des Ursprungs und der Fortdauer des Arianismus.*

[3] E.g., Rev 22.8-9 and Heb 1.4-14; see *Studien zur frühchristlichen Trinitätstheolgie*, 222.

[4] *Arius judaizans?*, 141-180.

[5] For an exhaustive treatment of the background of the Gnostic Demiurge in angelomorphic traditions, see Fossum, *Name of God*.

spokesmen of the Christian Church in this period used angelomorphic traditions in their Christological formulations. A few examples of this will suffice here.[6]

1. *Justin Martyr*

Justin, whose writings date from ca. 140-160 CE, is often viewed as the starting point for the clear expression of Angelomorphic Christology. Based upon the messianic "Angel of Great Counsel" in Isa 9.6 (LXX), he uses the designation "Angel" as one of the primary titles given to the Messiah by the prophets.[7] Especially noteworthy is his interpretation of OT theophanies as evidence of the Son's existence before the incarnation.[8] For example, in *Dialogue with Trypho* he argues for the Son's presence in various OT theophanies or angelophanies: the pillar of cloud (37.4); the Burning Bush (59.1); as one of the three men at Mamre (56.1-23); as the angel who wrestled with Jacob (58.4-13); and as the warrior angel who appeared to Joshua (62.5). He is careful to distinguish between the Angel who was begotten of the Father and the other "angels" who were created (128.4). Towards the end of this apologetic treatise, he outlines the principle which guides his exegesis of these theophanies, namely the invisibility of the Father:

> [127.4] Therefore, neither Abraham, nor Isaac, nor Jacob, nor any man saw the Father and ineffable Lord of absolutely all things and of Christ Himself, but [saw] only Him who, according to His [God's] will, is both God, his Son, and Angel, from the fact that He ministers to His purpose. Whom he also has willed to be born through the Virgin, and who once became fire for that conversation with Moses in the bush.

The significance of this idea should not be underestimated. Justin is not merely looking for the Angel of the Lord and then interpreting this figure Christologically; he is reading all possible visible manifestations of God as the Son, who is the visible

---

[6] See Barbel, *Christos Angelos*, esp. 50-108.
[7] See *Dial. Trypho* 76.3; 86.3; 93.2; 116.1; 126.6; 127.4; 128.1, 2, 4.
[8] See O. Skarsaune, *The Proof From Prophecy. A Study in Justin Martyr's Proof-Text Tradition: Text-Type, Provenance, Theological Profile* (SupNovT 56; Leiden: Brill, 1987) esp. 409-423; D. Trakatellis, *The Pre-existence of Christ in the Writings of Justin Martyr* (HDR 6; Missoula: Scholars Press, 1976); B. Kominiak, *The Theophanies of the Old Testament in the Writings of St. Justin* (Washington: The Catholic University of America Press, 1948).

manifestation of the Father. Justin also understands the Son in this pre-incarnate state as the Word (ὁ λόγος). Erwin Goodenough, among others, has argued that Justin's Christologically-oriented interpretation of OT theophanies is dependent on Hellenistic Jewish exegesis, such as Philo's interpretation of the OT theophanies as manifestations of the Word (e.g., *Conf* 146).[9] Justin was not limited to exegesis of Pentateuchal theophanies, as we see in this text:

> [*Dial. Trypho* 61.1] God begat before all creatures a Beginning, [who was] a certain rational Power [proceeding] from Himself, who is called by the Holy Spirit, now the Glory of the Lord, now the Son, again Wisdom, again an Angel, then God, and then Lord and Word; and on another occasion He calls Himself Captain, when he appeared in human form to Joshua the son of Nave.

2. *Theophilus of Antioch*

The identification of the Son with the concepts "the Word" (ὁ λόγος) and "Wisdom" (σοφία) is the dominant Christology in Theophilus of Antioch, who focuses much of his attention on teaching about the creation of the world by means of the Word. Writing in the years ca. 169-180 CE, he also emphasizes that the contact that human beings had with God was not with the Father, but with the Word:

> [*To Autolycus* 2.22] The God and Father, indeed, cannot be contained, and is not found in a place, for there is no place of His rest; but His Word, through whom He made all things, being His Power and His Wisdom, assuming the role of the Father and Lord of all, went to the garden and conversed with Adam [. . .]. John says, "In the beginning was the Word, and the Word was with God," showing that at first God was alone, and the Word was in Him. Then he says, "The Word was God; all things came into existence through Him; and apart from Him not one thing came into existence." The Word, then, being God, and being naturally produced from God, whenever the Father of the universe wills, He sends Him to any

---

[9] *The Theology of Justin Martyr* (Amsterdam: Philo Press, 1968 [repr.]) 139-75. Nuancing Goodenough's argument, L. W. Barnard emphasized the indirect nature of such influence through the exegetical practices of Hellenistic Judaism; see *Justin Martyr: His Life and Thought* (Cambridge: CUP, 1967) 85-100. Skarsaune also argues against direct Philonic influence; see *Proof from Prophecy*, 409-423, esp 416. See also the discussion of the angelomorphic roots of Philo's Word on 107-112 above.

place; and He, coming, is both heard and seen, being sent by Him, and is found in a place.

As with Justin, Theophilus emphasizes the action of the Word as God's visible communicator: "and He, coming, is *both* heard *and seen*, being sent by Him [God], and is found in a place". This indicates that Theophilus is not only drawing on "philosophical" concepts in his Christological use of Word and Wisdom; he is also dependent on angelomorphic traditions. The Word, according to Theophilus, has personhood that can be seen. This communication by means of the Word with the prophets is discussed earlier when Theophilus speaks of the generation of the Word, who is associated with, and identified as, Wisdom, and is also known as Beginning, Power, and Spirit[10]:

> [*To Autolycus* 2.10] God, having his own Word innate in his own bowels, begot him, together with his own Wisdom, by "vomiting him forth" [Ps 45.1] before everything else. He is called "Beginning" because he leads and dominates everything fashioned through him. It was he, "Spirit of God" [Gen 1.2] and "Wisdom" [Prov 8.22] and "Power of the Most High God" [Luke 1.35], who came down into the prophets and spoke through them of the creation of the world and all other things. For the prophets did not exist when the world came into existence; there was the Wisdom of God which is in him and his holy Word who is always present with him. For this reason she [Wisdom] speaks thus through the prophet Solomon: "When he prepared the heaven, I was present with him [. . .]".

The latter portion of this text shows that Theophilus understood Christ as a divine hypostasis who is known in two manners: as the angelomorphic "Word" who is present *with* God and appears to speak with humans (2.22) and the pneumatic "Wisdom" who is present *in* God and came into the prophets in order to speak (2.10).

3. *Irenaeus of Lyons*

Irenaeus, whose writings date ca. 177-203 CE, also follows the principle articulated by Justin that all visible manifestations of God are evidence of the Son of God and not the Father, including those

---

[10] For the dependence of this depiction on the Hellenistic mythology of the generation of Athena and Metis from Zeus, see R. Grant, *Jesus After the Gospels: The Christ of the Second Century* (Louisville: Westminster/John Knox, 1990) 72-74.

where God appears as an angel. With reference to God's appearance to Jacob, he states the following in his *Proof of the Apostolic Preaching*:

> [45] And all visions of this kind signify the Son of God in his speaking with men and his being with them. For it is not the Father of all, who is not seen by the world, the Creator of all, who said: Heaven is my throne and the earth is my footstool; what manner of house will you build for me, or what is the place of my rest? And who holds the land in his fist and the heavens in his span [...] it is not He who would stand circumscribed in space and speak with Abraham, but the Word of God who is always with mankind.

The terse listing of various OT manifestations (angelomorphic and otherwise) which was seen in Justin's writings, is also present in the following fragment from Irenaeus' lost writings. Especially noteworthy in this fragment are what appear to be creedal or doxological angelomorphic designations: "Angel of angels", "Man of men", "Chief of the cherubim", "Prince of the angelic powers":

> With regard to Christ, the law and the prophets and the evangelists have proclaimed that He was born of a virgin, that He suffered upon a beam of wood, and that He appeared from the dead; that he also ascended to the heavens, and was glorified by the Father, and is the Eternal King; that He is the perfect Intelligence, the Word of God, who was begotten before the light; that he was the Founder of the universe, along with it (light), and the Maker of man; that He is All in all; Patriarch among the patriarchs; Law in the laws; Chief Priest among the priests; Ruler among kings; the Prophet among prophets; the Angel among angels; the Man among men; Son in the Father; God in God; King to all eternity. For it was He who sailed along with Noah, and who guided Abraham; who was bound along with Isaac, and was a Wanderer with Jacob; the Shepherd of those who are saved, and the Bridegroom of the Church; the Chief also of the cherubim, the Prince of the angelic powers; God of God; Son of the Father; Jesus Christ; King for ever and ever. Amen.[11]

---

[11] This is the translation of a Syriac fragment as in *The Ante-Nicene Fathers*, 1.577 (Frag. LIII). The fragment is dependent on Wisdom of Solomon 10 in its depiction of Christ's presence with the patriarchs. It is significant that in a similar fragment (Frag. LIV), the designation "the Chief also of the cherubim" is listed as "the Charioteer of the cherubim"; this is probably a reference to the *Merkabah* and the Glory seated upon it (cf. Ezek 1). Clement of Alexandria calls Christ the "Charioteer of Israel"; see *Paid.* XII.

4. Tertullian

The idea that all visible manifestations of God are the Son had a pervasive influence on many of the church's leading exegetes. Tertullian, whose writings date from ca. 193-220 CE, is also guided by this principle. He, too, assigns all judgment and revelatory activity, including that carried out by the Angel of the Lord, to the Son:

> [*Adv. Prax.* 16] It is the Son, therefore, who has been from the beginning administering judgment, throwing down the haughty tower [Babel], and dividing the tongues, punishing the whole world by the violence of the waters, raining upon Sodom and Gomorrah fire and brimstone, as the Lord from the Lord. For He it was who at all times came down to hold converse with men, from Adam on to the patriarchs and the prophets, in vision, in dream, in mirror, in dark saying; ever from the beginning laying the foundation of the course of His dispensations, which He meant to follow out to the very last. Thus was He ever learning even as God to converse with men upon earth, being no other than the Word which was to be made flesh [cf. *Adv. Mar.* 2.27].

Tertullian is also careful to state that the use of angel terminology in Christology does not imply angelic nature:

> [*De carne Christi* 14] He is indeed called "Angel of Great Counsel", that is, messenger, by a word that refers to office rather than nature. For he had as his mission to announce to the world the great purpose of the Father, namely that concerning the restitution of humanity. He is not, however, on this account to be understood as an actual angel like Gabriel or Michael [cf. Novatian, *De Trinitate* 28].

It is very likely that this clarification by Tertullian came about because such a distinction between *office* and *nature* was not being maintained by all who expressed an Angelomorphic Christology. Already with someone as prominent and learned as Justin Martyr one can find evidence that this distinction was not made:

> [*I Apol.* 6.1-2] So then, we are called godless. We certainly confess that we are godless with reference to beings like these who are commonly thought of as gods, but not with reference to the most true God, the Father of righteousness and temperance and the other virtues, who is untouched by evil. But him, and the Son who came from him, and taught us these things, and the army of the other good angels who follow him and are made like him, and the prophetic Spirit, we worship and adore (σεβόμεθα καὶ προσκυνοῦμεν).

What is striking about this text is both Justin's acknowledgement that angels are made like Christ (i.e., of the same nature) and the inclusion of angels as receiving "worship and adoration" in a sequence after the Father and the Son and before the (prophetic) Spirit.

5. *Clement of Alexandria*

With Clement of Alexandria, whose writings date ca. 180-215 CE, the understanding of "the Word" in his pre-incarnate state as an angel is more explicit. The Word, as an angel who later became incarnate in Jesus, is the one who gave face to face instruction to the nation Israel through Moses:

> [*Paid.* I.7] For it is really the Lord [the Son] that was the instructor of the ancient people by Moses; but He is the instructor of the new people by himself, face to face. "For behold," He says to Moses, "My angel shall go before thee," representing the evangelical and commanding power of the Word, but guarding the Lord's prerogative. [. . .] Formerly the older people had an old covenant, and the law disciplined the people with fear, and the Word was an angel; but to the fresh and new people has also been given a new covenant, and the Word has appeared, and fear is turned to love, and that mystic angel is born—Jesus.

6. *Hippolytus of Rome*

The pre-incarnate Christology of Hippolytus, writing c. 200-235 CE, also is dominated by "the Word" and his participation in creation. It is intriguing to read in Hippolytus' exegetical works of his identification of the Angel of Daniel 10 with the Word.[12] Regarding the golden girdle of this angel (Dan 10.5), Hippolytus remarks: "For the Word was to bear us all, binding us like a girdle round his body [. . .] The complete body was His, but we are members of His body, united together, and sustained by the Word himself".[13] Another example of the Christological identification of the Word with a familiar OT angel tradition is prominently featured in the Eucharistic Prayer of Hippolytus' *Apostolic Tradition*:

> We render thanks to you, O God, through your beloved child Jesus Christ, whom in the last times you sent to us as Savior and Redeemer, and Angel of Your Counsel; who is your inseparable

---

[12] Babel, *Christos Angelos*, 68-70.
[13] *Fragments from Commentaries, On Daniel*, Frag. 25; see *The Ante-Nicene Fathers* 5.182.

Word, through whom you made all things, and in whom you were well pleased.[14]

7. Origen

The prolific exegete Origen, writing ca. 203-254 CE, is more distinctive in his use of angelomorphic traditions for Christology. He identifies the Son with an angel in two different ways. First, on several occasions he makes the bold identification of a pair of angels as the Son and the Holy Spirit. For example, in his *Commentary on Romans* he explains the two Cherubim of the Ark in the Tabernacle (cf. Exod 25.22) as the Son and Holy Spirit:

> [111.8] What are we to think of them as a symbol? Cherubim means fullness of knowledge. Where do we find fullness of knowledge if not in him of whom the Apostle says "in whom are all the treasures of wisdom and knowledge" [Col 2.3]? And the Apostle says that of the Word. He also writes the same things of the Holy Spirit when he says: "The Spirit scrutinizes all things, even the deep things of God" [1 Cor 2.10].

Origen uses this same identification in his exegesis of the two seraphim that are present in Isaiah 6. Although he is typically dependent on Alexandrian exegesis, here he claims that the source of his exegesis is "the Hebrew" (i.e., a Jewish Christian)[15]:

> [*Princ.* I.3.4] The Hebrew said that the two Seraphim with six wings in Isaiah who cry to one another and say, "Holy, Holy, Holy is the Lord Sabaoth," are the only Son of God and the Holy Spirit. For our part we believe that the expression in the *Psalm of Habakkuk* [Hab. 3.2 LXX], "In the midst of the two living creatures," refers to Christ and the Holy Spirit [cf. *Princ.* IV.3.14, *Hom. Is.* I.2; IV.1].

The other manner in which Origen identifies Christ as an angel is in his repeated Christological use of the designation "Angel of Great Counsel" (Isa 9.6 LXX). With it he emphasizes Christ's role as a revealer (*Comm. on Joh.* 1.277) and distinguishes him from the leagues of created angels (*Contra Celsum* 5.8). Joseph Trigg has recently demonstrated that Origen especially uses this

---

[14] Section 4 in *Hippolytus: A Text for Students* (trans. G. Cuming; Bramcote: Grove Books, 1976) 10.

[15] Kretschmar finds antecedents of this identification in the *Ascension of Isaiah* and in Philo, who equates the Seraphim of Isa 6.2 with the two Cherubim of the Ark and explains them as the kingly and creative "Powers" of God (*Quaes Ex* 2.68); see *Studien zur frühchristlichen Trinitätstheolgie*, 62-94. See also Stroumsa, "Le couple de l'ange et de l'esprit", 42-61.

title in expressing his understanding of Christ as the guardian angel for himself and the other enlightened Christians.[16]

8. *Novatian*

One of the most prominent discussions of Angelomorphic Christology is found in Novatian (ca. 250 CE). He also speaks of how the invisible God is only visible through his Image, the Son:

> [*De Trinitate* 18] We are led to understand that it was not the Father, who never has been seen, that was here seen, but the Son, who repeatedly descended to this earth and so was seen. For he is the image of the invisible God [Col 1.15], being so in order that weak and frail human nature might in time become accustomed to see, in Him, who is the Image of God, that is, in the Son of God, God the Father.

In conjunction with his treatment of the early theophanies of Genesis, Novatian explains how the Son can be called both God and Angel:

> [*De Trinitate* 19] Moreover it is written simply in the place of God, for it is not said in the place of the angel and God, but only of God; and He who promises those things is manifested to be both God and Angel, so that reasonably there must be a distinction between Him who is called God only, and Him who is declared to be not God simply, but Angel also. Whence if so great an authority cannot here be regarded as belonging to any other angel, that He should also avow Himself to be God, and should bear witness that a vow was made to Him, except to Christ alone, to whom not as angel only, but as to God, a vow can be vowed; it is manifest that it not be received as the Father, but as the Son, God and Angel. Moreover, if this is Christ, as it is, he is in terrible risk who says that Christ is either man or angel alone, withholding from him the power of the Divine name,—an authority which he has constantly received on the faith of the heavenly Scriptures, which continually say that He is both Angel and God.

This use of angelomorphic traditions, however, is carefully augmented by clear confessions about the divinity of the Son and his unity with the Father:

> [31] He therefore is God, but begotten for this special result, that He should be God. He is also the Lord, but born for this very purpose of the Father, that He might be Lord. He is also an Angel, but He was destined of the Father as an Angel to announce the Great Counsel

---

[16] "The Angel of Great Counsel: Christ and the Angelic Hierarchy in Origen's Theology", *JTS* 42 (1991) 42-51.

of God [cf. Isa 9.6 LXX]. And His divinity is thus declared, that it may not appear by any dissonance or inequality of divinity to have caused two Gods.

9. *Lactantius*

The Divine Institutes of Lactantius, written around 311, is principally an apologetic work defending Christianity against the attacks it faced after the Diocletian persecution. There is some evidence of his understanding of Christology's roots in the OT. In talking about the origin of the Son, he states:

> [4.6.1] God, therefore, the contriver and founder of all things, as we have said in the second book, before he commenced this excellent work of the world, begat a pure and incorruptible Spirit, whom he called his Son. [2] And although he had afterwards created by himself innumerable other beings, whom we call angels, this First-Begotten, however, was the only one whom he considered worthy of being called by the Divine Name, as being powerful in his Father's excellence and majesty.

He speaks here of the origin of Christ and the angels in the same context. Two chapters later, however, he is careful to distinguish between Christ and the angels by asserting that Christ was begotten as a Word from God's mouth while the angels were spirits from the breath of his nostrils (*Institutes* 4.8.7). The First-Begotten terminology and the mention of the creation of angels both indicate the possibility that Lactantius is using angelomorphic categories in his Christology. Furthermore, the primary aspect of the Son which confers his divine status is his possession of the Divine Name, a thoroughly Jewish and angelomorphic idea. He even speaks of the secret and hidden aspect of the Name, an idea which he finds also in Hermetic literature. He explains its significance in the next chapter of *the Divine Institutes*:

> [4.7.1] Some one may perhaps ask who this is who is so powerful, so beloved by God, and what name he has, who was not only begotten at first before the world, but who also arranged it by his wisdom and constructed it by his might. First of all, it is befitting that we should know that his name is not known even to the angels who dwell in heaven, but to himself only, and to God the Father; nor will that name be published, as the sacred writings relate [cf. Rev 19.12], before that purpose of God should be fulfilled. In the next place, we must know that this name cannot be uttered with the mouth of man, as Hermes teaches, saying these things: "Now the cause of this cause is the will of the divine good which produced

God, whose name cannot be uttered by the mouth of man." And shortly afterwards to his Son: "There is, O Son, a secret word of wisdom, holy and respecting the only Lord of all things, and the God first perceived by the mind, to speak of whom is beyond the power of man." But although his name, which the supreme Father gave him from the beginning, is known to none but himself, nevertheless he has one name among the angels, and another among men, since he is called Jesus among men: for Christ is not a proper name, but a title of power and dominion.

10. *Eusebius of Caesarea*

Eusebius, writing his *Preparation for the Gospel* (*Praeparatio*) in the fourth century CE, shows the continued use of even explicit angelomorphic designations as he calls Christ: "the Image of God and Power of God and Wisdom of God and Word of God, nay further 'the great captain of the host of the Lord' and 'Angel of Great Counsel'" (7.5; cf. *Demonstratio* 5.10). He, too, emphasizes the visible/invisible distinction between the Father and the Son who is the "Angel of the Most High his Father":

> [*Demonstratio* 1.5] Remember how Moses calls the Being, who appeared to the patriarchs and often delivered to them the oracles written down in Scripture, sometimes God and Lord and sometimes the Angel of the Lord. He clearly implies that this was not the Omnipotent God but a secondary Being, rightly called the God and Lord of holy men, but the Angel of the Most High his Father. [...] And if it is not possible for the Most High God, the invisible, the Uncreated, and the Omnipotent to be said to be seen in mortal form, the being who was seen must have been the Word of God, whom we call Lord as we do the Father.

11. *The Apostolic Constitutions*

Although the following text from the *Apostolic Constitutions* is difficult to date with any precision, the prominence of angelomorphic traditions is readily apparent[17]:

> [5.20] To him [Christ] did Moses bear witness and said: "The Lord received fire from the Lord, and it rained down." Him did Jacob see as a man, and said: "I have seen God face to face, and my soul is

---

[17] K. Kohler (1893), W. Bousset (1915), and E. Goodenough (1935) all have argued that Books 7-8 of *Apostolic Constitutions* contain remnants of pre-Christian Jewish synagogal prayers which were incorporated into the document; see D. Fiensy, "Hellenistic Synagogue Prayers", *OTP* 2.671-672.

preserved." Him did Abraham entertain, and acknowledge to be the Judge, and his Lord. Him did Moses see in the bush; concerning Him did he speak in Deuteronomy: "A Prophet will the Lord your God raise up" [. . .]. Him did Joshua the son of Nun see, as the captain of the Lord's host, in armour, for their assistance against Jericho; to whom he fell down and worshipped, as a servant does to his master. [. . .] Ezekiel also, and the following prophets, affirm everywhere that he is the Christ, the Lord, the King, the Judge, the Lawgiver, the Angel of the Father, the only-begotten God. Him therefore do we also preach to you, and declare him to be God the Word, who ministered to his God and Father for the creation of the universe.

C. *An Introduction to Early Evidence (Pre-150 CE)*

This 150-325 CE evidence of Angelomorphic Christology is typically not challenged or debated by scholars. The same is not true for evidence that predates this period, especially that found in NT documents. It is reasonable, however, to hypothesize that there must be evidence of ideological links in the period between the pre-Christian antecedent traditions surveyed in Part II and their evident use by Christians from the mid-second through the third century. It is central to the thesis of this study to demonstrate that this trajectory of Angelomorphic Christology is visible long before 150 CE.

The survey of specific evidence that follows in the chapters below will focus on seven different documents or groupings of documents: the *Pseudo-Clementines*; the *Shepherd of Hermas*, the *Ascension of Isaiah*, the Revelation to John; the Gospel of John; the Epistle to the Hebrews; and the Pauline Epistles. As can be seen from this sequence, this survey will begin with the later documents that contain what is generally regarded as the more indisputable evidence and progress back to the earlier, and usually more disputed, evidence contained in NT documents.[18] This

---

[18] The dating of some of these documents is debated. *Pseudo-Clementines* is usually dated to the third (*Homilies*) and fourth century (*Recognitions*) in its present form, but it contains traditions that are undoubtably second century Jewish Christian ideas; see G. Strecker, *Das Judenchristentum in den Pseudoklementinen* (TU 70; rev. ed.; Berlin: Akademie-Verlag, 1981) 255-267. The *Shepherd of Hermas* is usually dated around 140, but there is evidence it could be as early as late first century; see J. Wilson, *Toward a Reassessment of the Shepherd of Hermas: Its Date and Its Pneumatology* (Lewistown, NY: Mellen, 1993) 9-61. The *Ascension of Isaiah* probably dates from the first half of the second

evidence is put forward in support of the thesis of this study stated above: Angelomorphic traditions, especially those growing from the Angel of the Lord traditions, had a significant impact on early expressions of Christology to the extent that evidence of an Angelomorphic Christology is discernible in several documents dated between 50 and 150 CE.

---

century, between 112-138 CE; see J. Knight, *The Ascension of Isaiah*, 21-23. The Revelation to John is usually dated in the last decade of the first century, but there is substantial evidence to read it as a pre-70 document; see J.C. Wilson, "The Problem of the Domitianic Date of Revelation", *NTS* 39 (1993) 587-605. A late first century date for John is usually postulated due to its high Christology, but the Jewish nature of this Christology and other elements of this Gospel make a pre-70 date very possible; see J.A.T. Robinson, *Redating the New Testament* (Philadelphia: Westminster, 1976) 254-311. *The Epistle to the Hebrews* was probably written in the decade before the destruction of the temple in 70; see Robinson, *Redating the NT*, 200-220. The Pauline Epistles date between 50 and 65, although several scholars argue that Ephesians and Colossians are post-70; see Robinson, *Redating the NT*, 31-85. The precise dating of these documents, however, has little impact on the validity of the research presented below.

CHAPTER EIGHT

THE *PSEUDO-CLEMENTINES*

The difficulty in dating the *Pseudo-Clementines* has caused diverse opinions about its value for understanding Ante-Nicene Christianity.[1] Even though *Pseudo-Clementines Homilies* is generally understood to be from the late-third century CE and *Recognitions* from the mid-fourth century, there is little doubt among scholars that the ideas in this collection—or even an underlying document incorporated into this collection—can be dated substantially earlier.[2] This is especially true of the complex Christology that has distinctive Jewish characteristics, usually considered to be Ebionite in nature, which are considerably older than the 3rd or 4th century CE.

The Christology of *Pseudo-Clementines* centers on the person identified primarily as the True Prophet.[3] The central building block of this True Prophet Christology is the Prophet-like-Moses tradition of Deut 18.15 which depicts Moses declaring: "YHWH your Elohim will raise up for you a prophet like me from among your own people; you shall heed such a prophet." The focus of the Christology in *Pseudo-Clementines* is the truth that the True Prophet imparts through his teaching about the Law. The person and message of the True Prophet, therefore, is seen as congruent with the person and message of the Prophet Moses:

---

[1] *Pseudo-Clementines* is ancient romance literature that combines the story of the supposed reunion of Clement's long-lost family with several theological ideas that are typically classified as Ebionite by scholars. *Pseudo-Clementines* is preserved as two distinct documents which parallel each other in some content and are identified as *Homilies* (Greek) and *Recognitions* (Latin). The critical editions of these texts were recently updated by G. Strecker, *Die Pseudoklementinen I: Homilien* (GCS 42; Berlin: Akademie-Verlag, 1992), and *Die Pseudoklementinen II: Rekognitionen* (GCS 51; Berlin: Akademie-Verlag, 1993). For a readable introduction to the multi-faceted history of research on *Pseudo-Clementines*, see F. Stanley Jones, "The Pseudo-Clementines: A History of Research", *SecCent* 2 (1982) 1-33, 63-96.

[2] Scholars have discerned sources like *Kerygmata Petrou* which date to the second century; see G. Strecker, *Das Judenchristentum in den Pseudoklementinen* (TU 70; rev. ed.; Berlin: Akademie-Verlag, 1981).

[3] E.g., *Hom.* III.53; *Rec.* I.26-40.

> [*Rec.* IV.5] It is therefore the peculiar gift bestowed by God upon the Hebrews, that they believe Moses; and the peculiar gift bestowed upon the Gentiles is that they love Jesus.
>
> [*Hom.* VIII.6] For on this account Jesus is concealed from the Jews, who have taken Moses as their teacher, and Moses is hidden from those who have believed Jesus. For there being one teaching by both, God accepts him who has believed either of these.

This Prophet-like-Moses tradition, however, is by no means the entire foundation for the Christology presented in *Pseudo-Clementines*. Indeed, the "True Prophet" figure functions as an umbrella for a rather diverse collation of Jewish mediator traditions which all influenced this Christology.[4] The focus of this chapter will be limited to those Christological traditions in *Pseudo-Clementines* that are specifically angelomorphic and developed from antecedent traditions such as those discussed in Part II of this study.

A. *The True Prophet as Adam and the Glory*

Pseudo-Clementines presents the True Prophet as the Son of God who existed long before the human Jesus. *Rec.* II.48 states:

> [Peter says] Yes, if our Jesus knows him [God], then Moses also, who prophesied that Jesus should come, assuredly could not himself be ignorant of him. For he was a prophet; and he who prophesied of the Son doubtless knew the Father. For if it is in the option of the Son to reveal the Father to whom he will, the Son, who has been with the Father from the beginning and through all generations, revealed the Father to Moses and to the other prophets.

Such a perspective is also visible in *Rec.* I.45, where the True Prophet is identified as the Son of God who is older than creation:

> Although he indeed was the Son of God and the Beginning of all things, he was made man. Him first God anointed with oil which was taken from the wood of the Tree of Life. From that anointing, therefore, he is called "Christ".

The "man" in the *Rec.* I.45 above does not refer to Jesus, but to Adam (cf. *Rec.* II.5). *Pseudo-Clementines* presents the pre-existent Son

---

[4] See C. Gieschen, "The Seven Pillars of the World: Ideal Figure Lists in the Christology of the *Pseudo-Clementines*", *JSP* 12 (1994) 67-82. A similar coalescence of Christological traditions takes place in the Fourth Gospel; see Bühner, *Gesandte und sein Weg*, 341-385.

of God as becoming incarnate in Adam, as evidenced in these texts:

> [*Hom.* VIII.10] The only good God having made all things well, and having handed them over to man, who was made after his image, he who has been made breathing of the divinity of him who made him, being True Prophet and knowing all things, for the honor of the Father who had given all things to him [. . .] showed them the way which leads to his friendship, teaching them by what deeds of men the one God and Lord of all is pleased [cf. *Hom.* III.20-21].

> [*Rec.* IV.9] When God had made man after his own image and likeness, he grafted into his work a certain breathing and odor of his divinity, that men, being partakers of his Only-Begotten, might through him be also friends of God and sons of adoption. Therefore he himself, as the True Prophet, knowing with what actions the Father is pleased, instructed them in what way they might obtain that privilege.

Therefore, Adam is the first incarnation of the Son of God or True Prophet who later became incarnate also in Jesus.

These two incarnations of the True Prophet do not mean that he was not active in the period between Adam and Jesus. While no other incarnations are noted in *Pseudo-Clementines*, the continuing presence and appearances of the True Prophet with "the pious" is affirmed. For example, *Rec.* I.52 states:

> Know then that Christ, who was from the beginning, and always, was ever present with the pious, though secretly, through all their generations; especially with those who waited for Him, to whom He frequently appeared.

Several texts support this assertion by testifying that the True Prophet appeared to the patriarchs and Moses. Moreover, his presence and appearances continue even after his incarnation in Jesus:

> [*Rec.* II.22] For the True Prophet himself also from the beginning of the world, through the course of time, hastens to rest. For he is present with us at all times; and if at any time it is necessary, he appears and corrects us, that he may bring to eternal life those who obey him.

This pattern of the True Prophet being incarnate in only Adam and Jesus, but appearing to, or being present with, other important individuals of biblical history is further substantiated by the testimony of the heresiologist Epiphanius concerning Ebionite doctrine:

> [*Panarion* 30.3.5] He [Christ] comes into the world when he wishes, for he came into Adam and appeared to the patriarchs clothed with a body. He is the same who was sent to Abraham, Isaac, and Jacob, and who came at the end of time and clothed himself with the body of Adam, and who appeared to men, was crucified, raised, and returned on high.

Epiphanius states that, according to the Ebionites, Christ "clothed himself" with the "body" of Adam when he became incarnate as Jesus. What is meant by the "body" of Adam? *Pseudo-Clementines* places significant emphasis on Adam as the "image" of God (cf. Gen 1:26). Because "image" was often understood to signify physical likeness, it is possible that Adam as the "image" of God has a direct relationship to Adam as the visible "body" of God in this literature.[5]

Pseudo-Clementines has clear evidence of the Jewish idea that God has a visible body or form as a glorious man.[6] *Hom.* XVII.7 contains a substantial detailing of this idea:

> Of his commandments this is the first and great one, to fear the Lord God, and to serve him only. But he meant us to fear that God whose angels they are who are the angels of the least of the faithful among us, and who stand in heaven continually beholding the face of the Father [cf. Matt 18.10]. For he has a form [μορφήν], and he has every limb primarily and solely for beauty's sake, and not for use. For he has not eyes that he may see with them; for he sees on every side, since he is incomparably more brilliant [λαμπρότερος] in his body [τὸ σῶμα] than the visual spirit which is in us, and he is more splendid [φωτός] than everything, so that in comparison with him the light of the sun may be reckoned as darkness. Nor has he ears that he may hear, for he hears, perceives, moves, energizes, acts on every side. But he has the most beautiful form [καλλίστην μορφήν] on account of man, that the pure in heart may be able to see him, that they may rejoice because they suffered [. . .] Therefore, judging that he is the universe, and that man is his image (for he is himself invisible, but his image man is visible), the man who wishes to worship him honors his visible form [αὐτοῦ μορφὴν ἐκδικεῖ], which is man.

---

[5] Fossum, "Jewish Christian Christology", 269-271. There is rabbinic evidence that the Messiah would possess the glorious appearance and height of Adam (e.g., *Num. Rab.* 13.12; cf. *Gen. Rab.* 12.6).

[6] See esp. *Hom.* XVII.7 (quoted here); cf. *Hom.* III.7; X.6; XI.4; XVI.19. See also the discussion of the Glory on 100-110 above. The connection between this text and *Shi'ur Qomah* mysticism was seen by G. Scholem; see *Jewish Gnosticism, Merkebah Mysticism and Talmudic Tradition* (2d ed.; New York: Jewish Theological Seminary, 1965) 41.

Fossum has convincingly argued that this description of God's beautiful and brilliant "Form" is based upon Jewish traditions about the Glory, the radiant "likeness of a man" in Ezek 1.26.[7] Furthermore, he sifts the evidence in *Pseudo-Clementines* and demonstrates that there is an identification between this visible "form" of God and the Son, who is the older "form" that is incarnate in Adam as noted in *Rec.* I.28:

> But after all these things [creation prior to man], he made man, on whose account he had prepared all things, whose internal form is older, and for whose sake all things that are were made [. . .].

Based upon this evidence, Fossum draws this pointed conclusion:

> The divine archetype of Adam thus obviously corresponds to his pre-existent "Form" in *Rec.* 1, 28, 4 and must be identical with the beautiful and bright bodily Form (*morphe, soma*) of God described in *Hom.* 17, 7, 2-4. Furthermore, since Adam is an incarnation of Christ, his pre-existent and internal "Form", even the Form or Body of God and thus the Kabod, must be the Son.[8]

B. *The True Prophet as Wisdom and the Spirit*

As discussed in Chapter 4, there is a close relationship or union of Wisdom and Spirit several places in Jewish literature. These two concepts are the basis for a significant portion of the Christology of the *Pseudo-Clementines*. For example, Christ is understood to be the Wisdom of God in a discussion found in Book One of *Recognitions*:

> [I.39] He [the True Prophet] instituted baptism by water amongst them, in which they might be absolved from all their sins on the invocation of His Name, and for the future, following a perfect life, might abide in immortality, being purified not by the blood of beasts, but by the purification of the Wisdom of God.
>
> [I.40] [Peter says] To such an extent does wickedness prevail by the agency of evil ones; so that, but for the Wisdom of God assisting those who love the truth, almost all would have been involved in impious delusion. Therefore He [Christ/the True Prophet/the Wisdom of God] chose us twelve.

Neither of these texts confirm that Wisdom is understood here as an angelomorphic being, such as in several Jewish texts.[9] One

---

[7] "Jewish Christian Christology", 260-287, esp. 264-265.
[8] "Jewish Christian Christology", 269.
[9] See discussion on 89-103 above.

could argue that these texts merely present Jesus as Wisdom personified. Later in *Recognitions*, however, there is a discussion which identifies Wisdom as a person who was involved in creation:

> [*Rec.* VIII.34] He [God] has doubtless a certain reason and evident causes why, and when, and how He made the world; but it were not proper that these should be disclosed to those who are reluctant to inquire into and understand the things which are placed before their eyes, and which testify of His providence. For those things which are kept in secret, and are hidden within the senses of Wisdom, as in a royal treasury, are laid open to none but those who have learned of Him [Wisdom/Christ], with whom these things are sealed and laid up.

This text clearly draws on Wisdom tradition that sees her as an hypostasis whom God used to carry out his creation. Elsewhere in *Pseudo-Clementines* the work of creation is carried out by the Spirit:

> [*Hom.* XI.22] [After quoting Gen. 1.3] Which Spirit, at the bidding of God, as it were his Hand, makes all things, dividing light from darkness, and after the invisible heaven spreading out the visible, that the places above might be inhabited by the angels of light, and those below by man, and all the creatures that were made for his use.

The Spirit is understood as a being with an identity that is distinct from God. Moreover, the Spirit is here identified as God's "Hand". This understanding is also present in *Rec.* VI.7: "Which Spirit [cf. Gen 1.3], as the Creator's Hand, by command of God separated light from darkness". This assertion draws on the idea of the creative "Hand" as the hypostasized Wisdom, expressed most clearly in Wis 11.17: "For your All-Powerful Hand, which created the world out of formless matter [. . .]".[10] The fact that Wisdom and Spirit can be equated in *Pseudo-Clementines* is made clear a few books later where what was earlier said of the Spirit is now said of Wisdom, including the identification of Wisdom as God's creative "Hand":

> [*Hom.* XVI.12] And Peter answered: "One is he who said to his Wisdom, 'Let us make a man.' But his Wisdom was that which he himself always rejoiced as with his own Spirit. It is united as soul to God, but it is extended by him, as Hand, fashioning the universe."

---

[10] This idea is also found in: *2 Clem.* 14.2-4; Theophilus, *Autolycus* 2.18; Irenaeus, *Adv. haer.* 4.20.2, 5.5.1; Lactantius, *Institutiones* 4.6. For the origins of this "Hand" theology, see 100-101 above.

The uniting of Wisdom and Spirit ideas, as well as their influence on Christology, can also be seen in the relationship between the True Prophet and the pious, especially the so-called "pillars of the world": Adam, Enoch, Noah, Abraham, Isaac, Jacob, and Moses.[11] The precise relationship between Wisdom and the OT pious ones of Wisdom of Solomon 10 is described in 7.27: "In every generation she [Wisdom] passes into holy souls and makes them friends of God and prophets". Similar language is used in *Pseudo-Clementines* to describe how the "Holy Spirit of Foreknowledge" was infused to Adam by the True Prophet:

> [*Hom.* VIII.10] The only good God having made all things well, and having handed them over to man, who was made after his image, he who had been made breathing of the divinity of Him who made him, being true prophet and knowing all things, for the honor of the Father who had given all things to him, and for the salvation of the sons born of him [. . .] showed them the way which leads to His friendship.

> [*Rec.* IV.9] When God had made man after his own image and likeness, he grafted into his work a certain breathing and odour of His divinity [operi suo spiramen quoddam et odorem suae divinitatis inseruit], that so men, being partakers of His Only-begotten, might through Him be also friends of God and sons of adoption. When also he Himself, as the true Prophet, knowing with what actions the Father is pleased, instructed them in what way they might obtain that privilege.

Such imagery is also used to describe how the Spirit is imparted by the True Prophet:

> [*Hom.* I.19] Now the Man who is the helper I call the True Prophet; and He alone is able to enlighten the souls of men, so that with our own eyes we may be able to see the way of eternal salvation [cf. *Hom.* II.5, 12; III.15; *Rec.* I.33, 44].

> [*Hom.* III.17-18] For every person is a bride, whenever, being sown with the True Prophet's whole word of truth, he is enlightened in his understanding [. . .]. Whenever the soul is sown by others,

---

[11] The idea of these individuals as "pillars of the world" is recorded in *Hom.* XVIII.13-14. These seven individuals are identified in lists found in: *Hom.* XVIII.13; II.16-17, 52; XVII.4; *Rec.* II.47; III.61. The background of these lists in Wisdom tradition and their polemical use is asserted by W. Staerk, "Die sieben Säulen der Welt und des Hauses der Weisheit", *ZNW* 35 (1936) 232-261. The use of these figures as a polemic (primarily against Marcionism) is also an argument of Schoeps, *Theologie und Geschichte*, 173-188; see also *Urgemeinde-Judenchristentum-Gnosis*, 61-67, or *Jewish Christianity*, 121-130. For analysis see Gieschen, "Seven Pillars of the World", 47-82.

then it is forsaken by the Spirit, as guilty of fornication or adultery; and so the living body, the life-giving Spirit, being withdrawn, is dissolved into dust [...].

This influence of Wisdom tradition on *Pseudo-Clementines'* understanding of the presence of the Holy Spirit in the pillars can be understood as a tradition similar to the one found in the *Gospel of the Hebrews*. Here the Spirit, speaking as the hypostatized Wisdom, tells of her presence in the prophets as she comes to dwell fully in Christ at his baptism[12]:

> And it came to pass when the Lord was come up out of the water, the whole fount of the Holy Spirit descended upon him and rested on him and said to him: "My Son, in all the prophets was I waiting for thee that thou shouldest come and I might rest in thee. For thou art my rest; thou are my first-begotten Son that reignest forever."

Some scholars make uncritical use of *Pseudo-Clementines* to illustrate transmigration or repeated incarnations.[13] The *modus operandi* of the True Prophet in *Pseudo-Clementines*, however, is not like the Pythagorean metempsychosis (or transmigration) of Wisdom in Wis 7.27 since the True Prophet is incarnate in Adam and he does not enter the other pillars.[14] The True Prophet is presented as the one who imparts the Spirit to the soul when he appears to individuals or is present with them. The strong pneumatic character of this Christology should not be denied; yet, the True Prophet himself does not pass into souls as Wisdom does according to Wis 7.27.[15] Therefore, it will be demonstrated below that the focus on the *appearances* of the True Prophet grows not from Wisdom traditions, but from the ancient Angel of the Lord traditions.[16]

---

[12] For the resting of the Spirit on the Messiah, see Isa 11.2 and John 1.32.

[13] Winston speaks of the True Prophet's "transmigration"; see *Wisdom of Solomon*, 188. Although O. Cullmann's inclusion of *Pseudo-Clementines* in his discussion of Prophet Christology should be lauded, his mention of "repeated incarnations" of the True Prophet in the pious has probably furthered this misconception in scholarship; see *The Christology of the New Testament* (Philadelphia: Westminster, 1959) 40, and this same error in S. Goranson, "Ebionites", *ABD* 2.261.

[14] Nor is this an Elchasaite Christology where Christ always manifests himself in the body of Adam (cf. Epiphanus, *Pan.* 53.1.8; Hippolytus, *Ref.* 9.9.2); see also Schoeps, *Jewish Christianity*, 69-71, and Fossum, "Jewish-Christian Christology", 269-271.

[15] J.N.D. Kelly terms this "Pneumatic Christology"; see *Early Christian Doctrines*, 142-145, and 223 below.

[16] See also Gieschen, "Seven Pillars of the World", 73-81.

A final area where the influence of Wisdom tradition on this True Prophet Christology can be discerned is the theme of "eschatological rest".[17] Both *1 En.* 42.1-2 and Sir 24.1-17 record the vivid tradition about Wisdom searching far and wide for a resting place in the world. In a manner similar to several fragments of the *Gospel of the Hebrews*, including the one cited above, *Pseudo-Clementines* adapts this tradition of Wisdom's eschatological rest to the True Prophet who has the Holy Spirit of Christ:

> [*Hom.* III.20] If anyone does not allow the man fashioned by the hands of God [Adam/TP] to have had the Holy Spirit of Christ, how is he ['anyone'] not guilty of the greatest impiety in allowing another born of an impure stock to have it? But he ['anyone'] would act most impiously, if he should not allow to another to have it [the Holy Spirit of Christ], but should say that he [Adam/TP] alone has it, who has changed his forms and his names from the beginning of the world, and so reappeared again and again in the world, until coming upon his own times, and being anointed with mercy for the works of God, he shall enjoy rest forever [cf. *Rec.* II.22].

The various "forms and names" in this text need not be regarded as other human beings such as "the prophets" in Wis 7.27 or the *Gospel of the Hebrews*, since the True Prophet is incarnate only in Adam and Jesus.[18] A preferable antecedent of "forms and names" in *Hom.* III.20 is the changing divine manifestations of Christ in the OT, such as those described by Justin (e.g., *Dial. Typhro* 61.1).[19] Although these various "forms and names" are not systematically discussed in *Pseudo-Clementines*, nevertheless there is clear evidence which follows that the True Prophet Christology drew on overt angelomorphic traditions as it developed.

C. *The True Prophet as the Chief Archangel*

One of the more overt angelomorphic traditions that influenced the True Prophet Christology of this document presents Christ as

---

[17] See J. Helderman, *Die Anapausis im Evangelium Veritatis* (NHS 18; Leiden: Brill, 1984) esp. 60-69.

[18] Μορφή should be understood as "outward appearance" or "shape", not as "being" or "person"; cf. Justin, *Dial. Trypho* 75.

[19] The True Prophet is clearly divine, but not equal to the Most High God (*Rec.* II.42). *Pseudo-Clementines* objects to the title "God" being used of some figures in the Scriptures: Moses, angels, he who spoke in the bush, he who wrestled with Jacob, and he who would be born Emmanuel (*Hom.* XVI.14).

the Chief Archangel, a role usually occupied by Michael.[20] This idea is evinced in a discussion of the Jewish teaching that angels are appointed to the seventy-two parts of the world[21]:

> [*Rec.* II.42] But to the one among the archangels who is greatest, was committed the government of that nation; and when one of these appears, although he be thought and called God by those over whom he presides, yet, being asked, he does not give such testimony to himself. For the Most High God, who alone holds the power of all things, has divided all the nations of the earth into seventy-two parts, and over these he has appointed angels as princes. But to the one among the archangels who is greatest, was committed the government of those who, before all others, received the worship and knowledge of the Most High God [. . .]. But Christ is god of princes, who is Judge of all.

This text unequivocally testifies that Christ is the greatest "archangel" and "god of princes" under the authority of "the Most High God", even though he is sometimes called "God" by those whom he serves.[22] Christ has been identified with, and has subsumed, Michael.[23] According to this testimony, Christ governs the people of God and rules over the other angelic princes as the ultimate "judge". This teaching is also found among the descriptions of the Ebionites that are presented by Epiphanius in his *Panarion*:

> [30.16.2] They teach, as I said, that there are two who are appointed by God, one of them Christ and the other the devil. They say that Christ has been allotted the future age, but to the devil has been entrusted the present one, by the decree of the Almighty according to the request of each of them. [3] For this reason Jesus was born of a man's seed and chosen, so they say, and thus by election called God's Son from the Christ who came into him from above in the form of a dove. [4] They do not say that he was begotten of God the Father, but created like one of the archangels. They say that he rules over angels and everything made by the Almighty [. . .].

This form of Angelomorphic Christology, which presents the True Prophet as the Chief Archangel, probably grew out of the more fundamental identification of Christ with the ancient Angel of the Lord traditions.

---

[20] See discussion of Michael on 126-131 above.
[21] See the discussion on 127-128 above.
[22] 11QMelch ascribes the designations El and Elohim to the angelomorphic Melchizedek (cf. Michael in 1QM 17.6).
[23] Daniélou, *Theology of Jewish Christianity*, 126-127.

D. *The True Prophet as the Angel of the Lord*

The angelomorphic traditions that had the greatest impact on the Christology of *Pseudo-Clementines* are those which the OT preserves concerning the Angel of the Lord. Evidence of Christ being identified with the Angel of the Lord is found in the several discussions of the appearances of the True Prophet to the pious "pillars" in the Pentateuch. For example, in *Rec.* I.32 the author recalls that "an angel" instructed Abraham (Gen 15.22) and then proceeds to identify this angel as the True Prophet in the next chapter. In addition, *Rec.* I.34 states that "[. . .] the True Prophet appeared to Moses and struck the Egyptians with ten plagues [. . .]". Wis 18.15 accords this action to the angelomorphic "Word of God" who is a union of Word, Wisdom, and the Angel of the Lord traditions (cf. 1 Chr 21.16).[24] Furthermore, as noted above, there is mention of *appearances* of the True Prophet to all the pious. After Simon Magus outlines the individuals who supposedly knew God and attempts to show that this contradicts the words of Jesus about only the Son knowing the Father, Peter responds:

> [*Rec.* II.47] For if it is the option of the Son to reveal the Father to whom He will, then the Son, who has been with the Father from the beginning, and through all generations, as He revealed the Father to Moses, so also to the other prophets; but if this be so, it is evident that the Father has not been unknown to any of them [cf. *Rec.* II.48].

This view of the "pillars" as prophets is also visible in Epiphanius: "But after these [the pillars and Aaron] they [the Ebionites] acknowledge no more of the prophets" (*Pan.* 30.18.4). The most compelling evidence, however, comes in *Hom.* II.15 where Peter is explaining the prophetic rule of pairs (female/male) and preparing to give his lengthy list of ten examples of these pairs in *Hom.* II.16-17. This text links several of the pillars with the concept of a "succession of prophets":

> For, since the present world is female, as a mother bringing forth the souls of her children, but the world to come is male, as a father receiving his children from their mother, therefore in this world there came a *succession of prophets*, as being sons of the world to come, and having knowledge of men.

---

[24] For a discussion of the adaptation of the Angel of the Lord traditions in Wisdom of Solomon, see 98-103 above (cf. Num 20.16; Isa 63.9; Philo *Vita Mos* 1.166).

If knowledge and truth cannot be gained apart from the True Prophet, as *Pseudo-Clementines* asserts (*Rec.* I.33, 44; *Hom.* II.5, 12), then all the pillars must have had some form of contact with him. This is affirmed in *Rec.* I.52, which was cited earlier: "Know then that Christ, who was from the beginning, and always, was ever present with the pious [. . .] to whom He frequently appeared".[25] A pre-existent Christology is clearly at work here as in the NT, but for a different purpose.[26] The NT uses pre-existent Christology to support the divinity of Jesus.[27] *Pseudo-Clementines* uses it to establish the credibility of a particular pentateuchal tradition against those groups attacking it. Therefore, the appearances of the True Prophet to the pillars and other pious individuals should be understood as influenced by Angel of the Lord traditions.

E. *Conclusion*

There are some complexities in the relationship between the pillars and the True Prophet that cannot be explained as a simple adaptation of angelomorphic traditions. Note that the author of *Recognitions* asserts an apparent contradiction when he twice emphasizes the True Prophet's simultaneous presence and appearances with the pious:

> [*Rec.* I.52] Know then the Christ, who was from the beginning, and always, was ever present with the pious, though secretly, through all their generations; especially with those who waited for Him, to whom He frequently appeared.

> [*Rec.* II.22] For He [the True Prophet] is present with us at all times; and if at any time it is necessary, He appears and corrects us, that He may bring to eternal life those who obey him.

The most promising way to understand this apparent contradiction of both *always present and yet appearing frequently* is the uniting of Angelomorphic Christology (frequent appearances) with Pneumatic Christology (always present).[28] A similar idea appears to be

---

[25] The pillars were considered the most pious people in the world; see *Hom.* XVIII.14. *Rec.* I.45 notes that Christ anoints the pious, giving the Holy Spirit. This is possibly an installation of the pious into the prophetic office.

[26] The involvement of the pre-existent Christ in the lives of the pillars is attested in the NT (John 8.56; 1 Cor 10.4; 1 Peter 3.18; Heb 11.26; John 1.1-3, Jude 5).

[27] E.g., Phil 2.6; Col 1.15-20; and John 1.1-18.

[28] This dichotomy between angel and spirit should not be stretched; the possibility exists that the continual presence of the True Prophet could also be

present in Theophilus of Antioch. He uses the combination of Wisdom (pneumatic and internal) and Word (angelomorphic and external)[29]:

> [*To Autolycus* 2.10] For the prophets did not exist when the world came into existence; there were the Wisdom of God which is in him [God] and his holy Word who is always present with him [God].

Elements of an Angelomorphic Pneumatology can be discerned in *Pseudo-Clementines*. Several of the texts above have demonstrated clear links between the True Prophet, Christ, and the Holy Spirit. Both texts cited immediately above (*Rec.* I.51 and II.22) present a contrast that implies the union of Spirit and Angel in the True Prophet: he is ever present with the pious (Spirit) and frequently appears to them (Angel). Such a union is visible in *Hom.* III.20 where "the Holy Spirit of Christ" is united with Adam/the True Prophet who has repeatedly reappeared since the beginning for the purpose of imparting the Holy Spirit to others.

One must carefully distinguish between the various traditions in early Christianity that evidence Pneumatology.[30] Unlike the *Gospel of the Hebrews* fragment and 1 Peter 1.11, which speak solely of the *presence* of the Spirit in the prophets as expressed in Wisdom tradition, *Pseudo-Clementines* also sets forth *appearances* to the prophets by the True Prophet who possesses and imparts the Spirit. As detailed above, *Pseudo-Clementines* presents the Spirit as enlightening the souls of the pillars through appearances of the True Prophet (*Hom.* I.19; II.5, 12; III.15; *Rec.* I.33, 44). Angelomorphic Pneumatological traditions provided this Angelomorphic Christology with a dimension that enabled the True Prophet to be *both* continually present with, and frequently appearing to, the pillars.

---

influenced by guardian angel traditions (cf. *Herm. Man.* XI). There is, however, only one specific guardian angel tradition in *Pseudo-Clementines*, similar to that found in Matt 18.10, and it is not associated with the True Prophet or pillars (*Hom.* XVII.7). Angels are more often associated with watching over nations (cf. *Rec.* II.42; VIII.50).

[29] *To Autolycus* 2.22 notes that the Word is sent into the world and is both heard and seen (i.e., angelomorphic appearances); see discussion on 190-191 above.

[30] For a more comprehensive survey of these traditions, see W.-D. Hauschild, *Gottes Geist und der Mensch* (München: Kaiser, 1972) 80-85, and G. Quispel, "Genius and Spirit", *Essays on the Nag Hammadi Texts* (NHS 6; ed. M. Krause; Leiden: Brill, 1975) 155-169. An example of the uniting of Christology and Pneumatology with no explicit connection to Angel traditions is the use of "the Spirit of Christ" in 1 Pet 1.10-12.

CHAPTER NINE

THE *SHEPHERD OF HERMAS*

Scholars have been both intrigued and frustrated by the variety of angelomorphic figures that the author of the *Shepherd of Hermas* adapted in recording these so-called revelations and developing the ideology of a "second repentance" in this early Christian writing.[1] Some previous studies have sought to explain this variety and apparent confusion of mediator figures in terms of multiple authors or sources.[2] While such research provides insight to our understanding of how *Hermas* could have developed, it is noteworthy that the author or final redactor who brought the document to its present form apparently thought that the text was cohesive as it stands.[3]

This chapter will summarize the evidence for Angelomorphic Christology in *Hermas* by examining the vast array of angelomorphic figures found in this document.[4] The central importance of Angelomorphic Pneumatology for understanding the Christology and Ecclesiology of *Hermas* will be demonstrated.[5]

---

[1] For a comprehensive commentary that is conversant with past research, see N. Brox, *Der Hirt des Hermas* (Kommentar zu den Apostolischen Vätern 7; Göttingen: Vandenhoeck & Ruprecht, 1991); see also L.W. Barnard, "The Shepherd of Hermas in Recent Research," *HeyJ* 9 (1968) 29-36, and J.C. Wilson, *Five Problems in the Interpretation of the Shepherd of Hermas* (MBPS 34; Lewiston, NY: Mellen, 1995).

[2] Such theories of multiple authorship abounded in the late nineteenth century; a more recent advocate is S. Giet, *Hermas et les pasteurs: Les trois auteurs du pasteur d'Hermas* (Paris: Presses universitaires du France, 1963).

[3] The unity of *Hermas* was recently and convincingly defended by P. Henne, *L'Unité du Pasteur d'Hermas: Tradition et rédaction* (Paris: J. Gabalda, 1992).

[4] The most extensive study of Christology in *Hermas* is the recent work of P. Henne, *La christologie chez Clément de Rome et dans le Pasteur d'Hermas* (Fribourg Suisse: Éditions Universitaires, 1992).

[5] The central and unifying role of the Spirit in *Hermas* is visible in *Sim.* V.6.5-7 and IX.1.1-2 as discussed below; see C. Gieschen, "The Angel of the Prophetic Spirit: Interpreting the Revelatory Experiences of the *Shepherd of Hermas* in Light of *Mandate* XI", *SBLSP* 33 (1994) 790-803.

A. The Various Angelomorphic Figures

The diversity of angelomorphic figures in *Hermas* is very apparent and difficult to systematize. Some of these figures are clearly Christological, some are ecclesiastical, and most have a pneumatic character. Furthermore, some of the varied figures share the same functions and appear to be manifestations of a single angelomorphic figure. To facilitate this discussion, all significant mediators are listed below with a summary of their functions in *Hermas*.

The Old Lady. This figure dominates the Visions of *Hermas*. In *Vis.* I.4-9 she appears as an old woman in shining garments on a white chair with a book in her hand as she reveals to Hermas why God is angry with him. In *Vis.* II.1 she appears again, walking and reading a book that reveals Hermas' family sins. She is identified as the protological Church in *Vis.* II.4.1. In *Vis.* III.1.4 Hermas meets her sitting on a couch (or bench) of ivory covered with linen. She bids the six men who are around her to go and build the tower which *Vis.* III.3.3 and *Sim.* IX.13.1 identify as the Church. *Sim.* IX.1.1 identifies this lady as the Holy Spirit who spoke in the form of the Church.

The Maiden Bride. In *Vis.* IV.2.1 the "old" lady appears as a radiant maiden bride in white.[6] In spite of her relatively youthful depiction, she still has her white hair, which is an indicator of her divine status.

The Shepherd. In *Vis.* V, which is an introduction to the *Mandates*, a glorious man appears to Hermas in the dress of a Shepherd. He claims to have been sent by the Most Revered Angel to dwell with Hermas. Hermas does not recognize him as the one to whom he has been handed over (a Guardian Angel or the Angel of Repentence who is not mentioned as being entrusted with Hermas earlier). The Shepherd then changes his appearance and is recognized by Hermas. The Shepherd is identified as the Angel of Repentance in *Vis.* V.7, *Sim.* IX.1.1 and *Sim.* IX.33.1. He is Hermas' *angelus interpres* throughout the *Mandates* and *Similitudes*.

---

[6] This is an image for the church in the NT (cf. Rev 19.6-9; Eph 5.25-32). For OT background of this image, see J. Galambush, *Jerusalem in the Book of Ezekiel: The City as Yahweh's Wife* (SBLDS 131; Atlanta: Scholars Press, 1992).

The Angel of Repentance. This angel is identified as the Shepherd who looked like a glorious man in *Vis.* V.7. He describes his work in *Man.* IV.2.2. He speaks with the authority of God when he states in *Man.* IV.2.4 (cf. *Sim.* IX.33.1): "You shall live if you keep my commandments and walk in them." He assures Hermas of his continued presence in *Man.* XII.4.7 (cf. *Man.* XII.6.1) and identifies himself as "the one who lords it over" (ὁ κατακυριεύων) Hermas. According to *Sim.* IX.1.1-3 he is a manifestation of the same Spirit who spoke in the form of the church, but who now is in the form of an angel. The Glorious Angel sent the Angel of Repentance to live at Hermas' house. The title "Angel of Repentance" also occurs three additional times in *Sim.* IX: 23.5; 31.3; 33.1.

The Angel/Shepherd of Punishment. *Sim.* VI.2.5 depicts him as appearing like the Shepherd, but also carrying a whip. He is recognized as a righteous angel. *Sim.* VII.1-6 refers to him as the "Shepherd of Punishment" and the "Angel of Punishment".

The Most Revered Angel. This figure is alluded to as the one who sent the Shepherd to Hermas in *Vis.* V.2 (cf. this action is accorded to the Glorious Angel in *Sim.* IX.31.3). *Man.* V.1.7 mentions that this angel justifies all the righteous. He seems to be the same one who appears to Hermas in *Similitude* X.

The Glorious Angel. *Sim.* VII.2-3 states that this angel directs the actions of the Angel of Punishment. *Sim.* IX.1.3 testifies that this angel directed the Shepherd to live at Hermas' home. There is a link between the Glorious Angel and the Angel of the Lord since *Sim.* VIII.1.2 describes the Angel of the Lord as "*glorious* and very tall". *Sim.* VII.3.3 identifies the Glorious Angel as Michael. "The one who handed Hermas over to the Shepherd" finally appears to Hermas in *Sim.* X.1.1 and directs Hermas to follow the commands imparted by the Shepherd.

The Glorious Man. *Sim.* IX.6.1 describes him as so tall that he was taller than the tower. *Sim.* IX.7.1 identifies him as Lord of all the tower. In this text he also commands the Shepherd to prepare stones for the tower. *Sim.* IX.12.8 explains that the Glorious Man is the Son of God and there are six "glorious angels supporting him on the right hand and on the left".

The Angel of the Lord. *Sim.* VII.5 identifies him as "that angel of the Lord" and *Sim.* VIII.1.5 speaks of him as "the angel of the Lord". *Sim.* VIII.1.2 describes a vision Hermas has of him as "glorious and very tall". Therefore, he appears to be the same angel as the Glorious Angel and possibly also the Glorious Man.

The Son of God. This figure has the form of a servant in *Sim.* V.2.1-11. *Sim.* V.6.2-3 explains that the Son of God appointed angels over people, cleansed people of their sins, and gave them the law. The Holy Spirit dwelt in him according to *Sim.* V.6.5-7 and he is equated with the Spirit in *Sim.* IX.1.1. This text also asserts his pre-existence. He is identified with the Rock and the Door/Gate in *Sim.* IX.12.2. He is further identified with the Name in *Sim.* IX.14.5-6.

Michael. The Glorious Angel is identified as Michael in *Sim.* VIII.3.3. He is not mentioned by name in any other context.

The Holy Spirit and the Angel of the Prophetic Spirit. Because Pneumatology is so central to the author's understanding of Christology and Eccelesiology, greater attention must be given to these figures. The only occurrence of ὁ ἄγγελος τοῦ προφητικοῦ πνεύματος in *Hermas* is found in *Man.* XI.9.[7] The content of *Mandate* XI addresses early Christian concerns regarding true or false prophecy and prophets. While its instructional form has some ties with the "Two Spirits" doctrine found in several of the preceding *Mandates*, this chapter is fundamentally an independent literary unit that has been woven into the progression of the *Mandates*. Its form parallels the recurrent concern for true prophecy found in biblical and related literature, and especially in the *Didache*.[8] The *Sitz im Leben* of this chapter is related in verses 1-7 which demonstrate that this *Mandate* is directed against situations involving false prophecy

---

[7] The fundamental examination of *Mandate* XI remains J. Reiling, *Hermas and Christian Prophecy: A Study of the Eleventh Mandate* (NovTSup 37; Leiden: Brill, 1973).

[8] For a discussion of the prophetic office in the early church, see Reiling, *Hermas and Christian Prophecy*, 4-20, and D. Aune, *Prophecy in Early Christianity*, 247-338. One of the most related texts in form is *Didache* 13. Although there are many obvious differences between their view of prophecy and its testing, both documents follow a similar form to deal with a community concern (cf. 1 Corinthians 14).

influenced by hellenistic divination.⁹ After discussing the character of a true prophet, the author details how God guides this type of prophet to speak:

> (9) Therefore, when the man who has the Divine Spirit [τὸ πνεῦμα τὸ θεῖον] comes into an assembly of righteous men who have faith in the Divine Spirit, and a prayer is made to God by the assembly of those men, then the Angel of the Prophetic Spirit which is assigned to him [ὁ ἄγγελος τοῦ προφητικοῦ πνεύματος ὁ κείμενος ἐπ' αὐτῷ] fills the man [πληροῖ τὸν ἄνθρωπον], and that man, having been filled by the Holy Spirit [τῷ πνεύματι τῷ ἁγίῳ], speaks to the group as the Lord [ὁ κυρίος] wills. (10) So in this way the Spirit of the Deity [τὸ πνεῦμα τῆς θεότητος] is known.

Who is this Angel of the Prophetic Spirit and what is its relationship to the Spirit? This angelic mediator is sometimes equated by scholars with an angel who is assigned a specific function, such as the Angel of Repentance in *Vis.* V.7 (cf. *Man.* IV.2.2) or with an angel who mediates visions, such as Remiel in *2 Baruch* 55:3.¹⁰ The context, however, shows that this angel is much more than another angel with a specific function. The Angel of the Prophetic Spirit is closely linked with "the Spirit" who is identified in several different ways in this chapter.¹¹ More significantly, this angel is directly identified with the Holy Spirit in verse 9: "then the Angel of the Prophetic Spirit who has charge of him fills the man and the man, being filled with the Holy Spirit, speaks [. . . .]" Therefore, "the Angel of the Prophetic Spirit" is equated with, and is a manifestation of, "the Holy Spirit".¹²

---

⁹ E. Peterson has shown convincingly the hellenistic elements that are blended with Jewish Christian theology; see *Frühkirche, Judentum und Gnosis* (Freiburg: Herder, 1959) 254-284.

¹⁰ M. Dibelius, *Der Hirt des Hermas* (Die Apostolichen Väter IV; Tübingen: Mohr/Siebeck, 1923) 541. A much better direction to look is to Gabriel and his associations with the work of the Holy Spirit; see Daniélou, *Theology of Jewish Christianity*, 127-131, and Reiling, *Hermas and Christian Prophecy*, 27-57.

¹¹ The Spirit is identified with the following titles: τὸ πνεῦμα τὸ θεῖον (vv. 2, 5, 7, 9a, 9b, 12); τὸ πνεῦμα τὸ ἅγιον (vv. 8, 9); τὸ πνεῦμα τοῦ θεότητος (vv. 10a, 10b, 14); τὸ πνεῦμα τὸ ἄνωθεν (v. 8); τὸ πνεῦμα τὸ ἐρχομένω ἀπὸ τοῦ θεοῦ (v. 17).

¹² This title should be understood as an appositional genitive: the angel who is the Prophetic Spirit. For a contrary view, see J.C. Wilson, *Toward a Reassessment of the Shepherd of Hermas: Its Date and Pneumatology* (Lewiston: Mellen, 1993) 97-98. It is clear that "Prophetic Spirit" was a term of some prominence that was used interchangeably with Holy Spirit. For this title in Justin, see *I Apol.* 6.2; 13.3; 31.1; *Dial. Trypho* 72.2. For the targumic use of this title, see Str-B II.127-134. For other examples of the angelomorphic Holy Spirit, see discussions on 231-236 (*Ascension of Isaiah*) and 260-269 (Revelation) below.

Our understanding of this angel is furthered by the observation that it is described in a manner characteristic of guardian angels in Jewish tradition: the Angel of the Prophetic Spirit is ὁ κείμενος ἐπ' αὐτῷ. This is best translated "the one who is assigned to him" or "the one who is in charge of him".[13] Although it is possible that there may be some influence from the δαίμων πάρεδρος model of hellenistic divination, as Reiling argues, there is sufficient evidence to support the prominence of Guardian Angel traditions in Jewish Christianity and their impact on this depiction of prophetic inspiration.[14] It is clear from *Vis.* V.1-3 that the Shepherd is Hermas' Guardian Angel:

> While I was praying at home and sitting on my bed, there entered a man glorious to look on, in the dress of a shepherd, covered with a white goatskin, with a bag on his shoulders and a staff in his hand. And he greeted me, and I greeted him back. And at once he sat down by me, and said to me, "I have been sent by the most revered angel to dwell with you the rest of the days of your life." I thought he was come tempting me, and I said to him, "Yes, but who are you? For," I said, "I know to whom I was handed over [ᾧ παρεδόθην]." He said to me, "Do you not recognize me?" "No," I said. "I," said he, "am the shepherd to whom you were handed over."[15]

Furthermore, the context speaks against such a hellenistic model. In *Hermas* the Angel of the Prophetic Spirit does not have to be summoned; he is present with or in the prophet and only needs to "fill the man" so that he may speak. A similar type of Guardian Angel tradition is visible with the Angel of Righteousness in *Hermas* who indwells the believer. Notice the parallel description of the Divine Spirit in the prophet according to *Man.* XI.8 and the Angel of Righteousness in the believer according to *Man.* VI.2.3:

---

[13] This translation follows the text of *The Apostolischen Väter I: Der Hirt des Hermas* (ed. M. Whittaker; GCS; Berlin: Akademie, 1956). Note the inferior emended text and translation in LCL (trans. K. Lake): "then the angel of the prophetic spirit rests upon him [πρὸς αὐτὸν] and fills the man."

[14] See Reiling, *Hermas and Christian Prophecy*, 58-95, 110. Guardian Angel traditions of the NT are visible in Acts 12.15 and Matt 18.10. For a fuller treatment of these Jewish Christian Guardian Angel traditions, see G. Quispel, "Genius and Spirit", 155-69. Quispel also shows how these traditions influenced Mani's understanding of revelation by means of the Spirit in the form of an angel.

[15] A similar type of relationship is described here with the verb παραδίδωμι as is described in *Man.* XI.9 with the verb κεῖμαι. See also *Man.* XII.4.7; *Sim.* IX.1.3; IX.33.1; X.1.1-2.

both describe the person who is indwelt or possessed as "meek and gentle" (πραΰς καὶ ἡσύχιος).

B. *The Relationship between Pneumatology, Christology, and Ecclesiology*

How does one understand these various angelomorphic figures and their interrelationship? Scholarly opinion is diverse. Martin Dibelius has influenced interpretation in this matter by asserting that the numerous and varied angels in *Hermas* function Christologically.[16] Furthermore, he sees an Angel Christology at work in *Hermas*, especially in the figures of the Glorious Angel of *Sim.* VIII (who is also identified as the Angel of the Lord) and the Glorious Man of *Sim.* IX. Dibelius asserts that these figures not only function Christologically, but they are manifestations of the Son of God, and thus, of Christ. He proposes that many of the inconsistencies, like the identification of the Glorious Angel as Michael in *Sim.* VIII.3.3, result from the underlying Jewish tradition of *Hermas* not being fully "Christianized" by the author. Most scholarship followed this Christological path that Dibelius established in his exegesis.[17] More recently Halvor Moxnes has argued the sweeping thesis that there is one supreme angel figure in Hermas: the Son of God, Christ.[18] Nobert Brox uses the term "angelomorphic" to describe the Christology of this document, then wisely states that it is developed in a very fragmentary manner and is, therefore, difficult to systematize.[19]

Other scholars have been hesitant to identify Angel Christology in these texts. In an article that downplays the role of Angel Christology in early Christianity, Adolphine Bakker attempts to steer clear of any direct linking of Michael and Christ.[20] Giet rejects the presence of Angel Christology in *Hermas* and distinguishes between the Glorious Angel and the Glorious Man; the latter he sees as Christological.[21] He also proposes a total of three

---

[16] *Hirt des Hermas*, 494, 572-576.
[17] E.g., Peterson, *Frühkirche*, 276-284.
[18] "God and his Angel in the Shepherd of Hermas", *ST* 28 (1974) 50.
[19] See his excursus on Christology in *Hirt des Hermas*, 485-495, esp. 490-492.
[20] "Christ an Angel?", 257.
[21] *Hermas et les pasteurs*, 228. Both of these figures, however, are clearly angelomorphic.

different authors in *Hermas* in order to account for the apparent literary inconsistencies. G. Snyder prefers to emphasize the Christological functions of the angels while not identifying any figure directly with Christ.[22] Lage Pernveden takes the discussion in another direction by downplaying the role of Christology and highlighting the Ecclesiology theme which he sees as dominating *Hermas*.[23]

While recognizing that earlier forms of *Hermas* may have contributed to its apparent inconsistencies, it is important to note the crucial and unifying role that Pneumatology plays in the Christology and Ecclesiology of this document. The central text for understanding this is *Sim.* V.6.5-7:

> The pre-existent Holy Spirit which created all creation, God caused to dwell in that flesh which he wished. Therefore this flesh, in which the Holy Spirit dwelled, served the Spirit well, walking in holiness and purity, and did not in any way defile the Spirit. When, therefore, it had lived nobly and purely, and had labored with the Spirit, and worked with it in every deed, behaving with power and bravery, he chose it as companion with the Holy Spirit; for the conduct of this flesh pleased him, because it was not defiled while it was bearing the Holy Spirit on earth. Therefore he took the Son and the glorious angels as counsellors, that this flesh also, having served the Spirit blamelessly, should have some place of sojourn, and not seem to have lost the reward of its service. For all flesh in which the Holy Spirit has dwelt shall receive a reward if it be found undefiled and spotless.

Already in the 19th century Adolph von Harnack recognized this text as "Adoptionist Christology" and Dibelius, among others, has affirmed this conclusion.[24] Because of a myopic focus on Christology, however, what has been lacking in assessments of this document is a synchronic treatment of its assertions regarding Pneumatology. J. Christian Wilson has expended effort in this direction and affirms that there are two distinct pneumatologies in *Hermas*: the dualistic pneumatology involving the Two Spirits and the pneumatic Christology involving the relationship between the Holy Spirit and the Son of God.[25]

---

[22] *The Shepherd of Hermas* (The Apostolic Fathers 6; ed. R. Grant; Camden, NJ: Nelson, 1968) 60-62, 105.

[23] *The Concept of the Church in the Shepherd of Hermas* (trans. I. and N. Reeves; STL 27; Lund: GWK Gleerup, 1966) 58-64.

[24] A. Harnack, *History of Dogma* (4 vols.; London: Williams & Norgate, 1894) 1.191-192; see also Dibelius, *Hirt des Hermas*, 572-576.

[25] *Towards a Reassessment*, 162-165. Wilson notes that Harnack and others

What is the relationship between the Holy Spirit and the Son of God in *Hermas*? As evidenced in *Sim.* V.6.5-7 above, the Holy Spirit is clearly pre-existent and a participant in the work of creation. The same is asserted of the Son of God in these two texts:

> [*Sim.* V.2.6] The Son of God is older than all of his creation, so that he was counsellor to his Father in his creation.
>
> [*Sim.* IX.12.2-3] [The Shepherd explains the Rock and the Door of *Sim.* IX.2.2] "The Son of God is older than all his creation, so that he was the counsellor of his creation to the Father, therefore the rock is also old." "But why is the door new, sir?" "Because he [the Son] was manifested in the last days of the consummation; for this reason the door is new, so that those who are to be saved may go through it into the kingdom of God."

The apparent contradiction is obvious: How can the Son of God be pre-existent (as in *Sim.* V.2.6 and IX.12.2) and also be adopted as the Son by virtue of his obedient life (as in *Sim.* V.6.5-7)? One cannot reasonably attribute this glaring contradiction within the present form of *Similitude* V to sources or authorial ineptitude. Jean Daniélou, for example, struggles with the contradiction in this manner:

> This is a matter of some importance for the trinitarian theology of Hermas, which seems to be characterised by the fact that he borrowed his theology of the Word and his theology of the Spirit from two different systems. That of the Word is in the same line of development as the figure of the seventh Angel of the apocalyptic, surrounded by six archangels. That of the Spirit is in the same tradition as the Prince of Light opposed to the Angel of Darkness, and comes from the *Rule of the Community*. This is the explanation of the apparent lack of coherence in his theology. There is one theology of the Word and another theology of the Spirit, both Jewish Christian, but no unified theology of the Word and the Spirit together; and when he does speak of them both at the same time his thought is confused, as in the *Fifth Similitude*.[26]

Our examination of the evidence brings us to a different conclusion. There is no "unified theology" of the Son and the Spirit specifically because the author's Jewish milieu leads him to proclaim the Spirit as the single divine mediator: the Son is a manifestation of the Spirit. The solution to understanding the relationship between the Son and the Spirit in *Hermas* is to stop reading this

---

incorrectly regard adoptionistic and pneumatic Christology as mutually exclusive.

[26] *Jewish Christianity*, 143-144.

document with a trinitarian mindset; it is more binitarian in its understanding of the pre-existent Son of God as the Spirit.[27] In *Hermas* the Son is pre-existent through the Holy Spirit who indwelt him. The description of the pre-existent nature of the Son is parallel to that of the Spirit because the Spirit indwells the Son. Further support for this understanding of the relationship between Pneumatology and Christology is found in the parallel usage of "Spirit" and "Lord" in *Man.* III.1:

> Again he [the Shepherd] said to me [Hermas], "Love truth: and let all truth proceed from your mouth, that the Spirit which God has made to dwell in the flesh may be found true by all men, and the Lord [ὁ κύριος] who dwells in you shall thus be glorified, for the Lord is true in every word and with him there is no lie."

J. N. D. Kelly has recognized the prominence of Pneumatology in the Christology of *Hermas* as well as other early Christian writings and calls it "Spirit or Pneumatic Christology".[28] Kelly offers this pointed analysis:

> Hermas clearly envisages three distinct personages [. . .]. The distinction between the three, however, seems to date from the incarnation; as pre-existent the Son of God is identified with the Holy Spirit, so that before the incarnation there would seem to have been but two divine Persons, the Father and the Spirit. The third, the Saviour or Lord, was elevated to be their companion as a reward for his merits, having cooperated nobly with the pre-existent Spirit which indwelt him. Hermas's theology is thus an amalgam of binitarianism and adoptionism, though it made an attempt to conform to the triadic formula accepted in the Church.[29]

There is much evidence for this Son/Spirit union or Pneumatic Christology in early Christianity.[30] Moreover, there are texts that attribute the inspiration of the prophets to Christ or the Spirit of Christ.[31]

Another item of internal evidence supporting these assertions regarding Pneumatic Christology is the Ecclesiology of *Hermas*.

---

[27] See J.N.D. Kelly, *Early Christian Doctrines*, 94.
[28] *Early Christian Doctrines*, 142-144.
[29] *Early Christian Doctrines*, 94.
[30] See 2 Cor 3.15-18; Rom 8.9-11; Gal 2.19-20; 5.24-25; Acts 16.6-8; Phil 1.18-19; *1 Clem.* 22.1; *Ign. Mag.* 16 (cf. John 14.16; 20.22; Rev 2.7, 11, 17, 29; 3.6, 13, 22). These texts are not touching the issue that the Son is spirit, but that the Son is the Spirit.
[31] E.g., 1 Pet 1.10-12; *1 Clem.* 22.1; and Justin, *I Apol.* 33.6-9, 36.1, 38.1.

The Church has a very significant part in *Hermas*, but it is not an independent figure: it is a manifestation of the Spirit. Unlike the Son who is pre-existent through the Spirit, *Vis.* II.4.1 asserts that the Church is protological ("the first-created"; cf. *Vis.* I.1.6; I.3.4). Notice how *Sim.* IX.1.1-2 unites Pneumatology and Christology as it presents the Spirit/Son manifest in the Church[32]:

> After I had written the commandments and parables of the shepherd, the angel of repentance, he came to me and said to me: "I wish to show you what the Holy Spirit which spoke with you in the form [μορφή] of the Church showed you, for that Spirit is the Son of God. For since you were too weak in the flesh, it was not shown you by an angel. But when you were strengthened by the Spirit, and made strong in your strength, so that you could also see an angel, then the building of the tower was shown to you by the Church. You saw all things well and holily as if from a virgin. But now you see them from an angel, yet through the same Spirit."

According to this text it was the "same Spirit" who manifested himself in various ways to Hermas, such as in the Old Lady, the Bride, the Shepherd, or the Angel of Repentance. In addition, the Spirit manifested himself through not only the Son of God and the Church, but also angels. *Sim.* V.6.7 states that: "he took the Son and the glorious angels as counsellors."

Given this close relationship between the Spirit and the Son of God, the other mediator figures in *Hermas* may be seen as the Spirit in a fluid Pneumatology that manifests itself in angelomorphic figures. There are instances where some of these mediator figures seem to be distinct, yet they remain related. For example, it is mentioned in *Vis.* V.2 that the Most Revered Angel has sent the Shepherd to Hermas. The Most Revered Angel also justifies the penitent (*Man.* V.1.7). This is also the work of the Glorious Angel who is said to have sent the Shepherd and given him orders regarding Hermas (*Sim.* VII.1-2; IX.1.3) and who is also referred to as the Angel of the Lord (*Sim.* VII.5). This Glorious Angel is Michael (*Sim.* VIII.3.3) and is closely identified with the Glorious Man with his six glorious angels who is identified as the Son of God (*Sim.* IX.12.8). Elsewhere it is stated that the Son of God sends angels, cleanses from sin, and gives the Law (*Sim.*V.6.2-3). Even the Shepherd/Angel of Repentance appears in a fashion similar to

---

[32] Snyder identifies this text as a possible later insertion in order to reconcile these figures; see *Shepherd of Hermas*, 127.

the Glorious Man (*Sim.* V.1). How can these different figures be so interrelated and coalesced? Moxnes is partially correct when he argues that there is *one figure* behind several of these angelophanies, the Son of God.[33] The pneumatic character of the various Son of God manifestations, however, must not be overlooked or marginalized when determining the identity of this figure: for it is the Spirit who is ultimately behind the angelomorphic figures of *Hermas*. These figures are of the same Spirit whose manifestations are primarily Christological and Ecclesiastical in a very fluid Angelomorphic Pneumatology.

C. *The Son as the Angel of the Lord, the Name and the Glory*

This emphasis on the role of Angelomorphic Pneumatology does not mean that Angelomorphic Christology plays a minor role in *Hermas*. On the contrary, it is one of the most visible aspects of this document since most of the angelomorphic figures are identified, in some manner, with the Son of God. Although the author shows evidence of adoptionism, nevertheless the Son is depicted as a full member of the divine triad by means of his exalted appearances. These appearances are an amalgamation of three angelomorphic traditions: the Angel of the Lord, the Glory, and the Name.[34]

As noted above, one of the angelomorphic figures in the *Similitudes* is identified as "that Angel of the Lord" (*Sim.* VII.5) and "the Angel of the Lord" (*Sim.* VIII.1.5; VIII.2.1). It could be argued that ὁ ἄγγελος τοῦ κυρίου is used here in a general way to speak of one of God's many angels. The functions and description of this angel speak against such an interpretation: this angel has authority over Hermas (*Sim.* VII.5), gives orders (*Sim.* VIII.1.5), bestows crowns (*Sim.* VIII.2.1), and is "glorious and very tall" (*Sim.* VIII.1.2). Therefore, this title is undoubtably harkening the reader back to the Angel of the Lord traditions of the Pentateuch, Joshua, and Judges. Furthermore, the description of this angel as "tall and glorious" means that he is probably to be identified with the Glorious Angel (*Sim.* VII.1-3; IX.1.3; X.1.1), who is also known as Michael (*Sim.* VIII.3.3) and probably also the Most Revered Angel (*Vis.* V.2; *Man.* V.1.7). The identification of this angel with Michael

---

[33] "God and His Angel", 50, 55-56.
[34] See Gieschen, "Angel of the Prophetic Spirit", 799-802.

may appear surprising at first, but is not unreasonable in light of Michael's exalted status in Judaism and early Christianity.[35]

The reference to this angel as ὁ ἔνδοξος ἄγγελος ("the Glorious Angel") could be understood as a general description of this angel as full of splendor. It is much more probable, however, to see this as a technical title that calls to mind the theophanic Glory tradition. If this angel is distinguished from the myriads of angels due to his glory, then it is no ordinary glory, but the very Glory of the Lord. The adjective indicates that the Glorious Angel can also be identified with ὁ ἔνδοξος ἀνήρ ("the Glorious Man" in *Sim.* IX.6.1; IX.7.1; IX.12.8). The probability of this identification is strengthened by the Glorious Man's appearance in the middle of six angels. This is a clear reference to this figure's status as the chief angelomorphic figure, a divine Michael among six other archangels. This Glorious Angel/Man is none other than the Son of God:

> [*Sim.* IX.12.8] "This Glorious man," he [i.e., the Shepherd] said, "is the Son of God, and those six are the glorious angels who surround him on his right and on his left. Not one of these glorious angels," he said, "enters God's presence without him; whoever does not receive his name will not enter the kingdom of God.

The Glorious Man in *Hermas* is described as "[. . .] a man so tall that he rose above the tower" (*Sim.* IX.6.1). This size is especially impressive if one remembers that the reader has already been told in *Sim.* IX.3.1 that the tower was built over the Rock, which is also identified as the Son of God (*Sim.* IX.12.1) and is described as "[. . .] higher than the mountains and square, so as to contain the entire world" (*Sim.* IX.2.1). In addition, the Son of God has already been identified with the Glorious Angel who is "very tall" (*Sim.* VIII.1.2).

A tradition of the Son and the Holy Spirit as huge angelomorphic figures who are paired closely together is found in Elchasai, a Jewish Christian sect leader who wrote in 101 CE.[36] Only a few portions of his book were preserved by Hippolytus, who recorded how Elchasai, according to the missionary Alkibiades, received his book of revelation:

---

[35] See discussion of Michael on 200-205 above.
[36] For texts, but not interpretation, see G. Luttikhuizen, *The Revelation of Elchasai* (TSAJ 8; Tübingen: Mohr-Siebeck, 1985); see also Daniélou, *Theology of Jewish Christianity*, 64-67.

> [*Ref.* 9.13.2-3] It had been revealed by an angel whose height was 24 schoenoi, which make 96 miles, and whose breadth was four schoenoi, and from shoulder to shoulder six schoenoi, and the tracks of his feet extend to the length of 3 1/2 schoenoi, which make 14 miles, while the breadth 1 1/2 schoenos and the height half a schoenos. There should also be a female with him whose dimensions, he says, are according to those already mentioned. The male is the Son of God, while the female is called the Holy Spirit.

Both the Son of God and the Holy Spirit are presented as angels of gigantic proportions. Their size indicates that this tradition is in continuity with descriptions of the Glory upon the *Merkabah* throne in Jewish mystical literature.[37] *Hermas* undoubtedly reflects similar traditions in his description of the Glorious Man/Angel.

The weight of evidence supporting the identification of the Son with the Angel of the Lord traditions grows dramatically when the Name theology of *Hermas* is taken into account.[38] The text cited immediately above mentions the importance of "receiving the name of the Son" (*Sim.* IX.12.8); this is an obvious reference to Baptism where the Name is invoked and the person is sealed. *Hermas* contains a very Jewish and highly developed theology of the Divine Name:

> [*Sim.* IX.14.5] "Listen," said he [i.e., the Shepherd], "the name of the Son of God is great and incomprehensible, and supports the whole world. If then the whole creation is supported by the Son of God, what do you think of those who are called by him, and bear the name of the Son of God, and walk in his commandments?

The Son of God's divine status is expressed by identifying him as the Name, or the one who possesses the Divine Name, which is the very word that brought creation into existence.[39] This identification of the Son of God as possessor of the Name is an unmistakable example of how the Divine Name Angel tradition of Exod 23.20-21 was used in early Christology and shows the roots of this Angelomorphic Christology in the ancient Angel of the Lord traditions.

---

[37] See Fossum, "Jewish-Christian Christology", 260-263.
[38] *Vis.* II.1.2; III.3.5; III.1.9; III.2.1; III.4.3; IV.1.3; IV.2.3-4; *Sim.* VI.2.3; VIII.1.1; VIII. 6.4; IX.12.4-8; IX.13;2-7; IX.14.5-6; IX.15.1-3; IX.16.3-7; IX.17.4; IX.21.3; IX.28.1-7. Most of these texts are related to Baptism, where the Christian receives, or is sealed with, the Divine Name.
[39] For the significance of the Divine Name, see 33 and 70-78 above.

D. *Conclusion*

Because *Hermas* is more binitarian than trinitarian in its final form, it provides a clear example of how adoptionism can stand beside a strongly pneumatic Christology that asserts Christ's pre-existence in the Spirit and greatly exalts the Christological angelomorphic figures of the *Similitudes*. This means that one cannot limit the influence of angelomorphic traditions to one particular figure in *Hermas*. The foundational influence of Angel of the Lord, Glory, and Name traditions on the Angelomorphic Christology of this document has become apparent.

Although Christology and Ecclesiology are the major topics in *Hermas*, Pneumatology unifies the diversity of figures: they are all manifestations of the same Spirit. Certainly there are distinctions among the angelomorphic figures, with the result that the Christological and Ecclesiastical figures usually capture center stage. It is Pneumatology, however, that allows for the frequent changes in appearance and the continued unity of this varied revelation. This phenomenon grew out of the tradition of one divine mediator who manifests himself in multiple forms.[40] This tradition fascinated many Jewish Christians, including the author(s) and audience of *Hermas*, and it served a legitimizing function for the message of repentance which this document imparts through exalted angelomorphic figures.

---

[40] Talbert, "Descending-Ascending Redeemer", 429-430.

CHAPTER TEN

THE *ASCENSION OF ISAIAH*

The *Ascension of Isaiah* is a Jewish Christian apocalypse written from the perspective of the biblical prophet Isaiah in order to give expression to an angelomorphic Christology which is experienced through mystical ascent.[1] Its present form, which dates from the second to the fourth century CE, is a compilation of Jewish traditions about Isaiah's martyrdom and Christian traditions about his vision(s).[2] Most scholars agree that a mid to early second century date for the principal portions of the document is probable.[3] References to the Samaritans in the martyrdom traditions (2.12, 14; 3.1, 3) as well as polemics against Jerusalem (2.7; 3.6) indicate that this writing probably originated in Palestine.[4] Study

---

[1] Recent research on this document has been done most extensively among Italian scholars who have produced a critical edition of the text with a full commentary; see *Ascensio Isaiae: Textus* (eds. and trans. P. Bettiolo, A. Giambelluca Kossova, L. Leonardi, E. Norelli, and L. Perrone; Corpus Christianorvm, Series Apocryphorum 7; Turnhout: Brepols, 1995), and E. Norelli, *Ascensio Isaiae: Commentarius* (Corpus Christianorvm, Series Apocryphorum 8; Turnhout: Brepols, 1995). See also the extensive collection of essays in *Isaia, il dilietto e la chiesa: Visione ed esegesi progfetica cristiano-primitiva nell' Ascensione di Isaia. Atti del Convegno di Roma, 9-10 Aprile 1981* (ed. M. Pesce; Brescia: Paidea, 1983). The English translation by M. Knibb with some notes is found in *OTP* 2.143-176. J. Knight has written a brief introduction and a more extensive work that focuses primarily on Christology; see *The Ascension of Isaiah* and *Disciples of the Beloved One* (cf. discussion on 24 above).

[2] For a discussion of its date and place in early Christianity, see R. Hall, "The *Ascension of Isaiah*: Community Situation, Date, and Place in Early Christianity", *JBL* 109 (1990) 289-306; cf. R. Hall, "Isaiah's Ascent to See the Beloved: An Ancient Jewish Source for the *Ascension of Isaiah*", *JBL* 113 (1994) 463-484.

[3] The composite nature and date of the document is discussed by Knibb "Martyrdom and Ascension of Isaiah", *OTP* 2.147-150. The martyrdom traditions in 1.1-3.12 and 5.1-16 are clearly the most ancient portion of the document. The prophecy about the church in 3.13-4.22 appears to be post-apostolic, yet is often dated in late first century since its discussion of the Antichrist contains a reference to the Nero *redivivus* myth prominent during the decades following his death in 68 CE. The Vision (6.1-11.28) could be from the late first century, but is most often thought to be second century. For a discussion of the author's sources in the apocalypse, see Knight, *Disciples of the Beloved One*, 28-32, and Hall, "Isaiah's Ascent", 463-484.

[4] See Knibb, "Martyrdom and Ascension of Isaiah", *OTP* 2.150.

of this document has been complicated by a difficult textual tradition in which an originally Greek (and possibly Hebrew) text is preserved primarily in Ethiopic.[5]

This document is rooted in a Jewish Christian community that revered mystical ascent and ascetic practices in deference to what the author(s) sees happening in the wider Christian church.[6] There is an emphasis on the Parousia with its eschatologial reward (4.14-18) and a signal that the contemporary situation of the church is deteriorating (3.21-31; 8.23-24).[7] The esteemed reverence for mystical ascent is visible not only in the general apocalyptic nature of the vision, but also in the specific content. For example, 2.9-11 states that after Isaiah withdrew from Jerusalem to a desert he and others engaged in ascent activity:

> [9] And Micah the prophet, and the aged Ananias, and Joel, and Habakkuk, and Josab his son, and many of the faithful who believed in the ascension into heaven, withdrew and dwelt on the mountain. [10] All of them were clothed in sackcloth and all of them were prophets; they had nothing with them, but were destitute, and they all lamented bitterly over the going astray of Israel. [11] And they had nothing to eat except wild herbs [. . .] And they dwelt on the mountains and on the hills for two years of days.[8]

These words reflect a high respect for the prophet as a mystic who ascends to heaven to receive revelation. This community which revered Isaiah may have understood him to be the only

---

[5] Only a fragmentary fourth-fifth century Greek version exists containing 2.4-4.4, but it has allowed scholars to confirm the basic accuracy of the Ethiopic translations which exist. For discussion see Knibb, *OTP* 2.144-47 and esp. Bettiolo et. al., *Ascensio Isaiae: Textus*, 3-43.

[6] See M. Himmelfarb, *Ascent to Heaven in Jewish and Christian Apocalypses* (Oxford: OUP, 1992) esp. 55-58. Himmelfarb's focus on the relationship between exegesis and ascent, however, leads her to downplay the evidence of actual ascent practices. Bauckham takes the evidence of end-of-life ascent to be proof that the author did not advocate mystical ascent; see *Climax of Prophecy*, 143. Based upon the absence of angel names and the refusal of worship by the *angelus interpres*, Bauckham also argues that the author is deliberately rejecting "the theurgic use of angelological lore" such as found in *Merkabah* mysticism. Although the mysticism is not as highly developed as later *Merkabah* texts, nevertheless this document does not contain a polemic against mystical ascent and probably reflects mystical experience.

[7] Hall, "Ascension of Isaiah", places this phenomenon in the context of early second century Christianity; see esp. 300-306.

[8] Living on mountains is related to the practice of mystical ascent. For reference to ascent from a mountain top, see *T. Levi* 2.5-7 and *Apoc. Peter* 17.

prophet who saw God. His exalted status above Moses is implied in the message of the false prophets to Manasseh:

> [3.8] And Isaiah himself has said, 'I see more than Moses the prophet.' [9] Moses said, 'There is no man who can see the LORD and live.' But Isaiah has said, 'I have seen the LORD, and behold I am alive.' [10] Know, therefore, O king, that they (are) false prophets.

This statement may well reflect a contemporary polemic against mystical ascent that this group is facing. They may have been accused of being false prophets, even as Isaiah was in their text. A vision of the divine throne room, like that of Isaiah (Isa 6.1-3), is the type of experience sought by the individuals who wrote and read this document. Other content of this document affirms this espousal of charismatic and mystical activity.[9] Indeed, the final words of Isaiah after relating his vision have that thrust: "But as for you, be in the Holy Spirit that you may receive your robes, and the thrones and crowns of glory, which are placed in the seventh heaven" (11.40).

The focus of the analysis of this document's Angelomorphic Christology will center on the depictions of the three principal angelomorphic figures whom Isaiah encounters during his visionary experience: the Angel of the Holy Spirit, the Beloved, and the Great Glory.

A. *The Angel of the Holy Spirit*

The Jewish roots of this document's pneumatology are overtly present in the frequent angelomorphic designations given to the Holy Spirit: he is called "the Angel of the Spirit" (4.21; [var. 8.14]; 9.39; 10.4; 11.4) or "the Angel of the Holy Spirit" (3.15; 7.23; 9.36, 40; 11.33).[10] He is also identified as "the Angel of the Church" (3.15; cf. *Herm. Sim.* IX.1.1). Although his physical appearance is not

---

[9] Other examples include: the mention of believers speaking through the Holy Spirit (3.19-20); the later church is characterized by prophecy and visions being rendered ineffective (3.21-31, esp. 3.31); and the repeated attention given prophecy and the Spirit leading up to the vision (6.6, 8, 10, 17). See the analysis of varied scholarly opinion in Hall, "Ascension of Isaiah", 300-306, and Knight, *Disciples of the Beloved One*, 186-273.

[10] This terminology is also present in Mandate XI of the *Shepherd of Hermas* and a fragment of Elchasai found in Hippolytus, *Ref.* 9.13.2-3.

detailed in any of these contexts where he is explicitly identified, he is acknowledged as a glorious being (9.33) who is surpassed in glory only by the Great Glory himself (9.37-38) and the Beloved (9.27, 33-36). This language indicates a hierarchy among these three primary figures of this document: the Angel of the Holy Spirit is understood to be "the second angel" (9.35) who is slightly less glorious than the Beloved (9.27, 33) and both are subordinate to the Great Glory (9.40).

The Angel of the Holy Spirit has angelomorphic functions. Jean Daniélou has demonstrated that this angel in *Ascension of Isaiah* has probably assumed characteristics of the angel Gabriel as Jewish angel traditions were adapted by the author(s) of this document to describe the Son and the Holy Spirit.[11] He set forth three observations that are the basis for this conclusion. First, the Angel of the Holy Spirit is given a position of distinction on the left side of the throne of the Great Glory, which is the position given to Gabriel in some Jewish texts:

> [*Ascen. Is.* 11.32] And I saw how he ascended into the seventh heaven, and all the righteous and all the angels praised him. And then I saw that he sat down at the right hand of that Great Glory, whose glory I told you I could not behold. [33] And also I saw that the Angel of the Holy Spirit sat on the left.
>
> [*2 En.* 24.1] The Lord called me [Enoch] and placed me at his left hand, next to Gabriel, and I adored the Lord.

Second, the Angel of the Holy Spirit guides the ascent of individuals through the heavens, a task which is often carried out by Gabriel or Michael in Jewish texts:

> [*Ascen. Is.* 7.23] And I rejoiced very much that those who love the Most High and his Beloved will at their end go up there through the Angel of the Holy Spirit.
>
> [*2 En.* 21.3] The Lord sent one of his Glorious Ones, Gabriel, who said to me: Take courage, Enoch, be not afraid, arise and come with me and stand before the face of the Lord for ever.

---

[11] *Theology of Jewish Christianity*, 128-30 (cf. *2 En.* 21.3-22.5; 24.4); contra Norelli, "Sulla pneumatologia dell' *Ascensione di Isaia*", *Isaia, il dilietto e la chiesa*, 215-220, and Bauckham, *Climax of Prophecy*, 146-147. Danielou's assertion that *Ascension of Isaiah* draws on Michael traditions in its portrayal of the Beloved is more difficult to prove; see section C on 241-243 below.

The Angel of the Holy Spirit's work with Michael to open the tomb of Christ and carry him forth is further evidence of the Angel of the Holy Spirit's assumption of Gabriel's functions (3.15-16). His guidance of Isaiah in 11.35 is done in the same manner in which Gabriel guides Enoch in *2 En* 21.3.

Third, the *Ascension of Isaiah* identifies the angel who communicated with Joseph in Matt 1.20-21 as the Angel of the Holy Spirit:

> [*Ascen. Is.* 11.4] But the Angel of the Spirit appeared in this world, and after this Joseph did not divorce Mary; but kept her as a holy virgin, although she was pregnant.

This role is often associated with Gabriel because his name is specifically mentioned in the appearance of an angel to Mary in Luke 1.26. It appears quite logical that the incarnation account in Luke would promote the union of Gabriel with the Holy Spirit in some Jewish Christian circles since it was Gabriel who announced that the conception "by the Holy Spirit" had taken place. A natural conclusion is to see Gabriel as the Holy Spirit who brought about this pregnancy. Some early Christian literature shows evidence for an even more complex union of Gabriel traditions, Pneumatology, and Christology on this occasion: these texts detail Christ taking the form of Gabriel and impregnating himself in Mary's womb.[12]

More could be said about the Angel of the Holy Spirit if a link with Isaiah's *angelus interpres* could be established. The evidence that speaks against this identification are the portions of the vision that describe Isaiah seeing the Angel of the Holy Spirit with the Great Glory while still having the *angelus interpres* at his side (9.36, 39; cf. 9.21). The *angelus interpres* also defers an honorific title such as "Lord" (8.5) and refuses worship (7.21; 8.15).[13]

In spite of this, there is evidence that closely associates the Angel of the Holy Spirit with Isaiah's *angelus interpres*. First, the Holy Spirit is mentioned as speaking with Isaiah immediately

---

[12] See the *Epistle of the Apostles* 14 and *Sibylline Oracles* 8.456-461; see also Daniélou, *Theology of Jewish Christianity*, 131-132. A similar Jewish Christian tradition surfaces in the Qur'ān where Gabriel appears to Mary in the likeness of a perfect man to bestow a son in her (cf. *Sura* 19.17). The *Gospel of the Hebrews* gives evidence of a tradition that Michael took the form of Mary and cared for Christ (frag. 1).

[13] See the refusal tradition in Bauckham, *Climax of Prophecy*, 140-148, and Stuckenbruck, *Angel Veneration and Christology*, 75-103.

before his vision begins and the *angelus interpres* appears (6.8, 10). A similar phenomenon is found in *Mandate* XI of the *Shepherd of Hermas* where the Angel of the Prophetic Spirit is present with and in the prophet, and on occasion fills him for prophecy.[14]

Second, the *angelus interpres* is described in a manner that is consonant with the Angel of the Holy Spirit elsewhere in this document. Several observations support this assertion. The *angelus interpres* is from the seventh heaven (6.13; 7.8; 8.25), which is the locale of the Angel of the Holy Spirit (9.33-36).[15] The Angel of the Holy Spirit speaks in a manner similar to the *angelus interpres* (11.34-35). Like the Angel of the Holy Spirit, Isaiah's *angelus interpres* has a glory that is distinct from the other angels (7.2, 8; cf. 9.33-36). The opening scene of Isaiah's vision describes the glory of his *angelus interpres*:

> [7.2] When I prophesied in accordance with the message which you have heard, I saw a glorious angel; his glory was not like the glory of the angels which I always used to see, but he had great glory, and an office, such that I cannot describe the glory of this angel. [3] And I saw when he took hold of me by my hand, and I said to him, "Who are you? And what is your name? And where are you taking me up? For strength had been given to me that I might speak with him. [4] And he said to me, "When I have taken you up through (all) the stages and have shown you the vision on account of which I was sent, then you will understand who I am; but my name you will not know, for you have to return into this body.

The question of the name of this angel indicates that this is a principal angel who possesses the Divine Name (cf. Exod 23.20-21).[16] This is also the case with the Beloved whose name is unknown and unlearnable (8.7; 9.5; cf. 7.37). This is evidence that some Jewish Christian groups bifurcated the idea of a single Divine Name Angel so that both the angelomorphic Christ and Holy Spirit were understood to possess the Divine Name. Such an understanding would have been the basis for distinguishing these two from other glorious angels.

---

[14] See further analysis in Gieschen, "Angel of the Prophetic Spirit", 790-793.

[15] The principal angel and Abraham's *angelus interpres* in the *Apocalypse of Abraham* is Yahoel, who is from the seventh heaven (10.8); this also appears to be the case with Michael (10.17).

[16] See the discussion on 66-67 and 70-78 above.

The third reason for an identification of Isaiah's *angelus interpres* with the Angel of the Holy Spirit is the lack of any reference to the Angel of the Holy Spirit by the *angelus interpres* when he describes that Isaiah will see Christ and the Father in the seventh heaven: "You will see one greater than me [. . .] and the Father of the one who is greater you will also see, because for this purpose I was sent from the seventh heaven, that I might make this clear to you" (7.7-8). The reference to "one greater than me" may indicate that Isaiah's *angelus interpres* had a glory close to that of the Beloved (cf. 9.33-38).

Fourth, the Angel of the Spirit is presented as the faciliator of heavenly ascent. For example, the Angel of the Spirit, along with Michael, initiates Christ's ascent after the resurrection (3.18). Even more important is that he facilitates the after-death or end-time ascension of the righteous to heaven (7.23; 8.14; cf. 11.40). The implication may be that ascension before death is also facilitated by the Angel of the Holy Spirit. If this is true, then Isaiah's (pre-death) ascension was facilitated by the Angel of the Holy Spirit who functioned as his *angelus interpres*.

Fifth, the link between Gabriel traditions and the Angel of the Holy Spirit furthers our understanding of how the Angel of the Holy Spirit could be understood as the *angelus interpres* for Isaiah as Gabriel was for Daniel. Although this evidence is not conclusive, the probability of understanding the *angelus interpres* as the Angel of the Holy Spirit must be given due attention.[17]

Central to the theology of this document is the relationship between the two principal angels (the Beloved and the Angel of the Holy Spirit) as well as the veneration of these angels alongside the Great Glory. The Angel of the Holy Spirit is certainly more than a ministering angel with a pneumatic function. In spite of polemics against angel worship in this document (7.21; cf. 8.5), Isaiah is encouraged to worship the Angel of the Holy Spirit (9.37). This angel also claims divine authority when he declares to Isaiah "I have saved you" (11.34 Ethiopic).

Although there are clear associations uniting Christ, the Holy Spirit, and the Father as the foci of worship (8.18; 9.27-42), there is also a clear distinction between the two angelomorphic figures and the Great Glory: the former are subordinate to the latter. The

---

[17] There is evidence for the *angelus interpres* in Revelation being the Holy Spirit; see discussion on 260-269 below.

following text shows Isaiah's "LORD" (Christ) and the Angel of the Holy Spirit worshipping "the LORD":

> [9.36] And I asked the angel who led me and I said to him, "Who is this one?" And He said to me. "Worship him, for this is the Angel of the Holy Spirit who has spoken in you and also in the other righteous." [37] And I saw the Great Glory while the eyes of my spirit were open, but I could not thereafter see, nor the angel who was with me, nor any of the angels whom I have seen worship my LORD. [38] But I saw the righteous as they beheld with great power the glory of that one. [39] And my LORD approached me, and the Angel of the Spirit, and said, "See how it has been given to you to see the LORD, and how because of you power has been given to the angel who is with you." [40] And I saw how my LORD and the Angel of the Holy Spirit worshiped and both together praised the LORD.

In spite of these distinctions between the Beloved and the Angel of the Holy Spirit, they appear here to be of similar—not the same—status: they both are worshipped and both, in turn, offer worship to the Great Glory as angelomorphic beings who share in his divinity as subordinates.

B. *The Beloved*

The understanding of Christ as an angelomorphic being in this document is not accepted by all scholars. Wilhelm Michaelis, among others, has argued that Christ is carefully distinguished from the angels in *Ascension of Isaiah* and thus should not be understood as an angel.[18] There are, however, several aspects of the depiction of Christ that affirm the author clearly understood and depicted him as an angelomorphic figure.

The strongest evidence for this phenomenon is the identification of the Holy Spirit as "the second angel" in 9.35-36. This statement follows a description of how Christ "was transformed and became like an angel" (9.30). Christ is unmistakably the first angel. Such references to Christ do not indicate that Christ shared the ontology of an angel; on the contrary, he is carefully distinguished from, and elevated over, the created angels.

This Angelomorphic Christology is also in Christ's partnership with the Holy Spirit who is, as has been demonstrated, explicitly

---

[18] *Engelchristologie*, 81-82; see also Bauckham, *Climax of Prophecy*, 147.

identified as an angel several times. There is a hierarchy in which Christ is more glorious than the Angel of the Holy Spirit and less glorious than the Great Glory:

> [7.7] And he [the *angelus interpres*] said to me [Isaiah], "You will see one greater than me, how he will speak kindly and gently with you; [8] and the Father of the one who is greater you will also see, because for this purpose I was sent from the seventh heaven, that I might make all this clear to you."

Nevertheless, the distinction between Christ and the Angel of the Holy Spirit is not pronounced. The latter never worships the former. In fact, a similar status of these two beings is visible in their side by side worship of the Great Glory:

> [9.40] And I saw how my LORD and the angel of the Holy Spirit worshiped and both together praised the LORD [i.e., the Great Glory].

Angelomorphic Christology is also visible in how this document describes and defines the Beloved in relation to the angels who fill the seven-tiered heaven. This can be illustrated from the first visionary glimpse that Isaiah has of the Beloved:

> [9.27] And I saw one standing (there) whose glory surpassed that of all, and his glory was great and wonderful. [28] And when they saw him, all the righteous whom I had seen and the angels came to him. And Adam and Abel and Seth and all the righteous approached first and worshiped him, and they all praised him with one voice, and I also was singing praises with them, and my praise was like theirs. [29] And then all the angels approached, and worshiped, and sang praises. [30] And he was transformed and became like an angel. [31] And then the angel who led me said to me, "Worship this one," and I worshiped and sang praises. [32] And the angel said to me, "This is the LORD of all the praise which you have seen."

There are links between the Glory tradition and this portrayal of Christ.[19] Glory is a central aspect of the depiction of angels here and throughout this document. There are many glorious angels, even some whom Isaiah mistakenly thinks are worthy of worship (cf. 7.21). That is the reason for the angel's directions here: "Worship this one" (9.31). Christ is in the typical angelic posture of "standing" and he is unmistakably the most glorious of these glorious ones (9.27). Although the Father is called "the Great

---

[19] See discussion on 78-88 above.

Glory", one cannot look upon the Father for more than a brief glance (9.37). The glory of the Son, however, does not preclude visual contact with his form.

In an elaborate development of the multiple throne scene in Daniel 7, there are many more "Glory" figures and thrones, all of which appear to derive their glory or significance from the Great Glory in the seventh heaven. The Beloved, however, is the principal *visible* Glory figure and he appears in "the form of a man" (3.13). This latter detail indicates that this depiction of the Beloved developed from the mystical tradition of the Glory in Ezek 1.26.[20]

The traditions in the *Ascension of Isaiah* that identify Christ as a possessor of the Divine Name are also an important aspect of this document's Angelomorphic Christology:

> [8.7] And he [the angel] said to me [Isaiah], "From the sixth heaven upwards there are no longer those on the left, nor is there a throne place in the middle, but they are directed by the power of the seventh heaven, where the One who is not named dwells, and his Chosen One, whose name is unknown, and no heaven can learn his name."
>
> [9.5] "And the one who turned to you, this is your LORD, the LORD, the LORD Christ, who is to be called in the world Jesus, but you cannot hear his name until you have come up from this body."

Christ here possesses the Divine Name.[21] This idea is a development from Exod 23.20-21 and principal angel traditions. There is the strong element of the secretness or hiddeness of the Divine Name.[22] This idea is also present in Revelation where Christ has "a Name inscribed which no one knows but himself" (19.12). Possession of the Divine Name may be reflected in the common designation "the LORD" which is given to both the Father and Christ in this document (4.14; 9.5; 10.14) since the Ethiopic term used here is the same one used to translate the Tetragrammaton.[23] Such usage is related to the use of ὁ κύριος for YHWH in the LXX and Christ in the NT.[24] Unlike most Christian documents, the

---

[20] See discussion on 80-84 above.
[21] Although Knight discusses the various titles, he does not elucidate the significance of the possession of the Divine Name; see *Disciples of the Beloved One*, 153-157.
[22] See discussion by Fossum, *Image of the Invisible God*, 111-116.
[23] See Knibb, "Martyrdom and Ascension of Isaiah", *OTP* 2.157 notes.
[24] Davis, *Name and Way*, 13-23, and Capes, *OT YHWH Texts*, 34-89.

Ascension of Isaiah clearly distinguishes between the Divine Name and the name "Jesus": Jesus is a designation applied to Christ only during his earthly state (9.5; 10.7). In a similar manner, "the Son" also appears to be a designation for Christ when he was in the world (9.14; 8.25).

The author's primary title for Christ is "the Beloved".[25] "Beloved Son" is the designation used by the heavenly voice in the Baptism and Transfiguration accounts of the canonical gospels.[26] "The Beloved" is used in Ephesians as a title for Christ (1.6) who is also called "the Glory" in the very same context (1.12, 14, 17). This designation should be understood as an adaptation from angelomorphic mystical traditions that developed from Canticles concerning the form of God (Cant 5.9). In mystical circles "the Beloved" of Canticles came to be understood as the man-like Glory in Ezek 1.26.[27] The author of the *Ascension of Isaiah* was certainly familiar with Jewish mysticism and probably adapted the use of this designation from that context. Finally, Christ is referred to as the "Elect One" in 8.7 (also translated "Chosen One"), another title with links to Jewish mysticism because of its prominent usage in the Similtudes of *1 Enoch* for the angelomorphic figure who is also designated "the Son of Man" and sits on the throne of glory.

The question arises: If the depiction of the Angel of the Holy Spirit is adapted from Gabriel traditions, is there evidence that the portrayal of the Beloved is adapted from Michael traditions? Although there is evidence that supports an affirmative answer, the situation is indisputably more complex than the author simply adapting Michael traditions and changing the name to Christ. That the author is cognizant of Michael as the principal archangel is obvious from his presence in the resurrection account of this document:

> [3.15] And the descent of the Angel of the Church which is in the heavens, whom he will summon in the last days; and that the

---

[25] 1.4, 5, 7, 13; 3.13, 17, 18; 4.3, 6, 9, 18, 21; 5.15; 7.17, 23; 8.18, 25; 9.12. For possible background of this title and its use in early Christianity, see R.H. Charles, *Asension of Isaiah* (London: A & C Black, 1900) 3-4, and Knight, *Disciples of the Beloved One*, 153-157.

[26] Matt 3.17; 17.5; Mark 1.11; 9.7; Luke 3.22; 9.35. The old Syriac version of Mark 1.11, however, renders "my beloved Son" as separate titles (i.e., "my Son and my Beloved"); see Charles, *Ascension of Isaiah*, 3.

[27] See C. Morray-Jones, "The Body of the Glory: *Shi'ur Qomah* and Transformational Mysticism in the Epistle to the Ephesians" (unpublished paper presented at the 1992 National SBL Meeting in San Francisco).

> Angel of the Holy Spirit [16] and Michael, the chief of the holy angels, will open his grave on the third day, [17] and that [Gk: the] Beloved, sitting on their shoulders, will come forth and send out his twelve disciples [. . .].

This resurrection account does not imply Christ needed help out of his grave. Rather, this depiction is in continuity with the Jewish idea that the one who is ascending was to be accompanied or met by two heavenly beings or angels.[28] This tradition of two angels ushering Christ forth from the tomb is also recorded in the *Gospel of Peter*:

> [39] And whilst they [the soldiers] were relating what they had seen [to the centurion and elders], they saw again three men come out of the sepulchre, and two of them sustaining the other, and a cross following them. [40] And of the heads of the two reaching to heaven, but that of him who was led of them by hand overpassing the heavens.[29]

In spite of the Angel of the Holy Spirit and the Beloved as the two focal angelomorphic figures in this document, these two do not eliminate Michael who continues to be identified here as "the chief of the holy angels" (3.16). The Angel of the Holy Spirit's role as Michael's partner in ushering Christ from the tomb is understandable in light of the background of this angel in Gabriel traditions and his (slight) subordination to the Beloved.

Central to the Angelomorphic Christology of this document is the ascent/decent motif found in chapters 10-11. *Ascen. Is.* 10.7-16 details how Christ is commissioned by the Father to descend through the various heavens, taking on a "form like that of the angels of the firmament and also like that of the angels who are in Sheol" (10.10). Jonathan Knight argues that this motif is dependent upon earlier Jewish angel ascent/decent traditions such as those present in Tobit.[30] There the following elements are found:

---

[28] Peterson, *Frühkirche*, 262-264. In *Hermas Vis.* I.4.3 two men (angels) usher the Lady (the Church) from a visionary encounter with Hermas; see also *2 En.* 1.4-9 where a pair of angels accompany Enoch during his ascent. In the transfiguration accounts, it is Moses and Elijah who attend Jesus (e.g., Mark 9.2); see Fossum, *Image of the Invisible God*, 86-89.

[29] This excerpt comes from a fragment that is dated as mid-second century CE; see also the *Martyrdom of Matthew* 30.

[30] *Disciples of the Beloved One*, 146-150. For a broader discussion of this pattern, see Talbert, "Myth of a Descending-Ascending Redeemer", 418-439. For a discussion of the relation of this tradition to the Gnosticism, see U. Bianchi, "L'Ascensione di Isaia. Tematiche soterilogiche di descensus/ascensus", *Isaia, il deletto e la chiesa*, 155-184.

Raphael is divinely comissioned (3.16-17); Tobit does not recognize Raphael as the Angel of the Lord (5.4-5); Raphael's nature had been hidden from Tobit as if Raphael were a vision (12.19); and Raphael's identity is revealed in conjunction with his ascent (12.13-15, 20). Knight does not, however, explain the relationship of this descent/ascent pattern to the Glory tradition. The Beloved is the most glorious "angel" who descends in order to reveal God's Glory to the earth. He functions as a theophanic angel. People who "see" him are saved and seek the climactic vision of the Great Glory upon death. The *Ascension of Isaiah* affirms the incarnation by mentioning the birth, crucifixion, and resurrection (11.1-21). Nevertheless, the angelomorphic elements of this Christology are unmistakable.

C. *The Great Glory*

In spite of the testimony that one may not see God and live (Exod 33.20), some Jewish and Christian documents contain not only visions of an angelomorphic figure who is the visible form of God but also brief glimpses of God who is invisible. For example, in Daniel 7 the prophet is given a vision of not only the "one like a son of man", but also the Ancient of Days. This phenomenon is present in the *Ascension of Isaiah* since, at the climax of Isaiah's vision in the seventh heaven, he is given a brief glimpse of "the Great Glory":

> [9.37] And I saw the Great Glory while the eyes of my spirit were open, but I could not thereafter see, nor the angel who (was) with me, nor any of the angels whom I had seen worship my Lord. [36] But I saw the righteous as they beheld with great power the glory of that one.

This text recalls the call vision in Isa 6.1-3 where Isaiah saw the Lord in the temple.[31] The obvious relationship between the visions of this document and Isaiah's call vision leads to the probability that the depictions of the Angel of the Holy Spirit, the Beloved, and

---

[31] See discussion on 81-82 above. *Isa. Tg.* Isa 6.1 states that Isaiah saw the Glory of YHWH. Unlike some early Christians who interpreted this as a Christophany (cf. John 12.42), the *Ascension of Isaiah* maintains it is a theophany of the Father.

the Great Glory are founded upon the vision of YHWH and the two seraphim in Isaiah 6. This identification of the two angelomorphic figures, in Isaiah 6 and elsewhere, with the Son and Holy Spirit is also found in Origen.[32] An antecedent for this tradition is found in the exegesis that the two cherubim of the Ark of the Covenant received in Jewish mystical groups. Philo, writing prior to Christian interpretations, explains the meaning of the Ark in this manner:

> [*Quaes Ex* 2.68] And from the divine Logos, as from a spring, there divide and break forth two powers. One is the creative (power), through which the Artificer placed and ordered all things; this is named "God." And (the other is) the royal (power), since through it the Creator rules over created things; this is called "Lord." And from these two powers have grown the other. For by the side of the creative (power) there grows the propitious, of which the name is "beneficent," while (beside) the royal (power there grows) the legislative, of which the apt name is "punitive." And below these (cherubim) and beside them is the ark.[33]

The clear distinction between Christ, the Angel of the Holy Spirit, and the Great Glory in *Ascension of Isaiah* is maintained not only through mention of the former two worshiping the latter, but also in the emphasis on the inability of humans and angels to see the Father: Isaiah's vision of him is through the open "eyes" of his spirit and even then it is very terse and what Isaiah specifically saw is not described.[34] The Son and Holy Spirit are less glorious and can be viewed without limit, but not the Father (10.2). This inability to see the enthroned Glory or lack of describing him are tendencies also present in other apocalypses of this period. For example, *1 Enoch* uses both the title "the Great Glory" and emphasizes the inability to see his face (cf. Exod 33.20):

> [14.20] And the Great Glory was sitting on it [i.e., the Merkabah] —as for his gown, which was shining more brightly than the sun, it was whiter than any snow. [21] None of the angels was able to come in and see the face of the Excellent and Glorious One; and no one of the flesh can see him—[22] the flaming fire was around

---

[32] *Princ.* I.3.4 and IV.3.14; *Hom. Isa.* I.2 and IV.1; see discussion on 195-196 above.

[33] "Powers" in Philo are equated with angels; see 119-120 above.

[34] This limit to the knowledge or "seeing" of angels is a theme found in Jewish and Christian literature. "Even angels long to look" into the mystery of the Gospel (1 Pet 1.12) and the time of Jesus' parousia is not known by the angels or the Son of Man (Mark 13.32).

him, and a great fire stood before him. No one could come near unto him from among those that surrounded the tens of millions (that stood) before him.

Ascen. Is. 9.38 makes it clear, however, that the eschatological reward of the righteous is to behold the Great Glory continually. This certainly indicates that those righteous who are in heaven have the privilege of eternally viewing God on his throne, a privilege not even enjoyed by the angels. Moreover, it is also the righteous (Adam, Abel, Seth, and company) who are the first to approach Christ when he appears (9.27-28) and they initiate the heavenly worship of Christ (the angels follow in 9.29).

This document goes on to state three times that Isaiah not only heard, but also "saw" the glory that was directed to the Great Glory whom he could not see (10.3, 4, 5). This indicates that glorification is of the essence of the presence of God or even the action that brings about a mystical vision of his presence. Note how the glorification (i.e., praise) that Isaiah "sees" is identified here[35]:

> [10.2] And all (praise) was directed to that Glorious One whose glory I could not see. [3] And I also heard and saw the praise (which was directed to) him, [4] and the LORD and the Angel of the Spirit heard everything and saw everything. [5] And all the praise which was sent (up) from the six heavens was not only heard, but seen. [6] And I heard the angel who led me, and he said to me, "This is the Most High of the high ones, who dwells in the holy world, who rests among the holy ones, who will be called by the Holy Spirit in the mouth of the righteous the Father of the LORD."

The Great Glory is variously known as "the LORD", "the Glorious One", "the Most High", and "the Father". Based upon 10.6, it appears that the latter title is cherished as a unique aspect of revelation in the Christian period. This type of distinction in titles is similar to the phenomenon of using "Jesus" to refer Christ in his earthly state. Furthermore, the use of "Father" seems to indicate that it was understood as a title descriptive of the relationship between the two LORDs: Isaiah's LORD (i.e., Christ) is the son of "the primal Father", who is also the LORD (8.18).

---

[35] "Praise" and "glorify" are translated by the same Ethiopic word.

D. Conclusion

There is no doubt that this document contains a Christology and a Pneumatology that are saturated with Jewish angelomorphic traditions. As seen with the pair of large angels in the *Book of Elchasai*, the Angel of the Holy Spirit and the Beloved are angelomorphic figures.[36] They both are even explicitly called angels. The influence of Gabriel traditions upon depiction of the Angel of the Holy Spirit is also clear. The traditions about the Divine Name Angel(s) and the angelomorphic Glory are foundational for the Christology and Pneumatology of this document. Lastly, the idea of the incarnation of an angel is vividly portrayed. This abundant use of Jewish angelology is not for the purpose of undermining the divine status of either Christ or the Spirit. On the contrary, angelology was used to display dramatically the divinity of these two persons alongside God.

---

[36] See discussion of Elchasai on 226-227 above.

CHAPTER ELEVEN

THE REVELATION TO JOHN

This examination of early evidence now moves to more "sacred ground" as the focus turns to first century CE documents that later became part of the New Testament. Of all the documents within the canon, the one most widely acknowledged to have drawn on angel traditions in its depiction of Christology is the Revelation to John.[1] The recognition of the influence of angelology on Christology in Revelation is not a recent phenomenon. The earliest extant commentary on Revelation (c. late third century) by Victorinus, Bishop of Pettau in Pannonia, interpreted the "mighty angel" of Revelation 10 as Christ.[2] Although the term "Angel Christology" has been resisted by most interpreters of Revelation over the centuries, nomenclature such as "Angelomorphic Christology" has gained increased acceptance and wider usage in recent discussions of this document.[3]

This chapter is not an examination of the Christology of the entire document.[4] For example, the prominent focus on the Lamb in Revelation 4-7, which usually dominates Christological discussions, is not addressed. Instead, the focus is on select Christological texts that exhibit the influence of the antecedent angelomorphic traditions examined in Part II above. This evidence will be presented by examining the depictions of Christ as: "one like a son

---

[1] Even a skeptic of Angelomorphic Christology like Dunn acknowledges its presence in Revelation; see *Christology in the Making* (2d ed.), xxvi, and the more promising work of his student Peter Carrell, *Jesus and the angels*.

[2] *Victorini Episcopi Petauionensis Opera, Corpus Scriptoum Ecclesiasticum Latinorum* (ed. J. Haussleiter; Leipzig: G. Freytag, 1916 [repr. 1965]) 46:88, or J. P. Migne, *Patrologia Latina*, 5:317-344.

[3] Four examples are: Rowland, "A Man Clothed in Linen"; Carrell, *Jesus and the angels*; Stuckenbruck, *Angel Veneration and Christology*; and Gundry, "Angelomorphic Christology in the Book of Revelation". Most scholars tend to emphasize a clear distinction between Christology and Angelology; see Bauckham, "The Worship of Jesus", 322-341.

[4] The most thorough treatment of the Christology of Revelation is T. Holtz, *Die Christologie der Apokalypse des Johannes* (TU 85; 2d ed; Berlin: Akademie Verlag, 1971). For a survey of scholarship, see Stuckenbruck, *Angel Veneration and Christology*, 22-41.

of man" (Rev 1.10-3.22; 14.14-16); "the Word of God" (Rev 19.11-13); and the "Mighty Angel" with the Scroll (Rev 10.1-11). Furthermore, the identity of "his [God's] Angel" in Rev 1.1 will be discussed because of its implications for this document's pneumatology.

A. *One Like a Son of Man*

The first chapter of Revelation contains this vivid epiphany of the Risen Christ:

> [12] Then I turned to see whose voice it was that spoke to me, and on turning I saw seven golden lampstands, [13] and in the midst of the lampstands one like a son of man, clothed with a long robe and with a golden girdle around his breast. [14] His head and his hair were white like white wool, as snow; his eyes were like a flame of fire, [15] his feet were like burnished bronze, refined as in a furnace, and his voice was like the sound of many waters. [16] In his right hand he held seven stars, from his mouth issued a sharp two-edged sword, and his face was like the sun shining in full strength. [17] When I saw him, I fell at his feet as though dead. But he laid his right hand upon me [. . .].

This is one of the few depictions of how early Christians visualized Christ after the ascension. Even though the effort to understand the author's use of texts in recording these visions is fraught with difficulty, scholars have shown that the description of this *Christophany* draws on, or shares much in common with, the *angelophany* detailed in Daniel 10:[5]

> [5] I lifted up my eyes and looked, and behold, a man clothed in linen, whose loins were girded with gold of Uphaz. [6] His body was like beryl, his face like the appearance of lightning, his eyes like flaming torches, his arms and legs like the gleam of burnished bronze and the sound of his words like the noise of a multitude [. . .]. [9b] When I heard the sound of his words, I fell on my face in a deep sleep with my face to the ground. [10] And behold, a hand touched me and raised me to my hands and knees.

---

[5] See esp. Rowland's work: "The Vision of the Risen Christ", 1-11; "A Man Clothed in Linen", 99-110; *Open Heaven*, 100-101; see also Stuckenbruck, *Angel Veneration and Christology*, 209-221. For the difficulty in discerning the use of texts in recording visions, see C. Rowland, "Apocalyptic Literature", *It is Written: Scripture Citing Scripture* (eds. D. Carsons and H. Williamson; Cambridge: CUP, 1988) 170-189, and G. Beale, "Revelation", *It is Written*, 318-336.

Some similar details in the Christophany of Revelation 1 are not sufficiently distinctive to assert that they are drawn directly from Daniel 10.[6] There are, however, at least three shared details which support the conclusion that the author of Revelation specifically drew on Daniel 10 as he recorded the experience of his Christophany:

1. *"the golden girdle"*
Rev 1.13: καὶ περιεζωσμένον πρὸς τοῖς μαστοῖς ζώνην χρυσᾶν
Dan 10.5 (LXX): καὶ τὴν ὀσφὺν περιεζωσμένος βυσσίνῳ
Dan 10.5 (Theod.): καὶ ἡ ὀσφὺς αὐτοῦ περιεζωσμένον ἐν χρυσίῳ Ωφαξ
Dan 10.5 (MT): ומתניו חגרים בכתם אופז

2. *"the eyes like flaming torches"*
Rev 1.14: καὶ οἱ ὀφθαλμοὶ αὐτοῦ ὡς φλὸξ πυρός
Dan 10.6 (LXX=Theod.): καὶ οἱ ὀφθαλμοὶ αὐτοῦ ὡσεὶ λαμπάδες πυρός
Dan 10.6 (MT): ועיניו כלפידי אש

3. *"the legs of burnished bronze"*
Rev 1.15: καὶ οἱ πόδες αὐτοῦ ὅμοιοι χαλκολιβάνῳ ὡς ἐν καμίνῳ πεπυρωμένης
Dan 10.6 (LXX): καὶ οἱ βραχίονες αὐτοῦ καὶ οἱ πόδες ὡσεὶ χαλκὸς ἐξαστράπτων
Dan 10.6 (MT): וזרעתיו ומרגלתיו כעין נחשת קלל

The use of such details specifically identified with the angel of Daniel 10 (i.e., Gabriel) in depicting the Christ of Revelation 1 must not be minimized: it is important support for the thesis that angelomorphic traditions significantly impacted early Christology.

Furthermore, these details of the angelophany in Daniel 10 are augmented with elements of the angelophany in Dan 7.13-14. The "one like a son of man" designation found in the angelophany of Dan 7.13 (MT: כבר אנש; LXX: ὡς υἱὸς ἀνθρώπου) is a centerpiece in

---

[6] E.g., Rev 1.13 has Christ in "a long robe" while the angel in Dan 10.5 is clothed in "white linen"; Rev 1.16 has Christ's face "bright like the sun in full force" while the angel of Dan 10.6 has a face "like lightning"; Rev 1.15 depicts Christ's voice "like the sound of many waters" while the angel's words in Dan 10.6 were "like the sound of the roar of a multitude". The fact that other texts were undoubtably influential will be discussed below.

the Christophany in Rev 1.13 (ὅμοιον υἱὸν ἀνθρώπου).⁷ Revelation 1 provides further evidence that the "one like a son of man" of Dan 7.13 could be and was identified with the angelomorphic "man" who appears in Daniel 8 and 10, and who is identified as the angel Gabriel (Dan 8.16; 9.21).⁸ Not only does the outward *form* of Christ in Revelation 1 align with the Gabriel in these Daniel texts, but also Christ's *function* as a prophetic revealer in Revelation 2-3.⁹ These observations lead to the pointed conclusion of A. Yarboro Collins: "[. . .] the evidence suggests that the author of Revelation considered Gabriel to be God's principal angel and the risen Christ to be identified with Gabriel".¹⁰

This conclusion, even though it may be correct, does not go far enough. The *theophany* in Ezekiel 1, because of its influence on the *angelophany* in Daniel 10, must not be overlooked as an important antecedent in the description of this Christophany in Revelation.¹¹ The Christ in Revelation 1 was not only understood as Gabriel (from Daniel), but as the Glory (from Ezekiel 1 and 8), the very man-like form of God. For example, the Christ of Rev 1.15 has "a voice like the sound of many waters".¹² This sound is found in two visions of the Glory in Ezekiel: in 1.24 it comes from the four living creatures (angels) who surround the divine throne, and in 43.2 it comes from the Glory himself.¹³ The linking of this detail associated with the Glory in Ezekiel to the Christ in Revelation 1 supports the interpretation that the seer understood Christ to be the Glory whom Ezekiel saw.¹⁴ Furthermore, the use of ὅμοιον υἱὸν

---

⁷ M. Casey has challenged the widespread position of Rev 1.13 dependence upon Dan. 7.13 by asserting that ὅμοιον υἱὸν ἀνθρώπου in Rev 1.13 and 14.14 is dependent upon Dan 10.16, 18; see *The Son of Man* (London: Hodder and Stoughton, 1979) 144. Such a position is difficult to defend given the link with the Ancient of Days of Dan 7.9 in Rev. 1.14 ("hair as white as wool") and the description of the "one like a son of man coming upon a cloud" (cf. Dan 7.13) in Rev 14.14.

⁸ See the discussion on 131-134 above.

⁹ This is in line with early Christian tradition that accorded Gabriel the role of *angelus interpres* (cf. Luke 1.26-38).

¹⁰ "The 'Son of Man' Tradition and the Book of Revelation", *The Messiah* (ed. J. H. Charlesworth; Philadelphia: Fortress, 1992) 558.

¹¹ For details supporting the dependence of Daniel 10 upon Ezekiel 1, see Rowland, "Vision of the Risen Christ", 2-4.

¹² These words are also used of the heavenly worship (cf. Rev 14.2; 19.6).

¹³ This tradition about the four living creatures is used in a similar manner in *Apoc. Ab.* 18.2-3 where a voice "like a voice of many waters, like a voice of the sea in uproar" beckons Abraham and Yahoel to worship.

¹⁴ This "sound of many waters" voice imagery is also applied to the voice

ἀνθρώπου in Rev 1.13 (instead of ὡς υἱὸς ἀνθρώπου from Dan 7.13) is probably due to the description of the Glory in Ezek 1.26 LXX: ὁμοίωμα ὡς εἶδος ἀνθρώπου.[15]

The influence of theophanies on the description of this Christophany is especially clear when it comes to the elements of Dan 7.9-12 that appear in Revelation 1.[16] The most prominent example is the description of the Christ of Rev 1.14 with "hair as white as wool". This is an undeniable allusion to the Ancient of Days in Dan 7.9 (cf. *1 En.* 46.1). Rowland has offered the most tenable explanation for how this distinctive characteristic of the Ancient of Days could be transferred to the one like a son of man:

> It seems likely that this transference of imagery from God to the Son of Man derives from a theological development in a variant found in the LXX version of Dan. vii. 13. In the Greek versions of this verse we find a bifurcating tradition with regard to the translation of the words עד עתיק יומיא. Theodotion follows the Masoretic Text and translates the Aramaic by ἕως τοῦ παλαιοῦ ἡμερῶν, whereas the LXX translates by ὡς παλαιὸς ἡμερῶν. The implication of the LXX reading is that the human figure is regarded as the embodiment of the divine, in so far as the characteristics of divinity have been transferred to him.[17]

Rowland goes on to emphasize that Revelation is not the only evidence of this divine characteristic present on an angelomorphic being. The exalted description of Yahoel's appearance in the *Apocalypse of Abraham* includes mention that "the hair of his head [was] like snow" (11.2).[18]

Another detail of the opening Christophany of Revelation points to the rich blend of angelophanic and theophanic details here: "his face was like the sun shining in full strength" (1.16). An early divine throne text, *1 En.* 14.20, describes the gown of the Great Glory as "shining more brightly than the sun". The face of the Great Glory, however, is not visible. Ezek 1.27 emphasizes the

---

from heaven in 14.1-5 and 19.1-8, but in each case there is a more extensive description of the voice. For a viable explanation of the use of a Christological attribute in these two texts, see Stuckenbruck, *Angel Veneration and Christology*, 222-226.

[15] Quispel, "Judaism, Judaic Christianity, and Gnosis", 50-51.
[16] See the discussion of Rowland, "The Vision of the Risen Christ", 1-11. Rowland argues that Ezekiel 1 directly influenced the portrayal in Daniel 7, and thus has indirect influence on Revelation 1.
[17] "Vision of the Risen Christ", 2-3.
[18] The Noahic addition of *1 Enoch* depicts Noah as miraculously born with "hair as white as wool" (106.2); see discussion on 158-159 above.

"brightness" around the Glory, but does not make reference to the sun. The overall *appearance* of an angel sometimes has the brightness of the sun (e.g., Abel and Dokiel in *T. Ab.* 12.5 and 13.1). Elsewhere it is more narrowly the *faces* of particular angels which are described in this manner (e.g., Eremiel in *Apoc. Zeph.* 6.11 and "the two men" who usher Enoch in *2 En.* 1.5) or their *eyes* (Michael in *Jos. Asen.* 14.9 and Noah in *1 En.* 106.2, 5).[19] This detail is an important link between Christ here and the angel in Rev 10.1.

There is one further aspect of the opening Christophany that is related to the Angelomorphic Christology presented later in the apocalypse. Christ declares to John that he has "the keys of Death and Hades" (1.18) and then towards the end of the apocalypse comes this scene which uses this same image:

> [20.1] Then I saw an angel coming down from heaven, holding in his hand the key of the bottomless pit and a great chain. [2] And he seized the dragon, that ancient serpent, who is the Devil and Satan, and bound him for a thousand years [. . .].

The implication of reading these texts in light of one another is that "the angel" of Rev 20.1 is Christ.[20]

The "one like a son of man" designation also appears in a scene that is less overtly Christological, namely Rev 14.14-16:

> [14] I looked, and there before me was a white cloud, and seated on the cloud was one like a son of man with a crown of gold on his head and a sharp sickle in his hand. [15] Then another angel came out of the temple and called in a loud voice to him who was sitting on the cloud, "Take your sickle and reap, because the time to reap has come, for the harvest of the earth is ripe". [16] So he who was seated on the cloud swung his sickle over the earth, and the earth was harvested.

This is a visionary realization of the prophetic request for the eschatological judgment in Joel 3.13 (MT 4.13):

> Put in the sickle, for the harvest is ripe. Go in, tread, for the wine press is full. The vats overflow, for their wickedness is great.

It has already been demonstrated from Daniel 7 that "one like a son of man" was used as a designation for an angelomorphic

---

[19] Other angelophanies mention faces shining with lightning (Gabriel in Dan 10.6) or chrysolite (Yahoel in *Apoc. Ab.* 11.2).

[20] Christ's binding or defeat of Satan is a strong NT tradition: Matt 12.29; Luke 10.17-18; John 12.31-32; 16.8, 11; 1 John 3.8; Heb 2.14; Mark 12.24-29; 3.22-27.

being. The angelomorphic depiction of this figure is visible in several details of the text. First, his reception of a command from an angel (14.15; cf. 14.17-18) portrays him as an angel functioning with the other six angels in this sequence (Rev 14.6, 8, 9, 15, 17, 18). Secondly, the imagery of being seated on a cloud and wearing a crown in Rev 14.14, joined with the designation "one like a son of man", recalls the judgment scene of Dan 7.13: "I saw one like a son of man coming with the clouds of heaven" (cf. Rev 1.7, "He [Jesus] is coming with the clouds"). Although the image of being *seated on* the cloud(s) is not present in Daniel, nevertheless the Synoptic Gospels record an amalgamation of the traditions in Dan 7.13 and Ps 110.1 in the words Jesus spoke to the High Priest: "You will see the Son of Man *seated* at the right hand of the Power *and coming on the clouds* of heaven".[21] Thirdly, the use of a "sickle" is based upon the prophecy of Joel 3.13, but the "sword" of the Destroying Angel traditions are probably related to this sickle imagery.[22] Lastly, the gigantic size of this figure is obvious: he harvests the whole earth with one swipe of his sickle (14.16).[23]

In addition to this angelomorphic designation and description, this figure appears to be identified explicitly as an angel through the reference to "*another* angel [ἄλλος ἄγγελος]" (14.15) immediately after this "one like a son of man" is described.[24] Either John understood the "one like a son of man" to be an angel in some respect, or he is making a general comment about "another angel" in light of the angels whom he has described *before* the "one like a son of man". The former appears to be the logical conclusion based upon three observations. First, "the one like a son of man" is the

---

[21] Mark 14.62 and Matt 26.64; cf. Luke 22.69. J. Schaberg asserts that the combination of being seated and coming on clouds draws on the imagery of the *Merkabah*; see "Mark 14.62: Early Christian Merkabah Imagery?", *Apocalyptic and the New Testament*, eds. J. Marcus and M. Soards (JSNTSup 24; Sheffield: Sheffield Academic Press, 1989), 69-94. Sir 24.3 states that Wisdom has a throne in the pillar of cloud. This image originates from the theophanic/angelophanic cloud of the Exodus. The "crown" and "sitting" imagery, however, are not exclusively christophanic or theophanic, as can be seen from the description of the 24 elders each wearing a gold crown and being seated on a throne (Rev 4.4).

[22] See Rev 1.16 and 19.15; cf. Wis 18.16.

[23] See the discussion of size on 32 above; cf. Rev 14.19.

[24] Charles drains the significance of this assertion by labeling 14.15-17 as an interpolation. He then interprets only the ἄλλος of the ἄλλος ἄγγελος in 14.18 as referring back to the Son of Man by translating it "another, an angel". The factor that controls this exegesis is stated here: "for nowhere throughout our author is the Son of Man conceived of as an angel"; see *Revelation*, 2.21.

closest and most natural antecedent to the phrase "another angel". Secondly, this "one like the son of man" comes in the middle of a sequence with six other angels (Rev 14.6, 8, 9, 15, 17, 18); thus, this figure would be the fourth angel in a sequence of seven. Thirdly, a similar phase is used in Rev 10.1 ("another mighty angel") for an angel who has a more theophanic description than that given to the "one like a son of man" in 14.14.[25]

In spite of these angelomorphic details, most scholars understand this harvesting angel to be a vision of Christ.[26] This conclusion is based primarily upon the designation "one like a son of man" in 14.14 which links this figure with the Christ of 1.13, who is described with the same designation, and with the Glory of Ezek 1.26.[27] Furthermore, it will now be demonstrated that Rev 14.14 is not the exclusive appearance of the angelomorphic Christ in the various scenes of the apocalypse proper (Rev 4.1-22.5).

B. *The Word of God and the Name of God*

An angelomorphic background is also discernable in the description of the rider on the white horse in Rev 19.11-16.[28] Note the imagery used in these verses:

> [12] His eyes are like blazing fire, and on his head are many crowns. He has a Name written on him that no one but he himself knows. [13] He is dressed in a robe dipped in blood and his name is the Word of God [ὁ λόγος τοῦ θεοῦ]. [14] The armies of heaven were following him, riding on white horses and dressed in fine linen, white, and clean. [15] Out of his mouth comes a sharp sword with which to strike down the nations.

---

[25] See Fossum, *Name of God*, 279 n.61.

[26] See the summary of scholarly opinions in Stuckenbruck, *Angel Veneration and Christology*, 240-245.

[27] Carrell supports the Christological identification of this figure and acknowledges its angelomorphic characteristics, but argues that this is an example of Christ depicted as *temporarily* assuming angelic form and functions; see *Jesus and the angels*, 241-246. Given the angelomorphic form of Christ in chapters 1-3, it is not accurate to speak of temporarily assuming angelic form and function in 14.14.

[28] The identification of this figure as Christ is clear. This is not the case with Rev 6.2 where the rider on the white horse is a false Christ; see A. Kerkeslager, "Apollo, Greco-Roman Prophecy, and the Rider on the White Horse in Rev 6:2", *JBL* 112 (1993) 116-121.

Five details are especially important in understanding the influence of angelomorphic traditions upon this depiction. First, the visual and titular description of this figure links him with the Christ of Revelation 1-3. In both depictions Christ has "eyes like blazing fire" (1.14;19.12; cf. 2.18) and out of his mouth comes "a sharp sword" (1.16; 19.15, 21; cf. 2.12, 16).[29] Christ as "the faithful and true witness" in 3.14 is pictured in 19.11 as the judge and warrior who is called "Faithful and True". The Lamb and this warrior/judge are both identified as the "King of Kings and Lord of Lords" (17.14; 19.16). These texts unite the starkly different angelomorphic and Lamb depictions of Christ.[30]

Second, this text presents Christ as the possessor of a Hidden Name. As discussed previously, Exod 23.21 closely links the Tetragrammaton יהוה (i.e., the Divine Name) with Angel of the Lord traditions as well as other exalted angel traditions. This, most assuredly, is the Hidden Name which Christ bears according to Rev 19.12.[31] This interpretation is supported by the context which gives several titles or names by which Christ is identified: Faithful, True, the Word of God, King of Kings, Lord of Lords. None of these, obviously, is the Hidden Name he possesses which only he knows.[32]

The primary support for this interpretation is the other references to "the Name of God" in Revelation:

> [3.12] He who conquers, I will make him a pillar in the temple of my God; never shall he go out of it, and I will write on him the name of my God, and the name of the city of my God, the new

---

[29] Rev 1.16 and 2.14 both have the adjective "double-edged" (cf. Heb. 4.12-13). This sword of judgment is prominently featured in the Songs of Moses (Exod 15.9; Deut 32.24, 41, 42; cf. Gen 3.24). It is closely linked with angelomorphic traditions, esp. those developing about the Destroying Angel who wields a sword (Num 22.21-38; Josh 5.13-15; 2 Sam 24.16-17/1 Chr 21.15-16; 2 Kgs 19.35/Isa 37.33-37; Wis 18.15). A much different metaphorical meaning of "the sword of the Spirit" as "the word of God" is visible in Eph 6.17.

[30] Although the Lamb is the dominant Christological depiction in this document, the relationship between the angelomorphic and Lamb elements of this apocalypse has not been widely studied. For a preliminary attempt, see Stuckenbruck, *Angel Veneration and Christology*, 261-265.

[31] For further discussion of the Hidden or Secret Name, see Fossum, *Image of the Invisible God*, 111-116, and Segal, *Two Powers in Heaven*, 212-213. Neither scholar mentions the significance of Justin's remarks about the speaking of the Divine Name at Baptisms; see *I Apol.* 61.

[32] Those who assert that the Hidden Name of 19.12 is "the Word of God" in 19.13 miss the whole point of this text.

> Jerusalem which comes down from my God out of heaven, and my own new name.
>
> [14.1] Then I looked, and lo, on Mount Zion stood the Lamb, and with him a hundred and forty-four thousand who had his name and his Father's name written on their foreheads.
>
> [22.4] There shall no more be anything accursed, but the throne of God and of the Lamb shall be in it, and his servants shall worship him; they shall see his face, and his name shall be on their foreheads.

These texts evince the prominence of Name theology in Baptism where the symbol of the Divine Name was marked on the foreheads of the initiate.[33] The most logical way to understand the differences in these three texts—namely, the mention of one, two, or three names on the forehead—is to see these as the same name: the Divine Name.[34]

A third detail indicating the background of this depiction is his identification as ὁ λόγος τοῦ θεοῦ, a name which has significant links with angelomorphic traditions, especially "the All-Powerful Word" depicted in Wisdom of Solomon. The probability of a religio-historical relationship between the traditions found in Wis 18.14-25 and Rev 19.11-16 is supported by the graphic portrayal in both texts of the Word as *a warrior wielding a "sharp sword" who carries out God's "wrath"*: Wisdom 18 depicts the Word as the Destroyer who slew the firstborn of Egypt and delivered the devastating plague of Numbers 16, while Revelation 19 speaks about the Word of God as the leader of the eschatological battle.[35]

---

[33] See Daniélou, *Theology of Jewish Christianity*, 154-157. The placing of the Divine Name in Baptism is the idea behind the "sealing" mentioned in Rev 7.3 and 9.4. This sealing draws on the imagery of the marking the forehead of God's faithful people before the Passover style purge in Jerusalem that is depicted in Ezekiel's vision (9.4).

[34] The same idea is found in the baptismal formula: "In the Name of the Father, and of the Son, and of the Holy Spirit" (Matt 28.19); the (single) Divine Name is linked to the three persons (cf. Rev 3.12). The Baptism "in the Name of Jesus Christ" mentioned in Acts is not an alternate baptismal formula, but is a brief way of referring to Baptism in the Divine Name which Jesus possesses (e.g., Acts 10.48; cf. Rev 22.4).

[35] The linguistic relationships are striking: the use of "Word" (λόγος in both Wis 18.15 and Rev 19.13), "sharp sword" (ξίφος ὀξύ in Wis 18.15 and ῥομφαία ὀξεῖα in Rev 19.15), and "wrath" (τῆς ὀργῆς in both Wis 18.25 and Rev 19.15). The sharp sword *coming out his mouth* imagery obviously is built upon the opening Christophany (1,16; cf. 2.12, 16). See also T. Longman, "The Divine Warrior: The New Testament Use of an Old Testament Motif", *WTJ* 44 (1982) 290-307.

"The Word" as depicted in John 1.1-18 is not in immediate view here, yet neither is it absent from Revelation: Rev 3.14 calls the "faithful and true witness" (cf. 19.11) also "the Beginning of God's Creation" (cf. 21.6).[36] Furthermore, it should also be noted that there is a relationship between the reference to the Hidden Name and the name "the Word of God" or "the Word", since the creative Word was considered in some Jewish circles to be none other than יהוה, the Name of God.[37]

A fourth piece of evidence that this portrayal of Rev 19.11-16 is grounded in angelomorphic traditions is its relationship to Isaiah 63:

> [1] Who is this who comes from Edom, in crimsoned garments from Bozrah, he that is glorious in his apparel, marching in the greatness of his strength? "It is I, announcing vindication, mighty to save." [2] Why is thy apparel red, and thy garments like his that treads the wine press? [3] "I have trodden the wine press alone, and from the peoples no one was with me; I trod them in my anger and trampled them in my wrath; their lifeblood is sprinkled upon my garments, and I have stained all my raiment."

There is no question among scholars that this text provided some of the imagery found in the vision of Christ in Rev 19.11-16.[38] What scholars have not seen is how this portrayal of YHWH as a warrior in 63.1-6 could be interpreted as the same figure who is discussed in the verses which immediately follow: YHWH's "Angel of the Presence" who both protected and punished Israel following the Exodus (Isa 63.7-14).[39] Therefore, the use of the imagery from Isa 63.1-3 did not necessarily require the transfer of a description of YHWH to Christ; it could be seen as the adaption of imagery

---

[36] This astute observation is made by J. P. M. Sweet, *Revelation* (Pelican; Philadelphia: Westminster, 1979) 283. "The Beginning of God's Creation" calls Prov 8.22 to mind; see: Burney, "Christ as the APXH of Creation", 160-177; Daniélou, *Theology of Jewish Christianity*, 166-168; and G. Beale, "The Old Testament Background of Rev 3.14", *NTS* 42 (1996) 133-152. This idea is closely related to another title given Christ with obvious angel connotations: "the Morning Star" (Rev 2.28; 22.16; cf. 2 Pet 1.19; Isa 14.12-14). See also M. Moore, "Jesus Christ: Superstar", *NovT* 24 (1982) 82-91.

[37] See discussion on 74-76 above.

[38] The blood-stained robe, the treading the winepress of judgment, the mention of wrath and anger, and the use of Isa 63.2-3 in the imagery of Rev 14.19-20 all indicate a certain relationship; see the analysis of J. Fekkes, *Isaiah and Prophetic Traditions in the Book of Revelation* (JSNTSup 93; Sheffield: Sheffield Academic Press, 1994) 197-199.

[39] See the discussion of this text on 117-119 above.

already attributed to YḤWH's angel, whom John understood to be Christ.

The fifth angelomorphic aspect of this vision is the portrayal of Christ as the leader of the "armies of heaven" in battle (19.14). The armies that he leads could be made up of angels since they are identified as the army of "heaven" and are dressed in white linen (cf. Mark 8.38; 13.27; Matt 25.31). It is more probable, however, that this is a reference to the faithful saints or martyrs in heaven clothed in white as it is elsewhere in Revelation (7.9-17). This leadership role of a heavenly army is usually held by the Angel of the Lord (Josh 5.13) or an archangel such as Michael or Gabriel.[40] For example, earlier in this apocalypse Michael leads the angelic forces in the assault against Satan (Rev 12.7-9). These five observations lead to one conclusion: This picture of Christ in Rev 19.11-16 clearly draws on angelomorphic traditions, some of which were already introduced in the opening Christophany.

C. *The Mighty Angel with the Scroll*

Scholarly interest and debate has especially centered on the Mighty Angel of Revelation 10, since the angelomorphic being depicted there has at times been interpreted as Christ, even though this figure is overtly labeled an angel (10.1: ἄλλον ἄγγελον ἰσχυρόν "another mighty angel"). The unique combination of symbols used to describe this angel blurs the lines between calling this an angelophany, a Christophany, or even a theophany:

> [10.1] Then I saw another mighty angel coming down from heaven. He was robed in a cloud, with a rainbow above his head; his face was like the sun, and his legs were like fiery pillars. [2] He was holding a little scroll, which lay open in his hand. He planted his right foot on the sea and his left foot on the land, [3] and he gave a loud shout like the roar of a lion. When he shouted, the voices of the seven thunders spoke. [4] And when the seven thunders spoke, I was about to write; but I heard a voice from heaven say, "Seal up what the seven thunders have said and do not write it down." [5] Then the angel I had seen standing on the sea and on the land raised his right hand to heaven. [6] And he swore by him who lives for ever and ever, who created the heavens and all that is in it, and the sea and all that is in it, and said, "There will be no more delay!"

---

[40] See discussion on 124-134 above.

While the Christological identification of the figures already discussed in this chapter enjoy substantial scholarly consensus, such is not the case for this Mighty Angel in Revelation 10.[41] Most post-Reformation commentators, as well as the three extant Greek commentaries from the first millenium, interpret this angel as a created angel who has been given some theophanic characteristics to highlight his authority.[42] Others assert that this is not Christ, but the revelatory angel of God and Jesus (cf. Rev. 1.1; 22.6, 16).[43] Nevertheless, a Christological interpretation of this figure does have ancient precedent among the Latin Fathers, beginning with the earliest extant commentary on Revelation by Victorinus (Bishop of Pettau in Pannonia), which probably dates from the late third century.[44] Among several modern adherents of this Christological interpretation, no one has argued more vigorously and succintly in identifying this angel as Christ than Robert Gundry.[45]

There are several details used to describe this angel that must be examined with some caution because they do not *a priori* support a Christological interpretation. For example, several characteristics of this angel are not distinctively Christological: he "comes down from heaven", is "clothed with a cloud", "has feet like fiery pillars", and a voice "like seven thunders". Therefore, these details neither affirm, *nor deny*, that this angel is Christ.[46] Nevertheless, if these general characteristics help distinguish this angel from other angels, they can lend some support to a Christological interpretation.

The central detail that supports a Christological interpretation is the rainbow on the head of this angel. The detailing of the rainbow over the throne of God in Rev 4.3 demonstrates the author's awareness concerning the significance of this detail. This reference, as well as the one in Rev 10.1, both point back to Ezek 1.28 where the Glory appears as an angelomorphic "man" and one of his distinguishing characteristics is a rainbow:

---

[41] For a history of interpretation, see L. Brighton, "The Angel of Revelation: An Angel of God and an Icon of Jesus Christ" (Ph.D. diss., St. Louis University, 1991), 7-13.
[42] Brighton, "The Angel of Revelation", 7-13.
[43] E.g., Brighton, "The Angel of Revelation", 180-211, and Carrell, *Jesus and the angels*, 130-138.
[44] See note 2 above.
[45] "Angelomorphic Christology in Revelation", 662-678.
[46] This point asserted several times by Gundry in his "Angelomorphic Christology in Revelation".

Like the bow in a cloud on a rainy day, so was the appearance of the brightness round about. Such was the appearance of the likeness of the Glory of YHWH.

As noted in the analysis of Revelation 1, the visionary John was clearly aware of Ezek 1.26-28. Thus, he would be aware that any figure whom he described with a rainbow would be understood as divine. While many of the other details do not speak conclusively, the ascription of a rainbow on this angel leads to the conclusion that this figure was understood to be a depiction of the Glory.[47] Some may argue from Ezekiel 1 and Revelation 4 that this angel cannot be understood as the Glory because he is not depicted on the throne. It has already been demonstrated, however, that the Glory *does appear apart from the throne*.[48] Furthermore, such a characteristic on an exalted angel depicted as the Glory apart from the throne is seen with Yahoel in the *Apoc. Ab.* 11.3: "And a kidaris (was) on his head, its look that of a rainbow".[49] The gigantic size of this angel also speaks of his exalted status.[50]

The description that the angel's face "was like the sun" (10.1) is a second detail strongly supporting a Christological interpretation. It is not the appearance of this angel's face that is distinctive, but the fact that the author has previously described the appearance of the Glorified Christ in a similar manner: "his face was like the sun shining in its power" (Rev 1.16). As happens with the reference to "the one like a son of man" in 14.14, the appearance of this angel's face points the reader/hearer back to that angelomorphic being who has already been described in this manner: the Risen Christ.

The scroll imagery in Revelation 10 also supports a Christological interpretation of this angel.[51] This position is based upon the relationship between this scroll and the scroll that was taken by the Lamb (Christ) earlier in the apocalypse in order that its seven seals would be opened (Rev 5.2, 3, 4, 5, 9).[52] Once the Lamb took the

---

[47] This may be interpreted as some kind of "downsized" rainbow from the one that surrounds the divine throne, as noted in Rev 4.3. It must be remembered, however, that this angel is gigantic and a rainbow around his head is a very substantial rainbow.
[48] E.g., the man-like Glory appears apart from the throne in Exod 33.17-34.8 and Ezek 3.23, 8.2; see 80-84 above.
[49] See discussion on 142-144 above.
[50] See discussion on 32 above.
[51] See argument of Gundry, "Angelomophic Christology in Revelation", 665-666.
[52] The variation in Greek terms for the scrolls is the primary argument

scroll, he opened it seal by seal (Rev 6.1, 2, 5, 7, 9, 12; 8.1). This now-opened scroll appears to be the same "open" scroll that the Mighty Angel has in his hand (10.2). Notice that the Voice from heaven commands John to *seal* his own written scroll (10.4), but to take this open scroll: "Go take the scroll that lies *open* in the hand of the angel" (10.8). The imagery of eating the scroll and then prophesying most certainly draws on Ezek 2.8-3.11. There the Glory of YHWH, who appears as a man, hands the scroll to the prophet. The identification of Christ as the Glory of Ezekiel 1 in the opening Christophany makes a similar identification here probable. What Ezekiel is to prophesy, however, was shown to him after eating the scroll, whereas John has already seen the scroll opened and then eats it now because he "must prophesy again" (10.11). As in the opening Christophany where the angelomorphic Christ appeared to commission John to write the prophecy imparted in the letters and vision of heaven (1.3, 11, 19), in Revelation 10 the angelomorphic Christ appears *again* (10.1) to commission John to prophesy *again* (10.11). This scroll of prophecy is not imparted by an angel unknown to John; it is imparted by Christ himself (cf. Rev 1.1).

The influence of Gabriel traditions from Daniel upon the description of the opening Christophany has already been demonstrated. The Gabriel tradition from Daniel 12 appears to have influenced the portrait of the Mighty Angel swearing in Rev 10.6:

> [Dan 12.7] The man clothed in linen, who was upstream, raised his right hand and his left hand toward heaven. And I heard him swear by the One who lives forever that it would be a time, two times, and half a time, and that when the shatterng of the power of the holy people comes to an end, all these things would be accomplished.

This act of swearing by God has been viewed as evidence precluding a Christological interpretation.[53] While such an action certainly poses some distinction between this angel and God, it does not preclude an interpretation of this angel as Christ. Moreover, support

---

used against equating the scrolls in Revelation 5 and 10. Against such a position Gundry points out that both βιβλαρίδιον (5.1, 2, 3, 4, 5, 7, 8, 9) and βιβλίον (10.2) are diminutives of βίβλος. Furthermore, he notes the variation in this document between βιβλίον (13.8 [C]; 17.8; 20.12; 21.27) and βίβλος (3.5; 13.8 [𝔓47, ℵ, et.al.]; 20.15) with reference to the Scroll of Life. See his "Angelomophic Christology in Revelation", 665-666.

[53] E.g., R. Mounce, *The Book of Revelation* (NICNT; Grand Rapids: Eerdmans, 1977) 207.

for such an action accorded to a divine being is found in the Song of Moses (Deut 32.40-41). There, in a manner similar to Revelation 10, it is a divine action of God himself signaling his judgment:

> [40] For I lift up my hand to heaven and swear: As I live forever, [41] when I whet my flashing sword and my hand takes hold on judgment; I will take vengeance on my adversaries, and will repay those who hate me.

The Christological interpretation of this angel is significant for this study, not only on account of the use of angelomorphic characteristics and functions, but especially because of the overt use of angel terminology to identify this figure as "another mighty angel". This evidence should neither be ignored nor marginalized; it points to how Jewish angelology influenced the portrayal of Revelation's Christology. Furthermore, in light of the rich heritage of angelic theophanies in the OT and Jewish apocalyptic literature, this angelomorphic Christology only serves to exalt the divine status of Christ, who is clearly paired with God throughout Revelation.[54]

D. *God and His Angel*

The Revelation to John begins with a prologue indicating the content of this document was communicated to John by means of an angel:

> Ἀποκάλυψις Ἰησοῦ Χριστοῦ ἣν ἔδωκεν αὐτῷ ὁ θεὸς δεῖξαι τοῖς δούλοις αὐτοῦ ἃ δεῖ γενέσθαι ἐν τάχει, καὶ ἐσήμανεν ἀποστείλας διὰ τοῦ ἀγγέλου αὐτοῦ τῷ δούλῳ αὐτοῦ Ἰωάννῃ, ὃς ἐμαρτύρησεν τὸν λόγον τοῦ θεοῦ καὶ τὴν μαρτυρίαν Ἰησοῦ Χριστοῦ ὅσα εἶδεν.

The difficult task in translating this sentence is determining the subject of ἐσήμανεν and the referent(s) to the many personal pronouns, which are mostly ambiguous from a purely syntactical analysis; other than the first pronoun, they can refer either to God or to Jesus Christ. The subject of the sentence, however, is clearly ὁ θεός. That God is the one who sent his angel is confirmed in Rev 22.6: "The Lord, the God of the spirits of the prophets, sent *his angel*

---

[54] Such pairing is found in Rev 6.17; 7.10; 11.15; 12.10; 14.4; 20.6; 21.22; 21.23; 22.1; 22.3. For discussions of this pairing as a reflection of the author's monotheistic concerns, see Stuckenbruck, *Angel Veneration and Christology*, 261-265, and Bauckham, "The Worship of Jesus", 330-331.

to show his servants what must happen soon". Thus, the context favors seeing God as the referent of the ambiguous pronouns and the subject of ἐσήμανεν. With this understanding, a possible translation of this prologue reads:

> An apocalypse of Jesus Christ, which God gave him [Jesus Christ] to show his [God's] servants what must happen soon and he [God] made it known by sending his [God's] angel to his [God's] servant John, who [John] testifies to the word of God, namely to the testimony of Jesus Christ, [that is] to everything he [John] saw.

It is intriguing to consider if Jesus is the angel God sent to John.[55] Support for this conclusion is found in the two accounts where Christ imparts revelation. The first angelomorphic figure whom John encounters in 1.13-3.22 appears to be the angelomorphic Christ who imparts the seven letters. Furthermore, the angelomorphic Christ in Revelation 10 imparts the opened scroll to John in order that he may prophesy again.

This interpretation of Christ as God's Angel in 1.1, however, faces some substantial problems. Only a short while after 22.6 makes mention of God sending his angel, John records "Jesus" speaking in the first person as the one who sent the angel: "I, Jesus, have sent *my angel* to give you this testimony for the churches" (22.16). This indicates that Jesus does not consider himself to be the angel sent; rather, he too, like God, has sent this angel. This angel is God's angel and at the same time the angel of Jesus. Thus, the word of this angel is *both* the word of God and the testimony of Jesus (1.2).[56] He even speaks as Jesus in the first person in 22.7, which appears to be one of the reasons John falls to worship him (22.8). In light of Jesus' words in 22.16, it is very doubtful that John understood Jesus to be the referent of "God's angel" in 1.1. The evidence can be graphically summarized as follows:

---

[55] This position is argued by E. Schmidt, "Die Christologische Interpretation als das Grundlengende der Apokalypse", *TQ* 140 (1960) 257-290, esp. 262; see also Gundry, "Angelomorphic Christology in Revelation", 674-678. Gundry takes this attempt too far by interpreting several angels in Revelation Christologically.

[56] See J. Ramsey Michaels, "Revelation 1.19 and the Narrative Voices of the Apocalypse", *NTS* 37 (1991) 604-620, esp. 619, and also Gundry, "Angelomorphic Christology in Revelation", 674-678.

Text	Sender	Messenger	Recipient(s)
1.1a	God ——→	Jesus ——→	his servants
1.1b	He (God or Jesus)–>	his angel ——→	his servant John
22.6	God ——→	his angel ——→	his servants
22.16	Jesus ——→	his angel ——→	John for the churches
Thus,	God/Jesus ——→	their angel ——→	John and other servants

The natural question arises: Who, then, is this angel? Answers usually center around the *angelus interpres* found in 17.1-19.10 and 21.9-22.6. This angel is similarly identified at the start of both sequences: "one of seven angels who had the seven bowls" (17.1) and "one of the seven angels who had the seven bowls full of the seven last plagues" (21.9). Loren Stuckenbruck has done an extensive form-critical study of these textual sequences in the context of the angelic worship refusal tradition and notes the following parallel form in these texts[57]:

> The Invitation (17.1/21.9) "Come, I will show you . . ."
> The Movement (17.3/21.10) "And he carried me away in the Spirit"
> The Revelatory Activity (17.6-18/21.15-17; 21.1) Babylon/New Jerusalem
> The Concluding Speech (19.9/22.6) "These words are true . . ."
> John's Response (19.10a/22.8b) "I fell down at his feet to worship . . ."
> The Angel's Refusal (19.10b/22.9) "Do not do it. . .Worship God!"

This angel identifies himself in both refusals as "a fellow servant with you and your brothers" (19.10; 22.9). This qualified identification and the refusal of worship unmistakably distinguishes these angelophanies from the opening Christophany where the Risen Christ responds to John's prostration with: "Do not fear! I AM the First and the Last" (1.17). The significance of John's attempt to worship this revealing angel, however, should not be dismissed. Even though he is not to be worshiped like Christ along with God, nevertheless he is an angel of substantial significance whom John thought worthy of worship.

In fact, Rev 15.5-8 depicts him as one of the seven angels who wear shining linen and golden girdles and come out of the heavenly temple from the very presence of the divine throne

---

[57] *Angel Veneration and Christology*, 245-261. Stuckenbruck argues that the refusal tradition is used in Revelation to safeguard monotheism against an exalted view of angelic mediation and to legitimate the prophetic message.

room, which was filled with smoke from the Glory of God and his Power (the Lamb):

> [5] After this I looked, and the temple of the tent of witness in heaven was opened, [6] and out of the temple came the seven angels with the seven plagues, robed in pure bright linen, and their breasts girded with golden girdles. [7] And one of the four living creatures gave the seven angels seven golden bowls full of the wrath of God who lives for ever and ever; [8] and the temple was filled with smoke from the Glory of God and from his Power, and no one could enter the temple until the seven plagues of the seven angels were ended.

Interpreters readily acknowledge that the (Holy) Spirit is depicted in Revelation as the sevenfold Spirit who is before God's throne (1.4; 3.1; 4.5; 5.6; cf. Isa 11.2). This is especially clear from terminology in the "Trinitarian" greeting of 1.4:

> χάρις ὑμῖν καὶ εἰρήνη ἀπὸ ὁ ὢν καὶ ὁ ἦν καὶ ὁ ἐρχόμενος καὶ ἀπὸ τῶν ἑπτὰ πνευμάτων ἃ ἐνώπιον τοῦ θρόνου αὐτοῦ καὶ ἀπὸ Ἰησοῦ Χριστοῦ
> (Grace to you and peace from the One who is and who is to come, and from the Seven Spirits which are before his [God's] throne, and from Jesus Christ).

Rev 4.5 visually depicts the Spirit as seven torches of fire that burn before the throne (4.5; cf. Exod 40.25). The sevenfold Spirit is also linked closely with the Lamb (Christ) who has seven horns and seven eyes which are said to be "the seven spirits of God sent out into all the earth" (Rev 5.6). While the sevenfold gifts of the Spirit in Isa 11.2 form some of the basis for this pneumatology, the depictions of the Spirit in the Apocalypse are primarily an exegesis of Zech 4.1-14 where the Lord assures the prophet in a vision that he will conquer "not by might, nor by power, but by my Spirit" (Zech 4.6).[58] This vision to Zechariah depicts a golden lampstand with seven lamps which are interpreted as "the eyes of YHWH, which range through the whole earth" (Zech 4:10b).[59] The text of Zechariah clearly impacted the visual depiction of the Spirit in Revelation.

---

[58] See esp. R. Bauckham, *The Theology of the Book of Revelation* (Cambridge: CUP, 1993) 110-112.

[59] The specifications and construction of the seven branched lampstand in the temple is detailed in Exod 25.31-40 and 37.17-24. It is probable that this lampstand took on a much more significant role as a visible representation of God's presence in post-exilic Judah due to the absence of the Ark of the Covenant.

What interpreters have not seen consistently is the identification of this sevenfold spirit with the seven angels before the throne featured several times in Revelation.[60] Richard Bauckham, for example, argues against such an identification:

> The seven Spirits, called in 1:4 'the Seven Spirits who are before [God's] throne', have sometimes been identified, not as the divine Spirit, but as the seven principal angels who, in Jewish angelology, stand in the presence of God in heaven (e.g. Tob. 12:15). But Revelation itself refers to these seven angels (8:2) in terms quite different from the way it refers to these seven Spirits. Moreover, although the term 'spirit' could certainly be used of angels (as frequently in the Dead Sea Scrolls), it very rarely has this meaning in early Christian literature and never in Revelation.[61]

Bauckham does not provide evidence for his assertion that there is a sharp distinction in Revelation between the seven spirits and the seven principal angels. Rev. 8:2 does not indicate a sharp distinction between spirits and angels; it actually supports the view that the seven spirits are the seven principal angels since these angels are depicted as occupying the same privileged position given the seven spirits: "Then I saw *the seven angels who stand before God* [. . .]".[62] These seven are the angels who ring out the trumpets (Rev 8.2-11.19) and appear to be the same seven who later exit the throne room (Rev 15.5-8) to pour out the seven plagues (Rev 16.1-21).[63] The actions of these seven angels as they go about the earth appear to fit the description of the seven spirits whom "God sent out into all the earth" (Rev 5.6).[64] Furthermore, contrary to Bauckham's assertion,

---

[60] E. Schwiezer finds the religio-historical antecedent for the sevenfold Spirit in the seven archangels of Jewish Literature; see his "πνεῦμα", *TDNT* 6.450 and "Die sieben Geister in d. Apk.", *ET* 11 (1951/52) 506. Schwiezer stops short of concluding that the sevens spirits are the seven principal angels in Revelation. F. F. Bruce considers this possibility, but then concludes that John simply uses the seven lamps and seven eyes from Zechariah as symbols for the one Spirit; see "The Spirit in the Apocalypse", *Christ and Spirit in the New Testament*, (eds. B. Lindars and S. Smalley; Cambridge: CUP, 1973) 333-344.

[61] *Theology of Revelation*, 110.

[62] The presence of the sevenfold Spirit and the Lamb (5.6) before the throne is similar to the depiction of the Beloved (Christ) and the Angel of the Holy Spirit before the throne in *Ascension of Isaiah* (9.33-42).

[63] See the interrelationships between these two ideas and their background in G. Dix, "The Seven Archangels and the Seven Spirits", *JTS* 28 (1927) 245-250. Note the objections to this that force Charles to assign this greeting to the hand of an interpolator; see his *Revelation*, 1.11-12.

[64] Bauckham's sharp distinction between the Seven Spirits (whose activities are in the world) and the Spirit (who is active in the Church) is not

the Spirit is identified as an angel in several early Christian texts, including the two depictions of John being carried by an angel when he is "in the Spirit"[65]:

> [17.1] Then one of the seven angels who had the seven bowls came and said to me, "Come, I will show you the judgment of the great harlot [. . .]. [3] And he carried me away in the Spirit into the wilderness [. . .].

> [21.9] Then came one of the seven angels who had the seven bowls full of the seven last plagues, and spoke to me, saying, "Come, I will show you the Bride, the wife of the Lamb." [10] And in the Spirit he carried me away to a great, high mountain, and showed me the holy city Jerusalem coming down out of heaven from God.

Therefore, this evidence leads to the conclusion that these seven angels, both individually and corporately, should be understood as manifestations of the Holy Spirit.[66]

It seems odd that Rev 1.1 speaks of God sending his angel (the Spirit) to impart revelation and then this angel does not appear in action until 17.1.[67] One would expect that this angel would be the

---

apparent from the document; see *Theology of Revelation*, 115.

[65] It is puzzling that Bauckham would assert that identification of a spirit as an angel happens "very rarely in early Christian literature". Five examples will suffice. Acts 8.26-29 identifies the figure that speaks to Philip as both the Angel of the Lord and the Spirit. The *Ascension of Isaiah* unites these two ideas very prominently in its frequent depictions of "the Angel of the Spirit" (3.15; 4.21; 9.36, 39, 40; 10.4; 11.4, 33) as does the *Shepherd of Hermas*, especially in the figure of "the Angel of the Prophetic Spirit" (*Man.* XI.9). Elchesai speaks of the Son of God as a huge angel, who has a female counterpart, the Holy Spirit (in Hippolytus, *Ref.* 9.13.2-3). Origen identified Christ and the Holy Spirit as two supreme Angels of the Presence through a creative exegesis of Isa 6.3 (*Princ.* I.3.4).

[66] This is seldom emphasized by commentators. An exception is G. Quispel, *The Secret Book of Revelation* (New York: McGraw-Hill, 1979) 35. For further discussion of Angel Pneumatology, see Quispel, "Genius and Spirit", 155-169. The refusal of worship by the *angelus interpres* (19.10; 22.9) does not preclude the identification of this angel as the Holy Spirit since the foci of worship in Revelation is God and the Lamb who now shares the throne. Furthermore, I am not asserting that all the angels in Revelation are manifestations of the Holy Spirit. There is a distinction between the seven angels before the throne (8.2; 15.6) and other angels who sometimes act alone or are grouped in fours or sevens, as can be seen in these examples: 8.3-5 refers to an angel who independently handles the golden censer; 9.13-14 mentions the four angels bound at the Euphrates; 14.6-20 has a sequence of 7 angels which includes Christ as the fourth angel.

[67] Bauckham argues that the Spirit is distinct from the chain of revelation mentioned in 1:1 (God - Christ - Angel - John); see *Theology of Revelation*, 116. In early Christian contexts of revelation, however, the Holy Spirit faciliates the revelation, even when numerous angelomorphic figures are involved; see

first figure mentioned in conjunction with the first vision. This, in fact, is what happens. Upon examining the opening Christophany, the first figure who is mentioned is the Spirit: "On the Lord's Day I [John] was in the Spirit and I heard behind me a loud voice like a trumpet who said, 'Write what you see and send it to the seven churches'" (1.10-11). John then turns "to see the Voice" (1.12) and sees the "one like a son of man" in all his splendor (1.13) who identifies himself as the Risen Christ (1.18). Some commentators hurriedly link the Voice with the one like a son of man.[68] This voice "like a trumpet", however, should be distinguished from the Christ's voice which is "like the sound of rushing water" (1.15). The hypostatic Voice in 1.12 clearly does not belong to Christ.

The Voice is the Spirit who facilitates this vision of Christ. This conclusion is based upon the following observations. First, after John has heard the different voice of the Risen Christ ("like the sound of rushing waters") dictate the seven letters, he sees the open door and again hears "the voice I had first heard speaking to me like a trumpet" (4.1). Such a distinguishing remark precludes interpreting the Voice in 1.10 as that of Christ. Second, although traditions about the Voice in apocalyptic literature are by no means uniform, the understanding of the Voice in 1.10 as the Spirit is supported by a clear link between a voice and the Spirit in Rev 14.13: "Then I heard *a voice from heaven say*, 'Write: Blessed are the dead who die in the Lord from now on. Yes', *says the Spirit*, 'they will rest from their labor and their deeds will follow them'". Rather than seeing these messages as being spoken by two different figures, it is more understandable to view them as spoken by the same figure who is identified as both "a voice from heaven" and "the Spirit".[69] Third, the lack of an overt explanation that the

---

the discussion of this phenomenon on 220-225 above.

[68] J.H. Charlesworth, in the most substantial and helpful discussion of this topic, laments other interpreters' lack of attention to the Voice as an hypostasis and then (mistakenly) interprets its use in Revelation as Christological; see "The Jewish Roots of Christology: The Discovery of the Hypostatic Voice", *SJT* 39 (1986) 19-41.

[69] "Voice" (ἡ φωνή) is used frequently by John as he records his visionary experience. Although there is no absolute pattern how and with whom these voices are identified, there are some general patterns. Most occurances of the noun have some form of adjectival qualifier. The majority of individual angels as well as the whole company of angels are frequently described as speaking or singing with a "loud voice" (5.2, 12; 6.10; 7.2, 10; 14.7, 9, 15, 18; 19.1, 17) or as "a loud voice in heaven" (11.15; 12.10-12). Some exceptions: one angel is described as speaking with "a voice of thunder" (6.1); an eagle

Voice of 1.10 and 4.1 is God's/Jesus' angel (i.e., the Spirit) may indicate an awareness of the religio-historical tradition of the Voice being understood as the Spirit.[70] It is widely acknowledged that Ezekiel's visionary experience had a pervasive influence on how the visionary John recorded his apocalypse.[71] One of the similar ideas found in both documents is the understanding of the Voice as the Spirit who both enters and transports the visionary:

> [1.28] I heard the voice of one speaking and he said to me, "Son of man, stand on your feet and I will speak with you." [2.1] And when he spoke to me, the Spirit entered into me and set me on my feet; and I heard him speaking to me.
>
> [3.14] The Spirit lifted me up and took me away.

---

speaks with a loud voice (8:13); and the company of angels is described as "the voice of harpists playing their harps" (14.2; 18.22) as well as the sound of many waters/thunders (14.2; 19.6). Christ is identified with a "voice like the sound of many waters" (1.15; 3.20; cf. 14.2; 19.6) and also with "a loud voice, like a lion roaring" (10.3; cf. 5.5) which causes thunder (10.3; cf. 6.1; 14.2). His voice also appears to be described as "a loud voice coming from the temple, from the throne" (16.17; cf. 16.1; 19.5; 21.3-4). Based upon the identification of "the voice from heaven" as "the Spirit" in 14.13, the presence of this designation elsewhere can be interpreted as the voice of the Spirit (10.4, 8; 18.4). This interpretation fits with what the voice from heaven/the Spirit says since this voice commands John to write (14.13) or to seal up his writing (10.4) or to take the scroll (10.8) or to ascend to heaven (11.12; cf. 18.4). These specific commands of the Spirit/voice from heaven give additional warrant for identifying the voice of the opening Christophany, who commands John to write what he sees in a book (1.10-11) and to ascend (4.1), as none other than the Spirit. This functional link with the Spirit is also apparent with the *angelus interpres* who commands John to write (19.9) and not to seal up the words of the prophecy (22.10). One further significant link between the voice described as "like a trumpet" (1.10; 4.1) with the seven spirits/angels is the fact that the seven principal angels are given trumpets in the course of the apocalypse and they do blow them (8.2-15.19).

[70] Cf. *Ascen. Is.* 6.6-7.8; *Apoc. Sedr.* 2.1-5; see Charlesworth, "Jewish Roots of Christology", 24-37, who gives other examples of the so-called hypostatic Voice in literature. Also worthy of attention is *Hermas Man.* XI which details how the Angel of the Prophetic Spirit enables revelation.

[71] Both Ezekiel and Revelation begin with a vision on earth of the Glory, then comes the voice and the visionary movement by the Spirit (although in Revelation we are introduced to the voice before the Christophany). Ezekiel uses the angelomorphic expression "the Hand of the Lord" as another title for the Spirit who transports him to his next vision (3.22; 8.1, 3; 40.1). In the last of these visions Ezekiel encounters "a man whose appearance was like bronze" (40.3) who measures the temple (40.5-48.35); this man may be the Glory who is also described earlier as having a bronze appearance (1.27). In Revelation it is the *angelus interpres* who both transports John (21.10) and also measures the temple (21.15-17).

Another vivid example of this idea is found in *Ascen.Is.* 6.6-7.8.[72] The first portion of this account mentions the key elements also found in Revelation (the Voice, the open door, and the visionary ascent):

> [6.6] And when Isaiah spoke with Hezekiah the words of righteousness and faith, they [Hezekiah and the others] all heard a door being opened and the voice of the Spirit.
>
> [6.8] And when they all heard the voice of the Holy Spirit, they all worshiped him on their knees, and they praised the God of righteousness, the Most High, the One who (dwells) in the upper world and who sits on high, the Holy One, the One who rests among the holy ones, [6.9] and they ascribed glory to the One who had thus graciously given a door to an alien world, had graciously given it to a man. [6.10] And while he was speaking with the Holy Spirit in the hearing of them all, he became silent, and his mind was taken from him, and he did not see the men who were standing before him. [6.11] His eyes indeed were open, but his mouth was silent, and the mind in his body was taken up from him. [6.12] But his breath was (still) in him, for he was seeing a vision. [6.13] And the angel who was sent to show him (the vision) was not of this firmament, nor was he from the angels of glory of this world, but he came from the seventh heaven.

One last piece of evidence supports the identification of the Voice as the Spirit in the early chapters of Revelation with the angel who is the Spirit in the latter chapters. The form used by the Voice in Rev 4.1-2 begins in the same manner as the form used by the *angelus interpres* (17.1; 21.9):

> The Invitation (4.1) "Come, I will show you . . ."
> The Movement (4.2) "At once I was in the Spirit. . ."
> The Revelatory Activity (4.1-15.21) Divine Throne and Seven Seals

Although there is no concluding speech, response by John, or refusal of worship here, as in 19.9-10 and 22.6-11, nevertheless the pattern of invitation and movement to revelation leads to the probability that the Voice of 1.10 and 4.1 is also the *angelus interpres* of 17.1 and 21.9. Therefore, we see the Spirit extremely active in this experience as: the Voice who facilitates the opening Christophany; the seven angels who blow their trumpets and pour out

---

[72] This glorious *angelus interpres* in *Ascension of Isaiah* may be the Angel of the Holy Spirit; see argument on 231-236 above. Also instructive is *Apoc. Ab.* 9.1-11.6 where the Voice is God himself and the revealing angel he sends to Abraham is Yahoel.

their bowls of wrath, which cause significant events recorded in chapters 8-11 and 16; and the *angelus interpres* who carries John and interprets his visions of the whore of Babylon and the Bride of Christ.

E. Conclusion

A very intriguing interrelationship between Angelomorphic Christology and Pneumatology is present in Revelation. The Spirit speaks as Christ and Christ as the Spirit.[73] The presence of the Spirit is almost imperceivable because of the emphasis that this message is directly from God through Christ to John. This emphasis is brought out by means of the opening Christophany with its "commissioning" of John (1.13-3.22) and the later "recommissioning" (10.1-11). Furthermore, not only does Christ commission John, but Christ is the content of the visionary experience: as the triumphant Lamb, as the angelomorphic Reaper, and as the angelomorphic Word of God.

One would think that an apocalypse of Jesus would be imparted by the Spirit and not by Jesus. This is not the case. The Spirit of prophecy is declared to be the testimony of Jesus (19.10). The particular Pneumatology and the commissioning scenes, especially the powerful opening Christophany, place the imprimatur of Christ's direct revelation upon the entire experience and resulting document: everything John sees and hears is "the word of God and the testimony of Jesus Christ" (1.2; cf. 1.9).

---

[73] The first person speech of Christ at the conclusion of the document (22.7, 12-16) appears to have been spoken by the Angel who is the Spirit (cf. 16.15); see also the analysis by Michaels, "Revelation 1.19", 618-619. Conversely, Christ repeatedly speaks in the opening Christophany as the Spirit (2.7, 11, 17, 29; 3.6, 13, 22). Moreover, the Voice that beckons John to his ascent through "a door standing open" to view heaven, "Come up here, and I will show you what must take place after this" (4.1), appears to have some link with the Risen Christ who makes this promise in the seventh letter: "I stand at *the door* and knock. If anyone *hears my voice* and *opens the door*, I will come in and eat with him and he with me".

CHAPTER TWELVE

THE GOSPEL OF JOHN

The background of the Fourth Gospel, especially its Prologue, has been the subject of considerable study and debate for several decades.[1] The importance of Jewish Mysticism and angelomorphic traditions for addressing this question has been set forth by several scholars in the past, but has not received widespread endorsement.[2] This appears to be changing. For example, the widely read Johannine scholar John Ashton has even argued recently that the missing link in modern interpretations of Jesus in the Fourth Gospel is Angel Christology.[3]

Jesus is never called an angel in John. It will be demonstrated, however, that angelomorphic terminology, traditions, and functions are integral components of Johannine Christology. Moreover, the relationship between Jesus and the Paraclete in John 14-16 can further our understanding of the religio-historical background for both Johannine Christology and Pneumatology in angelomorphic traditions. Therefore, this chapter will investigate the question of Angelomorphic Christology and Pneumatology in the Gospel of John by focusing on four groupings of ideas: The Word, the Name,

---

[1] C. Evans summarizes issues and texts of the debate in *Word and Glory: On the Exegetical and Theological Background of John's Prologue* (JSNTSS 89; Sheffield: Sheffield Academic Press, 1993).

[2] In addition to himself, P. Borgen notes the research of Odeberg, Quispel, and Dahl; see "God's Agent in the Fourth Gospel", *Religions in Antiquity: Essays in Memory of Erwin Ramsdell Goodenough* (ed. J. Neusner; NumenSup 14; Leiden: Brill, 1968) 137-148, esp. 144, n.5. This article has been reprinted in *Logos was the True Light and Other Essays on the Gospel of John* (Trondheim: Tapir, 1983) 121-132. Since this article was originally written in 1968, it does not mention the important study on John by W. Meeks, *The Prophet-King*, which was published in 1967.

[3] "Bridging Ambiguities", *Studying John: Approaches to the Fourth Gospel* (Oxford: OUP, 1994) 71-89. Other examples of this direction in Johannine studies, some of which Ashton draws upon, include: Bühner, *Gesandte und sein Weg*; Rowland, "John 1.51, Jewish Apocalyptic and Targumic Tradition"; A. Segal, "Ruler of this World: Attitudes about Mediator Figures and the Importance of Sociology for Self-Definition", *Jewish and Christian Self-Definition II* (eds. E.P. Sanders, A. Baumgarten, and A. Mendelson; Philadelphia: Fortress, 1981) 245-268, and Fossum, *Image of the Invisible God*, 109-133.

and the Glory; the Descending and Ascending Son of Man; the Apostle; and the Paraclete(s).

A. *The Word, the Name, and the Glory*

One of the problems that has plagued the study of the Prologue is too narrow a focus on the term ὁ λόγος, rather than a broad focus on the conceptual background of 1.1-18. "The Word" (ὁ λόγος) appears only four times in the Prologue and three of these occur in the first verse:

> [1] In the beginning was the Word [ὁ λόγος], and the Word [ὁ λόγος] was with God, and God was the Word [ὁ λόγος]. [2] He was with God in the beginning. [3] Through him all things were made; without him nothing was made that has been made.
>
> [14a] And the Word [ὁ λόγος] became flesh and tabernacled [ἐσκήνωσεν] among us, and we beheld his Glory.

Four things are asserted about the Word in these verses: he was present with/as God in the beginning; he functioned as creator; he later became incarnate in flesh; and he "tabernacled" among humans.

The tendency among scholars is to race to Wisdom tradition in order to explain the origin of these characteristics or actions of the Word in John.[4] There is significant documentation for the idea of Wisdom being present with God in the beginning during the creation, but there is less evidence of her actually functioning as creator.[5] There is also some evidence of her "tabernacling" among men.[6] No text, however, speaks of her becoming incarnate and no where is she ever called "God".[7] Furthermore, Wisdom does not have a prominent focus in Johannine Christology, except in the sense that Jesus becomes the locus of truth and revelation, a position often occupied by Wisdom/Torah in Judaism.[8] Rather

---

[4] This position is widespread; see Evans, *Word and Glory*, 83-99.

[5] Prov 8.23, 27, 30; Sir 1.1; 24.9; Wis 8.3, 5-6; 9.4, 9.

[6] Sir 1.10; 24.4, 8, 10; Bar 3.37; *1 En.* 42.1-3. The cosmogenic role of Wisdom is discussed on 89-93 above.

[7] There is no evidence of incarnation, only of transmigration (Wis 7.27); see also Evans, *Word and Glory*, 93.

[8] The author appears to be carrying out a polemic against how Torah was being interpreted; see S. Pancaro, *The Law in the Fourth Gospel* (NovTSup 42; Leiden: Brill, 1975). Because of the conceptual links and actual identification of Wisdom and Torah in several texts, a polemic against the Jewish interpre-

than turning to Wisdom traditions for answers, it is methodologically sounder to look at the Word and his relationship with two other angelomorphic traditions that have a prominent place within the Prologue and the rest of the Gospel: Name and Glory.

The Name (τὸ ὄνομα) is mentioned already in the Prologue: "But to all who received him, who believe in his Name [. . .]" (1.12). That this is a reference to the Divine Name which belongs to the Father, and not the name "Jesus", can be deduced from Jesus' words elsewhere in the Gospel: "I have come in my Father's Name" (5.43). Jesus also identified himself as the one who is an hypostasis of the Divine Name: "Father, glorify *your Name*" (12.28). This is not simply a pious prayer about the Divine Name; it is Jesus' self-identification as the hypostatized Divine Name. This conclusion is based upon the announcement Jesus makes shortly before the prayer "glorify your Name": "The hour has come for *the Son of Man* to be glorified" (12.23). Thus, "the Son of Man" is equated with the designation "Your Name"; these are both designations for Jesus who will be glorified when he is lifted up on the cross (12.32).

"The Name" in the absolute form is used to identify Jesus elsewhere in the Johannine corpus and other early Christian literature.[9] This Name nomenclature is closely linked with the use of ἐγώ εἰμι in the LXX as a name for YHWH.[10] Jesus uses ἐγώ εἰμι to identify himself on several occasions in John, including

---

tation of Torah can also be seen as a polemic against their understanding of Wisdom. Instead, Jesus takes on the vivid images of Torah/Wisdom in this Gospel (Living Water, Bread of Life, Light of the World, etc.); see R. Brown, *The Gospel According to John I-XII* (AB 29; New York: Doubleday, 1966) cxxii-cxxv.

[9] 3 John 7 refers to Jesus as "the Name" and is the only reference to Jesus in this short letter. 1 John 5.13 mentions "the Name of the Son of God"; this is a reference to the Divine Name and not the name "Jesus". Numerous allusions to Christ as possessor of the Divine Name are discussed in this study. Christ is also specifically called "the Name" or "Your [the Father's] Name" in some documents that are not the focus of our study: Acts 5.41, 15.17; *Didache* 10.1-3; *1 Clem* 58.1-60.4; *Gos. Phil.* 54.5-8; *Apos. Con.* 7.26.1-3; and esp. *Gos. Truth* 38.7-40.29. The referent of "Thy Name" in the Lord's Prayer may even be Jesus.

[10] P. Harner, *The "I Am" of the Fourth Gospel: A Study in Johannine Usage and Thought* (Philadelphia: Fortress, 1970) esp. 6-17. Although Harner downplays the significance of Exod 3.14 for John, the LXX translation of אהיה אשר אהיה is important for understanding Jesus' words in John: ἐγώ εἰμι ὁ ὤν. The Tetragrammaton follows in Exod 3.15. See also D. Ball, *'I Am' in John's Gospel Literary Function, Background and Theological Implications* (JSNTSup 124; Sheffield: Sheffield Academic Press, 1996) esp. 33-45.

epiphanies where the power of the Divine Name is visible in actions, such as the stilling of the storm (6.20) and the falling back of the arresting crowd in the Garden of Gethsemane (18.5).[11]

The identification of Jesus with the Glory (ἡ δόξα) is also present in the Prologue:

> [1.14] And the Word became flesh and tabernacled [ἐσκήνωσεν] among us, and we have seen his Glory [τὴν δόξαν αὐτοῦ], the Glory [δόξαν] as of the Father's Only-Begotten [μονογενοῦς παπὰ πατρός], full of grace and truth.

The adjectival use of δόξα here does not negate the fact that John is drawing on the angelomorphic implications which this term receives in an absolute form within the LXX.[12] This is clear from the personalizing of this term by linking it to a person: ὁ μονογενής (the Only-Begotten).[13] That the Prologue understands the Only-Begotten as the Glory whom privileged individuals of Israel's past have seen is implied in 1.18: "No one has ever seen God; it is the Only-Begotten of God, who is close to the Father's bosom, who made him known" (cf. 6.46). This is a profound interpretation of the Israelite and Jewish theophanic traditions: God (the Father) has never been seen by man (cf. Exod 33.20), but the Only-Begotten (Son) has seen him and makes him known.[14] This assertion implies that the Only-Begotten was *seen* before the incarnation since he is the one who makes God known, not only *in* the incarnation, but also *before* the incarnation (cf. 6.46). Therefore, he has always been the visible manifestation of God.

---

[11] The absolute use of ἐγώ εἰμι is also found in 8.24, 28, 58; 13.19. The predicate nominative usages are probably allusions to the Divine Name (6.35, 51; 8.12; 10.7, 9, 11, 14; 11.25; 14.6; 15.1, 5). See also Fossum, *Image of the Invisible God*, 128-129.

[12] See the discussion on 78-88 above, and G. Kittel, "δόξα", *TDNT* 2.242-245. The use of the term δόξα in John is distinctive. Jesus' glory is not revealed primarily in the transfiguration or the resurrection, as it is in the Synoptics; his glory is visible in his person (1.14; 12.41; 17.24), miracles (2.11; 11.40; 17.4), and especially in his crucifixion (12.23, 28; 13.32; 17.1, 5).

[13] ὁ μονογενής is an important term which is similar to ὁ πρωτότοκος (the Firstborn), a title found more frequently in the NT (Rom 8.29; Col 1.15; Heb 1.6; 12.23). ὁ μονογενής may even be a polemical term which speaks for mediatorial exclusivity that is not explicit in the more common ὁ πρωτότοκος or ὁ πρωτόγονος (for latter term, see Philo *Conf* 62-63, 146; *Agr* 51; *Somn* 1.215; cf. *Pr. Jos.*, 3). This terminology also had an impact on Gnosticism; see *Apocryphon of John* 6.15-24.

[14] See Segal, *Two Powers in Heaven*, 213-214.

This identification of Christ as the Glory, who is God's visible form and has his Name, appears to be behind the polemical discussion recorded in John 5.19-47. This is seen especially in these verses:

> [37] And the Father who sent me has himself borne witness to me. His voice you have never heard, his form you have never seen [οὔτε εἶδος αὐτοῦ ἑωράκατε]; [38] and you do not have his Word abiding in you, for you do not believe in him whom he has sent.

> [43] I have come in my Father's Name, and you do not receive me; if another comes in his own name, him you will receive. [44] How can you believe, who receive glory from one another and do not seek the Glory [τὴν δόξαν] that comes from the only God.

Here Jesus chides the Jews because they do not hear him as the same "voice" that Israel heard at the Sinai revelation: "Then YHWH spoke to you out of the midst of the fire; you heard the sound of words, but saw no form; there was only a voice" (Deut 4.12).[15] Even more important is the assertion in 5.37 that these Jews who do not acknowledge Jesus are rejecting the "form" that spoke to Moses:

> [Num 12.6] "If there be a prophet among you, I YHWH make myself known to him in a vision, I speak with him in a dream. [7] Not so with my servant Moses; he is entrusted with all my house. [8] With him I speak mouth to mouth, clearly, and not in dark speech; and he beholds the form of YHWH.

The variation in the LXX translation of 12.8 further clarifies the background of Jesus' statement: στόμα κατὰ στόμα λαλήσω αὐτῷ, ἐν εἴδει καὶ οὐ δι' αἰνιγμάτων, καὶ τὴν δόξαν κυρίου εἶδεν ("I spoke to him mouth to mouth, in form, and not by riddles, and he saw the Glory of the Lord"). Therefore, Jesus is understood to be "the Glory that comes from God" (5.44), who has the Father's Name (5.43), and who is the very voice which Israel heard and the form who spoke to Moses when he beheld the Glory.

This identification of Christ as the Glory is made explicit in John 12.39-40. There it states that Christ was the figure whom the prophet Isaiah saw in his call vision (Isa 6.1-3)[16]:

---

[15] Hanson mentions this text, but argues that Num 12.6-8 is the primary background for this conversation; see *Jesus Christ in the OT*, 113-117.

[16] See discussions in: Segal, *Two Powers in Heaven*, 213-214; Rowland, "John 1.51", 499; and Fossum, "Glory", 665. Exegetical interest in Isaiah 6 flourished long before the first century; see F. W. Young, "A Study of the Relation of Isaiah to the Fourth Gospel", ZNW 46 (1955) 215-221.

[12.39] For this reason they could not believe, because, as Isaiah says elsewhere: [40] "It has blinded their eyes and deadened their hearts, so they can neither see with their eyes, nor understand with their hearts, nor turn—and I would heal them" [Isa 6.10]. [41] Isaiah said these things because he saw his [Jesus'] Glory and he spoke concerning him [Jesus].[17]

Further evidence that supports this interpretation is found in the use of Glory (Aramaic: יקרא) and *Memra* (Aramaic: מימרא) in the Targumim.[18] Usage of these terms in theophanies or instances of direct speech protect the truth that "man shall not see me [God] and live" (Exod 33.20). This usage opens the door to the possibility of interpreting these as divine hypostases: now the seer hears and sees "the Glory of YHWH" or "*Memra* YHWH" and not simply "YHWH". For example, the *Tg. Neb.* Isa. 6.1-8 reads: "I saw the Glory of the Lord [. . .] my eyes have seen the Glory of the Shekinah of the eternal king, the Lord of hosts" [. . .] and I heard the voice of the *Memra* of the Lord"[19] Such an exegetical tradition could have contributed to the Christological interpretation of Isaiah 6 found in John 12.41 as well as to the Christological use of Glory, Word, and Name in the Prologue and elsewhere in John.

Nor is the Prologue the only place in the Gospel where these three ideas are brought together. Especially significant is their combined presence in John 17[20]:

[5] So now, Father, glorify me in your own presence with THE GLORY that I had in your presence before the world began. [6] I have made YOUR NAME known to those you gave me from the world. They were yours, and you gave them to me, and they have kept YOUR WORD [τὸν λόγος σου]. [7] Now they know that

---

[17] The origin of this "quotation" from Isaiah is notoriously difficult to trace; see B. Schuchard, *Scripture Within Scripture: The Interrelationship of Form and Function in the Explicit Old Testament Citations in the Gospel of John* (SBLDS 133; Atlanta: Scholars Press, 1992) 91-106. Schuchard convincingly argues that the subject of 12.40 in its Johannine context is the "report" in 12.38, which is a reference to Jesus' proclamation in words and sign. Thus, the third person singular is translated as "it" (i.e., Jesus' proclamation) in 12.40.

[18] The translation of *Memra* as "Word" is too restrictive; it does not reflect the rich exegetical focus on the Divine Name which appears to be an intregal part of this term in the Targumim. Furthermore, *Memra* does not have an uniform conceptualization and usage in the various Targumim; see 112-114 above.

[19] See the discussion of Isaiah 6 on 81-82 above; see also C. Evans, *Word and Glory*, 133.

[20] Paschal's unpublished dissertation brings this conceptual background to light; see "The Farewell Prayer of Jesus", esp. 262-274.

everything you have given me is from you; [8] for the words [τὰ ῥήματα] that you gave to me I have given to them.

[11b] Holy Father, protect them in YOUR NAME that you have given me, so that they may be one, as we are one. While I was with them, I protected them in YOUR NAME that you have given me.

[14] I have given them YOUR WORD, and the world hated them.

[17] Sanctify them in the truth; YOUR WORD is truth.[21]

[22] THE GLORY that you have given me I have given them, so that they may be one, as we are one.

[24] Father, I desire that those also whom you have given me, may be with me where I am, to see MY GLORY, which you have given me because you loved me before the foundation of the world.

[26] I made YOUR NAME known to them and will continue to make it known.

These verses present all three designations as interrelated items given to Jesus from the Father: "Now they know that everything [i.e., Glory, Name, Word] you have given me is from you" (cf. 17.11b, 24). The use of "Glory" here affirms what was asserted above: Glory refers to the preexistent visible manifestation of God. This is apparent in 17.24 where there is a prayer that future disciples "see" the Glory that Jesus possessed since "before the foundation of the world" (cf. 17.5). The interrelation between Word and Name is especially intriguing: "I made your Name known to them [. . .] they have kept your Word" (17.6). One would expect to read: "I made your Name known to them [. . .] they have kept your *Name*". Gilles Quispel argues convincingly that "the Word" here is "the Name" that was hidden which Jesus revealed (cf. 17.26).[22] Thus, 17.14 reads: "I have given them Your Word" (i.e., God's hidden or secret Name).[23] This is another example of the hidden or secret Name idea.[24] The *Gospel of Philip* (ca. late second century) states:

---

[21] The interpretation of "Your Word" in 17.17 as a self-designation of Christ that refers to the Divine Name is supported by Jesus' claim: "I AM [. . .] the truth" (14.6).

[22] "John and Jewish Christianity", *Gnostic Studies*, 2.288. This idea may also be in John 5.38; the Jews do not believe so they do not have the Word (i.e., the Son as the Divine Name) abiding in them. See also Fossum, *Image of the Invisible God*, 125-129, and 1 Pet 4.14.

[23] The Hidden or Secret Name is the Name of the Father; see references to Jesus coming and acting in the Name of the Father (e.g., John 5.43; 10.25).

[24] See the discussion of Rev 19.11-16 on 252-256 above. For an example of another angelomorphic figure imparting the Divine Name to others, see *Apoc. Ab.* 10.6-14.

[54.5-12] One single name is not uttered in the world, the Name which the Father gave to the Son, the Name above all things: the Name of the Father. The Son would not become Father unless he put on the name of the Father. Those who possess this Name know it [in truth], but do not utter it [...].

This understanding of the Word being the Divine Name has profound implications for the interpretation of ὁ λόγος in the Prologue. Based upon his conversations with Quispel, Jean Daniélou made the following proposal in a footnote to his discussion of the Divine Name:

Is it not possible that the expression: 'The Word...dwelt among us' may be based on an older form: 'The Name...dwelt among us'? In the Old Testament such dwelling is in fact the property of the Name, and not of the Word.[25]

Building on this research direction, Jarl Fossum has emphasized that there indeed are close conceptual parallels between what is ascribed to the Name in Jewish, Christian, and Gnostic literature with what is ascribed to the Word in John's Prologue.[26] As shown in Chapter 4, there is evidence that the Name existed before creation, it was the word used in creation, and it dwelt or "tabernacled" with Israel.[27] The continued prominence of this Name theology with its elements of preexistence, creating, and tabernacling is visible in early Jewish Christian texts such as this one from *Didache* 10.1[28]:

But after you are satisfied with food, thus give thanks: "We give thanks to you, O holy Father, for your Holy Name which you made to tabernacle in our hearts [...] You, Lord Almighty, created all things for the sake of your Name."

Furthermore, indisputable evidence has already been presented which demonstrates that an angelomorphic being can possess the Name of God.[29] This means that the Name is inseparable from a personal being. This is true of such texts where angelomorphic beings such as Metatron (*3 En.* 12.5), Israel/Jacob (*Pr. Jos.* 9), Michael

---

[25] *Theology of Jewish Christianity*, 150 n.15. Quispel's influence is clear from Daniélou's notes.
[26] See *Image of the Invisible God*, 109-133.
[27] See discussion of the Name on 70-78 above.
[28] The preexistence of the Name is implied by the assertion that all things were created for or by the Name. In *1 En.* 48.2 the Name is given to the Son of Man/Elect One before creation and remains hidden.
[29] See discussion on 76-78 above.

(*1 En.* 69.15), and Yahoel (*Apoc. Ab.* 10.8) possess the Divine Name. The principal text which links together Name and Angel traditions, as has been repeatedly stated, is Exod 23.20-21. This union of the Name with an angelomorphic figure means that the Divine Name is not simply an attribute of God, albeit an hypostatized attribute. Therefore, the angelomorphic Name as a personal figure provides a more likely religio-historical background than Wisdom for the Only-Begotten in the Prologue who has seen God and makes him known.

Finally, unlike Wisdom traditions, there is evidence of the angelomorphic being who is considered the Name and the Glory becoming incarnate in a human being.[30] The *Prayer of Joseph* is the clearest evidence of this phenomenon. In this text the pre-existent Firstborn or First-Begotten (πρωτόγονος) Angel Israel who is said to be the Power (i.e., the Glory) and who bears the Inextinguishable Name descended (κατέβην) and tabernacled (κατεσκήνωσα) among men and is known by the name Jacob.[31] The assertion Israel/Jacob existed before the great patriarchs Abraham and Isaac who "were created before any work" (*Pr. Jos.* 2), as well as Israel/Jacob's possession of the Divine Name, provide a religio-historical background for Jesus' claim in this verbal exchange of John 8:

> [56] "Your ancestor Abraham rejoiced that he would see my day; he saw it and was glad." [57] Then the Jews said to him, "You are not yet fifty years old, and have you seen Abraham?" [58] Jesus said to them, "Amen, amen, I say to you, before Abraham was, I AM [ἐγώ εἰμι; cf. 8.24, 28]."

This evidence about the Name brings an important question to the forefront: Is there any literary evidence that confirms the Christological identification of "the Word" being "the Name"? As discussed in the previous chapter, Rev 19.12-13 makes such an identification. This text states that Christ has a Name "[. . .] which no one knows but himself". This is an obvious reference to the Divine Name which is characterized as secret or hidden. Moreover, because he cannot be identified by this secret Name (Rev 19.12), the name or title by which he is known to the world is "the Word of God" (Rev 19.13). "The Word of Life" (1 John 1.1) or

---

[30] For evidence of angelomorphic humans, see Chapter 6 on 153-183 above.
[31] This is incarnation language. For the understanding of "the Power" as the equivalent of "the Glory", see 120-121 above.

simply "the Word" (John 1.1, 14) appear to be alternate and synonomous titles for identifying Christ. The fact that "the Word of God" in Revelation 19 could be identified simply as "the Word" is clear from the similar, and earlier, Destroying Angel tradition in Wis 18.15-16: "Your all-powerful Word (λόγος) lept from heaven [. . .] a stern warrior carrying the sharp sword of your authentic command [. . .]". This text confirms that an angelmorphic figure identified as "the Word" was known before the Gospel of John and Revelation.

The writings of Philo attest to the existence of exegesis concerning the angelomorphic Word and Name in Jewish groups contemporary with the Fourth Gospel. As can be seen from the well-known and previously cited text, one of the titles Philo assigned to the Word, "who holds eldership among the angels", was "the Name of God" (*Conf* 146).[32] Some scholars have argued that Philo may have been influenced by targumic traditions in his adoption or adaptation of the Word.[33] The *Memra* of the Targumim could have been a catalyst for such adaptation of the Word among Jews because *Memra* is closely related to the Divine Name and the Angel of the Lord.[34] The probability that Philo is drawing on an existing tradition in *Conf* 146 is supported by one seemingly redundant title he gives the Word: "His [God's] Word" (cf. "My [God's] *Memra*" of the Targumim). Building upon the insights of Bühner, Craig Evans expresses the implications of the Angel of the Lord being identified by Philo as the Word:

> If the *logos* could be identified as the angel that walked the earth and was seen by the patriarchs, then it would not be too difficult [for John and others] to equate the *logos* with Jesus who walked the earth and taught his disciples.[35]

---

[32] See the evidence of Philo identifying the Angel of the Lord with the Word on 107-112 above.

[33] Barker argues for the links between Philo's Word and the Targumim's *Memra* in *The Great Angel*, 146-148; see also Evans, *Word and Glory*, 125-134.

[34] See the discussion of *Memra* on 112-114 above; see also Evans, *Word and Glory*, 114-134, and C. Hayward, "The Holy Name of the God of Moses and the Prologue of St John's Gospel", *NTS* 25 (1978) 16-32.

[35] *Word and Glory*, 107. For the broader application of Philo to the Prologue, see T. Tobin, "The Prologue of John and Hellenistic Jewish Speculation", *CBQ* 52 (1990) 252-269. Evans builds on the work of Tobin and Borgen by suggesting links between Philo's and John's Word; see *Word and Glory*, 102-114.

In light of this evidence, why did the Fourth Gospel use "the Word"? The exegetical circles in which the author was involved had undoubtedly reflected upon the identity of the Glory, YHWH's visible manifestation, and knew this hypostasis to be the Name as well as the Word. Indeed, the use of the Word in John may reflect concern for treating discussion of the Name with due respect. This usage could also mirror an effort to ground speculation about the Word in the biblical concept of the Name. It is most probable, however, that the Word was used in the Prologue because it had already become a more popular designation for the angelomorphic Glory within hellenistic Jewish groups, as well as an established title for Christ in some Christian groups.

B. *The Descending and Ascending Son of Man*

The identification of Jesus as the Glory in John is not limited to those texts which specifically speak of δόξα. The lengthy litany of titles ascribed to Jesus in John 1 climactically concludes with a very significant example of his self-identification with the Glory. Jesus says to Nathanael: "You will see greater things than these [. . . .] Amen, amen, I tell you, you will see heaven opened and the angels of God ascending and descending upon the Son of Man" (1.50b-51).

This saying is a clear allusion to Jacob's so-called "ladder" which he saw in a dream (Gen 28.12). Christopher Rowland has demonstrated that the Targumim on this text are particularly helpful in understanding the meaning of these words of Jesus. *Targum Ps-Jonathan, Targum Neofiti I*, and the *Fragmentary Targum* (cf. *Gen. Rab.* 68.12) all testify that an image of Jacob was engraved on, or near, the divine throne.[36] Therefore, the angels ascended to see this engraved image of Jacob and then descended to see Jacob himself. John Ashton has strengthened Rowland's argument by discussing the *Prayer of Joseph*, which testifies to the exalted nature of Jacob as the preexistent Angel Israel who is said to be the Archangel of the Power of the Lord.[37] Peder Borgen has emphasized that interpreters should not overlook the links between the Johannine

---

[36] "John 1.51", 498-507.
[37] *Understanding the Fourth Gospel*, 343-345. Ashton, however, does not understand the Angel Israel/Jacob to be the Glory.

Jesus and Philo's Word, since both are associated with the vision of God/the Father, ascent into heaven, and the second birth.[38] He notes that there are links between Philo's Word being called "'he who sees' that is Israel" (*Conf* 146) and Jesus who is the only one who sees the Father (John 1.18; 6.46). Jarl Fossum has probed more deeply into the question of Jacob's image engraved on the throne and has found evidence of what may be an earlier tradition that understood Jacob's likeness to be on—not engraved on—the throne.[39] This evidence testifies that traditions developed which understood Jacob's likeness to be the enthroned Glory, namely, the very likeness or image of God. Therefore, angels who longed to look upon the Glory ascended to see Jacob's likeness upon the throne and then descended to see him in flesh on earth.[40]

Given these exegetical traditions surrounding Gen 28.12, one can come to a fuller understanding of the saying of Jesus in John 1.50-51. Jesus is presented here as the angelomorphic Son of Man, namely, the Glory who has "the appearance like a man" (Ezek 1.26; Dan 7.13) and whom angels desire to see. Therefore, the "greater things" Jesus is promising that Nathanael, a true "Israelite" (cf. Philo's etymology of Israel = "he who sees God"), will see are those things associated with the visible manifestation of the Glory who is the Son of Man, upon whom all the heavenly host wish to gaze.[41] Rowland concludes:

> For the Fourth Evangelist, however, it was not Jacob whose form and person disclosed the nature of God but Jesus, the Son of Man [. . .] He is not anxious to portray Jesus merely as the recipient of angelic revelations, for he wants to stress that Jesus is himself the embodiment of the revelation of the divine *Kabod*. Nathanael is thus offered a vision which will go much further than the evidence upon which he has confessed Jesus as the Son of God. He will be

---

[38] "God's Agent", 144-147.

[39] "The Son of Man's Alter Ego: John 1.51, Targumic Tradition, and Jewish Mysticism", *The Image of the Invisible God*, 135-151. The Fragmentary Targum Gen 1.28 (MS Vatican) and the *editio princeps* (Venice), reprinted in the London Polyglot, states that the image of Jacob was upon the throne of glory (not engraved on it as in the other Targumim). Especially significant is Targum Ezekiel 1.26 (MS Montefiore No. 7) which states that some understand the Glory above the throne in Ezek 1.26 to be the form of Jacob.

[40] *Image of the Invisible God*, 135-142.

[41] N. Dahl, "The Johannine Church and History", *Current Issues in New Testament Interpretation* (ed. W. Klassen and G. Snyder; New York: Harper, 1962) 136-137.

shown that the one whom he has acknowledged is in fact the one whom angels desire to look upon.[42]

Not only does Jesus point to angels ascending and descending upon the Son of Man, he also speaks in several places of himself as the only mode of heavenly revelation by means of the descent-ascent motif (καταβαίνειν/ἀναβαίνειν). This is made very clear in the conversation with Nicodemus:

> [3.11] Amen, amen, I say to you, that we speak of what we know and testify to what we have seen, and you do not accept our testimony. [12] If I told you of the things on earth and you do not believe, what if I tell you of the things of heaven how will you believe? [13] The fact is that no one has ascended [ἀναβέβηκεν] into heaven except the son who descended [καταβάς] from heaven, the Son of Man.

The ascent portion of this pattern is especially intriguing. Already in his commentary on John written in 1929, Hugo Odeberg emphasized reading John 3.13 in light of Jewish mysticism and asserted that the discussion of Jesus' exclusive ascent into heaven has a polemical function against the claims that particular patriarchs or prophets had ascended to heaven.[43] Peder Borgen and Wayne Meeks find the background for such claims in Philo, especially concerning Moses' Sinai theophany.[44]

The descent/ascent pattern is by no means an isolated portion of the Gospel. It is prominent in other parts of the document and is also expressed in terms of coming from and going to the Father:

> [6.42] How does he now say, "I have come down from heaven"?

> [6.46] Not that any one has seen the Father except him who is from God; he has seen the Father.

> [6.62] What if you should see the Son of Man ascending where he was before?

> [16.28] I came from the Father and have come into the world; again, I am leaving the world and going to the Father.

> [20.17] I am ascending to my Father and your Father, to my God and your God.

---

[42] "John 1.51", 505.
[43] *The Fourth Gospel*, 72-98. For an intriguing discussion of competing mediator figures and Johannine sociology, see Segal, "Ruler of This World", 245-268.
[44] Borgen, "God's Agent", 146, and Meeks, *Prophet-King*, 241-245.

The importance of this descent/ascent pattern has long been recognized, especially in the work of Rudolph Bultmann.[45] What Bultmann and others missed was the need to look no further than Jewish angelomorphic traditions for evidence of this pattern. In an article on this subject, Charles Talbert points to these traditions, among others, as pre-Christian evidence of this pattern.[46] He demonstrates how this pattern is present in Jewish texts such as Tobit, *Joseph and Aseneth*, *Testament of Job*, the *Apocalypse of Moses* (L.A.E.), the *Testament of Abraham*, the *Prayer of Joseph*, and *2 Enoch* 69-73. It is J.-A. Bühner, however, who has painstakingly pointed to links between angel and prophet traditions in Johannine Christology.[47] After discussing this research direction, John Ashton concludes:

> I believe that a reasonable case has already been made for the view that the מלאך יהוה tradition provides the most plausible and obvious explanation of John's presentation of Jesus as the emissary of God.[48]

This ascent/descent pattern nuances the depiction of the Son of Man in a significant way.[49] The Son of Man in John is not primarily a future and hidden eschatological judge who is waiting to be revealed (cf. 5.29); he is the Glory or the heavenly man who has descended, is revealing himself, and is bringing about judgment now in the world (9.35; cf. 9.39). For John, Jesus is revealed as the Son of Man when Jesus is "exalted" (ὑψόω) on the cross (3.14; 8.28; 12.32-34). Bultmann brings out this point most lucidly:

> Yet they [the Jews] do not suspect that by "lifting him up" they themselves make him their judge. The double-meaning of 'lifting up' is obvious. They lift up Jesus by crucifying him; but it is precisely through his crucifixion that he is lifted up to his heavenly glory as the Son of Man. At the very moment when they think they are passing judgement on him, he becomes their judge.[50]

---

[45] See his *The Gospel According to John* (trans. G. R. Beasley-Murray, R. W. N. Hoare, J. K. Riches; Philadelphia: Fortress, 1974). The function of this motif, which will not be discussed here, has been carefully articulated in an essay that continues to exercise considerable influence: W. Meeks, "The Man From Heaven in Johannine Sectarianism", *JBL* 91 (1972) 44-72.
[46] "Descending-Ascending Redeemer", 418-439; cf. Ashton's comments on Talbert in *Understanding the Fourth Gospel*, 350-352.
[47] *Gesandte und sein Weg*.
[48] *Studying the Fourth Gospel*, 82.
[49] U. Müller emphasizes how angel traditions contributed to this motif in John; see *Menschenwerdung des Gottessohnes* (SBS 140; Stuttgart: KBW, 1990) 62-67, 80-83.
[50] *John*, 350.

C. *The Apostle*

While the title "Apostle" is not explicitly given to Jesus in John, the understanding of Jesus as the "Sent One" pervades this Gospel.[51] The noun is used once in John. In the context of the foot-washing during the Farewell Discourse, Jesus says: "Amen, Amen, I say to you, a servant is not greater than his master; nor the apostle [ἀπόστολος] greater than the one who sent him [τοῦ πέμψαντος αὐτόν]" (13.16). Although Jesus is addressing his disciples as ones whom he will send out, his self-identification as the Apostle sent by the Father is implicit. That Jesus understands himself to be the Apostle can also be concluded from an earlier saying of Jesus: "He who sees me sees the one who sent me [τὸν πέμψαντά με]" (12.45).

The verbal forms of ἀποστέλλω especially show the prominence of this theme throughout the Gospel:

[3.17] God sent the Son into the world.
[3.34] He whom God sent speaks the words of God.
[5.36] These works [...] testify that the Father has sent me.
[5.37] The Father who sent me has testified to me.
[5.38] You do not believe in him whom he [the Father] has sent.
[6.29] That you believe in him whom he [God] has sent.
[6.57] The living Father sent me.
[7.28] He [God] who sent me is true.
[7.29] I know him, for I am from him, and he [God] has sent me.
[8.42] I did not come of myself, but he [God] sent me.
[10.36] The Father has sanctified and sent [me] into the world.
[11.42] That they might believe that you [the Father] sent me.
[17.3] This is eternal life; that they know you, the only true God, and Jesus Christ whom you have sent.
[17.8] They believed that you [the Father] sent me.
[17.18] As you [the Father] sent me into the world, so have I sent them into the world.
[17.21, 23] [Let them be one] so that the world believes that you [the Father] sent me.
[17.25] These know that you [the Father] sent me.
[20.21] As the Father has sent me, I also send you.

---

[51] This title is used of Jesus in Heb 3.1; see 303-304 below. G. Buchanan discusses this aspect of Christology, but does not stress its relationship to angel traditions; see "Apostolic Christology", *SBLSP* 25 (1986) 172-182.

The roots of the apostle concept and terminology in angel and prophet traditions has already been demonstrated.[52] It should be stated, once again, that this conception developed in two paths: the angel/prophet/apostle direction and the Angel of the Lord/Prophet-Like-Moses/the Apostle direction.[53] The Johannine emphasis on Jesus as the One Sent (Apostle) from the Father provides invaluable first century evidence of the development of the latter concept. Although John does not speak of Jesus as "the Angel of YHWH", he nevertheless uses angelomorphic traditions associated with this principal angel (Word, Name, Glory). The Johannine emphasis on the Sent One serves as an antecedent of the Apostle concept which reaches full bloom in the Christology of Justin Martyr (*I Apol.* 63.5).[54]

This apostle terminology is closely related to the descent/ascent pattern: Jesus is sent from heaven by the Father (descent) and will return there (ascent). A very important aspect of this descent/ascent and send/return terminology in John is its exclusivity. Jesus is not one of many who descended from the Father and will ascend; he is the only one (John 3.13). Jesus is not one of many who are sent from the Father and will return; he is the only one (John 1.18). The Father sends "the Apostle" who, in turn, sends out "the apostles" (John 17.18; 20.21).

Why did John emphasize that Jesus is the "Sent one" (i.e., the Apostle)? One distinct possibility, especially in light of Hebrews 3, is that it is a polemic against Moses as the Apostle.[55] This was an emphasis in some groups, especially in Samaritanism. As previously mentioned, this Gospel appears to evince a polemic against the veneration of Moses:

> [1.17-18] For the Law was given through Moses; grace and truth came through Jesus Christ. No one has ever seen God, but God's only Son.
>
> [5.45] Moses, on whom you set your hope, is your accuser.
>
> [9.28-29] You [the blind man] are his disciple, but we [the Jews] are

---

[52] The angelomorphic background of this title is presented on 176-180 above.
[53] See Fossum, *Name of God*, 148-149.
[54] See the discussion of this text on 177-178 above.
[55] Moses was vested with the Divine Name, was understood to be the Angel of YHWH in some texts, and had the title Apostle; see evidence in Fossum, *Name of God*, 144-147.

disciples of Moses. We know that God has spoken to Moses, but as for this man [Jesus], we do not know where he comes from.

This concern for authentic revelation or interpretation is a vital part of the significance of the Paraclete, whom the Sent One would send (John 14.26; 15.26; 16.7).

D. *The Paraclete(s)*

Several scholarly attempts to understand the religio-historical background of the Johannine testimony about the Paraclete have focused on the influence of angel traditions.[56] Seldom has this evidence, however, been used to shed light on the background of this Gospel's Christology.[57] The validity of such an effort is founded upon the exceptionally close links between Christology and Pneumatology in John as well as on the explicit textual evidence within the Johannine corpus which affirms that Jesus was understood to be a paraclete. For example, he is specifically called a paraclete, albeit in a forensic sense, in 1 John 2.1: "But if anyone does sin, we have a Paraclete with the Father [παράκλητον ἔχομεν πρὸς τὸν πατέρα], Jesus Christ the Righteous". The Gospel also indicates that Jesus is a paraclete: "I will ask the Father, and he will give you *another* paraclete [ἄλλον παράκλητον], to be with you forever" (14.16). Thus, this look at the possibility of an "angelomorphic" Paraclete can inform an investigation of the Gospel's Angelomorphic Christology.

Discussion of the coming Paraclete is found exclusively in Jesus' farewell discourse:

> [14.16] And I will ask the Father, and he will give you another paraclete, to be with you forever. This is the Spirit of Truth, whom the world cannot receive, because it neither sees him nor knows him. [17] You know him, because he abides with you, and he will be in you. [18] I will not leave you orphaned; I am coming to you.
>
> [14.25] I have said these things to you while I am still with you. [26] But the Paraclete, the Holy Spirit, whom the Father will send

---

[56] For a history of research on the Paraclete, see G. Burge, *The Anointed Community: The Holy Spirit in the Johannine Tradition* (Grand Rapids: Eerdmans, 1987) and J. Ashton, "Paraclete", *ABD* 5.152-154.

[57] An exception is Quispel, "John and Jewish Christianity", *Gnostic Studies* 2.220-224.

in my Name, will teach you everything, and remind you of all that I have said to you.

[15.26] When the Paraclete comes, whom I will send to you from the Father, the Spirit of Truth who comes from the Father, he will testify on my behalf.

[16.7] Nevertheless I tell you the truth; it is to your advantage that I go away, for if I do not go away, the Paraclete will not come to you; but if I go I will send him to you. [8] And when he comes, he will prove the world wrong about sin and righteousness and judgment: [9] about sin, because they do not believe in me; [10] about righteousness, because I am going to the Father and you will see me no longer; [11] about judgment, because the Ruler of this World has been condemned. [12] I still have many things to say to you, but you cannot bear them now. [13] When the Spirit of Truth comes, he will guide you into all the truth; for he will not speak on his own, but will speak whatever he hears, and he will explain to you the things that are to come. [14] He will glorify me, because he will take what is mine and declare it to you. [15] All that the Father has is mine. For this reason I said that he will take what is mine and declare it to you.

The following conclusions can be drawn about the identity and work of the Paraclete from these texts. First, he is not only identified as "another paraclete" (14.16) or "the Paraclete" (14.26; 15.26; 16.7), but also as "the Holy Spirit" (14.26) and "the Spirit of Truth" (14.16; 15.26; 16.13). Second, the Paraclete has a very close relationship with Jesus and the Father: he will come if Jesus departs; the Father gives or sends the Paraclete at Jesus' request or in Jesus' Name; Jesus sends the Paraclete and even comes as the Paraclete. This latter point shows the degree of indistinguishability between these two paracletes (cf. 14.18). Third, the Paraclete will have a unique personal relationship with the disciples: they will "recognize" him; he will be "in" them; he will teach and guide them in all truth; and he will explain the things to come. Fourth, the Paraclete has a antagonistic relationship with the world: it cannot accept or recognize him; he will prove the world wrong with regard to sin, justice, and judgment. This last point shows that the Paraclete has some forensic functions. One can see that John contains a very developed understanding of the Paraclete and his relationship with the other paraclete, Jesus.

The background for the use of this title in the Farewell Discourse has eluded scholars. The verbal adjective παράκλητος, derived from παρακαλέω, is found only in the Johannine corpus: John 14.16; 14.26; 15.26; 16.7; and 1 John 2.1. The 1 John text is unique among these because there "Paraclete" is used in its classical forenic sense of "a legal aide, advocate, or intercessor" as a descriptive role for Jesus who intercedes in heaven for God's people.[58] This forensic sense is not central to its usage in the Gospel texts, yet neither is it totally absent.[59] In the Gospel it is used primarily as a distinct name for the Holy Spirit/Spirit of Truth, that hypostatic person who will be sent by Jesus and the Father.[60] This usage was probably adapted from the use of this title in forensic contexts.[61]

Contemporary literature sheds some light on the background for this title. Mowinckel has pointed out that the *Targum on Job* interpreted/translated the angelic *melîs* (witness) of Job 16.19 (cf. 19.25; 33.23, 26) with *peraqlêtâ* (paraclete).[62] The understanding of *melîs* as "interpreter" or "teacher" is found several times in the Qumran literature (1QH 2.13, 31; 4.7, 9; 6.13). Philo's writings also contain some examples that could have (indirectly) contributed to the use of the title in John. Philo calls the High Priest a paraclete in a manner that is very close to the forensic nature of 1 John 2.1: "For it was necessary for the one consecrated to the Father of the world to act as a paraclete, that sins will no more be remembered" (*Vita Mos* 2.134). It is noteworthy that Philo also gives the Word the role of a paraclete: "He thought it best to be called, not a servant of God, but an attendant of the Paraclete [i.e., the Word]; the Paraclete is a servant of the Creator of all and Father" (*Quaes Gen* 4.114). Moreover, the idea of a single principal angelic intercessor is a significant component of Philo's Word (cf. *Heres* 205).

A conceptual background for the Paraclete is not as elusive. A substantial amount of research on this topic has focused on the fruitful field of angel traditions.[63] The most closely scrutinized

---

[58] See the helpful discussion of primary literature by Kobleski, *Melchizedek and Melchireša'*, 100-103.
[59] See esp. 15.27 and 16.8; cf. Kobelski, *Melchizedek*, 103-105.
[60] J. Behm, "παράκλητος", *TDNT* 5.800-814.
[61] Quispel, "John and Jewish Christianity", 220-224.
[62] "Die Vorstellung des Spätjudentums vom heiligen Geist als Fürsprecher und der johanneische Paraklet", *ZNW* 52 (1934) 97-130.
[63] The background for the Paraclete in Jewish intercessary angel traditions was already argued by H. Windisch; see discussion on 11 above, esp. n. 12. In addition to Windisch and Mowinckel, a focus on angel traditions is also found in N. Johannson, *Parakletoi: Vorstellung von Fürsprechern für die Menschen vor Gott in der alttestamentlichen Religion, im Spätjudentum, und Urchristentum* (Lund: CWK Gleerup, 1940); J. Behm, "παράκλητος", *TDNT* 5.800-814; and esp. O. Betz, *Der Paraklet: Fürsprecher im häertischen Spätjudentum, im*

documents have been Jewish texts about intercessory angels.[64] Several texts present the idea of an advocate angel interceding in heaven for humans:

> [Job 16.19] Even now, in fact, my witness is in heaven,
> and he that vouches for me is on high [cf. Job 33.23].

> [Job 33.23] Then, if there should be for one of them an angel,
> a mediator, one of a thousand, who declares a person upright,
> [24] and he is gracious to that person, and says,
> "Deliver him from going down into the Pit; I have found a ransom;
> let his flesh become fresh with youth;
> [25] let him return to the days of his youthful vigor."[65]

> [Zech 3.1] Then he [the angel of his vision] showed me [Zechariah] the high priest Joshua standing before the Angel of YHWH, and the Adversary standing at his right hand to accuse him. [2] And the Lord said to the Adversary, "YHWH rebuke you, O Adversary! YHWH who has chosen Jerusalem rebuke you! Is not this man a brand plucked from the fire?" [3] Now Joshua was dressed with filthy clothes as he stood before the angel. The angel said to those who were standing before him, "Take off his filthy clothes." [4] And to him he said, "See, I have taken your guilt away from you, and I will clothe you with festal apparel."

> [T. Levi 5.5] And I [Levi] said to him [the angel], "I beg you, Lord, teach me your name, so that I may call on you in the day of tribulation." [6] And he said, "I am the angel who makes intercession for the nation Israel, that they might not be beaten." [cf. Jub. 1.29]

> [T. Dan 6.1] And now fear the Lord, my children, be on guard against Satan and his spirits. [2] Draw near to God and to the angel who intecedes for you, because he is the mediator between God and men for the peace of Israel. [3] He shall stand in opposition to the kingdom of the enemy. [4] Therefore the enemy is eager to trip up all who call on the Lord, because he knows that on the day in which Israel trusts, the enemy's kingdom will be brought to an end. [5] This angel of peace will strengthen Israel so that it will not succumb to an evil destiny. [6] But in Israel's period of lawlessness it will be the Lord who will not depart from her and therefore she will seek to do his will, for none of the angels is like him.

Johannes-Evangelium und in neu gefundenen gnostischen Schriften (AGJUZ; Leiden: Brill, 1963).

[64] Quispel, "John and Jewish Christianity", 220-224.
[65] Note Job 33.29: "Elohim indeed does all these things". It is possible that the angel of 33.23 is also Elohim here.

This is evidence of a single principal angel who is the mediator or intercessor between God and his people. An angel functions in a forensic sense in the first three texts above. These texts reflect the mediator/judgment roles from the Angel of YHWH traditions. Zech 3.1-4 brings in the noteworthy element of the adversary (angel). The *Shepherd of Hermas* identifies the two opposing angels as the Angel of Righteousness and the Angel of Wickedness (*Man.* VI.2). In the two testament literature texts, the angel appears to function as a guardian angel or protector for Israel (i.e., Michael). One can perceive the development of angel pneumatology as the features of these advocate and adversary angels are transferred to the Spirit of God/Truth and the Spirit of Deceit. This is visible in *T. Judah* 20:

> [1] Know therefore, my children, that two spirits wait upon man—the Spirit of Truth and the Spirit of Deceit. [2] And in the midst is the Spirit of Understanding of the mind, to which it belongs to turn whithersoever it will. [3] And the works of truth and the works of deceit are written upon the hearts of men, and each one of them the Lord knoweth. [4] And there is no time at which the works of men can be hid; for on the heart itself they have been written down before the Lord. [5] And the Spirit of truth testifieth to all things, and accuseth all; and the sinner is burnt up by his own heart, and cannot raise his face to judge.

Documents from the QL provide further support for this development.[66] There one reads about an angel who is identified as the Prince of Lights (1QS 3.20; CD 5.18; 1QM 13.10, 14), the Angel of Truth (1QS 3.24), and the Spirit of Truth (1QS 3.19; 4.21; cf. 1QM 13.10, 14). This angel is identified as Michael (1QM 17.6-8; cf. 13.10).[67] He rules and helps the sons of light in the battle against the Angel of Darkness who is also the Spirit of Falsehood (1QS 3.18-26).

Although there is not direct dependence, three important parallels to the Paraclete are found in this figure. First, John identifies the Paraclete as the Spirit of Truth (John 14.17; 15.26; 16.13); Qumran identifies the Angel of Truth as the Spirit of Truth. Secondly, the context of both John and the Qumran texts is one of conflict

---

[66] See Betz, *Der Paraklet*, 147-170, and A. Leaney, "The Johannine Paraclete and the Qumran Scrolls", *John and Qumran* (ed. J.H. Charlesworth; London: Chapman, 1979) 38-61.

[67] In 11QMelch the divine and angelomorphic Melchizedek carries out some of the functions usually associated with Michael in the QL; see 171-172 above.

where the Paraclete will judge the Ruler of the World (John 16.11) and the Prince of Light (Michael) will indict the Angel of Darkness (1QS 3.14). Thirdly, the Paraclete remains with, teaches, and guides the disciples in truth (Jn 14.17, 26; 16.13); the Prince of Light/Angel of Truth/Spirit of Truth succors, rules, enlightens, and imparts truth to the Qumran community (1QS 3.19-25; 4.1-7). This latter role is similar to the *angelus interpres* figure, prominent in apocalyptic literature, who is especially helpful for our understanding of the ideas used to describe the Paraclete.[68]

Correct teaching is a vital concern with the Paraclete in John (14.26; 15.26; 16.14-15). Such a concern is found in the Angel Pneumatology of *Hermas*, especially *Mandate* XI.[69] The Angel of the Prophetic Spirit discussed there, in addition to the various other angelomorphic figures, is equated with, and is a manifestation of, the Holy Spirit (cf. the union of Paraclete, Spirit of Truth, and Holy Spirit in John). This angel functions as an *angelus interpres* to instruct those assigned to him in a manner similar to the Paraclete/Spirit of Truth in John 16:

> [12] I still have many things to say to you, but you cannot bear them now. [13] When the Spirit of Truth comes, he will guide you into all the truth; for he will not speak on his own, but will speak whatever he hears, and he will explain to you the things that are to come. [14] He will glorify me, because he will take what is mine and declare it to you. All that the Father has is mine. [15] For this reason I said that he will take what is mine and declare it to you.

Our understanding of the Angel of the Prophetic Spirit in *Hermas* was furthered by the observation that he is described in a manner characteristic of guardian angels in Jewish tradition (cf. Acts 12.15): the Angel of the Prophetic Spirit is ὁ κείμενος ἐπ' αὐτῷ ("the one who is assigned to him" or "the one who is in charge of him"). Although individual guardian angel traditions were not a major influence on how the Paraclete is understood, it is very probable that the Paraclete was considered the guardian angel of the Christian church much like Michael was the guardian of Israel (Dan 10.13) or the True Prophet/Christ was the guardian of the Ebionite Christians (cf. *Ps-Clem. Rec.* II.42). A guardian angel is recognized by the person or congregation over whom he watches:

---

[68] This is proposed by Ashton, *Understanding the Fourth Gospel*, 392-394.
[69] See the discussion of this text on 217-220 above.

This is the Spirit of Truth, whom the world cannot receive, because it neither sees him nor knows him. You know him, because he abides with you, and he will be in you (John 14.17; cf. *Hermas Vis.* V.4).

One can also see a parallel development of angel traditions being united with Wisdom/Spirit traditions in the True Prophet of the Ebionite *Pseudo-Clementines* examined above.[70] According to this literature, long before and after the earthly Jesus ascended, the True Prophet was and is ever present (Spirit) with the pious and even appears (Angel) to them (*Rec.* I.52; II.22; cf. II.48). Notice how this *True* Prophet imparts the *truth* in ways similar to the way the Paraclete, the Spirit of *Truth*, functions in John:

> Now the Man who is the helper [τὸν Βόηθον] I call the True Prophet; and He alone is able to enlighten the souls of men, so that with our own eyes we may be able to see the way of eternal salvation [*Hom.* I.19; cf. *Hom.* II.5, 12; III.15, 17-18; *Rec.* I.33, 44].

> I have said these things to you while I am still with you. But the Paraclete, the Holy Spirit, whom the Father will send in my name, will teach you everything, and remind you of all that I have said to you [John 14.25-26].

Unlike the paracletes in John, however, we do not find two parallel angels clearly distinct and yet complementary in these texts. Gilles Quispel, informed by the research of Kretschmar, proposed a background for the two paracletes, Jesus and the Spirit, which has been largely ignored by Johannine scholars.[71] A conceptual parallel to the two paracletes in John is found in the Jewish Christian literature of Elchasai and the *Ascension of Isaiah*. In these texts the single principal angel, the Angel of the Lord, is developed into two principal angelomorphic figures who are exalted above others: Christ and the Angel of the Holy Spirit. It is worthy to note, in light of the Paraclete abiding "in" Jesus' followers and guiding them into truth (John 14.17), that in the *Ascension of Isaiah* the Angel of the Holy Spirit was speaking "in" the prophet Isaiah and others in some manner and did not only "appear" to them (9.36-37). The "inspiration" of Isaiah the prophet, other righteous ones, and the Psalmists is also credited to this angel

---

[70] See the discussion on 269-271 above.
[71] "John and Jewish Christianity", 220-224. See the foundational work of Kretschmar, *Studien zur frühchristlichen Trinitätstheologie*, 62-93, and more recently Stroumsa, "Le couple de l'ange et de l'esprit", 42-61.

elsewhere in the *Ascension of Isaiah* (4.21). Antecedents of this bifurcation of the principal angel tradition have already been proposed.[72]

This evidence shows that the phenomenon of two paracletes in John is probably closely related to traditions surrounding a pair of principal angels, and is dependent in various ways upon this imagery. It has also been argued that the background for the Johannine Paraclete is to be found in the matrix of traditions surrounding an intercessory angel or an *angelus interpres* (name and basic concept) and Angel Pneumatology (two paracletes and functions). This conclusion lends additional contour to the angelomorphic portrait of Jesus found in this Gospel.

E. *Conclusion*

Although John never calls Jesus an angel, this analysis of evidence has demonstrated that angelomorphic terminology, traditions, and functions are an integral part of his Christology. Once again, we see the prominence of the angelomorphic traditions related to the Glory, the Name, and the Word form a substantial foundation for the Christology of this document. The roots of several ideas in Angel of the Lord traditions have been shown: Christ as the visible form of the Father, his descending and ascending, as well as his being sent from the Father. Furthermore, the evidence concerning the Paraclete further underscores the parallel impact these traditions also had upon Pneumatology.

---

[72] These antecedents are founded in Michael and Gabriel traditions or the exegesis concerning the two angels at the throne (cherubim of the Ark or the seraphim of Isa 6.6); see 126-134 and 195-196 above.

CHAPTER THIRTEEN

THE EPISTLE TO THE HEBREWS

This homiletical letter is the example most often cited as indisputable evidence that first century Christianity did not embrace an Angel Christology, or even an Angelomorphic Christology. Indeed, some argue that chapters 1-2 contain a polemic against Angel Christology.[1] This conclusion is based upon the extended argument in the first two chapters of this epistle concerning Christ's superiority over the angels. This point is poignantly asserted in Heb 1.4b-5:

> When he [the Son] had made purification for sins, he sat down at the right hand of the Majesty on high, having become as much superior to angels as the Name he has obtained is more excellent than theirs.

An argument, however, that emphasizes a clear distinction between Christ and angels is not necessarily a disavowal of Angelomorphic Christology, much less a polemic against it. The opening chapters of Hebrews unambiguously affirm that Christ is distinct from "the angels" (cf. 1.4, 5, 6, 7, 13, 14; 2.5). There may have been some veneration of angels since the presence of polemics often presupposes the practice.[2] The evidence below will demonstrate that this author's efforts to distinguish clearly between Christ and the angels does not preclude the presence of Angelomorphic Christology.[3] Moreover, it will be shown that this evidence proves the author's dependence upon, and embracing of, angelomorphic terminology and traditions in his efforts to distinguish more carefully between Christ and the angelic hosts.

---

[1] This opinion is widespread. H. Attridge considers a polemic against some form of Angel Christology as one of the more attractive reasons for this portion of the argument in Hebrews; see his *The Epistle to the Hebrews* (Hermenia; Philadelphia: Fortress, 1986), 50-54.

[2] See the discussion of angel veneration on 33-36 above.

[3] This was seen already a century ago by Lueken, *Michael*, 139-148; see also Segal, *Two Powers in Heaven*, 213, and Rowland, *Open Heaven*, 112-113.

A. Creator, Name, Firstborn, Glory, and Enthroned Son

The opening lines of this epistle lay a clear and forceful foundation for the Christology that is presented in the body of the letter:

> [1.2] In these days he [God] has spoken to us by a Son, whom he appointed heir of all things, through whom he also created the universe, [3] who, being the Radiance of the Glory [ὃς ὢν ἀπαύγασμα τῆς δόξης] and the exact imprint of his [the Glory's] very person [καὶ χαρακτὴρ τῆς ὑποστάσεως αὐτοῦ], sustaining all things by his Word of Power [φέρων τε τὰ πάντα τῷ ῥήματι τῆς δυνάμεως αὐτοῦ]. When he had made purification for sins, he sat down at the right hand of the Majesty on high, [4] because he became as much superior to the angels as a Name he has obtained [κεκληρονόμηκεν ὄνομα] is more excellent than theirs.

> [6] And again, when he brings the Firstborn [τὸν πρωτότοκον] into the world, he says, "Let all of God's angels worship him" [cf. Deut 32.43 LXX; Ps 97.7].

> [8] But of the Son he says, "Your Throne, O God [ὁ θεός], is for ever and ever; the righteous scepter is the scepter of your kingdom" [cf. Ps 45.6].

> [10] But of the Son he says, "In the beginning, Lord, you founded the earth, and the heavens are the work of your hands" [cf. Ps 102.25].

In light of antecedents and evidence already discussed, one can readily see that the ideas and terminology in these verses have been influenced by, and adopted from, angelomorphic traditions. Five ideas or terms show this to be true: the Son's role in creation, the possession of the Divine Name, the designation of the Son as "the Firstborn", his description as "the Radiance of the Glory", and his enthronement.

The first idea is the Son as creator of the universe (1.2-3, 10; cf. 2.10). The Son is not only present at creation, he is the agent of creation: "through [διά] whom he [God] also created the world" (1.2). Because of the prominence of Wisdom in the discussion of creation in Prov 8.22-31, Wisdom tradition had a significant impact on later depictions of a second figure present at, and involved in, creation.[4] The use of Wisdom tradition for this description of Jesus is founded upon the observation that Christ as an ἀπαύγασμα τῆς

---

[4] Attridge, *Hebrews*, 40. See also: Prov 8.27; Sir 24.1-12; *1 En.* 42; Wis 7.12, 21; 8.4; and discussion on 89-93 above.

δόξης (Heb 1.2) may be a development of Wis 7.25-26, where Wisdom is said to be an ἀπόρροια τῆς τοῦ παντοκράτορος δόξης εἰλικρινής ("a pure emanation of the Glory of the Almighty) and an ἀπαύγασμα γάρ ἐστιν φωτὸς ἀιδίου ("a radiance of eternal light"). In this same context Wisdom is said to be "the Fashioner of all things" (Wis 7.22).

Wisdom tradition need not be the only, nor the primary, source for Hebrews' depiction of Christ as the creator. The possession of the Divine Name is the second angelomorphic idea in these opening verses and it, too, has cosmogenic associations. Heb 1.3 mentions that this universe is sustained by "his [the Son's] Word of Power" (τῷ ῥήματι τῆς δυνάμεως αὐτοῦ; cf. Heb 11.3). In light of previous discussion of the creative "Word", this should be understood as a reference to the Divine Name as the Son's "Word of Power" (cf. 1.4). Already a century ago, Wilhelm Lueken perceptively pointed to *1 Enoch* 69 as a conceptual background for the Divine Name as this sustaining "Word of Power" (Heb 1.3).[5] In *1 Enoch* the following statement is found in the long list of things of the universe that the Name has created:

> [16] Through his oath [i.e., the Divine Name] the firmament and the heavens were suspended before the world was created and for ever. [17] And through it the earth was founded upon the waters; and from the secret recesses of the mountains comes sweet water, for the creation of the world and unto eternity.

This idea that the Divine Name is the creative and sustaining "Word of Power" is also found in connection with the angel Yahoel of the *Apocalypse of Abraham*. He declares to Abraham that he is "a Power through the medium of his Ineffable Name in me" (10.8). His sustaining work with creation includes an appointment "to restrain the threats of living creatures [. . . .] to hold the Levithans" (10.9-10). Moreover, the prayer that Abraham recites in praise to God and Yahoel includes these words about Yahoel: "you make the light shine before the morning light upon your creation from your face" (17.18). *3 Enoch* uses the Exod 23.20-21 tradition to identify Metatron as the angel who possesses the Divine Name (12.5). The creative power of the Divine Name is found in a discussion of the letters inscribed upon Metatron's crown:

---

[5] *Michael*, 139-141. See the earlier discussion of *1 En.* 69.13-25 on 75-76 above.

[3 En. 1] R. Ishmael said: The angel Metatron, Prince of the Divine Presence, the glory of highest heaven, said to me: Out of the abundant love and great compassion wherewith the Holy One, blessed be he, loved and cherished me more than all the denizens of the heights, he wrote with his finger, as with a pen of flame, upon the crown which was on my head: the letters by which heaven and earth were created; the letters by which seas and rivers were created; the letters by which mountains and hills were created; the letters by which stars and constellations, lightning and wind, thunder and thunderclaps, snow and hail, hurricane and tempest were created; the letters by which all the necessities of the world and all the orders of creation were created.

Hebrews uses this idea to affirm the exalted status of Jesus: he possesses the Divine Name which is the "Word of Power" that creates and sustains the world.[6] This interpretation of the "Word of Power" in Heb 1.3 is founded upon the overt reference to "a name" in 1.4: "because he became as much superior to the angels as a Name he has obtained is more excellent than theirs". There is only one Name that surpasses all other names: the Divine Name.[7] That the author understood the Son/Jesus as the possessor of the Divine Name is also supported by the quotations found in this opening chapter: the Son is said to be both "God [θέος]" (1.2; cf. Ps 45.6) and "Lord [κύριος]" (1.10; cf. Ps 102.25).[8]

A third angelomorphic idea in these verses is the Son as τὸν πρωτότοκον ("the Firstborn", Heb 1.6; cf. 12.23).[9] It is used in Hebrews as an exalted title given to one who existed from the beginning and participated in the creation. This usage is not found in the OT. Psalm 89.27 (LXX 88.28) uses it as the title of the most exalted king by stating that God will make King David "the Firstborn [LXX: πρωτότοκον], the highest of the kings of the earth". In Exod 4.22-23 the nation Israel is called YHWH's "Firstborn Son" (LXX: υἱὸς πρωτότοκός μου). This latter text provides a clue for understanding its usage in Hebrews. In Second Temple Judaism this title was interpreted as applying to the *patriarch* Jacob as

---

[6] Philo assigns the sustaining of creation to the Word; see *Somn* 1.241; *Migr* 6; *Spec Leg* 1.81; *Plant* 8. See also Fossum's discussion of creation through the Name; *Name of God*, 77-84.
[7] See discussion on 70-78 above.
[8] The Tetragrammaton is translated in the LXX with ὁ κύριος.
[9] ὁ πρωτότοκος is also used as a designation for Christ in the Pauline Epistles (Rom 8.29; Col 1.15). John uses the epithet ὁ μονογενής (John 1.18), which may have a polemical function in light of the use of πρωτότοκος and πρωτόγονος elsewhere. See also 273 above, esp. n. 13.

"Israel", not to the *nation* Israel (*Jub.* 19.29; *Exod. Rab.* 19.7; *3 En.* 44.10). It has already been demonstrated that the *Prayer of Joseph* and Philo are evidence that the closely related term πρωτόγονος was used as a designation for the Angel Israel, who is a protological angelomorphic figure who receives many other epithets.[10] Although the *Prayer of Joseph* depicts Uriel's challenge to the "firstborn" angel Israel, the latter is clearly above all other angels in rank and significance.[11] Jonathan Smith has demonstrated that Jewish mystical literature contains evidence that Israel was a designation for the angel who is before the throne and leads the heavenly liturgy.[12] Hebrews gives some evidence of this idea being conferred upon Christ when it mentions "the Firstborn" again towards the end of the letter:

> [12.22] But you have come to Mount Zion and to the city of the living God, the heavenly Jerusalem, and to innumerable angels in festal gathering, [23] and to the assembly of the Firstborn [καὶ ἐκκλησίᾳ πρωτότοκων] who are enrolled in heaven, and to a Judge who is God of all, and to the spirits of just men made perfect [...].

The angelomorphic connotations of the "firstborn" terminology did not preclude its use in other prominent Christian texts. Two texts use the term to emphasize Christ's soteriological role among humanity: "firstborn among many brethren" (Rom 8.29) and "firstborn from the dead" (Col 1.18). Earlier in the Colossians hymn, however, the term is used in a way similar to the *Prayer of Joseph* in order to emphasize Christ's preeminence before and over all creation: "the Firstborn of all creation; for in him all things were created, in heaven and on earth, visible and invisible, whether thrones or dominions or principalities or authorities—all things were created through him and for him" (Col 1.15b-16).[13] Furthermore, Justin explicitly articulates the angelomorphic associations of this term by identifying the Angel Israel as the Son who is God "inasmuch as he is the Firstborn of all creation [πρωτότοκον τῶν ὅλων κτισμάτων]" (*Dial. Trypho* 125.3).

The "Firstborn" terminology is used in Heb 1.6 to distinguish the Son as an object of worship for the angels: "When he [God]

---

[10] See *Pr. Jos* 3. The designation is also in Philo (*Conf* 146; 62-63; *Agr* 51; *Somn* 1.215); see also 110 above.

[11] See the discussion of this text on 137-142 above.

[12] "Prayer", 262-265.

[13] See esp. Fossum, *Image of the Invisible God*, 24-28.

brings the Firstborn into the world, he says, 'Let all God's angels worship him.'" This worship by angels does not preclude Angelomorphic Christology since it has already been demonstrated that angels can and do worship an angelomorphic being in some texts. The author's quotation of the LXX version of Deut 32.43 (with slight modifications) appears to be used to support the idea that "the Firstborn" was revealed as an object of worship at the incarnation.[14] The visibility of Christ to the angels at the incarnation is indicated by the line "was seen by angels" in the hymn of 1 Tim 3.16 (cf. Luke 2.14). The incarnation initiating the worship of the angels is a prominent element of this intriguing text from Ignatius of Antioch (early second century), especially when one remembers that "star" is a popular term for "angel" in apocalyptic literature[15]:

> [*Ign. Eph.* 19.1] Now the virginity of Mary and her giving birth were hidden from the ruler of this age, as was also the death of the Lord—three mysteries to be loudly proclaimed, yet which were accomplished in the silence of God. [2] How, then, were they revealed to the ages? A star shone forth in heaven brighter than all the stars; its light was indescribable and its strangeness caused amazement. All the rest of the constellations, together with the sun and moon, formed a chorus around the star, yet the star itself far outshone them all, and there was perplexity about the origin of this strange phenomenon which was so unlike others. [3] Consequently all magic and every kind of spell were dissolved, the ignorance so characteristic of wickedness vanished, and the ancient kingdom was abolished, when God appeared in human form to bring the newness of eternal life; and what had been prepared by God began to take effect.

The fourth angelomorphic idea in these verses is "the Glory", namely, the visible manifestation of God as documented in Ezek 1.26 and related texts.[16] Heb 1.3 identifies the Son with this idea: "who, being the Radiance of the Glory [ὃς ὢν ἀπαύγασμα τῆς δόξης] and the exact imprint of his [the Glory's] very person [καὶ

---

[14] The emphasis on incarnation ("when he brings him into the world") stands in contrast to some Christian texts which emphasize the revelation of Christ to the angels and the reception of their worship upon his exaltation (Phil 2.9-11; 1 Pet 1.12; *Ign. Tr.* 9.1). The *Ascension of Isaiah* goes into great detail about how the angels did not recognize Christ in his incarnation (10.17-31), but then depicts how they worshipped him during his ascension through the heavens in his exalted state (11.22-32; cf. the Son of Man in *1 En.* 48.6-7; 62.7).

[15] See discussion on 28 above, esp. n.4.

[16] See discussion on 77-88 above.

χαρακτὴρ τῆς ὑποστάσεως αὐτοῦ]". Most scholars ignore the definite article and translate "the Glory" as a divine characteristic: "being the radiance of *God's* [or *his*] glory".[17] This interpretation is founded upon the influence of Wisdom tradition upon Hebrews: "She [Wisdom] is a breath of the power of God, and a pure emanation of the glory of the Almighty [...] a reflection [ἀπαύγασμα] of eternal light, a spotless mirror of the working of God, and an image [εἰκών] of his goodness" (Wis 7.25-26).[18] The purpose of ἀπαύγασμα and χαρακτήρ in Hebrews, however, is to emphasize the intimate and inseparable connection between *Christ and the Glory*, not *Christ and the Father* as many scholars conclude.[19]

The author's use of τῆς μεγαλωσύνης ("the Majesty") at the end of 1.3 (cf. 8.1) indicates a distinction between "the Glory" and "the Majesty":

> [3] who, being the Radiance of the Glory [ὃς ὢν ἀπαύγασμα τῆς δόξης] and the exact imprint of his [the Glory's] very person [καὶ χαρακτὴρ τῆς ὑποστάσεως αὐτοῦ], sustaining all things by his Word of Power [φέρων τε τὰ πάντα τῷ ῥήματι τῆς δυνάμεως αὐτοῦ]. When he had made purification for sins, he sat down at the right hand of the Majesty on high.

If the Son is distinct from the Glory, why did the author not say in 1.3 that the Son sat down at the right hand of "the Glory"? Given the evidence that Christians often interpreted Christ to be the Glory, Heb 1.3 appears to also identify Christ with the Glory (i.e., the radiance and imprint of the Glory) who is distinct from "the Majesty".[20] Käsemann makes the helpful comment that "Radiance of

---

[17] In the other portions of this letter "glory" is a characteristic of the Son, rather than a designation for an angelomorphic figure (2.7, 9; 3.3; 13.21). It is also a term used of the eschatological goal of God's people (2.10).

[18] For the tendency to look to Wisdom tradition to understand these concepts see Attridge, *Hebrews*, 41-47, and Lane, *Hebrews* (WBC; Dallas: Word, 1991) 14-15.

[19] See Attridge, *Hebrews*, 43, and W. Lane, *Hebrews*, 13. ἀπαύγασμα ("reflection") and χαρακτήρ ("imprint") appear to be used in synonymous parallelism. Their usage here is similar to εἰκών ("image") in the NT (cf. 2 Cor 4.4; Rom 8.29; Col 1.15). The relationship between these ideas becomes clearer if one sees the "Image of God" as a distinct angelomorphic figure who existed before the incarnation (cf. Col 1.15-20 and *Somn* 1.238)

[20] This distinction between the Majesty and Glory may also be present in 2 Peter 1.17 where "the Majestic Glory" (τῆς μεγαλορεποῦς δόξης) is a title for the Father at the Transfiguration. This title does not indicate that Christ was not identified as the Glory; rather it is a title similar to "the Great Glory" given to the Father in *Ascen. Is.* 9.37 (cf. *1 En.* 14.20).

the Glory" should be understood as similar to the Hellenistic and Pauline teaching about the "Image" (εἰκών).[21]

The phrases ὃς ὢν ἀπαύγασμα τῆς δόξης καὶ χαρακτὴρ τῆς ὑποστάσεως αὐτοῦ pose the possibility that the author is also making a fine distinction between the Glory and the Radiance of the Glory. Depending on the referant of the personal pronoun, a threefold structure may also be indicated in the phrase: χαρακτὴρ τῆς ὑποστάσεως αὐτοῦ ("the exact imprint [Christ] of the hypostasis [the Glory] of him [God]"). A similar phenomenon is visible in some later Jewish writings which identify the Glory or visible manifestation of God as "the *Yeqara* of the *Shekinah* [יקר שכינת] of God" ("the Glory of the Presence of God").[22] For example, *Tg. Neb.* Isa 6.5 states that Isaiah saw "*Yeqara* of the *Shekinah* of the King of the worlds" (cf. *Tg. Ps-.* Exod 24.9). Furthermore, *Midrash ha-Gadol* Exod 24.10 states that Rabbi Eliezer opposed the translation "*Yeqara* of the *Shekinah* of the God of Israel" in Exod 24.10 because this phrase implied a triad. Therefore, if Hebrews indeed indicates that the Glory is somewhat distinct from the Radiance or Imprint of the Glory, then the incarnate Son is understood to be the latter in this epistle. The theological motivation for such a distinction certainly grows from the invisibility of the Glory's face (cf. Exod 33.20).

A fifth image that the author uses to demonstrate the exalted status of Jesus over the angels is enthronement. The enthronement motif, however, does not preclude the presence of Angelomorphic Christology since there is significant Jewish literary evidence that describes the enthronement of angelomorphic figures. A noteworthy example which parallels the Christology of Hebrews 1-2 is the depiction of Metatron in *3 Enoch* 10-14.[23] These chapters portray God making a glorious throne for Metatron, revealing all mysteries to him, fashioning and vesting him with kingly appointments (robe, cloak, and crown), and bestowing upon him the Divine Name ("the Lesser YHWH" in *3 En.* 12.5). Metatron also receives

---

[21] *The Wandering People of God* (trans. R. Harrisville and I. Sandberg; Minneapolis: Augsburg, 1984) 101-106. Käsemann, however, uses this idea to support an understanding of Jesus as the Gnostic *Anthropos* in Hebrews. For use of "Image" in the Pauline Epistles, see 333-346 below.

[22] J. Fossum provided this insight and these texts in a personal conversation. Although these texts are significantly later than Hebrews, they may reflect a similar tradition.

[23] Käsemann compares the portrayals of Christ and Metatron; see *Wandering People of God,* 115-117

homage from the ranks of angels (*3En.* 14.5; cf. 10.3). Enthronement in this text and others distinguishes the enthroned angelomorphic being from the other angels. It does not, however, eliminate the angelomorphic features of the enthroned figure.

One of the ways the author of Hebrews articulates the idea of enthronement is through his emphasis on "sitting on the right hand" (1.3, 13). Elsewhere in the epistle the author makes it clear that this means nothing less than sharing the divine throne:

> [8.1] We have such a high priest, one who is seated at the right hand *of the throne of the Majesty in heaven*, [2] a minister in the [heavenly] sanctuary and the true tent which is made up not by man but by the Lord.
>
> [12.2] Looking to Jesus, the pioneer and perfecter of our faith, who for the joy that was set before him endured the cross, despising the shame, and is seated at the right hand *of the throne of God.*

Enthronement is also used to express Angelomorphic Christology by means of quotations from Psalm 45 (Heb 1.8-9) and Psalm 8 (Heb 2.6-8). What is important to observe about the quotation of Ps 45.6-7 are the implications of ascribing a text about YHWH, his throne, and his scepter to the Son: "But of the Son he says, 'Your throne, O God, is for ever and ever, the righteous scepter is the scepter of your kingdom'" (1.8). The quotation of Ps 8.4-6 is an even more intregal part of the enthronement emphasis in Hebrews:

> [Heb 2.5] For it was not to angels that God subjected the world to come, of which we are speaking. [6] It has been testified somewhere, "What is man that you are mindful of him, or the son of man, that you care for him? [7] You made him for a little while lower than the angels, you have crowned him with glory and honor, [8] putting everything in subjection under his feet." Now in putting everything in subjection to him, he left nothing outside his control. As it is, we do not yet see everything in subjection to him. [9] But we see Jesus, who for a little while was made lower than the angels, crowned with glory and honor because of the suffering of death, so that by the grace of God he might taste death for every one.

Rather than understanding "man" in Psalm 8 corporately as the one to whom the creation has been subjected, the author of Hebrews interprets this psalm Christologically as an enthronement text which depicts the subjection of the cosmic powers to Christ.[24] Justification for this is found in the language of the psalm that

---

[24] See esp. M. Kinzer, "'All Things Under His Feet': The Use of Psalm 8 in the New Testament in Light of Its Use in Other Jewish Literature of Late Antiquity" (Ph.D. diss., University of Michigan, 1995).

speaks of the "son of man" being "crowned" with glory and honor. "Son of man" had taken on obvious angelomorphic connotations from the enthronement in Dan 7.13-14.

B. *Apostle, High Priest, and Son of God's House*

Hebrews 3-4 turn the reader's focus to the superiority of Christ over Moses. This is brought out most clearly at the beginning of the argument through the use of three designations which have their roots in angelomorphic traditions: Apostle, High Priest, and Son of God's House. Hebrews 3 begins by introducing all three designations to the reader:

> [1] Therefore, holy brothers, who share in a heavenly calling, consider Jesus, the Apostle and High Priest of our confession. [2] He was faithful to him who appointed him, just as Moses also was faithful in God's House. [3] Yet Jesus has been counted worthy of as much more glory than Moses as the builder of a house has more honor than the house. [4] For every house is built by someone, but the builder of all things is God. [5] Now Moses was faithful in all God's House as a servant, to testify to the things that were to be spoken later, but Christ was faithful over God's House as a son. [6] And we are his house if we hold fast our confidence and rejoicing of the hope until the end.

This is the only place in the NT where Jesus is overtly called "the Apostle [ὁ ἀπόστολος]".[25] It has already been demonstrated that there is a close relationship between the Angel and Apostle concepts and ascriptions in some Jewish, Samaritan, and early Christian texts.[26] Hebrews shows some awareness of this link in 1.14 where "angels" are said to be "sent" (ἀποστέλλω). Because of a possible Samaritan background for the content of Hebrews, the Samaritan texts which link Angel and Apostle traditions are especially pertinent.[27] For example, in Samaritanism the Apostle designation began to replace the Angel of YHWH, as is visible in the *Samaritan Targum* to Exod 23.20-23:

---

[25] The apostle concept, however, is prominent to John (esp. 13.16); see 284-286 above.

[26] For an introduction to the Angel-Apostle question with relevant bibliography, see 176-180 above.

[27] Fossum argues for a Samaritan background; see *Name of God*, 150-152. Here he builds on the research of H. Kippenberg, *Garizim und Synagoge* (RGVV 30; Berlin, 1971), esp. 317.

> Behold! I send My Apostle before you in order to keep you and protect you on the way, and to bring you into the place which I have prepared. Give heed to him and obey his voice. Do not rebel against him, because he will not pardon your transgressions; for My Name is in him. But if you hearken attentively to his voice and do all that I say, then I will be an enemy to your enemies and an adversary to your adversaries. For My Apostle shall go before you [. . .].

An important portion of the argument for the superiority of Christ over Moses in Heb 3.1-6 is the fact that Moses was considered the Apostle *par excellence* by some Jews and Samaritans; thus, he had angelic status.[28] For example, *Memar Marqa* V.3 records this plea on the lips of the people as Moses prepared to die:

> By your life, O Apostle of God, remain with us a little longer!
> By your life, O Seal of the prophets, stay with us a little longer!

Therefore, the use of this designation in Hebrews solely for Jesus serves to emphasize Jesus' status as an angelomorphic being who is superior to Moses.

A second aspect of the superiority of Christ over Moses is the emphasis on Jesus as High Priest. This theme is introduced already in Heb 1.3 and 2.17 where his priestly role is described as "to make expiation for sins". The angelomorphic aspects of the priestly office have already been demonstrated.[29] The natural compliment to an angelomorphic priestly office is a heavenly counterpart to the Jerusalem temple.[30] The author of Hebrews certainly considers Jesus to be the High Priest in the heavenly sanctuary:

> [4.14] Since we have a great high priest who has passed through the heavens, Jesus, the Son of God, let us hold fast our confession.
>
> [8.1] We have such a high priest, one who is seated at the right hand of the throne of the Majesty in heaven, [2] a minister in the [heavenly] sanctuary and the true tent which is set up not by man but by the Lord.
>
> [9.24] For Christ has entered, not into a sanctuary made with hands, a copy of the true one, but into heaven itself, now to appear in the presence of God on our behalf [cf. 9.11-14].

---

[28] See Fossum, *Name of God*, 144-148.
[29] See discussion on 169-175 above.
[30] For an overview of the texts which detail this phenomenon and their origins, see C. Rowland, "The Second Temple: Focus of Ideological Struggle", *Templum Amicitiae: Essays in Honor of Ernst Bammel* (ed. W. Horbury; JSNTSup 48; Sheffield: Sheffield Academic Press, 1991), 175-198. For a perusal of scholarly opinion of the background and meaning of the heavenly sanctuary in Hebrews, see L. Hurst, *The Epistle to the Hebrews: Its Background of Thought* (SNTSMS 65; Cambridge: CUP, 1990) 24-42.

Heb 8.4-5 makes it clear that this heavenly sanctuary is the one that Moses merely saw and of which he built a copy (cf. 6.19-20). The contrast underlying Christ's superiority over Moses is this distinction between Christ as the priest of the heavenly sanctuary and Moses as the builder of the earthly tabernacle. This is a polemical assertion since, according to some Jewish and Samaritan groups, Moses did not perform priestly duties exclusively in the earthly tabernacle, as is evident in this Samaritan text:

> [*Memar Marqa* IV.6] Where is there the like of Moses, and who can compare with Moses, the Faithful One of His house, who dwelt with the angels in the Sanctuary of the unseen [. . .]. He was holy priest in two sanctuaries.

Jesus as High Priest is synonymous with the third designation "Son of God's House".[31] This is clear from Heb 12.21: "Since we have a great high priest over the House of God". The "House of God" is closely related to the heavenly sanctuary. It may also be connected with the builder (i.e., creator) idea that is in Heb. 3.3 and elsewhere: "Yet Jesus has been counted worthy of as much more glory than Moses as the builder of a house has more honor than the house" (cf. 11.10; 13.14). This idea of the heavenly sanctuary is brought out most vividly in 12.22-24:

> [22] But you have come to Mount Zion and to the city of the living God, the heavenly Jerusalem, and to innumerable angels in festal gathering, [23] and to the assembly of the Firstborn who are enrolled in heaven, and to a Judge who is God of all, and to the spirits of just men made perfect, [24] and to Jesus, the mediator of new covenant, and to the sprinkled blood that speaks more graciously than the blood of Abel.

The use of these designations (Apostle, High Priest, Son of God's House) not only forms a portion of the author's argument for the superiority of Christ over Moses, but probably is also a polemic against veneration of Moses in Jewish and Samaritan groups. In his discussion of Hebrews 3, Jarl Fossum has gathered evidence that demonstrates these epithets of Christ in Heb 3.1-6 are ascribed to Moses in Samaritanism.[32] Included in his analysis are the following Samaritan texts from *Memar Marqa*:

---

[31] See the discussion in Fossum, *Name of God*, 151.
[32] *Name of God*, 150-152.

[IV.1] Where is there anyone like Moses, and who can compare with Moses, who was glorifed in the unseen things even more than in the revealed things, — the Son of His house, the Faithful One of God, to whom God revealed himself, with whom God spoke?

[IV.1] Where is there a prophet like Moses, and who can compare with Moses, the Servant of God, the Son of the house of God?

[VI.3] Where is there anyone like Moses, Apostle of the Truth [i.e., of God], Faithful One of the house of God, and His Servant?

These texts testify to Moses being called "the Son of the house of God", "Priest", the "Faithful One", "Servant", and "Apostle". Each of these titles plays an important role in the comparison and contrast of Jesus with Moses in Heb 3.1-6. There the titles "Apostle", "High Priest" and "Son of the house of God" are ascribed solely to Jesus. Even though Moses was confessed as "Son of the house of God" in Samaritanism (as the texts above indicate), the author of Hebrews sets up a superior/inferior contrast in his use of the adjective "faithful" with regard to Jesus as "the Son" and Moses as "the Servant": "Now Moses was faithful *in* [ἐν] all God's house *as a servant*, to testify to the things that were to be spoken [in the future], but Christ was faithful *over* [ἐπί] God's house *as a son*" [3.5-6]. The use of these epithets for Moses (by Samaritans) and Jesus (by Christians) indicates that they are drawing on common angelomorphic antecedents, but ascribing them to different persons.

The idea of an angelomorphic high priest who serves in a non-earthly temple is also found in Philo. He speaks of two temples and states that one is staffed by the Word, God's Firstborn, as High Priest:

[*Somn* 1.215] For there are, as is evident, two temples of God: one of them this universe, in which there is also as High Priest His Firstborn, the divine Word, and the other the rational soul, whose Priest is the real Man [cf. *Fug.* 118].

Elsewhere Philo states that the priestly role of the Word is that of a two-way intercessor:

[*Heres* 205] To His Word, His archangel, Highest Image and Honor, the Father of all has given the special prerogative, to stand on the border and separate the creature from the Creator. This same Word both pleads with the immortal as supplicant for afflicted mortality and acts as ambassador of the ruler to the subject.

In light of the understanding of Jesus as the Name (1.4) as well as the Creator (1.2) and sustainer of creation (1.3), two other details about Philo's description of the High Priest are worthy of note.[33] First, Philo indicates that the turban of the High Priest held a golden plate with the four letters of the Divine Name (יהוה). In this manner he literally possessed and bore the Divine Name.[34] Second, Philo sees the Word as the High Priest performing the role of sustaining creation. He founds this understanding upon the robe of the High Priest, which contained an elaborate depiction of the world (*Somn* 1.215; cf. Wis 18.24):

> [*Fug* 110] Now the garments which the supreme Word of Him that IS puts on as raiment are the world, for He arrays Himself in earth and air and water and fire and all that comes from these.

> [*Fug* 112] And the oldest Word of God has put on the universe as a garment [. . .]. "He does not tear his garments," for the Logos of God is the bond of all things, as has been said, and holds together all parts, and prevents them by its constriction from breaking apart and becoming separated.

In light of this close relationship between the visible and material world in Philo, it is significant that he allegorizes both Moses and Melchizedek as the High Priest who is the Word.[35]

C. *A High Priest After the Order of Mechizedek*

In Heb 5.5-10 the author further defines the uniqueness of Jesus' High Priesthood by bringing the enigmatic priest Melchizedek into the argument through a quotation of Ps 110.4, which leads to the conclusion that Jesus was "designated by God a high priest after the order of Melchizedek" (5.10). The Melchizedek tradition found in subsequent chapters is among the several foils used in developing the elevated Christology of this document.[36] The author

---

[33] See M. Barker, "Temple Imagery in Philo: An Indication of the Origin of the Logos?", *Templum Amicitiae: Essays in Honor of Ernst Bammel* (ed. W. Horbury; JSNTSup 48; Sheffield: Sheffield Academic Press, 1991) 70-102.

[34] See *Vita Mos* 2.114; cf. *Migr* 103, *Letter of Aristeas* 98, Josephus, *Ant* 3.331. This tradition varies slightly from the testimony of Exod 28.36 which indicates that the words on this plate were קדש ליהוה ("Holy to YHWH").

[35] See the discussion in Meeks, *Prophet-King*, 117-125.

[36] For research on Melchizedek, see the bibliography mentioned on 171 above (esp. nn. 59 and 61). See also C. Gieschen, "The Different Functions of a Similar Melchizedek Tradition in *2Enoch* and the Epistle to the Hebrews",

of Hebrews was writing to people who had respect for the priestly sacrificial cult and were probably tempted to go back to it as the source of the forgiveness of sins.[37] To these Christians who were becoming discouraged, the author is showing Jesus to be the faithful High Priest who offered the ultimate sacrifice for sin and whose priesthood supersedes all that the Levitical priesthood offers. Therefore, the purpose of Hebrews is not to develop the story of Melchizedek in its own right; rather, the author uses a known non-Levitical priesthood tradition (Melchizedek via Psalm 110) to show that Christ's priesthood is more ancient than (7.10), and superior to (7.7), the Aaronic/Levitical priesthood, which appears to have been luring some Christians back. Moreover, the antiquity and superiority of the Melchizedek priesthood are supported, in part, by the author's use of exisiting traditions which depict Melchizedek as an eternal angelomorphic priest. This is significant in light of the research of Yigael Yadin which compares the QL with Hebrews since the QL elevates the status of the priestly messiah (Messiah of Aaron) over the royal Messiah (Messiah of Israel), but still has Michael (who appears to be identified with Melchizedek) as the ultimate authority above these messiahs.[38]

To demonstrate the legitimacy and superiority of the priesthood of Jesus, who was not a Levite, the author makes repeated use of Psalm 110 in which a kingly messianic figure is declared to be "[. . .] a priest forever according to the order of Melchizedek" (5.6; 5.10; 6.20; 7.11, 15, 17, 21). The importance of this psalm in Hebrew's use of the Melchizedek traditions is difficult to overemphasize.[39] The link between a Davidic messiah and a priestly role in Psalm 110 formed the basis for the unique High Priest aspect of the Christology in Hebrews.[40]

Early Christian Interpretation of the Scriptures of Israel: Investigations and Proposals (eds. C. Evans and J.A. Sanders; JSNTSup 148/SSEJC 5; Sheffield: Sheffield Academic Press, 1997) 364-379.

[37] Hebrews reflects the period before the destruction of the Temple in 70 CE; see Robinson, *Redating the NT*, 200-220.

[38] "The Dead Sea Scrolls and the Epistle to the Hebrews", *Scripta Hierosolymitana* (Vol 4; eds. C. Rabin and Y. Yadin; Jerusalem: Magnes, 1958) 36-55.

[39] See D. Hay, *Glory at the Right Hand*, 143-53, and Hengel, *Studies in Early Christology*, 119-226.

[40] See also Attridge's excursus on "The Antecedents and Development of the High-Priestly Christology" in *Hebrews*, 83-96.

It was not enough, however, for the author simply to assert that Jesus was associated with Melchizedek and to hope that his readers recognized the superiority of Jesus' priesthood. In Hebrews 7 the status of Melchizedek is carefully evaluated and elevated through a creative exegesis of Gen 14.18-20 and Psalm 110. The author points out the obvious significance of Melchizedek's kingship (7.2), his name (7.2), his city (7.2), his blessing of Abraham (7.6), and the tithe Abraham gave to him (7.4). The blessing and the tithe are then used to support the superiority of Melchizedek over the Levites (who also bestow blessings and receive tithes) since Levites are descendants of Abraham:

> [7.7] It is beyond dispute that the inferior [τὸ ἔλαττον] is blessed by the superior [ὑπὸ τοῦ κρείττονος]. [8] In the one case, tithes are received by those who are mortal; in the other, by one of whom it is testified that he lives [ζῇ].

The primary assertion Hebrews makes about Melchizedek in relationship to Jesus, however, concerns the eternal nature of Melchizedek's priesthood: "Without father [ἀπάτωρ], without mother [ἀμήτωρ], without genealogy [ἀγενεαλόγητος], having neither beginning of days nor end of life, but who was made like [ἀφωμοιωμένος] the Son of God, he remains a priest forever" (7.3). That this verse implies the eternal nature or immortality of Melchizedek and his priesthood is substantiated by 7.8 ("tithes are received [. . .] by one of whom it is testified that he lives") and 7.15-16 ("another priest arises, according to the likeness [κατὰ τὴν ὁμοιότητα] of Melchizedek, one who has become a priest [. . .] through the power of an indestructible life"). This reciprocal relationship between Melchizedek and Christ can be summarized as follows: Melchizedek *was made like* the (Firstborn) Son, thus the (fleshly High Priest) Christ *is according to the likeness* of Melchizedek.

Fred Horton, and others who follow his position, see the statement that Melchizedek lacks a genealogy to be the result of an argument from the silence of Gen 14.18-20, such as is found in Philo and Rabbinism.[41] The testimony of Psalm 110, however,

---

[41] Horton, *Melchizedek Tradition*, 153; see Philo, *Leg All* 2.55; 3.79 (Melchizedek) and *Abr* 31 (Noah). For the rabbinic argument that what is not stated in the Torah is just as important as what is stated, see H. Strack and P. Billerbeck, *Kommentar zum Neuen Testament aus Talmud und Midrash* (4 vols; München: C. H. Beck'sche, 1922) 3.694-95.

"silences" this argument since it shows a highly developed understanding of Melchizedek which greatly influenced the author of Hebrews. The exegesis of Psalm 110 probably also impacted a first century CE document like *2 Enoch* 69-73, which is anything but "silent" about Melchizedek's genealogy: it testifies that Melchizedek is an angelomorphic figure without human geneology.[42] The exalted status of Melchizedek is also visible in the Qumran fragment 11QMelch, which portrays him as a divine priest-king who will wage the eschatological battle against Belial and the sons of darkness.[43] Furthermore, it is probable that Hebrews drew on the rich Jewish traditions regarding the angelic liturgy in heaven, some of which have priestly angels offering bloodless sacrifices for sinners.[44]

The author's awareness of the traditions of Melchizedek as an angelomorphic priest is apparent from his interpretation of Psalm 110. He draws on Psalm 110.4 as the primary text for asserting the eternal nature of Melchizedek in 7.3 and 7.8. The author of Hebrews understood the "eternal nature" of the messiah's priestly status in Psalm 110.4 ("You are a priest *forever*") as a defining characteristic of Melchizedek: "he [Melchizedek] remains a priest *forever*" (7.3). Thus, for the author of Hebrews, "a priest forever" defines "the order of Melchizedek" set forth in Psalm 110. This interpretation is corroborated by the language of 7.8: "of whom it is testified that he [Melchizedek] lives". The "testimony" to which the author refers is not the "silence" of Genesis, but the testimony of Ps 110.4 as it was interpreted by him and others (i.e., the messiah is a priest forever in a manner like Melchizedek who is a priest forever).[45] "The order [τάξιν] of Melchizedek" should not be interpreted as having a technical meaning in Hebrews. Note that the author himself interprets the meaning of "according to the *order* of Melchizedek" with his paraphrase of 7.15: "according to the *likeness* [ὁμοιότητα] of Melchizedek" (cf. 7.3).[46] Jesus is also a

---

[42] Horton dismisses *2 Enoch*; see *The Melchizedek Tradition*, 81. See also the discussion of *2 En.* 69-73 on 172-173 above, and Gieschen, "Similar Melchizedek Tradition", 364-379.

[43] See discussion on 172-173 above.

[44] *T. Levi* 3:1-4. For further evidence and a treatment of this influence upon Hebrews, see Attridge, *Hebrews*, 99-100.

[45] Horton, *Melchizedek Tradition*, 153.

[46] For further discussion of this understanding see Hay, *Glory at the Right Hand*, 146-48, and P. Kobelski, *Melchizedek and Melchireša'*, 118-119.

priest forever because of his resurrection: "Consequently, he is able for all time to save those who approach God through him, since he always lives to make intercession for them" (7.25; cf. 7.16).

What must be kept in mind as one sorts out the ideology of these verses is how the author clearly maintains the spotlight on Jesus even as he elevates Melchizedek. *Jesus is the angelomorphic priest of Hebrews, not Melchizedek.*[47] The elevation of Melchizedek serves the purpose of elevating Jesus. Although the precise relationship between these two is not defined beyond Melchizedek being "made like the Son of God" (7.3) and Jesus being "according to the likeness of Melchizedek" (7.15), Jesus is certainly not Melchizedek incarnate according to Hebrews; he is the Son of God incarnate.[48] The relationship between Melchizedek and Jesus is best described in terms of typology.[49] The author maintains a delicate balance in his use of Melchizedek: to delimit Melchizedek in relation to Jesus would downplay the status of the Melchizedek priesthood and discredit the argument that the author constructed against the Levitical priesthood; to put more focus on Melchizedek as an eternal angelomorphic priestly mediator would take Jesus from the center stage of this epistle.

D. *The Word of God*

The Epistle to the Hebrews is filled with exhortations that are coupled with warnings. One of the vivid warnings found in this letter is the depiction of "the Word of God" as Judge:

> [4.11] Let us therefore strive to enter that rest, that no one fall by the same sort of disobedience [i.e., Israel's rebellion in the wilderness;

---

[47] See Gieschen, "Similar Melchizedek Tradition", 374-379.

[48] Since the mediator Melchizedek is already named, it is less probable that he would be equated with Jesus. It is easier to equate an unnamed mediator figure (e.g., Son of Man) with a historical personage. Furthermore, it is possible that the author of Hebrews did not see Melchizedek as an eternal angelomorphic priest, but uses these Jewish traditions as the means to express the surperiority of the high priesthood of Christ over that of Levi.

[49] L. Goppelt ably articulates typology as an central way early Christians appropriated the OT, but fails to see a Melchizedek-Christ typology in Hebrews; see *Typos: The Typological Interpretation of the Old Testament in the New* (Grand Rapids: Erdmanns, 1982) 163-170, esp. 164.

cf. Heb 3.16-19]. [12] For the Word of God [ὁ λόγος τοῦ θεοῦ] is living and active, sharper than any two-edged sword, piercing to the division of soul and spirit, of joints and marrow, and discerning the thoughts and intensions of the heart. [13] Namely, no creature is hidden before him, but all creatures are bare and laid open to his eyes, whom for us is the Word [πρὸς ὃν ἡμῖν ὁ λόγος].

Harold Attridge considers the possibility of a Christological interpretation of this text, but concludes that it focuses on God as the all-seeing Judge and "does not involve any inference to Jesus as the Logos".[50] This conclusion is usually based upon the limited testimony in Hebrews that judgment is the exclusive role of God (i.e., the Father).[51] The interpreter is left with a text that describes God as the angelomorphic "Word" (or "Word of God") who is a personal eschatological Judge.[52]

The conclusion that God is "the Word of God", however, is far from certain for four reasons. First, there is abundant testimony in early Christianity that Jesus is the eschatological judge. This fact alone weakens the claim that the author—much less the readers—of this epistle would not have understood Christ to be the judge depicted here. Second, the focus on *God as Judge* occurs primarily toward the end of the epistle (10.31; 12.23; 13.4) as a counterbalance to the dominant portrait of *Christ as the merciful priest*. Christ is not placed on the judgment throne in the closing chapters because such an image would detract from the picture painted of Christ before the mercy seat in the heavenly Holy of Holies. Third, there is internal evidence that the author associated Jesus with end-time judgment:

> [9.27] And just as it is appointed for men to die once, and after that comes judgment, [28] so Christ, having been offered once to bear the sins of many, will appear a second time, not to deal with sin but to save those who are eagerly waiting for him.

---

[50] Attridge, *Hebrews*, 133-134.
[51] For judgment depicted as God's role, see 10.31; 12.23; 13.4. Psalm 110, which speaks of YHWH carrying out judgment through his priest-king, is also frequently applied to Christ in Hebrews (1.3, 13; 5.6, 10; 6.20; 7.11, 15, 17, 21). Although the Psalm is primarily used to assert a priestly order after Melchizedek, the portion which speaks of judgment is quoted and applied to Christ in 1.13.
[52] Although there is some distinction in Hebrews between use of ῥῆμα (1.3; 6.5; 11.3; 12.19) and λόγος (2.2; 4.2, 12, 13; 5.11, 13; 6.1; 7.28; 12.19; 13.7, 17, 22), little can be said about this usage except that λόγος is used in its technical sense as a divine title. For historical background, see 103-113 above.

Although not explicit, the second coming of Christ to save those who are waiting for him also involves the condemnation of those who are not waiting for him. Fourth, it is much easier to explain why the author would refer to ὁ λόγος τοῦ θεοῦ as a designation for Christ, than it is to explain why he would refer to θεός as ὁ λόγος τοῦ θεοῦ. This evidence, although not conclusive, supports a Christological interpretation of this text.

This conception of the Word of God as Judge, which developed from the Destroyer Angel traditions (e.g., Wis 18.14-16), is especially visible in Rev 19.11-16, where the one who "judges in righteousness" and who has a "sharp sword" is described:

> [12] His eyes are like a flame of fire, and on his head are many diadems; and he has a Name inscribed which no one knows but himself. [13] He is clad in a robe dipped in blood, and the name by which he is called is the Word of God.[53]

The Targumim may have been instrumental in joining the Destroying Angel traditions together with "the Word".[54] In the discussion about the Word as a Divine Hypostasis, it was noted that the *Memra* replaces the figure of the Angel of the Lord in some texts, such as in the Exodus Passover account (*Tg. Neof.* Exod 12.12; cf. *Tg. Neof.* Exod 11.4 and 12.13). There is also evidence that the *Memra* carries out tasks of judgment:

> [*Tg. Ps-J.* Num 24.23] Woe to them that are alive at the time when the *Memra* of Yahweh shall be revealed to give the good reward to the righteous and to take vengence on the wicked.

> [*Tg. Neb.* Isa 8.14] His *Memra* will be among you for vengeance.

There is also evidence in Philo of the Word functioning as a judge. The basis for this understanding appears to be the oft-quoted Exod 23.20-21 about the angel whom God would send ahead of Israel to guide and discipline them. Philo makes the following comments in his discussion of Exod 23.20-21:

> [*Quaes Ex* 2.13] Therefore of necessity was the Logos appointed as judge and mediator [μεσίτης], who is called "angel." Him He sets "before the face," there where the place of the eyes and senses is, in order that by seeing and receiving sense it [i.e., humanity] may

---

[53] For detailed discussion, see 252-256 above.
[54] See the discussion and bibliography on 112-114 above. In the context of this discussion of the Word of God as Judge is the disobedience and punishment of ancient Israel in the wilderness (Heb 3.16-19).

follow the leadership of virtue, not unwillingly but willingly [. . .]. And this is the most sovereign and principal [being] which the heaven and earth and the whole world knows. And he who has so great a power must necessarily be filled with all-powerful wisdom.

Elsewhere Philo describes the dividing action of the Word in a non-judgment context (cf. Heb 4.12):

[*Heres* 130] He [Moses] wishes you to think of God who cannot be shewn, as severing through the Severer of all things, that is his Word, the whole succession of things material and immaterial whose natures appear to us to be knitted together and united. That severing Word whetted to an edge of utmost sharpness never ceases to divide.

Therefore, Heb 4.11-13 appears to be using angelomorphic terminology and tradition in its description of the eschatological Judge who is probably Christ, but could be God (the Father). These verses can be viewed as preserving a theologically-centered idea of God as Judge which often becomes a Christologically-centered idea in early Christianity.

E. *Conclusion*

Several ideas from angelomorphic terms and traditions that have been present in other documents are vital to the fabric of this epistle: the Name, Firstborn, the Glory, Enthroned Son, Apostle, and Creator. No disavowal or polemic against these angelomorphic traditions was found. Instead, the author embraced Angelomorphic Christology as support for the superiority of Christ. Furthermore, the prominent focus on Christ as the High Priest in Hebrews is the door through which some unique Jewish traditions about angelomorphic high priests enter the NT. Finally, the depiction of the "Word of God" as Judge—whether or not one sees its as Christological—shows that this angelomorphic tradition certainly impacted early Christian understandings of the eschatological theophany and judgment.

CHAPTER FOURTEEN

THE PAULINE EPISTLES

This examination of early evidence for Angelomorphic Christology climaxes with the Pauline corpus since it is widely accepted among scholars that the Apostle Paul wrote the earliest documents in the NT. Because the primary purpose of this examination is not to define the Christology of the Apostle Paul, evidence from the entire Pauline corpus will be considered, including those epistles many scholars consider to be Deutero-Pauline.[1] The purpose of this chapter, as with the others in Part III, is to set forth evidence which demonstrates that angelomorphic traditions such as those discussed in Part II played a formative role in the Christology expressed in some of the earliest extant documents of Christianity.

A perusal of the Pauline corpus indicates that angelmorphic traditions played a substantial role in Pauline Christology. This evidence will be examined in the following order: God's Angel; the Destroyer; the Heavenly Man; the Power of God and the Wisdom of God; the Image, the Glory, and the Spirit; the Form of God and the Name; the Body; and the Image of the Invisible God, the Head of the Body, the Firstborn, and the Beginning.

A. *God's Angel*

Galatians 4.14 is the one place in the Pauline corpus where there is an overt reference to Jesus as God's Angel. There Paul makes the curious claim that the Christians he had visited and now is writing to had welcomed him "as God's Angel, as Christ Jesus." Most exegetes interpret this phrase as a hypothetical comparison: the Galatians received Paul *as if* he were an angelic mediator, indeed *as if* he were Christ himself; supposedly, they knew that he was

---

[1] Ephesians, Colossians, 1-2 Timothy and Titus are considered to be Deutero-Pauline by many scholars; see H. Conzelmann and A. Lindemann, *Interpreting the New Testament* (trans. S. Schwatzmann; Peabody: Hendrickson, 1988) 199-213. Although I side with scholars who defend Pauline authorship, the answer to this question is not vital to the research below.

neither.² This position emphasizes that if he did use the title "God's Angel" for himself, then he used it metaphorically or in its basic meaning of "messenger".³ A few scholars have asserted that Paul is identifying himself as an angelic being of sorts.⁴ Still fewer have done more than hint that this text implies an Angelomorphic Christology.⁵ There is, however, support for a more literal exegesis of Gal 4.14b: Paul understood that the Galatians had received him as an angelic being. It will be argued that this understanding was based upon Paul's conviction that he had been united with a very specific angel: God's Angel, Christ Jesus.⁶

It is clear that some at the Galatian church had undermined the authority of Paul and had led other members astray from his teaching by returning them to works of the Law and circumcision as the means to life with God (cf. 1.6-9; 3.1-15; 6.12-17).⁷ Paul's authority as the source of revelation had been seriously questioned and eroded. The immediate context of Paul's claim in 4.14b is a

---

² Several commentaries can be cited as examples of this position: H. Meyer, *Galatians and Ephesians* (6th ed.; London: T&T Clark, 1885) 187; G. Duncan, *Galatians* (New York: Harper, 1934) 140; F.F. Bruce, *Galatians* (Exeter: Paternoster, 1982) 209; R. Fung, *The Epistle to the Galatians* (NICNT; Grand Rapids: Eerdmans, 1988) 198; H. Betz, *Galatians* (Hermenia; Philadelphia: Fortress, 1979) 226.

³ Bousset takes the position that "[. . .] in Gal. 4.14 ἄγγελος is simply 'emissary'[. . .]"; see *Kyrios Christos*, 257 n.68; see also Dunn, *Christology in the Making*, 155-156.

⁴ Commentators who argue a position that follows the text more closely include J. de Zwaan, "Gal 4,14 aus dem Neugrieschen erklärt", *ZNW* 10 (1909) 246-250; H. Schlier, "ἐκπτύω" *TDNT* 2.448, and *Der Breif an die Galater* (Meyer's 13th ed.; Göttingen: Vandenhoeck and Ruprecht, 1965) 210-211; U. Borse, *Der Standort des Galaterbriefs* (Köln: Peter Hanstein, 1972) 102-103. The texts which provide support are: Gal 1.11-12; 1.15-16; 2.20; 2 Cor 11.3-6.

⁵ Longenecker implies this possibility in his earlier writings, but distances himself from it in his more recent commentary on Galatians; see: "Some Distinctive Early Christological Motifs", 532; *Christology of Early Jewish Christianity*, 31; and *Galatians* (WBC; Waco: Word, 1990) 192. Barker makes a more forceful, but unsupported, assertion in *The Great Angel*, 223. Scheidweiler argues for Angel Christology in Gal 4.14; see "Novatian und die Engelchristologie", 138-139.

⁶ Although Paul does not overtly label Christ as "the Angel of the Lord" in any of his letters, Paul does identify Christ as "the Power", "Wisdom", "the Heavenly Man", and especially as "the Glory", all of which have angelomorphic roots closely linked with the Angel of the Lord; see Quispel, "Ezekiel 1.28 in Jewish Mysticism", 7-13, Segal, *Paul the Convert*, 35-71, and Newman, *Paul's Glory-Christology*, 241-247.

⁷ On the occasion of Galatians, see Betz, *Galatians*, 1-9, and J. H. Schütz, *Paul and the Anatomy of Apostolic Authority* (Cambridge: CUP, 1975) 114-158.

reminder of how positively the Galatians had received him and his message when he visited.[8] They had welcomed Paul as a divine mediator, even though his physical condition had apparently put them to the test[9]:

> [4.11] I am afraid that my work for you may have been wasted. [12] Brothers, I beg you, become as I am, for I also have become as you are. [13] You have done me no wrong. You know that it was because of a physical infirmity that I first announced the gospel to you; [14] though my condition put you to the test, you did not scorn or despise me, but as God's Angel you welcomed me, as [namely] Christ Jesus. What has become of the good will you felt?

Hans Dieter Betz gives an informed exegesis of 4.14b that, like much of current scholarship, hesitates to link Paul directly with an angel or Christ:

> The ὡς ("as if") expresses a distinction, since Paul does not intend to say that he actually came as an angel. No doubt, as an apostle of Christ he considers himself *the* messenger sent by God to the Galatians for the sake of their salvation. Indeed they did welcome him as if he were Jesus Christ himself. This statement is also more than a simple exaggeration, since Paul, as the apostle and "imitator" of Christ, represents Christ. Those who welcome him welcome Christ. And yet, the statements Paul makes about himself are exaggerations. They amount to a praise of the Galatians, corresponding to the common "praise among true friends."[10]

From these comments it is clear that Betz recognizes the boldness of what Paul is asserting, but he weakens the forcefulness of Paul's statements by labeling them "exaggerations". Margaret Mitchell goes further in this direction by stating that "[. . .] there is nothing in this passage to suggest that Paul likens himself to the supernatural envoys, angels."[11] Although the Pauline epistles reflect a

---

[8] There is a direct relationship between how people received an envoy and their feelings/thoughts about the person/God who sent the envoy; see M. Mitchell, "New Testament Envoys in the Context of Greco-Roman Diplomatic and Epistolary Conventions: The Example of Timothy and Titus", *JBL* 111 (1992) 641-662. Mitchell's research builds on, and is a corrective for, that of R. Funk, "The Apostolic *Parousia*: Form and Significance", in *Christian History and Interpretation: Studies Presented to John Knox* (ed. W. Farmer, C. Moule, and R. Niebuhr; Cambridge: CUP, 1967) 249-269.

[9] For the possible origin of this physical condition as the result of persecution, see A. Goddard and S. Cummins, "Ill or Ill-Treated? Conflict and Persecution as the Context of Paul's Original Ministry in Galatia", *JSNT* 20 (1993) 93-126.

[10] Betz, *Galatians*, 226.

[11] "New Testament Envoys", 646 n.17.

thorough awareness of Greco-Roman diplomatic conventions, Paul's understanding of apostleship is not limited to such conventions. The comparisons in 4.14b are more than simple similes. The common conclusion of scholarship that Paul did not, in a very significant way, conceive of himself as an angelic being—even Christ himself—needs to be challenged.

The first question that confronts the reader in 4.14b is: What does Paul mean by ἄγγελον θεοῦ? While the basic meaning of ἄγγελος is "one who brings a message, messenger, envoy, or emissary", in Jewish, Christian, and even in many Greco-Roman contexts it was a *terminus technicus* used to identify a spirit or heavenly being who mediates between the human and divine realms.[12] The LXX employed ἄγγελος to translate מלאך, which is used in the MT to identify such mediator figures. In Greco-Roman mythology Hermes is the primary ἄγγελος of Zeus in the realm of the gods, even though other divine ἄγγελοι are mentioned.[13] The incident recorded in Acts 14.12, in which Paul was hailed as Hermes and Barnabas was received as Zeus, is instructive for how people in the region of Galatia possibly perceived and received Paul as a divine being.[14]

The Pauline epistles use ἄγγελος in the same technical sense as in the LXX; an ἄγγελος is a spirit who mediates between the heavenly and earthly realms.[15] This word appears 13 times in the Pauline corpus.[16] Exegetes generally interpret ἄγγελος in its

---

[12] In addition to the standard lexicons, see W. Grundmann, G. von Rad, and G. Kittel, "ἄγγελος", *TDNT* 1.74-87.

[13] For primary sources, see Grundmann, "ἄγγελος", *TDNT* 1.74-76.

[14] Acts 14 clearly reflects the story of Baucis and Philemon who were visted by Zeus and Hermes in that general region (Ovid, *Metam.* 8.626). Most modern scholars downplay any link between Acts 14 and Galatians 4 because they question the reliabilty of Acts and because the people of Lystra subsequently turned against Paul according to Acts 14.19 (cf. Fung, *Galatians*, 198 n.17). Windisch, however, uses both Gal 4.14b and Acts 14.8, as well as Acts 28.3, for evidence of how early Christians received Paul as a Divine Man; see *Paulus und Christus* (Leipzig: J. C. Hinrichs'sche, 1934) 279-286.

[15] This definition does not exclude "fallen" angels, since they also were created as heavenly spirits. See the foundational studies by O. Everling, *Die paulinishe Angelolgie and Dämonologie* (Göttingen: Vandenhoeck & Ruprecht, 1888), and M. Dibelius, *Die Geisterwelt in Glauben des Paulus* (Göttingen: Vandenhoeck & Ruprecht, 1909). Paul does teach a pronounced demonology; see P. Benoit, "Pauline Angelology and Demonology", *RSB* 3 (1983) 1-18, but contra W. Carr, *Angels and Principalities* (Cambridge: CUP, 1981). See summary and critique of research in C. Arnold, *Ephesians: Power and Magic* (Grand Rapids: Baker, 1992) 42-51.

[16] Rom 8.38; 1 Cor 4.9; 6.3; 11.10; 13.1; 2 Cor 11.14; 12.7; Gal 1.8; 3.19; 4.14;

technical sense, except in one instance: "the thorn-in-the-flesh" ἄγγελος τοῦ σατανᾶ in 2 Cor 12.7 (usually translated "messenger of Satan"). Recent research, however, has explicated the Jewish mystical experience described by Paul and supports a more literal interpretation of ἄγγελος τοῦ σατανᾶ as an "angel of Satan" who hindered Paul during his visionary ascent.[17]

Moreover, Paul's other uses of ἄγγελος in Galatians support the technical meaning in 4.14b. Paul contrasts himself with an angel from heaven in 1.8: "But even if *we or an angel from heaven* should proclaim to you a gospel contrary to what we proclaimed, let that one be accursed" (cf. 2 Cor 11.4). This text presents the possibility that Paul considered himself to be an angel (from earth). Literary evidence for the equation or identification of an apostle as an angel has already been shown.[18] Paul does associate the realms of apostles and angels in his ringing condemnation of false apostles in 2 Corinthians:

> [11.13] For such boasters are false apostles, deceitful workers, disguising themselves as apostles of Christ. [14] And no wonder! Even Satan disguises himself as an angel of light. [15] So it is not strange if his ministers also disguise themselves as ministers of righteousness.

He makes one other reference to angels as spiritual beings in Galatians, one which is well-known, when he notes in 3.19 that the Law "[. . .] was ordained through angels by a mediator [Moses]".

Further support for this exegesis of 4.14b is found in 4.14a where Paul describes how the Galatians could have "scorned or rejected" him because his physical situation put them to the test. While the precise meaning of the idiomatic phrase καὶ τὸν περρασμὸν ὑμῶν ἐν τῇ σαρκί μου is difficult to ascertain, it definitely refers to the physical condition mentioned in 4.13.[19] With regard to the

---

2 Thess 1.7; Col 2.28; 1 Tim 5.21.

[17] Morray-Jones, "Paradise Revisited", esp. 282. For this idea he is dependent on the exegesis of R.M. Price, "Punished in Paradise (An Exegetical Theory on II Corinthians 12.1-10)", *JSNT* 7 (1980) 33-40.

[18] See discussion on 176-180 above.

[19] H. Seesemann, "πεῖρα", *TDNT* 6.32, renders this verse "You did not succumb to the temptation to despise me because of the weakness of my flesh". He also mentions the possiblity that it means: "[. . .] the Galatians did not fall victim to the tempter, who sought to exploit the apostle's sickness" (cf. 1 Cor 7.5; 2 Cor 2.11; 1 Thess 3.5). Based upon the practice of physiognomy in

Galatians' possible rejection of Paul, Albert Schweitzer comments on the verb ἐκπτύω ("to spit out or despise") in 4.14a: "[. . .] it was usual to spit out in the presence of men who had mysterious illnesses in order to protect oneself against the demon to whom the sickness in question was attributed".[20] This implication sets up a stark contrast in 4.14: rather than rejecting Paul as demon-possessed, the Galatians welcomed him as Christ-possessed; rather than reject him as Satan's demon, they received him as God's Angel.[21] Earlier in this epistle Paul speaks of Christ living in him: "I have been crucified with Christ; it is no longer I who live, but Christ who lives in me" (Gal 2.20). Paul also refers to the Christ in Christians as the "Spirit of Christ": "Any one who does not have the Spirit of Christ does not belong to him; but if Christ is in you, although your bodies are dead because of sin, your spirits are alive because of righteousness" (Rom 8.9b-10).[22]

The broader context of this pericope also encourages the understanding of Paul as an angelic being. Paul accuses the Galatians in 4.9 of leaving their freedom in Christ (who is the *Spirit*) and returning to the slavery of the *elemental spirits of the world* (τὰ στοιχεῖα τοῦ κόσμου; cf. 4.3). In this contrast Paul reveals his world view: Based on Greco-Roman and Jewish syncretism, Paul affirmed that demonic entities of cosmic proportions are active and hostile towards humans.[23] They are not only at work inside of humans, but also visit and manifest themselves in various ways from the outside. In short, Paul has a world view which is dominated by spiritual beings such as angels of God and Satan.

---

antiquity (the practice of judging inward spirit by outward appearance; e.g., Aristotle, *Physiognomy* 805a), it is possible that after Paul's visit some Galatians judged Paul's inward spirit based upon his outward appearance or suffering, whatever its cause.

[20] *The Mysticism of Paul the Apostle* (New York: Seabury, 1968 repr. [1931]) 152-53. For a similar explanation, see Schlier, "ἐκπτύω", 448, or de Zwaan, "Gal 4.14", 247-248.

[21] This kind of contrast is also found in 2 Cor 6.15, where Paul contrasts Christ with Beliar (i.e., Satan). There is evidence that speaks of Beliar as a spirit who can dwell within a person; see T. Lewis, "Belial", *ABD* 1.654-656.

[22] Conversely, Paul indicates that Satan can possess a person to the point where he is seen as an incarnation of Satan; see "the man of lawlessness" in 2 Thess 2.1-12. For a tradition-history of this figure, see G. Jenks, *The Origins and Early Development of the Antichrist Myth* (BZNW 59; Berlin: de Gruyter, 1991).

[23] See Betz, *Galatians*, 204-205, and note 15 above.

Thus, it is a natural consequence that Paul notes how the Galatians, who had been freed from the elemental spirits, acknowledged him as God's Angel (one in whom Christ dwells and speaks) in spite of his outward appearance or suffering. Paul is alluding to the familiar motif of the ready welcome of a heavenly being who suddenly appears. He purposely links this motif with the welcome that the Galatians gave him.[24]

Paul's discussion of his source of revelation in Gal 1.11-12 is additional evidence supporting the interpretation of ἄγγελος in its technical sense in 4.14b. After clearly stating that his apostleship is not of human origin but directly from Jesus Christ (1.1-2), he writes:

> [11] For I would have you know, brethren, that the gospel that was proclaimed by me is not of human origin; [12] for I did not receive [παρέλαβον] it from a human source, nor was I taught it, but I received it through a revelation [ἀποκαλύψεως] of Jesus Christ.

The use of ἀποκαλύψεως here indicates that Paul conceives of himself in a line of continutity with other Jewish prophets or mystics who were given a glimpse of the chariot-throne of God as depicted in Ezekiel 1, which only a select few were privileged to behold.[25] This aspect of Paul's experience is explicitly discussed in 2 Corinthians 12. Evidence of a mystical experience can also be seen in the accounts of Paul's conversion Christophany recorded

---

[24] Betz, *Galatians*, 226. For textual examples, see Gen 18.1-19.22; Heb 13.2; *Didache* 12; *1 Clem.* 10.7; 12.1.

[25] W. Bousset pointed in this direction already with "Die Himmelsreise der Seele", *ARW* 4 (1901) 136-169. This aspect of Paul's thought is being given increased attention by scholars; see J. Bowker, "'Merkabah' Visions and the Visions of Paul", *JSS* 16 (1971) 157-173; Rowland, *Open Heaven*, 368-386; J. Tabor, *Things Unutterable: Paul's Ascent to Paradise in its Greco-Roman, Judaic and Early Christian Contexts* (London: Lanham, 1986); B. Young, "The Ascension Motif of 2 Corinthians in Jewish, Christian and Gnostic Texts", *GTJ* 9 (1988) 73-108; Segal, *Paul the Convert*, 34-71, Newman, *Paul's Glory-Christology*, 164-212; Morray-Jones, "Paradise Revisited"; and J. Scott, "The Triumph of God in 2 Cor 2.14: Additional Evidence of Merkabah Mysticism in Paul", *NTS* 42 (1996) 260-281. P. Schäfer has challenged this direction; see "New Testament and Hekhalot Literature: The Journey into Heaven in Paul and in Merkabah Mysticism", *JJS* 35 (1984) 19-35. This mystical aspect of Paul's revelations/visions is supported by testimony from Acts regarding his conversion experience (Acts 9.3-8; 22.6-11; 26.12-18) and other visions (Acts 16.9-10; 18.9-10; and 22.17-21). It is probable that 2 Corinthians 12 is not a reference to Paul's Damascus road conversion, but could be related to the vision recorded in Acts 22; see Morray-Jones, "Paradise Revisited", 284-290.

in Acts.[26] Therefore, Paul's claim that he was received as an angel of God is very understandable and natural if he had, as this epistle indicates, received a direct revelation or vision of Jesus Christ.[27]

Paul's claim becomes even more plausible when one realizes that visionary ascent experiences can involve the transformation of the seer into the likeness of the Divine Image. Christopher Morray-Jones has traced the origins of this transformation idea in Paul and other early Christians to apocalyptic-*merkabah* tradition where "[. . .] the ascent into heaven and the vision of the *kabod* (whom Paul identifies as Christ) involves a transformation of the visionary into an angelic or supra-angelic likeness of this glory or divine image".[28] There are a number of instances in apocalyptic/mystical literature where a human is transformed into an angelic being. For example, *2 Enoch* states:

> [22.8] And the Lord said to Michael, "Go, and extract Enoch from [his] earthly clothing. And anoint him with my delightful oil, and put him into the clothes of my glory." [9] And so Michael did, just as the Lord had said to him. He anointed me and he clothed me. And the appearance of that oil is greater than the greatest light and its ointment is like sweet dew, and its fragrance myrrh; and it is like the rays of the glittering sun. [10] And I looked at myself, and I had become like one of his glorious ones, and there was no observable difference.

This text clearly asserts that Enoch was transformed into an angelic being after his visionary ascent to behold the *Merkabah*. Similar ideas appear to be the basis for Paul's understanding of his transformation which resulted from his vision of Christ on the road to Damascus and the transformation which Christians experience in baptism.[29]

---

[26] Note the use of ἀποκαλύψεως in 2 Cor 12.1 and 12.6. Links between Ezekiel 1 and Paul's conversion experience as recorded in Acts (9.3-8; 22.6-11; 26.12-18) have been shown by several scholars; see Quispel, "Ezekiel 1.26 in Jewish Mysticism", 8.

[27] Gal 1.1; 1.12; 2.7; 2.20; cf. 2 Cor 4.6; 10.8; 13.10; 1 Cor 9.1; 15.8.

[28] "Paradise Revisited (Part 2)", 273; see esp. his "Transformational Mysticism", 1-31, where much textual evidence is perused.

[29] Paul's understanding of transformation is not limited to mystics who ascend to the *Merkabah*. For Paul this transformation into the image of Christ happens in all who through baptism and believing behold the Glory in the face of Jesus Christ (2 Cor 3.18); see De Conick and Fossum, "Stripped Before God", 123-150, and Morray-Jones, "Paradise Revisted", 273 n.27; and Morray-Jones "Transformational Mysticism", 28. Furthermore, for Paul this transformation does not preclude carrying in his body the outward image of Christ's sufferings (cf. Gal 6.17; 2 Cor 4.10; Phil 3.10).

Now that the meaning of ἄγγελος has been clarified, a second important question which arises from Gal 4.14b involves what is meant by the parallel ὡς clauses: ἀλλὰ ὡς ἄγγελον θεοῦ ἐδέξασθε με, ὡς Χριστὸν Ἰησοῦν. It is well-known that ὡς can be used in wide variety of ways. It is used here as an adverb of manner (a relative meaning "as, like as, just as").[30] Such clauses, obviously, do not imply that the comparison is hypothetical. If Paul wanted to emphasize a hypothetical comparison he would have used ὡς ἄν (cf. 1 Thess 2.7).

Philemon 17 is often used to support a hypothetical interpretation of ὡς in Gal 4.14b. In a manner similar to Gal 4.14b, Philemon 17 contains a statement of Paul regarding the act of welcoming someone: "Therefore, if you have fellowship with me, welcome him [Onesimus] as me [προσλαβοῦ αὐτὸν ὡς ἐμέ]". This, too, is more than a simple simile. Paul is not urging Philemon to welcome Onesimus *as if* this slave were Paul; he is exhorting him to welcome Onesimus *as* Paul, because both are truly "brothers" in Christ (vs. 16).

Didache 11.3-4 provides an even closer contextual parallel: "And concerning the Apostles and Prophets, act thus according to the ordinance of the Gospel. Let every Apostle who comes to you be received as the Lord [δεχθήτω ὡς κύριος]". This is even stronger language than Jesus' words: "Whoever welcomes you, welcomes me" (Matt 10.40). Paul is saying that the Galatians recognized and received him as a true apostle in whom Christ lives and speaks: "you received me [. . .] as Christ Jesus".

It has been demonstrated that there is firm literary ground for the conclusion that the Apostle Paul could have been regarded and could have regarded himself as "an angel". A closer reading of 4.14b, however, indicates that Paul is being more specific about the angel of God with whom he was identified. As discussed above, in Gal 1.8 Paul contrasts the authority of his original proclamation of the gospel with that of an angel from heaven: "But even if we or an angel from heaven should proclaim to you a gospel contrary to what we proclaimed, let that one be accursed". This assertion follows Paul's statement about the origin of his apostleship as direct

---

[30] LSJ (2d ed.) 2038, sec. Ab, and BAGD (2d ed.) 898, sec. III.1; BDF sec. 453; H. Smyth, *A Greek Grammar* (Cambridge, MA: HUP, 1956), sec. 2463; A. T. Robertson, *A Grammar of the Greek New Testament* (Nashville: Broadman, 1934) 967-969.

from Jesus Christ and God the Father (1.1) and precedes his discussion of the origin of the gospel he preached as a direct revelation from Jesus Christ (1.11-12). Therefore, Paul places the authority of his office as an apostle and the authority of his original proclamation above that of "an angel from heaven". Based upon 1.8 and its context, Paul does not assert in 4.14b that the Galatians received him as "an" angel from among the myriads in God's service in heaven and on earth; rather, they received Paul as the most authoritative angel who not only sent him (Gal 1:1), but also lives in him (Gal 2:20) and speaks in him (2 Cor 13:3): God's Angel, Christ Jesus. J. de Zwaan emphasizes that Paul specifically mentioned that the Galatians received him as Christ because Paul also bore the marks which ordinary angels of God do not bear, but which Christ bears (cf. 2 Cor 1.5; Phil 3.10; Gal 6.17).[31]

The *crux* in this exegesis of 4.14b is the relationship between the two ὡς clauses: ἀλλὰ ὡς ἄγγελον θεοῦ ἐδέξασθε με, ὡς Χριστὸν Ἰησοῦν. The clauses are clearly in apposition to each other: "as God's Angel, as Christ Jesus". Most exegetes interpret this positioning in terms of distinct and increasing comparisons. To paraphrase: "You Galatians received me as if I were an angel of God. Actually, that is not stating things strongly enough; you received me as if I were Christ himself speaking to you". This interpretation ignores the very real possibility that Paul is associating himself with one person holding both titles: God's Angel and Christ Jesus. Therefore, instead of seeing the clauses in terms of distinct and increasing comparisons, this appositional structure understands the second ὡς clause as epexegetical (i.e., it explains or elaborates on the first clause). Thus, the translation: "You received me as God's Angel, namely Christ Jesus."

There are only two other instances of appositional ὡς clauses in the Pauline corpus: 1 Cor 3.1 and 2 Cor 2.17. All three occurences are shown here in order to illustrate how Paul uses this grammatical construction:

> [1 Cor 3.1] I could not speak to you as [ὡς] spiritual people, but as [ἀλλ' ὡς] people of the flesh, namely [ὡς] infants in Christ ["infants in Christ" clarifies "people of the flesh"].

---

[31] "Gal 4.14", 247-248. Paul may have seen his suffering as the "seal" or "sign" of his apostleship, much like a "sign" or "seal" was placed upon archangels (cf. *Odes Sol.* 4.6-8); cf. Fossum, *Name of God*, 95-105.

[2 Cor 2.17] For we are not as [ὡς] the many who peddle God's word; but as [ἀλλ' ὡς] men of sincerity we speak, namely [ἀλλ' ὡς] men from God, the presence of God in Christ ["men from God, the presence of God in Christ" further clarifies "men of sincerity"].[32]

[Gal 4.14] Though my condition put you to the test, you did not scorn or despise me, but as [ἀλλ' ὡς] God's Angel you received me, namely [ὡς] Christ Jesus ["Christ Jesus" clarifies "God's Angel"].

In the first two examples, both ὡς clauses follow an adversative (ἀλλά), both support the conclusion that the second clause is epexegetical, and both clauses deal with descriptions of the same people groups (i.e., people of the flesh=infants in Christ; men of sincerity=men from God). As there is an organic connection between the clauses in the first two examples, so there is an organic connection between "God's Angel" and "Christ Jesus" in Gal 4.14b. Why does Paul put these two figures in apposition? Because they belong to the same person: Paul understood Christ Jesus as God's Angel (i.e., the Angel of YHWH).[33]

This exegesis and conclusion is not given in a vacuum. In the sections below further evidence will show that these letters reflect various angelomorphic traditions which support the position that Paul understood Jesus as God's Angel. Moreover, it will be demonstrated that there is explicit evidence in 1 Cor 10.1-10 that Paul understood the Angel of the Lord to be the preexistent Christ.

B. *The Destroyer*

In 1 Cor 10.1-10 Paul acknowledges the presence of Christ in the life of Israel as they traveled through the wilderness after the Exodus.[34] Discussion of this Christological presence has tended to focus on Christ as "the spiritual Rock" who followed Israel (10.4),

---

[32] See the helpful explanation of this text by Scott, "The Triumph of God", 275.

[33] It is very improbable that Paul would use the actual title ὁ ἄγγελος τοῦ κυρίου since one of his primary exalted confessions of Jesus is ὁ κύριος. This confession probably prompted his use of ἄγγελον θεοῦ instead of ἄγγελον τοῦ κυρίου in Gal 4.14. One other instance of very explicit Angelomorphic Christology in Paul is found in 1 Thess 4.16: "the Lord *himself* will descend from heaven with a summons, [namely] *with a voice of an archangel* and with the trumpet of God, and the dead in Christ will be raised first".

[34] Hanson argues for a simple picture of Christ active in the OT; see *Jesus Christ in the OT*, 10-25.

which is evidence for how Paul identified the figure of Wisdom with Christ.[35] Even more significant for evidence of Angelomorphic Christology in this pericope, however, is the mention that "Christ" was the one whom Israel put "to the test" with their disobedience:

> [7] Do not become idolaters as some of them did; as it is written, "The people sat down to eat and drink, and they rose up to play" [cf. Exod 32.4-6] [8] We must not indulge in sexual immorality as some of them did, and twenty-three thousand fell in a single day [cf. Num 25.2-9]. [9] We must not put Christ to the test [μηδὲ ἐκπειράζωμεν τὸν Χριστόν], as some of them did, and were destroyed by serpents [cf. Num 21.5-6]. [10] And do not complain as some of them did, and were destroyed by the Destroyer [cf. Num 16.41-50].

The problematic nature of this assertion of Christ's presence with ancient Israel is visible in textual emendations: several texts have substituted τὸν κυρίον or τὸν θεόν for τὸν Χριστόν in 10.9.[36] Such emendations eliminate the perceived problem. The more difficult reading, however, leaves the exegete with the probing question: How, according to Paul, was "Christ" present with Israel that they could "put him to the test"?

There are two primary answers to this question. One possibility is that since Paul confessed "Jesus is κύριος" (1 Cor 12.3; Phil 2.11), he saw Christ as active in OT narratives where κύριος was active.[37]

---

[35] See: Exod 17.1-7; Num 20.7-13; 21.17; Ps 77.20; 104.41; 113.8; Isa 48.21; 26.4. For a discussion of this tradition, see E.E. Ellis, *Prophecy and Hermeneutic in Early Christianity* (WUNT 1/18; Tübingen: Mohr/Siebeck, 1978) 209-212. The Christological identification of the Rock as Christ probably grew from the Hellenistic Jewish exegesis, such as found in Philo, which identified this Rock as Wisdom; see *Quod Det* 115; *Leg All* 2.86; *Ebr* 112; *Somn* 2.270. It should be remembered that Wisdom is an angelomorphic tradition in Philo and elsewhere. "The Rock" is a title used for Christ in other early Christian literature which also identifies him as "Angel" (e.g., *Hermas Sim.* IX.12.2; Justin, *Dial. Trypho* 34). Another impetus for this Christological identification may have been the confession that Jesus is κύριος (1 Cor 12.3; Phil 2.11). The Song of Moses, apart from discussion of the traveling rock, identifies YHWH/ κύριος as "the Rock" (Deut 32.4, 18).

[36] The reading of τὸν Χριστόν is supported by 𝔓46 D F G Ψ 𝔐 latt sy co. τὸν κυρίον also has substantial support (ℵ B C P 33. 104. 326. 365. 1175. 2464. *pc* syhmg); support for τὸν θεόν is minimal (A 81 *pc*). For a text-critical argument in support of the more difficult reading (τὸν Χριστόν), see C. D. Osburn, "The Text of I Corinthians 10:9", *New Testament Textual Criticism, Its Significance for Exegesis. Essays in Honor of Bruce M. Metzger* (eds. E.J. Epp and G.D. Fee; Oxford: OUP, 1981) 201-212. This same problem can be seen in the text of Jude 5; see Fossum, *Image of the Invisible God*, 67-69.

[37] See Capes, *OT Yahweh Texts*. Although Capes does not discuss this text, he does offer substantial evidence that Paul did vascillate between Christ and God

The incident Paul is referring to in 1 Cor 10.9 is recorded in Num 21.4-9. There the people spoke against "God" (21.5: אלהים/θεός) and then they were punished by venomous snakes sent by "the Lord" (21.6, 7, 8: יהוה/κύριος). There is no mention of "testing" in this account. In light of this it is worth noting the uniting of various wilderness incidents in Deuteronomy 8:

> [14] The Lord your God [. . .], [15] who led you through the great and terrible wilderness, with its venomous serpents and scorpions and thirsty ground where there was no water, who brought you water out of the flinty rock, [16] who fed you in the wilderness with manna which your fathers did not know, that he might humble you and test [ἐκπειράσῃ] you, to do you good in the end.

The union of the "testing" theme with the "venomous serpents" and "the rock" all in the context of Moses' warning speech may have provided some impetus for Paul's joining of these events and ideas in his words of warning in 1 Cor 10.1-10.[38]

A second possibility, not wholly exclusive of the first, is that Paul identified Christ with the visible manifestation of YHWH, namely, the Angel of the Lord. It has already been shown that this angel is often associated with actions of judgment.[39] There is the familar tradition in Exod 23.21 that YHWH gave his angel the charge to bring Israel into the promised land and the authority to punish transgressions which happened along the way: "Be attentive to him and listen to his voice; do not rebel against him, for he will not pardon your transgression [. . .]".

The theory that Paul understood Christ to be present with Israel as this angel is supported by his mention in 1 Cor 10.10 of "the Destroyer" (a *hapax legomenon*: ὁ ὀλοθρευτής). Nowhere does the account of this incident in Num 16.41-50 (MT) mention "the Destroyer", but it does mention another angelomorphic tradition: "the Glory of YHWH" (16.42). In spite of the slight variation in the spelling, Paul's reference to ὁ ὀλοθρευτής is certainly indirectly dependent upon its usage in the OT for the angelomorphic figure

---

as the referent of YHWH in his explicit quotations of OT YHWH texts (i.e., Paul considered Jesus to be a manifestation of YHWH); see also L. Kreitzer, *Jesus and God in Paul's Eschatology* (JSNTSup 19; Sheffield: Sheffield Academic Press, 1987).

[38] Philo discusses Deut 8.15-16 in *Leg All* 2.84-88. Exod 17.1-7 also emphasizes the theme of "testing the Lord" (LXX Exod 17.2: τί πειράζετε κύριον; cf. 17.7), but it has no links to the serpent incident.

[39] See the discussion of the Destroying Angel on 63-67 above, and S. Meier, "Destroyer", *DDD* 456-453.

who carried out the 10th Plague (Exod 12.23: הַמַּשְׁחִית/ὁ ὀλεθρεύων) and destruction in Jerusalem at time of David (1 Chr 21.12, 15: וּמַלְאָךְ יהוה מַשְׁחִית/ὁ ἄγγελος ὁ ἐξολεθρεύων). Even though this title is linked with YHWH (Exod 12.23) and the Angel of YHWH (1 Chr 21.12, 15; cf. 2 Sam 24.16), none of these incidents are directly related to Paul's discussion of punishing Israel in the wilderness.

There is, however, the prominent tradition in Wis 18.14-25, already cited several times, which links the angelomorphic "Word" (18.15) with "the Destroyer" (18.25: ὁ ὀλεθρεύων) who bloodily executed the 10th plague *and the plague Paul refers to in 1 Cor 10.10*. The use of similar distinctive terminology with reference to the same event makes this tradition the most likely source of Paul's usage.[40] Paul draws from the foreboding description of this angelomorphic warrior to paint the placard of warning which he is posting for the Corinthians. The pattern of punishment in this pericope prompts the assertion that Paul understood "Christ" (10.9) to be the agent of punishment against Israel's disobedience and against the disobedience of the church in his day. The content of 10.9 leads to the conclusion that Paul understood Christ to be "the Destroyer" of 10.10.

Paul is not alone in this understanding. The presence of Christ with Ancient Israel as the delivering and destroying angel is a tradition which also influenced the author of Jude.[41] This short letter maintains that Jesus is the Angel of YHWH who detained the fallen angels, destroyed Sodom and Gommorah, and *also struck the unfaithful Israelites in the wilderness*:

> [5] Though you already know all this, I want to remind you that Jesus delivered his people out of Egypt, but later destroyed those who did not believe. [6] And the angels that did not keep their own position but left their proper dwelling have been kept by him in eternal chains in the nether gloom until the judgment of the great day; [7] just as Sodom and Gomorrah and the surrounding cities, which likewise acted immorally and indulged in unnatural lust, serve as an example by undergoing a punishment of eternal fire.

---

[40] *Tg. Ps-.* Num 17.11 also inserts the Destroyer into this account. 4 Macc 7.11 identifies "a fiery angel" as the one who brought this plague.

[41] See a complete presentation of the evidence in Fossum, *Image of the Invisible God*, 41-69. The translation of Jude above follows the more difficult reading "Jesus" in verse 5 (instead of "the Lord" or "God"); see Fossum's text-critical argument, esp. 67-69.

Such traditions impacted depictions of Christ as the Destroying Angel carrying out eschatological judgment, as has already been seen in discussion of Rev 19.11-16.[42] With such a background to the Christology in 1 Cor 10.1-10, one can readily understand the intimidating force of Paul's exhortation: "We must not put *Christ* to the test [...]" (10.9).

C. *The Heavenly Man*

Paul's understanding of the pre-incarnate angelomorphic Christ is by no means limited to his visible manifestation with ancient Israel. Congruent with Paul's involvement in Jewish Mysticism, he also understood Christ to be the visible appearance of God in heaven as an angelomorphic Man.[43] This understanding is articulated in Paul's discussion of the Heavenly Man in 1 Corinthians 15:

> [44b] If there is a physical body, there is also a spiritual body. [45] Thus it is written, "The first man [ἄνθρωπος], Adam, became a living being"; the Eschatological Adam became a life-giving Spirit. [46] But it is not the spiritual that is first, but the physical, and then the spiritual. [47] The first man was from the earth, a man of dust; the second man is from heaven [ὁ δεύτερος ἄνθρωπος ἐξ οὐρανοῦ]. [48] As was the man of dust, so are those who are of dust; and as is the Heavenly Man, so are those who are of heaven. [49] Just as we have borne the image [τὴν εἰκόνα] of the man of dust, we will also bear the image of the Heavenly Man.

This pericope provides evidence that Paul was conversant with teaching about the Heavenly Man (ὁ ἐπουράνοις), namely the Ἄνθρωπος tradition.[44] He contrasts the *first* man (Adam, 15.45), the one of the earth who is a living *soul* (ψυχὴν ζῶσαν), with the *second* man (Eschatological Adam, 15.45), the one from heaven who is a life-giving *spirit* (πνεῦμα ζῳοποιοῦν). What is the background for Paul's understanding of the Heavenly Man?

---

[42] See discussion of this text 252-256 above.
[43] For the importance of Jewish Mysticism in reading Paul, see Segal, *Paul the Convert*, 34-71, and Morray-Jones, "Paradise Revisited, 265-292.
[44] This Heavenly Man tradition is found in much Jewish, Christian, and Gnostic literature of this period; see Quispel, "Ezekiel 1:26 in Jewish Mysticism", 6-13. Also very helpful are Quispel, "Hermetism and the NT", and Fossum, "The Figure of the Heavenly Man in Recent Research"; both are forthcoming publications in *ANRW* II.22.

Philo's exegesis of two ἄνθρωποι created at the beginning, one heavenly and one earthly, is helpful for understanding the background of the Heavenly Man in Paul since it is an example of contemporaneous exegesis on the subject[45]:

> [*Leg All* 1.31] There are two types of men; one a heavenly man, the other earthly. The heavenly man, being made after the image of God, is altogether without part or lot in the corruptible and terrestrial substance; but the earthly one was compacted out of the matter scattered here and there, which Moses calls "clay." For this reason he says that the heavenly man was not molded; but was stamped with the image of God; while the earthly is a molded work of the Artificer, but not His offspring [cf. *Op* 134-139].

Philo's version is merely one example of the many variations of the Ἄνθρωπος tradition. In the *Corpus Hermeticum* and Gnostic literature, the idea of two Adams was used to explain how the body (Jewish influence) of the Earthly Man was formed after the idea (Hellenistic influence) of the Heavenly Man.[46] Although Paul's direct dependency upon any of the versions of this tradition cannot be traced, nevertheless we can conclude that Paul is conversant with exegesis about a Heavenly Man. A significant difference between Paul and other versions is the ordering of the two men: Although the Heavenly Man usually precedes the Earthly Man, Paul states, "The first man was from the earth [. . .] the second man is from heaven". Paul's placing of the Heavenly Man in second position probably has a polemical edge which is motivated by his eschatological concerns: Now Paul bears the *earthly body* of Adam, but in the future he will bear the *spiritual body* of the Heavenly Man.[47]

Gilles Quispel has extensively researched Paul's adaptation and nuance of the Ἄνθρωπος tradition.[48] From a vast array of literary parallels Quispel concludes that Heavenly Man or Ἄνθρωπος traditions, including the Pauline tradition, can be traced back to the pervasive influence of Ezek 1.26, which records the prophet's vision

---

[45] This text indicates that the creation of the heavenly (ideal) man is recorded in Gen 1.26 and the creation of the earthly (material) man is recorded in Gen 2.7. Philo also links the origin of the Heavenly Man with the Word before creation; see the discussion of this inconsistency on 110 above.

[46] Quispel, "Hermetism and the NT"; see also J. Fossum, "Gen. 1,26 and 2,7 in Judaism, Samaritanism, and Gnosticism", *JSJ* 16 (1985) 202-239.

[47] Contra R. Scroggs, who argues that there is no polemic here; see *The Last Adam: A Study in Pauline Anthropology* (Philadelphia: Fortress, 1966) 75-122.

[48] "Hermetism and the NT".

of the Glory of YHWH appearing as a man.[49] The conclusion that Paul's understanding of Christ as the Heavenly Man is fundamentally founded upon Ezek 1.26-28 is supported by his explicit identification of Christ as the Glory (2 Cor 3.18; 4.6; 1 Cor 2.8; cf. Eph 1.17).[50]

A feature of Paul's Heavenly Man that is not founded upon Ezek 1.26-28 is the Man's description as "a life-giving Spirit". Quispel has shown that there is often a twofold aspect to the Heavenly Man in Hellenistic sources since he is usually understood to be androgynous.[51] For example, in *Poimandres* the divine Ἄνθρωπος is made up of Φῶς (Adam/Man or Light) and Ζωή (Eve or Life) and is the "Image" and "Form" of God.[52] Paul's Heavenly Man also has a twofold aspect: He is both Ἄνθρωπος and Πνεῦμα. Christians bear the Image of Christ (the Heavenly Man of Ezek 1.26) who as Πνεῦμα lives within them and as Ἄνθρωπος has them within himself as his divine body. This twofold aspect of Pauline Christology is also behind the Christological pairing of Power and Wisdom (1 Cor 1.24).

D. *The Power of God and the Wisdom of God*

In the opening chapter of 1 Corinthians Paul refers to the "power of God" and "the wisdom of God" in two distinct manners. The first is in a soteriological manner:

> [18] For the word of the cross is folly to those who are perishing, but to us who are being saved it is the power of God.

> [21] For since, in the wisdom of God, the world did not know God through wisdom, it pleased God through the folly of what we preach to save those who believe.

---

[49] "Hermetism and the NT"; see also the discussion on 104-109 above. The influence of Ezek 1.26-28 on Paul was already argued by O. Procksch, "Die Berufungsvision Hesekiels", 141-150; see also Fossum, "Jewish Christian Christology", 260-287.
[50] See Newman, *Paul's Glory-Christology*, 157-247, and 333-337 below.
[51] These texts are all cited by Quispel in "Hermetism and the NT".
[52] This pair is noted in chapters 6, 9, 12, 17, 21, 32; see B. Covenhaver, *Hermetica: The Greek Corpus Hermeticum and the Latin Asclepius in a New English Translation with Notes and Introduction* (Cambridge: CUP, 1992). Christ is also called the "image" of God and "form" of God (cf. 2 Cor 4.4; Phil 2.6; Col 1.15). Quispel points to several other examples in "Hermetism and the NT".

Paul is using terms with a philosophical background (power and wisdom) as part of his effort to show the surpassing significance of the "word [message] of the cross" for salvation. This philosophical focus is also clear in the summary of 1.25: "For the foolishness of God is wiser than men, and the weakness of God is stronger than men".

What is said about the "word of the cross" as God's power and wisdom is also asserted of Christ in 1.23-24: "But we preach Christ crucified [. . .] Christ the Power [δύναμις] of God and the Wisdom [σοφία] of God". Paul is not, as some commentators assert, simply saying that Christ is the soteriological content of the word of the cross.[53] He is also making a significant *Christological* statement which reflects his Jewish understanding of these concepts. The hypostatization of the Power of God and the Wisdom of God as Christ would not go unnoticed by those familiar with traditions surrounding divine hypostases like Power and Wisdom in biblical and extra-biblical literature.[54]

We have already shown that "the Power of God" is another title for the visible bodily manifestation of God in heavenly visions (i.e., a virtual synonym for "the Glory").[55] Examples of the identification of a fleshly being on earth as the Power of God have also been given.[56] Moreover, "the Power" is a noteworthy title for Christ among some Jewish Christian groups, as is visible in these two texts[57]:

> [*Acts of Thomas* 10] You are the Beginning, and you put on the first man, <u>You are the Great Power, and the Wisdom</u>, and the Knowledge, and the Will and the Rest of your Father [. . .].

> [Justin, *I Apol.* 33.6] It is, therefore, wrong to understand <u>the Spirit and the Power of God</u> as anything else than the Word, who is also the Firstborn of God, as the foresaid prophet Moses declared.

Although Wisdom is best known for her links with Spirit and

---

[53] E.g., G. Fee emphasizes that this statement in 1.24 is not about Christology, but soteriology; see *The First Epistle to the Corinthians* (NICNT; Grand Rapids: Eerdmans, 1987) 77.
[54] See discussions about Wisdom and Power on 89-103 and 119-121 above.
[55] See discussion on 121 above; see also discussion of Eph 1.19 on 341 below.
[56] E.g., Jacob/Israel in the *Prayer of Joseph*, Simon Magus in Acts 8.10, and Elchasai in Epiphanius, *Pan.* 19.2.10.
[57] See Fossum, *Image of the Invisible God*, 24-28; see also Matt 22.29, Rev 15.8, and Rom 1.18. The Power can also refer to the Spirit; see Luke 1.35, *Gos. Peter* 19.

Torah, her roots in angelomorphic traditions have been demonstrated with textual evidence in chapter 4 above.[58] There it was shown that *1 Enoch* identifies the Son of Man/Elect One as the Glory ("whose countenance had the appearance of a man" in 46.1) and as Wisdom (49.1-3). This Man was hidden from the general populous, but revealed to the righteous according to *1 Enoch* 48:

> [6] For this purpose he [the Son of Man] became the Elect One; he was concealed in the presence of (the Lord of the Spirits) prior to the creation of the world, and for eternity. [7] And he has revealed the Wisdom of the Lord of the Spirits to the righteous and the holy ones, for he has preserved a portion of the righteous [...].

A similar matrix of ideas is central to Paul's depiction of Christ as Wisdom and *the Glory* shortly after his initial discussion of Christ as the Wisdom of God and *the Power* of God. In 1 Cor 2.7-8 he writes about Christ as the hidden Wisdom of God who has now been revealed and then links her with Christ as the Glory (cf. 2 Cor 4.3-4; Eph 3.8-10):

> [1 Cor 2.7] But we speak <u>a mysterious and hidden Wisdom of God</u> which God decreed before the ages for our glorification. [8] None of the rulers of this age understood this; for if they had, they would not have crucified <u>the Lord of Glory</u> [τὸν κύριον τῆς δόξης].[59]

Although the Corinthian congregation probably did not understand all these nuances of Angelomorphic Christology, Paul certainly did. This can be seen from his use of other angelomorphic traditions. Furthermore, Quispel argues that there is a consistent pattern in Paul's Christological pairings: in 1 Cor 1.24 Christ is both the Δύναμις (another title for the Glory whose appearance is as a Man) and Σοφία (another [feminine] title for the Spirit), even as in 1 Cor 15.45 he is both Ἄνθρωπος and Πνεῦμα.[60]

E. *The Glory, the Image of God, and the Spirit*

Significant support for Paul's understanding of Christ as the Heavenly Man of Ezek 1.26-28 and related texts is found in his

---

[58] See discussion on 89-103 above.
[59] The Lord of the Spirits in *1 Enoch* 37-71 is also called "the Lord of Glory" (40.3; 63.2) and "the Lord of Wisdom" (63.2); see Fossum, *Image of the Invisible God*, 18 n.21.
[60] "Ezekiel 1.26 in Jewish Mysticism", 10-11, and Fossum, *Name of God*, 177-181. See also Justin Martyr, *I Apol.* 33.6.

identification of Christ as the Glory. Paul's most overt and extensive use of the Glory tradition occurs in 2 Cor 3.4-4.6.[61] His argument against the false teachers who subverted the Gospel with a return to Moses culminates with these words:

> [4.3] And even if our gospel is veiled, it is veiled only to those who are perishing. [4] In their case the god of this world has blinded the minds of the unbelievers, to keep them from seeing the light of the gospel of the Glory of Christ [τὸν φωτισμὸν τοῦ εὐαγγελίου τῆς δόξης τοῦ Χριστοῦ], who is the Image of God [ὅς ἐστιν εἰκὼν τοῦ θεοῦ]. [5] For what we preach is not ourselves, but Christ Jesus as Lord, with ourselves as your servants for Jesus' sake. [6] For it is the God who said, "Let light shine out of darkness," who has shone in our hearts to give the light of the knowledge of the Glory of God in the face of Christ [τῆς δόξης τοῦ θεοῦ ἐν προσώπῳ Ἰησοῦ Χριστοῦ].

These verses make it eminently clear that Paul understood Christ to be the Glory. This is put no more pointedly than in 4.6: the Glory of God is beheld in the very "face of Christ". This is an allusion to Exod 33.20 where Moses (and others) could not see the face of the Glory. In stating the result of beholding the Glory of God in Christ a few verses earlier, Paul again identifies Christ (i.e., "the Lord") as the Glory: "And all of us, with unveiled faces, reflect as in a mirror the Glory of the Lord" (3.18). This revelation of the Glory is facilitated through the Spirit in the reading of "the old covenant" or "Moses" (3.14, 15), since Christ as the Spirit has removed the veil from the minds of Christians (3.14-17). Paul even refers to his message in 2 Cor 4.4 as the "the gospel of the Glory of Christ". There is an additional allusion to the Glory as the "heavenly dwelling" in 2 Cor 4.17: "For this slight momentary affliction is preparing us for an eternal weight of glory [βάρος δόξης]".[62]

The identification of Christ as the Glory is further reinforced in these verses with Paul's explanation of Christ in 2 Cor 4.4: "Christ, who is the Image of God [ὅς ἐστιν εἰκὼν τοῦ θεοῦ]". Εἰκών (Heb: צלם) is a term that is used as another designation for δόξα: Christ is the Glory of God who is also the Image of God (cf. Col 1.15; 2.9). The term carries an emphasis on material or visual likeness.[63]

---

[61] See Newman, *Paul's Glory-Christology*, 229-35 for a more detailed exegesis and bibliography.

[62] The Hebrew word כבוד literally means "weightiness" in a material sense; see also Fossum, "Glory", 659-660.

[63] See esp. S. Kim, *The Origin of Paul's Gospel 1* (WUNT 2/4; Tübingen: Mohr/Siebeck, 1984), 193-268. Kim sees this as a central aspect of Paul's

Paul's quotation of Gen 1.3 in 2 Cor 4.6 may indicate his understanding of the revealing of the Glory in the creation of Φῶς ("light" or "man") on the first day, an idea that has some prominence in Hellenistic Jewish groups.[64] As noted earlier, already in the second century BCE *Ezekiel the Tragedian* records Moses' supposed dream vision in *Exāgōgē* 68-72 about the great throne in heaven upon which a noble Man was seated (φῶτα γενναῖον).[65] Paul's linking of the Glory with the creation of light indicates that Paul understood the Glory to be protological. Therefore, the Glory is involved in creation, which includes functioning as the Image in whom Adam was created (Gen 1.26).

Paul's understanding of Christ as the Glory and Image of God in these verses is actually introduced already in 2 Cor 3.17-18. There Paul speaks about the transformation produced by the reading of scripture in the lives of those who are possessed by the Lord who is the Spirit:

> [17] Now the Lord is the Spirit, and where the Spirit of the Lord is, there is freedom. [18] And all of us, with unveiled faces [προσώπῳ], reflect as in a mirror the Glory of the Lord [τὴν δόξαν κυρίου] and are transformed into the same Image [εἰκόνα] from one degree of glory to another; for this comes from the Lord [who is] the Spirit.

The complexity of Paul's pneumatology and its intimate connections with his Christology has long been recognized.[66] "The Lord *is* the Spirit" forms the foundation of Paul's idea of the believer's union with Christ.[67] Therefore, the Christian is simultaneously *in*

---

theology, but founds his understanding of antecedents in Wisdom and Adam traditions, rather than the Glory of Ezek 1.26-28 and related texts.

[64] See the evidence of this idea presented by Fossum, *Image of the Invisible God*, 15-24; see also the discussion on 110 above.

[65] See discussion of this text on 163-165 above.

[66] To realize this complexity, one needs only to try to systematize what is said of the Spirit in Paul's epistles or read E. Schweizer, "πνεῦμα", *TDNT* 6.415-437. For a brief helpful introduction, see R. Bultmann, *The Theology of the New Testament* (trans. K. Grobel; New York: Scribner's Sons, 1950 and 1955) 203-210.

[67] The entry of a human into the Deity and the Deity into a human are the fundamental tenets of Hellenistic Mysticism; R. Reitzenstien, *Hellenistic Mystery Religions*, 73 and 381 (for his discussion of Paul, see 426-500). Reitzenstein had been inspired by Bousset in the old *religionsgeschichtliche Schule* approach to Pauline mysticism; see *Kyrios Christos*, 153-205. More recent scholarship has justly criticized their complete focus on Hellenistic parallels (with origins in Oriental religion of Persia and Iran) and has shifted to interpreting Paul from the perspective of Judaism, especially apocalypticism and rabbinism; see M.C. de Boer, *The Defeat of Death: Apocalyptic Eschatology in*

Christ (as Ἄνθρωπος) and Christ (as Πνεῦμα) is *in him*.[68] There is an interdependent, reciprocal, and circular relationship between these two ideas; neither reality functions independently of the other.

The impact of Paul's understanding of Christ as the Glory and Image of God also impacts his pneumatology. The most prominent metaphor for understanding Paul's concept of "Christ in me" is that of the Glory or the Name "dwelling" or "tabernacling" in the temple. He uses this metaphor as a model to describe the indwelling of the Spirit/Christ in the believer/congregation. For example:

> [1 Cor. 6.15b] Or do you not know that your body is a temple of the Holy Spirit within you, which you have from God, and that you are not your own?
>
> [2 Cor 6.16] For we are the temple of the living God; as God said, "I will live in them and walk among them and I will be their God" [cf. Lev. 26.12].
>
> [1 Cor 3.16-17] Do you not know that you are God's temple and that God's Spirit dwells in you? If anyone destroys God's temple, God will destroy that person. For God's temple is holy, and you are that temple.

A probable reason for Paul's adaptation of this metaphor is that this idea from the OT readily illustrates how YHWH, whom "heaven and earth cannot contain" (2 Sam 8.27) and who has a large visible body as the Glory, can dwell within a confined object (i.e., body= individual or community). The reception of the Spirit happens in baptism where one is invested with the Divine Name and becomes a habitat for the Son/Spirit.[69] This "dwelling in" by the Spirit is a guarantee of what will come in the future since one day the believer will "dwell in" a heavenly body.[70]

---

1 Corinthians 15 and Romans 5 (JSNTSup 22; Sheffield: Sheffield Academic Press, 1988) 15-37, and W.D. Davies, *Paul and Rabbinic Judaism* (4th ed.; Philadelphia: Fortress, 1980) 175-226. In spite of this criticism, a balanced reassessment of Hellenistic aspects of Paul's expression of theology, in light of recent scholarship and new manuscripts, is proper and needed. See the dated work of A. Wikenhauser, *Pauline Mysticism* (trans. J. Cunningham; New York: Herder and Herder, 1960) 163-242.

[68] All the various nuances of these phrases will not be discussed here; see Wikenhauser, *Pauline Mysticism*, 17-108.

[69] See Fossum, *Name of God*, 103, 180 n.320, 185 n.330.

[70] Unlike the hellenistic emphasis on leaving the material body (i.e., being "naked" before God), Paul is very concerned in 2 Cor. 5.1-10 with not being found "naked" but "putting on" the heavenly dwelling; see De Conick and Fossum, "Stripped Before God, 130-131, and Fossum, *Image of the Invisible God*, 99-102.

The result of this intimate indwelling of Christ for Paul is nothing less than union with Christ: the believer is one πνεῦμα with him. Notice how Paul expresses this in Rom 8.29:

> For those whom he foreknew he also predestined to be conformed to the Image of his Son, in order that he might be the Firstborn [i.e., the eldest son of God] of a large family [i.e., fellow sons of God].

F. *The Form and the Name of God*

The Philippians Hymn, which has received much exegetical attention over the years, also presents an Angelomorphic Christology in terms of Christ as the "Form of God" who has been invested with the Divine "Name"[71]:

> [2.5] Have this mind among yourselves, which is yours in Christ Jesus, [6] who, though he was in the Form of God [ὃς ἐν μορφῇ θεοῦ ὑπάρχων], did not count equality with God a thing to be grasped, [7] but emptied himself [ἀλλὰ ἑαυτὸν ἐκένωσεν], taking on the Form of a servant [μορφὴν δούλου λαβών], being born in likeness of men [ἐν ὁμοιώματι ἀνθρώπων γενόμενος]. [8] And being found in appearance as a man [καὶ σχήματι εὑρεθεὶς ὡς ἄθρωπος], he humbled himself and became obedient unto death, even death on a cross. [9] Therefore God has highly exalted him and bestowed on him the Name [τὸ ὄνομα] which is above every name, that at the name of Jesus every knee should bow, in heaven and on earth and under the earth, [11] and every tongue confess that Jesus Christ is Lord, to the glory of God the Father.

One of the difficulties that exegetes have struggled with in this hymn is the prevalent μορφή ("form") terminology. Jarl Fossum has argued persuasively, with extensive textual evidence, that there is an interchangeability and common semantic field between the following terms: δόξα ("glory"), εἰκών ("image"), ὁμοίωμα ("likeness"), and μορφή ("form").[72] For example, the interchangeability

---

[71] M. Bockmuehl recently discussed the secondary literature on this hymn and examined the "Form of God" theme; see "'The Form of God' (Phil. 2:6): Variations on a Theme of Jewish Mysticism", *JTS* 48 (1997) 1-23. See also: R. Martin, *Carmen Christi: Philippians ii. 5-11 in Recent Interpretation and in the Setting of Early Christian Worship* (SNTSMS 4; Cambridge: CUP, 1967); J. T. Sanders, *New Testament Christological Hymns: Their Historical Background* (SNTSMS 15; Cambridge: CUP, 1971), 58-74; and Lueken, *Michael*, 138-139.

[72] See the following: "Jewish-Christian Christology", 266-70; *Name of God*, 269-70, 284; *Image of the Invisible God*, 35, esp. n.83. See also John 5.37 and discussion on 274 above.

of εἰκών and μορφή is illustrated well in this second century CE text from *Poimandres*:

> [12] Nous, the Father of all, who is Life and Light, brought forth Man like unto Himself, whom he loved as His own child, for he was very beautiful and was his Father's image [εἰκόνα]. Even God indeed loved His own form [μορφῆς] and handed over to him all His works.

Both Quispel and Fossum have drawn attention to the relevance of Jewish Christian traditions in the *Pseudo-Clementines* about the "Form of God" for the exegesis of the Philippians hymn.[73] The description of God in *Hom.* XVII.7 is based upon Jewish traditions about the Glory.[74] Furthermore, Fossum sifted the evidence in *Pseudo-Clementines* and demonstrated that there is an identification between this visible "form" of God and the Son, who is the older "form" that is incarnate in Adam (*Rec.* I.28). Based upon these philological and tradition-history insights, one can see a Christology in Philippians which understands the pre-incarnate Christ to be the visible manifestation or "Form" of God: the Glory in "the likeness of a man" as depicted in Ezek 1.26-28 and related texts.[75]

This exegesis of Christ as the Glory is further supported by Phil 3.21 which speaks of Christ's "Body of Glory": "who will transform our body of lowliness to be of one form with his Body of Glory [ὃς μετασχηματίσει τὸ σῶμα τῆς ταπεινώσεως ἡμῶν σύμμορφον τῷ σώματι τῆς δόξης αὐτοῦ]". Following the suggestion of Scholem that the *Shi'ur Qomah* notion of *guf ha-kavod* or *guf ha-shekhinah* ("the body of the Glory" or "the body of the Divine Presence") appears to related to this idea in Philippians, Stroumsa has asserted that scholars should consider this as evidence of Jewish *makranthropos* traditions which antedate Christianity.[76] This understanding of the pre-incarnate Form of God has led Stroumsa to theorize that the "emptying" of the Form of God (ἀλλὰ ἑαυτὸν ἐκένωσεν) probably meant giving up his form or body when he became incarnate:

> Despite numerous studies this *kenosis* of Christ has remained obscure [...]. In my opinion, the notion can be best understood as

---

[73] Quispel, "Ezekiel 1.26 in Jewish Mysticism", 9, and Fossum, "Jewish-Christian Christology", 269-270; see also 204-205 above.

[74] "Jewish Christian Christology", 260-287, esp. 264-265.

[75] Fossum presents a brief exposition of this hymn in "The Magharians", 341-343.

[76] "Form(s) of God", 269-288, esp. 279-280. Bockmuehl was apparently not aware of this research; see "Form of God", 1-23.

reflecting an original mythical conception, rather than being simply metaphorical. We may assume that according to this original conception, when Christ was "in the form of God," his cosmic body filled the whole world and was identical to the *pleroma*. Incarnation, therefore, literally implied that Christ emptied the world (or the *pleroma*) that is, in a sense, himself.[77]

Stroumsa, however, goes too far by shifting from talk about a *gigantic* body to discussion of a *cosmic* body. Further evidence from Ephesians and Colossians does not support this shift.[78]

The second prominent angelomorphic tradition in this pericope is the teaching of the Divine Name and its investiture: "Therefore God has highly exalted him and bestowed on him the Name [τὸ ὄνομα] which is above every name". The referent of "the Name" is not the name "Jesus", but the Divine Name. This is clear from his inclusion of κύριος, which the LXX uses to translate the Tetragrammaton, in the confession of 2.11: κύριος Ἰησοῦς Χριστὸς. The significance of this ascription cannot be overestimated. It is indisputable evidence that lays bare the ancient roots of this Christology in angelomorphic traditions that grew from the Divine Name Angel of Exod 23.20-21. The unparalleled status and enthronement of the one who possesses the Divine Name is also emphasized in Eph 1.12-23:

> [. . .] the riches of his glorious inheritance in the saints [. . .] which he accomplished in Christ when he raised him from the dead and made him sit at his right hand in the heavenly places, far above all rule and authority and power and dominion, and above every name that is named, not only in this age but also in that which is to come.

G. *The Body*

The discussion of the Philippians hymn asserted, but did not examine in detail, that the prominent idea of Christ as head of the

---

[77] Stroumsa, "Form(s) of God", 269-288, esp. 283-284. He presents a parallel idea from *Odes Sol.* 7.3 to support his assertion.

[78] E.g., Col 1.18 speaks of the church as the body of Christ, not the cosmos. C. Arnold mounts a persuasive argument against a cosmic interpretation of the body; see "Jesus Christ: 'Head' of the Church", *Jesus of Nazareth: Lord and Christ. Essays on the Historicla Jesus and New Testament Christology* (eds. M. Turner and J. Green; Grand Rapids: Eerdmans, 1994) 346-366. Arnold, however, does not see or discuss any connection of this imagery with Jewish traditions about the divine body.

Body is dependent upon Jewish understandings of the Divine Body, such as those found later in *Shi'ur Qomah* Mysticism.[79] Research on this idea was stimulated several decades ago by Gershom Scholem, but has not enjoyed much attention until the past fifteen years.[80] The common expression, "in Christ", also "into Christ" or "with Christ", reflects being incorporated *into* the "Body of Christ" and can be best understood if one accepts that Paul believed Christ to be the manifestation of God with a mystical body of gigantic proportions.[81]

This idea of the Church as Christ's Body is prominent throughout the Pauline corpus; it is not only found in the so-called Deutero-Pauline epistles (cf. 1 Cor 12.12-13; Rom 12.4-5; Gal 3.28). Paul states the following concerning this mystical "Body of Christ", which he equates with "the church":

> [1 Cor 12.12] For just as the body is one and has many members, and all the members of the body, though many, are one body, so it is with Christ. [13] For in the one Spirit we were all baptized into one body—Jews or Greeks, slaves or free—and we were all made to drink of one Spirit.

According to Paul, incorporation into this body happens through baptism which is linked with believing the Gospel (Gal 3.2). In baptism the individual dies and is buried with Christ (Rom 6.1-4; Col 2.12-15). Then Christ as Ἄνθρωπος revives that person and raises him to new life by breathing his Πνεῦμα into him (1 Cor. 15.45; Rom 6.11).

The "Body of Christ" image forms a central part of the Christology in Ephesians, as is evident from this text[82]:

> [1.17] I pray that the God of our Lord Jesus Christ, the Father of the Glory [ὁ πατὴρ τῆς δόξης] may give you a spirit of wisdom and revelation in fuller knowledge of him, [18] so that, the eyes of your heart having been enlightened, you may know what is the hope to

---

[79] See discussion of this "Measure of the Body" Mysticism on 29 and 32 above.

[80] Scholem, *Major Trends in Jewish Mysticism*, 1-79. His research was an impetus to Quispel, Fossum, Segal, Stroumsa, and Morray-Jones, among others.

[81] This understanding probably resulted, in part, from his Christophany on the road to Damascus in which Paul's persecution of *the church* is aggression against *Christ*: "Saul, Saul, why do you persecute *me?*" (Acts 9.4-5; cf. 22.7-8; 26.14-15).

[82] This analysis of Ephesians draws heavily on the research of Morray-Jones, "The Body of Glory".

which he has called you, what is the wealth of his glorious inheritance among the holy ones, [19] and what is the immeasurable greatness of His Power [τὸ ὑπερβάλλον μέγεθος τῆς δυνάμεως] for us who believe, according to the working of His mighty strength, [20] which he exerted in Christ when he raised him from the dead and seated him at his right hand in the heavenly heights, [21] far above all rule and authority and power and lordship and every name that is named, not only in this world but also in the world to come. [22] And he placed all things under his feet and appointed him the head over all things for the church, [23] which is his Body, the fullness [τὸ πλήρωμα] of him who fills all in all.

Several details in this text indicate Paul was cognizant of Angelomorphic Christology. First and foremost, the parallelism between "the God of our Lord Jesus Christ, the Father of the Glory" in 1.17 strongly implies that Paul understood Jesus Christ to be the Glory. Indeed, what 1.23 states about the Body seems to be an allusion to Isa 6.4: "The whole earth is filled with his Glory". Second, the linking of "immeasurable greatness" with "Power" in 1.19 indicates that Power in this context is to be understood as the Glory (i.e., the immeasurable visible manifestation of God). Third, 1.21 indicates that Christ has been given authority that is "far above every name that is named"; this is a transparent reference to Christ's possession of the Divine Name. Fourth, 1.22 is an obvious allusion to Ps 8.4-6 ("placed all things under his feet"), a psalm which was often interpreted as an expression of the Heavenly Man/Son of Man idea.[83]

The central focus of this epistle is the Church as the Body of Christ/the Glory and "fullness of him [God] who fills all in all" (1.23; cf. Col 1.19; 2.9). The nature of this Body is described further in Ephesians:

[3.17] And that Christ may dwell in your hearts through faith; that you, being rooted and grounded in love, [18] may have power to comprehend with all the saints what is the breadth and length and height and depth, [19] and to know the love of Christ which surpasses knowledge, that you may be filled with all the fullness of God.

[4.4] There is one Body and one Spirit, just as you were called to the one hope that belongs to your call, [5] one Lord, one faith, one baptism, [6] one God and Father of all, who is above all and through all and in all. [7] But to each one of us was given grace according to the measure [τὸ μέτρον] of the gift of Christ.

---

[83] See Kinzer, "All Things Under His Feet", 217-225.

> [4.15] Let us in every way grow up into him who is the head, Christ, from whom the whole body, [16] being fitly joined together and united through every joint with which it is supplied, according to the working in measure [ἐν μέτρῳ] of each single part, promotes the body's building up of itself in love.

A term that is prominent in *Shi'ur Qomah* mysticism, "the measure" (τὸ μέτρον), is found twice in these verses (4.7, 16). The criticism of reading the later ideas of *Shi'ur Qomah* mysticism back into the interpretation of the Pauline corpus can be answered by emphasizing that the idea of a huge divine body which is measurable can be dated to the centuries before the NT.[84] Furthermore, there are other first century CE Jewish and Christian texts which evince this idea. For example, *2 En* 39.6 (Rec. A) reads: "You see the extent [measure] of my body, the same as your own, but I have seen the extent [measure] of the LORD, without measure and without analogy, who has no end".[85] The Jewish Christian sect leader Elchasai, writing in 101 CE, gives specific measurements of the huge body of the Son.[86] Nor did this idea disappear from Christianity in the second century. W. C. van Unnik has found references to Christ as the "measure" of God in the *Gospel of Philip* and Ireaneus[87]:

> [*Gos. Phil.* 62.7-18] The apostles who were before us had these names for him: "Jesus, the Nazorean, Messiah", that is, "Jesus, the Nazorean, the Christ." The last name is "Christ," the first is "Jesus" that in the middle is "the Nazarene". Messiah has two meanings, both "the Christ" and <u>"the measured"</u>. "Jesus" in Hebrew is "the redemption." "Nazara" is "the truth." "The Nazarene," then, is "the

---

[84] Quispel argues for the Orphic Makranathropos as an antecedent of the idea of a huge visible Divine Body in Judaism and Christianity; see "Hermetism and the NT". For evidence see the Orphic Hymn to Zeus in the Derveni Papyrus (4th century CE; cf. Plato, *Laws* IV.715E-716C) and the hymn to Zeus in Orphic Fragment 168 (3d century CE), in *Orphicorum Fragmenta* (ed. O. Kern; 2d ed.; Berlin, 1963) 201-202. More probable antecedents are the biblically related traditions of a gigantic man on the divine throne (note the size of the Glory in Ezek 1.26-28 if one takes the size of the rainbow seriously) or gigantic angels (see 1 Chr 21.16, Wis 18.16, and discussion on 32 above).

[85] This text is discussed by Scholem (he refers to it as *2 En.* 13.8) in *Kabbalah* (Jerusalem: Keter, 1974) 17. *2 Enoch* is considered by scholars to be originally written in the 1st century CE, probably before 70; see discussion on 173 n.64 above.

[86] This fragment of the *Book of Elchasai* is preserved in Hippolytus, *Ref.* 9.13.2-3; see the discussion of this text on 226-227 above.

[87] "Three Notes on the 'Gospel of Philip'", *NTS* 10 (1963-64) 466-469; see also Stroumsa, "Form(s) of God", 285-287. Stroumsa notes that the immeasurability of God is also mentioned by Irenaeus in *Adv. haer.* 4.20.1 and 4.20.4.

truth." "Christ"[. . .] been measured. It is "the Nazarene" and "Jesus" who have been measured."

[*Adv. haer.* 4.4.2] For God does all things by measure and in order; nothing is unmeasured with him, because nothing is out of order. He spoke well, who said that the unmeasureable Father was himself subjected to measure in the Son; for the Son is the measure of the Father, since he also comprehends him [μέτρον γὰρ τοῦ πατρὸς ὁ υἱος, ἐπεὶ καὶ χωρεῖ αὐτόν].

As with the idea of Christ being "in" the believer, the body and temple imagery are also vital to Paul's idea of being "in Christ". Morray-Jones states that, "'Body' and 'Temple' are complementary expressions of the same paradoxical and mystical reality: the Glory of the LORD, the Divine Image, is enthroned at the centre 'within' but, at the same time, He comprehends all things within Himself".[88] Eph 2.21-22 illustrates this reciprocal idea extremely well:

[21] In him [Christ] the whole structure is joined together and grows into a holy temple in the Lord; [22] in whom you also are built together into a dwelling place for God in the Spirit.

H. *The Image of the Invisible God, the Head of the Body, the Firstborn, and the Beginning*

Nowhere in the Pauline corpus is the language and imagery of Angelomorphic Christology more densely concentrated than in the Colossians Hymn (1.15-20).[89] This hymn draws together several of the angelomorphic ideas that have surfaced and been discussed in other texts: "the Image", "the Body", "the Firstborn", and "the Beginning":

---

[88] "The Body of Glory".
[89] E. Norden wrote the form-critical study which emphasized the hymnic nature of this text, which probably existed before the epistle and was appropriated into the content of Colossians; see *Agnostos Theos: Untersungen zur Formengeschichte religiöser Rede* (2d ed.; Leipzig: Teubner, 1923). Scholars have continued to recognize the hymnic nature of this text, even if disagreeing on its use before this epistle. For the abundant scholarly research on this text, see: J. Gabathuler, *Jesus Christ: Haupt der Kirche—Haupt her Welt* (ATANT 45; Zürich: Zwingli, 1965) 11-124; P. Benoit, "L'hymne christologique de Col 1,15-20. Jugement critique sur l'état des recherches", *Christianity, Judaism and Other Greco-Roman Cults: Festschrift for Morton Smith*, (SJLA 12; Leiden: Brill, 1975) 1.226-263; and L. Helyer, "Recent Research on Col 1:15-20 (1980-1990)", *GTJ* 12 (1992) 51-67.

[15] He is the Image of the Invisible God,
the Firstborn of all creation;
[16] for in him all things in heaven and on earth were created,
things visible and invisible,
whether thrones or dominions or rulers or powers
—all things have been created through him and for him.
[17] He himself is before all things, and in him all things hold together.
[18] He is the head of the Body, the Church;
he is the Beginning, the Firstborn from the dead,
so that he might have first place in everything.

The hymn's prominent emphasis on Christ as the creator, which is seen to echo Wisdom's presence and participation in creation, has led the majority of scholarship to argue that Wisdom tradition is the primary background for this hymn's language and imagery.[90] Wisdom, however, is only described as "an Image of God's goodness" (Wis 7.26), which is considerably different than what is being asserted about Christ in Colossians.[91] The testimony that Christ is "the Image of God" in 2 Cor 4.4 appears here with even more boldness: Christ is the εἰκὼν τοῦ θεοῦ τοῦ ἀοράτου ("the Image of the Invisible God"). This is more than Adam Christology. The text states that Christ is not merely *in* or *after* the image of God; he *is* the Image of God. Moreover, God is specifically "invisible". This implies that Christ is not the image of God's visible manifestation, as is the case with Jewish ideas about Adam being created in the image of the Glory; Christ *is* the only visible Image. As noted above, εἰκών has material connotations and belongs to the same semantic field as δόξα.[92] Therefore, this text is additional testimony that Christ is understood to be the Glory, the enthroned man of Ezek 1.26.

This understanding of Christ as the Glory is supported by the "Head of the Body" imagery in 1.18-19. The background of the "Body" imagery was discussed in the previous section above; here "Head" is combined with body imagery to emphasize Christ's supremacy and control over his body, the church.[93] As in Ephesians,

---

[90] See the discussion and bibliography in Arnold, *Colossian Syncretism*, 246-270.
[91] See Fossum's extensive treatment of this text, *Image of the Invisible God*, 13-39, esp. 18.
[92] See 337 above, and Fossum, *Image of the Invisible God*, 34-35.
[93] Arnold argues this on the basis of Greek physiological explanations about the function of the head of a physical body; see "Jesus Christ: 'Head' of

this text reflects a mystical body with gigantic portions, but is not simply an adaptation of Hellenistic tradition about the cosmic body.[94] This is affirmed by Col 1.19 ("for in him all the fulness was pleased to dwell") which should be interpreted in light of 2.9: ὅτι ἐν αὐτῷ κατοικεῖ πᾶν τὸ πλήρωμα τῆς θεότητος σωματικῶς ("For in him the whole fulness *of God* dwells *bodily*").

The titles "Firstborn of all creation" (1.15) and "the Beginning" (1.18) are both closely related to the theme of Christ as the creator of the cosmos: "for in him all things in heaven and on earth were created, visible and invisible" (1.16). The "Firstborn" title has surfaced several times in earlier chapters: it is one of the designations of Philo's Word (*Conf* 146), a title for the Angel Israel/Jacob in the *Prayer of Joseph*, and of Christ in Hebrews (1.6; 12.23).[95] As the Firstborn, Christ is the creator and ruler over the various angelic ranks: Thrones, Dominions, Rulers, Powers (1.16).[96] "The Beginning", a title which arises from Gen 1.1 and Prov 8.22, was previously encountered in the study of Philo's Word (*Conf* 146) and the Christophany in the opening chapters of Revelation (3.12).[97] Here it is used as an additional title which emphasizes Christ's existence before, and participation in, creation. Its pairing with "Firstborn of the dead" (1.18), however, indicates that it could be adapted to the resurrection/new creation context.[98]

There are two implications of the Angelomorphic Christology expressed in these verses. First, the language and imagery used in this text gives this Christology a polemical edge which reasserts the centrality and supremacy of Christ among the "angels" which were clearly the subject of interest—even veneration—in the Colossian church.[99] Secondly, the invisibility of God, as stated in this text, expresses a conviction concerning how some early Christians understood OT theophanies as well as their own mystical experiences. If God cannot be seen, then who was making himself visible on so many occasions in the OT? Who is the Angel of the

---

the Church", 346-366.

[94] Fossum argues for a background in cosmic body traditions, but does not emphasize the significant difference between the cosmos and the church as God's Body; see *Image of the Invisible God*, 32-38.

[95] See discussions above on 110-111, 140, and 297-299.

[96] See the excellent discussion by Arnold, *Colossian Syncretism*, 251-260.

[97] See discussions on 111 and 255 above.

[98] This is similar to the transferring the "firstborn" nomenclature to the resurrection; see Rom 8.29, Heb 11.28, and Rev 1.5.

[99] See Arnold, *Colossian Syncretism*, esp. 90-102.

Lord or the Glory of the Lord that was visible in various ways? This text gives one answer: the Son, who is the *visible* Image of the Invisible God.[100]

I. *Conclusion*

In the Pauline corpus Christ is identified as God's Angel, the Destroyer, the Heavenly Man, the Power of God, the Wisdom of God, the Glory, the Image, the Spirit, the Form, the Name, the Firstborn, the Beginning, the Head, and the Body. This Angelomorphic Christology, dating from the mid-first century, is crucial evidence for the Christological appropriation of angelomorphic language and imagery which we examined in Part II. The Pauline corpus can and should be viewed as part of a varied Christological continuum which stretches from the earliest expressions of Christology to Nicea. In fact, this examination shows that the Christology of the Pauline corpus is not ideologically distant from the Angelomorphic Christology found in the frequently-cited mid-second century apologist Justin Martyr, who called Christ by several names, including: the Beginning, a Power, the Glory of the Lord, the Son, Wisdom, an Angel, God, Lord, Word, and Captain (*Dial. Trypho* 61).

---

[100] There may be additional language related to angelomorphic traditions in Col 1.25-28. Paul talks about making "the Word of God" full known and then further defines this Word as "the mystery hidden for ages" (1.26), "which is Christ in you" (1.27). Thus, Christ is not only the content of the word of God, he is the hypostatized Word of God: "Him we proclaim" (1.28).

PART FOUR

CONCLUSION

CHAPTER FIFTEEN

IMPLICATIONS FOR THE STUDY OF EARLY CHRISTOLOGY

[*Gos. Thom.* 13] Jesus said to his disciples: "Make a comparison to me and tell me whom I am like". Simon Peter said to him: "You are like a righteous angel".

Most people who read this comparison of Jesus to a righteous angel conclude that angels have little to do with Christ; thus, Peter is making a rather weak Christological statement. This study, however, has demonstrated that angelomorphic traditions played a significant role in early Christology, including the Christology found on the pages of the NT. Moreover, it has also been shown that these traditions were used to assert that Christ is the visible manifestation of God, who has been seen over centuries of time in various forms and by various means. What remains, therefore, is to delineate four implications of this research for the continued study of early Christology.

First and foremost, this study, building on recent research, has defined and illustrated more extensively the existence of angelomorphic traditions which were profoundly employed in the earliest extant expressions of Christology. This signifies that the study of Angelomorphic Christology has been broadened far beyond the simplistic confines of the question: Did any early Christians understand Jesus to be an angel from among the myriads of created angels? This ontological question has greatly inhibited past research. The question that was repeatedly asked above, and which should continue to be asked and researched in future studies of early Christology, is much broader and more nuanced: Where and how did early Christians use the variegated angelomorphic traditions from the OT and other sources to express their Christology? The evidence of the last four chapters, as well as the supporting evidence from the pages which precede them, has shown that this question is not one that should be confined to second and third century CE documents. Furthermore, this evidence has rendered the pronouncement that "no NT writer thought of Christ as an angel" to be both simplistic and false.[1]

---

[1] Dunn, *Christology in the Making*, 158; see discussion on 2 above.

Second, this study has reasserted the importance of Angel of the Lord traditions for early Christology, especially in light of how these traditions contributed to the expression of experiences and ideas concerning Divine Hypostases and Principal Angels. As was stressed repeatedly, "[the] identification of the Angel of the Lord and the Glory of God by means of a personal name, whether that of one of the archangels or that of a human being, was a very significant step".[2] Indeed, such an important, even gigantic, step was taken when the earliest Christians made the confession Κύριος Ιησοῦς ("Jesus is Lord"; i.e., "Jesus is YHWH").[3] This enabled them to link one or more of the unnamed angelomorphic figures intimately identified with YHWH (i.e., the Angel, the Glory, the Name, the Word, Wisdom) to the fleshly Jesus who had ascended and was now enthroned. It has also been demonstrated that the threat of Arianism effectively veiled and virtually buried the important contribution which angelomorphic traditions made to the origin and development of Christology. This process was also furthered by the distancing of Christianity and its Christology, in both time and ideology, from its Jewish roots.

Third, in spite of the *variety* of textual traditions examined, this study has shown that there are *interrelationships* among both the various antecedent traditions and the subsequent Christological expressions. Caution must be exercised in studying the significance of one mediator figure (e.g., Wisdom) apart from its dependence upon, or its relationship to, other mediator figures. The Pauline and Johannine evidence, as well as second century CE texts, has shown the affinity of early Christians for employing different, but related, mediator traditions for the same figure.[4] That the interrelationship and uniting of such angelomorphic figures are pre-Christian phenomena is visible in the many-named mediator of Philo who is most frequently identified as the Word. Therefore, this study does not seek to spawn a "new" Christology among the many individual—sometimes conflicting—Christologies which claim to be definitive.[5] On the contrary, it presents a Christology that

---

[2] Fossum, *Name of God*, 337.
[3] E.g., 1 Cor 12.3; Phil 2.11; Rev 17.14; 19.16; see Capes, *OT Yahweh Texts*.
[4] Hengel discusses the Many-Named Mediator tradition in *Son of God*, 57-58 n.109.
[5] This criticism is mentioned by Hengel, *Son of God*, 57.

highlights the interrelationship and interdependence of various Christological traditions.

Fourth, the invisibility of God is a concept that greatly contributed to the development of angelomorphic traditions. Scholarship earlier this century tended to emphasize the transcendence of God as the key theological shift that contributed to the growth of mediator traditions. The growth of a pre-incarnation Christology and a Christological interpretation of the OT sought to answer the ambiguity which already existed in the text of the OT: people were interacting face to face with a God who said "man shall not see me and live" (Exod 33.20). The visibility of God as man is present in the panorama of angelomorphic traditions which depict God, or his visible manifestation, as a man enthroned in heaven or even walking on earth. This evidence is an important, although often unappreciated, precursor for the early Christian belief in the incarnation. Furthermore, this evidence has also emphasized the probability that angelomorphic traditions were not only used to understand the Risen Christ decades later, but were also used from the early days of Christianity to understand the fleshly Jesus and his preexistence.

The seeds that were needed to express a sophisticated Christology were sown in the Israelite and Jewish texts from which early Christianity sought to understand Jesus as Lord. It has been repeatedly demonstrated that the angelomorphic traditions of this literature, among which the Angel of the Lord texts are foundational, were some of the oldest and most significant traditions that inspired the Christology which we now find in early Christian literature, including the New Testament.

BIBLIOGRAPHY

I. *Primary Sources*

Amidon, Philip R., ed. *The Panarion of St. Epiphanius, Bishop of Salamis*. New York: Oxford University Press, 1990.
Ben-Ḥayyim, Z., ed. *The Liturgy and Oral Tradition of Hebrew and Aramaic amongst the Samaritans*. Academy of the Hebrew Language: Texts and Studies 6. Five volumes. Jerusalem, 1957-77.
Black, Matthew, ed. *The Book of Enoch or 1 Enoch*. SVTP 7. Leiden: Brill 1985.
Bettiolo, P., A. Giambelluca Kossova, L. Leonardi, E. Norelli, and L. Perrone, eds. *Ascensio Isaiae: Textus*. Corpus Christianorvm, Series Apocryphorum 7. Turnhout: Brepols, 1995.
Braude, William G., ed. *The Midrash on Psalms*. Two Volumes. Yale Judaica Series XIII. New Haven: Yale University Press, 1959.
Cathcart, Kevin J., and Robert P. Gordon, eds. *The Targum of the Minor Prophets*. The Aramaic Bible 14. Wilmington: Michael Glazier, 1989.
Charles, R. H., ed. *The Apocrypha and Pseudepigrapha of the Old Testament*. Two volumes. Oxford: Oxford University Press, 1913.
———. *The Ascension of Isaiah*. London: Adam and Charles Black, 1900.
Charlesworth, James H., ed. *The Old Testament Pseudepigrapha*. Two volumes. New York: Doubleday, 1983/1985.
———. *The Dead Sea Scrolls, Volume 1: Rules: Rule of the Community and Related Documents*. Louisville: Westminster/John Knox, 1993.
———. *The Dead Sea Scrolls, Volume 2: Rules: Damascus Document, War Scroll, and Related Documents*. Louisville: Westminster/John Knox, 1995.
———. *The Dead Sea Scrolls, Volume 4: Angelic Liturgy, Prayers, and Psalms*. Louisville: Westminster/John Knox, 1997.
Chilton, Bruce, ed. *The Isaiah Targum*. The Aramaic Bible 11. Wilmington: Michael Glazier, 1987.
Cohen, M. S., ed. *The Shi'ur Qomah: Texts and Recensions*. TSAJ 9. Tübingen: Mohr/Siebeck, 1985.
Colson, F. H., G. H. Whitaker, J. W. Earp, and R. Marcus, eds. *Philo*. LCL. Thirteen volumes. Cambridge, MA: Harvard University Press, 1927-1962.
Copenhaver, Brian P., ed. *Hermetica: The Greek Corpus Hermeticum and the Latin Asclepius in a New English Translation with Notes and Introduction*. Cambridge: Cambridge University Press, 1992.
Cowley, A. E., ed. *The Samaritan Liturgy*. Oxford: Oxford University Press, 1909.
Cuming, G., ed. *Hippolytus: A Text for Students*. Bramcote: Grove Books, 1976.
Danby, Herbert, ed. *The Mishnah*. Oxford: Oxford University Press, 1933.
Drower, Ethel S., ed. *The Canonical Prayerbook of the Mandaeans*. Leiden: Brill, 1959.
Ellinger, K. and W. Rudolph, eds. *Biblia Hebraica Stuttgartensia*. Stuttgart: Deutsche Bibelgesellschaft, 1984.
Epstein, I., ed. *The Babylonian Talmud*. 31 volumes. Translated by M. Simon. London: Soncino Press, 1935-52; reprints.
Evans, Ernest, ed. *Tertullian: Adversus Marcionem*. Two volumes. Oxford: Oxford University Press, 1972.

Freedman, H. and M. Simon, eds. *Midrash Rabbah.* 10 volumes. London: Soncino Press, 1939; reprint, 1961.
Friedlander, Gerald, ed. *Pirkê de Rabbi Eliezer.* London: Hegan Paul, Trench, Trubner, 1916.
Ginzberg, Louis. *The Legends of the Jews.* Seven volumes. Philadelphia: Jewish Publication Society, 1909-1938.
Grossfeld, Bernard, ed. *The Targum Onqelos to Genesis.* The Aramaic Bible 6. Wilmington: Michael Glazier, 1988.
——. *The Targum Onqelos to Exodus.* The Aramaic Bible 7. Wilmington: Michael Glazier, 1988.
Haussleiter, J., ed. *Victorini Episcopi Petauionensis Opera, Corpus Scriptorum Ecclesiasticorum Latinorum.* Leipzig: G. Freytan, 1916; reprint 1965.
Jacobson, Howard. *The Exagoge of Ezekiel.* Cambridge: Cambridge University Press, 1983.
de Jonge, M., ed. *The Testaments of the Twelve Patriarchs: A Critical Edition of the Greek Text.* PVTG 1/2. Leiden: Brill, 1978.
Kern, O., ed. *Orphicorum Fragmenta.* 2d ed. Berlin: Walter de Gruÿter, 1963.
Klein, M., ed. *The Fragment-Targums of the Pentateuch according to their Extant Sources.* AnBib 76. Two volumes. Rome: Pontifical Biblical Institute Press, 1980.
Koetschau, P., ed. *Origenes, Gegen Celsus.* Two volumes. GCS 2-3. Leipzig: Hinriches, 1899.
Kropp, A. M., ed. *Ausgewählte koptische Zaubertexte.* Three volumes. Bruxelles: Foundation Egyptologique Reine Elisabeth, 1930-31.
Lake, Kirsopp, ed. *The Apostolic Fathers.* LCL. Two volumes. Cambridge, MA: Harvard University Press, 1913.
——. *Eusebius: The Ecclesiastical History.* LCL. Cambridge, MA: Harvard University Press, 1926.
Levey, Samson H., ed. *The Targum of Ezekiel.* The Aramaic Bible 13. Wilmington: Michael Glazier, 1987.
Lidzbarski, Mark, ed. *Ginza: Der Schatz oder Das Grosse Buch der Mandäer.* Göttingen: Vandenhoeck & Ruprecht, 1925.
Macdonald, J., ed. *Memar Marqah.* Two volumes. BZAW 84. Berlin: Töpelmann, 1963.
Maher, Michael, ed. *Targum Pseudo-Jonathan: Genesis.* The Aramaic Bible 1B. Wilmington: Michael Glazier, 1992.
Mangan, Céline, John F. Healey, and Peter S. Knobel. *The Targum of Job, The Targum of Proverbs,* and *The Targum of Qohelet.* The Aramaic Bible 15. Wilmington: Michael Glazier, 1991.
Martínez, Florentino García, ed. *The Dead Sea Scrolls Translated.* Leiden: Brill, 1994.
McNamara, Martin, ed. *Targum Neofiti 1: Genesis.* The Aramaic Bible 1A. Wilmington: Michael Glazier, 1992.
McNamara, Martin and Ernest G. Clarke, eds. *Targum Neofiti 1: Numbers* and *Targum Pseudo-Jonathan: Numbers.* The Aramaic Bible 4. Wilmington: Michael Glazier, 1995.
McNamara, Martin, and Robert Hayward, eds. *Targum Neofiti 1: Exodus.* The Aramaic Bible 2. Wilmington: Michael Glazier, 1994.
——. *Targum Neofiti 1: Leviticus.* The Aramaic Bible 3. Wilmington: Michael Glazier, 1994.
Metzger, Bruce M., ed. *The Oxford Annotated Bible with Apocrypha* (RSV). New York: Oxford University Press, 1965.
Migne, J. P., ed. *Patrologia Graeca.* Paris: J. P. Migne, 1857-66.
——. *Patrologia Latina.* Paris: J. P. Migne, 1844-64.

Mras, K., ed. *Eusebius: Praeparatio Evangelica*. Two volumes. GCS 43/1-2. Berlin: Akademie-Verlag, 1954/1958.
Nestle, Erwin, and Kurt Aland, eds. *Novum Testamentum Graece*. 26th ed. Stuttgart: Deutsche Bibelstiftung, 1979.
Neusner, Jacob, ed. *Pesiqta de Rab Kahana: An Analytical Translation*. Two Volumes. Atlanta: Scholars Press, 1987.
———. *The Talmud of the Land of Israel. Volume 34: Horayot and Niddah*. Chicago: University of Chicago Press, 1982.
———. *The Talmud of the Land of Israel. Volume 31: Sanhedrin and Makkot*. Chicago: University of Chicago Press, 1984.
Newson, Carol, ed. *Songs of the Sabbath Sacrifice: A Critical Edition*. HSS 27. Atlanta: Scholars Press, 1985.
Odeberg, Hugo, ed. *3 Enoch or The Hebrew Book of Enoch*. Cambridge: Cambridge University Press, 1928; reprint, New York: KTAV, 1973.
Peterman, H. *Thesaurus sive Liber Magnus, vulgo "Liber Adamai" appellatus*. Leipzig, 1867.
Polotsky, H. J. ed. *Manichäische Homilien*. Manichäische Handscriften der Sammlung A. Chester Beatty I. Stuttgart: W. Kohlhammer, 1934.
Polotsky, H. J., and A. Böhlig, eds. *Kephalaia I*. Manichäische Handschriften der Staatlichen Museen Berlin I. Stuttgart: W. Kohlhammer, 1940.
Philonenko, M., ed. *Joseph et Asénath*. SPB 13. Leiden: Brill, 1968.
Rahlfs, Alfred, ed. *Septuaginta*. Stuttgart: Deutsche Bibelgesellschaft, 1935.
Roberts, Alexander, and James Donaldson, eds. *The Ante-Nicene Fathers*. Eight volumes. Grand Rapids: Eerdmans, 1885; reprints.
Robinson, James M., ed. *The Nag Hammadi Library*. San Francisco: Harper and Row, 1978.
Sacchi, P., ed. *Apocrifi dell'Antico Testamento*. Two volumes. Turin: Union Tipografico-Editrice Torinese, 1989.
Schneemelcher, Wilhelm, ed. *New Testament Apocrypha*. Translated by R. McL. Wilson. Two volumes. Philadelphia: Westminster, 1992.
Sperber, A., ed. *The Bible in Aramaic*. Five volumes. Leiden: Brill, 1959-73.
Stählin, O., ed. *Clemens Alexandrinus, Opera*. Three volumes. GCS 12, 15, and 16. Berlin: Akademie-Verlag, 1936-72.
Strecker, Georg, ed. *Die Pseudoklementinen I: Homilien*. 3d ed. GCS 42. Berlin: Akademie-Verlag, 1992.
———. *Die Pseudoklementinen II: Rekognitionen*. 2d ed. GCS 51. Berlin: Akademie-Verlag, 1993.
Thackery, H., R. Marcus, and L. Feldman, eds. *Josephus*. LCL. Ten volumes. Cambridge, MA: Harvard, 1927-1965.
Vaillant, A., ed. *Le livre des secrets d'Hénoch*. Testes publiés par l'Institut d'Études Slaves 4. 2d ed. Paris, 1952.
Wendland, P., ed. *Hippolytus: Refutatio omnium haeresium*. GCS 26. Leipzig: Hinrichs, 1916; reprint, Hildesheim: Olm, 1977.
Wittaker, Molly, ed. *Die Apostolischen Väter I: Der Hirt des Hermas*. GCS 48. Berlin: Akademie-Verlag, 1956.
Zahavy, Tzvee, ed. *The Talmud of the Land of Israel. Volume 1: Berakot*. Chicago: University of Chicago Press, 1989.

II. *Secondary Sources*

Adler, William. "Enoch in Early Christian Literature". *SBLSP* 17 (1978) 271-276.
Agnew, F. H. "The Origin of the NT Apostle-Concept: A Review of Research". *JBL* 105 (1986) 75-96.
Alexander, Phillip. "The Historical Setting of the Hebrew Book of Enoch". *JJS* 28 (1977) 156-177.
Arnold, Clinton E. *Ephesians: Power and Magic*. SNTSMS 63. Cambridge: Cambridge University Press, 1989. Reprinted Grand Rapids: Baker, 1992.
——. *The Colossian Syncretism: The Interface Between Christianity and Foldk Belief in Colossae*. WUNT 2/77. Tübingen: Mohr/Siebeck, 1995. Reprinted Grand Rapids: Baker, 1996.
——. "Jesus Christ: 'Head' of the Church (Colossians and Ephesians)". In *Jesus of Nazareth: Lord and Christ*, eds. Joel B. Green and Max Turner, 346-366. Grand Rapids: Eerdmans, 1994.
Ashton, John. "Paraclete." *ABD* 5.152-154.
——. *Studying John: Approaches to the Fourth Gospel*. Oxford: Oxford University Press, 1994.
——. *Understanding the Fourth Gospel*. Oxford: Oxford University Press, 1991.
Attridge, Harold. *The Epistle to the Hebrews*. Hermeneia. Philadelphia: Fortress, 1989.
Aune, David E. *Prophecy in Early Christianity and the Ancient Mediterranean World*. Grand Rapids: Eerdmans, 1983.
Bakker, Adolphine. "Christ an Angel? A Study of Early Christian Docetism". *ZNW* 32 (1933) 255-265.
Ball, David Mark. *'I Am' in John's Gospel: Literary Function, Background and Theological Implications*. JSNTSup 124. Sheffield: Sheffield Academic Press, 1996.
Barbel, Joseph. *Christos Angelos: Die Anschauung von Christus als Bote und Engel in der gelehrten und volkstümlichen Literatur des christlichen Altertums*. Bonn: Peter Hanstein, 1941. Nackdruck 1964 mit einem Anhang.
Barker, Margaret. *The Gate of Heaven*. London: SPCK, 1991.
——. *The Great Angel: A Study of Israel's Second God*. Louisville: Westminster/John Knox, 1992.
——. "Temple Imagery in Philo: An Indication of the Origin of the Logos?". In *Templum Amicitiae: Essays in Honor of Ernst Bammel*, 70-102. JSNTSup 48. Sheffield: Sheffield Academic Press, 1991.
Barnard, L.W. *Justin Martyr: His Life and Thought*. Cambridge: Cambridge University Press, 1967.
——. "The Shepherd of Hermas in Recent Study". *Heythrop Journal* 9 (1968), 29-36.
Barr, James. "Hypostatization of Linguistic Phenomena in Modern Theological Interpretation". *JSS* 7 (1962) 85-92.
——. "Theophany and Anthropomorphism in the Old Testament". In *Congress Volume: Oxford 1959*, 31-38. VTSup 7. Leiden: Brill, 1960.
Barton, G. "The Origin of the Names of Angels and Demons in the Extra-Canonical Apocalyptic Literature to 100 A.D." *JBL* 31 (1912) 156-167.
Bauckham, Richard. *The Climax of Prophecy*. Edinburgh: T&T Clark, 1993.
——. *The Theology of the Book of Revelation*. Cambridge: Cambridge University Press, 1993.
——. "The Worship of Jesus in Apocalyptic Christianity". *NTS* 27 (1980/81) 322-341.

Beale, G. K. "Revelation". In *It is Written: Scripture Citing Scripture*, eds. D. A. Carsons and H. G. M. Williamson, 318-336. Cambridge: Cambridge University Press, 1988.
——. "The Old Testament Background of Rev. 3.14". *NTS* 42 (1996) 133-152.
Behm, J. "παράκλητος". *TDNT* 5.800-814.
Benoit, P. "L'hymne christologique de Col 1,15-20. Jugement critique sur l'état des recherches". In *Christianity, Judaism and Other Greco-Roman Cults: Festschrift for Morton Smith*, 1.226-263. SJLA 12. Leiden: Brill, 1975.
——. "Pauline Angelology and Demonology". *RSB* 3 (1983) 1-18.
Betz, Hans Dieter. "Dynamis". In *Dictionary of Deities and Demons in the Bible*, eds. K. van der Toorn, Bob Becking, and Pieter W. van der Horst, 509-515. Leiden: Brill, 1995.
——. *Galatians*. Hermeneia. Philadelphia: Fortress, 1979.
Betz, Otto. *Der Paraklet: Fürsprecher im häretischen Spätjudentum, im Johannes-Evangelium und in neu gefundenen gnostischen Schriften*. AGJU 2. Leiden: Brill, 1963.
Bianchi, U. "L'Ascensione di Isaia. Tematiche soterilogiche di descensus/ascensus". In *Isaia, il dilietto e la chiesa: Visione ed esegesi profetica cristiano-primitiva nell' Ascensione di Isaia. Atti del Convegno di Roma, 9-10 Aprile 1981*, ed. M. Pesce, 155-184. Brescia: Paidea, 1983.
Black, Matthew. "The Messianism of the Parables of Enoch: Their Date and Contribution to Christian Origins". In *The Messiah: Developments in Early Judaism and Christianity*, ed. J.H. Charlesworth, 145-168. Minneapolis: Fortress, 1992.
——. "Two Unusual Nomina Dei in the Second Vision of Enoch". In *The New Testament Age: Essays in Honor of Bo Reicke*, ed. W. Weinrich, 1.53-59. Macon, GA: Mercer, 1984.
Boccaccini, Gabriele. "Middle Judaism and Its Contemporary Interpreters (1986-1992): Methodological Foundations for the Study of Judaisms, 300 BCE to 200 CE". *Henoch* 15 (1993) 207-233.
——. *Middle Judaism: Jewish Thought 300 BCE to 200 CE*. Minneapolis: Fortress, 1991.
Bockmuehl, Markus. "'The Form of God' (Phil. 2:6): Variation on a Theme of Jewish Mysticism". *JTS* 48 (1997) 1-23.
de Boer, Martinus. *The Defeat of Death: Apocalyptic Eschatology in 1 Corinthians 15 and Romans 5*. JSNTSup 22. Sheffield: Sheffield Academic Press, 1988.
Borgen, Peder. *Bread From Heaven: An Exegetical Study of the Concept of Manna in the Gospel of John and the Writings of Philo*. SupNovT 10. Leiden: Brill, 1965.
——. "God's Agent in the Fourth Gospel". In *Religions in Antiquity: Essays in Memory of Erwin Ramdell Goodenough*, ed. J. Neusner, 137-148. Supplements to *Numen* 14. Leiden: Brill, 1968.
——. "Heavenly Ascent in Philo: An Examination of Selected Passages". In *The Pseudepigrapha and Early Biblical Interpretation*, eds. J.H. Charlesworth and C. Evans, 246-268. JSPSup 14. Sheffield: Sheffield Academic Press, 1991.
——. *Logos was the True Light and Other Essays on the Gospel of John*. Trondheim: Tapir, 1983.
——. "Philo of Alexandria". *ANRW* II.21.1, 99-154.
Borse, U. *Der Standort des Galaterbriefes*. Köln: Peter Hanstein, 1972.
Bousset, D. Wilhelm. *Der Antichrist in der Überlieferung des Judentums, des neuen Testaments, und der alten Kirche: Ein Beitrag zur Erklärung der Apocalypse*. Göttingen: Vandenhoeck & Ruprecht, 1895.
——. "Die Himmelsreise der Seele". *Archiv für Religionswissenschaft* 4 (1901) 136-169.

———. *Kyrios Christos*. Translated by J. Steely. 5th ed. Nashville: Abingdon, 1970.
Bousset, D. Wilhelm, and H. Gressman. *Die Religion des Judentums im Späthellenistischen Zeitalter*. 4th ed. Tübingen: Mohr/Siebeck, 1966.
Bowker, J. "'Merkabah' Visions and the Visions of Paul". *JSS* 16 (1971) 157-173.
Box, G. H. "The Idea of Intermediation in Jewish Theology: A Note on Memra and Shekinah". *JQR* 23 (1932/33) 103-119.
———. "The Jewish Environment of Early Christianity". *Exp Tim* 42 (1916) 1-25.
Brighton, Louis. "The Angel of Revelation: An Angel of God and an Icon of Jesus Christ". Ph.D. diss., St. Louis University, 1991.
Brown, Raymond. *The Gospel According to John I-XII*. AB 29. New York: Doubleday, 1966.
Brox, Norbert. *Der Hirt Des Hermas*. Kommentar zu den Apostolischen Vätern 7. Göttingen: Vandenhoeck & Ruprecht, 1991.
Bruce, F. F. *Galatians*. Exeter: Paternoster, 1982.
———. "Holy Spirit in the Qumran Texts". *The Annual of Leeds University Oriental Society* 6 (1969) 49-55.
Buchanan, George. "Apostolic Christology". *SBLSP* 25 (1986) 172-182.
Bühner, Jan-A. *Der Gesandte und sein Weg im 4. Evangelium*. WUNT 2/2. Tübingen: Mohr/Siebeck, 1977.
Bultmann, Rudolph. *The Gospel of John*. Translated by G. R. Beasley-Murray, R. W. N. Hoare, J. K. Riches. Philadelphia: Fortress, 1974.
———. *The Theology of the New Testament*. Two volumes. Translated by K. Grobel. New York: Scribner's Sons, 1950/1955.
Burge, G. *The Anointed Community: The Holy Spirit in the Johannine Tradition*. Grand Rapids: Eerdmans, 1978.
Burney, C. "Christ as the APXH of Creation". *JTS* 27 (1926) 161-177.
Capes, David. *Old Testament Yahweh Texts in Paul's Christology*. WUNT 2/47. Tübingen: Mohr/Siebeck, 1992.
Carr, W. *Angels and Principalities: The Background, Meaning, and Development of the Pauline Phrase "Hai Archai kai hai Exousai"*. SNTSMS 42. Cambridge: Cambridge University Press, 1981.
Carrell, Peter R. *Jesus and the angels: Angelology and the christology of the Apocalypse of John*. SNTSMS 95. Cambridge: Cambridge University Press, 1997.
Casey, Maurice. *The Son of Man*. London: Hodder and Stoughton, 1979.
Casey, P. M. *From Jewish Prophet to Gentile God: The Origins and Development of New Testament Christology*. Philadelphia: Westminister/John Knox, 1991.
Charles, R. H. *The Revelation to St. John*. ICC. Two volumes. Edinburgh: T & T Clark, 1920.
Charlesworth, James H. "The Jewish Roots of Christology: The Discovery of the Hypostatic Voice". *SJT* 39 (1986) 19-41.
———. "The Portrayal of the Righteous as an Angel". In *Ideal Figues in Ancient Judaism*, SCS 12, eds. J.J. Collins and G. Nickelsburg, 135-151. Chico, CA: Scholars Press, 1980.
Cherus, I. *Mysticism in Rabbinic Judaism*. SJ 11. Berlin: Walter de Gruyter, 1982.
Chester, Andrew. *Divine Revelation and Divine Titles in the Penteuchal Targumim*. TSAJ 14. Tübingen: Mohr/Siebeck, 1986.
———. "Jewish Messianic Expectations and Mediatorial Figures and Pauline Christology". In *Paulus und das antike Judentum*, eds. M. Hengel and U. Heckel, 17-89. Tübingen: Mohr/Siebeck, 1991.
Chilton, Bruce. "Recent and Prospective Discussion of *Memra*". In *From Ancient Israel to Modern Judaism: Intellect in Quest of Understanding*, ed. J. Neusner, 119-137. BJS 173. Atlanta: Scholars Press, 1989.

Cohen, M. *The Shi'ur Qomah: Liturgy and Theurgy in Pre-Kabbalistic Jewish Mysticism*. New York: University Press of America, 1983.
Conzelmann, H. and A. Lindemann. *Interpreting the New Testament*. Translated by S. Schwatzmann. Peabody: Hendrickson, 1988.
Collins, A. Yarboro. "The 'Son of Man' Tradition and the Book of Revelation". In *The Messiah: Developments in Early Judaism and Christianity*, ed. J.H. Charlesworth, 536-568. Minneapolis: Fortress, 1992.
Collins, John J. *Daniel*. Hermenia. Philadelphia: Fortress, 1993.
——. "The Heavenly Representative: The 'Son of Man' in the Similitudes of Enoch". In *Ideal Figures in Ancient Judaism*, eds. G. Nickelsburg and J.J. Collins, 111-133. SCS 12. Chico, CA: Scholars Press, 1980.
Culianu, Ioan P. "The Angels of the Nations and the Origins of the Gnostic Myth". In *Studies in Gnosticism and Hellenistic Religions: Studies presented to Gilles Quispel*, eds. R. van den Broek and M. J. Vermaseren, 78-91. Leiden: Brill, 1981.
Cullmann, Oscar. *The Christology of the New Testament*. Rev. ed. Philadelphia: Westminster, 1963.
Dahl, N. A. "Sources of Christological Language". *Jesus the Christ: The Historical Origins of Christological Doctrine*, ed. Donald Juel, 113-136. Minneapolis: Fortress, 1991.
——. "The Johannine Church and History". In *Current Issues in New Testament Interpretation*, eds. W. Klassen and G. Synder, 124-142. New York: Harper, 1962.
Daniélou, Jean. *The Development of Christian Doctrine before the Council of Nicea. Volume I: The Theology of Jewish Christianity*. Translated by J. Baker. Philadelphia: Westminster, 1964.
Davidson, Maxwell J. *Angels at Qumran: A Comparative Study of 1 Enoch 1-36, 72-108 and the Sectarian Writings from Qumran*. JSPSup 11. Sheffield: Sheffield Academic Press, 1992.
Davies, W. D. "A Note on Josephus, Antiquities 15.136". *HTR* 47 (1954) 135-140.
——. *Paul and Rabbinic Judaism*. 4th ed. Philadelphia: Fortress, 1980.
Davis, Carl. *The Name and Way of the Lord: Old Testament Themes, New Testament Christology*. JSNTSup 129. Sheffield: Sheffield Academic Press, 1996.
Decock, P. B. "Holy ones, sons of God, and the transcendent future of the righteous in 1 Enoch and the New Testament". *Neot* 17 (1983) 70-82.
De Conick, April. *Seek to See Him: Ascent and Vision Mysticism in the Gospel of Thomas*. VCSup 33. Leiden: Brill, 1996.
De Conick, April, and Jarl Fossum. "Stripped Before God: A New Interpretation of Logion 37 in the Gospel of Thomas". *VC* 45 (1991) 123-150.
Dibelius, Martin. *Die Geisterwelt in Glauben des Paulus*. Göttingen: Vandenhoeck & Ruprecht, 1909.
——. *Die apostolischen Väter IV: Der Hirt des Hermas*. HNT. Tübingen: Mohr/Siebeck, 1923.
Dix, G. H. "The Heavenly Wisdom and the Divine Logos in Jewish Apocalyptic". *JTS* 26 (1924) 1-12.
——. "The Influence of Babylonian Ideas on Jewish Messianism." *JTS* 26 (1925) 241-256.
——. "The Seven Archangels and the Seven Spirits." *JTS* 28 (1927) 233-250.
Drower, Ethel S. *The Secret Adam*. Oxford: Oxford University Press, 1960.
Duhaime, J. "Dualistic Reworking in the Scrolls from Qumran". *CBQ* 49 (1987) 32-56.
Duncan, G. *Galatians*. New York: Harper, 1934.
Dunn, James D. G. *Christology in the Making: An Inquiry into the Origins of the Doctrine of the Incarnation*. 2d ed. London: SCM, 1989.

———. *The Parting of the Ways between Christianity and Judaism and their Significance for the Character of Christianity*. London: SCM, 1991.
Dupont-Sommer, A. "Adam. 'Père du Monde" dans la Sagesse de Solomon (10,1.2)". *RHR* 119 (1939) 182-191.
Eichrodt, Walter. *Theology of the Old Testament*. Translated by J. Baker. Two volumes. London: SCM, 1967.
Ellis, E. E. *Prophecy and Hermeneutic in Early Christianity*. WUNT 1/18. Tübingen: Mohr/Siebeck, 1978.
Evans, Craig. A. *Word and Glory: On the Exegetical and Theological Background of John's Prologue*. JSNTSup 89. Sheffield: Sheffield Academic Press, 1993.
Everling, O. *Die paulinische Angelologie und Dämonologie*. Göttingen: Vandenhoeck & Ruprecht, 1888.
Fee, Gordon. *The First Epistle to the Corinthians*. NICNT. Grand Rapids: Eerdmans, 1987.
Fekkes, Jan. *Isaiah and Prophetic Traditions in the Book of Revelation*. JSNTSS 93. Sheffield: Sheffield Academic Press, 1994.
Fletcher-Louis, Crispin H. T. *Luke-Acts: Angels, Christology and Soteriology*. WUNT 2/94. Tübingen: Mohr/Siebeck, 1997.
Fossum, Jarl E. "Colossians 1.15-18a in the Light of Jewish Mysticism and Gnosticism". *NTS* 35 (1989) 183-201.
———. "Glory". In *Dictionary of Deities and Demons in the Bible*, eds. K. van der Toorn, Bob Becking, and Pieter W. van der Horst, 659-668. Leiden: Brill,1995.
———. "Jewish-Christian Christology and Jewish Mysticism". *VC* 37 (1983) 260-287.
———. "Kyrios Jesus as the Angel of the Lord in Jude 5-7". *NTS* 33 (1987) 226-243.
———. "The Adorable Adam of the Mystics and the Rebuttals of the Rabbis". In *Geschichte-Tradition-Reflexion: Festschrift für Martin Hengel zum 70. Geburtstag*, eds. H. Cancik, H. Lichtenberger, and P. Schäfer, I.529-539. Tübingen: Mohr/Siebeck, 1996.
———. "The Apostle Concept in the Qur'an and Pre-Islamic Near Eastern Literature". In *Literary Heritage of Classical Islam: Arabic and Islamic Studies in Honor of James A. Bellamy*, ed. M. Mir with J. Fossum, 149-167. Princeton: Darwin, 1993.
———. "The Figure of the Heavenly Man in Recent Research". *ANRW* II.22, forthcoming.
———. *The Image of the Invisible God: Essays on the Influence of Jewish Mysticism on Early Christology*. NTOA 30. Universitätsverlag Freiburg, Schweiz, and Vandenhoeck & Ruprecht, Göttingen, 1995.
———. "The Magharians: A Pre-Christian Jewish Sect and Its Significance for the Study of Gnosticism and Christianity". *Henoch* 9 (1987) 303-344.
———. *The Name of God and the Angel of the Lord: Samaritan and Jewish Concepts of Intermediation and the Origin of Gnosticism*. WUNT 1/36. Tübingen: Mohr/Siebeck, 1985.
———. "The New *Religionsgeschichtliche Schule*: The Quest for Jewish Christology". *SBLSP* 30 (1991) 638-646.
———. "Sects and Movements". In *The Samaritans*, ed. Alan Crown, 293-389. Tübingen: Mohr/Siebeck, 1989.
———. "Son of God". *ABD* 6.1128-1137.
Fretheim, Terrance. "Word of God". *ABD* 6.961-968.
Fung, R. *The Epistle to the Galatians*. NICNT. Grand Rapids: Eerdmans, 1988.
Funk, R. "The Apostolic *Parousia*: Form and Significance". In *Christian History and Interpretation*, eds. W. R. Farmer, C. F. D. Moule, and R. Niebuhr, 249-269. Cambridge: Cambridge University Press, 1967.

Gabathuler, J. *Jesus Christ. Haupt der Kirche—Haupt der Welt.* ATANT 45. Zürich: Zwingli, 1965.
Galambush, Julie. *Jerusalem in the Book of Ezekiel: The City as Yahweh's Wife.* SBLDS 130. Atlanta: Scholars Press, 1992.
Gemser, B. *Spruche Salomos.* HAT 16. Tübingen: Mohr/Siebeck, 1963.
Gianotto, C. *Melchisedek e la sua tipologia: tradizioni giudaiche, cristiane e gnostiche.* Brescia: Paideia Editrice, 1984.
Gibson, Arthur. *Biblical Semantic Logic: A Preliminary Analysis.* Oxford: Basil Blackwell, 1981.
Gieschen, Charles A. "The Angel of the Prophetic Spirit: Interpreting Revelatory Experiences in the *Shepherd of Hermas* in Light of *Mandate* XI". *SBLSP* 33 (1994) 790-803.
———. "The Different Functions of a Similar Melchizedek Tradition in *2 Enoch* and the Epistle to the Hebrews". In *Early Christian Interpretations of the Scriptures of Israel: Investigations and Proposals,* eds. C.A. Evans and J.A. Sanders, 364-379. JSNTSup 148/SSEJC 5. Sheffield: Sheffield Academic Press, 1997.
———. "The Seven Pillars of the World: Ideal Figure Lists in the Christology of the Pseudo-Clementines". *JSP* 12 (1994) 47-82.
Giet, S. *L'énigme de la Didachè.* Paris: Les Éditions Ophrys, 1970.
———. *Hermas et les pasteurs: Les trois auteurs du pasteur d'Hermas.* Paris: Presses universitaires du France, 1963.
Goddard, A. J. and S. A. Cummins. "Ill or Ill-Treated? Conflict and Persecution as the Context of Paul's Original Ministry in Galatia (Galatians 4.12-20)". *JSNT* 52 (1993) 93-126.
Goetz, Karl. *Das antichristliche und das christliche, geschichtliche Jesusbild von heute.* Basel: Helbing & Lichtenhahn, 1944.
Goldin, J. "Not by Means of an Angel and not by Means of a Messenger". In *Religions in Antiquity Essays in Memory of Erwin Ramsdell Goodenough,* ed. J. Neusner, 412-424. Supplements to *Numen* 14. Leiden: Brill, 1968.
Goodenough, Erwin R. *By Light, Light: The Mystic Gospel of Hellenistic Judaism.* New Haven: Yale University Press, 1935.
———. *The Theology of Justin Martyr.* Jena: Formmansche Buchhandlung, 1923; reprint, Amsterdam: Philo Press, 1968.
Goodman, D. "Do Angels Eat?" *JJS* 37 (1986) 160-175.
Goppelt, L. *Typos: The Typological Interpretation of the Old Testament in the New.* Grand Rapids: Erdmanns, 1982.
Goranson, S. "Ebionites". *ABD* 2.261.
Grant, Robert M. *Jesus After the Gospels: The Christ of the Second Century.* Louisville: Westminster/John Knox, 1990.
Grether, O. *Name und Wort Gottes im Alten Testament.* BZAW 64. Giessen: Töpelmann, 1934.
Grillmeier, Aloys. *Christ in the Christian Tradition.* Volume 1: From the Apostolic Age to Chalcedon. Translated by John Bowdon. 2d ed. Atlanta: John Knox, 1975.
Gruenwald, Ithamar. *Apocalyptic and Merkavah Mysticism.* AGJU 14. Leiden: Brill, 1980.
Gundry, Robert. "Angelomorphic Christology in the Book of Revelation". *SBLSP* 33 (1994) 662-678.
Hall, Robert. "Isaiah's Ascent to See the Beloved: An Ancient Jewish Source for the *Ascension of Isaiah*". *JBL* 113 (1994) 463-484.
———. "The *Ascension of Isaiah*: Community Situation, Date, and Place in Early Christianity". *JBL* 109 (1990) 289-306.
Handy, Lowell K. *Among the Host of Heaven: The Syro-Palestinian Pantheon as Bureaucracy.* Winona Lake, IN: Eisenbrauns, 1994.

Hanson, Anthony Tyrrel. *Jesus Christ in the Old Testament*. London: SPCK, 1965.
von Harnack, Adolph. *History of Dogma*. Six volumes. Translated by Neil Buchanan. London: Williams and Norgate, 1894-1887.
Harner, P. *The "I Am" of the Fourth Gospel: A Study in Johannine Usage and Thought*. Philadelphia: Fortress, 1970.
Hauschild, Wolf-Dieter. *Gottes Geist und der Mensch: Studien zur frühchristlichen Pneumatologie*. München: Chr. Kaiser Verlag, 1972.
Hay, David. *Glory at the Right Hand: Psalm 110 in Early Christianity*. Nashville: Abingdon, 1973.
Hayward, C.T.R. "The Holy Name of the God of Moses and the Prologue of St John's Gospel". *NTS* 25 (1978) 16-32.
Hayward, Robert. *Divine Name and Presence: The Memra*. Oxford: Allanheld & Osum, 1991.
Heidt, W. *Angelology of the Old Testament: A Study in Biblical Theology*. SST 2/24. Washington: Catholic University of America Press, 1949.
Helderman, J. *Die Anapausis im Evangelium Veritatis*. NHS 18. Leiden: Brill, 1984.
Helyer, L. "Recent Research on Col 1:15-20 (1980-1990)", *GTJ* 12 (1992) 51-67.
Hengel, Martin. *Between Jesus and Paul*. Translated by J. Bowden. London: SCM, 1983.
——. *Judaism and Hellenism: Studies in their Encounter in Palestine in the Early Hellenistic Period*. Translated by J. Bowden. Two volumes. Philadelphia: Fortress, 1974.
——. *Studies in Early Christology*. Edinburgh: T&T Clark, 1995.
——. *The Son of God: The Origin of Christology and the History of Jewish-Hellenistic Religion*. Translated by J. Bowden. London: SCM, 1983.
Hengstenberg, E. W. *Christologie des Alten Testaments und Commentar über die Messianischen Weissagungen*. Three volumes. Berlin: L. Oehmigke, 1854-57.
Henne, P. *La christologie chez Clément de Rome et dans le Pasteur d' Hermas*. Fribourg Suisse: Éditions Universitaires, 1992.
——. *L'Unité du Pasteur d'Hermas: Tradition et rédaction*. Parish: J. Gabalda, 1992.
van Henten, J. "Angel II". In *Dictionary of Deities and Demons in the Bible*, eds. K. van der Toorn, Bob Becking, and Pieter W. van der Horst, 90-96. Leiden: Brill, 1995.
Himmelfarb, Martha. *Ascent to Heaven in Jewish and Christian Apocalypses*. Oxford: Oxford University Press, 1992.
Hirth, Volkmar. *Gottes Botten im Alten Testament*. Theologische Arbeiten 32. Berlin: Evangelische Verlagsanstalt, 1975) 25-31.
Holladay, Carl. *Theios Aner in Hellenistic Judaism*. SBLDS 40. Missoula, MT: Scholars Press, 1977.
Holtz, Traugott. *Die Christologie der Apokalypse des Johannes*. TU 85. 2d ed. Berlin: Akademie Verlag, 1971.
van der Horst, Pieter. "Moses' Throne Vision in Ezekiel the Dramatist". *JJS* 34 (1983) 19-29.
——. "Some Notes on the *Exagoge* of Ezekiel". In *Essays on the Jewish World of Early Christianity*, 72-93. NTOA 14. Universitätsverlag Freiburg, Schweiz, and Vandenhoeck & Ruprecht, Göttingen, 1990.
Horton, Fred. *The Melchizedek Tradition: A Critical Examination of the Sources to the Fifth Century A.D. and in the Epistle to the Hebrews*. Cambridge: Cambridge University Press, 1976.
Hurst, L. *The Epistle to the Hebrews: Its Background of Thought*. SNTSMS 65. Cambridge: Cambridge University Press, 1990.
Hurtado, Larry W. "New Testament Christology: A Critique of Bousset's Influence". *TS* 40 (1979) 306-317.

―――. *One God, One Lord: Early Christian Devotion and Ancient Jewish Monotheism.* Philadelphia: Fortress, 1988.
―――. "What Do We Mean by 'First Century Jewish Monotheism'?". *SBLSP* 32 (1993) 348-368.
Jenks, Gregory C. *The Origin and Early Development of the Antichrist Myth.* BZNW 59. New York: Walter de Gruyter, 1991.
Jeremias, Joachim. "Ἡλ(ε)ίας". *TDNT* 2.928-941.
Johannson, N. *Parakletoi: Vorstellung von Fürsprechern für die Menschen vor Gott in der alttestamentlichen Religion, im Spätjudentum, und Urchristum.* Lund: CWK Gleerup, 1940.
Jones, F. Stanley. "The Pseudo-Clementines: A History of Research". *SecCent* 2 (1982) 1-33, 63-96.
de Jonge, M. and A. S. van der Woude. "11Q Melchizedek and the New Testament". *NTS* 12 (1965/66) 301-326.
Käsemann, Ernst. *The Wandering People of God.* Trans. R. Harrisville and I. Sandberg. Minneapolis: Augsburg, 1984.
Kelly, J. N. D. *Early Christian Doctrines.* Rev. ed. San Francisco: Harper, 1978.
Kerkeslager, A. "Apollo, Greco-Roman Prophecy, and the Rider on the White Horse in Rev. 6:2". *JBL* 112 (1993) 116-121.
Kim, Seyoon. *The Origin of Paul's Gospel.* WUNT 2/4. Tübingen: Mohr/Siebeck, 1984.
Kinzer, Mark. "'All Things Under His Feet': The Use of Psalm 8 in the New Testament in Light of Its Use in Other Jewish Literature of Late Antiquity". Ph.D. diss., University of Michigan, 1995.
Kippenberg, H. G. *Garizim und Synagoge.* REVV 30. Berlin: Walter de Gruyter, 1971.
Kittel, G. "ἄγγελος". *TDNT* 1.80-87.
―――. "εἰκών". *TDNT* 2.392-397.
Klijn, A. F. J. "The 'Single One' in the Gospel of Thomas". *JBL* 81 (1962) 271-278.
Knibb, M. "The Date of the Parables of Enoch: A Critical Review". *NTS* 25 (1975) 345-359.
Knight, Jonathan. *Disciples of the Beloved One: The Christology, Social Setting and Theological Context of the Ascension of Isaiah.* JSPSup 18. Sheffield: Sheffield Academic Press, 1996.
―――. *The Ascension of Isaiah.* Sheffield: Sheffield Academic Press, 1995.
Kobelski, P. *Melchizedek and Melchireš{a}ᶜ.* CBQMS 10. Washington: Catholic Biblical Association of America, 1981.
Kominiak, B. *The Theophanies of the Old Testament in the Writings of St. Justin.* Washington: The Catholic University of America Press, 1948.
Kreitzer, L. *Jesus and God in Paul's Eschatology.* JSNTSup 19. Sheffield: Sheffield Academic Press, 1987.
Kretschmar, Georg. *Studien zur frühchristlichen Trinitätstheologie.* Beiträge zur historischen Theologie 21. Tübingen: Mohr/Siebeck, 1956.
Lane, W. *Hebrews.* WBC. Dallas: Word, 1991.
Leaney, A. R. C. "The Johannine Paraclete and the Qumran Scrolls". In *John and Qumran*, ed. J. Charlesworth, 38-61. London: Chapman, 1979.
Lelli, F. "Star". In *Dictionary of Deities and Demons in the Bible*, eds. K. van der Toorn, Bob Becking, and Pieter W. van der Horst, 1530-1540. Leiden: Brill, 1995.
Levison, John R. "Josephus' Interpretation of the Divine Spirit". *JJS* 47 (1996) 234-255.
―――. *Portraits of Adam in Early Judaism: From Sirach to 2 Baruch.* JSPSup 1. Sheffield: Sheffield Academic Press, 1988.

———. "The Angelic Spirit in Early Judaism". *SBLSP* 34 (1995) 464-493.
———. "The Debut of the Divine Spirit in Josephus's Antiquities". *HTR* 87 (1994) 123-139.
———. "The Prophetic Spirit as an Angel According to Philo". *HTR* 88 (1995) 189-207.
———. *The Spirit in First Century Judaism*. AGJU 29. Leiden: Brill, 1997.
Lewis, T. "Belial". *ABD* 1.654-656.
Liddon, H. P. *The Divinity of Our Lord and Savior Jesus Christ*. 6th ed. London Rivingtons, 1872.
Lieberman, Saul. "Metatron, the meaning of his name and his functions". Appendix 1 in Ithamar Gruenwald, *Apocalyptic and Merkavah Mysticism*, 235-241. AGJU 14. Leiden: Brill, 1980.
Loader, J. *A Tale of Two Cities: Sodom and Gomorrah in the Old Testament, Early Jewish and Early Christian Traditions*. Contributions to Biblical Exegesis and Theology 1. Kampen: Kok, 1990.
Lods, Adolphe. "L'Ange de Yahvé et l'âme extérieure". *BZAW* 27 (1913) 265-278.
Longenecker, Richard N. *The Christology of Early Jewish Christianity*. Grand Rapids: Baker, 1970.
———. "Some Distinctive Early Christological Motifs". *NTS* 14 (1968) 536-545.
Longman, T. "The Divine Warrior: The New Testament Use of an Old Testament Motif". *WTJ* 44 (1982) 290-307.
Lorenz, Rudolf. *Arius judaizans? Untersuchungen zur dogmengeschichtlichen Einordnung des Arius*. Göttingen: Vandenhoeck & Ruprecht, 1979.
Luedemann, Gerd. *Opposition to Paul in Jewish Christianity*. Translated by M. Boring. Philadelphia: Fortress, 1989.
Lueken, Wilhelm. *Michael: Eine Darstellung und Vergleichung der jüdischen und der morgenlandisch-christlichen Tradition vom Erzengel Michael*. Göttingen: Vanderhoeck & Ruprecht, 1898.
Luttikhuizen, G. *The Revelation of Elchasai*. TSAJ 8. Tübingen: Mohr/Siebeck, 1985.
Macdonald, J. "The Tetragrammaton in Samaritan Liturgical Compositions". *Transactions. Glasgow University Oriental Society* 17 (1959) 37-47.
Mach, Michael. *Entwicklungsstadien des jüdischen Engelglaubens in vorrabbinischer Zeit*. TSAJ 34. Tübingen: Mohr/Siebeck, 1992.
———. "Michael". In *Dictionary of Deities and Demons in the Bible*, eds. K. van der Toorn, Bob Becking, and Pieter W. van der Horst, 1065-1072. Leiden: Brill,1995.
———. "Raphael". In *Dictionary of Deities and Demons in the Bible*, eds. K. van der Toorn, Bob Becking, and Pieter W. van der Horst, 1299-1300. Leiden: Brill,1995.
Mack, Burton. *Logos und Sophia: Untersuchungen zur Weisheitstheologie im hellenistischen Judentum*. Göttingen: Vandenhoeck & Ruprecht, 1973.
MacRae, G. The Jewish Background of the Gnostic Sophia Myth". *NovT* 12 (1970) 86-101.
Marcus, Ralph. "On Biblical Hypostases of Wisdom". *HUCA* (1950/51) 157-71.
Martin, Ralph. *Carmen Christi: Philippians ii. 5-11 in Recent Interpretation and in the Setting of Early Christian Worship*. SNTSMS 4. Cambridge: Cambridge University Press, 1967.
McDonald, William. "Christology and 'The Angel of the Lord'". In *Current Issues in Biblical and Patristic Interpretation: Studies in Honor of Merrill C. Tenney Presented by His Former Students*, ed. G. Hawthorne, 324-335. Grand Rapids: Eerdmans, 1975.
McKane, W. *Proverbs*. Old Testament Library. London: SCM, 1970.

Meeks, Wayne A. "Moses as God and King". In *Religions in Antiquity: Essays in Memory of Erwin Ramdell Goodenough*, ed. J. Neusner, 354-371. Supplements to *Numen* 14. Leiden: Brill, 1968.
——. "The Man From Heaven in Johannine Sectarianism". *JBL* 91 (1972) 44-72.
——. *The Prophet-King: Moses Traditions and the Johannine Christology*. NovTSup 14. Leiden: Brill, 1967.
Meier, Samuel. "Angel". In *Dictionary of Deities and Demons in the Bible*, eds. K. van der Toorn, Bob Becking, and Pieter W. van der Horst, 81-90. Leiden: Brill, 1995.
——. "Angel of Yahweh". In *Dictionary of Deities and Demons in the Bible*, eds. K. van der Toorn, Bob Becking, and Pieter W. van der Horst, 96-108. Leiden: Brill, 1995.
——. "Destroyer". In *Dictionary of Deities and Demons in the Bible*, eds. K. van der Toorn, Bob Becking, and Pieter W. van der Horst, 456-458. Leiden: Brill, 1995.
——. *The Messenger in the Ancient Semitic World*. HSM 45. Atlanta: Scholars Press, 1988.
Menzies, Robert. *The Development of Early Christian Pneumatology: With Special Reference to Luke-Acts*. JSNTSup 54. Sheffield: Sheffield Academic Press, 1991.
Mettinger, Tryggve N. D. *The Dethronement of Sabaoth: Studies in the Shem and Kabod Theologies*. ConBOT 18. Lund: CWK Gleerup, 1982.
Meyer, Heinrich. *Galatians and Ephesians*. 6th ed. London: T & T Clark, 1885.
Michaelis, Wilhelm. "στύλος". *TDNT* 7.732-736.
——. *Zur Engelchristologie im Urchristentum*. Basel: Majer, 1942.
Michaels, J. Ramsey. "Revelation 1.19 and the Narrative Voices of the Apocalypse". *NTS* 37 (1991) 604-620
Miller, Patrick. *The Divine Warrior in Early Israel*. Cambridge, MA: Harvard University Press, 1973.
Mitchell, Margaret. "New Testament Envoys in the Context of Greco-Roman Diplomatic and Epistolary Convention: The Example of Timothy and Titus". *JBL* 111 (1992) 641-662.
Moore, George Foot. "Christian Writers on Judaism". *HTR* 14 (1921) 197-254.
——. "Intermediaries in Jewish Theology". *HTR* 15 (1922) 41-85.
Moore, M. "Jesus Christ: Superstar". *NovT* 24 (1982) 82-91.
Morray-Jones, Christopher R.A. "Merkabah Mysticism and Talmudic Tradition". Ph.D. diss., University of Cambridge, 1988.
——. "Paradise Revisited (2 Cor 12:1-12): The Jewish Mystical Background of Paul's Apostolate" *HTR* 86 (1993) 177-217 ("Part 1: The Jewish Sources") and 265-292 ("Part 2: Paul's Heavenly Ascent and Its Significance").
——. "The Body of the Glory: *Shi'ur Qomah* and Transformational Mysticism in the Epistle to the Ephesians". Unpublished paper presented at the 1992 National SBL Meeting in San Francisco (USA).
——. "Transformational Mysticism in the Apocalyptic-Merkabah Tradition". *JJS* 43 (1992) 1-31.
Mounce, R. *The Book of Revelation*. NICNT. Grand Rapids: Eerdmans, 1977.
Mowinkel, S. "Die Vorstellung des Spätjudentums vom heiligen Geist als Fürsprecher und der johanneische Paraklet". *ZNW* 52 (1934) 97-130.
Moxnes, Halvor. "God and His Angel in the Shepherd of Hermas." *Studia Theologie* 28 (1974) 49-56.
Mullen, E. "Divine Assembly". *ABD* 2.214-217.
Müller, U. B. *Menschenwerdung des Gottessohnes*. SBS 140. Stuttgart: KBW, 1990.
Munoa, Phillip. "Four Powers in Heaven: Exegesis of Daniel 7 in the *Testament of Abraham*". Ph.D. diss., University of Michigan, 1993.

Muñoz, D. Leon. *Memra en los Targumim del Pentateuco.* Institución San Jerónimo 4. Granada, 1974.
Murmelstein, B. "Adam, ein Beitrag zur Messiaslehre". *WZKM* 35 (1928) 242-275 and 36 (1929) 51-86.
Neusner, Jacob. "The Formation of Rabbinic Judaism: Yavneh (Jamnia) from A.D. 70-100." *ANRW* II, 19.2 (1979) 3-42.
——. *The Systemic Analysis of Judaism.* Atlanta: Scholars Press, 1988.
Newman, Carey. *Paul's Glory-Christology: Tradition and Rhetoric.* NovTSup 69. Leiden: Brill, 1992.
Newsom, Carol. "'He has Established for Himself Priests': Human and Angelic Priesthood in the Qumran *Sabbath Shirot*". In *Archaeology and History in the Dead Sea Scrolls,* ed. L. Schiffman, 101-120. JSPSup 8. Sheffield: Sheffield Academic Press, 1990.
——. "Uriel". *ABD* 6.769.
Norden, E. *Agnostos Theos: Untersungen zur Formengeschichte religiöser Rede.* Second edition. Leipzig: Teubner, 1923.
Norelli, E. *Ascensio Isaiae: Commentarius.* Corpus Christianorvm, Series Apocryphorum 8. Turnhout: Brepols, 1995.
Noth, Martin. *Die israelitischen Personennamen im Rahmen der gemeinsemitischen Namengebung.* BWANT 3/10. Stuttgart, 1928.
Odeberg, Hugo. *The Fourth Gospel Interpreted in Its Relation to Contemporaneous Religious Currents in Palestine and the Hellenistic-Oriental World.* Chicago: Argonaut, 1929.
Olyan, Saul M. *A Thousand Thousands Served Him: Exegesis and the Naming of Angels in Ancient Judaism.* TSAJ 36. Tübingen: Mohr/Siebeck, 1993.
Osburn, C.D. "The Text of I Corinthians 10:9". In *New Testament Textual Criticism, Its Significance for Exegesis: Essays in Honor of Bruce M. Metzger,* eds. E.J. Epps and G.D. Fee, 201-212. Oxford: Oxford University Press, 1981.
Pancaro, Stephen. *The Law in the Fourth Gospel.* NovTSup 42. Leiden: Brill, 1975.
Paschal, Robert Jr. "The Farewell Prayer of Jesus: A Study of the Gattung and the Religious Background of John 17". Ph.D. diss., University of Cambridge, 1983.
Perdue, Leo. *Wisdom and Creation: The Theology of Wisdom Literature.* Nashville: Abingdon, 1994.
Pernveden, Lage. *The Concept of the Church in the Shepherd of Hermas.* Lund: CWK Gleerup, 1966.
Pesce, M., ed. *Isaia, il dilietto e la chiesa: Visione ed esegesi profetica cristiano-primitiva nell' Ascensione di Isaia. Atti del Convegno di Roma, 9-10 Aprile 1981.* Brescia: Paidea, 1983.
Peterson, Erik. *Frühkirche, Judentum, und Gnosis.* Freiburg: Herder, 1959.
Pfeifer, G. *Ursprung und Wesen der Hypostasenvorstellungen im Judentum.* Arbeiten zum Theologie 31. Stuttgart: Calwer, 1967.
Plooij, D. *Studies in the Testimony-Book.* Verhandelingen der Koninklijke Akademie van Wetenschappen te Amsterdam 32/2. Amsterdam: Noord-Hollandsche Uitgevers-Maatschappij, 1932.
Price, R. M. "Punished in Paradise (An Exegetical Theory on II Corinthians 12.1-10)". *JSNT* 7 (1980) 33-40.
Procksch, O. "Die Berufungsvision Hesekiels". In *Karl Budde Festschrift,* 141-149. BZAW 34. Giessen: Töpelmann, 1920.
Quispel, Gilles. "Ezekiel 1.26 in Jewish Mysticism and Gnosis". *VC* 34 (1980) 1-13.
——. "Genius and Spirit". In *Essays on the Nag Hammadi Texts,* ed. M. Krause, 155-69. NHS 6. Leiden: Brill, 1975.

———. *Gnostic Studies*. Two volumes. Istanbul: Nederlands Historisch-Archaeologisch Instituut, 1974/1975.
———. "Hermes Trismegistus and the Origins of Gnosticism". *VC* 46 (1992) 1-19.
———. "Hermetism and the New Testament, Especially Paul". *ANRW* II.22, forthcoming.
———. "Het Johannesevangelie en de Gnosis", *NedTTs* 11 (1956/57) 173-202.
———. "John and Jewish Christianity", In *John and Qumran*, ed. J.H. Charlesworth, 137-155. London: Chapman, 1972.
———. "Judaism, Judaic Christianity and Gnosis". In *The New Testament and Gnosis: Essays in honour of Robert McL Wilson*, ed. A. Logan and A. Wedderburn, 47-68. Edinburgh: T & T Clark, 1983.
———. *The Secret Book of Revelation*. New York: McGraw-Hill, 1979.
von Rad, Gerhard. "ἄγγελος" (D. מַלְאָךְ in the OT). *TDNT* 1.76-80.
———. *Genesis*. Translated by J. Marks. Old Testament Library. 3d rev. ed. London: SCM, 1972.
———. *Old Testament Theology*. Translated by D. Stalker. Two volumes. London: Oliver and Boyd, 1962.
———. *Studies in Deuteronomy*. Translated by D. Stalker. London: SCM, 1953.
———. *Wisdom in Israel*. Translated by J. Martin. London: SCM, 1972.
Reiling, J. *Hermas and Christian Prophecy: A Study of the Eleventh Mandate*. SupNovT 37. Leiden: Brill, 1973.
Reitzenstein, Richard. *Hellenistic Mystery Religions: Their Basic Ideas and Significance*. Translated by J. Steely. 3d. ed. Pittsburgh Monograph Series 15. Pittsburgh: Pickwick, 1978.
Rengstorf, Karl. "ἀπόστολος". *TDNT* 1.407-447.
Ringgren, Helmer. "Geister, Dämonen, Engel". In *Die Religion in Geschichte und Gegenwart*, 3d ed., 2.1301-2.
———. "Hypostasen". In *Die Religion in Geschichte und Gegenwart*, 3d ed., 3.504.
———. *Israelite Religion*. Translated by D. Green. London: SPCK, 1966.
———. *Word and Wisdom: Studies in the Hypostatization of Divine Qualities and Functions in the Ancient Near East*. Lund: Hakan Ohlssons, 1947.
Robinson, John T. *Redating the New Testament*. Philadelphia: Westminster, 1976.
Rohland, J. P. *Der Erzengel Michael: Arzt und Feldherr*. BZRGG 29. Leiden: Brill, 1977.
Röttger, H. *Mal'ak Jahwe - Bote von Gott*. Regensburger Studien zur Theologie 13. Frankfurt: Peter Lang, 1978.
Rowland, Christopher C. "A Man Clothed in Linen: Daniel 10.6ff and Jewish Angelology". *JSNT* 24 (1985) 99-110.
———. "Apocalyptic Literature". In *It is Written: Scripture Citing Scripture*, eds. D. A. Carsons and H. G. M. Williamson, 170-189. Cambridge: Cambridge University Press, 1988.
———. "Apocalyptic Visions and the Exaltation of Christ in the Letter to the Colossians". *JSNT* 19 (1983) 73-83.
———. *Christian Origins: From Messianic Movement to Christian Religion*. Minneapolis: Augsburg, 1985.
———. "John 1.51, Jewish Apocalyptic and Targumic Tradition". *NTS* 30 (1984) 498-507.
———. *The Open Heaven: A Study of Apocalyptic in Judaism and Early Christianity*. New York: Crossroad, 1982.
———. "The Influence of the First Chapter of Ezekiel on Judaism and Early Christianity". Ph.D. diss., University of Cambridge, 1975.
———. "The Second Temple: Focus of Ideological Struggle?". In *Templum Amicitiae: Studies in Honor of Ernst Bammel*, ed. W. Horbury, 175-198. JSNTSup 48. Sheffield: Sheffield Academic Press, 1991.

——. "The Vision of the Risen Christ in Rev. i.13 ff.: The Debt of an Early Christology to an Aspect of Jewish Angelology". *JTS* 31 (1980) 1-11.
——. "The Visions of God in Apocalyptic Literature". *JSJ* 10 (1979) 137-154.
Rowley, H. *The Biblical Doctrine of Election*. London: Lutterworth, 1950.
Runia, David. T. "Logos". In *Dictionary of Deities and Demons in the Bible*, eds. K. van der Toorn, Bob Becking, and Pieter W. van der Horst, 988-989. Leiden: Brill, 1995.
Sanders, Jack T. *The New Testament Christological Hymns: Their Historical Background*. SNTSMS 15. Cambridge: Cambridge University Press, 1971.
Sandmel, S. "Parallelomania". *JBL* 81 (1962) 1-13.
Schaberg, Jane. "Mark 14.62: Early Christian Merkabah Imagery?". *Apocalyptic and the New Testament*, eds. J. Marcus and M. Soards, 69-94. JSNTSup 24. Sheffield: Sheffield Academic Press, 1989.
Schäfer, Peter. *Rivalität zwischen Engeln und Menschen*. SJ 8. Berlin: Walter de Gruyter, 1975.
——. *The Hidden and Manifest God: Some Major Themes in Jewish Mysticism*. Translated by A. Pomerance. Albany: SUNY, 1992.
Scheidweiler, Felix. "Novatian und die Engelchristologie". *ZKG* 66 (1954/55) 126-139.
——. "Zur Christologie des Paulus". *Deutsches Pfarrerblatt* 10/11 (1952) 292.
Schlier, H. *Der Brief an die Galater*. 13th ed. Göttingen: Vandenhoeck & Ruprecht, 1965.
——. "ἐκπτύω". *TDNT* 2.448-449.
Schmidt, Euge. "Die Christologische Interpretation als das Grundlengende der Apokalypse". *TQ* 14O (1960) 257-290.
Schoeps, Hans Joachim. *Jewish Christianity: Factional Disputes in the Early Church*. Translated by D. Hare. Philadelphia: Fortress, 1969.
——. *Theologie und Geschichte des Judenchristentums*. Tübingen: Mohr/Siebeck, 1949.
——. *Urgemeinde-Judenchristentum-Gnosis*. Tübingen: Mohr/Siebeck, 1956.
Scholem, Gershom G. *Jewish Gnosticism, Merkebah Mysticism, and Talmudic Tradition*. Second edition. New York: Jewish Theological Seminary, 1965.
——. *Kabbalah*. Jerusalem: Keter, 1974.
——. *Major Trends in Jewish Mysticism*. 3d ed. New York: Schocken, 1954.
——. "Metatron". *Encyclopedia Judaica* 11.1443-1446.
Schuchard, Bruce. *Scripture Within Scripture: The Interrelationship of Form and Function in the Explicit Old Testament Citations in the Gospel of John*. SBLDS 133. Atlanta: Scholars Press, 1992.
Schütz, J. H. *Paul and the Anatomy of Apostolic Authority*. Cambridge: Cambridge University Press, 1975.
Schürer, Emil. *The History of the Jews in the Age of Jesus Christ*. Revised edition edited by G. Vermes, F. Miller, M. Goodman. Four volumes. Edinburgh: T & T Clark, 1983.
Schweitzer, Albert. *The Mysticism of Paul the Apostle*. Translated by W. Montgomery. New York: Seabury, 1931.
Schweizer, E. "Die sieben Geister in d. Apk". *ET* 11 (1951/52) 506.
Scott, J. "The Triumph of God in 2 Cor 2.14: Additional Evidence of Merkabah Mysticism in Paul". *NTS* 42 (1996) 260-281
Scroggs, Robin. *The Last Adam: A Study in Pauline Anthropology*. Philadelphia: Fortress, 1966.
Seesemann, H. "πεῖρα". *TDNT* 6.32.
Segal, Alan F. "Heavenly Ascent in Hellenistic Judaism, Early Christianity, and Their Environments". *ANRW* II.23.2 (1980) 1332-1392.
——. *Paul the Convert: The Apostolate and Apostasy of Saul the Pharisee*. New Haven: Yale University Press, 1990.

———. "The Risen Christ and Angelic Mediator Figures in Light of Qumran". In *Jesus and the Dead Sea Scrolls*, ed. James H. Charlesworth, 302-328. New York: Doubleday, 1992
———. *Rebecca's Children: Judaism and Christianity in the Roman World.* Cambridge, MA: Harvard University Press, 1986.
———. "Ruler of this World: Attitudes about Mediator Figures and the Importance of Sociology for Self-Definition". In *Jewish and Christian Self-Definition II*, eds. E. P. Sanders, A. I. Baumgarten, and A. Mendelson, 245-268. Philadelphia: Fortress, 1981.
———. *Two Powers in Heaven: Early Rabbinic Reports About Christianity and Gnosticism.* SJLA 25. Leiden: Brill, 1977.
Sekki, A. *The Meaning of Ruah at Qumran.* SBLDS 110. Atlanta: Scholars Press, 1989.
Seow, Choon-Leong. "Face". In *Dictionary of Deities and Demons in the Bible*, eds. K. van der Toorn, Bob Becking, and Pieter W. van der Horst, 612. Leiden: Brill, 1995.
Skarsaune, Oskar. *The Proof From Prophecy: A Study in Justin Martyr's Proof Text Tradition.* SupNovT 56. Leiden: Brill, 1987.
Smith, Jonathan Z. "The Prayer of Joseph". In *Religions in Antiquity: Essays in Memory of Erwin Ramsdell Goodenough*, ed. J. Neusner, 253-294. Supplements to *Numen* 14. Leiden: Brill, 1970.
Smith, Morton. "Two Ascended to Heaven—Jesus and the Author of 4Q491". In *Jesus and the Dead Sea Scrolls*, ed. J. Charlesworth, 290-301. New York: Doubleday, 1992.
Snyder, Graydon F. *The Shepherd of Hermas. The Apostolic Fathers: Volume 6.* Camden, NJ: Thomas Nelson, 1968.
Spitta, F. *Studien zum Hirten des Hermas* in *zur Geschichte und Literatur des Urchristentums.* Two volumes. Göttingen: Vandenhoeck and Ruprecht, 1896.
Starek, W. *Die Erlösererwartung in den östlichen Religionen.* Berlin: Kohlhammer, 1938.
———. *Die sieben Säulen der Welt und des Hauses der Weisheit".* ZNW 35 (1936) 232-261.
Stead, Christopher. *Divine Substance.* Oxford: Oxford University Press, 1977.
Steenburg, David. "The Worship of Adam and Christ as the Image of God". *JSNT* 39 (1990) 95-109.
Stier, Fridolin. *Gott und sein Engel im Alten Testament.* Münster: Aschendorffschen, 1934.
Stone, Michael E. *A History of the Literature of Adam and Eve.* Atlanta: Scholars Press, 1992.
Strack H. and P. Billerbeck. *Kommentar zum Neuen Testament aus Talmud und Midrash.* Four volumes. München: C. H. Beck'sche, 1922.
Strecker, Georg. *Der Judenchristentum in den Pseudoklementinen.* TU 70. Rev. ed. Berlin: Akademie-Verlag, 1981.
Stroumsa, Gedaliahu G. "Forms of God: Some Notes on Metatron and Christ". *HTR* 76 (1983) 269-288.
———. "Le couple de l'ange et de l'esprit: traditions juives et chrétiennes". *RB* 88 (1981) 42-61.
———. "Polymorphie divine et transformations d'un mythologème: L' >>apocryphon de jean<< et ses sources". *VC* 35 (1981) 412-434.
Stuckenbruck, Loren. "An Angel Refusal of Worship: The Tradition and Its Function in the Apocalpyse of John". *SBLSP* 33 (1994) 679-696.
———. *Angel Veneration and Christology: A Study in Early Judaism and in the Christology of the Apocalypse of John.* WUNT 2/70. Tübingen: Mohr/Siebeck, 1995.

Sweet. J. P. M. *Revelation*. Pelican. Philadelphia: Westminster, 1979.
Tabor, James D. *Things Unutterable: Paul's Ascent to Paradise in its Greco-Roman, Judaic and Early Christian Contexts*. London: Lanham, 1986.
Talbert, Charles H. "The Myth of a Descending-Ascending Redeemer in Mediterranean Antiquity". *NTS* 22 (1976) 418-439.
Thompson, Michael. *Clothed with Christ: The Example and Teaching of Jesus in Romans 12.1-15.13*. JSNTSup 59. Sheffield: Sheffield Academic Press, 1991.
Tobin, Thomas. "Logos". *ABD* 4.348-356.
——. "The Prologue of John and Hellenistic Jewish Speculation". *CBQ* 52 (1990) 252-69.
Trigg, Joseph. "The Angel of Great Counsel: Christ and the Angelic Hierarchy in Origen's Theology". *JTS* 42 (1991) 35-51.
Trakatellis, D. C. *The Pre-existence of Christ in the Writings of Justin Martyr*. HDR 6. Missoula: Scholars Press, 1976.
van Unnik, W. C. "Three Notes on the 'Gospel of Phillip'". *NTS* 10 (1963-64) 466-469.
VanderKam, James C. "1 Enoch, Enochic Motifs, and Enoch in Early Christian Literature". In *The Jewish Apocalyptic Heritage in Early Christianity*, eds. W. Adler and J.C. Vanderkam, 33-101. CRINT III.4. Minneapolis: Fortress, 1996.
——. "Righteous One, Messiah, Chosen One, and Son of Man in 1 Enoch 37-71". In *The Messiah: Developments in Early Judaism and Christianity*, ed. J.H. Charlesworth, 169-191. Minneapolis: Fortress, 1992.
Volz, Paul. *Der Geist Gottes und die verwandten Erscheinungen im Alten Testament und im anschliessenden Judentum*. Tübingen: Mohr/Siebeck, 1910.
Watson, D. "Michael". *ABD* 4.811.
Wensick, A. J. "Muhammad und die Propheten". *Acta Orientalia* 2 (1924) 168-198.
Werner, Martin. *Die Entstehung des christlichen Dogma*. Tübingen: Katzmann, 1941.
——. *The Formation of Christian Dogma: An Historical Study of its Problem*. Translated by S. G. F. Brandon. London: Adam and Charles Black, 1957.
Whybray, R. N. *Wisdom in Proverbs: The Concept of Wisdom in Proverbs 1-9.45*. SBT 45. London: SPCK, 1965.
Widengren, Geo. *Muhammad, the Apostle of God, and His Ascension*. Uppsala: Almqvist & Wicksell, 1955.
——. *The Ascension of the Apostle and the Heavenly Book*. Uppsala: Almqvist & Wicksell, 1950.
——. *The Gnostic Attitude*. Translated by B. Pearson. Santa Barbara: Univeristy of CA, 1973.
——. *The Great Vohu Manah and the Apostle of God: Studies in Iranian and Manichean Religion*. Uppsala: Almqvist & Wiksell, 1950.
Wikenhauser, A. *Pauline Mysticism*. Translated by J. Cunningham. New York: Herder and Herder, 1960.
Wilson, Ian. *Out of the Midst of Fire: Divine Presence in Deuteronomy*. SBLDS 151. Atlanta: Scholars Press, 1995.
Wilson, John Christian. *Five Problems in the Interpretation of the Shepherd of Hermas*. MBPS 34. Lewiston, NY: Mellen, 1995.
——. "The Problem of the Domitianic Date of Revelation". *NTS* 39 (1993) 587-605.
——. *Towards a Reassessment of the Shepherd of Hermas: Its Date and Its Pneumatology*. Lewiston: Mellen, 1993.
Windisch, Hans. "Die fünf johanneischen Parakletsprüche". In *Festgabe für Adolf Jülicher*. Tübingen: Mohr/Siebeck, 1927.

——. Die göttliche Weisheit der Juden und die paulinische Christologie". In *Neutestamentliche Studien für G. Heinrici.* UNT 6. Leipzig, 1914.
——. "Jesus und der Geist im Johannesevangelium". In *Amicitiae Corolla.* London: University of London Press, 1933.
——. *Paulus und Christus.* Leipzig: Hinrichs'sche, 1934.
——. *The Spirit-Paraclete in the Fourth Gospel.* Translated by J. W. Cox. Philadelphia: Fortress, 1968.
Winston, David. *Logos and Mystical Theology in Philo of Alexandria.* Cincinnati: Hebrew Union College Press, 1985.
——. *The Wisdom of Solomon.* AB 43. New York: Doubleday, 1969.
——. "Wisdom in the Wisdom of Solomon". In *In Search of Wisdom: Essays in Memory of John G. Gammie,* eds. L. Perdue, B. Scott, and W. Wiseman, 149-164. Louisville: Westminster/John Knox, 1993).
van der Woude, A. S. "De *Mal'ak Jahweh*: Een Godsbode". *NedTTs* 18 (1963/64) 1-13.
Yadin, Yigael. "The Dead Sea Scrolls and the Epistle to the Hebrews". In *Scripta Hierosolymitana,* Vol. 4, Aspects of the Dead Sea Scrolls, eds. C. Rabin and Y. Yadin, 36-55. Jerusalem: Magnes Press, 1958.
Young, B. "The Ascension Motif of 2 Corinthians in Jewish, Christian and Gnostic Texts". *GTJ* 9 (1988) 73-108.
Young, F.W. "A Study of the Relation of Isaiah to the Fourth Gospel". *ZNW* 46 (1955) 215-221.
Zimmerli, W. *Ezekiel.* Hermenia. Two volumes. Philadelphia: Fortress, 1979.
de Zwaan, J. "Gal 4,14 aus dem Neugriechischen erklärt". *ZNW* 10 (1909) 246-250.

ANCIENT LITERATURE INDEX

OT and NT literature is listed in canonical order. Philo and Josephus are listed in the order found in LCL. All other literature is listed alphabetically or numerically within the respective literary collection.

OLD TESTAMENT

Genesis

1.1	345
1.3	110, 130, 206, 335
1.26-27	153
1.26	110, 154, 204, 330, 335
2.7	110, 330
3	153
3.24	64, 253
5.24	156
12.2	58
14	171
14.18-20	309
15.1-6	103
15.7-21	104
15.22	211
16.7-14	27, 52, 53, 57-58
16.13	68
18	103, 109, 120
18.1-19.1	58
18.1-19.22	321
18.1-19.23	98
18.1-32	127
18.1-3	52
18.1	148
18.2	160
18.16	108
19.1-22	160
19.1	52
19.24	58
21.17	27, 52
21.17-19	58
22.11-15	27, 52, 102
22.11	58, 148
22.15	58
22.16	58
28.10-27	159
28.12-17	102, 112
28.12	280, 281
28.22	166
31.1-3	102
31.2-13	53
31.11-13	102
31.11	27, 52
31.24	102
32.1-2	102
32.20	55
32.24-30	52, 60, 102, 127, 148
32.24-32	111
32.29	77
32.30	58
32.31	68, 139
48.9-49.28	138
48.15-16	60
48.15-17	66
48.16	52

Exodus

2.2-7	53
3	104
3.1-14	27, 52, 53, 58
3.2	28, 53, 62, 103, 107
3.5	65
3.13-14	77
3.14-15	272
3.14	78
3.16	53
4.2	140
4.16	163
4.22	140
4.22-23	180, 297
7.1	163, 166
12.1-30	125
12.21-29	63-64, 105
12.23	328
13.21-22	59, 79, 98
14.19-20	27, 52, 59, 79, 117
14.19	28, 94, 98, 99
14.22	87
14.24	59, 64, 79, 94, 98
15.1-18	100
15.1-19	98
15.3-18	63
15.3-6	101

15.3	28, 64	9.23-24	62
15.9	101, 253	26.12	336
15.10	64		
15.12	101	**Numbers**	
15.19	64		
15.21	64	12.6-8	274
16.9-10	79	12.8	68
17.1-7	326, 327	16	254
19.9	94	16.41-49	106
19.18	62	16.41-50	326, 327
20.19	68	16.42	327
23.20-21	33, 55, 56-57, 58, 65, 67, 68, 76, 77, 109, 111, 118, 124, 125, 127, 143, 147, 227, 234, 238, 278, 296, 313, 327, 339	20.7-13	326
		20.15-16	59, 98-99
		20.16	79, 211
		21.4-9	327
		21.5-6	326
		21.5	327
		21.6-8	327
23.20-23	117	21.17	326
23.20-24	66, 76, 117	22.21-38	64, 253
23.20	40, 79, 98, 168	22.22-35	27, 52
23.21	77, 149, 253	22.23	64
24	87	22.35	65
24.9-18	79	22.38	65
24.9-11	103, 164	23.12	65
24.10-11	68	23.16	65
24.10	82, 301	25.2-9	326
24.12	165		
24.16-17	62	**Deuteronomy**	
24.17	80		
24.47	159	4.12-15	68
25.22	195	4.12	274
25.31-40	263	4.24	68
28.4	144	4.36	71
28.36	144, 307	5.21	68
32.4-6	326	5.31	31, 166
32.34	66, 117	5.37	274
33	104-105	8.14-16	327
33.2	66, 117	11	71
33.14	117-118	12.5	71-72
33.14-15	117	12.11	72
33.17-34.8	80, 82, 258	14.1	180
33.18	81	14.23	71-72
33.18-23	81, 84	14.24	72
33.20	55, 58, 60, 68, 87, 241-242, 273, 275, 301, 334, 351	16.2	72
		16.6	72
		16.11	71-72
33.22	81	18.15	201
34.5-6	81	26.2	72
37.17-24	263	26.36	71
40.25	263	32.4	326
40.34-38	80	32.5	180
		32.6	180
Leviticus		32.8-9	127-128
		32.18	180, 326
9.22-24	80	32.19	180

32.24	253	**1 Kings (LXX: 3 Kgms)**	
32.39-42	63	3.2	71, 73
32.40-41	260	5.5	73
32.41-42	253	5.7	71
32.43	299	5.17	73
34.5-6	166	8.10-11	80
		8.12	71
Joshua		8.16	72
5.13-14	64	8.17	73
5.13-15	65, 127, 253	8.18	73
5.13	256	8.19	73
5.14	125, 141	8.20	73
23.3	65	8.43	73
23.9-10	65	8.44	73
		8.48	73
Judges		9.3	71, 72
2.1-4	27, 52, 66, 117, 162	9.7	71
2.1	59, 99	9.17	73
5.23	27, 52, 66	11.36	72
6.11-13	52	14.21	72
6.11-18	103	17.1 (LXX)	119
6.11-24	27, 52, 58	18.15 (LXX)	119
6.14	52	19.4-9	105
6.20	27, 52	19.11-18	105
6.20-21	131	22.13-23	163
6.22	52	22.19	28
13.3-21	27, 52-53		
13.3-22	160	**2 Kings**	
13.3	61	2.1-11	163
13.6	61-63	2.11	131
13.8-13	61	6.16	167
13.15-20	131	8.29	72
13.15-22	61-62	19.35	64, 253
13.17-18	77	21.4	72
16.14	119	21.7	71-72
		23.27	72
1 Samuel			
3.1	104	**1 Chronicles**	
3.6	104	13.6	73
3.10	104	21.12	328
3.21	104	21.14-16	65
11.4	51	21.15-16	64, 106, 253
		21.15-30	55
2 Samuel		21.15	328
7.13	71	21.16	32, 211, 342
8.27	336	21.17-30	65
14.11	66	22.5	72
14.17	175	22.7	73
14.20	175	22.8	73
24.15-17	65	22.10	73
24.16-17	64, 253	22.19	73
24.16	328	28.3	73
		28.5	175

29.20	175	7	172
29.26	73	7.8-9	172
		8	76

2 Chronicles

1.18	73	8.4-6	302, 341
2.3	73	18.6-15	63
3.1-2	65-66	20.1	71
6.5	72	24.9-10	119
6.6	72	29.1-11	32
6.7	73	33.6	107
6.8	73	34.7	66
6.9	73	35.5-6	66
6.10	73	42.12	119
6.20	72	44.5	71
6.33	73	45.6-7	302
6.34	73	45.6	297
6.38	73	45.7	176
7.16	72	51.11	118
7.20	73	54.3	71, 119
9.8	175	54.6-7	71
12.13	72	74.7	71
18.18-22	163	77.20	326
18.18	28	80.1	176
20.8	71, 73	82	172
20.9	72	82.1	171
33.4	72	82.2	172
33.7	72	88.28 (LXX)	140, 297
36.6-15	161	89.27	140, 297
		95.3-5	32

Ezra

		96.6	32
1.3	72	99.1	83
6.12	72	102.25	297
		103.20	51

Nehemiah

		103.21	28
		104.4	114, 116
1.9	72	104.41	326
9.6	28	110.1	85, 251
9.20	118	110.4	171, 307-310
		113.8	326
		118.10-14	71

Job

		124.8	72
1.6-12	163	147.4	165
2.1-7	163	148.13	71
16.19	128, 288, 289		
19.25	288	**Proverbs**	
28	38		
33.23-25	11, 289	1-9	89
33.23	66, 288	3.19-20	90
33.23-25	128	8.6	92
33.26	289	8.22-30	42
33.29	289	8.22-31	90, 188, 295
41.1-34	143	8.22	38, 111, 255, 295
		8.23	91, 271

Psalms

		8.27	94, 271, 295
		8.30	91, 271
2.6	91	18.10	74

Ecclesiastes
5.5	86
5.6	66

Canticles
5.9	239

Isaiah
1.18	161
6	87, 103, 242, 293
6.1-13	82, 163, 168-169
6.1-8	163
6.1-3	16, 231, 241, 274
6.1-4	19, 32
6.1	68, 81
6.2-7	28
6.2	195
6.3	115, 265
6.4	341
6.5	68, 81
6.10	275
9.6	176, 189, 194
11.2	208, 263
14.12-14	97, 255
18.7	72
24.21-22	127
26.4	326
30.27	74
33.14	68
37.33-37	64, 253
40.3	23
40.12	32
43.6	180
44.24	134
45.11	180
48.21	326
52.7	172
52.12	32
60.9	72
63.1-14	255
63.9	141, 211
63.9-14	117
63.10	118
63.14	118
65.9	180
65.15	180
66.1	32

Jeremiah
1	103
1.1	169
1.4-13	104
1.4	105
1.6-9	105
1.11	105
1.13	105
1.15	105
1.19	105
2.1	105
3.4	180
3.17	72
3.22	86
7.10	73
7.11	73
7.12	72
7.14	73
7.30	73
23.6	180
23.18-19	163
23.21-22	163
25.29	73
26.20	145
27.5	119
31.9-10	180
32.34	73
33.9	72
34.15	73
52.15	91

Ezekiel
1	84, 258, 259
1.1	169
1.1-28	19
1.4-14	28
1.5-11	124
1.22	80
1.24	248
1.26-27	83
1.26-28	19, 32, 40, 68, 82, 86, 132, 144, 159, 258, 331, 333, 338
1.26	17, 82, 84, 87-88, 95-96, 110, 130-131, 154, 160, 164, 205, 238-239, 249, 252, 281, 299, 330-331, 335, 342, 344
1.27	85, 87, 249, 267
1.28	257
2.1-13	82
2.8-3.11	259
3	84
3.22-24	83
3.22	267
3.23	258
3.24-5.17	83
8	83, 84, 248

8.1	267	10.9-10	246
8.2-4	40	10.11-16	126
8.2	19, 83, 87, 132-133, 258	10.13-21	126
8.3-4	86	10.13	65, 126-127, 291
8.3	83, 267	10.16	248
9.1-11	66, 124, 128	10.18	248
9.2	62	10.20-21	127
9.3-4	84	10.21	65
9.4	254	12.1	28, 65, 126, 128, 141
10.4	83	12.3	152, 180
10.8	101	12.6	133
10.18	83	12.7	133, 259
28.13	86, 144	54.6	126
40.1-48	19		
40.1	267	**Hosea**	
40.3	163	2.1	180
40.5-48.35	267	12.3-4	61
40.5	267		
46.1	87	**Joel**	
		2.26	71
Daniel		2.32	23
7	86, 95, 96, 238, 241, 250	3.5	23
		3.13	250-251
7.9-13	19, 85		
7.9-12	249	**Amos**	
7.9	31, 32, 144, 161, 249	3.7	163
7.10	91, 124	9.1-4	163
7.13-27	155		
7.13-14	121, 247, 303	**Habbakuk**	
7.13	18, 86, 133, 248, 249, 281	3.5	42
7.16-18	132	**Haggai**	
7.23-27	132	1.12-13	161
8.10	28	1.13	52
8.11	126	2.5	118
8.15-26	86, 132		
8.16	248	**Zechariah**	
9.2	133	1.1-6	19
9.3	133	1.7-21	62-63
9.11	133	1.9	163
9.18-19	73	1.20-22	63
9.21-27	132	3.1-4	120, 289-290
9.21	86, 248	3.1-7	163
10.2	133	3.3-7	169-170
10.4-6	132	3.6-10	63
10.4-12.13	132	4.1-14	263
10.5-6	127, 145, 246-247	12.7	175
10.5-9	40, 86		
10.5-10	19	**Malachi**	
10.5	62, 133, 194	1.11	71
10.6	133, 156, 158, 161, 250	2.7	169
10.7	133	3.1-5	168

3.1	113, 148, 167	9.35	239
4.5-6	168	10.17-18	250
		11.49	178
		20.36	152

NEW TESTAMENT

		22.69	97, 251
		24.3	156

Matthew

		John	
1.20-21	233		
3.17	239	1.1-18	212, 250, 271
10.40	179, 323	1.1-3	212
11.10	168	1.12	272
11.11	168	1.14	273
11.14	168	1.17-18	285
12.29	250	1.18	281, 285, 297
16.14	168	1.21	168
17.1-8	167	1.25	168
17.2	156	1.32	208
17.5	239	1.50-51	280-281
18.10	213, 219	2.11	273
22.30	180	3.11-13	282
25.31	256	3.13	136, 285
26.64	97, 121, 251	3.14	283
28.3	156	3.17	284
28.19	254	3.34	284
		5.19-47	274
Mark		5.29	283
		5.36	284
1.2	168	5.37	284, 337
1.11	239	5.38	276, 284
1.24	180	5.43	272, 276
3.22-27	250	5.44	16
6.15	168	5.45	285
8.28	168	6.20	273
8.38	256	6.29	284
9.2-8	167	6.35	273
9.2	28	6.42	282
9.7	239	6.46	273, 281-282
12.24-29	250	6.51	273
13.27	256	6.57	284
13.32	242	6.62	136, 282
14.62	121, 251	6.69	180
14.64	97	7.28	284
16.5	168	7.29	284
		8.12	273
Luke		8.24	273, 278
		8.28	273, 278, 283
1.26	233	8.56-58	278
1.35	180, 332	8.56	212
1.49	180	8.58	273
2.14	299	9.28-29	285-286
3.22	239	9.35	283
4.34	180	9.39	283
9.8	168	10.7	273
9.19	168	10.9	273
9.28-36	167		

378   ANCIENT LITERATURE INDEX

10.11	273	17.25	284
10.14	273	17.26	276
10.25	276	18.5	273
10.36	284	20.17	282
11.25	273	20.21	284-285
11.40	273	20.22	223
11.42	284		
12.23	272-273	**Acts**	
12.28	272-273	1.10	156
12.31-32	250	2.27	180
12.31	140	5.41	272
12.32-34	283	6.15	178
12.32	272	7.30	53
12.38	275	7.35	53
12.39-40	274	7.38	53, 128
12.39-41	275	7.53	128
12.41	273	7.55-56	31
12.42	241	8.10	121, 332
12.45	284	8.26-29	6, 265
13.16	284, 303	9.3-8	321, 322
13.19	273	9.4-5	340
13.32	273	10.48	254
14.6	273, 276	12.15	219, 291
14.16-18	286	13.35	180
14.16	223, 287	14.8	318
14.17	290-292	14.12	318
14.18	287	14.19	318
14.25-26	286-287, 292	15.17	272
14.26	286-287, 291	16.6-8	6, 223
15.1	273	16.9-10	321
15.5	273	18.9-10	321
15.26	286-287, 290-291	22.6-11	321-322
15.27	288	22.7-8	340
16.7-15	287	22.17-21	321
16.7	286	26.12-18	321-322
16.8	250, 288	26.14-16	340
16.11	140, 250, 291	28.3	318
16.12-15	291		
16.13	290-291	**Romans**	
16.14-15	291	6.1-4	340
16.28	282	6.11	340
17.1	273	8.9-10	320
17.3	284	8.29	273, 297-298, 300, 337
17.5-8	275-276	8.38	119, 318
17.5	273, 276	12.4-5	340
17.6	276		
17.8	284	**1 Corinthians**	
17.11	276	1.18	331
17.14	276	1.21	331
17.17	276	1.23-24	332
17.18	284-285	1.24	331, 333
17.21	284	1.25	332
17.22	276	2.7-8	333
17.23	284		
17.24	273, 276		

ANCIENT LITERATURE INDEX 379

2.8	331
3.1	324
3.16-17	332
4.9	318
6.3	318
6.15	336
7.5	319
9.1	322
10.1-10	325-329
10.4	212
10.9	16
11.10	318
12.3	326
12.7	319
12.12-13	340
12.28	178
13.1	318
14	217
15.8	322
15.24	119
15.44-49	329-331
15.45	333, 340

2 Corinthians

1.5	324
2.11	319
2.17	324-325
3.4-4.6	334-337
3.14-17	334
3.14	334
3.15-18	223
3.15	334
3.17-18	334
3.18	322, 331, 334
4.3-6	334
4.3-4	333
4.4	300, 331, 334
4.6	322, 331, 334
4.10	322
4.17	334
6.16	332
9.4	37
10.8	322
11.4	319
11.13-15	319
11.14	318
11.17	37
12.1-12	321
12.1	322
12.6	322
12.7	318
13.3	324
13.10	322

Galatians

1.1-2	321
1.1	322, 324
1.6-9	316
1.8	318, 319, 323-324
1.11-12	321, 324
1.12	322
2.7	322
2.19-20	223
2.20	320, 322, 324
3.1-15	316
3.2	340
3.19	128, 318
3.28	340
4.3	320
4.9	320
4.11-14	317
4.14	4, 179, 315-325
5.24-25	223
6.12-17	316
6.17	322, 324

Ephesians

1.6	239
1.12-23	339
1.17-23	340-341
1.17	331
1.21	119
2.20	178
2.21-22	343
3.5	178
3.8-10	333
3.17-19	341
4.4-7	341
4.7	342
4.15-16	342
5.25-32	215
6.17	253

Philipians

1.18-19	6, 223
2.5-11	11, 337-339
2.6	212, 331
2.9-11	299, 311
2.11	326, 339
3.10	322, 324

Colossians

1.15-20	212, 300, 343-346
1.15-19	11
1.15-16	298
1.15	273, 297, 300, 331, 334-345

1.16	345	2.9	300
1.18-19	344	2.10	295, 300
1.18	90, 298, 339, 345	2.14	250
1.19	341, 345	2.17	304
1.25-28	346	3	285
2.8	319	3.1-6	303-306
2.9	334, 341, 345	3.1	284
2.12-15	346	3.2	179
2.18	34	3.3	300, 305
2.28	4	3.14	37
		3.16-19	313

1 Thessalonians

		4.2	312
2.7	323	4.11-13	106, 311-312, 314
3.5	319	4.12-13	253
4.16	325	4.12	312, 314
		4.13	312
		4.14	136, 304

2 Thessalonians

		5.5-10	307
1.7	119, 319	5.6	312
2.1-12	320	5.10	308, 312
		5.11	312
		5.13	312

1 Timothy

		6.1	312
3.16	299	6.5	312
5.21	319	6.19-20	305
		6.20	308, 312

Philemon

		7.2	309
		7.3	309-311
16	323	7.4	309
17	323	7.6	309
		7.7-8	309

Hebrews

		7.7	308
1-3	4	7.8	309-310
1	11	7.10	308
1.2-4	295	7.11	308-312
1.2	296, 297, 307	7.15-16	309
1.3	37, 296-297, 300, 302, 304, 307, 312	7.15	308, 310-312
		7.16	311
1.4-14	188	7.17	308, 312
1.4-7	294	7.21	308, 312
1.4	115, 296-297, 307	7.25	311
1.5	115	7.28	312
1.6	273, 295, 297-298, 345	8.1	300, 302, 304
1.7	114-116	8.4-5	305
1.8-9	302	9.24	304
1.8	295	9.27-28	312
1.10	295, 297	10.19-20	136
1.13-14	294	10.31	312
1.13	115, 302, 312	11.1	37
1.14	116, 303	11.3	296, 312
2.2	312	11.10	305
2.5-9	302	11.26	212
2.5	294	12.2	302, 305
2.7	300	12.9	115, 312
		12.19	312

12.21	305	1.10-11	266-268
12.22-24	305	1.10-3.22	246
12.22-23	298	1.12-17	246
12.23	273, 297, 312, 345	1.12	266
12.29	68	1.13-16	23, 247
13.2	321	1.13-17	19
13.4	312	1.13-3.22	261, 269
13.7	312	1.13	28, 248-249, 252, 266
13.14	305	1.14	158, 161, 248-249, 253
13.17	312	1.15	248, 266
13.21	300	1.16	28, 119, 145, 156, 249, 251, 253-254
13.22	312	1.17	262
		1.18	250, 266
James		1.28	267
2.1	16	2-3	248
		2.1	251, 267
1 Peter		2.7	223, 269
1.10-12	218, 223	2.11	223, 269
1.11	213	2.12	253, 254
1.12	242, 299	2.14	253
1.19	255	2.16	253, 254
3.18	212	2.17	223, 269
3.22	119, 136	2.18	253
		2.28	255
2 Peter		2.29	223, 269
1.17	300	3.1	263
2.11	119	3.5	259
		3.6	223, 269
1 John		3.12	253-254
1.1	278, 279	3.13	223, 269
1.14	279	3.14	90, 253, 255, 267
2.1	286-288	3.21	91, 97
3.8	250	3.22	223, 267, 269
5.13	272	4	80
		4-7	97, 245
3 John		4.1-22.5	252
7	272	4.1-15.21	268
		4.1-2	268
Jude		4.1	266, 267, 269
5-7	328	4.2	80
5	16, 212	4.3	257, 258
9	125-126, 128	4.4	251
		4.5	263
Revelation		5	259
1	247	5.1	259
1-3	253	5.2-5	258
1.1	246, 257, 261-262, 265	5.2	259
1.2	261, 269	5.3	259
1.4	263-264	5.4	259
1.6	253	5.5	259, 267
1.7	251	5.6-7	91
1.9	269	5.6	263-264
		5.7	259
		5.8	259

5.9	258-259	14.14-15	4
6.1	259, 267	14.14	23, 32, 251-252, 258
6.2	252, 259	14.15-17	251
6.5	259	14.15	251-252, 266
6.6	268	14.17-18	251-252
6.7	259	14.18	266
6.8-13	268	14.19-20	255
6.9	259	15.5-8	262-264
6.12	259	15.6	265
6.17	260	16	269
7.3	254	16.1-21	264
7.9-17	256	16.1	267
7.10	260	16.15	269
7.15-17	31, 91, 97	16.17	267
8-11	269	17.1-19.10	262
8.1	259, 267	17.1	262, 265, 268
8.2-11.9	264	17.3	262, 265
8.2-15.19	267	17.6-18	262
8.2	124, 264-265	17.8	259
8.3-5	265	17.14	253
8.3	267	18.1-3	23
8.13	267	18.4	267
9.4	254	18.20	178
10	245, 257, 261	18.21-24	23
10.1-11	23, 32, 246, 269	18.22	267
10.1-6	256	19	259
10.1	4, 145, 156, 250, 252, 257-258	19.1-8	249
		19.1	266
10.2	259	19.5	267
10.3	267	19.6-9	215
10.4	259, 267	19.6	248, 267
10.6	259	19.9-10	268
10.8	259, 267	19.9	262
10.11	259	19.10	131, 146, 262, 265, 269
11	259		
11.3-13	167	19.11-16	23, 106, 252, 254, 255, 256, 276, 313, 329
11.12	267		
11.15	260, 266	19.11-13	246
12.4	28	19.11	253
12.7-8	125, 126	19.12-13	253, 278
12.7-9	140, 256	19.12	158, 161, 238, 253
12.7	128	19.13	254
12.10-12	266	19.15	253-254
12.10	260	19.16	253
13.8	259	19.17	266
14.1-5	249	19.21	253
14.1	23, 254	20.1-3	23
14.2	248, 267	20.1-2	250
14.4	260	20.1	4
14.6-20	265	20.6	260
14.6	251-252	20.12	259
14.7	266	20.15	259
14.8	251-252	21.1	262
14.9	251-252, 266	21.3-4	267
14.13	266-267	21.6	255

21.9-22.6	262	1.10	271
21.9-10	265	8.24-25	90
21.9	262, 268	17.17	128
21.10	262	24.1-12	295
21.15-17	262	24.1-7	91
21.22	260	24.2	91
21.23	260	24.3	90, 251
21.27	259	24.4	94, 100, 271
22.1-3	91	24.8	159, 271
22.1	80, 260	24.9	271
22.3	260	24.10	271
22.4	254	24.12	127
22.6-11	268	24.17	209
22.6	257, 260-262	24.23	103
22.7	261, 269	45.1-5	163
22.8-9	146, 188	48.1-11	167
22.8	261-262	49.16	153
22.9	262, 265	50.1-24	171
22.12-16	269		
22.16	255, 257, 261-262		

OLD TESTAMENT APOCRYPHA

Tobit

3.16-17	241
5.4-5	241
5.16	135
5.20-21	135
8.3	135
11.14-15	136
12.5	127
12.12-13	135
12.13-15	241
12.14	136
12.15	124, 135
12.19	59, 135, 241
12.20	136, 241
12.22	135

Baruch

2.26	73
3.37	271

Judith

16.14	114

1 Maccabees

7.37	73

2 Maccabees

3.1-40	66
3.24	115
10.24-32	66
11.6-13	66
11.6-8	126

Wisdom of Solomon

1.4-6	114
3.1	101
3.9	180
5.16-23	101
6.22	92
7.7	114
7.12	295
7.16	101
7.21-29	92
7.21	295
7.22	91, 114, 296
7.23	107
7.25-26	296, 300
7.26	344
7.27	207-209, 271
8.1	91
8.3	92, 271
8.4	295

4 Maccabees

7.11	328

Prayer of Manasseh

2	74

Sirach

1.1	271
1.4	90
1.8-9	91
1.9	90

8.5-6	271	10.17	144
8.5	91	11.2-4	19
9.1-2	91, 93-94, 106-107	11.2-3	144
9.1	101	11.2	156, 159, 161, 249-250
9.4-10	107	11.3	258
9.4	91, 94, 97, 271	17.1-21	144
9.9	271	17.13	144
9.10	94-95, 97	17.18	296
9.11	91	18	84
9.17	114	18.2-3	248
10	207	18.10-11	143
10.1-21	98	18.12-14	143
10.1	154	29.17	180
10.5	102		
10.6	101	*Apocalypse of Sedrach*	
10.10-12	101-102	2.1-5	84, 267
10.15-17	99		
10.17-21	100	*Apocalypse of Zephaniah*	
10.18-19	101	6.4-15	145-146
10.20	101	6.11-	156
11.17	101, 206	6.11	250
11.21	101	6.15	131
12.1	114	8.3-4	169
14.6	101		
16.21	37	*Ascension of Isaiah*	
18.14-25	253, 328	1.1-3.12	229
18.14-16	105-106, 313	1.3	120
18.15-21	32	1.4-5	239
18.15-16	279	1.7	239
18.15	64, 94, 101, 211, 253-254	1.12	239
18.16	251, 342	1.13	239
18.20-25	106	1.14	239
18.24	307	1.17	239
18.21-25	173	2.4-4.4	230
19.8	101	2.4	120
		2.9-11	230
		2.12	229

OLD TESTAMENT PSEUDEPIGRAPHA

		2.14	229
		3.1	229
Apocalypse of Abraham		3.3	229
9.1-11.6	268	3.8-10	231
10-11	67	3.13-18	136
10.1-17.21	133	3.13	229, 238-239
10.3-17	142-143	3.15-16	233
10.3-8	77	3.15-17	239-240
10.4	144	3.15	140, 231, 265
10.6-14	276	3.16	125, 240
10.8	120, 278, 296	3.17-18	239
10.9-10	143, 296	3.17	32
10.9	143	3.18	235
10.10-12	143	3.19-20	231
10.16	143	3.21-31	230-231
		4.3	239

4.6	239	9.38	243
4.9	239	9.39	140, 231, 233, 265
4.14-18	230	9.40	140, 231-232, 237, 265
4.14	238	10.2-6	243
4.18	239	10.2	242
4.21	140, 231, 239, 265, 293	10.4	140, 231, 265
		10.7-16	240
4.22	137	10.14	238
5.1-16	229	10.17-31	299
5.15	239	10.17	136
6.1-11.28	229	10.29	120
6.6-7.8	267, 268	11.1-21	241
6.6	231	11.4	140, 231, 233, 265
6.8	231, 234	11.22-32	299
6.10	231, 234	11.23	136
6.13	234	11.26	241
6.17	231	11.32-33	31
7.2-4	234	11.32	121, 232
7.7-8	235, 237	11.33	140, 231, 265
7.8	234	11.34-35	234
7.9-10	127	11.34	235
7.17	239	11.35	169, 233
7.21	146, 233, 235, 237	11.40	231, 235
7.23	140, 231, 232, 235, 239	*2 Baruch*	
7.25	169	2.9-4.4	103
7.37	234	3.14-15	91
8.5	146, 233, 235	3.16	127
8.7	234, 238-239	3.29	91
8.14	140, 235	30.2	180
8.15	233	36	84
8.18	235, 239, 243	51.5	152
8.23-24	230	51.10-13	180
8.25	234, 239	51.10	152
9.5	234, 238	51.12	152
9.9-10	31	53	84
9.9	156	55.3	145, 218
9.12	239	63.6	145
9.14	239	75.1	146
9.19-23	128	75.5	180
9.21	233		
9.27-28	243	*3 Baruch*	
9.27-32	237	10.1	124
9.27-42	235	11.1	126
9.27	232	11.6	141
9.29	243	11.7	124
9.30	236	13.3	141
9.31	146		
9.33-36	234	*1 Enoch*	
9.33-38	232, 235	9.1-3	128
9.33-42	264	9.1	124-125, 136
9.36-40	236	10.1-11	124, 135
9.36	140, 231, 233, 265	10.1	125
9.37-38	241	10.4-9	135
9.37	235, 238, 300		

ANCIENT LITERATURE INDEX

10.9-10	131	71	17
14.8-16.3	156	71.8-9	135
14.20-22	242-243	71.8	124
14.20	249, 300	71.9-13	124
16.1-5	148	71.14-17	156-157
18.14-19.2	137	71.14	180
18.14	28	71.34	173
20.1-7	124-125	72.1	137
20.2	137	74.2	137
20.3	135	75.3-4	137
20.5	126-127	78.10	137
20.8	145	79.6	137
21.5-6	137	81.5	124
21.9	137	82.7	137
22.3	135	87.2	124
32.6	135	88.1	124
37-71	157, 333	89.59-62	127
38.2-5	180	90.14	126
39.6-7	180	90.21-22	124
39.12	31	104.2-6	28
40.1-10	124	104.2	180
40.1	31	104.4	180
40.3	333	104.6	180
40.6	133	106.2-6	158
40.9	42, 133, 135	106.2	161, 249-250
41.2	180	106.5	250
42	159		
42.1-3	271	*2 Enoch*	
42.1-2	209, 295	1.4-5	145, 156
45.3	164	1.4-8	146
46.1	159, 161, 249, 333	1.4-9	240
46.3	180	1.5	250
47.3	31	21.1-22.6	132
48.1	180	21.1	31
48.2	277	21.3-22.5	232
48.6-7	299, 333	21.3	232-233
49.1-3	333	22.5-10	157
49.2	31	22.6	125-126, 141-142
51.1-5	180	22.8-10	322
51.3	164	22.10	31
54.6	124, 135	24.1	232
55.4	164	24.4	232
61.8	164	25.4	94
61.13	180	30.8	93
61.70	180	30.11-12	93, 153-154
62.7	173, 299	33.10	125-126, 128, 141
62.8	180	37.2	158
63.2	333	39.6	342
68.1-5	128	56.2	158
68.2	31	69-73	172, 283
69.11	152	69.1-72.5	310
69.13-25	296	71.17-19	173
69.14-26	127	71.17-21	159
69.15	126, 278	71.28	125
69.16-17	296	71.34	107, 120

72.5	125	69.29	95
72.9	173	70.27	96
		71	84

3 Enoch

		71.14	88, 96
		83.3	95
1-36	87		
1.4	176		
1.7	146	*Ezekiel the Tragedian*	
2.1-4	27, 52, 66, 162	68-80	31, 164
9.2-4	147	70-71	130
9.4	95	70	88
9.5	32	74	144
10-14	164	96-99	107
10.1-14.5	301	159	64
10.1	147	187	64
10.3	302		
10.4-5	147	*4 Ezra*	
10.9	67	2.38	180
12.1-16.5	96	4.1	137
12.1-5	146-147	4.36	125, 145
12.1	142	4.38	137
12.5-13.1	77	5.9-10	91
12.5	277, 296	5.20	137
13.1	297	5.40	137
14.5	147, 302	5.41	137
14.17-18	80	5.42	137
14.20-22	87	6.6	137
16.1-5	86, 146, 148	6.38	107
37-71	87	7.3	146
39.12	115	7.45	137
42.1-2	91, 97	7.58	137
44.10	298	7.75	137
45.3	95, 96	8.47	137
46.1-2	96, 165	9-13	84
46.1	88, 96	9.18-22	137
47.3	95, 96	13.37	137
48.2	76, 77, 96	16.74-78	180
48.6-7	96		
48.7	77	*Greek Apocalypse of Ezra*	
49.1-2	96	1.4	135, 141
51.3	95, 96	2.1	177
55.4	95, 96	4.24	141
60.2	95	6.2	124-125
61.7	107		
61.8	95, 96	*Joseph and Aseneth*	
62.1-6	97	passim	283
62.2-3	95	5.5-6	160
62.5-6	96	6.2	160
62.5	95	6.3	160
62.7	76	6.5	160
69.13-25	75-76	13.13	160
69.13-26	76	14.1-17.10	133
69.15	77	14.2-10	129
69.16	77	14.7	141
69.26-27	76		

14.8	124	19.9	150
14.9	130, 145, 156, 159-161, 250	25.1-2	150
		26.4	150
14.10	161	30.2	150
14.11	131	31.1	28
15.4	128	32.14-18	28
15.7-8	42	35.1-7	150
15.11-12	130	38.4	150
15.12	130-131	60.8-9	150
16.14	160		
17.3	131		
17.8	131		

Life of Adam and Eve [Vita]

3.1	153
13.1-15.3	154
14.2	154
48.1	124

17.9-10	131		
18.9	160-161		
18.11	160		
19.8	160		
21.4	160		
22.3	131		
22.6-8	160		
22.7	161		
23.10	160		

[Apocalypse]

passim	283
Preface	128

Jubilees

Lives of the Prophets

16.2-3	169

1.27-2.1	128
1.27	124, 141, 148
1.29	124, 148, 180, 289
2.1-2	124
2.1	105, 115, 141, 148
2.2	124, 141
2.18	124, 141
4.17-26	156
10.17	156
15.27	144
15.31-32	128
15.31	127
16.1	148
18.9-10	148
21.10	156
31.14	169
31.20	95
31.34	141
32.16-26	149
36.7	75
49.2	64

Odes of Solomon

4.6-8	324
7.3	339

Prayer of Jacob

19	160

Prayer of Joseph
Fragment A

passim	112, 137-142, 168, 283, 298, 332, 345
1	115, 138
2-3	140
2	140
3	139, 273
5	111, 138
7-8	140
7	115, 120, 140
9	67, 77, 139, 277

Letter of Aristeas

98	307
132	119
157	119

Pseudo-Philo

(See *Liber Antiquitatum Biblicarum*)

Sibylline Oracles

Liber Antiquitatum Biblicarum (Pseudo-Philo)

2.214-219	145
2.215-235	137
2.215	135

15.2	28

3.69	180
5.414-427	88
8.456-461	233

Testament of Abraham

1.4	126, 141
2.1-3.12	127
2.1-6	126
2.10	60
6.1-18a	60
7.11	31
8.1	31
10.1	131
11.1-13.7	155
11.4-12	88
11.4	155
11.8-9	155
12.4-13.3	88
12.4-5	155
12.5	250
13.1	156, 250
13.2-3	155
13.10	125, 156

Testament of Moses

10.1-5	66
10.2	126

Testament of Job

passim	283

Testament of Solomon

1.6	76
2.4	124

Testament of the Twelve Partiarchs

Testament of Benjamin
9.1	156

Testament of Dan
5.6	156
6.1-6	128, 289
6.1-3	129

Testament of Judah
18.1	156
20.1-5	290
25.2	141

Testament of Levi
2.5-7	230
2.10	170
3.5-7	141
3.5	141
5.5-6	128, 129, 289
8.1-4	170
8.2	124
10.5	156
14.1	156
18.1-14	170
18.35	171

Testament of Naphthali
4.1	156

Testament of Reuben
5.7	32

Testament of Simeon
5.4	156

Testament of Zebulun
3.4	156

QUMRAN LITERATURE

CD

2.19	32
3.20	180
4.2-4	180
5.15	126
5.18	116, 126, 176, 290

1QH

2.13	288
2.31	288
3.21-23	174
4.7	288
4.9	288
4.24	174
6.13	124, 174, 288
11.10-12	174

1QIsa

passim	118

1QM

9.14-16	124
10-19	101
12.8-9	115
13.9-14	128
13.10-12	172
13.10	116, 126, 290
13.14	101, 290
17.5-8	172
17.6-8	126, 290
17.6	210

1QpHab

5.4	180

9.12	180		**PHILO**

1QS

De Opificio Mundi

3.13-17	180	20	108, 111
3.14	291	29-31	110
3.18-26	290	72	108
3.19-25	291	134-139	330
3.19	116	134	110
3.20	101, 116, 126, 176		
3.24	116	*Legum Allegoriae*	
4.1-7	291	1.31	110, 330
4.21	116, 290	1.40-41	165
8.5-9	180	1.43	93, 111
11.7-8	180, 181	1.53-55	110
11.7	174	2.49	93
		2.55	309
1QSa		2.86	120, 326
2.3-11	174	3.79-82	173
		3.79	309
1QSb		3.96	108, 110, 111
4.25-26	174	3.169-178	109
4.25	124, 141	3.177	100
		3.217-219	108

4QDeut

De Cherubim

Frag.	128	27-30	120
		127	108, 111

4QShir-Shab

De Sacrificiis Abelis et Caini

passim	181	8-10	166
		8	108, 111

4Q181

Quod Deterius Potiori insidiari solet

Frag. 1.3-4	181	54	93
		115	326
4Q405		162	165
Frags. 20-22	95		
		De Posteritate Caini	
4Q491		27-28	166
Frag. 11	174	27-31	31

4Q511

De Gigantibus

Frag. 35	174	49	166

11QMelch

Quod Deus immutabilis sit

passim	116, 126, 290, 310	57	108, 111
2.7-14	171	143	109
2.15-16	172		

De Agricultura

51	109, 110, 140, 273
128-129	100

De Plantatione

8	297

De Ebrietate

30-31	93, 111
112	326

De Confusione Linguarum

41	110
62-63	110, 140, 273, 297, 298
95	79
146	77, 93, 109, 111, 139, 140, 190, 273, 279, 281, 298, 345
168-182	119

De Migratione Abrahami

6	297
84	165
103	103, 111, 173
173-174	108-109
174	77, 108

Quis Rerum Diviinarum Heres

130	314
201-205	59
203-204	99
205	11, 109, 288, 306

De Congressu quaerendae Eruditionis gratia

99	173

De Fuga et Inventione

63	109
66	100
94	108, 111
101	108, 110
109	93
110	307
112	307

De Mutatione Nominum

128-129	165

De Somniis

1.62	108
1.68-69	109
1.75	110
1.127-132	102
1.189	165
1.215	110, 140, 273, 306, 307
1.228-230	108
1.241	297
2.270	326

De Abrahamo

31	309
115	120
118	59
121	60
143-145	120
235	173

Vita Mosis

1.58	165
1.155-159	166
1.158	165
1.166	28, 59, 100, 211
1.269-279	116
1.277	116
1.283	116
2.99-199	120
2.114	111, 173, 307
2.134	288

De Specialibus Legibus

1.81	108, 111, 297

De Virtutibus

62	93

Quaestiones et Solutiones in Genesin

2.56	154
2.62	108, 110
4.8	166
4.114	288

Quaestiones et Solutiones in Exodum

2.13	111, 313-314
2.29	165
2.40	165
2.68	242

JOSEPHUS

The Jewish War

5.388.1	149

Jewish Antiquities

1.122	59
1.189.1	149
1.196.2	149
1.198	160
1.198.4	149
1.200.1	149
1.219.1	149
1.332.3	149
1.333.2-3	149
3.331	307
4.108	116, 149
4.108.1	149
4.109.2	149
4.110.2	149
4.118-121	116
5.213	149
5.277	149, 160
5.279.1	149
5.280.3-4	149
5.284.3	149
7.327.1-5	149
15.136	161

RABBINIC LITERATURE

Mishna

Hagiga
2.1   84

Megilla
4.10   84

Jerusalem Talmud

Berakot
13a   129

Horayot
3.1   64

Sanhedrin
2.1	64
38a	110
63a	78

Babylonian Talmud

Aboda Zara
42b   129

Berakot
48.9   125

Hagiga
| 14.a | 85 |
| 15.a | 86, 97 |

Pesahim
54a   77, 94

Sanhedrin
38b   85

Sukka
45b   78

Yoma
77a   126

Midrash Rabbah

Genesis Rabbah
1.1	93
1.3	134
1.4	94
3.8	134
12.6	204
12.10	74
18.1	125
51.2	60
68.12	161, 280

Exodus Rabbah
| 19.7 | 298 |
| 43.3 | 78 |

Leviticus Rabbah
1.1   162

Numbers Rabbah
13.12   204

Judges Rabbah
16.1   162

Other Rabbinic Works

Hekaloth Rabbati
9   74

Midrash ha-Gadol
Exod 24.10   301

Midrash Psalms
72.2   97

Mekilta Pisha
| 7 | 64 |
| 13 | 64 |

Pesiqta Rabbiti
44.10   126

Pirque Rabbi Eliezer
3   77
73   59

Shi'ur Qomah
passim   29, 204, 338, 340, 342

TARGUMIM

Fragmentary Targum

Gen 1.1	93
Exod 3.14	74

Samaritan Targum
(See Samaritan Literature)

Targum Neofiti

Gen 1.1	93, 114
Gen 32.29	61
Gen 32.31	61
Gen 33.29	61
Exod 3.14	74
Exod 11.4	113, 313
Exod 12.12	113, 313
Exod 12.13	113, 313
Exod 14.19	59
Lev 24.16	113
Num 6.27	113

Targum Onqelos

Gen 32.29	61
Gen 32.31	61
Exod 14.19	59

Targum Pseudo-Jonathan

Gen 28.12	159
Gen 32.25	61,127
Gen 32.31	61
Gen 33.29	61
Exod 12.29	64
Exod 14.19	59
Exod 24.9	301
Num 24.23	313
Deut 31.6	113
Deut 32.9	127

Targum of the Prophets

Isa 6.1-8	275
Isa 6.1	81-82, 241
Isa 6.5	82, 301
Isa 6.6	82
Isa 8.14	313
Ezek 1.26	281
Mal 3.1	113

Targum of the Writings

Ps 137.7	126
Prov 8.22	111

SAMARITAN LITERATURE

Defter
passim   121

Memar Marqa

passim	121
I.1	167
I.3	167
I.9	167
II.12	167
III.5	99
IV.1	78, 306
IV.2	74
IV.3	306
IV.6-7	167
IV.6	305
IV.12	31
V.3	304

Samaritan Liturgy
passim   31, 167

Samaritan Targum

Exod 23.20-22	177
Exod 23.20-23	304-305

APOSTOLIC FATHERS

1 Clement

10.7	321
12.1	321
22.1	223
58.1-60.4	272
59.3	74

2 Clement
14.2-4	101, 206

Didache
10.1-3	272
10.1	277
11.3-9	178
11.3-4	323
12	321
13	217

Ignatius of Antioch

Magnesians
16	6, 223

Ephesians
19.1-3	299

Trallians
9.1	299

Shepherd of Hermas

Visions
I.1.6	224
I.3.4	224
I.4-9	215
I.4.3	240
II.1	215
II.1.2	227
II.4.1	215, 224
III.1.4	215
III.1.9	227
III.2.1	227
III.3.3	215
III.3.5	227
III.4.3	227
IV.1.3	227
IV.2.1	215
IV.2.3-4	227
V	215
V.1-3	219
V.2	216, 224-225
V.4	292
V.7	215-216, 218
V.8	42

Mandates
III.1	233
IV.2.2	216, 218
IV.2.4	216
V.1.7	216, 224-225
VI.2	290
VI.2.3	219
XI	213, 217, 231, 234, 267, 291
XI.8	219
XI.9-10	218
XI.9	140, 219, 265
XII.4.7	216, 219
XII.6.1	216

Similitudes
V.1	225
V.2.1-11	217
V.2.6	222
V.6.2-3	217, 224
V.6.5-7	214, 217, 221-222
V.6.7	224
VI.2.3	227
VI.2.5	216
VII.1-2	224
VII.1-3	225
VII.1-6	216
VII.1.2	32
VII.2-3	216
VII.3.3	216
VII.5	217, 224-225
VIII	220
VIII.1.1	227
VIII.1.2	216-217, 225-226
VIII.1.5	217, 225
VIII.2.1	225
VIII.3.3	128, 217, 220, 224-225
VIII.6.4	227
IX	220
IX.1.1-2	214, 224
IX.1.1-3	216
IX.1.1	215, 217, 231
IX.1.3	216, 219, 224-225
IX.2.1	32
IX.2.2	222
IX.3.1	32, 226
IX.6.1	32, 216, 226
IX.7.1	216, 226
IX.12.1	226
IX.12.2-3	222
IX.12.2	217, 326
IX.12.4-8	227
IX.12.8	216, 224, 226-227
IX.13.1	215
IX.13.2-7	227
IX.14.5-6	217, 227
IX.14.5	227
IX.15.1-3	227
IX.16.3-7	227
IX.17.4	227
IX.21.3	227
IX.28.1-7	227
IX.31.3	216
IX.33.1	215-216, 219

X	216	18	31, 182
X.1.1-2	219	22	182
X.1.1	216, 225	23	182
		49	182
		75	182
		88	178
		106	182

NEW TESTAMENT APOCRYPHA
(Includes Nag Hammadi Codices)

Acts of Andrew and Matthias
30   59, 127

Acts of Thomas
9   179
10   332

Apocalypse of Peter
17   230

Apocryphal Gospel of Matthew
3.3   146

Apocryphon of John
(NHC II)
6.15-24   273

Book of Elchesai
(See Hippolytus)

Eugnostos the Blessed
(NHC III)
76.15-24   110

Gospel of Peter
19   332
39-40   240
40   32

Gospel of Philip
(NHC II)
54.5-12   272
52.5-8   277
62.7-18   342

Gospel of Thomas
(Logion)
4   182
11   182
13   349
16   31, 182

Gospel of Truth
(NHC I)
38.7-40.29   272

Gospel of Hebrews
Frag. 1   120, 233

Epistle of the Apostles
14   233

On the Origin of the World
(NHC II)
105.20-25   139

Pseudo-Clementines
Homilies
I.19   207, 213, 292
II.5   207, 212-213, 292
II.12   207, 212-213, 292
II.15   211
II.16-17   207, 211
II.22   31, 101
II.52   207
III.7   204
III.15   207, 292
III.17-18   207-208, 292
III.20-21   203
III.20   209, 213
III.53   201
VIII.6   202
VIII.10   203, 207
X.6   204
XI.4   204
XI.22   101, 206
XVI.12   206
XVI.14   209
XVI.19   204
XVII.4   207
XVII.7   204, 212
XVIII.13-14   207
XVIII.14   212

Recognitions
I.26-40   201

I.28	205	1.5	198
I.32	211	5.10	198
I.33	207, 212-213, 292	*Historia Ecclesiastica*	
I.34	211	II.23.13	121
I.39-40	205	*Praeparatio Evangelica*	
I.44	207, 212-213, 292	7.5	198
I.45	202, 212		
I.51	213	**Hippolytus**	
I.52	203, 212, 292	*Apostolic Tradition*	
II.5	202, 207	4	194-195
II.22	203, 209, 212-213, 292	*Comm. on Daniel*	
II.42	209, 212-213, 292	Frag. 25	194
II.47	207, 211	*Refutation* (Re: *Book of Elchasai*)	
II.48	202, 211, 292	9.9.2	208
III.61	207	9.13.2-3	32, 140, 227, 231, 265, 342
IV.5	202		
IV.9	203		
VI.7	101, 206	**Irenaeus**	
VIII.34	206	*Adversus Haereses*	
VIII.50	213	4.4.2	343
X.72	178	4.20.1	101, 342
		4.20.2	206
Teachings of Silvanus		4.20.4	342
(NHC VII)		5.5.1	101, 206
106.21-28	123	*Proof of the Apostolic Preaching*	
		45	192
		Fragments	
PATRISTIC LITERATURE		LIII	192
		LIV	192
Apostolic Constitutions			
5.20	198-199	**Justin Martyr**	
7.26.1-3	272	*Dialogue with Trypho*	
7.34.5-6	93	34	326
8.12.7-8	93	37.4	189
8.12.9	176	56	60
8.12.16	93	56.1-23	189
		58.4-13	189
Clement of Alexandria		59.1	189
Paidagogus		61	346
I.7	77, 194	61.1	123, 190, 209
XII	192	62.5	189
		72.2	218
Epiphanius		75	177
Panarion		76.3	189
19.2.10	121	86.3	189
30.3.5	204	93.2	189
30.16.2	210	116.1	189
30.18.4	211	125.3	139, 298
53.1.8	208	126.6	189
		127.4	189
Eusebius		128.1	189
		128.2	189
Demonstratio		128.4	189

I Apology
6.1-2	193
6.2	218
13.3	218
31.1	218
33.6-9	223
33.6	332-333
36.1	223
38.1	223
61	253
63.5	177, 285

Lactantius

Divinae Institutiones
4.6	101, 206
4.6.1-2	197
4.7.1	197-198
4.8.7	197

Novatian

De Trinitate
18	196
19	196
31	196-197

Origen

Comm. In Ioannem
I.277	195
II.31	168

Comm. In Romanum
III.8	195

Contra Celsum
5.8	195

Homilies on Isaiah
I.2	195, 242
I.3.4	195
IV.1	195, 242
IV.3.14	195

De Principiis
I.3.4	242, 265
IV.3.14	242

Tertullian

Adversus Marcionem
2.27	193

Adversus Praxeam
16	193

De Carne Christi
14	28, 193

Theophilus

To Aulotycus
2.10	191, 213
2.18	101, 206
2.22	190, 213

GRECO-ROMAN LITERATURE

Aristotle

Physiognomy
805a	320

Corpus Hermeticum

I (Poimandres)
6	331
9	331
12	331, 338
21	331
32	331

Derveni Papyrus
passim	342

Homer

Iliad
4.443	106

Orphic Fragment
168	342

Ovid

Metamorphoses
8.626	318

Plato

Laws
IV.715E-716C	342

Testament of Orpheus
33-34	106

Virgil

Aeneid
4.177	106

MANDEAN LITERATURE

Right Ginza
passim	179
93.19	134

MANICHEAN LITERATURE

Homilies 179
Kephalaia 179

ISLAMIC LITERATURE

Qurʾan
  passim 179-180
  Sura 19.17 233

MODERN AUTHOR INDEX

Adler, W. 156
Agnew, F. H. 177
Alexander, P. 146
Andersen, F. 173
Arnold, C. 33-35, 129, 318, 339, 344-345
Ashton, J. 20, 137-138, 280, 283, 286, 291
Attridge, H. 294-295, 300, 308, 310, 312
Aune, D. 163, 169

Baillet, M. 175
Bakker, A. 13, 220
Ball, D. 272
Bammel, E. 304, 307
Barbel, J. 5, 8, 15, 188-189, 194
Barker, M. 24, 112, 170, 176, 279, 307, 316
Barnard, L. W. 189, 214
Barr, J. 43; 54-55
Barton, G. 125
Bauckham, R. 22, 30, 131, 146, 230, 232-233, 236, 245, 260, 263-265
Baumgarten, A. 270
Beale, G. 246, 255
Beasley-Murray, G. R. 283
Behm, J. 288
Benoit, P. 318, 343
Bettiolo, P. 229-230
Betz, H. D. 119, 316-317, 320-321
Betz, O. 288-290
Bianchi, U. 240
Billerbeck, P. 309
Black, M. 75, 115, 157
Boccaccini, G. 8, 26
Bockmuehl, M. 337-338
de Boer, M. 335
Böhlig, A. 179
Borgen, P. 109, 111, 270, 280, 282
Borse, U. 316
Bousset, W. 9-12, 37-38, 125, 198, 316, 321, 335
Bowden, J. 5
Bowker, J. 321
Box, G. H. 12-13, 38, 112
Brandon, S. 14
Brighton, L. 257
van den Broek, R. 127

Brown, R. 272
Brox, N. 214, 220
Bruce, F. F. 264, 316
Budde, K. 19
Buchanan, G. 284
Buchanan, N. 9
Bühner, J.-A. 19, 152, 162, 177, 202, 270, 283
Bultmann, R. 283, 335
Burchard, C. 128, 130-131
Burge, G. 286
Burney, C. 90, 255

Canick, H. 153
Capes, D. 23, 144, 238, 326, 350
Carr, W. 318
Carrell, P. 24-25, 83, 245, 252, 257
Casey, M. 248
Casey, P. 5
Charles, R. H. 12, 115, 239, 251, 264
Charlesworth, J. H. 12, 18, 21, 96, 109, 152, 175, 248, 266-267, 290.
Cherus, I. 182
Chester, A. 23, 43-44, 113
Chilton, B. 113
Cohen, M. 29
Conzelmann, H. 315
Collins, A. Y. 248
Collins, J. J. 125, 127, 132, 152, 157
Covenhaver, B. 331
Cowley, A. E. 31, 167
Cox, J. 11
Culianu, I. P. 127, 145-146
Cullman, O. 208
Cuming, G. 195
Cunningham, J. 336

Dahl, N. 20-21, 270, 281
Daniélou, J. 16, 70, 90, 141, 210, 218, 222, 226, 232-233, 254-255, 277
Davies, W. D. 161, 336
Davis, C. 23, 172, 238
Decock, P. 180
De Conick, A. 31, 180-182, 322, 336
Dibelius, M. 218, 220-221, 318

Dix, G. H.   13, 125, 176, 264
Duhaime, J.   100
Duncan, G.   316
Dunn, J.   3, 41, 89, 245, 316, 349
Dupont-Sommer, A.   154

Eichrodt, W.   55, 70-71
Ellis, E. E.   326
Epp, E. J.   326
Evans, C.   109, 270, 275, 279, 308
Everling, O.   318

Farmer, W.   317
Fee, G.   326, 332
Fekkes, J.   255
Fiensy, D.   198
Fletcher-Louis, C.   25, 175, 183
Fossum, J.   3, 5, 18, 20-22, 29, 31, 40-42, 45-46, 57, 60, 64, 67, 70-71, 74, 76-78, 80-81, 87-89, 99, 101, 107-108, 110, 121, 125, 127-134, 138, 140-141, 143, 149-151, 153-154, 159, 161, 167, 176-180, 188, 204-205, 227, 238, 252-253, 270, 273-274, 276-277, 281, 285, 297-298, 301, 303-305, 322, 324, 326, 328-332, 334-338, 340, 344-345, 350
Fretheim, T.   103
Fung, R.   316, 318
Funk, R.   317

Gabathuler, J.   343
Galambush, J.   215
Gemser, B.   39
Gianotto, C.   171
Gibson, A.   43
Gieschen, C.   202, 207, 214, 225, 234, 307, 310-311
Giet, S.   214
Goddard, A.   317
Goetz, K.   14
Goldin, J.   64, 118
Goodenough, E.   64, 111, 160, 190, 198, 270
Goodman, D.   59
Goodman, M.   100
Goppelt, L.   311
Goranson, S.   208
Grant, R.   191
Green, J.   339
Greenfield, J.   13
Gressmann, H.   10, 38
Grether, G.   71, 103
Grobel, K.   335

Gruenwald, I.   29, 147
Grundmann, W.   318
Gundry, R.   25, 245, 257-259, 261

Hall, R.   229-231
Handy, L.   51
Hanson, A. T.   16, 274, 325
von Harnack, A.   9, 221
Harner, P.   272
Harrisville, R.   301
Hauschild, W.-D.   213
Haussleiter, J.   245
Hawthorne, G.   4
Hay, D.   171, 308, 310
Hayward, R.   113, 279
Heckel, V.   23
Heidt, W.   53-55
Helderman, J.   209
Helyer, L.   343
Hengel, M.   5, 18, 22-23, 38, 40, 89-91, 95, 138, 308, 350
Hengstenberg, E.   9
Henne, P.   214
van Henten, J.   51, 124
Himmelfarb, M.   230
Hirth, V.   52-53
Hoane, N.   283
Hofius, O.   337
Holladay, C.   165
Holtz, T.   245
Horbury, W.   304, 307
van der Horst, P.   164-165
Horton, F.   171, 309-310
Hurst, L.   304
Hurtado, L.   3, 10-11, 22-23, 30, 36, 39, 41-43, 84, 131, 143-144, 163

Isaac, E.   158

Jacobson, H.   163
Jenks, G.   320
Jeremias, J.   167-168
Johannson, N.   288
Jones, F. S.   210
de Jonge, M.   171
Juel, D.   20
Jülicher, A.   11, 288

Käsemann, E.   300-301
Kelly, J. N. D.   37, 208, 223
Kerkeslager, A.   252
Kim, S.   335
Kinzer, M.   302, 341
Kippenberg, H.   303
Kittel, G.   153, 273, 318

Klassen, W. 21
Klijn, A. F. J. 182
Knibb, M. 157, 229-230, 238
Knight, J. 24, 136, 229, 231, 238-240
Knox, J. 317
Kobelski, P. 171-172, 288, 310
Kohler, K. 198
Kominiak, B. 189
Kossova, A. G. 229
Krause, M. 213
Kreitzer, L. 327
Kretschmar, G. 15-16, 188, 195, 292
Kroop, A. M. 141

Lake, K. 219
Lane, W. 300
Leaney, A. 290
Lelli, F. 28
Leonardi, L. 229
Levison, J. 6, 114, 116-119, 150, 153
Lewis, T. 320
Lichtenberger, H. 153
Liddon, H. P. 9
Lieberman, S. 147
Lindars, B. 264
Lindemann, A. 315
Loader, J. 59
Lods, A. 56
Logan, A. 17
Longenecker, R. 16, 316
Longman, T. 254
Lorenz, R. 8, 188
Lueken, W. 11, 65, 125-129, 294, 296, 337
Luttikhuizen, G. 226

Macdonald, J. 74
Mach, M. 51, 126, 135
MacRae, G. 91
Marcus, J. 251
Marcus, R. 39-40
Martin, R. 337
Martínez, F. 172
Martyn, J. L. 168
McDonald, W. 3
McKane, W. 89, 91
Meeks, W. 160, 163-164, 167, 270, 282-283, 307
Meier, S. 51-52, 54, 327
Menzies, R. 61
Mendelson, A. 270
Mettinger, T. 71-73, 78

Metzger, B. 326
Meyer, H. 316
Michaelis, W. 3, 14-15, 236
Michaels, J. R. 261, 269
Miller, F. 100
Miller, P. 63
Migne, J. P. 245
Mir, M. 133
Mitchell, M. 317
Moore, G. F. 11-12, 38, 112
Moore, M. 255
Morray-Jones, C. 22, 146, 148, 151-152, 170, 239, 319, 321-322, 329, 340, 343
Moule, C. 317
Mounce, R. 259
Mowinckel, S. 38-39
Moxnes, H. 220, 225
Mullen, E. 163
Müller, U. 283
Munoa, P. 155
Muñoz-Leon, D. 113
Murmelstein, B. 153

Neusner, J. 8, 46, 64, 111, 113, 137, 270
Newman, C. 23, 42, 78, 80, 105, 316, 321, 331, 334
Newsom, C. 137, 181
Nickelsburg, G. 152, 157
Niebuhr, R. 317
Norden, E. 343
Norelli, E. 229, 232
Noth, M. 131

Odeberg, H. 13, 146, 270, 282
Oesterley, W. O. E. 38
Olyan, S. 10-11, 30, 36, 42-43
Osburn, C. D. 326

Pancaro, S. 271
Paschal, R. 20, 42, 275
Pearson, B. 179
Perdue, L. 89, 92
Pernveden, L. 221
Perrone, L. 229
Pesce, M. 232
Peterman, H. 179
Peterson, E. 218, 220, 240
Pfeifer, G. 38-39
Piper, O. 21
Polotsky, H.J. 179
Pooij, D. 177
Price, R. M. 319
Procksch, O. 19, 331

Quispel, G. 15-17, 21, 70, 93, 133, 213, 219, 249, 265, 270, 276-277, 288-289, 292, 316, 322, 329-331, 333, 338, 340, 342

Rabin, C. 308
von Rad, G. 51, 54, 73, 89, 318
Reicke, B. 115
Reiling, J. 217-219
Reitzenstein, R. 10, 335
Rengstorf, K. 177
Riches, J. K. 283
Ringgren, H. 38-41, 55, 114
Robertson, A. T. 323
Robinson, J. A. T. 200, 308
Rohland, J. P. 126
Röttger, H. 51
Rowland, C. 3-5, 19, 22, 28-30, 40-41, 83-84, 86-87, 94, 115, 132-133, 138, 143, 148, 159, 161, 245-246, 248-249, 270, 274, 280-281, 294, 304, 321
Rowley, H. 180
Runia, D. 107, 112

Sacchi, P. 173
Sandberg, I. 301
Sanders, E. P. 270
Sanders, J. A. 308
Sanders, J. T. 337
Sandmel, S. 46
Schaberg, J. 251
Schäfer, P. 29, 124, 153, 321
Scheidweiler, F. 14, 316
Schiffman, L. 181
Schlier, H. 316, 320
Schmidt, E. 261
Schoeps, H. J. 15, 207-208
Scholem, G. 17, 29, 146-147, 204, 338, 340
Schuchard, B. 275
Schürer, E. 100
Schütz, J. H. 316
Schwatzmann, S. 315
Schweitzer, A. 320
Schweizer, E. 264
Scott, B. 92
Scott, J. 321, 325
Scroggs, R. 330
Seesemann, H. 319
Segal, A. 3, 6, 21-23, 26, 40, 42, 64, 70, 76, 85-86, 92, 97, 100, 108-109, 120, 134, 138, 140, 148, 168, 253, 270, 273-274, 282, 294, 316, 321, 329, 340

Sekki, A. 115
Seow, C. 118
Skarsaune, O. 189
Smalley, S. 264
Smith, J. 111, 137-140, 290
Smith, M. 175, 343
Smyth, H. 323
Snyder, G. 21, 221, 224
Soards, M. 251
Staerk, W. 153, 207
Stead. C. 37
Steely, J. 10
Steenburg, D. 154
Stone, M. 153
Strack, H. 309
Strecker, G. 199, 201
Stroumsa, G. 20, 147, 195, 292, 338, 340
Stuckenbruck, L. 24-25, 30, 33-35, 129, 131, 136, 146, 233, 245-246, 249, 252-253, 260, 262
Sweet, J. P. M. 255

Tabor, J. 321
Talbert, C. 20, 159, 228, 283
Tenney, M. 3
Thompson, M. 46
Tobin, T. 107, 108, 279
Trakatellis, D. 189
Trigg, J. 175, 195-196
Turner, M. 339

van Unnick, W. C. 342

VanderKam, J. 96, 156-157
Vermaseren, M. J. 127
Vermes, G. 100
Volz, P. 114

Watson, D. 126
Wedderburn, W. 17
Weinrich, W. 115
Wensick, A. J. 179-180
Werner, M. 14-15, 187
Whybray, R. N. 39, 89, 91
Whittaker, M. 219
Widengren, G. 179
Wikenhauser, A. 336
Wilson, I. 72-73
Wilson, J. C. 199-200, 214, 218, 221
Windisch, H. 11, 138, 288, 318.
Winston, D. 92, 106-107, 109, 111, 208
Wiseman, W. 92
Wolfson, H. 150

Wood, H. 11, 288
van der Woude, A. S. 53, 56, 171

Yadin, Y. 308
Young, B. 321

Young, F. W. 274

Zimmerli, W. 83
de Zwaan, J. 316, 320

ARBEITEN ZUR GESCHICHTE
DES ANTIKEN JUDENTUMS UND DES URCHRISTENTUMS

MARTIN HENGEL Tübingen · PETER SCHÄFER Berlin
PIETER W. VAN DER HORST Utrecht · MARTIN GOODMAN Oxford
DANIEL R. SCHWARTZ Jerusalem

1 M. Hengel. *Die Zeloten.* Untersuchungen zur jüdischen Freiheitsbewegung in der Zeit von Herodes I. bis 70 n. Chr. 2. verbesserte und erweiterte Auflage. 1976. ISBN 90 04 04327 6
2 O. Betz. *Der Paraklet.* Fürsprecher im häretischen Spätjudentum, im Johannes-Evangelium und in neu gefundenen gnostischen Schriften. 1963. ISBN 90 04 00109 3
5 O. Betz. *Abraham unser Vater.* Juden und Christen im Gespräch über die Bibel. Festschrift für Otto Michel zum 60. Geburtstag. Herausgegeben von O. Betz, M. Hengel, P. Schmidt. 1963. ISBN 90 04 00110 7
6 A. Böhlig. *Mysterion und Wahrheit.* Gesammelte Beiträge zur spätantiken Religionsgeschichte. 1968. ISBN 90 04 00111 5
7 B. J. Malina. *The Palestinian Manna Tradition.* The Manna Tradition in the Palestinian Targums and its Relationship to the New Testament Writings. 1968. ISBN 90 04 00112 3
8 J. Becker. *Untersuchungen zur Entstehungsgeschichte der Testamente der zwölf Patriarchen.* 1970. ISBN 90 04 00113 1
9 E. Bickerman. *Studies in Jewish and Christian History.*
  1. 1976. ISBN 90 04 04396 9
  2. 1980. ISBN 90 04 06015 4
  3. 1986. ISBN 90 04 07480 5
11 Z. W. Falk. *Introduction to Jewish Law of the Second Commonwealth.*
  1. 1972. ISBN 90 04 03537 0
  2. 1978. ISBN 90 04 05249 6
12 H. Lindner. *Die Geschichtsauffassung des Flavius Josephus im Bellum Judaicum.* Gleichzeitig ein Beitrag zur Quellenfrage. 1972. ISBN 90 04 03502 8
13 P. Kuhn. *Gottes Trauer und Klage in der rabbinischen Überlieferung.* Talmud und Midrasch. 1978. ISBN 90 04 05699 8
14 I. Gruenwald. *Apocalyptic and Merkavah Mysticism.* 1980. ISBN 90 04 05959 8
15 P. Schäfer. *Studien zur Geschichte und Theologie des rabbinischen Judentums.* 1978. ISBN 90 04 05838 9
16 M. Niehoff. *The Figure of Joseph in Post-Biblical Jewish Literature.* 1992. ISBN 90 04 09556 X
17 W. C. van Unnik. *Das Selbstverständnis der jüdischen Diaspora in der hellenistisch-römischen Zeit.* Aus dem Nachlaß herausgegeben und bearbeitet von P. W. van der Horst. 1993. ISBN 90 04 09693 0

18 A.D. Clarke. *Secular and Christian Leadership in Corinth.* A Socio-Historical and Exegetical Study of 1 Corinthians 1-6. 1993. ISBN 90 04 09862 3
19 D.R. Lindsay. *Josephus and Faith.* Πίστις and πιστεύειν as Faith Terminology in the Writings of Flavius Josephus and in the New Testament. 1993. ISBN 90 04 09858 5
20 D.M. Stec (ed.). *The Text of the Targum of Job.* An Introduction and Critical Edition. 1994. ISBN 90 04 09874 7
21 J.W. van Henten & P.W. van der Horst (eds.). *Studies in Early Jewish Epigraphy.* 1994. ISBN 90 04 09916 6
22 B.S. Rosner. *Paul, Scripture and Ethics.* A Study of 1 Corinthians 5-7. 1994. ISBN 90 04 10065 2
23 S. Stern. *Jewish Identity in Early Rabbinic Writings.* 1994. ISBN 90 04 10012 1
24 S. Nägele. *Laubhütte Davids und Wolkensohn.* Eine auslegungsgeschichtliche Studie zu Amos 9:11 in der jüdischen und christlichen Exegese. 1995. ISBN 90 04 10163 2
25 C.A. Evans. *Jesus and His Contemporaries.* Comparative Studies. 1995. ISBN 90 04 10279 5
26 A. Standhartinger. *Das Frauenbild im Judentum der hellenistischen Zeit.* Ein Beitrag anhand von 'Joseph und Aseneth'. 1995. ISBN 90 04 10350 3
27 E. Juhl Christiansen. *The Covenant in Judaism and Paul.* A Study of Ritual Boundaries as Identity Markers. 1995. ISBN 90 04 10333 3
28 B. Kinman. *Jesus' Entry into Jerusalem.* In the Context of Lukan Theology and the Politics of His Day. 1995. ISBN 90 04 10330 9
29 J.R. Levison. *The Spirit in First Century Judaism.* 1997. ISBN 90 04 10739 8
30 L.H. Feldman. *Studies in Hellenistic Judaism.* 1996. ISBN 90 04 10418 6
31 H. Jacobson. *A Commentary on Pseudo-Philo's* Liber Antiquitatum Biblicarum. With Latin Text and English Translation. Two vols. 1996. ISBN 90 04 10553 0 (Vol.1); ISBN 90 04 10554 9 (Vol.2); ISBN 90 04 10360 0 (Set)
32 W.H. Harris III. *The Descent of Christ.* Ephesians 4:7-11 and Traditional Hebrew Imagery. 1996. ISBN 90 04 10310 4
33 R.T. Beckwith. *Calendar and Chronology, Jewish and Christian.* Biblical, Intertestamental and Patristic Studies. 1996. ISBN 90 04 10586 7
34 L.H. Feldman & J.R. Levison (eds.). *Josephus'* Contra Apionem. Studies in its Character and Context with a Latin Concordance to the Portion Missing in Greek. 1996. ISBN 90 04 10325 2
35 G. Harvey. *The True Israel.* Uses of the Names Jew, Hebrew and Israel in Ancient Jewish and Early Christian Literature. 1996. ISBN 90 04 10617 0
36 R.K. Gnuse. *Dreams and Dream Reports in the Writings of Josephus.* A Traditio-Historical Analysis. 1996. ISBN 90 04 10616 2
37 J.A. Draper. *The* Didache *in Modern Research.* 1996. ISBN 90 04 10375 9
38 C. Breytenbach. *Paulus und Barnabas in der Provinz Galatien.* Studien zu Apostelgeschichte 13f.; 16,6; 18,23 und den Adressaten des Galaterbriefes. 1996. ISBN 90 04 10693 6
39 B.D. Chilton & C.A. Evans. *Jesus in Context.* Temple, Purity, and Restoration. 1997. ISBN 90 04 10746 0
40 C. Gerber. *Ein Bild des Judentums für Nichtjuden von Flavius Josephus.* Untersuchungen zu seiner Schrift *Contra Apionem*. 1997. ISBN 90 04 10753 3

41 T. Ilan. *Mine and Yours are Hers.* Retrieving Women's History from Rabbinic Literature. 1997. ISBN 90 04 10860 2
42 C.A. Gieschen. *Angelomorphic Christology.* Antecedents and Early Evidence. 1998. ISBN 90 04 10840 8

www.ingramcontent.com/pod-product-compliance
Lightning Source LLC
Chambersburg PA
CBHW021814300426
44114CB00009BA/172